Euge[...] [...]nt
force[...] [...]ly
Amer[...] [...]us
dram[...] of
the U[...] [...]nd
two l[...] [...]er
One-act Plays (1914) was originally published. From this point on, O'Neill's work falls roughly into three phases: the early plays, written from 1914 to 1921 (*The Long Voyage Home, The Moon of the Caribbees, Beyond the Horizon, Anna Christie*); a variety of full-length plays for Broadway (*Desire Under the Elms; Great God Brown; Ah, Wilderness!*); and the last, great plays, written between 1938 and his death (*The Iceman Cometh, Long Day's Journey Into Night, A Moon for the Misbegotten*). Eugene O'Neill is a four-time Pulitzer Prize winner, and he was awarded the Nobel Prize in literature in 1936.

Jeffrey H. Richards, professor of English at Old Dominion University, teaches early American literature and early through contemporary American drama. He is the author of *Theater Enough: American Culture and the Metaphor of the World Stage, 1607–1789*, and *Mercy Otis Warren*, and most recently the editor of *Early American Drama*, published in Penguin Classics.

EARLY PLAYS

EUGENE O'NEILL

EDITED WITH AN
INTRODUCTION BY
JEFFREY H. RICHARDS

PENGUIN BOOKS

PENGUIN BOOKS

Published by the Penguin Group

Penguin Group (USA) Inc., 375 Hudson Street, New York, New York 10014, U.S.A.

Penguin Group (Canada), 90 Eglinton Avenue East, Suite 700, Toronto,
Ontario, Canada M4P 2Y3 (a division of Pearson Penguin Canada Inc.)

Penguin Books Ltd, 80 Strand, London WC2R 0RL, England

Penguin Ireland, 25 St Stephen's Green, Dublin 2, Ireland (a division of Penguin Books Ltd)

Penguin Group (Australia), 250 Camberwell Road, Camberwell,
Victoria 3124, Australia (a division of Pearson Australia Group Pty Ltd)

Penguin Books India Pvt Ltd, 11 Community Centre, Panchsheel Park, New Delhi – 110 017, India

Penguin Group (NZ), cnr Airborne and Rosedale Roads,
Albany, Auckland 1310, New Zealand (a division of Pearson New Zealand Ltd)

Penguin Books (South Africa) (Pty) Ltd, 24 Sturdee Avenue,
Rosebank, Johannesburg 2196, South Africa

Penguin Books Ltd, Registered Offices: 80 Strand, London WC2R 0RL, England

First published in Penguin Books 2001

5   7   9   10   8   6   4

Introduction and notes copyright © Jeffery H. Richards, 2001
All rights reserved

ISBN 0 14 11.8670 4
CIP data available

Printed in the United States of America
Set in Sabon

ACKNOWLEDGMENTS

The editor wishes to thank the graduate students in his O'Neill seminar at Old Dominion University, John Seelye, and Michael Millman for their critique and encouragement of the project; research assistants Ruth Barrineau Brooks and Elisabeth Simmons for their invaluable sleuthing of bibliographical items; and Stephanie Sugioka, Aaron Richards, and Sarah Richards for their unfailing support.

CONTENTS

INTRODUCTION

The fame accorded to Eugene O'Neill lies largely with his late plays, especially *The Iceman Cometh* (1940) and *Long Day's Journey into Night* (1941), as well as those of his middle period, including *Desire Under the Elms* (1924), *The Great God Brown* (1925), and *Strange Interlude* (1927). Those plays were only made possible, of course, by the work he produced between 1913 and 1922, the first phase of his career as a playwright. For the most part, scholars have examined these early plays as material to be considered as predictive of the later, in the way that New Testament theologians often read the Old. Certainly, such reading of early into late is inevitable for readers of the whole corpus of O'Neill's work: one cannot help, for instance, but connect the barroom scene in *Anna Christie* to that in *Iceman* or see the family conflicts in *Beyond the Horizon* as harbingers of the Tyrones' troubles in *Long Day's Journey*. Unfortunately, such readings often obscure what O'Neill was doing when plays like *Ile* or *Moon of the Caribbees* were the newest things he wrote, and critics were hailing him as the most innovative playwright in the American theater.

This volume brings to readers a selection of O'Neill's early work, written between 1914 and 1921 and produced for the stage between 1916 and 1922. The last play printed here, *The Hairy Ape*, was O'Neill's forty-first written drama—an enormous output of something like four plays a year from 1913. Indeed, by the time he wrote *Bound East for Cardiff* (1914), the earliest play in this Penguin edition, he had already written seven plays; the next earliest in this book, *In the Zone* (1917), was O'Neill's twenty-first. The point of such numbers is to suggest that even with much of his early work, O'Neill was a practiced playwright, not simply an apprentice waiting to write *A Moon for the Misbegotten* (1943). Rather, he was a late Victorian who took the theater of his day and wrestled it into modes as yet unexploited or unexplored, producing dramas that still have the power to move and provoke. The challenge for readers and scholars of American drama is to be able to see these plays as something more than a source of motifs for the dramas of O'Neill's last years.

LIFE

Eugene Gladstone O'Neill was born in a hotel in New York on October 16, 1888, the third child of Mary Ellen Quinlan and James O'Neill. His father, a noted actor, had been born in Ireland and was making his career as the star of a vehicle play, *Monte Cristo*. His mother, daughter of an Irish-American merchant family from Cleveland, had difficulties during Eugene's birth and began taking morphine. She soon became addicted, unbeknownst to Eugene until he was a teenager, and only overcame the habit in 1914. A brother, Edmund, had died of measles before Eugene was born. His oldest brother, James Jr. (Jamie), became a member of his father's acting company and took other bit roles in theatrical performances but led a dissolute life before dying in late 1923, at age forty-five. The transience of a life on the road with his father, the tensions in the family occasioned by his mother's addiction, and his brother's failure to make his mark would profoundly influence Eugene's dramatic thinking in later years.

O'Neill's scholastic career was checkered. Much of what he learned he picked up from acquaintances in New York City, including the radical politics of socialists and anarchists; the philosophy of Nietzsche; drama by Ibsen and later Strindberg; and poetry by the decadent writers Baudelaire, Dowson, Swinburne, and Wilde. Suspended after one year at Princeton University, O'Neill lived a bohemian existence. An affair with Kathleen Jenkins in 1909 led to a secret marriage, then O'Neill's sudden departure on a mining trip to Honduras. When he returned stateside, after a bout with malaria, he shipped out on a sailing vessel, the *Charles Racine*, not bothering to visit his wife or new son, Eugene Jr. This trip took him to Buenos Aires, an experience that haunts the fringes of some of his early plays like a nightmare; eventually, he departed South America on board a British steamer, the *Ikala*, the model for the SS *Glencairn* in several plays. He returned to New York in April 1911, without any interest in taking up again with Kathleen.

The next five years would be greatly formative for O'Neill the playwright. He lived for several months at a flophouse tavern run by James "Jimmy the Priest" Condon, fitting in last voyages as a seaman on the luxury liners *New York* and *Philadelphia* in 1911. After a suicide attempt at Condon's in 1912, he spent more time with his parents in New London, Connecticut. The onset of tuberculosis led to commitment to a county sanatorium, then a private one, Gaylord, at the end of 1912. His months there, he said later, were the impetus to his becoming a playwright. Beginning with *A Wife for a Life*, O'Neill took to writing one-act and a few full-length plays, publishing five of his one-acts in 1914. In that year, too, he entered Harvard as a special student in George Pierce Baker's English 47 class on playwriting, learning craft elements that remained with him his whole career. With his father in financial trouble, O'Neill left Harvard after the spring 1915 term, and returned to New York, resuming such long-term bad habits as heavy drinking and consorting with prostitutes.

In the summer of 1916, O'Neill and an anarchist friend, Terry Carlin, took a boat from Boston to Provincetown at the tip of Cape Cod. There he met a group of writers and actors, the Provincetown Players, who hoped to challenge what they saw as a moribund American theater through new, more intimate forms of presentation. Led by George Cram Cook, his wife Susan Glaspell, Neith Boyce, and her husband Hutchins Hapgood, the group attracted a number of talented, innovative writers and artists, including Louise Bryant, with whom O'Neill would have an affair. For their second summer bill, played at the old wharf they had converted to a theater space, the group chose O'Neill's *Bound East for Cardiff*; later, the Players put on an even earlier O'Neill play, *Thirst*. The combination of O'Neill's compelling one-act maritime drama and a timely fog gave the group a sense that in their midst was someone with the force to carry out their program of theatrical reform.

For the next several years, O'Neill would retain connections with the Provincetown group. During winters, they would retreat to New York and put on seasons of plays there, in a small theater at 139, then later, 133 Macdougal Street in Greenwich Village. The group would eventually stage many of the plays printed in this volume. But O'Neill also began to move independently toward more ambitious works that would outgrow the Players. In 1918, he married again, this time to the prose writer Agnes Boulton and with whom he would have two children, Shane and Oona. By 1921, *Beyond the Horizon*, *The Emperor Jones*, *Anna Christie*, and *The Straw* would all be in production, with *The Hairy Ape* following in 1922. O'Neill was now a nationally known innovator in the drama. Perhaps it is strangely fitting that as his success grew, his original family died—father in 1920, mother in 1922, and Jamie the year after. After 1923, O'Neill was alone with his ghosts, and the plays he wrote about them became world famous.

Following the acclaim he garnered for *Desire under the Elms*, *The Great God Brown*, *Strange Interlude*, and *Mourning Becomes Electra*, O'Neill in 1936 became the first American playwright to be awarded the Nobel Prize in literature. Despite this recognition, he struggled with a play cycle, then wrote several dramas, the fame of which was only achieved either after World War II or his death: *The Iceman Cometh, Long Day's Journey into Night,* and *Moon for the Misbegotten.* By this time long divorced from Agnes and married to actress Carlotta Monterey, O'Neill went into a physical decline sparked by several conditions, including a thyroid problem and a tremor from what was diagnosed as Parkinson's disease (though it appears to have been something rarer), not to mention whatever damage years of heavy alcohol abuse had done before he quit drinking in the late 1920s. Further problems developed from overmedication. With his writing career effectively at an end by 1944, O'Neill could only attend to the performance of *Iceman* in 1946 and his deteriorating family situation, which included the suicide of his son Eugene Jr.; the death of his grandson, Eugene III; the arrest of his son Shane for heroin possession; and his estrangement from daughter Oona over her marrying Charlie Chaplin. On November 27, 1953, he died as he was born, in a hotel, the irony of which O'Neill was well aware in his last hours.

No American playwright of the twentieth century has had the exhaustive biographical treatment that O'Neill has received. From Barrett H. Clark's 1927 biography to the large works by Arthur and Barbara Gelb (1962; rev. 1973 and 2000), Louis Sheaffer (two volumes, 1968, 1973), and Stephen Black (1999)—to all of which I am indebted for information—as well as many smaller studies, scholars know the essential details of the author's life. A number of books contain selections of his correspondence and research libraries, notably that of Yale University, hold significant collections of his papers. Many recent critical studies of O'Neill's plays have been enriched by reference to this biographical record. But such riches create their own interpretive problems. As will be seen in the commentary on individual plays, many of the author's works grow out of personal experience. In many ways, O'Neill's use of autobiographical elements marks a departure from dramaturgical practice in the years before he began writing. If we survey the major works of eighteenth- and nineteenth-century drama in America, we might see portraits of a world somewhat like that the author knew, but rarely the intimate details of personal life inscribed in drama. If we take but one example, Anna Cora Mowatt's *Fashion* (1845), a reader might see how the drawing room world of the Tiffanys would be familiar to the elite-born Mowatt and the use of French would reflect her own early childhood in Bordeaux. But Mowatt's personal struggles, her husband's failure in business, and her own illness find only the faintest of expressions in her popular play, if they can be seen at all. Thus the large-scale insertion of the personal marked a sea change in drama that redefined the drama of the 1900s.

Nevertheless, the hunt for the particularities of the playwright's life can also lead to a critical distortion of his work. The tendency among many O'Neill scholars is to see O'Neill in the plays rather than see the plays for themselves. Of course, we cannot ignore information; once out in the public arena, biographical episodes become part of the general critical dialogue. Indeed, we cannot pretend, as extreme New Criticism used to, that things like personal lives of authors do not exist or have no bearing on the work. Yet even acknowledging that O'Neill's real-life voyages play directly into his sea plays, for example, we can still search for elements of the play as play. Given the enormous amount of writing on the Tyrone–O'Neill connections in *Long Day's Journey*, one has to work diligently and consciously not simply to read the play as O'Neill's life on stage.

THE BEGINNING PLAYWRIGHT

The first and most lasting influence on O'Neill as a developing dramatist was the theater of his father. James O'Neill was one of the last of the old-style matinee idols, who traded in whatever credit he had toward being a wide-ranging actor to become a one-play celebrity. *Monte Cristo* resembles many another star vehicle of the nineteenth century— full of intrigue, action, stage business, and crowd-pleasing declamations, but notoriously short on complexity of character and subtlety of language. Not surprisingly, Eugene's early plays reflect his proximity to the lingering melodrama of the late nineteenth century. This was a theater he absorbed as a stage brat, not one he consciously sought to emulate. One might even argue that his whole oeuvre is an attempt to write against his father's stage, an attempt that only succeeded in transmuting *Monte Cristo* to modernist terms.

By the time O'Neill began writing plays in earnest, he knew the works of Shakespeare, the social realist dramas of Ibsen, the psychologically acute plays of Strindberg, and the Irish and German experimental theaters. Most notably, he saw that drama should do more than just entertain; it should seek after truths of human experience, uncomfortable though they be. In some ways, he is the inheritor of ideas propounded in the 1890s by James Herne, author of the first modern American drama, *Margaret Fleming* (1890). In an 1897 article for *Arena*, Herne called for an "art for truth's sake" aesthetic, one that suborned the beautiful for its own sake and replaced it with the often rough, but far truer elements of life as it is lived. Herne's understanding of drama leaned toward socialism, and, as we have seen, many of O'Neill's early associations in New York were with political radicals. Although he never became a truly political playwright, O'Neill often blended dimensions of both the melodramatic and modernist stages with philosophy (primarily Nietzschean), politics, and plain life observed. These early plays show him experimenting with the proportions of his influences as he strives for a voice all his own.

FIRST PLAYS

Eugene O'Neill decided to become a playwright while a patient at the Gaylord Sanatorium. There he dashed off what he later dismissively referred to as a vaudeville skit, *A Wife for a Life*, sometime in spring 1913. In one act, an Older Man, a miner, learns that Jack, his younger companion, is in love with a woman whom he realizes is his estranged wife. The Older Man reacts silently to this news, making the sort of grimaces that audiences for over a century recognized as part and parcel of the popular theater. A telltale artifact (that is, an object in a play, like a will in a melodrama, that increases in meaning over the narrative), a telegram from Yvette, the woman for whom the men are rivals, also plays its usual revelatory role. In the end, without telling Jack that the presumed lout of a husband is himself, the Older Man symbolically relinquishes his claim to his wife with the line, "Greater love hath no man than this that he giveth his wife for his friend" (*Complete Plays* 1:11). So bad did this effort seem to O'Neill himself later, that he presumed he had destroyed it—in fact, he had had it copyrighted—and would not even dignify it with the word "play."

Nevertheless, O'Neill set off in directions that will reappear in the plays in this volume. The world of *Wife for a Life* is a homosocial one, where women are referred to by men or speak only at a remove (the telegram). Because O'Neill himself had done mining, he makes use of direct personal experience in the setting. As someone who had married, then left a wife to go adventuring, he may also have written something of himself into the Older Man. The plot moves toward violence and is saved from it only by the Older Man's ability to see Jack's innocence and recognize his own bitterness. And Jack as an idealist who seeks a better world through the force of his desires and dreams is only the first of many such figures to populate O'Neill plays.

True enough, if this had been O'Neill's only play, it would barely rate a footnote in historical surveys of drama. The moral is crude, the coincidences the type that were already stock, and one of the characters, Old Pete, a mere plot device. Even so, *A Wife for a Life* smolders with barely expressed resentments. Unlike its forebears on the stage of O'Neill's father, this skit reveals darker, more inchoate motivations for action. The Older Man is no villain, but a drifter who still harbors some unrealizable hope for his own redemption. In a portrayal O'Neill would struggle with his whole career, the woman is more symbol than being, a bodiless voice in this case, a name given to a gold mine, a divisive force between two male friends—not someone with autonomy or integrity.

His other plays from 1913–1915 suffer from some of the same ills, but also show O'Neill pulling away from melodramatic technique if not altogether from sensationalism. Suicide, murder, or disease appear frequently, providing abrupt if ruthlessly logical endings to his mostly one-act dramas. *The Web* was the effort the author acknowledged as his first "play." Appropriately, the main character, the prostitute Rose, has tuberculosis. Throughout the play, she coughs (the play was originally entitled "The Cough"), a technique that will appear later, but the sort of device that would not normally have appeared on a stage that was reluctant to offend its audience with too-close an approximation to the reality of sickness and poverty. In addition, her child is hungry, her pimp brutal, her circumstances cause for despair. A safecracker, Tim Moran, offers to help her get a start on a new life, but he's gunned down by the pimp, and Rose, with her baby taken by the police, is arrested for Tim's murder. The grimness of it all is naturalism, the literary depiction of pathetic individuals wincing under the cruel blows of an uncaring universe. As Rose cries to the air, "Gawd! Gawd! Why d'yuh hate me so?" (*CP* 1:28), an audience may be left to wonder the same thing. One of the differences, then, between his first skit and this play is the introduction of philosophical issues to the depiction of human struggles. Not content merely to entertain his fellow inmates of hospital Earth, O'Neill saw that drama must do more: boil life down to its essential agonies, then have his characters make of them the best that they can. In that sense, the author was working more in the tradition of the writers of Job than of *Monte Cristo*.

In these and other O'Neill plays, the choking by circumstance mirrors the gasping for breath by tuberculosis, with both given force by the inexorability extracted from a naturalistic vision of life. Some of this vision came from such plays as Ibsen's *A Doll's House* or Strindberg's *Miss Julie*, as in the short play *Recklessness* (1913). But much of the energy behind O'Neill's naturalism seems to have its origins in novels and stories by American prose writers, notably Frank Norris, Stephen Crane, and Jack London. In their works, the playwright could find stories unlike those on the stage of his day, the struggles and failings of working stiffs, the uneducated, the beguiled, the animalistic men, and sometimes women, who made up huge segments of the population but who rarely got anything except comic treatment in the theater. To name just one example, Norris's novel *McTeague* (1899) chronicles a would-be dentist whose mechanic's approach to his job and limited ability to understand his circumstances leave him helpless to avoid the forces that push him toward brutish behavior, murder, greed, and his own grim death. The confinement of McTeague's marriage and apartment, his ultimate entrapment in a world of No Exit, as Jean-Paul Sartre would later imagine, might have given to O'Neill a vocabulary of situation with which to challenge the limited range of dramatic narratives being used by early twentieth-century playwrights.

Another classic work of literary naturalism is Stephen Crane's "The Open Boat," the largely true-life story of that author's experience in a lifeboat. The universe Crane depicts is not actively hostile but instead is indifferent to the outcome of the four men's attempt to beach their craft safely. To some extent, O'Neill's response to the claustrophobia of life in a closed room is also the open boat, under the broad skies, but even there, too, a sense of enclosure often suffocates its victims. In one-act plays such as *Thirst* and *Fog*, life rafts provide a sort of "microcosm," as Margaret Loftus Ranald notes (52), where life on the wide sea turns inward or desperate. If the hospital or sick room lies behind O'Neill's early depictions of enclosed space, the forecastle of a ship may be the template, even for drifting rafts. In *Thirst*, for instance, three people—a female Dancer from a luxury liner, a Gentleman, and a West Indian sailor are adrift and desperately thirsty in shark-infested waters. In these circumstances, the singing and then silence of the West Indian become unbearable to the white characters, who imagine he is hoarding drinking water. After the woman goes insane, performs a grim striptease, and dies, the sailor proposes that the two men eat her to save themselves. All are reduced to primal urges and fears; in quick succession, the Gentleman throws her body overboard, the men fight, and both fall into the sea.

In *Fog*, two men, a woman, and her dead child are in a lifeboat. With a keen sense of the power of sound on stage, the playwright opens with darkness—they are surrounded by fog—and only the voices of the two men, who themselves can't see each other or anything else, punctuate the stage. Two worldviews, that of the Businessman and of the Poet, come into conflict in the constricted space of the boat. Forced to deal with other, the Businessman insists on his America First ideology, where immigrants, like the foreign woman, be damned, while the Poet, more sensitive to the sufferings of the poor people in steerage, is a nihilist, unafraid of his own death, even as he helps others. Unlike the sudden violence of *Thirst*, *Fog* ends with a rescue, although when the fog lifts, the men discover that the mother has also died in the night. Their survival seems as much an accident as that of the deaths in *Thirst*, but O'Neill holds out the possibility of opening up the enshrouded world of the boat to another reality, where hope cannot be discounted even in the face of death.

In these first plays, O'Neill experiments with a variety of circumstances and situations, not always successfully. *The Movie Man* (1914), for instance, is remarkably prescient in anticipating the linkage between the new media and the events that make news. But the situation—two movie newsreel men in Mexico, covering a Pancho Villa–type insurrection—brings out some of O'Neill's worst writing, including the stage Spanglish spoken by the Mexican characters. In *The Sniper*, O'Neill again moves out of the world of his personal knowledge, this time to wartime Belgium. He establishes some effective ironies but sacrifices subtlety when Rougon, a Belgian peasant grieving for his son, turns killer, and the Prussian officer, who had earlier expressed some slight sympathy for him, is forced to have him executed quickly. The naturalistic power of what seems from early in the play as inevitable is undercut by the obvious trajectory of the plot. As with *Movie Man*, O'Neill chooses a setting and situation where complexity of action will be sacrificed to the inevitability of violence.

In later plays, O'Neill would restrict the display of violent acts so frequently shown in his first dramatic pieces. Nevertheless, the playwright indicates that he is willing to explore darker dimensions of social situation and individual consciousness. Not content with the simpleminded assignment of violence to purely evil villains, he finds that ordinary people, caught in war or the slums or trapped in a life raft with no water to drink are likely to act as other than the angels they should be onstage. As he moved into the next phase of his writing, 1916–1918, O'Neill would retain this belief in the human capacity for violence, even if only expressed as language, but would look for demonstrations of it beyond the pistol to the head.

THE MATURING PLAYWRIGHT

ONE-ACT PLAYS

SS Glencairn *Series*

O'Neill would make use of all of his maritime voyages in his plays, but the four plays gathered as the *Glencairn* plays are based primarily on his experiences aboard the British steamer SS *Ikala* in 1911. The order of composition suggests that O'Neill only thought of putting them together later; three years separate the first draft of *Bound East for Cardiff* (1914) and the three others: *In the Zone*, *The Moon of the Caribbees*, and *The Long Voyage Home*. As with James Fenimore Cooper's Leatherstocking Tales, the order of events in the *Glencairn* plays does not match composition; when finally played as a set, *Moon* was acted first, *Bound East* next, and *In the Zone* last. Through all four plays, the one binding character is Driscoll, the Irish stoker. Others enter or reappear, but Driscoll—a hard-living, hard-drinking, dominating but good-hearted, superstitious, and ignorant man—persists in all conditions. He is no hero, though; just a man with the same biases and strengths of other men. The dramatic focus may be pointed to another character—Yank or Smitty or Olson, for instance; still, Driscoll continues as best he can, a limited man in a rough, hauntingly beautiful, often crushing world.

The Moon of the Caribbees

Written in early 1917, *The Moon of the Caribbees* remained the author's personal favorite of the *Glencairn* plays. O'Neill thought *The Moon* "was my first real break with theatrical traditions," and "an attempt to achieve a higher plane of bigger, finer values" (Sheaffer *Playwright*, 383–84). Most commentators have recognized it as a mood-driven rather than plot-driven drama, an attempt to generate interest from a story other than a typical linear one about two or three main characters. As Margaret Ranald remarks, it is "his first truly multicultural play [and it] foreshadows also his interest in 'total theatre' "(Ranald 55). Although its first performance (December 20, 1918) at the Provincetown theater in New York was something of a bust—someone had left the painted scenery outside in the rain—*The Moon* had better luck in a professional production of all four *Glencairn* plays in 1924. Although considered dull by its first viewers, *The Moon* is now recognized as one of O'Neill's best short plays.

According to Louis Sheaffer, O'Neill based the action of the play on an otherwise undescribed incident while the future playwright was a seaman on board the SS *Ikala*, anchored a half-mile off the shallow-water harbor of Port of Spain, Trinidad, in 1911 (*Playwright* 187). Here, though, O'Neill is after something other than gritty verisimilitude. In contrast to the earlier written *Bound East for Cardiff*, the motif of the enclosed forecastle is muted; most of the men sit on the hatch, outside in the full moon, listening to the singing of West Indians on shore. One level of action deals with the pent-up emotions of men eager for release. As the sounds of the men drinking and cavorting with the women grow louder and effectively drown out the "melancholy," and perhaps funereal, music, the otherwise unobserved forecastle seems like a subconscious from which demons violently erupt. The libido is in full gear; when Bella, a voice of socially conscious reason, tries to stop their riot, Driscoll grabs her to force her to dance. Once opened and emptied, the forecastle will not reclaim its demons until blood has been spilled.

At the other end of the psychological spectrum are the two quiet ones, Smitty and Tom ("Donk") the donkeyman (steam engine operator). Donk cannot drink, under doctor's orders, but he is untroubled by the past. Smitty, by contrast, an Englishman of somewhat higher class background than the others, finds that the music brings up "beastly memories" that haunt him. Unlike the other men who can put aside their racism at the prospect of pleasure, Smitty recoils in disgust at Pearl. Even after the chaos on deck, he seems untouched by what's immediately around him. Instead, he reacts more powerfully to his own personal demons than to the chastened demons of the forecastle. The price of articulation—Smitty is a "gentleman"—is self-censorship and lingering internal strife.

For O'Neill, the evocative setting of the moon, the island, and the quiet sea highlights Smitty's self-conscious pose as the intellectual in despair: "[H]is silhouetted gestures of self-pity," he wrote to Barrett Clark, "are reduced to their proper insignificance" (Sheaffer, *Playwright* 384). In other words, Smitty's own sense of gloom should not be taken as the message of the play. As Stephen Black summarizes, "Beauty and truth were manifest in the sea. . . . [H]umanity is simply part of the picture." Therefore, he continues, the play is "neither pessimistic nor optimistic" (200). This view suggests that O'Neill has moved away from his hostile universe of *The Web* and other early works and closer to Crane's "The Open Boat," but even there he goes a step further: It is the very mystery of the sea's beauty rather than its flat grayness, as Crane describes it, that exacerbates Smitty's feelings of alienation.

Bound East for Cardiff

The most famous of O'Neill's one-act plays, *Bound East for Cardiff*, is also the only play of his from before 1916 that has had more than occasional stage life beyond the decade in which it was written. *Bound East*, originally titled "Children of the Sea," was written in spring 1914 and copyrighted on May 14 of that year. Its fame rests largely on the fact that it is the first O'Neill play to be performed by an acting company, the Provincetown Players at the wharf theater on Cape Cod. Most accounts of this key moment in American theatrical history include Susan Glaspell's 1927 remark about hearing the actor Frederick Burt read the script to the company: "Then we knew what we were for" (Sheaffer, *Playwright* 347). When *Bound East* premiered on July 28, 1916, with himself in the cast, O'Neill's career as a public playwright was launched.

Whatever its relative worth or predictive value, *Bound East* packs a lot into a short space. Set entirely in the cramped forecastle, the play emphasizes the fears and awe of the men in the presence of a dying, then dead comrade. In this homosocial world, domestic life is strangely recreated, brought on by an event all of them hope to avoid. Driscoll, the powerful Irishman stoker, becomes nursemaid to Yank, while the others do their best to go about their business. The two have been together for five years; they have fought, seen dirty movies in Argentina, and drifted together in a lifeboat, with Yank saving Driscoll from drowning himself. Now, the stage Irish in Driscoll wants to sentimentalize the moment, lie to Yank about his imminent recovery—but Yank rejects all such attempts: "What're yuh all lyin' for?" he asks. Later, however, Yank brings up his own fantasy of a farm, one he would share with Driscoll, a happy, cozy pair, no doubt, to paraphrase Ishmael's characterization of his time in bed with Queequeg in Herman Melville's *Moby-Dick*. Indeed, this imagined rural utopia for two anticipates a similar fantasy in another prose naturalist's work, John Steinbeck's *Of Mice and Men* (1937), a novel that was successfully adapted for the stage.

Whereas in many of O'Neill's plays from 1913–1915 endings come abruptly with violence, *Bound East* leaves its violence offstage. Instead, it is the more basic act of dying that draws attention. Driscoll dreads Yank's death not only because it leaves him bereft of a friend, but also because it exposes the danger of being on board a ship for long periods. Reality is scraping rust—and falling off ladders—not little farms for old sailors. The only woman who enters the scene is the "pretty lady dressed in black" whom Yank sees at the end. Even the hard-bitten Cocky is chastened. In the compressed world of the forecastle, the sudden appearance of death leaves no escape hatch. "Gawd blimey!" is the only articulated response.

The Long Voyage Home

Although the death of Yank induces "*horror*" and "*awe*" in the men, *Bound East* is not an entirely depressing play. *The Long Voyage Home*, however, is another matter. Fat Joe's bar on the London waterfront represents the nadir of such establishments for O'Neill, a place where poor, benighted sailors are exploited and seduced and, at best, left with nothing. Only the solace—the fog—of drink makes their lot bearable. The men claim to be going home, but the playwright forces us to question whether such men as these have any home beyond the forecastle of a tramp steamer.

Fat Joe keeps prostitutes and a "crimp" in his place. Nick's "job" is to shanghai men for sailing ships—impress them into service against their will. Olson makes an easy mark: with money in his pocket, his service commitment finished, he drinks happily, dreaming of home. Women and whiskey are pleasures impossible for many of the seamen to resist; but what makes this especially poignant is Olson's brief moment of lucidity, when he hears the name of the ship on which he will unwittingly be put once his pockets are empty. There is no "home" for these sailors—only more voyages on bad ships. Sea life has always been shown to be a tough one in O'Neill's work; here, though, it turns into absolute futility. Alcohol is the enemy disguised as a friend, desired but stupefying, leaving the men witless, transparently exploitable, forever in bondage to a rotten system. Dreamers like Olson are doomed losers, fools to believe they can return home or recover what they have lost— the farm, mother, an imaginary wife and kids. Mostly, it's the cynical who persist—they have no illusions about who they are or the morality of what they do.

Written earlier in the year, the play opened on November 2, 1917, and was performed, in Ronald Wainscott's description, "in a set so horribly executed that it could stand as an exemplar of the worst aspects of some amateur theatre" (Wainscott, "Notable" 98). The play fared better in the 1924 omnibus production of the *Glencairn* series. Olson was based on a seaman whom O'Neill met on board the SS *Ikala* in 1911 and about whom he wrote in 1920, "The great sorrow and mistake of his life, he used to grumble, was that as a boy he had left the small paternal farm to run away to sea." On the *Ikala*, the seaman would spin a perfect fantasy of farm life right there in the forecastle, then "having got rid of his farm inhibitions for the time being would grin resignedly, and take up his self-appointed burden of making a rope mat for some 'gel' in Barracas" (Sheaffer, *Playwright* 186–87). In the play a Swede, in O'Neill's remembrance a Norwegian, the original was probably Danish, as if Nordic nationality were interchangeable. Regardless, the playwright suggests that the Irish stoker, Driscoll, will never be conned as easily as Olson. The most important character across the four *Glencairn* plays, Driscoll drinks hard, demands his Irish whiskey, and at the end is oblivious to Olson's fate. But he's still standing; earlier in the play he also had the ability to put down his glass and carry off his drunken shipmate, Ivan, before the latter turned worse. That's still only a small consolation in the desolate landscape of forecastle society, but it is all that O'Neill will let us have.

In the Zone

Another of O'Neill's early 1917 plays, *In the Zone* is unique among the *Glencairn* series in that it is set in wartime. Although O'Neill was as physically distant from World War I as he was from the Pancho Villa actions in Mexico, his use of a familiar setting, the tramp steamer, and a psychological approach to war make *In the Zone* a more compelling drama than *The Movie Man* or *The Sniper*. Louis Sheaffer surmises that the drama is based in part on a 1912 episode familiar to the playwright when he was a reporter for the New London *Telegraph*; a box discovered in an Italian grocery, thought to contain something deadly, was found to have only clothes (*Playwright* 381–82). Converted into a story about wartime paranoia, *In the Zone* was given a strong presentation by the Washington Square Players on October 31, 1917—in wartime—and soon became part of the Orpheum vaudeville circuit, touring for thirty-four weeks. That latter development provided O'Neill with his first steady income from his craft, enabling him to marry Agnes Boulton and reduce the chronic worry about finances.

O'Neill, once arrested himself on Cape Cod as a suspected German spy, again focuses on his sensitive young man among the roughs. Smitty, whose anxieties come close to being exposed in *Moon*, appears this time as a man with a secret the others feel they need to know. They have entered a war zone—the time is 1915—and with that comes heightened vigilance. Smitty has always been different. Based on an alcoholic son of a nobleman whom O'Neill met in a bar in Buenos Aires called the Sailor's Opera, Smitty has the education and complex personality that put him at odds with his simpler, louder, more superstitious shipmates. As a consequence, his black box becomes an object of suspicion, standing for the man who has never quite fit in and does not reveal his secrets.

As with the nineteenth-century plays O'Neill watched as a boy, a telltale artifact reveals the truth. It is also another instance in O'Neill (*Wife for a Life* is the first such) in which a woman speaks but is not seen. Edith's personal letters to "Sidney Davidson," read through the medium of Driscoll, become a public spectacle when the men suspect Smitty of being a German spy. Her letters are quoted—and like the lady in black that Yank thinks he sees in *Bound East*, the physically absent Edith, through her devastating words, becomes a figure who shatters illusion as surely as death. Smitty's urban life, his alcoholism, his failed romance, all become grist for the forecastle mill. But as with *Bound*, the sight of a man in private agony is too much for the others. In their shame and odd sympathy, they find the slaughter of a shipmate's dignity "in the zone" leaves them all wounded.

Ile

Written at the same time as *Moon*, *Zone*, and *Voyage*, *Ile* marks O'Neill's departure from the *Glencairn* but not from the sea. During his time in Provincetown, he no doubt heard stories of residents there, including Captain John Cook and his wife Viola. Cook, a whaling captain who was rumored once to have killed a mutineer, had taken his wife along on at least one voyage. The experience damaged her psyche and her relation with her husband; afterward, she became known as a frightening figure to local children, someone who sang hymns at odd times and sharpened the kitchen knives as if they were to be murder weapons. Captain Cook, while home, kept his bedroom door locked at night (Sheaffer, *Playwright* 384–85).

That radical estrangement informs the text of *Ile*. Keeney's monomania, like Captain Ahab's, divorces him from his men and his wife. Although the setting, a whaler, and the date of the action, 1895, puts the immediate circumstances of the play out of O'Neill's personal experience, commentators have seen much of the private in this play. Readers familiar with *Long Day's Journey into Night* quickly connect Annie Keeney's mad scene at the end with Mary Tyrone's; by extension, then, given the proximity of *Long Day's Journey* to O'Neill biography, Annie represents an early version of the playwright's use of his mother, Ella, as a haunted figure in his drama. Stephen Black, following Sheaffer, suggests further that Keeney stands for James O'Neill and that *Ile* is a statement about "alienation" from a wandering father who dragged his wife hither and yon. If that is so, then there is some irony in an episode from January 1920. James O'Neill, then dying and attended by his playwright son, was entertained by George Tyler and Will Connor, who staged a debate about whether *Ile* or *The Rope* was the "best one-act play ever written" (O'Neill to Agnes Boulton, January 14, 1920, in King 64). The son's success was a source of pride to the father, not evidence of James's failings.

The play opened on November 30, 1917, at the Provincetown in New York, with Nina Moise directing. It seems appropriate that a woman should have directed *Ile*; heretofore, women in O'Neill's nautical dramas have been either absent entirely, spoken only through signs, or been taken largely as sexual objects, but in *Ile*, Annie, like Smitty in the *Glencairn* plays, absorbs more of the human interest than the blustering males in the world of ships. There seems to be a strong dose of Glaspell's *Trifles* in Annie's plea to her husband: "Oh, I want to be home in the old house once more and see my own kitchen again, and hear a woman's voice talking to me and be able to talk to her." Unlike the real-life Viola Cook and Glaspell's Mary Wright, however, Annie does not turn her frustration into murderous thoughts. Instead, as Jean Chothia notes, Annie's revenge, if one wants to use that word, comes in the way she excludes her husband from access to her private being (Chothia, "Trying" 194). There may be something wild in her playing the organ, signs of an Ophelia-like madness (Pfister 204), but it comes from the frozen wasteland of passion thwarted. As such, it is her final protest, as Egil Törnqvist rightly describes, "against the brutal, implacable silence of the universe" (182)—and against the patriarchal will, inarticulate but unmoveable.

Where the Cross Is Made

Written sometime in early fall 1918 and based on an unpublished short story by Agnes Boulton, "The Captain's Walk," *Where the Cross Is Made* moved quickly into production, directed by Ida Rauh and presented by the Provincetowners on November 22, 1918 (Black 224). Although O'Neill seemed pleased with it at the time, it rapidly fell in importance in his own eyes as well as the eyes of others. He tried a full-length version in *Gold* (1920), but not even that treatment could really save the play. As with nearly all his longer plays through 1920, *Gold* was abandoned by O'Neill when it came time to collect a set of his full-length work in 1932. If *Gold* shows its flaws rather easily, *Where the Cross Is Made* can more readily be viewed through the playwright's intention. This tale of a mad retired captain, his adult children, and a set of ghosts seems pulled from the nineteenth-century stage, but O'Neill imagined that he was creating an experiment whereby the audience could be brought into the madness suggested by the haunting. "It was great fun to write," he told George Jean Nathan, "theatrically very thrilling, an amusing experiment in treating the audience as insane—that is all it means or ever meant to me" (Sheaffer, *Playwright* 443).

Theatrically, this use of ghosts hardly seems tenable in a stage world being reshaped by such plays as *Bound East for Cardiff*. Yet O'Neill understood that madness is not always an isolated individual's peculiar situation but something that can affect, even transform others. Behind this lies Shakespeare's *King Lear*, a play about a monarch deserted by all but his most loyal daughter, Cordelia. Lear protests to the elements and strips down to naked manhood before the forces, including other family members, arrayed against him; yet even in his aloneness, Lear ironically defines the world around him in its attempts to bring him at bay. Bartlett does not obviously have Lear's stature, but the dynamic in the play is a complex of the captain's personal psychology—guilt over crimes committed in the treasure hunting coincidental with lust for lucre—and family domestic politics that are affected by one individual's madness. In other ways, the situation resembles Norris's *McTeague*, when the dentist fixes on his wife's gold coins and cannot imagine himself without them. With Bartlett's wife dead, the one clear-eyed character, Sue, is no match for her father and her brother, once the gold fever takes hold.

Sue's loyalty and rationality keep her removed from the treasure story, but Nat swings wildly from pole to pole. Like Eugene O'Neill himself, who both rejected his father and his famous parent's theatrical milieu at the same time as he sought James's approval, Nat wants the old man out of the way, then suddenly takes up his mad cause. It is surely no accident that the father's obsession with ill-gotten treasure mirrors James O'Neill's own wealth generated from a play about a character fixated on treasure, *Monte Cristo*. Did Eugene himself fear that he would fall under his father's spell and sell out his art for the hope of commercial success? Oddly enough, this play comes closer to pandering to popular effects than many of his others from this period; it is almost as if once turning to the issue of ambivalent son and doddering but once domineering father, O'Neill found himself in a trap from which he could not extricate himself. Killing the father but then maddening the son seemed to him the only way out, at a time when O'Neill's father still lived and the son was feeling quite sane.

This doesn't mean that the play is only or even primarily autobiography. As Törnqvist notes, for instance, *Where the Cross* is filled with interesting lighting directions as ways of suggesting psychological states (86–88). He adds that having an unobserving observer (Sue) mitigates the mass effects suggested by the lights or at least makes their effectiveness problematic; even so, "the green glow" that Nat begins to see near the end "seems to signify Captain Bartlett's *idée fixe*" (87). More importantly, the use of ghosts, throwback though it is, obviously meant a great deal to the playwright for this particular drama. When others tried to dissuade him from using them in the small space of the Provincetown theater, he insisted they remain. For O'Neill, family dramas are filled with ghosts. In *Long Day's Journey* he will use the ghost motif more effectively by having Mary Tyrone come into the room holding her wedding dress, the shade of her former self, but even here, the Banquolike projections of Bartlett's obsession attempt to give reality to the inner demons of a character more talked about than talking. As an experiment, *Where the Cross* curiously mixes the modern interest in psychology with styles of dramatic presentation from the melodramatic era; that it is not entirely successful does not lessen the insights we gain into O'Neill's dramaturgical practice through such transparent devices as green light and ghosts. In addition, as a play about the search for metaphoric treasure, *Where the Cross* captures an essential problem of the artist in a mass culture devoted to attaining wealth: how literal is the gold one seeks and where is it to be found?

The Rope

As with *Where the Cross Is Made*, *The Rope* has attracted little attention from critics since its first appearance on the Provincetown Players stage on April 26, 1918 (although it was performed on television in 1989 [Eisen, "O'Neill" 117]). This may reflect the quick turnaround time between composition and first performance; O'Neill only finished the play on March 18. He appears not to have done much with it afterward, and the story of a miserly farmer father he would reconceive in the more justly famous *Desire Under the Elms*. Nevertheless, it continues a naturalist theme from *McTeague* that recurs in the playwright's work: greed and its effects through the generations. As with another play he was working on during this period, *Beyond the Horizon*, *Rope* takes place not at sea but at its edge. There's no comfort at the boundary—only extremity and varieties of discontent. In this play, it seems, all gold is fool's gold, all discoveries ironic jokes.

Once again, the farm becomes a potent symbol. For a few of O'Neill's sailing men, as we have seen in *Bound East* and *Long Voyage*, "farm" is the fantasy space in which all the ills of being at sea can be solved, a kind of land paradise visible only from the middle of the ocean. For Pat, Luke's return threatens his attaining the Bentley farm—it has been willed to the prodigal, it seems; but when Luke arrives, the wanderer disdains being in one fixed place. "I ain't made to be no damned dirt puncher—not me!" he tells Pat. After all, he's seen the noose—the play's telltale artifact—and realized the old man, Abraham, would be pleased to have him swing in it. The son only wants revenge: the farm is nothing more than a square of dirt, and the money is merely the agency for his getting back at the father, not an end in itself. If in *Where the Cross* the son becomes intoxicated by obtaining an ill-gotten patrimony, in *Rope* Luke disdains patrimony; a ritual killing of the father, in the form of torturing the whereabouts of the money from him (another motif from *McTeague*), allows him to obliterate inheritance and reenter life as a free, fatherless, utterly independent man.

The ending is full of irony, of course, but it is also a plot trick more in keeping with stage entertainments than serious drama. That Mary is implicated, however, reveals something else going on with the play. As with *Ile*, *Rope* was directed by Nina Moise; although it is not as centered on a woman as *Ile* is with Annie Keeney, *Rope* hints more about women than it tells. Annie Sweeney—an interesting name echo—accuses her father of destroying their mother, then carrying on with a woman who slept around; that woman, Luke's mother—much younger than Abraham—is also gone. As in other early O'Neill plays, the rigid patriarch leaves no space for the feminine in his life, unless it suits his comfort. Though Annie has some importance to the story, the absent women, who speak only through signs or remembrances, take up more of the thematic space. One task in reading O'Neill is to find women's voices when they are only scantily provided; perhaps other writers, as Sena Naslund has done with Melville's *Moby-Dick* in her novel *Ahab's Wife* (1999), will give new voice to the loud silences of absent women that punctuate O'Neill's plays. As it is, many of O'Neill's one-act plays almost contain shadow stories of unseen characters—ghost plays, perhaps, psychologically present if not physically represented on stage. In that sense, he follows in the tradition of the naturalists Crane and Norris, for whom women are at best victims or nags and hardly credible characters in their own right.

FULL-LENGTH PLAYS

Beyond the Horizon (1918)

Beginning serious writing of *Beyond the Horizon* in New York the fall of 1917, O'Neill did not finish his first important full-length play until the early months of 1918, after going to Provincetown. During that period, the story evolved from that of a literally roaming character to one who dreams about it but stays home. Stephen Black suggests that the suicide of his friend Louis Holladay played a role in O'Neill's retreating from depicting someone who abandons all old relationships (213). Whatever the cause, the playwright had a moment of inspiration, apparently, and shifted gears to write essentially the current text. He gave the manuscript to John D. Williams to produce; when Williams failed to do anything, the actor Richard Bennett read it and finally prodded Williams into putting it into production, though the latter initially planned only a short run. Opening at the Morosco Theater on February 3, 1920, the play moved to the Criterion and Little Theaters, with a total of over one hundred performances. Despite multiple problems with the actual production, as Ronald Wainscott enumerates, including poorly prepared scenery and acting styles that did not meet the demands of O'Neill's play, it nevertheless inspired audiences enough to see it and critics to have it chosen for a Pulitzer Prize, O'Neill's first (Wainscott, *Staging* 9–29).

O'Neill claims to have developed the idea for the play in the summer of 1917, with Ibsen's *Peer Gynt* as a model, but the germ may have come before that. In 1916, after the Provincetown Players had gone to New York for their winter season, O'Neill's short play *Before Breakfast* appeared on the same November 17 bill as that of his associate at the time, Neith Boyce. Her one-act play *Two Sons* features brothers at a seashore house, Paul and Karl, who are in an unstated rivalry over Paul's ostensible girlfriend Stella. The mother, Hilda, worries out loud to the artist, Paul, that Karl, a man comfortable with the physical world and just returned home after an absence, will steal Stella from him. Paul doesn't see it, but Hilda forces a confrontation between the brothers that leads to Karl's denunciation of women and his expression of love for his brother. It is quite likely that O'Neill, a conflicted brother and son himself, may have stored the basic story and simply switched the roles for *Beyond the Horizon*, with the sensitive brother, Robert, taking the girl from the practical worldly one, Andrew. Because *Before Breakfast* and *Two Sons* were also printed together in *Provincetown Plays, Third Series* (1916), O'Neill would have owned a copy of Boyce's drama. *Beyond the Horizon* is certainly the more ambitious of the two plays, but it must be remembered that O'Neill was also aware of and perhaps borrowing from his lesser-known contemporaries.

Despite its great importance in theater history as a play that began to change mass audience taste away from melodrama and toward serious drama, *Beyond the Horizon* has had relatively few theatrical revivals since the 1920s. Even while the play was in production, Richard Bennett complained of the length of the dialogue and argued O'Neill into making significant cuts for the stage. The playwright's own father, no doubt proud to see his son's work on Broadway, is supposed to have asked Eugene if his point was to drive everyone in the audience to suicide (Sheaffer, *Playwright* 477). Others have questioned the purpose of Robert Mayo's transformation from potential poet wanderer to stay-at-home farmer. Yet there is no doubt that despite the production problems, the play had a powerful effect on its first viewers. In Black's words, the dramatist had "created the first play written in North America that deserves to be thought of as a tragedy in the tradition of the Greeks" (215). The very idea of a true American tragedy struck critics as something new—exciting to some; threatening, even incomprehensible to others. O'Neill had struck a blow for dramatic modernism and began to drag a reluctant American stage kicking and screaming with him.

The play opens in May at the Mayo farm. As readers will quickly see, O'Neill spends considerable time on the first stage direction, with very precise delineations of set and costume. One of his innovations in dramatic writing is the inclusion of highly developed, "literary" stage directions, even though often they would not, or could not, be followed in actual theatrical production. As many writers on O'Neill have noted, the author may have aimed his plays as much to readers as to viewers, a practice not particularly common in the American theater of this time. Indeed, one of the great problems in studying early American drama is the paucity of texts—we have names for many plays and entertainments but no scripts. For O'Neill, however, drama demanded its own place in print along with other literary forms. That first stage direction is almost a manifesto of sorts, announcing that American drama will be written on other principles than pleasing an account-book producer or Mrs. Grundy.

As Kurt Eisen reminds us, O'Neill very consciously sought in *Beyond the Horizon* to blend the novel with drama (*Inner Strength* 9–10, 33); the playwright himself, in a letter to *The New York Times* in 1920, speaks of recreating performance expectations in order for audiences to endure longer productions and thereby allowing the writer to bring out values then only possible in the discursive length of the novel. Robert Mayo's problem and the conflicts he enters with his father, brother, and wife cannot be reduced to a few artifacts and stock situations; there is no villain, no forged will, no seducing tavern that leaves him trembling with delirium tremens, to cite only a few of the techniques for creating crises in the older theater. Rather, Robert wrestles with his own nature and its inevitable clash with others' expectations. A vulnerable dreamer with no skill for farming or supplying a family's material wants, Robert must look inside himself while the audience must take into account numerous complicating factors—the kind normally associated with long prose fiction—for the play to make sense. Having made his choice, however, Robert cannot escape its consequences; there will not be a sudden infusion of cash or a miracle cure for his illness or an inexplicable, sentimental outburst of saving love from Ruth. These things cannot happen in the dynamic established by O'Neill; there is no force of goodness to rescue a falling man in Act 3 when such a force cannot be seen in Act 1.

Andrew and Robert illustrate a dichotomy that appears in several O'Neill plays, that of the materialist and the dreamer. In *Fog*, for instance, the men in the lifeboat are a Poet and a Businessman, with appropriately different worldviews. Right from their first interchange, the brothers in *Beyond* are set in stark contrast: Robert, with his year in college, reads poetry; Andy, having just finished high school, works the land. They still care for each other, however, and accept their differences. Not surprisingly in O'Neill, a woman brings crisis, the disruption of the otherwise amicable male-male bond. Robert imagines that he can transform life with Ruth on the farm by his poetic gaze into the very beyond he has long dreamed of possessing.

Although it may seem artificial, the shift between interior and exterior scenes—one each in the three separate acts—produces its own rhythm. Each recreation of the interior space particularly signals a change downward in Mayo fortunes. Simply by adjusting people and props in the household space, O'Neill can jump narrative time and fill in the blanks without excessive dialogue devoted to history. The love talk from Act 1, scene 2, quickly shifts in stage time to something else, but the set allows us the transition. Ruth's bitter attack on Robert, "If I hadn't been such a fool to listen to your cheap, silly, poetry talk that you learned out of books," and his bitter response, make sense when the mothers-in-law bicker in a room made dingy by time and inattention. The dreamer fails to inscribe his idealized horizon on the rest of the world.

In the last act, Robert's tuberculosis, coupled with the brute difficulty of wresting a living from a hardscrabble New England farm, leads him toward death. His final appeal to the sun, a last gasp romance of rescuing his incipient dream, has the pathos of the striving failure of tragedy. Scholars have likened the ending to *Oedipus at Colonnus* or Ibsen's *Ghosts*, where the syphilitic and dying Osvald Alving repeats, "The sun—the sun" (Ibsen 275–6), and something similar will appear at the end of *Desire Under the Elms*. But it also bears some resemblance to a contemporary play, Lula Vollmer's prize-winning *Sun-Up* (1918). Vollmer, originally from North Carolina, was one of the first playwrights to capitalize on folk materials for modern drama; her fellow Carolinians, Paul Green in drama and Thomas Wolfe in fiction, are more likely to be remembered in this vein, but Vollmer's play of a mountain family and the death of a farmer son who is caught up by the false romance of World War I also deals with some of the same dynamics as *Beyond*. It ends with sunrise, and the mother, angry over the death of her son in France, comes to an affirmative resolution in the raw poetic power of the sun over the land. Whether or not he was aware of Vollmer's successful play or whether it had any influence on him, he went his own way with the device. In O'Neill, of course, the sunrise is both ironic and tragic—the reality of death in a ditch is too stark to give the audience anything special to cheer about. And yet perhaps there was something to affirm after all—the development of a dramatic idiom, capable of playing on Broadway, that refused to sentimentalize even the most sentimental of characters.

The Straw (1919)

Whereas plays like *The Web*, *Long Day's Journey into Night*, and *Beyond the Horizon* reflect O'Neill's own bout with tuberculosis, no play recreates his experience at Gaylord Farm Sanatorium as fully as *The Straw*. O'Neill wrote it in early 1919 while living with Agnes Boulton at her house in West Point Pleasant, New Jersey, but he was thinking of events from six years previous to that year, during his confinement at Gaylord. O'Neill's biographers note the parallels between Stephen Murray and himself; Eileen Carmody and a fellow Gaylord patient, Kitty

MacKay; and Dr. Stanton with his own doctor, David R. Lyman. Given that his intensive reading in drama and his developing a sense that playwriting was his life's work happened as a result of his illness, O'Neill was drawn to reimagine the context under which a muse might be engaged while one is seriously ill.

At the time of composition, O'Neill thought he had a winner. "I honestly believe my play would have a good fighting chance because it is at bottom a message of the significance of human hope—even the most hopeless hope," he wrote to his agent in 1919 (Sheaffer, *Playwright* 465). Unfortunately for the history of *The Straw*, the hopelessness of hope was not something that producers were flocking to produce, either then or later. It took well over two years to bring *The Straw* to its first night on November 10, 1921; as produced by George Tyler, with an inadequate actress as Eileen and stock sets, the play limped along and died after twenty performances. Apparently the playwright lost even hopeless hope for it after that; he never expressed interest in rewriting or reviving the play, and it has largely faded from the O'Neill repertoire and critical commentary.

Of all of O'Neill's early plays, *The Straw* is the most seriously undervalued. Despite its seeming conventional realism on the surface, this drama experiments with theatrical space, seeking to create multiple levels of interest within the confines of a single set. Hill Farm Sanatorium confines its patients in order to make them well, and, even more than *Beyond the Horizon*, functions well as a potential stage set—in other words, it both encloses and intensifies. For Eileen, the common room represents something larger and more hopeful than her cramped, crowded home, but her space at the hospital shrinks as time goes by, reduced finally to her porch and probable deathbed at the end of the play. O'Neill portrays a space that is both refuge and constriction, a place of recovery and virtual burial, sentimental hope and deepest despair. For Stephen, the sanatorium allows him distance from the tendium of small-town newspaper reporting; for Eileen, it is a haven from the cruelties of a cloddish father and demanding family. But as their fortunes shift, so does the reading of place. Stephen has a destination away— Eileen does not. No matter how benign the staff of Hill Farm, nothing can reverse the darkening meaning of that narrowing interior except the melodramatic cure that refuses to arrive in time.

Unfortunately, the producer in 1921 did not realize the scenic intent that O'Neill writes into *The Straw* in the use of space. Neither did Tyler understand the powerfully theatrical elements of the weighing scene in Act 2, scene 1. In that episode, all the patients at Hill Farm are weighed as a measure of their progress; to gain a little is good, to lose is bad. A long period of losses spells doom, the diagnosis of "incurable," and removal from Hill Farm to a public facility. Stephen and Eileen take the dramatic center in the scene, but Dr. Stanton throughout weighs each patient, the sounds of which activity punctuate the talk between the two principals. In his staging, Tyler chose only to enlist a group of supernumeraries (house extras) without direction, and have them merely go through their paces (Wainscott, *Staging* 94). This kind of inept, late Victorian staging could only make the scene tedious instead of filled with tension, which it should be. An innovative, postmodern director, someone like Leon Ingelsrud, for instance, might give the scene a Suzuki touch, pacing the weighing in a deliberately artificial way, as a contrast to the more natural interchange between Eileen and Stephen. Without the history of an effective staging, readers need to imagine a set with multiple points of interest to bring the scene to life.

The play begins in the home of the Irish Carmodys, run with petty tyranny by the father, Bill. O'Neill's love-hate relationship with things Irish comes out starkly in the first scene. Whereas Eileen is the sainted virgin, worn by disease and overwork, Bill is transplanted shanty Irish, patriarchal, stereotypical, a selfish whiner—a product as much of the stage Irishman as observed life among Irish Americans. Stephen Murray scorns Carmody's low-bred behavior. Irish himself, Murray has no family as far as the play goes and thus has discarded whatever baggage Irishness brings. Nevertheless, for all the pain her family brings to her, Eileen is used to being in relations with people. Murray, however, is a solo operator, cynical but one whose hopes lie in his own talents, not in a connection with another person. To some extent, the play criticizes both the smothering Irish family and the stance of casting the family off. One gets the feeling in this and other plays that Irishness in O'Neill is a disease like tuberculosis—something from which one despairs of being cured and yet which is painfully familiar, even perversely lovable, for all that.

Whatever his quarrels with his ancestry, O'Neill makes the real tuberculosis the pall that hangs over the entire play. Called consumption in previous centuries, TB remained a dangerous and pervasive disease in early twentieth-century America. It is communicated among humans and animals through a bacterium, *Mycobacterium tuberculosis*, which leaves lungs scarred. For mild cases, such as O'Neill had, the rest cure of a Gaylord Farm seemed to work well, even in Connecticut; later, many patients would be sent to drier or more hospitable climates in the West. Now, of course, TB can be prevented through inoculation, but at the time of the play, no one could assure a patient that treatment would always be successful. Eileen has been allowed to go too long without medical help; Murray thrives under the care of the sanatorium regimen, as O'Neill himself did. The play uses their crisscrossing medical trajectories to bring them together and pull them apart.

This leads to a great problem with the play: Who is it about? Eileen begins the action, but Stephen's consciousness takes over; she cannot force events, only react to them. O'Neill pushes us to see Eileen's situation as tragic, but only insofar as her life connects to Stephen's. The last act makes some attempt to restore Eileen to prominence, but the ending scene makes that difficult. One might argue that there are two protagonists, but in the Greek plays, whose dramatic vision lies behind *The Straw*, only one usually commands the final and ultimate attention of the audience—Oedipus, Medea. The revelation at the end belongs to Stephen. Even so, Eileen has more depth than many O'Neill female characters. In most of his plays, women's suffering falls well short of the men's; here, the physical illness and accompanying despair fully rival Stephen's more spiritual concerns about who he is. Eileen's consciousness may not be rendered as fully as Stephen's, but her sensibility of loss, coupled with a "hopeless hope," overpowers her lover's latter-day realization of his own feelings, leaving her the emotional center of the play.

Still, he will be the one to persist past the time of the drama. Kurt Eisen suggests that Eileen's strength and demise are reflections of the playwright's struggle for form. The playwright situates the action in a location like that in which his own writing path was established. "If this play recreates the beginning of O'Neill's career as a dramatist," Eisen remarks, "the death of Eileen Carmody inaugurates his almost compulsive need to free himself from the old aesthetic of melodrama even as he continues to draw upon its life-giving powers" (*Inner* 100). Both lover and mother, Eileen embodies pain and takes it away. She is the Victorian self-sacrificing virgin and modernist phantom of the unconscious, the desired but diseased mother-lover. That paradox cannot be resolved by declarations of love, even as O'Neill never sheds his own duplicitous embrace of the theater he loved to scorn.

The Emperor Jones (1920)

Heretofore, O'Neill had experimented with new ways to present essentially realist material. With *The Emperor Jones*, he employed a more openly expressionistic style that led to his biggest formal breakthrough.

Of all his full-length early plays, however, none is quite as controversial as this one. Beyond the scenic devices he calls for, the play also centers an African American character as something other than a comic butt. As such, the play has earned both praise for its pioneering effort and condemnation for its ultimately racist treatment of a black subject. Its attempt to incorporate a history of blacks within the psychological experience of a single individual is both daring and damning. The staging of *Jones* represents a significant moment in theatrical history, even as the play makes for uncomfortable reading many decades after its opening.

O'Neill seems to have developed the narrative from several sources. He claims to have heard a story about the dictatorial Guillaume Sam of Haiti, who said his enemies would never get him with a lead bullet. The silver bullet he reserved for himself inspired O'Neill's original title for the play, *The Silver Bullet*. O'Neill could also draw on his own experiences in a jungle, specifically the Honduras of his gold-digging days. More important, the playwright would have been exposed to more materials on African ritual and art than earlier Western writers had available. Artists like Picasso, for instance, were being influenced in their work by African masks, which were making their way into art collections in Europe and later the United States. Books on such ritual acts as drumming as well as picture books of masks, both of which O'Neill encountered, showed him non-European forms of representation and worldview. In addition, the psychological theories of Jung and the notion of racial memory permeate *Jones* (Gelb and Gelb 435, 438–39). One of the best-known American poems of the time was Vachel Lindsay's "The Congo" (1914), a deliberate attempt to capture "primitivism" in verse and written as if accompanied by drums. Yet as Travis Bogard carefully elucidates, O'Neill was still indebted to earlier influences, including Ibsen's *Peer Gynt*, a play whose narrative provides numerous parallels to the unfolding story of *Jones*, and Joseph Conrad's novel of the primitivism at the human core, *The Heart of Darkness* (136, 139).

Whatever the number and particularity of O'Neill's sources, the actual drama has rarely been discussed outside the context of its original production. There are two good reasons for this. The first has to do with scene design. For the November 1, 1920, opening, the director of the play, George Cram Cook, expended the entire treasury of the always poor Provincetown Players on the construction of a concrete and iron quarter-spherical dome to be used instead of the traditional backdrops and flats. He also employed a new designer to the New York theater scene, Cleon Throckmorton, to develop an effective use of the reduced space. Going for painted strips rather than standard issue prop palms, Throckmorton created a landscape more psychological than natural, reinforcing the play's direction of depicting a jungle of the imagination. The combination of eerie lighting effects generated by the dome and Throckmorton's sets made the New York theater critics, who often ignored Provincetown productions, sit up and take notice.

One other scenic effect of that first production is also worth noting: the drum. Ronald Wainscott has attempted to track down how exactly the tom-tom was employed. At first it stopped during scene changes, and some of the effect was lost. As the Provincetown Players got more skilled at scene transitions, the drumming continued across scene breaks. O'Neill's directions indicate that the beat speeds up at points during the performance, beginning at a normal human pulse rate, then increasing. Not only are we to hear the drum as the sign of Jones's more rapidly beating heart, but as with his attempt at ghosts in *Where the Cross Is Made*, O'Neill wanted to use drumming to pull the audience into the play in the same way, perhaps, that Lindsay uses "Boomlay, boomlay, boomlay, boom" in "The Congo." In any event, the tom-tom worked; the criticism and recorded memories of the early productions all mention the power of the drum. When the bugs had been worked out, the Provincetown Players put on the most effective performance ever for the essentially amateur and experimentalist group (Wainscott 38–58). As Wainscott remarks, "*The Emperor Jones* remains Cook's glorious moment in the sun" as a director (57). At the same time, this highly effective combination of visual and aural devices ensured the play's fame and continued success throughout the 1920s and beyond.

The other reason why *Jones* the play is linked to *Jones* the 1920 production has to do with a casting decision made by Cook and O'Neill. Although it seems ridiculous now even to imagine that this was a problem, the fact remains that in 1920, black actors did not appear in legitimate drama on stages aimed at white audiences (except rarely as the occasional servant), even when the play identified characters as "negro." The revolutionary decision of Cook and O'Neill to hire Charles Gilpin to play Jones made that production the first of its kind in New York to feature an African-American actor playing a main character role in the otherwise all-white theater. Gilpin, who had had a career in the Harlem all-black theater, was found operating an elevator in a department store, but once on the set, struck the play's producers as the ideal man for the role. Reviews of the play are filled with paeans to Gilpin's mesmerizing performance of the tortured Emperor Jones, and O'Neill himself, no fan of actors generally, remembered Gilpin as one of only three actors whose performance in one of the playwright's dramas matched O'Neill's expectations for the part in any way. The combination of play and actor made it possible for Broadway theaters (*Jones* moved uptown to the Selwyn Theater after its run at the Provincetown) to incorporate black actors into casts and to encourage playwrights to write with black actors in mind.

History aside, Gilpin's developing performance, however, pointed out problems with the play itself. If 1920 is a year in which white artists and intellectuals were paying more attention to African culture, it was also a year in which their black counterparts were developing a much more politically and socially conscious movement to elevate the status of black cultural achievement in America. Called later the Harlem Renaissance, and in the mid-1920s the New Negro movement, this awakening of pride in African American artistic and intellectual expression, led by such powerful figures as W. E. B. DuBois and encouraged by writers such as Claude McKay and Langston Hughes, may not have developed enough yet to claim Gilpin as a member, but it most certainly would have exerted some influence. He identified himself as one proud of his race, and this pride led him to make some artistic decisions of his own on how Jones should be played. Privately objecting to the use of "nigger" in the text, Gilpin began to use substitute words, such as "Negro" or "black baby"; this brought about a legendary confrontation between playwright and actor in which the former threatened to beat up the latter if he kept making changes. The end result of this conflict, inflamed by Gilpin's problems with alcohol, was O'Neill's demand to substitute another actor for future main stage productions—Paul Robeson, whose London and Broadway performances and his film version of *Jones* ensured his association with the play in the public mind. Having brought Gilpin to prominence, O'Neill effectively exiled the actor to new, and perhaps harsher obscurity. In the struggle between white playwright and independent-minded black actor, the power cards were dealt only to one hand. In an irony straight out of the playwright's rural idyl plays, Gilpin retired from acting and died in straitened circumstances on a New Jersey chicken farm in 1930, while O'Neill had before him further theatrical triumphs and the Nobel Prize.

This conflict between actor and dramatist represents more than an interesting episode in theater history—it goes to the core of the play itself. What exactly is it about and what attitudes does it finally demonstrate toward the character Jones? The expressionist style, so striking to the play's first audiences, tends toward universalizing the problems faced by Jones. Expressionism, the external representation of internal states, began as an artistic style in early twentieth-century European art, drama, and film, but has antecedents in literary naturalism, including the work of Crane and Norris. While probably not the first American expressionist play, *Emperor Jones* is certainly one of the first and the most prominent of early American expressionist experiments. By representing Jones's anxieties in the Formless Fears, for instance, O'Neill articulates another medium for the expression of deep states on stage besides endless diagnostic dialogue in the realist mode. As Jones moves from his scarlet throne into the forest, he is caught, in Egil Törnqvist's deft phrase, between "the natives that hunt him and the visions that haunt him" (233). This dual pursuit, external and internal, seems the kind of experience any criminal with a conscience might have. This dimension of the play has led some commentators to suggest that Jones's race is more incidental than essential; "O'Neill was not appealing on behalf of the black," one pair of critics remark: "The message is much broader and more universal, having nothing to do with race or racism" (Miller and Fraser 53). But it is clear that Gilpin thought otherwise, for good reasons.

At the same time as the New Negro asserted itself as a fresh image for blacks in America, other older, persistent depictions remained that undermined the cause of black pride. Joel Pfister notes the numerous contradictions that O'Neill evokes in the play. In 1920, white New Yorkers would recall recent events, including race riots in East St. Louis and Houston, that would conjure something threatening about the presence of a large and growing population of African Americans in their midst. Marcus Garvey, the uniformed Jamaican and black nationalist often spoken of in kingly or imperial rhetoric, was a prominent figure caricatured in the white-dominated media. Other mocking stereotypes in the popular press, including racist images of powerful alligators or crocodiles pulling the pants off frightened blacks, eerily inform O'Neill's own use of the crocodile and other devices in *Jones*. Looked at from the perspective of Garvey and other progressive black writers, the play hardly represented a step forward for race equality; instead, as Pfister summarizes, "[T]he black people whom O'Neill thought of himself as uplifting through drama were, at times, white theatrical, psychological, and commercial stereotypes of black people" (135). Certainly, O'Neill does not help his cause with some of the stage directions, particularly his description of the insurrectionist Lem: *"ape-faced old savage of the extreme African type."* Whatever totemic power the dramatist seeks to evoke with the use of the drum or the Congo witch doctor, he qualifies it enormously by the suggestions that blacks are a race imbued with savagery and superstition.

As with his depiction of Irish characters, O'Neill's portrait of blacks has less to do with actual persons he knew than theatrical types—in this case, the history of black portraiture (or rather caricature) on Anglo-American stages. O'Neill inherited a centuries-old tradition of simple-minded, crudely drawn images of dark-skinned characters, most prominently recognized in the black-faced minstrel shows but predating those 1840s performances with the stage Negro of the eighteenth and early nineteenth centuries. Despite his great originality and daring, the author of *Emperor Jones* often capitulated to traditional stage idioms, even if he brushed them up a bit. Jones has much more going for him than many stage-blackened characters in earlier plays, as Gilpin's early, enthusiastic performances indicate. He makes the white trader Smithers fearful in scene 1, and makes no apologies—initially—for having killed the white guard at the prison. Once in the jungle, however, Jones increasingly resembles white popular culture notions of the fearful, trembling black. His line, "Feet, do yo' duty!" all too painfully anticipates the film actor Mantan Moreland's trademark exit from a stressful situation, "Feets, do your stuff." To be mounted today, the play would require very careful translation; that is, it would need to be staged in such a way that audiences did not interpret Jones's behavior as racially essentialist.

This could be done by stressing the reverse history of Africans in America that the middle scenes provide. Brutus Jones envisions not only his own violent history but the history of violence against his ancestors. In those scenes, O'Neill shows awareness that Jones's behavior is as much culturally conditioned as it is the product of some atavistic yearning for or fear of the jungle. Jones differs from Lem in this sense; where the latter is at home in the forest, Jones sees his salvation back in the United States, its racism notwithstanding. This makes him more "civilized," and to some extent, his fears more understandable to a white audience who are themselves fearful of atavism. Obviously informed by Jung's concept of racial memory, *Emperor Jones* both reaches for a new stage expression of psychological torment and exploits comfortable (to whites) if demeaning (to blacks) stereotypes of the theater. As a play, it brings new resources to the theater, but all too painfully carries in its belly the carcass of a discarded and hurtful concept of race.

Anna Christie (1921)

When *Anna Christie* opened at the Provincetown Theatre on November 2, 1921, just eight days before the premiere of *The Straw*, it became an instant hit. Critics praised the acting, the set, and for the most part the play itself. Audiences came as well, extending the run to 177 performances. Within two years, it had been made into a film, and in 1930 would receive a talking picture treatment, this time with Greta Garbo as Anna. For this play, O'Neill would earn his second Pulitzer Prize, cementing his position as a leading figure in New York theater. Despite this success, however, the playwright would dismiss the play as a failure. In 1932, when asked by Joseph Wood Krutch to help select his best plays for a collection to be published by the Modern Library, O'Neill omitted *Anna Christie*.

The opposition of public and playwright opinion indicates problems the play poses for readers and performers alike, some of which have to do with O'Neill's composing process. He appears to have begun writing the play in the early months of 1919, then rewrote it over the summer. As *Chris Christophersen* (spelled thus originally), the drama primarily featured the old sea captain, with his daughter a prim, British-born typist and her lover a ship's officer. When it premiered in March 1920, it was directed by an old friend of the author's father, George C. Tyler, and featured a very young Lynn Fontanne, but with its "overproduced settings" (Wainscott, "Notable" 100) and its perceived lack of dramatic action, *Chris* only played Atlantic City and Philadelphia and closed after a few performances. Not ready to let it go, O'Neill wrote a second version with a much revised and more prominent Anna character and called it *The Ole Davil*, after Chris's frequent remark about the sea. This, too, was rewritten, until it became the *Anna Christie* of the 1921 performance.

The problem all along had been the ending. What O'Neill apparently sought was to leave audiences with the feeling at the end that nothing was fully resolved; he even suggested to the drama critic George Jean Nathan that he really wanted to entitle the play "Comma" (*Selected Letters* 148). But as several commentators have observed, the playwright was at something like cross-purposes with himself about what exactly he wanted to show in the play. Originally, Chris was to dominate. He was based on a Norwegian seaman by that name whom O'Neill knew from his days at Jimmy the Priest's saloon on Fulton Street in New York. The early Chris, also a coal barge captain, had been at sea since age fourteen and had come from a long line of drowned sailing men. Though muttering curses to the "ole davil" sea, the real Chris also provided well for his family back home—none apparently dropped into disrepute. In October 1917, he fell into the harbor and died, probably the result of drinking too much at Jimmy the

Priest's. O'Neill heard the story and in barely more than a year from his acquaintance's drowning began writing the play about him (Sheaffer, *Playwright* 202–3). His first intentions seem to have been to capture the ambivalence of Chris, cursing the sea in one breath and being drawn to it the next.

Between the *Chris* version and the play that became *Anna Christie*, O'Neill's father died. Stephen Black sees that event as affecting the rewriting, turning the play away from a relatively benign portrait of a father figure and more into a father-child conflict, reflecting the author's conflicted feelings toward James O'Neill (272). Be that as it may, O'Neill acknowledged that "Anna forced herself on me" (*Selected Letters* 148) as a character and began to take up more space. Her feminist militancy is an Ibsenesque rebellion against her father and restrictive gender roles; after all, women's suffrage only became law in 1920, as O'Neill was working on the play. But once having admitted Anna into a more privileged position in the text, she made her own demands, in essence, on the meaning of the play. If *Chris* seemed noncommittal to its audiences, *Anna* in turn was deeply divided. When the play opened, audiences read the ending as a happy one, the lovers reunited and Anna to be waiting patiently to create a loving domesticity with her father and husband.

When he saw the reviews, O'Neill was most unhappy. In a letter to critics printed in the *New York Times*, the playwright challenged the response to his play:

> I wanted to have the audience leave with a deep feeling of life flowing on, of the past which is never the past—but always the birth of the future—of a problem solved for the moment but by the very nature of its solution involving new problems.
> I must have failed in this attempt. (Gelb and Gelb 481)

Regardless of O'Neill's attempt to distance himself from the play, it hardly warrants the failure label. As with his one-act plays of the sea or rural life, *Anna Christie* too makes considerable use of the resources of what Jean Chothia calls "low colloquial" speech (*Forging* 61). The power of this kind of language can be measured on several levels. Unlike the slick, upper-class dialogue of a Clyde Fitch, for example, where no one struggles with articulation and witty surface covers for a lack of depth in the characters, the speech in *Anna Christie* shows the torment of people with powerful emotions and few words with which to express them. When Mat calls Anna a "slut," the word stings Anna but also projects the speaker's inadequacy to express his conflicted feelings of attraction and horror at her revelation of her past. Chris, too, a foreign-born man, speaks in formulas rather than with freshly conceived language to describe his shifting moods. By calling the sea "ole davil," Chris succumbs to a philosophy of a hostile universe, personally out to get him even as it seduces, like a prostitute. His anger with Anna is as much his rage at the sea inarticulately shifted to his daughter as anything directly connected to her.

But Anna best shows the possibilities of this low-colloquial speech. Her language is part immigrant, part Minnesota farm girl, part city hooker, not always blended with consistency. No matter: her opening line in Act 1, "Gimme a whiskey—ginger ale at the side. And don't be stingy, baby," shows what few plays of the time offered—a forceful woman who is neither saint nor virgin. Indeed, her language allows her to avoid the pat contrition of middle-class stage women who stray. In her conversation with Marthy, Chris's wheezing—and no doubt tubercular—mistress, Anna is blunt about her change of career from "nurse girl" to prostitute: "It was all men's fault—the whole business." Later, in Act 3, when she finally tells Mat and Chris about her past, that same bluntness comes to her aid again. To Burke, she shouts, "But, damn it, shut up! Let me talk for a change!" Burke responds, out of his inability to express anything between black and white, "'Tis quare, rough talk, that—for a decent girl the like of you!" He's right, ironically: it is rough talk, for a stage heroine. But given the thickness of skull in the two men, Anna has no other choice. Even in her *"weariness"* at their inability to understand her situation—that she didn't turn tricks just for a lark—she can still tell Burke, "You're just like the rest!" She takes no prisoners, but in the world of this play, the now confined and claustrophobic space of the coal barge, she talks herself into stark aloneness.

Barbara Voglino observes that the play creates its ambiguity in the conflict between Anna's feminism and the overall fatalism that O'Neill evokes (35–45). Anna's blunt language does not need words like "patriarchy" to make her point clearly enough, but as with her father and Mat, Anna finds herself swept by forces beyond her ability to speak them. Like Rose in *The Web*, Anna always has in her mind a "Gawd" who will strike her dead; and when Mat shows his obtuseness again in Act 4, she mutters, in words reminiscent of Hurstwood's suicide in Dreiser's novel *Sister Carrie* (1900), the ultimate naturalistic cry: "What's the use of me talking? What's the use of anything?" When Mat relents at last, she chooses love over ideology. The fog that she has embraced as a health-giving phenomenon of the open air then settles around them. For Anna, the fog that is love resists fatalism more resolutely than feminist assertion. For Chris, who speaks the last words, the fog remains a sign of uncontrollable force, "dat old davil, sea." O'Neill refuses to commit to a single reading of the choking/liberating atmosphere.

The Hairy Ape (1921)

As *Anna Christie* was opening in New York, O'Neill began work on another play that he thought of as an extension of *The Emperor Jones*. Written largely in an intense burst in November and December 1921, *The Hairy Ape* premiered at the Provincetown on March 9, 1922, ostensibly directed by James Light but with a strong dose of O'Neill himself and some help from Arthur Hopkins. As with *Jones*, *Hairy Ape* proved a critical success; its star, Louis Wolheim as Yank, gave a legendary performance as the increasingly tormented stoker and helped propel the play into the O'Neill canon. This story of natural man in a machine world remains one of the best-known of all American dramas from this period.

In some ways, *The Hairy Ape* represents the end of an era; although not the last O'Neill play to be presented by the Provincetown Players, it brought about the dissolution of the original group that first welcomed the playwright in 1916. Despite the fact that O'Neill may have been strongly influenced in this play by Provincetowner Susan Glaspell's expressionist drama *The Verge* (1920), not everyone among the company was happy with the marquee dramatist in their midst (Ben-Zvi). According to O'Neill's several biographers, George Cram "Jig" Cook, whose involvement with *The Emperor Jones* had been key to that play's success, came to resent O'Neill's prominence. Cook felt that the dramatist was only using the Players until such time as he could be an uptown—that is, Broadway—playwright. The period between play's completion and first staging saw Cook grow estranged from the production, from O'Neill and the rest of the company. He finally went with wife Susan Glaspell to Greece. The era of deliberate innocence, of anything-goes experimentation, was over. O'Neill emerged as top dog, without any illusions that anybody with a clever idea could be a playwright.

To some extent, *The Hairy Ape* is a play about the price of innocence and ignorance. Robert Smith, the Yank of this play—and not to be confused with the Yank of the *Glencairn* one-acts—thrives in the stokehole of a luxury ocean liner. He, too, is a top dog, or to nudge the metaphor, top ape, the alpha male whose raw power and brute belief in his unlimited control over his environment rules below deck. In some ways, Yank is O'Neill, full steam ahead in the modern world, louder and brasher than the others but not entirely ready to separate from them, either. Paddy, the mooning Irishman, represents the old ways. He recalls with lyrical nostalgia the days of the sailing ships, the freedom of the wind and waves and flapping canvas, someone like Cook, trying desperately to hold on to an ideal whose time has inexorably passed. If this is Good Ship Theater, however, the message is not simply the triumph of the savvy modernist over the Greek shepherd wannabe, but also the perils encountered by anyone who tests social assumptions, particularly a playwright, when he or she confronts the larger and largely unaccepting world.

But Yank's importance is much more than as a substitute dramatist. He wants to belong, and in the beginning he does. In a peculiar use of expressionist staging, O'Neill both stresses the animal nature of the men, with their gorillalike postures, and their denaturalization, with their brazen, phonographlike noises (Bogard 239–52). Is Yank, then, a product of devolution, some social Darwinian survival—again, very much like McTeague—whose only function is to shovel coal, thoughtlessly, and forever? For his part, Paddy is a living fossil, soon to be extinct (O'Neill was interested in anthropology and wrote a play, *The First Man*, on the subject). Yank, however, feels the force of the large ship engines. To stress Yank's feelings, Cleon Throckmorton, with help from the set designer Robert Edmond Jones, shaped a two-tier stage with glowing coal furnaces. The compressed space of the stokehole in the lower tier, like the forecastle of earlier plays and scene 4 of this play, intensifies the action and exaggerates Yank's size relative to the others. But like the sickroom of other plays, the stokehole also magnifies the illness affecting all the men, their complete separation from the natural world. Whereas in *Moon of the Caribbees* the multiple voice gives the whole a winsome roughness, in *The Hairy Ape* multiculturalism only means hostility and impotence, the imprisonment of many nations by the forces of modernity. The ghastly light, the bars, the low ceiling as outlined in O'Neill's expressionist set directions serve to distort and disturb perceptions of the stokers as men at all (Wainscott, *Staging* 107–23).

The upper tier of the stage represents the passenger deck. There, the pale, grotesquely spoiled Mildred and her enervated aunt snipe and bitch at each other, both deformed creatures of the artificial world engendered by industrial capitalism. The inevitable meeting of Yank and

Mildred is the climax of the play. Her posing gets its comeuppance when she goes below deck to the forecastle and faces one of the creatures shaped by daddy's money machine; at the same time, Yank's bravado deflates rapidly in the sudden confrontation with one who does not see his power as beauty and strength. Suddenly, Yank realizes in the acorn of consciousness he possesses that he does not belong, at least to her world. For the rest of the play, he seeks another society, one that will take him back.

Scenes five through eight trace Yank's attempt to find something like home. He does not search in the poetic way that Robert Mayo looks "beyond the horizon" for his salvation, but he's heard things and tried to think about them in his Rodin posture. The street, radical politics, and prison all prove soulless places or organizations. Yank can bend jail cell bars but not harm a top-hatted Manhattanite whose wealth and position leave him unaffected by Yank's pathetic rage. When he goes to the International Workers of the World (IWW) headquarters, he finds that this workers' organization has no room for his incendiary solution to the exploitation of the working class. It is as if O'Neill rejects all institutional solutions: capitalism may foster the conditions that divide human beings from themselves, but neither socialism, anarchism, nor any other social-political force can provide a ready answer. Yank's fate resists what Clifford Odets would offer his characters later in his propagandistic, though highly effective *Waiting for Lefty* (1935)—solidarity among the toiling masses (although, ironically, Joel Pfister argues that Odets was influenced by *Hairy Ape* [Pfister 118]). Out of his stark, animalized alienation, one that anticipates that of Richard Wright's Bigger Thomas or Hollywood's King Kong, the stoker seeks solace and self-obliteration in the embrace of an ape. As Kurt Eisen explains, O'Neill casts Yank in terms of Nietzsche's *The Birth of Tragedy*, placing him between Mildred's "Apollonian dream world of money and power" and "the gorilla's annihilating Dionysian frenzy," leaving Yank a "posthumous person," more alive dead than quick (Eisen 71). In fact, for Robert Mayo, Eileen Carmody, and Robert Smith, death offers possibilities for belonging that are unrealized among the living.

As Louis Sheaffer notes, the contemporary commentary largely supported the feeling held by the playwright and other theater insiders that *The Hairy Ape* was a major watershed for O'Neill; no longer on the rise, he was "the best this country had yet produced" (Sheaffer, *Artist* 89). If *The Hairy Ape* was a beginning of O'Neill's second career, as an established rather than experimental playwright, it also marked an end of his own youth. Just days before the play was to open in New York, on February 28, 1922, his mother, Ella Quinlan O'Neill, died in California. O'Neill's brother Jamie accompanied the body back east, arriving with the coffin the night *The Hairy Ape* premiered. The death of his mother would open up troubled feelings about women that would be reflected in his plays and turn his style more toward the psychological and away from the sociological or political. At age thirty-three, both parents dead, his career certain, O'Neill could no longer afford to pretend that something external to himself would allow him to belong. He would have to create his own sense of belonging out of the raw materials of his own internal landscape and his observations of men and women around him. Unlike Yank, O'Neill did not die after a couple of rebuffs but emerged from the stokehole of genius to try to make it on the top deck. That he succeeded as America's first Nobel Prize playwright has everything to do with his early work. With a little more thought, the Hairy Ape could decide to wear a business suit and pretend to speak and act like the very ones who made him feel for a terrible moment as if he were a despised and rejected monster. Robert Smith may not have had the wherewithal to fight the forces arrayed against him, but his creator certainly did.

A NOTE ON THE TEXTS

The seven one-act plays—*The Moon of the Caribbees, Bound East for Cardiff, The Long Voyage Home, In the Zone, Ile, The Rope,* and *Where the Cross Is Made*—are printed as they appear in *The Moon of the Caribbees and Six Other Plays of the Sea* (New York: Boni and Liveright, 1921). The texts for *Beyond the Horizon* and *The Straw* are reproduced here as they were published in a volume that also contained *Before Breakfast* (New York: Random House, 1921). *The Emperor Jones* is printed as it appeared in a volume with *Diff'rent* (New York: Boni and Liveright, 1921). *Anna Christie* and *The Hairy Ape* come from a collection that included *The First Man* (New York: Boni and Liveright, 1922). I have made only minimal corrections to the printed texts in the case of obvious errors.

SELECTED BIBLIOGRAPHY

The bibliography by and about O'Neill is extensive. I have restricted the references below to items cited in the introduction and other works of direct relevance to the study of early O'Neill plays and to his life; even then I have not included all the studies available. For some works, however, such as *The Straw*, there are virtually no discussions outside of contemporary reviews or more general books on O'Neill. In addition to checking the updated listings in such periodical indexes as the *MLA International Bibliography*, those interested in further reading on the plays in this volume will want to consult Madeline Smith and Richard Eaton, *Eugene O'Neill: An Annotated Bibliography* (New York: Garland Publishing, 1988).

EDITIONS

There are many editions of O'Neill plays, including volumes published in O'Neill's lifetime. The standard edition of all available O'Neill plays is *O'Neill: Complete Plays*, edited by Travis Bogard, three volumes (New York: Library of America, 1988). References to early plays in the introduction that are not included in the Penguin edition are to the Library of America volumes, abbreviated here as *CP*.

BIOGRAPHICAL AND GENERAL STUDIES

Note: The following works usually contain extended discussions of more than one of the plays in this volume. There are many more secondary works on O'Neill than can be listed here, including articles on individual plays.

Barlow, Judith. "O'Neill's Female Characters." Manheim, 164–73.
Ben-Zvi, Linda. "Susan Glaspell and Eugene O'Neill: The Imagery of Gender." *Eugene O'Neill Newsletter*, 10:1 (1986): 22–27.
Berlin, Normand. *Eugene O'Neill*. New York: Grove, 1982.

Black, Stephen A. *Eugene O'Neill: Beyond Mourning and Tragedy*. New Haven: Yale University Press, 1999. Biography.

Bogard, Travis. *Contour in Time: The Plays of Eugene O'Neill*. New York: Oxford University Press, 1972. Revised 1988.

Chothia, Jean. *Forging a Language: A Study of the Plays of Eugene O'Neill*. Cambridge: Cambridge University Press, 1979.

———. "Trying to Write the Family Play: Autobiography and the Dramatic Imagination." Manheim, 192–205.

Eisen, Kurt. *The Inner Strength of Opposites: O'Neill's Novelistic Drama and the Melodramatic Imagination*. Athens: University of Georgia Press, 1994.

Gelb, Arthur, and Barbara Gelb. *O'Neill*. London: Jonathan Cape, 1962. Biography. Revised in 1973.

Ibsen, Henrik. *The Complete Major Prose Plays*. Translated by Rolf Fjelde. New York: Farrar Straus Giroux, 1978.

King, William Davies, ed. *"A Wind is Rising": The Correspondence of Agnes Boulton and Eugene O'Neill*. Madison, N.J.: Fairleigh Dickinson University Press, 2000.

Manheim, Michael, ed. *The Cambridge Companion to Eugene O'Neill*. Cambridge: Cambridge University Press, 1998.

Miller, Jordan G., and Winifred L. Frazer. *American Drama between the Wars: A Critical History*. Boston: Twayne Publishers, 1991.

Murphy, Brenda. *American Realism and American Drama, 1880–1940*. Cambridge: Cambridge University Press, 1987. See especially pages 112–24.

O'Neill, Eugene. *Selected Letters*. Edited by Travis Bogard and Jackson R. Bryer. New Haven: Yale University Press, 1988.

Pfister, Joel. *Staging Depth: Eugene O'Neill and the Politics of Psychological Discourse*. Chapel Hill: University of North Carolina Press, 1995.

Ranald, Margaret Loftus. "From Trial to Triumph: The Early Plays." Manheim. 51–68.

Sheaffer, Louis. *O'Neill: Son and Artist*. Boston: Little, Brown, 1973. Volume 2 of a biography, covering years 1920 and later.

———. *O'Neill: Son and Playwright*. Boston: Little, Brown, 1968. Volume 1 of a biography, covering years to 1920.

Törnqvist, Egil. *A Drama of Souls: Studies in O'Neill's Supernaturalistic Technique*. Uppsala: Uppsala University, 1968.

Voglino, Barbara. *"Perverse Mind": Eugene O'Neill's Struggle with Closure*. Madison, N.J.: Fairleigh Dickinson University Press, 1999. One chapter each on *Beyond the Horizon* and *Anna Christie*.

Wainscott, Ronald. "Notable American Stage Productions." Manheim, 96–115.

————. *Staging O'Neill: The Experimental Years, 1920–1934.* New Haven: Yale University Press, 1988.

Watermeier, Daniel J. "O'Neill and the Theatre of His Time." Manheim. 33–50.

THE MOON OF THE CARIBBEES

A PLAY IN ONE ACT

CHARACTERS

YANK
DRISCOLL
OLSON
DAVIS
COCKY
SMITTY
PAUL

} *Seamen of the British tramp steamer,* Glencairn.

LAMPS, *the lamptrimmer.*

CHIPS, *the carpenter.*

OLD TOM, *the donkeyman.*

BIG FRANK
DICK
MAX
PADDY

} *Firemen on the* Glencairn.

BELLA
SUSIE
VIOLET
PEARL

} *West Indian Negresses.*

THE FIRST MATE

Two other seamen—SCOTTY and IVAN—and several other
members of the stokehole-engine-room crew.

NOTE.—With the exception of "In the Zone," the action of all the plays in this
volume takes place in years preceding the outbreak of the World War. [O'Neill's
note.]

THE MOON OF THE CARIBBEES

SCENE—*A forward section of the main deck of the British tramp steamer* Glencairn, *at anchor off an island in the West Indies. The full moon, half-way up the sky, throws a clear light on the deck. The sea is calm and the ship motionless.*

On the left two of the derrick booms of the foremast jut out at an angle of forty-five degrees, black against the sky. In the rear the dark outline of the port bulwark is sharply defined against a distant strip of coral beach, white in the moonlight, fringed with coco palms whose tops rise clear of the horizon. On the right is the forecastle with an open doorway in the center leading to the seamen's and firemen's compartments. On either side of the doorway are two closed doors opening on the quarters of the Bo'sun, the ship's carpenter, the messroom steward, and the donkeyman—what might be called the petty officers of the ship. Near each bulwark there is also a short stairway, like a section of fire escape, leading up to the forecastle head (the top of the forecastle)—the edge of which can be seen on the right.

In the center of the deck, and occupying most of the space, is the large, raised square of the number one hatch, covered with canvas, battened down for the night.

A melancholy negro chant, faint and far-off, drifts, crooning, over the water.

Most of the seamen and firemen are reclining or sitting on the hatch. PAUL *is leaning against the port bulwark, the upper part of his stocky figure outlined against the sky.* SMITTY *and* COCKY *are sitting on the edge of the forecastle head with their legs dangling over. Nearly all are smoking pipes or cigarettes. The majority are dressed in patched suits of dungaree. Quite a few are in their bare feet and some of them, especially the firemen, have nothing on but a pair of pants and an undershirt. A good many wear caps.*

There is the low murmur of different conversations going on in the separate groups as the curtain rises. This is followed by a sudden silence in which the singing from the land can be plainly heard.

DRISCOLL: [*A powerfully built Irishman who is sitting on the edge of the hatch, front—irritably.*] Will ye listen to them naygurs? I wonder now, do they call that keenin' a song?

SMITTY: [*A young Englishman with a blond mustache. He is sitting on*

3

the forecastle head looking out over the water with his chin supported on his hands.] It doesn't make a chap feel very cheerful, does it? [*He sighs.*]

COCKY: [*A wizened runt of a man with a straggling gray mustache—slapping* SMITTY *on the back.*] Cheero, ole dear! Down't be ser dawhn in the marf, Duke. She loves yer.

SMITTY: [*Gloomily.*] Shut up, Cocky! [*He turns away from* COCKY *and falls to dreaming again, staring toward the spot on shore where the singing seems to come from.*]

BIG FRANK: [*A huge fireman sprawled out on the right of the hatch—waving a hand toward the land.*] They bury somebody—py chiminy Christmas, I tink so from way it sound.

YANK: [*A rather good-looking rough who is sitting beside* DRISCOLL.] What d'yuh mean, bury? They don't plant 'em down here, Dutchy. They eat 'em to save fun'ral expenses. I guess this guy went down the wrong way an' they got indigestion.

COCKY: Indigestion! Ho yus, not 'arf! Down't yer know as them blokes 'as two stomacks like a bleedin' camel?

DAVIS: [*A short, dark man seated on the right of hatch.*] An' you seen the two, I s'pect, ain't you?

COCKY: [*Scornfully.*] Down't be showin' yer igerance be tryin' to make a mock o' me what has seen more o' the world than yeself ever will.

MAX: [*A Swedish fireman—from the rear of hatch.*] Spin dat yarn, Cocky.

COCKY: It's Gawd's troof, what I tole yer. I 'eard it from a bloke what was captured pris'ner by 'em in the Solomon Islands. Shipped wiv 'im one voyage. 'Twas a rare treat to 'ear 'im tell what 'appened to 'im among 'em. [*Musingly.*] 'E was a funny bird, 'e was—'ailed from Mile End, 'e did.

DRISCOLL: [*With a snort.*] Another lyin' Cockney, the loike av yourself!

LAMPS: [*A fat Swede who is sitting on a camp stool in front of his door talking with* CHIPS.] Where you meet up with him, Cocky?

CHIPS: [*A lanky Scotchman—derisively.*] In New Guinea, I'll lay my oath!

COCKY: [*Defiantly.*] Yus! It *was* in New Guinea, time I was shipwrecked there. [*There is a perfect storm of groans and laughter at this speech.*]

YANK: [*Getting up.*] Yuh know what we said yuh'd get if yuh sprung any of that lyin' New Guinea dope on us again, don't yuh? Close that trap if yuh don't want a duckin' over the side.

COCKY: Ow, I was on'y tryin' to edicate yer a bit. [*He sinks into dignified silence.*]

YANK: [*Nodding toward the shore.*] Don't yuh know this is the West Indies, yuh crazy mut? There ain't no cannibals here. They're only common niggers.

DRISCOLL: [*Irritably.*] Whativir they are, the divil take their cryin'. It's enough to give a man the jigs listenin' to 'em.

YANK: [*With a grin.*] What's the matter, Drisc? Yuh're as sore as a boil about somethin'.

DRISCOLL: I'm dyin' wid impatience to have a dhrink; an' that blarsted bumboat naygur woman took her oath she'd bring back rum enough for the lot av us whin she came back on board tonight.

BIG FRANK: [*Overhearing this—in a loud eager voice.*] You say the bumboat voman vill bring booze?

DRISCOLL: [*Sarcastically.*] That's right—tell the Old Man about ut, an' the Mate, too. [*All of the crew have edged nearer to* DRISCOLL *and are listening to the conversation with an air of suppressed excitement.* DRISCOLL *lowers his voice impressively and addresses them all.*] She said she cud snake ut on board in the bottoms av thim baskets av fruit they're goin' to bring wid 'em to sell to us for'ard.

THE DONKEYMAN: [*An old gray-headed man with a kindly, wrinkled face. He is sitting on a camp stool in front of his door, right front.*] She'll be bringin' some black women with her this time—or times has changed since I put in here last.

DRISCOLL: She said she wud—two or three—more, maybe, I dunno. [*This announcement is received with great enthusiasm by all hands.*]

COCKY: Wot a bloody lark!

OLSON: Py yingo, we have one hell of a time!

DRISCOLL: [*Warningly.*] Remimber ye must be quiet about ut, ye scuts—wid the dhrink, I mane—ivin if the bo'sun is ashore. The Old Man ordered her to bring no booze on board or he wudn't buy a thing off av her for the ship.

PADDY: [*A squat, ugly Liverpool Irishman.*] To the divil wid him!

BIG FRANK: [*Turning on him.*] Shud up, you tamn fool, Paddy! You vant make trouble? [*To* DRISCOLL.] You und me, ve keep dem quiet, Drisc.

DRISCOLL: Right ye are, Dutchy. I'll split the skull av the first wan av ye starts to foight. [*Three bells are heard striking.*]

DAVIS: Three bells. When's she comin', Drisc?

DRISCOLL: She'll be here any minute now, surely. [*To* PAUL, *who has returned to his position by the bulwark after hearing* DRISCOLL'*s news.*] D'you see 'em comin', Paul?

PAUL: I don't see anyting like bumboat. [*They all set themselves to wait, lighting pipes, cigarettes, and making themselves comfortable. There is a silence broken only by the mournful singing of the negroes on shore.*]

SMITTY: [*Slowly—with a trace of melancholy.*] I wish they'd stop that song. It makes you think of—well—things you ought to forget. Rummy go, what?

COCKY: [*Slapping him on the back.*] Cheero, ole love! We'll be 'avin our rum in arf a mo', Duke. [*He comes down to the deck, leaving* SMITTY *alone on the forecastle head.*]

BIG FRANK: Sing someting, Drisc. Den ve don't hear dot yelling.

DAVIS: Give us a chanty, Drisc.

PADDY: Wan all av us knows.

MAX: We all sing in on chorus.

OLSON: "Rio Grande," Drisc.

BIG FRANK: No, ve don't know dot. Sing "Viskey Johnny."

CHIPS: "Flyin' Cloud."

COCKY: Now! Guv us "Maid o' Amsterdam."

LAMPS: "Santa Anna" iss good one.

DRISCOLL: Shut your mouths, all av you. [*Scornfully.*] A chanty is ut ye want? I'll bet me whole pay day there's not wan in the crowd 'ceptin' Yank here, an' Ollie, an' meself, an' Lamps an' Cocky, maybe, wud be sailors enough to know the main from the mizzen on a windjammer. Ye've heard the names av chanties but divil a note av the tune or a loine av the words do ye know. There's hardly a rale deep-water sailor lift on the seas, more's the pity.

YANK: Give us "Blow The Man Down." We all know some of that. [*A chorus of assenting voices:* Yes!—Righto!—Let 'er drive! Start 'er, Drisc! *etc.*]

DRISCOLL: Come in then, all av ye. [*He sings:*]
        As I was a-roamin' down Paradise Street—

ALL: Wa-a-ay, blow the man down!

DRISCOLL: As I was a-roamin' down Paradise Street—

ALL: Give us some time to blow the man down!

CHORUS

        Blow the man down, boys, oh, blow
            the man down!
        Wa-a-ay, blow the man down!
        As I was a-roamin' down Paradise
            Street—
            Give us some time to blow the
                man down!

DRISCOLL: A pretty young maiden I chanced for to meet.
ALL: Wa-a-ay, blow the man down!
DRISCOLL: A pretty young maiden I chanced for to meet.
ALL: Give us some time to blow the man down!

CHORUS

> Blow the man down, boys, oh, blow
>   the man down!
> Wa-a-ay, blow the man down!
> A pretty young maiden I chanced
>   for to meet.
> Give us some time to blow the
>   man down!

PAUL: [*Just as Driscoll is clearing his throat preparatory to starting the next verse.*] Hay, Drisc! Here she come, I tink. Some bumboat comin' dis way. [*They all rush to the side and look toward the land.*]
YANK: There's five or six of them in it—and they paddle like skirts.
DRISCOLL: [*Wildly elated.*] Hurroo, ye scuts! 'Tis thim right enough. [*He does a few jig steps on the deck.*]
OLSON: [*After a pause during which all are watching the approaching boat.*] Py yingo, I see six in boat, yes, sir.
DAVIS: I kin make out the baskets. See 'em there amidships?
BIG FRANK: Vot kind booze dey bring—viskey?
DRISCOLL: Rum, foine West Indy rum wid a kick in ut loike a mule's hoind leg.
LAMPS: Maybe she don't bring any; maybe skipper scare her.
DRISCOLL: Don't be throwin' cold water, Lamps. I'll skin her black hoide off av her if she goes back on her worrd.
YANK: Here they come. Listen to 'em gigglin'. [*Calling.*] Oh, you kiddo!
[*The sound of women's voices can be heard talking and laughing.*]
DRISCOLL: [*Calling.*] Is ut you, Mrs. Old Black Joe?
A WOMAN'S VOICE: Ullo, Mike! [*There is loud feminine laughter at this retort.*]
DRISCOLL: Shake a leg an' come abord thin.
THE WOMAN'S VOICE: We're a-comin'.
DRISCOLL: Come on, Yank. You an' me'd best be goin' to give 'em a hand wid their truck. 'Twill put 'em in good spirits.
COCKY: [*As they start off left.*] Ho, you ain't 'arf a fox, Drisc. Down't drink it all afore we sees it.

DRISCOLL: [*Over his shoulder.*] You'll be havin' yours, me sonny bye, don't fret. [*He and Yank go off left.*]

COCKY: [*Licking his lips.*] Gawd blimey, I can do wiv a wet.

DAVIS: Me, too!

CHIPS: I'll bet there ain't none of us'll let any go to waste.

BIG FRANK: I could trink a whole barrel mineself, py chimminy Christmas!

COCKY: I 'opes all the gels ain't as bloomin' ugly as 'er. Looked like a bloody organ-grinder's monkey, she did. Gawd, I couldn't put up wiv the likes of 'er!

PADDY: Ye'll be lucky if any of thim looks at ye, ye squint-eyed runt.

COCKY: [*Angrily.*] Ho, yus? You ain't no bleedin' beauty prize yeself, me man. A 'airy ape, I calls yer.

PADDY: [*Walking toward him—truculently.*] Whot's thot? Say ut again if ye dare.

COCKY: [*His hand on his sheath knife—snarling.*] 'Airy ape! That's wot I says! [PADDY *tries to reach him but the others keep them apart.*]

BIG FRANK: [*Pushing* PADDY *back.*] Vot's the matter mit you, Paddy. Don't you hear vat Driscoll say—no fighting?

PADDY: [*Grumblingly.*] I don't take no back talk from that deck-scrubbin' shrimp.

COCKY: Blarsted coal-puncher! [DRISCOLL *appears wearing a broad grin of satisfaction. The fight is immediately forgotten by the crowd who gather around him with exclamations of eager curiosity.* How is it, Drisc? Any luck? Vot she bring, Drisc? Where's the gels? *etc.*]

DRISCOLL: [*With an apprehensive glance back at the bridge.*] Not so loud, for the love av hivin! [*The clamor dies down.*] Yis, she has ut wid her. She'll be here in a minute wid a pint bottle or two for each wan av ye—three shillin's a bottle. So don't be impashunt.

COCKY: [*Indignantly.*] Three bob! The bloody cow!

SMITTY: [*With an ironic smile.*] Grand larceny, by God! [*They all turn and look up at him, surprised to hear him speak.*]

OLSON: Py yingo, we don't pay so much.

BIG FRANK: Tamn black tief!

PADDY: We'll take ut away from her and give her nothin'.

THE CROWD: [*Growling.*] Dirty thief! Dot's right! Give her nothin'! Not a bloomin' 'apenny! etc.

DRISCOLL: [*Grinning.*] Ye can take ut or lave ut, me sonny byes. [*He casts a glance in the direction of the bridge and then reaches inside his shirt and pulls out a pint bottle.*] 'Tis foine rum, the rale stuff. [*He drinks.*] I slipped this wan out av wan av the baskets whin they wasn't lookin'. [*He hands the bottle to* OLSON *who is nearest him.*]

Here ye are, Ollie. Take a small sup an' pass ut to the nixt. 'Tisn't much but 'twill serve to take the black taste out av your mouths if ye go aisy wid ut. An' there's buckets more av ut comin'. [*The bottle passes from hand to hand, each man taking a sip and smacking his lips with a deep "Aaah" of satisfaction.*]

DAVIS: Where's she now, Drisc?

DRISCOLL: Up havin' a worrd wid the skipper, makin' arrangements about the money, I s'pose.

DAVIS: An' where's the other gels?

DRISCOLL: Wid her. There's foive av thim she took aboard—two swate little slips av things, near as white as you an' me are, for that gray-whiskered auld fool, an' the mates—an' the engineers too, maybe. The rist av thim'll be comin' for'ard whin she comes.

COCKY: 'E ain't 'arf a funny ole bird, the skipper. Gawd blimey! 'Member when we sailed from 'ome 'ow 'e stands on the bridge lookin' like a bloody ole sky pilot? An' 'is missus dawn on the bloomin' dock 'owlin' fit to kill 'erself? An' 'is kids 'owlin' an' wavin' their 'andkerchiefs? [*With great moral indignation.*] An' 'ere 'e is makin' up to a bleedin' nigger! There's a captain for yer! Gawd blimey! Bloody crab, I calls 'im!

DRISCOLL: Shut up, ye insect! Sure, it's not you should be talkin', an' you wid a woman an' childer weepin' for ye in iviry divil's port in the wide worrld, if we can believe your own tale av ut.

COCKY: [*Still indignant.*] I ain't no bloomin' captain, I ain't. I ain't got no missus—reg'lar married, I means. I ain't——

BIG FRANK: [*Putting a huge paw over Cocky's mouth.*] You ain't going talk so much, you hear? [COCKY *wriggles away from him.*] Say, Drisc, how ve pay dis voman for booze? Ve ain't got no cash.

DRISCOLL: It's aisy enough. Each girl'll have a slip av paper wid her an' whin you buy anythin' you write ut down and the price beside ut and sign your name. If ye can't write have some one who can do ut for ye. An' rimimber this: Whin ye buy a bottle av dhrink or [*With a wink.*] somethin' else forbid, ye must write down tobaccy or fruit or somethin' the loike av that. Whin she laves the skipper'll pay what's owin' on the paper an' take ut out av your pay. Is ut clear to ye now?

ALL: Yes—Clear as day—Aw right, Drisc—Righto—Sure. etc.

DRISCOLL: An' don't forgit what I said about bein' quiet wid the dhrink, or the Mate'll be down on our necks an' spile the fun. [*A chorus of assent.*]

DAVIS: [*Looking aft.*] Ain't this them comin'? [*They all look in that direction. The silly laughter of a woman is heard.*]

DRISCOLL: Look at Yank, wud ye, wid his arrm around the middle av wan av thim. That lad's not wastin' any toime. [*The four women enter from the left, giggling and whispering to each other. The first three carry baskets on their heads. The youngest and best-looking comes last.* YANK *has his arm about her waist and is carrying her basket in his other hand. All four are distinct negro types. They wear light-colored, loose-fitting clothes and have bright bandana handkerchiefs on their heads. They put down their baskets on the hatch and sit down beside them. The men crowd around, grinning.*]

BELLA: [*She is the oldest, stoutest, and homeliest of the four—grinning back at them.*] 'Ullo, boys.

THE OTHER GIRLS: 'Ullo, boys.

THE MEN: Hello, yourself—Evenin'—Hello—How are you? etc.

BELLA: [*Genially.*] Hope you had a nice voyage. My name's Bella, this here's Susie, yander's Violet, and her there [*Pointing to the girl with* YANK] is Pearl. Now we all knows each other.

PADDY: [*Roughly.*] Never mind the girls. Where's the dhrink?

BELLA: [*Tartly.*] You're a hawg, ain't you? Don't talk so loud or you don't git any—you nor no man. Think I wants the ole captain to put me off the ship, do you?

YANK: Yes, nix on hollerin', you! D'yuh wanta queer all of us?

BELLA: [*Casting a quick glance over her shoulder.*] Here! Some of you big strapping boys sit back of us on the hatch there so's them officers can't see what we're doin'. [DRISCOLL *and several of the others sit and stand in back of the girls on the hatch.* BELLA *turns to* DRISCOLL.] Did you tell 'em they gotter sign for what they gits—and *how* to sign?

DRISCOLL: I did—what's your name again—oh, yis—Bella, darlin'.

BELLA: Then it's all right; but you boys has gotter go inside the fo'castle when you gits your bottle. No drinkin' out here on deck. I ain't takin' no chances. [*An impatient murmur of assent goes up from the crowd.*] Ain't that right, Mike?

DRISCOLL: Right as rain, darlin'. [BIG FRANK *leans over and says something to him in a low voice.* DRISCOLL *laughs and slaps his thigh.*] Listen, Bella, I've somethin' to ask ye for my little friend here who's bashful. Ut has to do wid the ladies so I'd best be whisperin' ut to ye meself to kape them from blushin. [*He leans over and asks her a question.*]

BELLA: [*Firmly.*] Four shillin's.

DRISCOLL: [*Laughing.*] D'you hear that, all av ye? Four shillin's ut is.

PADDY: [*Angrily.*] To hell wid this talkin'. I want a dhrink.

BELLA: Is everything all right, Mike?

DRISCOLL: [*After a look back at the bridge.*] Sure. Let her droive!

BELLA: All right, girls. [*The girls reach down in their baskets in under the fruit which is on top and each pulls out a pint bottle. Four of the men crowd up and take the bottles.*] Fetch a light, Lamps, that's a good boy. [LAMPS *goes to his room and returns with a candle. This is passed from one girl to another as the men sign the sheets of paper for their bottles.*] Don't you boys forget to mark down cigarettes or tobacco or fruit, remember! Three shillin's is the price. Take it into the fo'castle. For Gawd's sake, don't stand out here drinkin' in the moonlight. [*The four go into the forecastle. Four more take their places.* PADDY *plants himself in front of* PEARL *who is sitting by* YANK *with his arm still around her.*]

PADDY: [*Gruffly.*] Gimme thot! [*She holds out a bottle which he snatches from her hand. He turns to go away.*]

YANK: [*Sharply.*] Here, you! Where d'yuh get that stuff? You ain't signed for that yet.

PADDY: [*Sullenly.*] I can't write me name.

YANK: Then I'll write it for yuh. [*He takes the paper from* PEARL *and writes.*] There ain't goin' to be no welchin' on little Bright Eyes here—not when I'm around, see? Ain't I right, kiddo?

PEARL: [*With a grin.*] Yes, suh.

BELLA: [*Seeing all four are served.*] Take it into the fo'castle, boys. [PADDY *defiantly raises his bottle and gulps down a drink in the full moonlight.* BELLA *sees him.*] Look at 'im! Look at the dirty swine! [PADDY *slouches into the forecastle.*] Wants to git me in trouble. That settles it! We all got to git inside, boys, where we won't git caught. Come on, girls. [*The girls pick up their baskets and follow* BELLA. YANK *and* PEARL *are the last to reach the doorway. She lingers behind him, her eyes fixed on* SMITTY, *who is still sitting on the forecastle head, his chin on his hands, staring off into vacancy.*]

PEARL: [*Waving a hand to attract his attention.*] Come ahn in, pretty boy. Ah likes you.

SMITTY: [*Coldly.*] Yes; I want to buy a bottle, please. [*He goes down the steps and follows her into the forecastle. No one remains on deck but the* DONKEYMAN, *who sits smoking his pipe in front of his door. There is the subdued babble of voices from the crowd inside but the mournful cadence of the song from the shore can again be faintly heard.* SMITTY *reappears and closes the door to the forecastle after him. He shudders and shakes his shoulders as if flinging off some-*

*thing which disgusted him. Then he lifts the bottle which is in his
hand to his lips and gulps down a long drink.* THE DONKEYMAN
watches him impassively. SMITTY *sits down on the hatch facing him.
Now that the closed door has shut off nearly all the noise the singing
from shore comes clearly over the moonlit water.*]

SMITTY: [*Listening to it for a moment.*] Damn that song of theirs. [*He
takes another big drink.*] What do you say, Donk?

THE DONKEYMAN: [*Quietly.*] Seems nice an' sleepy-like.

SMITTY: [*With a hard laugh.*] Sleepy! If I listened to it long—sober—I'd
never go to sleep.

THE DONKEYMAN: 'Tain't sich bad music, is it? Sounds kinder pretty
to me—low an' mournful—same as listenin' to the organ outside o'
church of a Sunday.

SMITTY: [*With a touch of impatience.*] I didn't mean it was bad music.
It isn't. It's the beastly memories the damn thing brings up—for some
reason. [*He takes another pull at the bottle.*]

THE DONKEYMAN: Ever hear it before?

SMITTY: No; never in my life. It's just a something about the rotten
thing which makes me think of—well—oh, the devil! [*He forces a
laugh.*]

THE DONKEYMAN: [*Spitting placidly.*] Queer things, mem'ries. I ain't
ever been bothered much by 'em.

SMITTY: [*Looking at him fixedly for a moment—with quiet scorn.*] No,
you wouldn't be.

THE DONKEYMAN: Not that I ain't had my share o' things goin' wrong;
but I puts 'em out o' me mind, like, an' fergets 'em.

SMITTY: But suppose you couldn't put them out of your mind? Suppose
they haunted you when you were awake and when you were
asleep—what then?

THE DONKEYMAN: [*Quietly.*] I'd git drunk, same's you're doin'.

SMITTY: [*With a harsh laugh.*] Good advice. [*He takes another drink.
He is beginning to show the effects of the liquor. His face is flushed
and he talks rather wildly.*] We're poor little lambs who have lost our
way, eh, Donk? Damned from here to eternity, what? God have
mercy on such as we! True, isn't it, Donk?

THE DONKEYMAN: Maybe; I dunno. [*After a slight pause.*] Whatever
set you goin' to sea? You ain't made for it.

SMITTY: [*Laughing wildly.*] My old friend in the bottle here, Donk.

THE DONKEYMAN: I done my share o' drinkin' in my time. [*Regret-
fully.*] Them was good times, those days. Can't hold up under drink
no more. Doctor told me I'd got to stop or die. [*He spits content-
edly.*] So I stops.

SMITTY: [*With a foolish smile.*] Then I'll drink one for you. Here's your health, old top! [*He drinks.*]

THE DONKEYMAN: [*After a pause.*] S'pose there's a gel mixed up in it someplace, ain't there?

SMITTY: [*Stiffly.*] What makes you think so?

THE DONKEYMAN: Always is when a man lets music bother 'im. [*After a few puffs at his pipe.*] An' she said she threw you over 'cause you was drunk; an' you said you was drunk 'cause she threw you over. [*He spits leisurely.*] Queer thing, love, ain't it?

SMITTY: [*Rising to his feet with drunken dignity.*] I'll trouble you not to pry into my affairs, Donkeyman.

THE DONKEYMAN: [*Unmoved.*] That's everybody's affair, what I said. I been through it many's the time. [*Genially.*] I always hit 'em a whack on the ear an' went out and got drunker'n ever. When I come home again they always had somethin' special nice cooked fur me to eat. [*Puffing at his pipe.*] That's the on'y way to fix 'em when they gits on their high horse. I don't s'pose you ever tried that?

SMITTY: [*Pompously.*] Gentlemen don't hit women.

THE DONKEYMAN: [*Placidly.*] No; that's why they has mem'ries when they hears music. [SMITTY *does not deign to reply to this but sinks into a scornful silence.* DAVIS *and the girl* VIOLET *come out of the forecastle and close the door behind them. He is staggering a bit and she is laughing shrilly.*]

DAVIS: [*Turning to the left.*] This way, Rose, or Pansy, or Jessamine, or black Tulip, or Violet, or whatever the hell flower your name is. No one'll see us back here. [*They go off left.*]

THE DONKEYMAN: There's love at first sight for you—an' plenty more o' the same in the fo'c's'tle. No mem'ries jined with that.

SMITTY: [*Really repelled.*] Shut up, Donk. You're disgusting. [*He takes a long drink.*]

THE DONKEYMAN: [*Philosophically.*] All depends on how you was brung up, I s'pose. [PEARL *comes out of the forecastle. There is a roar of voices from inside. She shuts the door behind her, sees* SMITTY *on the hatch, and comes over and sits beside him and puts her arm over his shoulder.*]

THE DONKEYMAN: [*Chuckling.*] There's love for you, Duke.

PEARL: [*Patting* SMITTY's *face with her hand.*] 'Ullo, pretty boy. [SMITTY *pushes her hand away coldly.*] What you doin' out here all alone by yourself?

SMITTY: [*With a twisted grin.*] Thinking and,—[*He indicates the bottle in his hand.*]—drinking to stop thinking. [*He drinks and laughs maudlinly. The bottle is three-quarters empty.*]

PEARL: You oughtn't drink so much, pretty boy. Don' you know dat? You have big, big headache come mawnin'.

SMITTY: [*Dryly.*] Indeed?

PEARL: That's true. Ah knows what Ah say. [*Cooingly.*] Why you run 'way from me, pretty boy? Ah likes you. Ah don' like them other fellahs. They act too rough. You ain't rough. You're a genelman. Ah knows. Ah can tell a genelman fahs Ah can see 'im.

SMITTY: Thank you for the compliment; but you're wrong, you see. I'm merely—a ranker. [*He adds bitterly.*] And a rotter.

PEARL: [*Patting his arm.*] No, you ain't. Ah knows better. You're a genelman. [*Insinuatingly.*] Ah wouldn't have nothin' to do with them other men, but [*She smiles at him enticingly.*] you is diff'rent. [*He pushes her away from him disgustedly. She pouts.*] Don' you like me, pretty boy?

SMITTY: [*A bit ashamed.*] I beg your pardon. I didn't mean to be rude, you know, really. [*His politeness is drunkenly exaggerated.*] I'm a bit off color.

PEARL: [*Brightening up.*] Den you do like me—little ways?

SMITTY: [*Carelessly.*] Yes, yes, why shouldn't I? [*He suddenly laughs wildly and puts his arm around her waist and presses her to him.*] Why not? [*He pulls his arm back quickly with a shudder of disgust, and takes a drink. PEARL looks at him curiously, puzzled by his strange actions. The door from the forecastle is kicked open and YANK comes out. The uproar of shouting, laughing and singing voices has increased in violence. YANK staggers over toward SMITTY and PEARL.*]

YANK: [*Blinking at them.*] What the hell—oh, it's you, Smitty the Duke. I was goin' to turn one loose on the jaw of any guy'd cop my dame, but seein' it's you— [*Sentimentally.*] Pals is pals and any pal of mine c'n have anythin' I got, see? [*Holding out his hand.*] Shake, Duke. [*SMITTY takes his hand and he pumps it up and down.*] You'n me's frens. Ain't I right?

SMITTY: Right it is, Yank. But you're wrong about this girl. She isn't with me. She was just going back to the fo'c's'tle to you. [*PEARL looks at him with hatred gathering in her eyes.*]

YANK: Tha' right?

SMITTY: On my word!

YANK: [*Grabbing her arm.*] Come on then, you, Pearl! Le's have a drink with the bunch. [*He pulls her to the entrance where she shakes off his hand long enough to turn on SMITTY furiously.*]

PEARL: You swine! You can go to hell! [*She goes in the forecastle, slamming the door.*]

THE DONKEYMAN: [*Spitting calmly.*] There's love for you. They're all the same—white, brown, yeller 'n' black. A whack on the ear's the only thing'll learn 'em. [SMITTY *makes no reply but laughs harshly and takes another drink; then sits staring before him, the almost empty bottle tightly clutched in one hand. There is an increase in volume of the muffled clamor from the forecastle and a moment later the door is thrown open and the whole mob, led by Driscoll, pours out on deck. All of them are very drunk and several of them carry bottles in their hands.* BELLA *is the only one of the women who is absolutely sober. She tries in vain to keep the men quiet.* PEARL *drinks from* YANK's *bottle every moment or so, laughing shrilly, and leaning against* YANK, *whose arm is about her waist.* PAUL *comes out last carrying an accordion. He staggers over and stands on top of the hatch, his instrument under his arm.*]

DRISCOLL: Play us a dance, ye square-head swab!—a rale, Godforsaken son av a turkey trot wid guts to ut.

YANK: Straight from the old Barbary Coast in Frisco!

PAUL: I don' know. I try. [*He commences tuning up.*]

YANK: Ataboy! Let 'er rip! [DAVIS *and* VIOLET *come back and join the crowd.* THE DONKEYMAN *looks on them all with a detached, indulgent air.* SMITTY *stares before him and does not seem to know there is any one on deck but himself.*]

BIG FRANK: Dance? I don't dance. I trink! [*He suits the action to the word and roars with meaningless laughter.*]

DRISCOLL: Git out av the way thin, ye big hulk, an' give us some room. [BIG FRANK *sits down on the hatch, right. All of the others who are not going to dance either follow his example or lean against the port bulwark.*]

BELLA: [*On the verge of tears at her inability to keep them in the forecastle or make them be quiet now they are out.*] For Gawd's sake, boys, don't shout so loud! Want to git me in trouble?

DRISCOLL: [*Grabbing her.*] Dance wid me, me cannibal quane. [*Someone drops a bottle on deck and it smashes.*]

BELLA: [*Hysterically.*] There they goes! There they goes! Captain'll hear that! Oh, my Lawd!

DRISCOLL: Be damned to him! Here's the music! Off ye go! [PAUL *starts playing "You Great Big Beautiful Doll" with a note left out every now and then. The four couples commence dancing—a jerk-shouldered version of the old Turkey Trot as it was done in the sailor-town dives, made more grotesque by the fact that all the couples are drunk and keep lurching into each other every moment. Two of the men start dancing together, intentionally bumping into the others.* YANK *and* PEARL *come around in front of* SMITTY *and, as they pass him,* PEARL *slaps him across the side of the face with all her might, and laughs viciously. He jumps to his feet with his fists clenched but sees who hit him and sits down again smiling bitterly.* YANK *laughs boisterously.*]

YANK: Wow! Some wallop! One on you, Duke.

DRISCOLL: [*Hurling his cap at* PAUL.] Faster, ye toad! [PAUL *makes frantic efforts to speed up and the music suffers in the process.*]

BELLA: [*Puffing.*] Let me go. I'm wore out with you steppin' on my toes, you clumsy Mick. [*She struggles but Driscoll holds her tight.*]

DRISCOLL: God blarst you for havin' such big feet, thin. Aisy, aisy, Mrs. Old Black Joe! 'Tis dancin'll take the blubber off ye. [*He whirls her around the deck by main force.* COCKY, *with* SUSIE, *is dancing near the hatch, right, when* PADDY, *who is sitting on the edge with* BIG FRANK, *sticks his foot out and the wavering couple stumble over it and fall flat on the deck. A roar of laughter goes up.* COCKY *rises to his feet, his face livid with rage, and springs at* PADDY, *who promptly knocks him down.* DRISCOLL *hits* PADDY *and* BIG FRANK *hits* DRISCOLL. *In a flash a wholesale fight has broken out and the deck is a surging crowd of drink-maddened men hitting out at each other indiscriminately, although the general idea seems to be a battle between seamen and firemen. The women shriek and take refuge on top of the hatch, where they huddle in a frightened group. Finally there is the flash of a knife held high in the moonlight and a loud yell of pain.*]

DAVIS: [*Somewhere in the crowd.*] Here's the Mate comin'! Let's git out o' this! [*There is a general rush for the forecastle. In a moment there is no one left on deck but the little group of women on the hatch;* SMITTY, *still dazedly rubbing his cheek;* THE DONKEYMAN *quietly smoking on his stool; and* YANK *and* DRISCOLL, *their faces battered up considerably, their undershirts in shreds, bending over the still form of* PADDY, *which lies stretched out on the deck between them. In the silence the mournful chant from the shore creeps slowly out to the ship.*]

DRISCOLL: [*Quickly—in a low voice.*] Who knoifed him?

YANK: [*Stupidly.*] I didn't see it. How do I know? Cocky, I'll bet. [*The* FIRST MATE *enters from the left. He is a tall, strongly-built man.*]

THE MATE: [*Angrily.*] What's all this noise about? [*He sees the man lying on the deck dressed in a plain blue uniform.*] Hello! What's this? [*He bends down on one knee beside* PADDY.]

DRISCOLL: [*Stammering.*] All av us—was in a bit av a harmless foight, sir,—an'—I dunno—[*The* MATE *rolls* PADDY *over and sees a knife wound on his shoulder.*]

THE MATE: Knifed, by God. [*He takes an electric flash from his pocket and examines the cut.*] Lucky it's only a flesh wound. He must have hit his head on deck when he fell. That's what knocked him out. This is only a scratch. Take him aft and I'll bandage him up.

DRISCOLL: Yis, sor. [*They take* PADDY *by the shoulders and feet and carry him off left. The* MATE *looks up and sees the women on the hatch for the first time.*]

THE MATE: [*Surprised.*] Hello! [*He walks over to them.*] Go to the cabin and get your money and clear off. If I had my way, you'd never—— [*His foot hits a bottle. He stoops down and picks it up and smells of it.*] Rum, by God! So that's the trouble! I thought their breaths smelled damn queer. [*To the women, harshly.*] You needn't go to the skipper for any money. You won't get any. That'll teach you to smuggle rum on a ship and start a riot.

BELLA: But, Mister——

THE MATE: [*Sternly.*] You know the agreement—rum—no money.

BELLA: [*Indignantly.*] Honest to Gawd, Mister, I never brung no——

THE MATE: [*Fiercely.*] You're a liar! And none of your lip or I'll make a complaint ashore tomorrow and have you locked up.

BELLA: [*Subdued.*] Please, Mister—

THE MATE: Clear out of this, now! Not another word out of you! Tumble over the side damn quick! The two others are waiting for you. Hop, now! [*They walk quickly—almost run—off to the left.* THE MATE *follows them, nodding to* THE DONKEYMAN, *and ignoring the oblivious* SMITTY.]

[*There is absolute silence on the ship for a few moments. The melancholy song of the negroes drifts crooning over the water.* SMITTY *listens to it intently for a time; then sighs heavily, a sigh that is half a sob.*]

SMITTY: God! [*He drinks the last drop in the bottle and throws it behind him on the hatch.*]

THE DONKEYMAN: [*Spitting tranquilly.*] More mem'ries? [SMITTY *does not answer him. The ship's bell tolls four bells.* THE DONKEYMAN *knocks out his pipe.*] I think I'll turn in. [*He opens the door to his cabin, but turns to look at* SMITTY—*kindly.*] You can't hear it in the fo'c's'tle—the music, I mean—an' there'll likely be more drink in there, too. Good night. [*He goes in and shuts the door.*]

SMITTY: Good night, Donk. [*He gets wearily to his feet and walks with bowed shoulders, staggering a bit, to the forecastle entrance and goes in. There is silence for a second or so, broken only by the haunted, saddened voice of that brooding music, faint and far-off, like the mood of the moonlight made audible.*]

[*The Curtain Falls*]

BOUND EAST FOR CARDIFF

A PLAY IN ONE ACT

CHARACTERS

YANK
DRISCOLL
COCKY
DAVIS
SCOTTY
OLSON
PAUL
SMITTY
IVAN
THE CAPTAIN
THE SECOND MATE

BOUND EAST FOR CARDIFF

SCENE—*The seamen's forecastle of the British tramp steamer* Glencairn *on a foggy night midway on the voyage between New York and Cardiff. An irregular shaped compartment, the sides of which almost meet at the far end to form a triangle. Sleeping bunks about six feet long, ranged three deep with a space of three feet separating the upper from the lower, are built against the sides. On the right above the bunks three or four port holes can be seen. In front of the bunks, rough wooden benches. Over the bunks on the left, a lamp in a bracket. In the left foreground, a doorway. On the floor near it, a pail with a tin dipper. Oilskins are hanging from a hook near the doorway.*

The far side of the forecastle is so narrow that it contains only one series of bunks.

In under the bunks a glimpse can be had of seachests, suit cases, seaboots, etc., jammed in indiscriminately.

At regular intervals of a minute or so the blast of the steamer's whistle can be heard above all the other sounds.

Five men are sitting on the benches talking. They are dressed in dirty patched suits of dungaree, flannel shirts, and all are in their stocking feet. Four of the men are pulling on pipes and the air is heavy with rancid tobacco smoke. Sitting on the top bunk in the left foreground, a Norwegian, Paul, is softly playing some folk song on a battered accordion. He stops from time to time to listen to the conversation.

In the lower bunk in the rear a dark-haired, hard-featured man is lying apparently asleep. One of his arms is stretched limply over the side of the bunk. His face is very pale, and drops of clammy perspiration glisten on his forehead.

It is nearing the end of the dog watch—about ten minutes to eight in the evening.

COCKY: [*A weazened runt of a man. He is telling a story. The others are listening with amused, incredulous faces, interrupting him at the end of each sentence with loud derisive guffaws.*] Makin' love to me, she was! It's Gawd's truth! A bloomin' nigger! Greased all over with cocoanut oil, she was. Gawd blimey, I couldn't stand 'er. Bloody old cow, I says; and with that I fetched 'er a biff on the ear wot knocked 'er silly, an'— [*He is interrupted by a roar of laughter from the others.*]

21

DAVIS: [*A middle-aged man with black hair and mustache.*] You're a liar, Cocky.

SCOTTY: [*A dark young fellow.*] Ho-ho! Ye werr neverr in New Guinea in yourr life, I'm thinkin'.

OLSON: [*A Swede with a drooping blond mustache—with ponderous sarcasm.*] Yust tink of it! You say she wass a cannibal, Cocky?

DRISCOLL: [*A brawny Irishman with the battered features of a prize-fighter.*] How cud ye doubt ut, Ollie? A quane av the naygurs she musta been surely. Who else wud think herself aqual to fallin' in love wid a beauthiful, divil-may-care rake av a man the loike av Cocky? [*A burst of laughter from the crowd.*]

COCKY: [*Indignantly.*] Gawd strike me dead if it ain't true, every bleedin' word of it. 'Appened ten year ago come Christmas.

SCOTTY: 'Twas a Christmas dinner she had her eyes on.

DAVIS: He'd a been a tough old bird.

DRISCOLL: 'Tis lucky for both av ye ye escaped; for the quane av the cannibal isles wad 'a died av the belly ache the day afther Christmas, divil a doubt av ut. [*The laughter at this is long and loud.*]

COCKY: [*Sullenly.*] Blarsted fat 'eads! [*The sick man in the lower bunk in the rear groans and moves restlessly. There is a hushed silence. All the men turn and stare at him.*]

DRISCOLL: Ssshh! [*In a hushed whisper.*] We'd best not be talkin' so loud and him tryin' to have a bit av a sleep. [*He tiptoes softly to the side of the bunk.*] Yank! You'd be wantin' a drink av wather, maybe? [*YANK does not reply. DRISCOLL bends over and looks at him.*] It's asleep he is, sure enough. His breath is chokin' in his throat loike wather gurglin' in a poipe. [*He comes back quietly and sits down. All are silent, avoiding each other's eyes.*]

COCKY: [*After a pause.*] Pore devil! It's over the side for 'im, Gawd 'elp 'im.

DRISCOLL: Stop your croakin'! He's not dead yet and, praise God, he'll have many a long day yet before him.

SCOTTY: [*Shaking his head doubtfully.*] He's bod, mon, he's verry bod.

DAVIS: Lucky he's alive. Many a man's light woulda gone out after a fall like that.

OLSON: You saw him fall?

DAVIS: Right next to him. He and me was goin' down in number two hold to do some chippin'. He puts his leg over careless-like and misses the ladder and plumps straight down to the bottom. I was scared to look over for a minute, and then I heard him groan and I scuttled down after him. He was hurt bad inside for the blood was drippin' from the side of his mouth. He was groanin' hard, but he never let a word out of him.

COCKY: An' you blokes remember when we 'auled 'im in 'ere? Oh, 'ell, 'e says, oh, 'ell—like that, and nothink else.

OLSON: Did the captain know where he iss hurted?

COCKY: That silly ol' josser! Wot the 'ell would 'e know abaht anythink?

SCOTTY: [Scornfully.] He fiddles in his mouth wi' a bit of glass.

DRISCOLL: [Angrily.] The divil's own life ut is to be out on the lonely sea wid nothin' betune you and a grave in the ocean but a spindleshanked, gray-whiskered auld fool the loike av him. 'Twas enough to make a saint shwear to see him wid his gold watch in his hand, tryin' to look as wise as an owl on a tree, and all the toime he not knowin' whether 'twas cholery or the barber's itch was the matther wid Yank.

SCOTTY: [Sardonically.] He gave him a dose of salts, na doot?

DRISCOLL: Divil a thing he gave him at all, but looked in the book he had wid him, and shook his head, and walked out widout sayin' a word, the second mate afther him no wiser than himself, God's curse on the two av thim!

COCKY: [After a pause.] Yank was a good shipmate, pore beggar. Lend me four bob in Noo Yark, 'e did.

DRISCOLL: [Warmly.] A good shipmate he was and is, none betther. Ye said no more than the truth, Cocky. Five years and more ut is since first I shipped wid him, and we've stuck together iver since through good luck and bad. Fights we've had, God help us, but 'twas only when we'd a bit av drink taken, and we always shook hands the nixt mornin'. Whativer was his was mine, and many's the toime I'd a been on the beach or worse, but for him. And now— [His voice trembles as he fights to control his emotion.] Divil take me if I'm not startin' to blubber loike an auld woman, and he not dead at all, but goin' to live many a long year yet, maybe.

DAVIS: The sleep'll do him good. He seems better now.

OLSON: If he wude eat something—

DRISCOLL: Wud ye have him be eatin' in his condishun? Sure it's hard enough on the rest av us wid nothin' the matther wid our insides to be stomachin' the skoff on this rusty lime-juicer.

SCOTTY: [Indignantly.] It's a starvation ship.

DAVIS: Plenty o' work and no food—and the owners ridin' around in carriages!

OLSON: Hash, hash! Stew, stew! Marmalade, py damn! [He spits disgustedly.]

COCKY: Bloody swill! Fit only for swine is wot I say.

DRISCOLL: And the dishwather they disguise wid the name av tea! And the putty they call bread! My belly feels loike I'd swalleyed a dozen rivets at the thought av ut! And sea-biscuit that'd break the teeth av a lion if he had the misfortune to take a bite at one! [*Unconsciously they have all raised their voices, forgetting the sick man in their sailor's delight at finding something to grumble about.*]

PAUL: [*Swings his feet over the side of his bunk, stops playing his accordion, and says slowly*]: And rot-ten po-tay-toes! [*He starts in playing again. The sick man gives a groan of pain.*]

DRISCOLL: [*Holding up his hand.*] Shut your mouths, all av you. 'Tis a hell av a thing for us to be complainin' about our guts, and a sick man maybe dyin' listenin' to us. [*Gets up and shakes his fist at the Norwegian.*] God stiffen you, ye squarehead scut! Put down that organ av yours or I'll break your ugly face for you. Is that banshee schreechin' fit music for a sick man? [*The Norwegian puts his accordion in the bunk and lies back and closes his eyes. DRISCOLL goes over and stands beside YANK. The steamer's whistle sounds particularly loud in the silence.*]

DAVIS: Damn this fog! [*Reaches in under a bunk and yanks out a pair of seaboots, which he pulls on.*] My lookout next, too. Must be nearly eight bells, boys. [*With the exception of OLSON, all the men sitting up put on oilskins, sou'westers, seaboots, etc., in preparation for the watch on deck. OLSON crawls into a lower bunk on the right.*]

SCOTTY: My wheel.

OLSON: [*Disgustedly.*] Nothin' but yust dirty weather all dis voyage. I yust can't sleep when weestle blow. [*He turns his back to the light and is soon fast asleep and snoring.*]

SCOTTY: If this fog keeps up, I'm tellin' ye, we'll no be in Carrdiff for a week or more.

DRISCOLL: 'Twas just such a night as this the auld Dover wint down. Just about this toime ut was, too, and we all sittin' round in the fo'castle, Yank beside me, whin all av a suddint we heard a great slitherin' crash, and the ship heeled over till we was all in a heap on wan side. What came afther I disremimber exactly, except 'twas a hard shift to get the boats over the side before the auld teakittle sank. Yank was in the same boat wid me, and sivin morthal days we drifted wid scarcely a drop of wather or a bite to chew on. 'Twas Yank here that held me down whin I wanted to jump into the ocean, roarin' mad wid the thirst. Picked up we were on the same day wid only Yank in his senses, and him steerin' the boat.

COCKY: [*Protestingly.*] Blimey but you're a cheerful blighter, Driscoll! Talkin' abaht shipwrecks in this 'ere blushin' fog. [*YANK groans and stirs uneasily, opening his eyes. DRISCOLL hurries to his side.*]

DRISCOLL: Are ye feelin' any betther, Yank?

YANK: [*In a weak voice.*] No.

DRISCOLL: Sure, you must be. You look as sthrong as an ox. [*Appealing to the others.*] Am I tellin' him a lie?

DAVIS: The sleep's done you good.

COCKY: You'll be 'avin your pint of beer in Cardiff this day week.

SCOTTY: And fish and chips, mon!

YANK: [*Peevishly.*] What're yuh all lyin' fur? D'yuh think I'm scared to— [*He hesitates as if frightened by the word he is about to say.*]

DRISCOLL: Don't be thinkin' such things! [*The ship's bell is heard heavily tolling eight times. From the forecastle head above the voice of the lookout rises in a long wail: Aaall's welll. The men look uncertainly at* YANK *as if undecided whether to say good-by or not.*]

YANK: [*In an agony of fear.*] Don't leave me, DRISC! I'm dyin', I tell yuh. I won't stay here alone with every one snorin'. I'll go out on deck. [*He makes a feeble attempt to rise, but sinks back with a sharp groan. His breath comes in wheezy gasps.*] Don't leave me, Drisc! [*His face grows white and his head falls back with a jerk.*]

DRISCOLL: Don't be worryin', Yank. I'll not move a step out av here— and let that divil av a bosun curse his black head off. You speak a word to the bosun, Cocky. Tell him that Yank is bad took and I'll be stayin' wid him a while yet.

COCKY: Right-o. [COCKY, DAVIS, *and* SCOTTY *go out quietly.*]

COCKY: [*From the alleyway.*] Gawd blimey, the fog's thick as soup.

DRISCOLL: Are ye satisfied now, Yank? [*Receiving no answer, he bends over the still form.*] He's fainted, God help him! [*He gets a tin dipper from the bucket and bathes* YANK's *forehead with the water.* YANK *shudders and opens his eyes.*]

YANK: [*Slowly.*] I thought I was goin' then. Wha' did yuh wanta wake me up fur?

DRISCOLL: [*With forced gayety.*] Is it wishful for heaven ye are?

YANK: [*Gloomily.*] Hell, I guess.

DRISCOLL: [*Crossing himself involuntarily.*] For the love av the saints don't be talkin' loike that! You'd give a man the creeps. It's chippin' rust on deck you'll be in a day or two wid the best av us. [YANK *does not answer, but closes his eyes wearily. The seaman who has been on lookout,* SMITTY, *a young Englishman, comes in and takes off his dripping oilskins. While he is doing this the man whose turn at the wheel has been relieved enters. He is a dark burly fellow with a round stupid face. The Englishman steps softly over to* DRISCOLL. *The other crawls into a lower bunk.*]

SMITTY: [*Whispering.*] How's Yank?

DRISCOLL: Betther. Ask him yourself. He's awake.

YANK: I'm all right, Smitty.

SMITTY: Glad to hear it, Yank. [*He crawls to an upper bunk and is soon asleep.*]

IVAN: [*The stupid-faced seaman who came in after* SMITTY *twists his head in the direction of the sick man.*] You feel gude, Jank?

YANK: [*Wearily.*] Yes, Ivan.

IVAN: Dot's gude. [*He rolls over on his side and falls asleep immediately.*]

YANK: [*After a pause broken only by snores—with a bitter laugh.*] Good-by and good luck to the lot of you!

DRISCOLL: Is ut painin' you again?

YANK: It hurts like hell—here. [*He points to the lower part of his chest on the left side.*] I guess my old pump's busted. Ooohh! [*A spasm of pain contracts his pale features. He presses his hand to his side and writhes on the thin mattress of his bunk. The perspiration stands out in beads on his forehead.*]

DRISCOLL: [*Terrified.*] Yank! Yank! What is ut? [*Jumping to his feet.*] I'll run for the captain. [*He starts for the doorway.*]

YANK: [*Sitting up in his bunk, frantic with fear.*] Don't leave me, Drisc! For God's sake don't leave me alone! [*He leans over the side of his bunk and spits.* DRISCOLL *comes back to him.*] Blood! Ugh!

DRISCOLL: Blood again! I'd best be gettin' the captain.

YANK: No, no, don't leave me! If yuh do I'll git up and follow you. I ain't no coward, but I'm scared to stay here with all of them asleep and snorin'. [DRISCOLL, *not knowing what to do, sits down on the bench beside him. He grows calmer and sinks back on the mattress.*] The captain can't do me no good, yuh know it yourself. The pain ain't so bad now, but I thought it had me then. It was like a buzz-saw cuttin' into me.

DRISCOLL: [*Fiercely.*] God blarst ut!

[*The captain and the second mate of the steamer enter the fore-castle. The captain is an old man with gray mustache and whiskers. The mate is clean-shaven and middle-aged. Both are dressed in simple blue uniforms.*]

THE CAPTAIN: [*Taking out his watch and feeling* YANK's *pulse.*] And how is the sick man?

YANK: [*Feebly.*] All right, sir.

THE CAPTAIN: And the pain in the chest?

YANK: It still hurts, sir, worse than ever.

THE CAPTAIN: [*Taking a thermometer from his pocket and putting it into* YANK's *mouth.*] Here. Be sure and keep this in under your tongue, not over it.

THE MATE: [*After a pause.*] Isn't this your watch on deck, Driscoll?

DRISCOLL: Yes, sorr, but Yank was fearin' to be alone, and——

THE CAPTAIN: That's all right, Driscoll.

DRISCOLL: Thank ye, sorr.

THE CAPTAIN: [*Stares at his watch for a moment or so; then takes the thermometer from* YANK's *mouth and goes to the lamp to read it. His expression grows very grave. He beckons the* MATE *and* DRISCOLL *to the corner near the doorway.* YANK *watches them furtively. The* CAPTAIN *speaks in a low voice to the* MATE.] Way up, both of them. [*To* DRISCOLL]: Has he been spitting blood again?

DRISCOLL: Not much for the hour just past, sorr, but before that—

THE CAPTAIN: A great deal?

DRISCOLL: Yes, sorr.

THE CAPTAIN: He hasn't eaten anything?

DRISCOLL: No, sorr.

THE CAPTAIN: Did he drink that medicine I sent him?

DRISCOLL: Yes, sorr, but it didn't stay down.

THE CAPTAIN: [*Shaking his head.*] I'm afraid—he's very weak. I can't do anything else for him. It's too serious for me. If this had only happened a week later we'd be in Cardiff in time to—

DRISCOLL: Plaze help him some way, sorr!

THE CAPTAIN: [*Impatiently.*] But, my good man, I'm not a doctor. [*More kindly as he sees* DRISCOLL's *grief.*] You and he have been shipmates a long time?

DRISCOLL: Five years and more, sorr.

THE CAPTAIN: I see. Well, don't let him move. Keep him quiet and we'll hope for the best. I'll read the matter up and send him some medicine, something to ease the pain, anyway. [*Goes over to* YANK.] Keep up your courage! You'll be better to-morrow. [*He breaks down lamely before* YANK's *steady gaze.*] We'll pull you through all right—and—hm—well—coming, Robinson? Dammit! [*He goes out hurriedly, followed by the* MATE.]

DRISCOLL: [*Trying to conceal his anxiety.*] Didn't I tell you you wasn't half as sick as you thought you was? The Captain'll have you out on deck cursin' and swearin' loike a trooper before the week is out.

YANK: Don't lie, Drisc. I heard what he said, and if I didn't I c'd tell by the way I feel. I know what's goin' to happen. I'm goin' to— [*He hesitates for a second—then resolutely.*] I'm goin' to die, that's what, and the sooner the better!

DRISCOLL: [*Wildly.*] No, and be damned to you, you're not. I'll not let you.

YANK: It ain't no use, Drisc. I ain't got a chance, but I ain't scared. Gimme a drink of water, will yuh, Drisc? My throat's burnin' up. [DRISCOLL *brings the dipper full of water and supports his head while he drinks in great gulps.*]

DRISCOLL: [*Seeking vainly for some word of comfort.*] Are ye feelin' more aisy loike now?

YANK: Yes—now—when I know it's all up. [*A pause.*] You must'nt take it so hard, Drisc. I was just thinkin' it ain't as bad as people think— dyin'. I ain't never took much stock in the truck them sky-pilots preach. I ain't never had religion; but I know whatever it is what comes after it can't be no worser'n this. I don't like to leave you, Drisc, but—that's all.

DRISCOLL: [*With a groan.*] Lad, lad, don't be talkin'.

YANK: This sailor life ain't much to cry about leavin'—just one ship after another, hard work, small pay, and bum grub; and when we git into port, just a drunk endin' up in a fight, and all your money gone, and then ship away again. Never meetin' no nice people; never gittin' outa sailor town, hardly, in any port; travellin' all over the world and never seein' none of it; without no one to care whether you're alive or dead. [*With a bitter smile.*] There ain't much in all that that'd make yuh sorry to lose it, Drisc.

DRISCOLL: [*Gloomily.*] It's a hell av a life, the sea.

YANK: [*Musingly.*] It must be great to stay on dry land all your life and have a farm with a house of your own with cows and pigs and chickens, 'way in the middle of the land where yuh'd never smell the sea or see a ship. It must be great to have a wife, and kids to play with at night after supper when your work was done. It must be great to have a home of your own, Drisc.

DRISCOLL: [*With a great sigh.*] It must, surely; but what's the use av thinkin' av ut? Such things are not for the loikes av us.

YANK: Sea-farin' is all right when you're young and don't care, but we ain't chickens no more, and somehow, I dunno, this last year has seemed rotten, and I've had a hunch I'd quit—with you, of course— and we'd save our coin, and go to Canada or Argentine or some place and git a farm, just a small one, just enough to live on. I never told yuh this cause I thought you'd laugh at me.

DRISCOLL: [*Enthusiastically.*] Laugh at you, is ut? When I'm havin' the same thoughts myself, toime afther toime. It's a grand idea and we'll be doin' ut sure if you'll stop your crazy notions—about—about bein' so sick.

YANK: [*Sadly.*] Too late. We shouldn'ta made this trip, and then— How'd all the fog git in here?

DRISCOLL: Fog?

YANK: Everything looks misty. Must be my eyes gittin' weak, I guess. What was we talkin' of a minute ago? Oh, yes, a farm. It's too late. [*His mind wandering.*] Argentine, did I say? D'yuh remember the times we've had in Buenos Aires? The moving pictures in Barracas? Some class to them, d'yuh remember?

DRISCOLL: [*With satisfaction.*] I do that; and so does the piany player. He'll not be forgettin' the black eye I gave him in a hurry.

YANK: Remember the time we was there on the beach and had to go to Tommy Moore's boarding house to git shipped? And he sold us rotten oilskins and seaboots full of holes, and shipped us on a skysail yarder round the Horn, and took two months' pay for it. And the days we used to sit on the park benches along the Paseo Colon with the vigilantes lookin' hard at us? And the songs at the Sailor's Opera where the guy played ragtime—d'yuh remember them?

DRISCOLL: I do, surely.

YANK: And La Plata—phew, the stink of the hides! I always liked Argentine—all except that booze, caña. How drunk we used to git on that, remember?

DRISCOLL: Cud I forget ut? My head pains me at the menshun av that divil's brew.

YANK: Remember the night I went crazy with the heat in Singapore? And the time you was pinched by the cops in Port Said? And the time we was both locked up in Sydney for fightin'?

DRISCOLL: I do so.

YANK: And that fight on the dock at Cape Town— [*His voice betrays great inward perturbation.*]

DRISCOLL: [*Hastily.*] Don't be thinkin' av that now. 'Tis past and gone.

YANK: D'yuh think He'll hold it up against me?

DRISCOLL: [*Mystified.*] Who's that?

YANK: God. They say He sees everything. He must know it was done in fair fight, in self-defense, don't yuh think?

DRISCOLL: Av course. Ye stabbed him, and be damned to him, for the skulkin' swine he was, afther him tryin' to stick you in the back, and you not suspectin'. Let your conscience be aisy. I wisht I had nothin' blacker than that on my sowl. I'd not be afraid av the angel Gabriel himself.

YANK: [*With a shudder.*] I c'd see him a minute ago with the blood spurtin' out of his neck. Ugh!

DRISCOLL: The fever, ut is, that makes you see such things. Give no heed to ut.

YANK: [*Uncertainly.*] You don't think He'll hold it up agin me—God, I mean.

DRISCOLL: If there's justice in hiven, no! [YANK *seems comforted by this assurance.*]

YANK: [*After a pause.*] We won't reach Cardiff for a week at least. I'll be buried at sea.

DRISCOLL: [*Putting his hands over his ears.*] Ssshh! I won't listen to you.

YANK: [*As if he had not heard him.*] It's as good a place as any other, I s'pose—only I always wanted to be buried on dry land. But what the hell'll I care—then? [*Fretfully.*] Why should it be a rotten night like this with that damned whistle blowin' and people snorin' all round? I wish the stars was out, and the moon, too; I c'd lie out on deck and look at them, and it'd make it easier to go—somehow.

DRISCOLL: For the love av God don't be talkin' loike that!

YANK: Whatever pay's comin' to me yuh can divvy up with the rest of the boys; and you take my watch. It ain't worth much, but it's all I've got.

DRISCOLL: But have ye no relations at all to call your own?

YANK: No, not as I know of. One thing I forgot: You know Fanny the barmaid at the Red Stork in Cardiff?

DRISCOLL: Sure, and who doesn't?

YANK: She's been good to me. She tried to lend me half a crown when I was broke there last trip. Buy her the biggest box of candy yuh c'n find in Cardiff. [*Breaking down—in a choking voice.*] It's hard to ship on this voyage I'm goin' on—alone! [DRISCOLL *reaches out and grasps his hand. There is a pause, during which both fight to control themselves.*] My throat's like a furnace. [*He gasps for air.*] Gimme a drink of water, will yuh, Drisc? [DRISCOLL *gets him a dipper of water.*] I wish this was a pint of beer. Oooohh! [*He chokes, his face convulsed with agony, his hands tearing at his shirt front. The dipper falls from his nerveless fingers.*]

DRISCOLL: For the love av God, what is ut, Yank?

YANK: [*Speaking with tremendous difficulty.*] S'long, Drisc! [*He stares straight in front of him with eyes starting from their sockets.*] Who's that?

DRISCOLL: Who? What?

YANK: [*Faintly.*] A pretty lady dressed in black. [*His face twitches and his body writhes in a final spasm, then straightens out rigidly.*]

DRISCOLL: [*Pale with horror.*] Yank! Yank! Say a word to me for the love av hiven! [*He shrinks away from the bunk, making the sign of the cross. Then comes back and puts a trembling hand on* YANK's *chest and bends closely over the body.*]

COCKY: [*From the alleyway.*] Oh, Driscoll! Can you leave Yank for arf a mo' and give me a 'and?

DRISCOLL: [*With a great sob.*] Yank! [*He sinks down on his knees beside the bunk, his head on his hands. His lips move in some half-remembered prayer.*]

COCKY: [*Enters, his oilskins and sou'wester glistening with drops of water.*] The fog's lifted. [COCKY *sees* DRISCOLL *and stands staring at him with open mouth.* DRISCOLL *makes the sign of the cross again.*]

COCKY: [*Mockingly.*] Sayin' 'is prayers! [*He catches sight of the still figure in the bunk and an expression of awed understanding comes over his face. He takes off his dripping sou'wester and stands, scratching his head.*]

COCKY: [*In a hushed whisper.*] Gawd blimey!

[*The Curtain Falls*]

THE LONG VOYAGE HOME

A PLAY IN ONE ACT

CHARACTERS

FAT JOE, *proprietor of a dive.*

NICK, *a crimp.*

MAG, *a barmaid.*

OLSON
DRISCOLL
COCKY
IVAN
} *Seamen of the British tramp steamer,* Glencairn.

KATE

FREDA

TWO ROUGHS

THE LONG VOYAGE HOME

SCENE—*The bar of a low dive on the London water front—a squalid, dingy room dimly lighted by kerosene lamps placed in brackets on the walls. On the left, the bar. In front of it, a door leading to a side room. On the right, tables with chairs around them. In the rear, a door leading to the street.*

A slovenly barmaid with a stupid face sodden with drink is mopping off the bar. Her arm moves back and forth mechanically and her eyes are half shut as if she were dozing on her feet. At the far end of the bar stands FAT JOE, *the proprietor, a gross bulk of a man with an enormous stomach. His face is red and bloated, his little piggish eyes being almost concealed by rolls of fat. The thick fingers of his big hands are loaded with cheap rings and a gold watch chain of cable-like proportions stretches across his checked waistcoat.*

At one of the tables, front, a round-shouldered young fellow is sitting, smoking a cigarette. His face is pasty, his mouth weak, his eyes shifting and cruel. He is dressed in a shabby suit, which must have once been cheaply flashy, and wears a muffler and cap.

It is about nine o'clock in the evening.

JOE: [*Yawning.*] Blimey if bizness ain't 'arf slow to-night. I donnow wot's 'appened. The place is like a bleedin' tomb. Where's all the sailor men, I'd like to know? [*Raising his voice.*] Ho, you Nick! [NICK *turns around listlessly.*] Wot's the name o' that wessel put in at the dock below jest arter noon?

NICK: [*Laconically.*] Glencairn—from Bewnezerry. (Buenos Aires).

JOE: Ain't the crew been paid orf yet?

NICK: Paid orf this arternoon, they tole me. I 'opped on board of 'er an' seen 'em. 'Anded 'em some o' yer cards, I did. They promised faithful they'd 'appen in tonight—them as whose time was done.

JOE: Any two-year men to be paid orf?

NICK: Four—three Britishers an' a square-'ead.

JOE: [*Indignantly.*] An' yer popped orf an' left 'em? An' me a-payin' yer to 'elp an' bring 'em in 'ere!

NICK: [*Grumblingly.*] Much you pays me! An' I ain't slingin' me 'ook abaht the 'ole bleedin' town fur now man. See?

JOE: I ain't speakin' on'y fur meself. Down't I always give yer yer share, fair an' square, as man to man?

35

NICK: [*With a sneer.*] Yus—b'cause you 'as to.

JOE: 'As to? Listen to 'im! There's many'd be 'appy to 'ave your berth, me man!

NICK: Yus? Wot wiv the peelers li'ble to put me away in the bloody jail fur crimpin', an' all?

JOE: [*Indignantly.*] We down't do no crimpin'.

NICK: [*Sarcastically.*] Ho, now! Not arf!

JOE: [*A bit embarrassed.*] Well, on'y a bit now an' agen when there ain't no reg'lar trade. [*To hide his confusion he turns to the barmaid angrily. She is still mopping off the bar, her chin on her breast, half-asleep.*] 'Ere, me gel, we've 'ad enough o' that. You been a-moppin', an' a-moppin', an' a-moppin' the blarsted bar fur a 'ole 'our. 'Op it aht o' this! You'd fair guv a bloke the shakes a-watchin' yer.

MAG: [*Beginning to sniffle.*] Ow, you do frighten me when you 'oller at me, Joe. I ain't a bad gel, I ain't. Gawd knows I tries to do me best fur you. [*She bursts into a tempest of sobs.*]

JOE: [*Roughly.*] Stop yer grizzlin'! An' 'op it aht of 'ere!

NICK: [*Chuckling.*] She's drunk, Joe. Been 'ittin' the gin, eh, Mag?

MAG: [*Ceases crying at once and turns on him furiously.*] You little crab, you! Orter wear a muzzle, you ort! A-openin' of your ugly mouth to a 'onest woman what ain't never done you no 'arm. [*Commencing to sob again.*] H'abusin' me like a dawg cos I'm sick an' orf me oats, an' all.

JOE: Orf yer go, me gel! Go hupstairs an' 'ave a sleep. I'll wake yer if I wants yer. An' wake the two gels when yer goes hup. It's 'arpas' nine an' time as some one was a-comin' in, tell 'em. D'yer 'ear me?

MAG: [*Stumbling around the bar to the door on left—sobbing.*] Yus, yus, I 'ears you. Gawd knows wot's goin' to 'appen to me, I'm that sick. Much you cares if I dies, down't you? [*She goes out.*]

JOE: [*Still brooding over* NICK's *lack of diligence—after a pause.*] Four two-year men paid orf wiv their bloody pockets full o' sovereigns—an' yer lorst 'em. [*He shakes his head sorrowfully.*]

NICK: [*Impatiently.*] Stow it! They promised faithful they'd come, I tells yer. They'll be walkin' in in 'arf a mo'. There's lots o' time yet. [*In a low voice.*] 'Ave yer got the drops? We might wanter use 'em.

JOE: [*Taking a small bottle from behind the bar.*] Yus; 'ere it is.

NICK: [*With satisfaction.*] Righto! [*His shifty eyes peer about the room searchingly. Then he beckons to* JOE, *who comes over to the table and sits down.*] Reason I arst yer about the drops was 'cause I seen the capt'n of the Amindra this arternoon.

JOE: The Amindra? Wot ship is that?

NICK: Bloody windjammer—skys'l yarder—full rigged—painted white—been layin' at the dock above 'ere fur a month. You knows 'er.

JOE: Ho, yus. I knows now.

NICK: The capt'n says as 'e wants a man special bad—ternight. They sails at daybreak termorrer.

JOE: There's plenty o' 'ands lyin' abaht waitin' fur ships, I should fink.

NICK: Not fur this ship, ole buck. The capt'n an' mate are bloody slave-drivers, an' they're bound down round the 'Orn. They 'arf starved the 'ands on the larst trip 'ere, an' no one'll dare ship on 'er. [*After a pause.*] I promised the capt'n faithful I'd get 'im one, and ternight.

JOE: [*Doubtfully.*] An' 'ow are yer goin' to git 'im?

NICK: [*With a wink.*] I was thinkin' as one of 'em from the Glencairn'd do—them as was paid orf an' is comin' 'ere.

JOE: [*With a grin.*] It'd be a good 'aul, that's the troof. [*Frowning.*] If they comes 'ere.

NICK: They'll come, an' they'll all be rotten drunk, wait an' see. [*There is the noise of loud, boisterous singing from the street.*] Sounds like 'em, now. [*He opens the street door and looks out.*] Gawd blimey if it ain't the four of 'em! [*Turning to JOE in triumph.*] Naw, what d'yer say? They're lookin' for the place. I'll go aht an' tell 'em. [*He goes out. JOE gets into position behind the bar, assuming his most oily smile. A moment later the door is opened, admitting DRISCOLL, COCKY, IVAN and OLSON. DRISCOLL is a tall, powerful Irishman; COCKY, a wizened runt of a man with a straggling gray mustache; IVAN, a hulking oaf of a peasant; OLSON, a stocky, middle-aged Swede with round, childish blue eyes. The first three are all very drunk, especially IVAN, who is managing his legs with difficulty. OLSON is perfectly sober. All are dressed in their ill-fitting shore clothes and look very uncomfortable. DRISCOLL has unbuttoned his stiff collar and its ends stick out sideways. He has lost his tie. NICK slinks into the room after them and sits down at a table in rear. The seamen come to the table, front.*]

JOE: [*With affected heartiness.*] Ship ahoy, mates! 'Appy to see yer 'ome safe an' sound.

DRISCOLL: [*Turns round, swaying a bit, and peers at him across the bar.*] So ut's you, is ut? [*He looks about the place with an air of recognition.*] 'An the same damn rat's-hole, sure enough. I remimber foive or six years back 'twas here I was sthripped av me last shillin' whin I was aslape. [*With sudden fury.*] God stiffen ye, come none av your dog's thricks on me this trip or I'll— [*He shakes his fist at JOE.*]

JOE: [*Hastily interrupting.*] Yer must be mistaiken. This is a 'onest place, this is.

COCKY: [*Derisively.*] Ho, yus! An' you're a bleedin' angel, I s'pose?

IVAN: [*Vaguely taking off his derby hat and putting it on again—plaintively.*] I don' li-ike dis place.

DRISCOLL: [*Going over to the bar—as genial as he was furious a moment before.*] Well, no matther, 'tis all past an' gone an' forgot. I'm not the man to be holdin' harrd feelin's on me first night ashore, an' me dhrunk as a lord. [*He holds out his hand, which* JOE *takes very gingerly.*] We'll all be havin' a dhrink, I'm thinkin'. Whiskey for the three av us—*Irish* whiskey!

COCKY: [*Mockingly.*] An' a glarse o' ginger beer fur our blarsted love-child 'ere. [*He jerks his thumb at* OLSON.]

OLSON: [*With a good-natured grin.*] I bane a good boy dis night, for one time.

DRISCOLL: [*Bellowing, and pointing to* NICK *as* JOE *brings the drinks to the table.*] An' see what that crimpin' son av a crimp'll be wantin'—an' have your own pleasure. [*He pulls a sovereign out of his pocket and slams it on the bar.*]

NICK: Guv me a pint o' beer, Joe. [JOE *draws the beer and takes it down to the far end of the bar.* NICK *comes over to get it and* JOE *gives him a significant wink and nods toward the door on the left.* NICK *signals back that he understands.*]

COCKY: [*Drink in hand—impatiently.*] I'm that bloody dry! [*Lifting his glass to* DRISCOLL.] Cheero, ole dear, cheero!

DRISCOLL: [*Pocketing his change without looking at it.*] A toast for ye: Hell roast that divil av a bo'sun! [*He drinks.*]

COCKY: Righto! Gawd strike 'im blind! [*He drains his glass.*]

IVAN: [*Half-asleep.*] Dot's gude. [*He tosses down his drink in one gulp.* OLSON *sips his ginger ale.* NICK *takes a swallow of his beer and then comes round the bar and goes out the door on left.*]

COCKY: [*Producing a sovereign.*] Ho there, you Fatty! Guv us another!

JOE: The saime, mates?

COCKY: Yus.

DRISCOLL: No, ye scut! I'll be havin' a pint av beer. I'm dhry as a loime kiln.

IVAN: [*Suddenly getting to his feet in a befuddled manner and nearly upsetting the table.*] I don' li-ike dis place! I wan' see girls—plenty girls. [*Pathetically.*] I don't li-ike dis place. I wan' dance with girl.

DRISCOLL: [*Pushing him back on his chair with a thud.*] Shut up, ye Rooshan baboon! A foine Romeo you'd make in your condishun. [IVAN *blubbers some incoherent protest—then suddenly falls asleep.*]

JOE: [*Bringing the drinks—looks at* OLSON.] An' you, matey?

OLSON: [*Shaking his head.*] Noting dis time, thank you.

COCKY: [*Mockingly.*] A-saivin' of 'is money, 'e is! Goin' back to 'ome an' mother. Goin' to buy a bloomin' farm an' punch the blarsted dirt, that's wot 'e is! [*Spitting disgustedly.*] There's a funny bird of a sailor man for yer, Gawd blimey!

OLSON: [*Wearing the same good-natured grin.*] Yust what I like, Cocky. I wus on farm long time when I wus kid.

DRISCOLL: Lave him alone, ye bloody insect! 'Tis a foine sight to see a man wid some sense in his head instead av a damn fool the loike av us. I only wisht I'd a mother alive to call me own. I'd not be dhrunk in this divil's hole this minute, maybe.

COCKY: [*Commencing to weep dolorously.*] Ow, down't talk, Drisc! I can't bear to 'ear you. I ain't never 'ad no mother, I ain't—

DRISCOLL: Shut up, ye ape, an' don't be makin' that squealin'. If ye cud see your ugly face, wid the big red nose av ye all screwed up in a knot, ye'd never shed a tear the rist av your loife. [*Roaring into song.*] We ar-re the byes av We-e-exford who fought wid hearrt an' hand! [*Speaking.*] To hell wid Ulster! [*He drinks and the others follow his example.*] An' I'll strip to any man in the city av London won't dhrink to that toast. [*He glares truculently at* JOE, *who immediately downs his beer.* NICK *enters again from the door on the left and comes up to* JOE *and whispers in his ear. The latter nods with satisfaction.*]

DRISCOLL: [*Glowering at them.*] What divil's thrick are ye up to now, the two av ye? [*He flourishes a brawny fist.*] Play fair wid us or ye deal wid me!

JOE: [*Hastily.*] No trick, shipmate! May Gawd kill me if that ain't troof!

NICK: [*Indicating* IVAN, *who is snoring.*] On'y your mate there was ar-skin' fur gels an' I thorght as 'ow yer'd like 'em to come dawhn and 'ave a wet wiv yer.

JOE: [*With a smirking wink.*] Pretty, 'olesome gels they be, ain't they, Nick?

NICK: Yus.

COCKY: Aar! I knows the gels you 'as, not 'arf! They'd fair blind yer, they're that 'omely. None of yer bloomin' gels fur me, ole Fatty. Me an' Drisc knows a place, down't we, Drisc?

DRISCOLL: Divil a lie, we do. An' we'll be afther goin' there in a minute. There's music there an' a bit av a dance to liven a man.

JOE: Nick, 'ere, can play yer a tune, can't yer, Nick?

NICK: Yus.

JOE: An' yer can 'ave a dance in the side room 'ere.

DRISCOLL: Hurroo! Now you're talkin'. [*The two women,* FREDA *and* KATE, *enter from the left.* FREDA *is a little, sallow-faced blonde.* KATE *is stout and dark.*]

COCKY: [*In a loud aside to* DRISCOLL.] Gawd blimey, look at 'em! Ain't they 'orrible? [*The women come forward to the table, wearing their best set smiles.*]

FREDA: [*In a raspy voice.*] 'Ullo, mates.

KATE: 'Ad a good voyage?

DRISCOLL: Rotten; but no matther. Welcome, as the sayin' is, an' sit down, an' what'll ye be takin' for your thirst? [*To* KATE.] You'll be sittin' by me, darlin'—what's your name?

KATE: [*With a stupid grin.*] Kate. [*She stands by his chair.*]

DRISCOLL: [*Putting his arm around her.*] A good Irish name, but you're English by the trim av ye, an' be damned to you. But no matther. Ut's fat ye are, Katy dear, an' I never cud endure skinny wimin. [FREDA *favors him with a viperish glance and sits down by* OLSON.] What'll ye have?

OLSON: No, Drisc. Dis one bane on me. [*He takes out a roll of notes from his inside pocket and lays one on the table.* JOE, NICK, *and the women look at the money with greedy eyes.* IVAN *gives a particularly violent snore.*]

FREDA: Waike up your fren'. Gawd, 'ow I 'ates to 'ear snorin'.

DRISCOLL: [*Springing to action, smashes* IVAN's *derby over his ears.*] D'you hear the lady talkin' to ye, ye Rooshan swab? [*The only reply to this is a snore.* DRISCOLL *pulls the battered remains of the derby off* IVAN's *head and smashes it back again.*] Arise an' shine, ye dhrunken swine! [*Another snore. The women giggle.* DRISCOLL *throws the beer left in his glass into* IVAN's *face. The Russian comes to in a flash, spluttering. There is a roar of laughter.*]

IVAN: [*Indignantly.*] I tell you—dot's someting I don' li-ike!

COCKY: Down't waste good beer, Drisc.

IVAN: [*Grumblingly.*] I tell you—dot is not ri-ight.

DRISCOLL: Ut's your own doin', Ivan. Ye was moanin' for girrls an' whin they come you sit gruntin' loike a pig in a sty. Have ye no manners? [IVAN *seems to see the women for the first time and grins foolishly.*]

KATE: [*Laughing at him.*] Cheero, ole chum, 'ows Russha?

IVAN: [*Greatly pleased—putting his hand in his pocket.*] I buy a drink.

OLSON: No; dis one bane on me. [*To* JOE.] Hey, you faller!

JOE: Wot'll it be, Kate?

KATE: Gin.

FREDA: Brandy.

DRISCOLL: An' Irish whiskey for the rist av us—wid the excipshun av our timperance friend, God pity him!

FREDA: [*To* OLSON.] You ain't drinkin'?

OLSON: [*Half-ashamed.*] No.

FREDA: [*With a seductive smile.*] I down't blame yer. You got sense, you 'ave. I on'y tike a nip o' brandy now an' agen fur my 'ealth. [JOE *brings the drinks and* OLSON's *change.* COCKY *gets unsteadily to his feet and raises his glass in the air.*]

COCKY: 'Ere's a toff toast for yer: The ladies, Gawd— [*He hesitates— then adds in a grudging tone.*]—bless 'em.

KATE: [*With a silly giggle.*] Oo-er! That wasn't what you was goin' to say, you bad Cocky, you! [*They all drink.*]

DRISCOLL: [*To* NICK.] Where's the tune ye was promisin' to give us?

NICK: Come ahn in the side 'ere an' you'll 'ear it.

DRISCOLL: [*Getting up.*] Come on, all av ye. We'll have a tune an' a dance if I'm not too dhrunk to dance, God help me. [COCKY *and* IVAN *stagger to their feet.* IVAN *can hardly stand. He is leering at* KATE *and snickering to himself in a maudlin fashion. The three, led by* NICK, *go out the door on the left.* KATE *follows them.* OLSON *and* FREDA *remain seated.*]

COCKY: [*Calling over his shoulder.*] Come on an' dance, Ollie.

OLSON: Yes, I come. [*He starts to get up. From the side room comes the sound of an accordion and a boisterous whoop from* DRISCOLL, *followed by a heavy stamping of feet.*]

FREDA: Ow, down't go in there. Stay 'ere an' 'ave a talk wiv me. They're all drunk an' you ain't drinkin'. [*With a smile up into his face.*] I'll think yer don't like me if yer goes in there.

OLSON: [*Confused.*] You wus wrong, Miss Freda. I don't—I mean I do like you.

FREDA: [*Smiling—puts her hand over his on the table.*] An' I likes you. Yer a genelman. You don't get drunk an' hinsult poor gels wot 'as a 'ard an' uneppy life.

OLSON: [*Pleased but still more confused—wriggling his feet.*] I bane drunk many time, Miss Freda.

FREDA: Then why ain't yer drinkin' now? [*She exchanges a quick, questioning glance with* JOE, *who nods back at her—then she continues persuasively.*] Tell me somethin' abaht yeself.

OLSON: [*With a grin.*] There ain't noting to say, Miss Freda. I bane poor devil sailor man, dat's all.

FREDA: Where was you born—Norway? [OLSON *shakes his head.*] Denmark?

OLSON: No. You guess once more.

FREDA: Then it must be Sweden.

OLSON: Yes. I wus born in Stockholm.

FREDA: [*Pretending great delight.*] Ow, ain't that funny! I was born there, too—in Stockholm.

OLSON: [*Astonished.*] You wus born in Sweden?

FREDA: Yes; you wouldn't think it, but it's Gawd's troof. [*She claps her hands delightedly.*]

OLSON: [*Beaming all over.*] You speak Swedish?

FREDA: [*Trying to smile sadly.*] Now. Y'see my ole man an' woman come 'ere to England when I was on'y a baby an' they was speakin' English b'fore I was old enough to learn. Sow I never knew Swedish. [*Sadly.*] Wisht I 'ad! [*With a smile.*] We'd 'ave a bloomin' lark of it if I 'ad, wouldn't we?

OLSON: It sound nice to hear the old talk yust once in a time.

FREDA: Righto! No place like yer 'ome, I says. Are yer goin' up to—to Stockholm b'fore yer ships away agen?

OLSON: Yes. I go home from here to Stockholm. [*Proudly.*] As passenger!

FREDA: An' you'll git another ship up there arter you've 'ad a vacation?

OLSON: No. I don't never ship on sea no more. I got all sea I want for my life—too much hard work for little money. Yust work, work, work on ship. I don't want more.

FREDA: Ow, I see. That's why you give up drinkin'.

OLSON: Yes. [*With a grin.*] If I drink I yust get drunk and spend all money.

FREDA: But if you ain't gointer be a sailor no more, what'll yer do? You been a sailor all yer life, ain't yer?

OLSON: No. I work on farm till I am eighteen. I like it, too—it's nice—work on farm.

FREDA: But ain't Stockholm a city same's London? Ain't no farms there, is there?

OLSON: We live—my brother and mother live—my father iss dead—on farm yust a little way from Stockholm. I have plenty money, now. I go back with two years' pay and buy more land yet; work on farm. [*Grinning.*] No more sea, no more bum grub, no more storms—yust nice work.

FREDA: Ow, ain't that luv'ly! I s'pose you'll be gittin' married, too?

OLSON: [*Very much confused.*] I don't know. I like to, if I find nice girl, maybe.

FREDA: Ain't yer got some gel back in Stockholm? I bet yer 'as.

OLSON: No. I got nice girl once before I go on sea. But I go on ship, and I don't come back, and she marry other faller. [*He grins sheepishly.*]

FREDA: Well, it's nice for yer to be goin' 'ome, anyway.

OLSON: Yes. I tank so. [*There is a crash from the room on left and the music abruptly stops. A moment later* COCKY *and* DRISCOLL *appear, supporting the inert form of* IVAN *between them. He is in the last stage of intoxication, unable to move a muscle.* NICK *follows them and sits down at the table in rear.*]

DRISCOLL: [*As they zigzag up to the bar.*] Ut's dead he is, I'm thinkin', for he's as limp as a blarsted corpse.

COCKY: [*Puffing.*] Gawd, 'e ain't 'arf 'eavy!

DRISCOLL: [*Slapping* IVAN's *face with his free hand.*] Wake up, ye divil, ye. Ut's no use. Gabriel's trumpet itself cudn't rouse him. [*To* JOE.] Give us a dhrink for I'm perishing wid the thirst. 'Tis harrd worrk, this.

JOE: Whiskey?

DRISCOLL: *Irish* whiskey, ye swab. [*He puts down a coin on the bar.* JOE *serves* COCKY *and* DRISCOLL. *They drink and then swerve over to* OLSON's *table.*]

OLSON: Sit down and rest for time, Drisc.

DRISCOLL: No, Ollie, we'll be takin' this lad home to his bed. Ut's late for wan so young to be out in the night. An' I'd not trust him in this hole as dhrunk as he is, an' him wid a full pay day on him. [*Shaking his fist at* JOE.] Oho, I know your games, me sonny bye!

JOE: [*With an air of grievance.*] There yer goes again—hinsultin' a 'onest man!

COCKY: Ho, listen to 'im! Guv 'im a shove in the marf, Drisc.

OLSON: [*Anxious to avoid a fight—getting up.*] I help you take Ivan to boarding house.

FREDA: [*Protestingly.*] Ow, you ain't gointer leave me, are yer? An' we 'avin' sech a nice talk, an' all.

DRISCOLL: [*With a wink.*] Ye hear what the lady says, Ollie. Ye'd best stay here, me timperance lady's man. An' we need no help. 'Tis only a bit av a way and we're two strong men if we are dhrunk. Ut's no hard shift to take the remains home. But ye can open the door for us, Ollie. [OLSON *goes to the door and opens it.*] Come on, Cocky, an' don't be fallin' aslape yourself. [*They lurch toward the door. As they go out* DRISCOLL *shouts back over his shoulder.*] We'll be comin' back in a short time, surely. So wait here for us, Ollie.

OLSON: All right. I wait here, Drisc. [*He stands in the doorway uncertainly.* JOE *makes violent signs to* FREDA *to bring him back. She goes over and puts her arm around* OLSON's *shoulder.* JOE *motions to* NICK *to come to the bar. They whisper together excitedly.*]

FREDA: [*Coaxingly.*] You ain't gointer leave me, are yer, dearie? [*Then irritably.*] Fur Gawd's sake, shet that door! I'm fair freezin' to death wiv the fog. [OLSON *comes to himself with a start and shuts the door.*]

OLSON: [*Humbly.*] Excuse me, Miss Freda.

FREDA: [*Leading him back to the table—coughing.*] Buy me a drink o' brandy, will yer? I'm sow cold.

OLSON: All you want, Miss Freda, all you want. [*To* JOE, *who is still whispering instructions to* NICK.] Hey, Yoe! Brandy for Miss Freda. [*He lays a coin on the table.*]

JOE: Righto! [*He pours out her drink and brings it to the table.*] 'Avin' somethink yeself, shipmate?

OLSON: No. I don't tank so. [*He points to his glass with a grin.*] Dis iss only belly-wash, no? [*He laughs.*]

JOE: [*Hopefully.*] 'Ave a man's drink.

OLSON: I would like to—but no. If I drink one I want drink one tousand. [*He laughs again.*]

FREDA: [*Responding to a vicious nudge from* JOE's *elbow.*] Ow, tike somethin'. I ain't gointer drink all be meself.

OLSON: Den give me a little yinger beer—small one. [JOE *goes back of the bar, making a sign to* NICK *to go to their table.* NICK *does so and stands so that the sailor cannot see what* JOE *is doing.*]

NICK: [*To make talk.*] Where's yer mates popped orf ter? [JOE *pours the contents of the little bottle into* OLSON's *glass of ginger beer.*]

OLSON: Dey take Ivan, dat drunk faller, to bed. They come back. [JOE *brings* OLSON's *drink to the table and sets it before him.*]

JOE: [*To* NICK—*angrily.*] 'Op it, will yer? There ain't no time to be dawdlin'. See? 'Urry!

NICK: Down't worry, ole bird, I'm orf. [*He hurries out the door.* JOE *returns to his place behind the bar.*]

OLSON: [*After a pause—worriedly.*] I tank I should go after dem. Cocky iss very drunk, too, and Drisc—

FREDA: Aar! The big Irish is all right. Don't yer 'ear 'im say as 'ow they'd surely come back 'ere, an' fur you to wait fur 'em?

OLSON: Yes; but if dey don't come soon I tank I go see if dey are in boarding house all right.

FREDA: Where is the boardin' 'ouse?

OLSON: Yust little way back from street here.

FREDA: You stayin' there, too?

OLSON: Yes—until steamer sail for Stockholm—in two day.

FREDA: [*She is alternately looking at* JOE *and feverishly trying to keep* OLSON *talking so he will forget about going away after the others.*] Yer mother won't be arf glad to see yer agen, will she? [OLSON *smiles.*] Does she know yer comin'?

OLSON: No. I tought I would yust give her surprise. I write to her from Bonos Eres but I don't tell her I come home.

FREDA: Must be old, ain't she, yer ole lady?

OLSON: She iss eighty-two. [*He smiles reminiscently.*] You know, Miss Freda, I don't see my mother or my brother in—let me tank— [*He counts laboriously on his fingers.*] must be more than ten year. I write once in while and she write many time; and my brother he write me, too. My mother say in all letter I should come home right away. My brother he write same ting, too. He want me to help him on farm. I write back always I come soon; and I mean all time to go back home at end of voyage. But I come ashore, I take one drink, I take many drinks, I get drunk, I spend all money, I have to ship away for other voyage. So dis time I say to myself: Don't drink one drink, Ollie, or, sure, you don't get home. And I want go home dis time. I feel homesick for farm and to see my people again. [*He smiles.*] Yust like little boy, I feel homesick. Dat's why I don't drink noting to-night but dis—belly-wash! [*He roars with childish laughter, then suddenly becomes serious.*] You know, Miss Freda, my mother get very old, and I want see her. She might die and I would never—

FREDA: [*Moved a lot in spite of herself.*] Ow, don't talk like that! I jest 'ates to 'ear any one speakin' abaht dyin'. [*The door to the street is opened and* NICK *enters, followed by two rough-looking, shabbily-dressed men, wearing mufflers, with caps pulled down over their eyes. They sit at the table nearest to the door.* JOE *brings them three beers, and there is a whispered consultation, with many glances in the direction of* OLSON.]

OLSON: [*Starting to get up—worriedly.*] I tank I go round to boarding house. I tank someting go wrong with Drisc and Cocky.

FREDA: Ow, down't go. They kin take care of theyselves. They ain't babies. Wait 'arf a mo'. You ain't 'ad yer drink yet.

JOE: [*Coming hastily over to the table, indicates the men in the rear with a jerk of his thumb.*] One of them blokes wants yer to 'ave a wet wiv 'im.

FREDA: Righto! [*To* OLSON.] Let's drink this. [*She raises her glass. He does the same.*] 'Ere's a toast fur yer: Success to yer bloomin' farm an' may yer live long an' 'appy on it. Skoal! [*She tosses down her brandy. He swallows half his glass of ginger beer and makes a wry face.*]

OLSON: Skoal! [*He puts down his glass.*]

FREDA: [*With feigned indignation.*] Down't yer like my toast?

OLSON: [*Grinning.*] Yes. It iss very kind, Miss Freda.

FREDA: Then drink it all like I done.

OLSON: Well— [*He gulps down the rest.*] Dere! [*He laughs.*]

FREDA: Done like a sport!

ONE OF THE ROUGHS: [*With a laugh.*] Amindra, ahoy!

NICK: [*Warningly.*] Sssshh!

OLSON: [*Turns around in his chair.*] Amindra? Iss she in port? I sail on her once long time ago—three mast, full rig, skys'l yarder? Iss dat ship you mean?

THE ROUGH: [*Grinning.*] Yus; right you are.

OLSON: [*Angrily.*] I know dat damn ship—worst ship dat sail to sea. Rotten grub and dey make you work all time—and the Captain and Mate wus Bluenose devils. No sailor who know anyting ever ship on her. Where iss she bound from here?

THE ROUGH: Round Cape 'Orn—sails at daybreak.

OLSON: Py yingo, I pity poor fallers make dat trip round Cape Stiff dis time year. I bet you some of dem never see port once again. [*He passes his hand over his eyes in a dazed way. His voice grows weaker.*] Py golly, I feel dizzy. All the room go round and round like I wus drunk. [*He gets weakly to his feet.*] Good night, Miss Freda. I bane feeling sick. Tell Drisc—I go home. [*He takes a step forward and suddenly collapses over a chair, rolls to the floor, and lies there unconscious.*]

JOE: [*From behind the bar.*] Quick, nawh! [NICK *darts forward with* JOE *following.* FREDA *is already beside the unconscious man and has taken the roll of money from his inside pocket. She strips off a note furtively and shoves it into her bosom, trying to conceal her action, but* JOE *sees her. She hands the roll to* JOE, *who pockets it.* NICK *goes through all the other pockets and lays a handful of change on the table.*]

JOE: [*Impatiently.*] 'Urry, 'urry, can't yer? The other blokes'll be 'ere in 'arf a mo'. [*The two roughs come forward.*] 'Ere, you two, tike 'im in under the arms like 'e was drunk. [*They do so.*] Tike 'im to the Amindra—yer knows that, don't yer?—two docks above. Nick'll show yer. An' you, Nick, down't yer leave the bleedin' ship till the capt'n guvs yer this bloke's advance—full month's pay—five quid, d'yer 'ear?

NICK: I knows me bizness, ole bird. [*They support* OLSON *to the door.*]

THE ROUGH: [*As they are going out.*] This silly bloke'll 'ave the s'prise of 'is life when 'e wakes up on board of 'er. [*They laugh. The door closes behind them.* FREDA *moves quickly for the door on the left but* JOE *gets in her way and stops her.*]

JOE: [*Threateningly.*] Guv us what yer took!

FREDA: Took? I guv yer all 'e 'ad.

JOE: Yer a liar! I seen yer a-playin' yer sneakin' tricks, but yer can't fool Joe. I'm too old a 'and. [*Furiously.*] Guv it to me, yer bloody cow! [*He grabs her by the arm.*]

FREDA: Lemme alone! I ain't got no—

JOE: [*Hits her viciously on the side of the jaw. She crumples up on the floor.*] That'll learn yer! [*He stoops down and fumbles in her bosom and pulls out the banknote, which he stuffs into his pocket with a grunt of satisfaction.* KATE *opens the door on the left and looks in— then rushes to* FREDA *and lifts her head up in her arms.*]

KATE: [*Gently.*] Pore dearie! [*Looking at* JOE *angrily.*] Been 'ittin' 'er agen, 'ave yer, yer cowardly swine!

JOE: Yus; an' I'll 'it you, too, if yer don't keep yer marf shut. Tike 'er aht of 'ere! [KATE *carries* FREDA *into the next room.* JOE *goes behind the bar. A moment later the outer door is opened and* DRISCOLL *and* COCKY *come in.*]

DRISCOLL: Come on, Ollie. [*He suddenly sees that* OLSON *is not there, and turns to* JOE.] Where is ut he's gone to?

JOE: [*With a meaning wink.*] 'E an' Freda went aht t'gether 'bout five minutes past. 'E's fair gone on 'er, 'e is.

DRISCOLL: [*With a grin.*] Oho, so that's ut, is ut? Who'd think Ollie'd be sich a divil wid the wimin? 'Tis lucky he's sober or she'd have him stripped to his last ha'penny. [*Turning to* COCKY, *who is blinking sleepily.*] What'll ye have, ye little scut? [*To* JOE.] Give me whiskey, *Irish* whiskey!

[*The Curtain Falls*]

IN THE ZONE

A PLAY IN ONE ACT

CHARACTERS

SMITTY
DAVIS
SWANSON
SCOTTY
IVAN   } *Seamen on the British Tramp Steamer* Glencairn
PAUL
JACK
DRISCOLL
COCKY

IN THE ZONE

SCENE—*The seamen's forecastle. On the right above the bunks three or four portholes covered with black cloth can be seen. On the floor near the doorway is a pail with a tin dipper. A lantern in the middle of the floor, turned down very low, throws a dim light around the place. Five men,* SCOTTY, IVAN, SWANSON, SMITTY *and* PAUL, *are in their bunks apparently asleep. It is about ten minutes of twelve on a night in the fall of the year 1915.*

SMITTY *turns slowly in his bunk and, leaning out over the side, looks from one to another of the men as if to assure himself that they are asleep. Then he climbs carefully out of his bunk and stands in the middle of the forecastle fully dressed, but in his stocking feet, glancing around him suspiciously. Reassured, he leans down and cautiously pulls out a suit-case from under the bunks in front of him.*

Just at this moment DAVIS *appears in the doorway, carrying a large steaming coffee-pot in his hand. He stops short when he sees* SMITTY. *A puzzled expression comes over his face, followed by one of suspicion, and he retreats farther back in the alleyway, where he can watch* SMITTY *without being seen.*

All the latter's movements indicate a fear of discovery. He takes out a small bunch of keys and unlocks the suit-case, making a slight noise as he does so. SCOTTY *wakes up and peers at him over the side of the bunk.* SMITTY *opens the suit-case and takes out a small black tin box, carefully places this under his mattress, shoves the suit-case back under the bunk, climbs into his bunk again, closes his eyes and begins to snore loudly.*

DAVIS *enters the forecastle, places the coffee-pot beside the lantern, and goes from one to the other of the sleepers and shakes them vigorously, saying to each in a low voice:* Near eight bells, Scotty. Arise and shine, Swanson. Eight bells, Ivan. SMITTY *yawns loudly with a great pretense of having been dead asleep. All of the rest of the men tumble out of their bunks, stretching and gaping, and commence to pull on their shoes. They go one by one to the cupboard near the open door, take out their cups and spoons, and sit down together on the benches. The coffee-pot is passed around. They munch their biscuits and sip their coffee in dull silence.*

DAVIS: [*Suddenly jumping to his feet—nervously.*] Where's that air comin' from? [*All are startled and look at him wonderingly.*]

SWANSON: [*A squat, surly-faced Swede—grumpily.*] What air? I don't feel nothing.

DAVIS: [*Excitedly.*] I kin feel it—a draft. [*He stands on the bench and looks around—suddenly exploding.*] Damn fool square-head! [*He leans over the upper bunk in which* PAUL *is sleeping and slams the porthole shut.*] I got a good notion to report him. Serve him bloody well right! What's the use o' blindin' the ports when that thickhead goes an' leaves 'em open?

SWANSON: [*Yawning—too sleepy to be aroused by anything—carelessly.*] Dey don't see what little light go out yust one port.

SCOTTY: [*Protestingly.*] Dinna be a loon, Swanson! D'ye no ken the dangerr o' showin' a licht wi' a pack o' submarines lyin' aboot?

IVAN: [*Shaking his shaggy ox-like head in an emphatic affirmative.*] Dot's right, Scotty. I don' li-ike blow up, no, by devil!

SMITTY: [*His manner slightly contemptuous.*] I don't think there's much danger of meeting any of their submarines, not until we get into the War Zone, at any rate.

DAVIS: [*He and* SCOTTY *look at* SMITTY *suspiciously—harshly.*] You don't, eh? [*He lowers his voice and speaks slowly.*] Well, we're in the war zone right this minit if you wants to know. [*The effect of this speech is instantaneous. All sit bolt upright on their benches and stare at Davis.*]

SMITTY: How do you know, Davis?

DAVIS: [*Angrily.*] 'Cos Drisc heard the First send the Third below to wake the skipper when we fetched the zone—bout five bells, it was. Now whata y' got to say?

SMITTY: [*Conciliatingly.*] Oh, I wasn't doubting your word, Davis; but you know they're not pasting up bulletins to let the crew know when the zone is reached—especially on ammunition ships like this.

IVAN: [*Decidedly.*] I don't li-ike dees voyage. Next time I ship on wind-jammer Boston to River Plate, load with wood only so it float, by golly!

SWANSON: [*Fretfully.*] I hope British navy blow 'em to hell, those submarines, py damn!

SCOTTY: [*Looking at* SMITTY, *who is staring at the doorway in a dream, his chin on his hands. Meaningly.*] It is no the submarines only we've to fear, I'm thinkin'.

DAVIS: [*Assenting eagerly.*] That's no lie, Scotty.

SWANSON: You mean the mines?

SCOTTY: I wasna thinkin' o' mines eitherr.

DAVIS: There's many a good ship blown up and at the bottom of the sea, what never hit no mine or torpedo.

SCOTTY: Did ye neverr read of the German spies and the dirrty work they're doin' all the war? [*He and* DAVIS *both glance at* SMITTY, *who is deep in thought and is not listening to the conversation.*]

DAVIS: An' the clever way they fool you!

SWANSON: Sure; I read it in paper many time.

DAVIS: Well— [*He is about to speak but hesitates and finishes lamely*] you got to watch out, that's all I says.

IVAN: [*Drinking the last of his coffee and slamming his fist on the bench explosively.*] I tell you dis rotten coffee give me belly-ache, yes! [*They all look at him in amused disgust.*]

SCOTTY: [*Sardonically.*] Dinna fret about it, Ivan. If we blow up ye'll no be mindin' the pain in your middle. [JACK *enters. He is a young American with a tough, good-natured face. He wears dungarees and a heavy jersey.*]

JACK: Eight bells, fellers.

IVAN: [*Stupidly.*] I don' hear bell ring.

JACK: No, and yuh won't hear any ring, yuh boob—[*Lowering his voice unconsciously.*] now we're in the war zone.

SWANSON: [*Anxiously.*] Is the boats all ready?

JACK: Sure; we can lower 'em in a second.

DAVIS: A lot o' good the boats'll do, with us loaded deep with all kinds o' dynamite and stuff the like o' that! If a torpedo hits this hooker we'll all be in hell b'fore you could wink your eye.

JACK: They ain't goin' to hit us, see? That's my dope. Whose wheel is it?

IVAN: [*Sullenly.*] My wheel. [*He lumbers out.*]

JACK: And whose lookout?

SWANSON: Mine, I tink. [*He follows* IVAN.]

JACK: [*Scornfully.*] A hell of a lot of use keepin' a lookout! We couldn't run away or fight if we wanted to. [*To* SCOTTY *and* SMITTY.] Better look up the bo'sun or the Fourth, you two, and let 'em see you're awake. [SCOTTY *goes to the doorway and turns to wait for* SMITTY, *who is still in the same position, head on hands, seemingly unconscious of everything.* JACK *slaps him roughly on the shoulder and he comes to with a start.*] Aft and report, Duke! What's the matter with yuh—in a dope dream? [SMITTY *goes out after* SCOTTY *without answering.* JACK *looks after him with a frown.*] He's a queer guy. I can't figger him out.

DAVIS: Nor no one else. [*Lowering his voice—meaningly.*] An' he's liable to turn out queerer than any of us think if we ain't careful.

JACK: [*Suspiciously.*] What d'yuh mean? [*They are interrupted by the entrance of* DRISCOLL *and* COCKY.]

COCKY: [*Protestingly.*] Blimey if I don't fink I'll put in this 'ere watch

ahtside on deck. [*He and* DRISCOLL *go over and get their cups.*] I
down't want to be caught in this 'ole if they 'its us. [*He pours out
coffee.*]

DRISCOLL: [*Pouring his.*] Divil a bit ut wud matther where ye arre. Ye'd
be blown to smithereens b'fore ye cud say your name. [*He sits down,
overturning as he does so the untouched cup of coffee which* SMITTY
*had forgotten and left on the bench. They all jump nervously as the
tin cup hits the floor with a bang.* DRISCOLL *flies into an unreason-
ing rage.*] Who's the dirty scut left this cup where a man 'ud sit
on ut?

DAVIS: It's Smitty's.

DRISCOLL: [*Kicking the cup across the forecastle.*] Does he think he's
too much av a bloody gentleman to put his own away loike the rist
av us? If he does I'm the bye'll beat that noshun out av his head.

COCKY: Be the airs 'e puts on you'd think 'e was the Prince of Wales.
Wot's 'e doin' on a ship, I arsks yer? 'E ain't now good as a sailor, is
'e?—dawdlin' abaht on deck like a chicken wiv 'is 'ead cut orf!

JACK: [*Good-naturedly.*] Aw, the Duke's all right. S'posin' he did ferget
his cup—what's the dif? [*He picks up the cup and puts it away—
with a grin.*] This war zone stuff's got yer goat, Drisc—and yours
too, Cocky—and I ain't cheerin' much fur it myself, neither.

COCKY: [*With a sigh.*] Blimey, it ain't no bleedin' joke, yer first trip,
to know as there's a ship full of shells li'ble to go orf in under
your bloomin' feet, as you might say, if we gets 'it be a torpedo or
mine. [*With sudden savagery.*] Calls theyselves 'uman bein's, too!
Blarsted 'Uns!

DRISCOLL: [*Gloomily.*] 'Tis me last trip in the bloody zone, God help
me. The divil take their twenty-foive percent bonus—and be drowned
like a rat in a trap in the bargain, maybe.

DAVIS: Wouldn't be so bad if she wasn't carryin' ammunition. Them's
the kind the subs is layin' for.

DRISCOLL: [*Irritably.*] Fur the love av hivin, don't be talkin' about ut.
I'm sick wid thinkin' and jumpin' at iviry bit av a noise. [*There is a
pause during which they all stare gloomily at the floor.*]

JACK: Hey, Davis, what was you sayin' about Smitty when they
come in?

DAVIS: [*With a great air of mystery.*] I'll tell you in a minit. I want to
wait an' see if he's comin' back. [*Impressively.*] You won't be callin'
him all right when you hears what I seen with my own eyes. [*He
adds with an air of satisfaction.*] An' you won't be feelin' no safer,
neither. [*They all look at him with puzzled glances full of a vague apprehension.*]

DRISCOLL: God blarst ut! [*He fills his pipe and lights it. The others, with an air of remembering something they had forgotten, do the same.* SCOTTY *enters.*]

SCOTTY: [*In awed tones.*] Mon, but it's clear outside the nicht! Like day.

DAVIS: [*In low tones.*] Where's Smitty, Scotty?

SCOTTY: Out on the hatch starin' at the moon like a mon half-daft.

DAVIS: Kin you see him from the doorway?

SCOTTY: [*Goes to doorway and carefully peeks out.*] Aye; he's still there.

DAVIS: Keep your eyes on him for a moment. I've got something I wants to tell the boys and I don't want him walkin' in in the middle of it. Give a shout if he starts this way.

SCOTTY: [*With suppressed excitement.*] Aye, I'll watch him. And I've somethin' myself to tell aboot his Lordship.

DRISCOLL: [*Impatiently.*] Out wid ut! You're talkin' more than a pair av auld women wud be standin' in the road, and gittin' no further along.

DAVIS: Listen! You 'member when I went to git the coffee, Jack?

JACK: Sure, I do.

DAVIS: Well, I brings it down here same as usual and got as far as the door there when I sees him.

JACK: Smitty?

DAVIS: Yes, Smitty! He was standin' in the middle of the fo'c's'tle there [*Pointing.*] lookin' around sneakin'-like at Ivan and Swanson and the rest 's if he wants to make certain they're asleep. [*He pauses significantly, looking from one to the other of his listeners.* SCOTTY *is nervously dividing his attention between* SMITTY *on the hatch outside and* DAVIS' *story, fairly bursting to break in with his own revelations.*]

JACK: [*Impatiently.*] What of it?

DAVIS: Listen! He was standin' right there—[*Pointing again.*] in his stockin' feet—no shoes on, mind, so he wouldn't make no noise!

JACK: [*Spitting disgustedly.*] Aw!

DAVIS: [*Not heeding the interruption.*] I seen right away somethin' on the queer was up so I slides back into the alleyway where I kin see him but he can't see me. After he makes sure they're all asleep he goes in under the bunks there—bein' careful not to raise a noise, mind!—an' takes out his bag there. [*By this time every one,* JACK *included, is listening breathlessly to his story.*] Then he fishes in his pocket an' takes out a bunch o' keys an' kneels down beside the bag an' opens it.

SCOTTY: [*Unable to keep silent longer.*] Mon, didn't I see him do that same thing wi' these two eyes. 'Twas just that moment I woke and spied him.

DAVIS: [*Surprised, and a bit nettled to have to share his story with any one.*] Oh, you seen him, too, eh? [*To the others.*] Then Scotty kin tell you if I'm lyin' or not.

DRISCOLL: An' what did he do whin he'd the bag opened?

DAVIS: He bends down and reaches out his hand sort o' scared-like, like it was somethin' dang'rous he was after, an' feels round in under his duds—hidden in under his duds an' wrapped up in 'em, it was—an' he brings out a black iron box!

COCKY: [*Looking around him with a frightened glance.*] Gawd blimey! [*The others likewise betray their uneasiness, shuffling their feet nervously.*]

DAVIS: Ain't that right, Scotty?

SCOTTY: Right as rain, I'm tellin' ye'!

DAVIS: [*To the others with an air of satisfaction.*] There you are! [*Lowering his voice.*] An' then what d'you suppose he did? Sneaks to his bunk an' slips the black box in under his mattress—in under his mattress, mind!—

JACK: And it's there now?

DAVIS: Course it is! [JACK *starts toward* SMITTY's *bunk.* DRISCOLL *grabs him by the arm.*]

DRISCOLL: Don't be touchin' ut, Jack!

JACK: Yuh needn't worry. I ain't goin' to touch it. [*He pulls up* SMITTY's *mattress and looks down. The others stare at him, holding their breaths. He turns to them, trying hard to assume a careless tone.*] It's there, aw right.

COCKY: [*Miserably upset.*] I'm gointer 'op it aht on deck. [*He gets up but* DRISCOLL *pulls him down again.* COCKY *protests.*] It fair guvs me the trembles sittin' still in 'ere.

DRISCOLL: [*Scornfully.*] Are ye frightened, ye toad? 'Tis a hell av a thing fur grown men to be shiverin' loike childer at a bit av a black box. [*Scratching his head in uneasy perplexity.*] Still, ut's damn queer, the looks av ut.

DAVIS: [*Sarcastically.*] A bit of a black box, eh? How big d'you think them—[*He hesitates*]—things has to be—big as this fo'c's'tle?

JACK: [*In a voice meant to be reassuring.*] Aw, hell! I'll bet it ain't nothin' but some coin he's saved he's got locked up in there.

DAVIS: [*Scornfully.*] That's likely, ain't it? Then why does he act so s'picious? He's been on ship near two year, ain't he? He knows damn well there ain't no thiefs in this fo'c's'tle, don't he? An' you know 's well 's I do he didn't have no money when he came on board an' he ain't saved none since. Don't you? [JACK *doesn't answer.*] Listen! D'you know what he done after he put that thing in under his mattress?—an' Scotty'll tell you if I ain't speakin' truth. He looks round to see if any one's woke up—

SCOTTY: I clapped my eyes shut when he turned round.

DAVIS: An' then he crawls into his bunk an' shuts his eyes, an' starts in *snorin', pretendin'* he was asleep; mind!

SCOTTY: Aye, I could hear him.

DAVIS: An' when I goes to call him I don't even shake him. I just says, "Eight bells, Smitty," in a'most a whisper-like, an' up he gets yawnin' an' stretchin' fit to kill hisself 's if he'd been dead asleep.

COCKY: Gawd blimey!

DRISCOLL: [*Shaking his head.*] Ut looks bad, divil a doubt av ut.

DAVIS: [*Excitedly.*] An' now I come to think of it, there's the porthole. How'd it come to git open, tell me that? I know'd well Paul never opened it. Ain't he grumblin' about bein' cold all the time?

SCOTTY: The mon that opened it meant no good to this ship, whoever he was.

JACK: [*Sourly.*] What porthole? What're yuh talkin' about?

DAVIS: [*Pointing over PAUL's bunk.*] There. It was open when I come in. I felt the cold air on my neck an' shut it. It would'a been clear's a lighthouse to any sub that was watchin'—an' we s'posed to have all the ports blinded! Who'd do a dirty trick like that? It wasn't none of us, nor Scotty here, nor Swanson, nor Ivan. Who would it be, then?

COCKY: [*Angrily.*] Must'a been 'is bloody Lordship.

DAVIS: For all's we know he might'a been signallin' with it. They does it like that by winkin' a light. Ain't you read how they gets caught doin' it in London an' on the coast?

COCKY: [*Firmly convinced now.*] An' wots 'e doin' aht alone on the 'atch—keepin' 'isself clear of us like 'e was afraid?

DRISCOLL: Kape your eye on him, Scotty.

SCOTTY: There's no a move oot o' him.

JACK: [*In irritated perplexity.*] But, hell, ain't he an Englishman? What'd he wanta—

DAVIS: English? How d'we know he's English? Cos he talks it? That ain't no proof. Ain't you read in the papers how all them German spies they been catchin' in England has been livin' there for ten, often as not twenty years, an' talks English as good's any one? An' look here, ain't you noticed he don't talk natural? He talks it too damn good, that's what I mean. He don't talk exactly like a toff, does he, Cocky?

COCKY: Not like any toff as I ever met up wiv.

DAVIS: No; an' he don't talk it like us, that's certain. An' he don't look English. An' what d'we know about him when you come to look at it? Nothin'! He ain't ever said where he comes from or why. All we knows is he ships on here in London 'bout a year b'fore the war starts, as an A. B.—stole his papers most lik'ly—when he don't know how to box the compass, hardly. Ain't that queer in itself? An' was he ever open with us like a good shipmate? No; he's always had that sly air about him 's if he was hidin' somethin'.

DRISCOLL: [*Slapping his thigh—angrily.*] Divil take me if I don't think ye have the truth av ut, Davis.

COCKY: [*Scornfully.*] Lettin' on be 'is silly airs, and all, 'e's the son of a blarsted earl or somethink!

DAVIS: An' the name he calls hisself—Smith! I'd risk a quid of my next pay day that his real name is Schmidt, if the truth was known.

JACK: [*Evidently fighting against his own conviction.*] Aw, say, you guys give me a pain! What'd they want puttin' a spy on this old tub for?

DAVIS: [*Shaking his head sagely.*] They're deep ones, an' there's a lot o' things a sailor'll see in the ports he puts in ought to be useful to 'em. An' if he kin signal to 'em an' they blows us up it's one ship less, ain't it? [*Lowering his voice and indicating* SMITTY's *bunk.*] Or if he blows us up hisself.

SCOTTY: [*In alarmed tones.*] Hush, mon! Here he comes! [SCOTTY *hurries over to a bench and sits down. A thick silence settles over the forecastle. The men look from one to another with uneasy glances.* SMITTY *enters and sits down beside his bunk. He is seemingly unaware of the dark glances of suspicion directed at him from all sides. He slides his hand back stealthily over his mattress and his fingers move, evidently feeling to make sure the box is still there. The others follow this movement carefully with quick looks out of the corners of their eyes. Their attitudes grow tense as if they were about to spring at him. Satisfied the box is safe,* SMITTY *draws his hand away slowly and utters a sigh of relief.*]

SMITTY: [*In a casual tone which to them sounds sinister.*] It's a good light night for the subs if there's any about. [*For a moment he sits staring in front of him. Finally he seems to sense the hostile atmosphere of the forecastle and looks from one to the other of the men in surprise. All of them avoid his eyes. He sighs with a puzzled expression and gets up and walks out of the doorway. There is silence for a moment after his departure and then a storm of excited talk breaks loose.*]

DAVIS: Did you see him feelin' if it was there?

COCKY: 'E ain't arf a sly one wiv 'is talk of submarines, Gawd blind 'im!

SCOTTY: Did ve see the sneakin' looks he gave us?

DRISCOLL: If ivir I saw black shame on a man's face 'twas on his whin he sat there!

JACK: [*Thoroughly convinced at last.*] He looked bad to me. He's a crook, aw right.

DAVIS: [*Excitedly.*] What'll we do? We gotter do somethin' quick or— [*He is interrupted by the sound of something hitting against the port side of the forecastle with a dull, heavy thud. The men start to their feet in wild-eyed terror and turn as if they were going to rush for the deck. They stand that way for a strained moment, scarcely breathing and listening intently.*]

JACK: [*With a sickly smile.*] Hell! It's on'y a piece of driftwood or a floatin' log. [*He sits down again.*]

DAVIS: [*Sarcastically.*] Or a mine that didn't go off—that time—or a piece o' wreckage from some ship they've sent to Davy Jones.

COCKY: [*Mopping his brow with a trembling hand.*] Blimey! [*He sinks back weakly on a bench.*]

DRISCOLL: [*Furiously.*] God blarst ut! No man at all cud be puttin' up wid the loike av this—an' I'm not wan to be fearin' anything or any man in the worrld'll stand up to me face to face; but this divil's trickery in the darrk— [*He starts for* SMITTY'*s bunk.*] I'll throw ut out wan av the portholes an' be done wid ut. [*He reaches toward the mattress.*]

SCOTTY: [*Grabbing his arm—wildly.*] Arre ye daft, mon?

DAVIS: Don't monkey with it, Drisc. I knows what to do. Bring the bucket o' water here, Jack, will you? [JACK *gets it and brings it over to* DAVIS.] An' you, Scotty, see if he's back on the hatch.

SCOTTY: [*Cautiously peering out.*] Aye, he's sittin' there the noo.

DAVIS: Sing out if he makes a move. Lift up the mattress, Drisc—careful now! [DRISCOLL *does so with infinite caution.*] Take it out, Jack—careful—don't shake it now, for Christ's sake! Here—put it in the water—easy! There, that's fixed it! [*They all sit down with great sighs of relief.*] The water'll git in and spoil it.

DRISCOLL: [*Slapping* DAVIS *on the back.*] Good wurrk for ye, Davis, ye scut! [*He spits on his hands aggressively.*] An' now what's to be done wid that black-hearted thraitor?

COCKY: [*Belligerently.*] Guv 'im a shove in the marf and 'eave 'im over the side!

DAVIS: An' serve him right!

JACK: Aw, say, give him a chance. Yuh can't prove nothin' till yuh find out what's in there.

DRISCOLL: [*Heatedly.*] Is ut more proof ye'd be needin' afther what we've seen an' heard? Then listen to me—an' ut's Driscoll talkin'— if there's divilmint in that box an' we see plain 'twas his plan to murrdher his own shipmates that have served him fair— [*He raises his fist.*] I'll choke his rotten hearrt out wid me own hands, an' over the side wid him, and one man missin' in the mornin'.

DAVIS: An' no one the wiser. He's the balmy kind what commits suicide.

COCKY: They 'angs spies ashore.

JACK: [*Resentfully.*] If he's done what yuh think I'll croak him myself. Is that good enough for yuh?

DRISCOLL: [*Looking down at the box.*] How'll we be openin' this, I wonder?

SCOTTY: [*From the doorway—warningly.*] He's standin' up.

DAVIS: We'll take his keys away from him when he comes in. Quick, Drisc! You an' Jack get beside the door and grab him. [*They get on either side of the door.* DAVIS *snatches a small coil of rope from one of the upper bunks.*] This'll do for me an' Scotty to tie him.

SCOTTY: He's turrnin' this way—he's comin'! [*He moves away from door.*]

DAVIS: Stand by to lend a hand, Cocky.

COCKY: Righto. [*As* SMITTY *enters the forecastle he is seized roughly from both sides and his arms pinned behind him. At first he struggles fiercely, but seeing the uselessness of this, he finally stands calmly and allows* DAVIS *and* SCOTTY *to tie up his arms.*]

SMITTY: [*When they have finished—with cold contempt.*] If this is your idea of a joke I'll have to confess it's a bit too thick for me to enjoy.

COCKY: [*Angrily.*] Shut yer marf, 'ear!

DRISCOLL: [*Roughly.*] Ye'll find ut's no joke, me bucko, b'fore we're done wid you. [*To* SCOTTY.] Kape your eye peeled, Scotty, and sing out if any one's comin'. [SCOTTY *resumes his post at the door.*]

SMITTY: [*With the same icy contempt.*] If you'd be good enough to ex- plain—

DRISCOLL: [*Furiously.*] Explain, is ut? 'Tis you'll do the explainin'—an' damn quick, or we'll know the reason why. [*To* JACK *and* DAVIS.] Bring him here, now. [*They push* SMITTY *over to the bucket.*] Look here, ye murrdherin' swab. D'you see ut? [SMITTY *looks down with an expression of amazement which rapidly changes to one of anguish.*]

DAVIS: [*With a sneer.*] Look at him! S'prised, ain't you? If you wants to try your dirty spyin' tricks on us you've gotter git up earlier in the mornin'.

COCKY: Thorght yer weren't 'arf a fox, didn't yer?

SMITTY: [*Trying to restrain his growing rage.*] What—what do you mean? That's only—How dare—What are you doing with my private belongings?

COCKY: [*Sarcastically.*] Ho yus! Private b'longings!

DRISCOLL: [*Shouting.*] What is ut, ye swine? Will you tell us to our faces? What's in ut?

SMITTY: [*Biting his lips—holding himself in check with a great effort.*] Nothing but— That's my business. You'll please attend to your own.

DRISCOLL: Oho, ut is, is ut? [*Shaking his fist in SMITTY's face.*] Talk aisy now if ye know what's best for you. Your business, indade! Then we'll be makin' ut ours, I'm thinkin'. [*To JACK and DAVIS.*] Take his keys away from him an' we'll see if there's one'll open ut, maybe. [*They start in searching SMITTY, who tries to resist and kicks out at the bucket. DRISCOLL leaps forward and helps them push him away.*] Try to kick ut over, wud ye? Did ye see him then? Tryin' to murrdher us all, the scut! Take that pail out av his way, Cocky. [*SMITTY struggles with all of his strength and keeps them busy for a few seconds. As COCKY grabs the pail SMITTY makes a final effort and, lunging forward, kicks again at the bucket but only succeeds in hitting COCKY on the shin. COCKY immediately sets down the pail with a bang and, clutching his knee in both hands, starts hopping around the forecastle, groaning and swearing.*]

COCKY: Ooow! Gawd strike me pink! Kicked me, 'e did! Bloody, bleedin', rotten Dutch 'og! [*Approaching SMITTY, who has given up the fight and is pushed back against the wall near the doorway with JACK and DAVIS holding him on either side—wrathfully, at the top of his lungs.*] Kick me, will yer? I'll show yer what for, yer bleedin' sneak! [*He draws back his fist. DRISCOLL pushes him to one side.*]

DRISCOLL: Shut your mouth! D'you want to wake the whole ship? [*COCKY grumbles and retires to a bench, nursing his sore shin.*]

JACK: [*Taking a small bunch of keys from SMITTY's pocket.*] Here yuh are, Drisc.

DRISCOLL: [*Taking them.*] We'll soon be knowin'. [*He takes the pail and sits down, placing it on the floor between his feet. SMITTY again tries to break loose but he is too tired and is easily held back against the wall.*]

SMITTY: [*Breathing heavily and very pale.*] Cowards!

JACK: [*With a growl.*] Nix on the rough talk, see! That don't git yuh nothin'.

DRISCOLL: [*Looking at the lock on the box in the water and then scrutinizing the keys in his hand.*] This'll be ut, I'm thinkin'. [*He selects one and gingerly reaches his hand in the water.*]

SMITTY: [*His face grown livid—chokingly.*] Don't you open that box, Driscoll. If you do, so help me God, I'll kill you if I have to hang for it.

DRISCOLL: [*Pausing—his hand in the water.*] Whin I open this box I'll not be the wan to be kilt, me sonny bye! I'm no dirty spy.

SMITTY: [*His voice trembling with rage. His eyes are fixed on* DRISCOLL's *hand.*] Spy? What are you talking about? I only put that box there so I could get it quick in case we were torpedoed. Are you all mad? Do you think I'm— [*Chokingly.*] You stupid curs! You cowardly dolts! [DAVIS *claps his hand over* SMITTY's *mouth.*]

DAVIS: That'll be enough from you! [DRISCOLL *takes the dripping box from the water and starts to fit in the key.* SMITTY *springs forward furiously, almost escaping from their grasp, and drags them after him half-way across the forecastle.*]

DRISCOLL: Hold him, ye divils! [*He puts the box back in the water and jumps to their aid.* COCKY *hovers on the outskirts of the battle, mindful of the kick he received.*]

SMITTY: [*Raging.*] Cowards! Damn you! Rotten curs! [*He is thrown to the floor and held there.*] Cowards! Cowards!

DRISCOLL: I'll shut your dirty mouth for you. [*He goes to his bunk and pulls out a big wad of waste and comes back to* SMITTY.]

SMITTY: Cowards! Cowards!

DRISCOLL: [*With no gentle hand slaps the waste over* SMITTY's *mouth.*] That'll teach you to be misnamin' a man, ye sneak. Have ye a handkerchief, Jack? [JACK *hands him one and he ties it tightly around* SMITTY's *head over the waste.*] That'll fix your gab. Stand him up, now, and tie his feet, too, so he'll not be movin'. [*They do so and leave him with his back against the wall near* SCOTTY. *Then they all sit down beside* DRISCOLL, *who again lifts the box out of the water and sets it carefully on his knees. He picks out the key, then hesitates, looking from one to the other uncertainly.*] We'd best be takin' this to the skipper, d'you think, maybe?

JACK: [*Irritably.*] To hell with the Old Man. This is our game and we c'n play it without no help.

COCKY: Now bleedin' horficers, I says!

DAVIS: They'd only be takin' all the credit and makin' heroes of theyselves.

DRISCOLL: [*Boldly.*] Here goes, thin! [*He slowly turns the key in the lock. The others instinctively turn away. He carefully pushes the cover back on its hinges and looks at what he sees inside with an expression of puzzled astonishment. The others crowd up close. Even* SCOTTY *leaves his post to take a look.*] What is ut, Davis?

DAVIS: [*Mystified.*] Looks funny, don't it? Somethin' square tied up in a rubber bag. Maybe it's dynamite—or somethin'—you can't never tell.

JACK: Aw, it ain't got no works so it ain't no bomb, I'll bet.

DAVIS: [*Dubiously.*] They makes them all kinds, they do.

JACK: Open it up, Drisc.

DAVIS: Careful now! [DRISCOLL *takes a black rubber bag resembling a large tobacco pouch from the box and unties the string which is wound tightly around the top. He opens it and takes out a small packet of letters also tied up with string. He turns these over in his hands and looks at the others questioningly.*]

JACK: [*With a broad grin.*] On'y letters! [*Slapping* DAVIS *on the back.*] Yuh're a hell of a Sherlock Holmes, ain't yuh? Letters from his best girl too, I'll bet. Let's turn the Duke loose, what d'yuh say? [*He starts to get up.*]

DAVIS: [*Fixing him with a withering look.*] Don't be so damn smart, Jack. Letters, you says, 's if there never was no harm in 'em. How d'you s'pose spies gets their orders and sends back what they finds out if it ain't by letters and such things? There's many a letter is worser'n any bomb.

COCKY: Righto! They ain't as innercent as they looks, I'll take me oath, when you read 'em. [*Pointing at* SMITTY.] Not 'is Lordship's letters; not be no means!

JACK: [*Sitting down again.*] Well, read 'em and find out. [DRISCOLL *commences untying the packet. There is a muffled groan of rage and protest from* SMITTY.]

DAVIS: [*Triumphantly.*] There! Listen to him! Look at him trying' to git loose! Ain't that proof enough? He knows well we're findin' him out. Listen to me! Love letters, you says, Jack, 's if they couldn't harm nothin'. Listen! I was readin' in some magazine in New York on'y two weeks back how some German spy in Paris was writin' love letters to some woman spy in Switzerland who sent 'em on to Berlin, Germany. To read 'em you wouldn't s'pect nothin'—just mush and all. [*Impressively.*] But they had a way o' doin' it—a damn sneakin' way. They had a piece o' plain paper with pieces cut out of it an' when they puts it on top o' the letter they sees on'y the words what tells them what they wants to know. An' the Frenchies gets beat in a fight all on account o' that letter.

COCKY: [*Awed.*] Gawd blimey! They ain't 'arf smart bleeders!

DAVIS: [*Seeing his audience is again all with him.*] An' even if these letters of his do sound all right they may have what they calls a code.
You can't never tell. [*To* DRISCOLL, *who has finished untying the
packet.*] Read one of 'em, Drisc. My eyes is weak.

DRISCOLL: [*Takes the first one out of its envelope and bends down to
the lantern with it. He turns up the wick to give him a better light.*]
I'm no hand to be readin' but I'll try ut. [*Again there is a muffled
groan from* SMITTY *as he strains at his bonds.*]

DAVIS: [*Gloatingly.*] Listen to him! He knows. Go ahead, Drisc!

DRISCOLL: [*His brow furrowed with concentration.*] Ut begins: Dearest
Man— [*His eyes travel down the page.*] An' thin there's a lot av
blarney tellin' him how much she misses him now she's gone away to
singin' school—an' how she hopes he'll settle down to rale worrk an'
not be skylarkin' around now that she's away loike he used to before
she met up wid him—and ut ends: "I love you betther than anythin'
in the worrld. You know that, don't you, dear? But b'fore I can agree
to live out my life wid you, you must prove to me that the black
shadow—I won't menshun uts hateful name but you know what I
mean—which might wreck both our lives, does not exist for you.
You can do that, can't you, dear? Don't you see you must for my
sake?" [*He pauses for a moment—then adds gruffly.*] Uts signed:
"Edith." [*At the sound of the name* SMITTY, *who has stood tensely
with his eyes shut as if he were undergoing torture during the reading, makes a muffled sound like a sob and half turns his face to the
wall.*]

JACK: [*Sympathetically.*] Hell! What's the use of readin' that stuff
even if—

DAVIS: [*Interrupting him sharply.*] Wait! Where's that letter from, Drisc?

DRISCOLL: There's no address on the top av ut.

DAVIS: [*Meaningly.*] What'd I tell you? Look at the postmark, Drisc,—
on the envelope.

DRISCOLL: The name that's written is Sidney Davidson, wan
hundred an'—

DAVIS: Never mind that. O' course it's a false name. Look at the postmark.

DRISCOLL: There's a furrin stamp on ut by the looks av ut. The mark's
blurred so it's hard to read. [*He spells it out laboriously.*] B-e-r—the
nixt is an l, I think—i—an' an n.

DAVIS: [*Excitedly.*] Berlin! What did I tell you? I knew them letters was
from Germany.

COCKY: [*Shaking his fist in* SMITTY's *direction.*] Rotten 'ound! [*The others look at* SMITTY *as if this last fact had utterly condemned him in their eyes.*]

DAVIS: Give me the letter, Drisc. Maybe I kin make somethin' out of it. [DRISCOLL *hands the letter to him.*] You go through the others, Drisc, and sing out if you sees anythin' queer. [*He bends over the first letter as if he were determined to figure out its secret meaning.* JACK, COCKY *and* SCOTTY *look over his shoulder with eager curiosity.* DRISCOLL *takes out some of the other letters, running his eyes quickly down the pages. He looks curiously over at* SMITTY *from time to time, and sighs frequently with a puzzled frown.*]

DAVIS: [*Disappointedly.*] I gotter give it up. It's too deep for me, but we'll turn 'em over to the perlice when we docks at Liverpool to look through. This one I got was written a year before the war started, anyway. Find anythin' in yours, Drisc?

DRISCOLL: They're all the same as the first—lovin' blarney, an' how her singin' is doin', and the great things the Dutch teacher says about her voice, an' how glad she is that her Sidney bye is worrkin' harrd an' makin' a man av himself for her sake. [SMITTY *turns his face completely to the wall.*]

DAVIS: [*Disgustedly.*] If we on'y had the code!

DRISCOLL: [*Taking up the bottom letter.*] Hullo! Here's wan addressed to this ship—S. S. Glencairn, ut says—whin we was in Cape Town sivin months ago— [*Looking at the postmark.*] Ut's from London.

DAVIS: [*Eagerly.*] Read it! [*There is another choking groan from* SMITTY.]

DRISCOLL: [*Reads slowly—his voice becomes lower and lower as he goes on.*] Ut begins wid simply the name Sidney Davidson—no dearest or sweetheart to this wan. "Ut is only from your chance meetin' wid Harry—whin you were drunk—that I happen to know where to reach you. So you have run away to sea loike the coward you are because you knew I had found out the truth—the truth you have covered over with your mean little lies all the time I was away in Berlin and blindly trusted you. Very well, you have chosen. You have shown that your drunkenness means more to you than any love or faith av mine. I am sorry—for I loved you, Sidney Davidson—but this is the end. I lave you—the mem'ries; an' if ut is any satisfaction to you I lave you the real-i-zation that you have wrecked my loife as you have wrecked your own. My one remainin' hope is that nivir in God's worrld will I ivir see your face again. Good-by. Edith." [*As he finishes there is a deep silence, broken only by* SMITTY's *muffled sob-*

bing. *The men cannot look at each other.* DRISCOLL *holds the rubber bag limply in his hand and some small white object falls out of it and drops noiselessly on the floor.* Mechanically DRISCOLL *leans over and picks it up, and looks at it wonderingly.*]

DAVIS: [*In a dull voice.*] What's that?

DRISCOLL: [*Slowly.*] A bit av a dried-up flower,—a rose, maybe. [*He drops it into the bag and gathers up the letters and puts them back. He replaces the bag in the box, and locks it and puts it back under* SMITTY'S *mattress. The others follow him with their eyes. He steps softly over to* SMITTY *and cuts the ropes about his arms and ankles with his sheath knife, and unties the handkerchief over the gag.* SMITTY *does not turn around but covers his face with his hands and leans his head against the wall. His shoulders continue to heave spasmodically but he makes no further sound.*]

DRISCOLL: [*Stalks back to the others—there is a moment of silence, in which each man is in agony with the hopelessness of finding a word he can say—then* DRISCOLL *explodes:*] God stiffen us, are we never goin' to turn in fur a wink av sleep? [*They all start as if awakening from a bad dream and gratefully crawl into their bunks, shoes and all, turning their faces to the wall, and pulling their blankets up over their shoulders.* SCOTTY *tiptoes past* SMITTY *out into the darkness . . .* DRISCOLL *turns down the light and crawls into his bunk as*

[*The Curtain Falls*]

ILE

A PLAY IN ONE ACT

CHARACTERS

BEN, *the cabin boy*

THE STEWARD

CAPTAIN KEENEY

SLOCUM, *second mate*

MRS. KEENEY

JOE, *a harpooner*

Members of the crew of the steam whaler Atlantic Queen.

ILE

SCENE—CAPTAIN KEENEY's *cabin on board the steam whaling ship* Atlantic Queen—*a small, square compartment about eight feet high with
a skylight in the center looking out on the poop deck. On the left [the
stern of the ship] a long bench with rough cushions is built in against
the wall. In front of the bench, a table. Over the bench, several cur-
tained portholes.*

*In the rear, left, a door leading to the captain's sleeping quarters. To
the right of the door a small organ, looking as if it were brand new, is
placed against the wall.*

*On the right, to the rear, a marble-topped sideboard. On the
sideboard, a woman's sewing basket. Farther forward, a doorway leading to the companion way, and past the officer's quarters to the main
deck.*

*In the center of the room, a stove. From the middle of the ceiling a
hanging lamp is suspended. The walls of the cabin are painted white.*

*There is no rolling of the ship, and the light which comes through
the skylight is sickly and faint, indicating one of those gray days of calm
when ocean and sky are alike dead. The silence is unbroken except for
the measured tread of some one walking up and down on the poop
deck overhead.*

*It is nearing two bells—one o'clock—in the afternoon of a day in the
year 1895.*

*At the rise of the curtain there is a moment of intense silence. Then
the* STEWARD *enters and commences to clear the table of the few dishes
which still remain on it after the* CAPTAIN's *dinner. He is an old, grizzled man dressed in dungaree pants, a sweater, and a woolen cap with
ear flaps. His manner is sullen and angry. He stops stacking up the
plates and casts a quick glance upward at the skylight; then tiptoes over
to the closed door in rear and listens with his ear pressed to the crack.
What he hears makes his face darken and he mutters a furious curse.
There is a noise from the doorway on the right and he darts back to the
table.*

BEN *enters. He is an over-grown, gawky boy with a long, pinched
face. He is dressed in sweater, fur cap, etc. His teeth are chattering with
the cold and he hurries to the stove, where he stands for a moment
shivering, blowing on his hands, slapping them against his sides, on the
verge of crying.*

THE STEWARD: [*In relieved tones—seeing who it is.*] Oh, 'tis you, is it? What're ye shiverin' 'bout? Stay by the stove where ye belong and ye'll find no need of chatterin'.

BEN: It's c-c-cold. [*Trying to control his chattering teeth—derisively.*] Who d'ye think it were—the Old Man?

THE STEWARD: [*Makes a threatening move—*BEN *shrinks away.*] None o' your lip, young un, or I'll learn ye. [*More kindly.*] Where was it ye've been all o' the time—the fo'c's'tle?

BEN: Yes.

THE STEWARD: Let the Old Man see ye up for'ard monkeyshinin' with the hands and ye'll get a hidin' ye'll not forget in a hurry.

BEN: Aw, he don't see nothin'. [*A trace of awe in his tones—he glances upward.*] He just walks up and down like he didn't notice nobody— and stares at the ice to the no'the'ard.

THE STEWARD: [*The same tone of awe creeping into his voice.*] He's always starin' at the ice. [*In a sudden rage, shaking his fist at the skylight.*] Ice, ice, ice! Damn him and damn the ice! Holdin' us in for nigh on a year—nothin' to see but ice—stuck in it like a fly in molasses!

BEN: [*Apprehensively.*] Ssshh! He'll hear ye.

THE STEWARD: [*Raging.*] Aye, damn him, and damn the Arctic seas, and damn this stinkin' whalin' ship of his, and damn me for a fool to ever ship on it! [*Subsiding as if realizing the uselessness of this outburst—shaking his head—slowly, with deep conviction.*] He's a hard man—as hard a man as ever sailed the seas.

BEN: [*Solemnly.*] Aye.

THE STEWARD: The two years we all signed up for are done this day. Blessed Christ! Two years o' this dog's life, and no luck in the fishin', and the hands half starved with the food runnin' low, rotten as it is; and not a sign of him turnin' back for home! [*Bitterly.*] Home! I begin to doubt if ever I'll set foot on land again. [*Excitedly.*] What is it he thinks he' goin' to do? Keep us all up here after our time is worked out till the last man of us is starved to death or frozen? We've grub enough hardly to last out the voyage back if we started now. What are the men goin' to do 'bout it? Did ye hear any talk in the fo'c's'tle?

BEN: [*Going over to him—in a half whisper.*] They said if he don't put back south for home today they're goin' to mutiny.

THE STEWARD: [*With grim satisfaction.*] Mutiny? Aye, 'tis the only thing they can do; and serve him right after the manner he's treated them—'s if they wern't no better nor dogs.

BEN: The ice is all broke up to s'uth'ard. They's clear water 's far 's you can see. He ain't got no excuse for not turnin' back for home, the men says.

THE STEWARD: [*Bitterly.*] He won't look nowheres but no'the'ard where they's only the ice to see. He don't want to see no clear water. All he thinks on is gittin' the ile—'s if it was our fault he ain't had good luck with the whales. [*Shaking his head.*] I think the man's mighty nigh losin' his senses.

BEN: [*Awed.*] D'you really think he's crazy?

THE STEWARD: Aye, it's the punishment o' God on him. Did ye ever hear of a man who wasn't crazy do the things he does? [*Pointing to the door in rear.*] Who but a man that's mad would take his woman—and as sweet a woman as ever was—on a stinkin' whalin' ship to the Arctic seas to be locked in by the rotten ice for nigh on a year, and maybe lose her senses forever—for it's sure she'll never be the same again.

BEN: [*Sadly.*] She useter be awful nice to me before— [*His eyes grow wide and frightened.*] she got—like she is.

THE STEWARD: Aye, she was good to all of us. 'Twould have been hell on board without her; for he's a hard man—a hard, hard man—a driver if there ever was one. [*With a grim laugh.*] I hope he's satisfied now—drivin' her on till she's near lost her mind. And who could blame her? 'Tis a God's wonder we're not a ship full of crazed people— with the damned ice all the time, and the quiet so thick you're afraid to hear your own voice.

BEN: [*With a frightened glance toward the door on right.*] She don't never speak to me no more—jest looks at me 's if she didn't know me.

THE STEWARD: She don't know no one—but him. She talks to him— when she does talk—right enough.

BEN: She does nothin' all day long now but sit and sew—and then she cries to herself without makin' no noise. I've seen her.

THE STEWARD: Aye, I could hear her through the door a while back.

BEN: [*Tiptoes over to the door and listens.*] She's cryin' now.

THE STEWARD: [*Furiously—shaking his fist.*] God send his soul to hell for the devil he is! [*There is the noise of some one coming slowly down the companionway stairs. THE STEWARD hurries to his stacked up dishes. He is so nervous from fright that he knocks off the top one, which falls and breaks on the floor. He stands aghast, trembling with dread. BEN is violently rubbing off the organ with a piece of cloth which he has snatched from his pocket. CAPTAIN KEENEY ap-*]

pears in the doorway on right and comes into the cabin, removing his fur cap as he does so. He is a man of about forty, around five-ten in height but looking much shorter on account of the enormous proportions of his shoulders and chest. His face is massive and deeply lined, with gray-blue eyes of a bleak hardness, and a tightly clenched, thin-lipped mouth. His thick hair is long and gray. He is dressed in a heavy blue jacket and blue pants stuffed into his seaboots.

[*He is followed into the cabin by the* SECOND MATE, *a rangy six-footer with a lean weather-beaten face. The* MATE *is dressed about the same as the captain. He is a man of thirty or so.*]

KEENEY: [*Comes toward the* STEWARD—*with a stern look on his face. The* STEWARD *is visibly frightened and the stack of dishes rattles in his trembling hands.* KEENEY *draws back his fist and the* STEWARD *shrinks away. The fist is gradually lowered and* KEENEY *speaks slowly.*] 'Twould be like hitting a worm. It is nigh on two bells, Mr. Steward, and this truck not cleared yet.

THE STEWARD: [*Stammering.*] Y-y-yes, sir.

KEENEY: Instead of doin' your rightful work ye've been below here gossipin' old woman's talk with that boy. [*To* BEN, *fiercely.*] Get out o' this, you! Clean up the chart room. [BEN *darts past the* MATE *to the open doorway.*] Pick up that dish, Mr. Steward!

THE STEWARD: [*Doing so with difficulty.*] Yes, sir.

KEENEY: The next dish you break, Mr. Steward, you take a bath in the Bering Sea at the end of a rope.

THE STEWARD: [*Tremblingly.*] Yes, sir. [*He hurries out. The* SECOND MATE *walks slowly over to the* CAPTAIN.]

MATE: I warn't 'specially anxious the man at the wheel should catch what I wanted to say to you, sir. That's why I asked you to come below.

KEENEY: [*Impatiently.*] Speak your say, Mr. Slocum.

MATE: [*Unconsciously lowering his voice.*] I'm afeard there'll be trouble with the hands by the look o' things. They'll likely turn ugly, every blessed one o' them, if you don't put back. The two years they signed up for is up to-day.

KEENEY: And d'you think you're tellin' me somethin' new, Mr. Slocum? I've felt it in the air this long time past. D'you think I've not seen their ugly looks and the grudgin' way they worked? [*The door is rear is opened and* MRS. KEENEY *stands in the doorway. She is a slight, sweet-faced little woman primly dressed in black. Her eyes are red from weeping and her face drawn and pale. She takes in the cabin with a frightened glance and stands as if fixed to the spot by some nameless dread, clasping and unclasping her hands nervously. The two men turn and look at her.*]

KEENEY: [*With rough tenderness.*] Well, Annie?

MRS. KEENEY: [*As if awakening from a dream.*] David, I— [*She is silent. The* MATE *starts for the doorway.*]

KEENEY: [*Turning to him—sharply.*] Wait!

MATE: Yes, sir.

KEENEY: D'you want anything, Annie?

MRS. KEENEY: [*After a pause, during which she seems to be endeavoring to collect her thoughts.*] I thought maybe—I'd go up on deck, David, to get a breath of fresh air. [*She stands humbly awaiting his permission. He and the* MATE *exchange a significant glance.*]

KEENEY: It's too cold, Annie. You'd best stay below today. There's nothing to look at on deck—but ice.

MRS. KEENEY: [*Monotonously.*] I know—ice, ice, ice! But there's nothing to see down here but these walls. [*She makes a gesture of loathing.*]

KEENEY: You can play the organ, Annie.

MRS. KEENEY: [*Dully.*] I hate the organ. It puts me in mind of home.

KEENEY: [*A touch of resentment in his voice.*] I got it jest for you.

MRS. KEENEY: [*Dully.*] I know. [*She turns away from them and walks slowly to the bench on left. She lifts up one of the curtains and looks through a porthole; then utters an exclamation of joy.*] Ah, water! Clear water! As far as I can see! How good it looks after all these months of ice! [*She turns round to them, her face transfigured with joy.*] Ah, now I must go upon deck and look at it, David.

KEENEY: [*Frowning.*] Best not today, Annie. Best wait for a day when the sun shines.

MRS. KEENEY: [*Desperately.*] But the sun never shines in this terrible place.

KEENEY: [*A tone of command in his voice.*] Best not today, Annie.

MRS. KEENEY: [*Crumbling before this command—abjectly.*] Very well, David. [*She stands there staring straight before her as if in a daze. The two men look at her uneasily.*]

KEENEY: [*Sharply.*] Annie!

MRS. KEENEY: [*Dully.*] Yes, David.

KEENEY: Me and Mr. Slocum has business to talk about—ship's business.

MRS. KEENEY: Very well, David. [*She goes slowly out, rear, and leaves the door three-quarters shut behind her.*]

KEENEY: Best not have her on deck if they's goin' to be any trouble.

MATE: Yes, sir.

KEENEY: And trouble they's goin' to be. I feel it in my bones. [*Takes a revolver from the pocket of his coat and examines it.*] Got your'n?

MATE: Yes, sir.

KEENEY: Not that we'll have to use 'em—not if I know their breed of dog—jest to frighten 'em up a bit. [*Grimly.*] I ain't never been forced to use one yit; and trouble I've had by land and by sea 's long as I kin remember, and will have till my dyin' day, I reckon.

MATE: [*Hesitatingly.*] Then you ain't goin'—to turn back?

KEENEY: Turn back! Mr. Slocum, did you ever hear 'o me pointin' s'uth for home with only a measly four hundred barrel of ile in the hold?

MATE: [*Hastily.*] No, sir—but the grub's gittin' low.

KEENEY: They's enough to last a long time yit, if they're careful with it; and they's plenty o' water.

MATE: They say it's not fit to eat—what's left; and the two years they signed on fur is up today. They might make trouble for you in the courts when we git home.

KEENEY: To hell with 'em! Let them make what law trouble they kin. I don't give a damn 'bout the money. I've got to git the ile! [*Glancing sharply at the* MATE.] You ain't turnin' no damned sea lawyer, be you, Mr. Slocum?

MATE: [*Flushing.*] Not by a hell of a sight, sir.

KEENEY: What do the fools want to go home fur now? Their share o' the four hundred barrel wouldn't keep 'em in chewin' terbacco.

MATE: [*Slowly.*] They wants to git back to their folks an' things, I s'pose.

KEENEY: [*Looking at him searchingly.*] 'N you want to turn back, too. [THE MATE *looks down confusedly before his sharp gaze.*] Don't lie, Mr. Slocum. It's writ down plain in your eyes. [*With grim sarcasm.*] I hope, Mr. Slocum, you ain't agoin' to jine the men agin me.

MATE: [*Indignantly.*] That ain't fair, sir, to say sich things.

KEENEY: [*With satisfaction.*] I warn't much afeard o' that, Tom. You been with me nigh on ten year and I've learned ye whalin'. No man kin say I ain't a good master, if I be a hard one.

MATE: I warn't thinkin' of myself, sir—'bout turnin' home, I mean. [*Desperately.*] But Mrs. Keeney, sir—seems like she ain't jest satisfied up here, ailin' like—what with the cold an' bad luck an' the ice an' all.

KEENEY: [*His face clouding—rebukingly but not severely.*] That's my business, Mr. Slocum. I'll thank you to steer a clear course o' that. [*A*

pause.] The ice'll break up soon to no'th'ard. I could see it startin'
today. And when it goes and we git some sun Annie'll perk up. [*Another pause—then he bursts forth:*] It ain't the damned money what's
keepin' me up in the Northern seas, Tom. But I can't go back to
Homeport with a measly four hundred barrel of ile. I'd die fust. I
ain't never come back home in all my days without a full ship. Ain't
that truth?

MATE: Yes, sir; but this voyage you been ice-bound, an'—

KEENEY: [*Scornfully.*] And d'you s'pose any of 'em would believe that—
any o' them skippers I've beaten voyage after voyage? Can't you
hear 'em laughin' and sneerin'—Tibbots 'n' Harris 'n' Simms and the
rest—and all o' Homeport makin' fun o' me? "Dave Keeney what
boasts he's the best whalin' skipper out o' Homeport comin' back
with a measly four hundred barrel of ile?" [*The thought of this
drives him into a frenzy, and he smashes his fist down on the marble
top of the sideboard.*] Hell! I got to git the ile, I tell you. How could
I figger on this ice? It's never been so bad before in the thirty year I
been acomin' here. And now it's breakin' up. In a couple o' days it'll
be all gone. And they's whale here, plenty of 'em. I know they is and
I ain't never gone wrong yit. I got to git the ile! I got to git it in spite
of all hell, and by God, I ain't agoin' home till I do git it! [*There is
the sound of subdued sobbing from the door in rear. The two men
stand silent for a moment, listening. Then* KEENEY *goes over to the
door and looks in. He hesitates for a moment as if he were going to
enter—then closes the door softly.* JOE, *the harpooner, an enormous
six-footer with a battered, ugly face, enters from right and stands
waiting for the captain to notice him.*]

KEENEY: [*Turning and seeing him.*] Don't be standin' there like a gawk,
Harpooner. Speak up!

JOE: [*Confusedly.*] We want—the men, sir—they wants to send a de-
pitation aft to have a word with you.

KEENEY: [*Furiously.*] Tell 'em to go to— [*Checks himself and continues
grimly.*] Tell 'em to come. I'll see 'em.

JOE: Aye, aye, sir. [*He goes out.*]

KEENEY: [*With a grim smile.*] Here it comes, the trouble you spoke of,
Mr. Slocum, and we'll make short shift of it. It's better to crush such
things at the start than let them make headway.

MATE: [*Worriedly.*] Shall I wake up the First and Fourth, sir? We might
need their help.

KEENEY: No, let them sleep. I'm well able to handle this alone, Mr.
Slocum. [*There is the shuffling of footsteps from outside and five of*

the crew crowd into the cabin, led by JOE. *All are dressed alike—
sweaters, seaboots, etc. They glance uneasily at the* CAPTAIN,
twirling their fur caps in their hands.]

KEENEY: [*After a pause.*] Well? Who's to speak fur ye?

JOE: [*Stepping forward with an air of bravado.*] I be.

KEENEY: [*Eyeing him up and down coldly.*] So you be. Then speak your
say and be quick about it.

JOE: [*Trying not to wilt before the* CAPTAIN'*s glance and avoiding his
eyes.*] The time we signed up for is done today.

KEENEY: [*Icily.*] You're tellin' me nothin' I don't know.

JOE: You ain't pintin' fur home yit, far 's we kin see.

KEENEY: No, and I ain't agoin' to till this ship is full of ile.

JOE: You can't go no further no'the with the ice afore ye.

KEENEY: The ice is breaking up.

JOE: [*After a slight pause during which the others mumble angrily to
one another.*] The grub we're gittin' now is rotten.

KEENEY: It's good enough fur ye. Better men than ye are have eaten
worse. [*There is a chorus of angry exclamations from the crowd.*]

JOE: [*Encouraged by this support.*] We ain't agoin' to work no more
less you puts back for home.

KEENEY: [*Fiercely.*] You ain't, ain't you?

JOE: No; and the law courts'll say we was right.

KEENEY: To hell with your law courts! We're at sea now and I'm the
law on this ship. [*Edging up toward the harpooner.*] And every
mother's son of you what don't obey orders goes in irons. [*There are
more angry exclamations from the crew.* MRS. KEENEY *appears in
the doorway in rear and looks on with startled eyes. None of the
men notice her.*]

JOE: [*With bravado.*] Then we're agoin' to mutiny and take the old
hooker home ourselves. Ain't we, boys? [*As he turns his head to look
at the others,* KEENEY'*s fist shoots out to the side of his jaw.* JOE *goes
down in a heap and lies there.* MRS. KEENEY *gives a shriek and hides
her face in her hands. The men pull out their sheath knives and start
a rush, but stop when they find themselves confronted by the re-
volvers of* KEENEY *and the* MATE.]

KEENEY: [*His eyes and voice snapping.*] Hold still! [*The men stand hud-
dled together in a sullen silence.* KEENEY'*s voice is full of mockery.*]
You've found out it ain't safe to mutiny on this ship, ain't you? And
now git for'ard where ye belong, and— [*He gives* JOE'*s body a contemptuous kick.*] Drag him with you. And remember the first man of
ye I see shirkin' I'll shoot dead as sure as there's a sea under us, and

you can tell the rest the same. Git for'ard now! Quick! [*The men leave in cowed silence, carrying* JOE *with them.* KEENEY *turns to the* MATE *with a short laugh and puts his revolver back in his pocket.*] Best get up on deck, Mr. Slocum, and see to it they don't try none of their skulkin' tricks. We'll have to keep an eye peeled from now on. I know 'em.

MATE: Yes, sir. [*He goes out, right.* KEENEY *hears his wife's hysterical weeping and turns around in surprise—then walks slowly to her side.*]

KEENEY: [*Putting an arm around her shoulder—with gruff tenderness.*] There, there, Annie. Don't be afeard. It's all past and gone.

MRS. KEENEY: [*Shrinking away from him.*] Oh, I can't bear it! I can't bear it any longer!

KEENEY: [*Gently.*] Can't bear what, Annie?

MRS. KEENEY: [*Hysterically.*] All this horrible brutality, and these brutes of men, and this terrible ship, and this prison cell of a room, and the ice all around, and the silence. [*After this outburst she calms down and wipes her eyes with her handkerchief.*]

KEENEY: [*After a pause during which he looks down at her with a puzzled frown.*] Remember, I warn't hankerin' to have you come on this voyage, Annie.

MRS. KEENEY: I wanted to be with you, David, don't you see? I didn't want to wait back there in the house all alone as I've been doing these last six years since we were married—waiting, and watching, and fearing—with nothing to keep my mind occupied—not able to go back teaching school on account of being Dave Keeney's wife. I used to dream of sailing on the great, wide, glorious ocean. I wanted to be by your side in the danger and vigorous life of it all. I wanted to see you the hero they make you out to be in Homeport. And instead— [*Her voice grows tremulous.*] All I find is ice and cold— and brutality! [*Her voice breaks.*]

KEENEY: I warned you what it'd be, Annie. "Whalin' ain't no ladies' tea party," I says to you, and "you better stay to home where you've got all your woman's comforts." [*Shaking his head.*] But you was so set on it.

MRS. KEENEY: [*Wearily.*] Oh, I know it isn't your fault, David. You see, I didn't believe you. I guess I was dreaming about the old Vikings in the story books and I thought you were one of them.

KEENEY: [*Protestingly.*] I done my best to make it as cozy and comfortable as could be. [MRS. KEENEY *looks around her in wild scorn.*] I even sent to the city for that organ for ye, thinkin' it might be

soothin' to ye to be playin' it times when they was calms and things
was dull like.

MRS. KEENEY: [*Wearily.*] Yes, you were very kind, David. I know that.
[*She goes to left and lifts the curtains from the porthole and looks
out—then suddenly bursts forth:*] I won't stand it—I can't stand it—
pent up by these walls like a prisoner. [*She runs over to him and
throws her arms around him, weeping. He puts his arm protectingly
over her shoulders.*] Take me away from here, David! If I don't get
away from here, out of this terrible ship, I'll go mad! Take me home,
David! I can't think any more. I feel as if the cold and the silence
were crushing down on my brain. I'm afraid. Take me home!

KEENEY: [*Holds her at arm's length and looks at her face anxiously.*]
Best go to bed, Annie. You ain't yourself. You got fever. Your eyes
look so strange like. I ain't never seen you look this way before.

MRS. KEENEY: [*Laughing hysterically.*] It's the ice and the cold and the
silence—they'd make any one look strange.

KEENEY: [*Soothingly.*] In a month or two, with good luck, three at the
most, I'll have her filled with ile and then we'll give her everything
she'll stand and pint for home.

MRS. KEENEY: But we can't wait for that—I can't wait. I want to get
home. And the men won't wait. They want to get home. It's cruel,
it's brutal for you to keep them. You must sail back. You've got no
excuse. There's clear water to the south now. If you've a heart at all
you've got to turn back.

KEENEY: [*Harshly.*] I can't, Annie.

MRS. KEENEY: Why can't you?

KEENEY: A woman couldn't rightly understand my reason.

MRS. KEENEY: [*Wildly.*] Because it's a stupid, stubborn reason. Oh, I
heard you talking with the second mate. You're afraid the other cap-
tains will sneer at you because you didn't come back with a full ship.
You want to live up to your silly reputation even if you do have to
beat and starve men and drive me mad to do it.

KEENEY: [*His jaw set stubbornly.*] It ain't that, Annie. Them skippers
would never dare sneer to my face. It ain't so much what any one'd
say—but— [*He hesitates, struggling to express his meaning.*] You
see—I've always done it—since my first voyage as skipper. I always
come back—with a full ship—and—it don't seem right not to—
somehow. I been always first whalin' skipper out o' Homeport,
and— Don't you see my meanin', Annie? [*He glances at her. She is
not looking at him but staring dully in front of her, not hearing a
word he is saying.*] Annie! [*She comes to herself with a start.*] Best
turn in, Annie, there's a good woman. You ain't well.

MRS. KEENEY: [*Resisting his attempts to guide her to the door in rear.*] David! Won't you please turn back?

KEENEY: [*Gently.*] I can't, Annie—not yet awhile. You don't see my meanin'. I got to git the ile.

MRS. KEENEY: It'd be different if you needed the money, but you don't. You've got more than plenty.

KEENEY: [*Impatiently.*] It ain't the money I'm thinkin' of. D'you think I'm as mean as that?

MRS. KEENEY: [*Dully.*] No—I don't know—I can't understand— [*Intensely.*] Oh, I want to be home in the old house once more and see my own kitchen again, and hear a woman's voice talking to me and be able to talk to her. Two years! It seems so long ago—as if I'd been dead and could never go back.

KEENEY: [*Worried by her strange tone and the far-away look in her eyes.*] Best go to bed, Annie. You ain't well.

MRS. KEENEY: [*Not appearing to hear him.*] I used to be lonely when you were away. I used to think Homeport was a stupid, monotonous place. Then I used to go down on the beach, especially when it was windy and the breakers were rolling in, and I'd dream of the fine free life you must be leading. [*She gives a laugh which is half a sob.*] I used to love the sea then. [*She pauses; then continues with slow intensity:*] But now—I don't ever want to see the sea again.

KEENEY: [*Thinking to humor her.*] 'Tis no fit place for a woman, that's sure. I was a fool to bring ye.

MRS. KEENEY: [*After a pause—passing her hand over her eyes with a gesture of pathetic weariness.*] How long would it take us to reach home—if we started now?

KEENEY: [*Frowning.*] 'Bout two months, I reckon, Annie, with fair luck.

MRS. KEENEY: [*Counts on her fingers—then murmurs with a rapt smile.*] That would be August, the latter part of August, wouldn't it? It was on the twenty-fifth of August we were married, David, wasn't it?

KEENEY: [*Trying to conceal the fact that her memories have moved him—gruffly.*] Don't *you* remember?

MRS. KEENEY: [*Vaguely—again passes her hand over her eyes.*] My memory is leaving me—up here in the ice. It was so long ago. [*A pause—then she smiles dreamily.*] It's June now. The lilacs will be all in bloom in the front yard—and the climbing roses on the trellis to the side of the house—they're budding. [*She suddenly covers her face with her hands and commences to sob.*]

KEENEY: [*Disturbed.*] Go in and rest, Annie. You're all wore out cryin' over what can't be helped.

MRS. KEENEY: [*Suddenly throwing her arms around his neck and cling-ing to him.*] You love me, don't you, David?

KEENEY: [*In amazed embarrassment at this outburst.*] Love you? Why d'you ask me such a question, Annie?

MRS. KEENEY: [*Shaking him—fiercely.*] But you do, don't you, David? Tell me!

KEENEY: I'm your husband, Annie, and you're my wife. Could there be aught but love between us after all these years?

MRS. KEENEY: [*Shaking him again—still more fiercely.*] Then you do love me. Say it!

KEENEY: [*Simply.*] I do, Annie.

MRS. KEENEY: [*Gives a sigh of relief—her hands drop to her sides. Keeney regards her anxiously. She passes her hand across her eyes and murmurs half to herself:*] I sometimes think if we could only have had a child. [KEENEY *turns away from her, deeply moved. She grabs his arm and turns him around to face her—intensely.*] And I've always been a good wife to you, haven't I, David?

KEENEY: [*His voice betraying his emotion.*] No man has ever had a bet-ter, Annie.

MRS. KEENEY: And I've never asked for much from you, have I, David? Have I?

KEENEY: You know you could have all I got the power to give ye, Annie.

MRS. KEENEY: [*Wildly.*] Then do this this once for my sake, for God's sake—take me home! It's killing me, this life—the brutality and cold and horror of it. I'm going mad. I can feel the threat in the air. I can hear the silence threatening me—day after gray day and every day the same. I can't bear it. [*Sobbing.*] I'll go mad, I know I will. Take me home, David, if you love me as you say. I'm afraid. For the love of God, take me home! [*She throws her arms around him, weeping against his shoulder. His face betrays the tremendous struggle going on within him. He holds her out at arm's length, his expression soft-ening. For a moment his shoulders sag, he becomes old, his iron spirit weakens as he looks at her tear-stained face.*]

KEENEY: [*Dragging out the words with an effort.*] I'll do it, Annie—for your sake—if you say it's needful for ye.

MRS. KEENEY: [*With wild joy—kissing him.*] God bless you for that, David! [*He turns away from her silently and walks toward the com-panionway. Just at that moment there is a clatter of footsteps on the stairs and the* SECOND MATE *enters the cabin.*]

MATE: [*Excitedly.*] The ice is breakin' up to no'the'ard, sir. There's a clear passage through the floe, and clear water beyond, the lookout

says. [KEENEY *straightens himself like a man coming out of a trance.*
MRS. KEENEY *looks at the* MATE *with terrified eyes.*]

KEENEY: [*Dazedly—trying to collect his thoughts.*] A clear passage? To
no'the'ard?

MATE: Yes, sir.

KEENEY: [*His voice suddenly grim with determination.*] Then get her
ready and we'll drive her through.

MATE: Aye, aye, sir.

MRS. KEENEY: [*Appealingly.*] David!

KEENEY: [*Not heeding her.*] Will the men turn to willin' or must we
drag 'em out?

MATE: They'll turn to willin' enough. You put the fear o' God into 'em,
sir. They're meek as lambs.

KEENEY: Then drive 'em—both watches. [*With grim determination.*]
They's whale t'other side o' this floe and we're going to git 'em.

MATE: Aye, aye, sir. [*He goes out hurriedly. A moment later there is the
sound of scuffling feet from the deck outside and the* MATE'*s voice
shouting orders.*]

KEENEY: [*Speaking aloud to himself—derisively.*] And I was agoin'
home like a yaller dog!

MRS. KEENEY: [*Imploringly.*] David!

KEENEY: [*Sternly.*] Woman, you ain't adoin' right when you meddle in
men's business and weaken 'em. You can't know my feelin's. I got to
prove a man to be a good husband for ye to take pride in. I got to git
the ile, I tell ye.

MRS. KEENEY: [*Supplicatingly.*] David! Aren't you going home?

KEENEY: [*Ignoring this question—commandingly.*] You ain't well. Go
and lay down a mite. [*He starts for the door.*] I got to git on deck.
[*He goes out. She cries after him in anguish:*] David! [*A pause. She
passes her hand across her eyes—then commences to laugh hysterically and goes to the organ. She sits down and starts to play wildly
an old hymn.* KEENEY *reënters from the doorway to the deck and
stands looking at her angrily. He comes over and grabs her roughly
by the shoulder.*]

KEENEY: Woman, what foolish mockin' is this? [*She laughs wildly and
he starts back from her in alarm.*] Annie! What is it? [*She doesn't answer him.* KEENEY'*s voice trembles.*] Don't you know me, Annie?
[*He puts both hands on her shoulders and turns her around so that
he can look into her eyes. She stares up at him with a stupid expression, a vague smile on her lips. He stumbles away from her, and she
commences softly to play the organ again.*]

KEENEY: [*Swallowing hard—in a hoarse whisper, as if he had difficulty in speaking.*] You said—you was a-goin' mad—God! [*A long wail is heard from the deck above.*] Ah bl-o-o-o-ow! [*A moment later the* MATE'*s face appears through the skylight. He cannot see* MRS. KEENEY.]

MATE: [*In great excitement.*] Whales, sir—a whole school of 'em—off the star'b'd quarter 'bout five mile away—big ones!

KEENEY: [*Galvanized into action.*] Are you lowerin' the boats?

MATE: Yes, sir.

KEENEY: [*With grim decision.*] I'm a-comin' with ye.

MATE: Aye, aye, sir. [*Jubilantly.*] You'll git the ile now right enough, sir. [*His head is withdrawn and he can be heard shouting orders.*]

KEENEY: [*Turning to his wife.*] Annie! Did you hear him? I'll git the ile. [*She doesn't answer or seem to know he is there. He gives a hard laugh, which is almost a groan.*] I know you're foolin' me, Annie. You ain't out of your mind— [*Anxiously.*] be you? I'll git the ile now right enough—jest a little while longer, Annie—then we'll turn hom'ard. I can't turn back now, you see that, don't ye? I've got to git the ile. [*In sudden terror.*] Answer me! You ain't mad, be you? [*She keeps on playing the organ, but makes no reply. The* MATE'*s face appears again through the skylight.*]

MATE: All ready, sir. [KEENEY *turns his back on his wife and strides to the doorway, where he stands for a moment and looks back at her in anguish, fighting to control his feelings.*]

MATE: Comin', sir?

KEENEY: [*His face suddenly grown hard with determination.*] Aye. [*He turns abruptly and goes out.* MRS. KEENEY *does not appear to notice his departure. Her whole attention seems centered in the organ. She sits with half-closed eyes, her body swaying a little from side to side to the rhythm of the hymn. Her fingers move faster and faster and she is playing wildly and discordantly as*

[*The Curtain Falls*]

WHERE THE CROSS IS MADE

A PLAY IN ONE ACT

CHARACTERS

CAPTAIN ISAIAH BARTLETT

NAT BARTLETT, *his son*

SUE BARTLETT, *his daughter*

DOCTOR HIGGINS

SILAS HORNE, *mate*
CATES, *bo'sun*   } *of the schooner* Mary Allen
JIMMY KANAKA, *harpooner*

WHERE THE CROSS IS MADE

SCENE—*Captain Bartlett's "cabin"—a room erected as a lookout post at the top of his house situated on a high point of land on the California coast. The inside of the compartment is fitted up like the captain's cabin of a deep-sea sailing vessel. On the left, forward, a porthole. Farther back, the stairs of the companionway. Still farther, two more portholes. In the rear, left, a marble-topped sideboard with a ship's lantern on it. In the rear, center, a door opening on stairs which lead to the lower house. A cot with a blanket is placed against the wall to the right of the door. In the right wall, five portholes. Directly under them, a wooden bench. In front of the bench, a long table with two straight-backed chairs, one in front, the other to the left of it. A cheap, dark-colored rug is on the floor. In the ceiling, midway from front to rear, a skylight extending from opposite the door to above the left edge of the table. In the right extremity of the skylight is placed a floating ship's compass. The light from the binnacle sheds over this from above and seeps down into the room, casting a vague globular shadow of the compass on the floor.*

The time is an early hour of a clear windy night in the fall of the year 1900. Moonlight, winnowed by the wind which moans in the stubborn angles of the old house, creeps wearily in through the portholes and rests like tired dust in circular patches upon the floor and table. An insistent monotone of thundering surf, muffled and far-off, is borne upward from the beach below.

After the curtain rises the door in the rear is opened slowly and the head and shoulders of NAT BARTLETT *appear over the sill. He casts a quick glance about the room, and seeing no one there, ascends the remaining steps and enters. He makes a sign to some one in the darkness beneath: "All right, Doctor."* DOCTOR HIGGINS *follows him into the room and, closing the door, stands looking with great curiosity around him. He is a slight, medium-sized professional-looking man of about thirty-five.* NAT BARTLETT *is very tall, gaunt, and loose-framed. His right arm has been amputated at the shoulder and the sleeve on that side of the heavy mackinaw he wears hangs flabbily or flaps against his body as he moves. He appears much older than his thirty years. His shoulders have a weary stoop as if worn down by the burden of his massive head with its heavy shock of tangled black hair. His face is long, bony, and sallow, with deep-set black eyes, a large aquiline nose,*

a wide thin-lipped mouth shadowed by an unkempt bristle of mustache.
His voice is low and deep with a penetrating, hollow, metallic quality.
In addition to the mackinaw, he wears corduroy trousers stuffed down
into high laced boots.

NAT: Can you see, Doctor?

HIGGINS: [*In the too-casual tones which betray an inward uneasiness.*]
Yes—perfectly—don't trouble. The moonlight is so bright—

NAT: Luckily. [*Walking slowly toward the table.*] He doesn't want any
light—lately—only the one from the binnacle there.

HIGGINS: He? Ah—you mean your father?

NAT: [*Impatiently.*] Who else?

HIGGINS: [*A bit startled—gazing around him in embarrassment.*] I suppose this is all meant to be like a ship's cabin?

NAT: Yes—as I warned you.

HIGGINS: [*In surprise.*] Warned me? Why, warned? I think it's very
natural—and interesting—this whim of his.

NAT: [*Meaningly.*] Interesting, it may be.

HIGGINS: And he lives up here, you said—never comes down?

NAT: Never—for the past three years. My sister brings his food up to
him. [*He sits down in the chair to the left of the table.*] There's a
lantern on the sideboard there, Doctor. Bring it over and sit down.
We'll make a light. I'll ask your pardon for bringing you to this
room on the roof—but—no one'll hear us here; and by seeing for
yourself the mad way he lives— Understand that I want you to get
all the facts—just that, facts!—and for that light is necessary. Without that—they become dreams up here—dreams, Doctor.

HIGGINS: [*With a relieved smile carries over the lantern.*] It is a trifle
spooky.

NAT: [*Not seeming to notice this remark.*] He won't take any note of
this light. His eyes are too busy—out there. [*He flings his left arm in
a wide gesture seaward.*] And if he does notice—well, let him come
down. You're bound to see him sooner or later. [*He scratches a
match and lights the lantern.*]

HIGGINS: Where is—he?

NAT: [*Pointing upward.*] Up on the poop. Sit down, man! He'll not
come—yet awhile.

HIGGINS: [*Sitting gingerly on the chair in front of table.*] Then he has
the roof too rigged up like a ship?

NAT: I told you he had. Like a deck, yes. A wheel, compass, binnacle
light, the companionway there [*He points.*], a bridge to pace up and

down on—*and keep watch.* If the wind wasn't so high you'd hear him now—back and forth—all the live-long night. [*With a sudden harshness.*] Didn't I tell you he's mad?

HIGGINS: [*With a professional air.*] That was nothing new. I've heard that about him from all sides since I first came to the asylum yonder. You say he only walks at night—up there?

NAT: Only at night, yes. [*Grimly.*] The things he wants to see can't be made out in daylight—dreams and such.

HIGGINS: But just what is he trying to see? Does any one know? Does he tell?

NAT: [*Impatiently.*] Why, every one knows what Father looks for, man! The ship, of course.

HIGGINS: What ship?

NAT: His ship—the Mary Allen—named for my dead mother.

HIGGINS: But—I don't understand— Is the ship long overdue—or what?

NAT: Lost in a hurricane off the Celebes with all on board—three years ago!

HIGGINS: [*Wonderingly.*] Ah. [*After a pause.*] But your father still clings to a doubt—

NAT: There is no doubt for him or any one else to cling to. She was sighted bottom up, a complete wreck, by the whaler John Slocum. That was two weeks after the storm. They sent a boat out to read her name.

HIGGINS: And hasn't your father ever heard—

NAT: He was the first to hear, naturally. Oh, he *knows* right enough, if that's what you're driving at. [*He bends toward the doctor—intensely.*] He *knows*, Doctor, he *knows*—but he won't *believe*. He can't—and keep living.

HIGGINS: [*Impatiently.*] Come, Mr. Bartlett, let's get down to brass tacks. You didn't drag me up here to make things more obscure, did you? Let's have the facts you spoke of. I'll need them to give sympathetic treatment to his case when we get him to the asylum.

NAT: [*Anxiously—lowering his voice.*] And you'll come to take him away tonight—for sure?

HIGGINS: Twenty minutes after I leave here I'll be back in the car. That's positive.

NAT: And you know your way through the house?

HIGGINS: Certainly, I remember—but I don't see—

NAT: The outside door will be left open for you. You must come right up. My sister and I will be here—with him. And you understand—

Neither of us knows anything about this. The authorities have been complained to—not by us, mind—but by some one. He must never know—

HIGGINS: Yes, yes—but still I don't— Is he liable to prove violent?

NAT: No—no. He's quiet always—too quiet; but he might do something—anything—if he knows—

HIGGINS: Rely on me not to tell him, then; but I'll bring along two attendants in case— [*He breaks off and continues in matter-of-fact tones.*] And now for the facts in this case, if you don't mind, Mr. Bartlett.

NAT: [*Shaking his head—moodily.*] There are cases where facts— Well, here goes—the brass tacks. My father was a whaling captain as his father before him. The last trip he made was seven years ago. He expected to be gone two years. It was four before we saw him again. His ship had been wrecked in the Indian Ocean. He and six others managed to reach a small island on the fringe of the Archipelago—an island barren as hell, Doctor—after seven days in an open boat. The rest of the whaling crew never were heard from again—gone to the sharks. Of the six who reached the island with my father only three were alive when a fleet of Malay canoes picked them up, mad from thirst and starvation, the four of them. These four men finally reached Frisco. [*With great emphasis.*] They were my father; Silas Horne, the mate; Cates, the bo'sun; and Jimmy Kanaka, a Hawaiian harpooner. Those four! [*With a forced laugh.*] There are facts for you. It was all in the papers at the time—my father's story.

HIGGINS: But what of the other three who were on the island?

NAT: [*Harshly.*] Died of exposure, perhaps. Mad and jumped into the sea, perhaps. That was the told story. Another was whispered—killed and eaten, perhaps! But gone—vanished—that, undeniably. That was the fact. For the rest—who knows? And what does it matter?

HIGGINS: [*With a shudder.*] I should think it would matter—a lot.

NAT: [*Fiercely.*] We're dealing with facts, Doctor! [*With a laugh.*] And here are some more for you. My father brought the three down to this house with him—Horne and Cates and Jimmy Kanaka. We hardly recognized my father. He had been through hell and looked it. His hair was white. But you'll see for yourself—soon. And the others—they were all a bit queer, too—mad, if you will. [*He laughs again.*] So much for the facts, Doctor. They leave off there and the dreams begin.

HIGGINS: [*Doubtfully.*] It would seem—the facts are enough.

NAT: Wait. [*He resumes deliberately.*] One day my father sent for me

and in the presence of the others told me the dream. I was to be heir
to the secret. Their second day on the island, he said, they discovered
in a sheltered inlet the rotten, water-logged hulk of a Malay prau—a
proper war prau such as the pirates used to use. She had been there
rotting—God knows how long. The crew had vanished—God knows
where, for there was no sign on the island that man had ever
touched there. The Kanakas went over the prau—they're devils for
staying under water, you know—and they found—in two chests—
[*he leans back in his chair and smiles ironically*]—Guess what,
Doctor?

HIGGINS: [*With an answering smile.*] Treasure, of course.

NAT: [*Leaning forward and pointing his finger accusingly at the other.*]
You see! The root of belief is in you, too! [*Then he leans back with a
hollow chuckle.*] Why, yes. Treasure, to be sure. What else? They
landed it and—you can guess the rest, too—diamonds, emeralds,
gold ornaments—innumerable, of course. Why limit the stuff of
dreams? Ha-ha! [*He laughs sardonically as if mocking himself.*]

HIGGINS: [*Deeply interested.*] And then?

NAT: They began to go mad—hunger, thirst, and the rest—and they began to forget. Oh, they forgot a lot, and lucky for them they did,
probably. But my father realizing, as he told me, what was happening to them, insisted that while they still knew what they were doing
they should—guess again now, Doctor. Ha-ha!

HIGGINS: Bury the treasure?

NAT: [*Ironically.*] Simple, isn't it? Ha-ha. And then they made a map—
the same old dream, you see—with a charred stick, and my father
had care of it. They were picked up soon after, mad as hatters, as I
have told you, by some Malays. [*He drops his mocking and adopts a
calm, deliberate tone again.*] But the map isn't a dream, Doctor.
We're coming back to facts again. [*He reaches into the pocket of his
mackinaw and pulls out a crumpled paper.*] Here. [*He spreads it out
on the table.*]

HIGGINS: [*Craning his neck eagerly.*] Dammit! This is interesting. The
treasure, I suppose, is where—

NAT: Where the cross is made.

HIGGINS: And here are the signatures, I see. And that sign?

NAT: Jimmy Kanaka's. He couldn't write.

HIGGINS: And below? That's yours, isn't it?

NAT: As heir to the secret, yes. We all signed it here the morning the
Mary Allen, the schooner my father had mortgaged this house to fit
out, set sail to bring back the treasure. Ha-ha.

HIGGINS: The ship he's still looking for—that was lost three years ago?

NAT: The Mary Allen, yes. The other three men sailed away on her. Only father and the mate knew the approximate location of the island—and I—as heir. It's— [*He hesitates, frowning.*] No matter. I'll keep the mad secret. My father wanted to go with them—but my mother was dying. I dared not go either.

HIGGINS: Then you wanted to go? You believed in the treasure then?

NAT: Of course. Ha-ha. How could I help it? I believed until my mother's death. Then *he* became mad, entirely mad. He built this cabin—to wait in—and he suspected my growing doubt as time went on. So, as final proof, he gave me a thing he had kept hidden from them all—a sample of the riches of the treasure. Ha-ha. Behold! [*He takes from his pocket a heavy bracelet thickly studded with stones and throws it on the table near the lantern.*]

HIGGINS: [*Picking it up with eager curiosity—as if in spite of himself.*] Real jewels?

NAT: Ha-ha! You want to believe, too. No—paste and brass—Malay ornaments.

HIGGINS: You had it looked over?

NAT: Like a fool, yes. [*He puts it back in his pocket and shakes his head as if throwing off a burden.*] Now you know why he's mad—waiting for that ship—and why in the end I had to ask you to take him away where he'll be safe. The mortgage—the price of that ship—is to be foreclosed. We have to move, my sister and I. We can't take him with us. She is to be married soon. Perhaps away from the sight of the sea he may—

HIGGINS: [*Perfunctorily.*] Let's hope for the best. And I fully appreciate your position. [*He gets up, smiling.*] And thank you for the interesting story. I'll know how to humor him when he raves about treasure.

NAT: [*Somberly.*] He is quiet always—too quiet. He only walks to and fro—watching—

HIGGINS: Well, I must go. You think it's best to take him tonight?

NAT: [*Persuasively.*] Yes, Doctor. The neighbors—they're far away but—for my sister's sake—you understand.

HIGGINS: I see. It must be hard on her—this sort of thing—Well.—[*He goes to the door, which NAT opens for him.*] I'll return presently. [*He starts to descend.*]

NAT: [*Urgently.*] Don't fail us, Doctor. And come right up. He'll be here. [*He closes the door and tiptoes carefully to the companionway. He ascends it a few steps and remains for a moment listening for some sound from above. Then he goes over to the table, turning the lantern very low, and sits down, resting his elbows, his chin on his hands, staring somberly before him. The door in the rear is slowly opened. It creaks slightly and* NAT *jumps to his feet—in a thick voice of terror.*] Who's there? [*The door swings wide open, revealing* SUE BARTLETT. *She ascends into the room and shuts the door behind her. She is a tall, slender woman of twenty-five, with a pale, sad face framed in a mass of dark red hair. This hair furnishes the only touch of color about her. Her full lips are pale; the blue of her wistful wide eyes is fading into a twilight gray. Her voice is low and melancholy. She wears a dark wrapper and slippers.*]

SUE: [*Stands and looks at her brother accusingly.*] It's only I. What are you afraid of?

NAT: [*Averts his eyes and sinks back on his chair again.*] Nothing. I didn't know—I thought you were in your room.

SUE: [*Comes to the table.*] I was reading. Then I heard some one come down the stairs and go out. Who was it? [*With sudden terror.*] It wasn't—Father?

NAT: No. He's up there—watching—as he always is.

SUE: [*Sitting down—insistently.*] Who was it?

NAT: [*Evasively.*] A man—I know.

SUE: What man? What is he? You're holding something back. Tell me.

NAT: [*Raising his eyes defiantly.*] A doctor.

SUE: [*Alarmed*] Oh! [*With quick intuition.*] You brought him up here—so that I wouldn't know!

NAT: [*Doggedly.*] No. I took him up here to see how things were—to ask him about Father.

SUE: [*As if afraid of the answer she will get.*] Is he one of them—from the asylum? Oh, Nat, you haven't—

NAT: [*Interrupting her—hoarsely.*] No, no! Be still.

SUE: That would be—the last horror.

NAT: [*Defiantly.*] Why? You always say that. What could be more horrible than things as they are? I believe—it would be better for him—away—where he couldn't see the sea. He'll forget his mad idea of waiting for a lost ship and a treasure that never was. [*As if trying to convince himself—vehemently.*] I believe this!

SUE: [*Reproachfully.*] You don't, Nat. You know he'd die if he hadn't the sea to live with.

NAT: [*Bitterly.*] And you know old Smith will foreclose the mortgage. Is that nothing? We cannot pay. He came yesterday and talked with me. He knows the place is his—to all purposes. He talked as if we were merely his tenants, curse him! And he swore he'd foreclose immediately unless—

SUE: [*Eagerly.*] What?

NAT: [*In a hard voice.*] Unless we have—Father—taken away.

SUE: [*In anguish.*] Oh! But why, why? What is Father to him?

NAT: The value of the property—our home which is his, Smith's. The neigbors are afraid. They pass by on the road at nights coming back to their farms from the town. They see *him* up there walking back and forth—waving his arms against the sky. They're afraid. They talk of a complaint. They say for his own good he must be taken away. They even whisper the house is haunted. Old Smith is afraid of his property. He thinks that *he* may set fire to the house—do anything—

SUE: [*Despairingly.*] But you told him how foolish that was, didn't you? That Father is quiet, always quiet.

NAT: What's the use of telling—when they believe—when they're afraid? [SUE *hides her face in her hands—a pause—*NAT *whispers hoarsely:*] I've been afraid myself—at times.

SUE: Oh, Nat! Of what?

NAT: [*Violently.*] Oh, him and the sea he calls to! Of the damned sea he forced me on as a boy—the sea that robbed me of my arm and made me the broken thing I am!

SUE: [*Pleadingly.*] You can't blame Father—for your misfortune.

NAT: He took me from school and forced me on his ship, didn't he? What would I have been now but an ignorant sailor like him if he had had his way? No. It's the sea I should not blame, that foiled him by taking my arm and then throwing me ashore—another one of *his* wrecks!

SUE: [*With a sob.*] You're bitter, Nat—and hard. It was so long ago. Why can't you forget?

NAT: [*Bitterly.*] Forget! You can talk! When Tom comes home from this voyage you'll be married and out of this with life before you—a captain's wife as our mother was. I wish you joy.

SUE: [*Supplicatingly.*] And you'll come with us, Nat—and father, too—and then—

NAT: Would you saddle your young husband with a madman and a cripple? [*Fiercely.*] No, no, not I! [*Vindictively.*] And not him, either! [*With sudden meaning—deliberately.*] I've got to stay here. My book is three-fourths done—my book that will set me free! But I know, I feel, as sure as I stand here living before you, that I must finish it here. It could not live for me outside of this house where it was born. [*Staring at her fixedly.*] So I will stay—in spite of hell! [SUE *sobs hopelessly. After a pause he continues:*] Old Smith told me I could live here indefinitely without paying—as caretaker—if—

SUE: [*Fearfully—like a whispered echo.*] If?

NAT: [*Staring at her—in a hard voice.*] If I have *him* sent—where he'll no longer harm himself—nor others.

SUE: [*With horrified dread.*] No—no, Nat! For our dead mother's sake.

NAT: [*Struggling.*] Did I say I had? Why do you look at me—like that?

SUE: Nat! Nat! For our mother's sake!

NAT: [*In terror.*] Stop! Stop! She's dead—and at peace. Would you bring her tired soul back to him again to be bruised and wounded?

SUE: Nat!

NAT: [*Clutching at his throat as though to strangle something within him—hoarsely.*] Sue! Have mercy! [*His sister stares at him with dread foreboding.* NAT *calms himself with an effort and continues deliberately:*] Smith said he would give two thousand cash if I would sell the place to him—and he would let me stay, rent free, as caretaker.

SUE: [*Scornfully.*] Two thousand! Why, over and above the mortgage its worth—

NAT: It's not what it's worth. It's what one can get, cash—for my book—for freedom!

SUE: So that's why he wants Father sent away, the wretch! He must know the will Father made—

NAT: Gives the place to me. Yes, he knows. I told him.

SUE: [*Dully.*] Ah, how vile men are!

NAT: [*Persuasively.*] If it were to be done—if it were, I say—there'd be half for you for your wedding portion. That's fair.

SUE: [*Horrified.*] Blood money! Do you think I could touch it?

NAT: [*Persuasively.*] It would be only fair. I'd give it you.

SUE: My God, Nat, are you trying to bribe me?

NAT: No. It's yours in all fairness. [*With a twisted smile.*] You forget I'm heir to the treasure, too, and can afford to be generous. Ha-ha.

SUE: [*Alarmed.*] Nat! You're so strange. You're sick, Nat. You couldn't talk this way if you were yourself. Oh, we must go away from here—you and father and I! Let Smith foreclose. There'll be something over the mortgage; and we'll move to some little house—by the sea so that father—

NAT: [*Fiercely.*] Can keep up his mad game with me—whispering dreams in my ear—pointing out to sea—mocking me with stuff like this! [*He takes the bracelet from his pocket. The sight of it infuriates him and he hurls it into a corner, exclaiming in a terrible voice:*] No! No! It's too late for dreams now. It's too late! I've put them behind me tonight—forever!

SUE: [*Looks at him and suddenly understands that what she dreads has come to pass—*letting her head fall on her outstretched arms with a long moan.*] Then—you've done it! You've sold him! Oh, Nat, you're cursed!

NAT: [*With a terrified glance at the roof above.*] Ssshh! What are you saying? He'll be better off—away from the sea.

SUE: [*Dully.*] You've sold him.

NAT: [*Wildly.*] No! No! [*He takes the map from his pocket.*] Listen, Sue! For God's sake, listen to me! See! The map of the island. [*He spreads it out on the table.*] And the treasure—where the cross is made. [*He gulps and his words pour out incoherently.*] I've carried it about for years. Is that nothing? You don't know what it means. It stands between me and my book. It's stood between me and life—driving me mad! *He* taught me to wait and hope with him—wait and hope—day after day. He made me doubt my brain and give the lie to my eyes—when hope was dead—when I knew it was all a dream—I couldn't kill it! [*His eyes starting from his head.*] God forgive me, I still believe! And that's mad—mad, do you hear?

SUE: [*Looking at him with horror.*] And that is why—you hate him!

NAT: No, I don't— [*Then in a sudden frenzy.*] Yes! I do hate him! He's stolen my brain! I've got to free myself, can't you see, from him—and his madness.

SUE: [*Terrified—appealingly.*] Nat! Don't! You talk as if—

NAT: [*With a wild laugh.*] As if I were mad? You're right—but I'll be mad no more! See! [*He opens the lantern and sets fire to the map in his hand. When he shuts the lantern again it flickers and goes out. They watch the paper burn with fascinated eyes as he talks.*] See how I free myself and become sane. And now for facts, as the doctor said. I lied to you about him. He was a doctor from the asylum. See how it burns! It must all be destroyed—this poisonous madness. Yes, I lied to you—see—it's gone—the last speck—and the only other map is the one Silas Horne took to the bottom of the sea with him. [*He lets the ash fall to the floor and crushes it with his foot.*] Gone! I'm free of it—at last! [*His face is very pale, but he goes on calmly.*] Yes, I sold him, if you will—to save my soul. They're coming from the asylum to get him— [*There is a loud, muffled cry from above, which sounds like "Sail-ho," and a stamping of feet. The slide to the companionway above is slid back with a bang. A gust of air tears down into the room. NAT and SUE have jumped to their feet and stand petrified. CAPTAIN BARTLETT tramps down the stairs.*]

NAT: [*With a shudder.*] God! Did he hear?

SUE: Ssshh! [CAPTAIN BARTLETT *comes into the room. He bears a strik-*

*ing resemblance to his son, but his face is more stern and formidable,
his form more robust, erect and muscular. His mass of hair is pure
white, his bristly mustache the same, contrasting with the weather-
beaten leather color of his furrowed face. Bushy gray brows over-
hang the obsessed glare of his fierce dark eyes. He wears a heavy,
double-breasted blue coat, pants of the same material, and rubber
boots turned down from the knee.]*

BARTLETT: [*In a state of mad exultation strides toward his son and
points an accusing finger at him.* NAT *shrinks backward a step.*] Bin
thinkin' me mad, did ye? Thinkin' it for the past three years, ye
bin—ever since them fools on the Slocum tattled their damn lie o'
the Mary Allen bein' a wreck.

NAT: [*Swallowing hard—chokingly.*] No—Father—I—

BARTLETT: Don't lie, ye whelp! You that I'd made my heir—aimin' to
git me out o' the way! Aimin' to put me behind the bars o' the jail
for mad folk!

SUE: Father—no!

BARTLETT: [*Waving his hand for her to be silent.*] Not you, girl, not
you. You're your mother.

NAT: [*Very pale.*] Father—do you think—I—

BARTLETT: [*Fiercely.*] A lie in your eyes! I bin a-readin' 'em. My curse
on you!

SUE: Father! Don't!

BARTLETT: Leave me be, girl. He believed, didn't he? And ain't he
turned traitor—mockin' at me and sayin' it's all a lie—mockin' at
himself, too, for bein' a fool to believe in dreams, as he calls 'em.

NAT: [*Placatingly.*] You're wrong, Father. I do believe.

BARTLETT: [*Triumphantly.*] Aye, now ye do! Who wouldn't credit their
own eyes?

NAT: [*Mystified.*] Eyes?

BARTLETT: Have ye not seen her, then? Did ye not hear me hail?

NAT: [*Confusedly.*] Hail? I heard a shout. But—hail what?—seen what?

BARTLETT: [*Grimly.*] Aye, now's your punishment, Judas. [*Explosively.*]
The Mary Allen, ye blind fool, come back from the Southern Seas—
come back as I swore she must!

SUE: [*Trying to soothe him.*] Father! Be quiet. It's nothing.

BARTLETT: [*Not heeding her—his eyes fixed hypnotically on his son's.*]
Turned the pint a half-hour back—the Mary Allen—loaded with
gold as I swore she would be—carryin' her lowers—not a reef in
'em—makin' port, boy, as I swore she must—too late for traitors,
boy, too late!—droppin' her anchor just when I hailed her.

NAT: [*A haunted, fascinated look in his eyes, which are fixed immovably on his father's.*] The Mary Allen! But how do you know?

BARTLETT: Not know my own ship! 'Tis you're mad!

NAT: But at night—some other schooner—

BARTLETT: No other, I say! The Mary Allen—clear in the moonlight. And heed this: D'you call to mind the signal I gave to Silas Horne if he made this port o' a night?

NAT: [*Slowly.*] A red and a green light at the mainmast-head.

BARTLETT: [*Triumphantly.*] Then look out if ye dare! [*He goes to the porthole, left forward.*] Ye can see it plain from here. [*Commandingly.*] Will ye believe your eyes? Look—and then call me mad! [NAT *peers through the porthole and starts back, a dumbfounded expression on his face.*]

NAT: [*Slowly.*] A red and a green at the mainmast-head. Yes—clear as day.

SUE: [*With a worried look at him.*] Let me see. [*She goes to the porthole.*]

BARTLETT: [*To his son with fierce satisfaction.*] Aye, ye see now clear enough—too late for you. [NAT *stares at him spellbound.*] And from above I saw Horne and Cates and Jimmy Kanaka plain on the deck in the moonlight lookin' up at me. Come! [*He strides to the companionway, followed by* NAT. *The two of them ascend.* SUE *turns from the porthole, an expression of frightened bewilderment on her face. She shakes her head sadly. A loud "Mary Allen, ahoy!" comes from above in* BARTLETT's *voice, followed like an echo by the same hail from* NAT. SUE *covers her face with her hands, shuddering.* NAT *comes down the companionway, his eyes wild and exulting.*]

SUE: [*Brokenly.*] He's bad tonight, Nat. You're right to humor him. It's the best thing.

NAT: [*Savagely.*] Humor him? What in hell do you mean?

SUE: [*Pointing to the porthole.*] There's nothing there, Nat. There's not a ship in harbor.

NAT: You're a fool—or blind! The Mary Allen's there in plain sight of any one, with the red and the green signal lights. Those fools lied about her being wrecked. And I've been a fool, too.

SUE: But, Nat, there's nothing. [*She goes over to the porthole again.*] Not a ship. See.

NAT: I saw, I tell you! From above it's all plain. [*He turns from her and goes back to his seat by the table.* SUE *follows him, pleading frightenedly.*]

SUE: Nat! You mustn't let this— You're all excited and trembling, Nat. [*She puts a soothing hand on his forehead.*]

NAT: [*Pushing her away from him roughly.*] You blind fool! [*Bartlett comes down the steps of the companionway. His face is transfigured with the ecstasy of a dream come true.*]

BARTLETT: They've lowered a boat—the three—Horne and Cates and Jimmy Kanaka. They're a-rowin' ashore. I heard the oars in the locks. Listen! [*A pause.*]

NAT: [*Excitedly.*] I hear!

SUE: [*Who has taken the chair by her brother—in a warning whisper.*] It's the wind and sea you hear, Nat. Please!

BARTLETT: [*Suddenly.*] Hark! They've landed. They're back on earth again as I swore they'd come back. They'll be a-comin' up the path now. [*He stands in an attitude of rigid attention.* NAT *strains forward in his chair. The sound of the wind and sea suddenly ceases and there is a heavy silence. A dense green glow floods slowly in rhythmic waves like a liquid into the room—as of great depths of the sea faintly penetrated by light.*]

NAT: [*Catching at his sister's hand—chokingly.*] See how the light changes! Green and gold! [*He shivers.*] Deep under the sea! I've been drowned for years! [*Hysterically.*] Save me! Save me!

SUE: [*Patting his hand comfortingly.*] Only the moonlight, Nat. It hasn't changed. Be quiet, dear, it's nothing. [*The green light grows deeper and deeper.*]

BARTLETT: [*In a crooning, monotonous tone.*] They move slowly—slowly. They're heavy, I know, heavy—the two chests. Hark! They're below at the door. You hear?

NAT: [*Starting to his feet.*] I hear! I left the door open.

BARTLETT: For them?

NAT: For them.

SUE: [*Shuddering.*] Ssshh! [*The sound of a door being heavily slammed is heard from way down in the house.*]

NAT: [*To his sister—excitedly.*] There! You hear?

SUE: A shutter in the wind.

NAT: There is no wind.

BARTLETT: Up they come! Up, bullies! They're heavy—heavy! [*The paddling of bare feet sounds from the floor below—then comes up the stairs.*]

NAT: You hear them now?

SUE: Only the rats running about. It's nothing, Nat.

BARTLETT: [*Rushing to the door and throwing it open.*] Come in, lads, come in!—and welcome home! [*The forms of* SILAS HORNE, CATES, *and* JIMMY KANAKA *rise noiselessly into the room from the stairs. The last two carry heavy inlaid chests.* HORNE *is a parrot-nosed, an-*

*gular old man dressed in gray cotton trousers and a singlet torn open
across his hairy chest.* JIMMY *is a tall, sinewy, bronzed young
Kanaka. He wears only a breech cloth.* CATES *is squat and stout and
is dressed in dungaree pants and a shredded white sailor's blouse,
stained with iron rust. All are in their bare feet. Water drips from
their soaked and rotten clothes. Their hair is matted, intertwined
with slimy strands of seaweed. Their eyes, as they glide silently into
the room, stare frightfully wide at nothing. Their flesh in the green
light has the suggestion of decomposition. Their bodies sway limply,
nervelessly, rhythmically as if to the pulse of long swells of the
deep sea.*]

NAT: [*Making a step toward them.*] See! [*Frenziedly.*] Welcome home,
boys!

SUE: [*Grabbing his arm.*] Sit down, Nat. It's nothing. There's no one
there. Father—sit down!

BARTLETT: [*Grinning at the three and putting his finger to his lips.*] Not
here, boys, not here—not before him. [*He points to his son.*] He has
no right, now. Come. The treasure is ours only. We'll go away with it
together. Come. [*He goes to the companionway. The three follow. At
the foot of it* HORNE *puts a swaying hand on his shoulder and with
the other holds out a piece of paper to him.* BARTLETT *takes it and
chuckles exultantly.*] That's right—for him—that's right! [*He ascends. The figures sway up after him.*]

NAT: [*Frenziedly.*] Wait! [*He struggles toward the companionway.*]

SUE: [*Trying to hold him back.*] Nat—don't! Father—come back!

NAT: Father! [*He flings her away from him and rushes up the companionway. He pounds against the slide, which seems to have been shut
down on him.*]

SUE: [*Hysterically—runs wildly to the door in rear.*] Help! Help! [*As she
gets to the door* DOCTOR HIGGINS *appears, hurrying up the stairs.*]

HIGGINS: [*Excitedly.*] Just a moment, Miss. What's the matter?

SUE: [*With a gasp.*] My father—up there!

HIGGINS: I can't see—where's my flash? Ah. [*He flashes it on her terror-
stricken face, then quickly around the room. The green glow disappears. The wind and sea are heard again. Clear moonlight floods
through the portholes.* HIGGINS *springs to the companionway.* NAT
is still pounding.] Here, Bartlett. Let me try.

NAT: [*Coming down—looking dully at the doctor.*] They've locked it. I
can't get up.

HIGGINS: [*Looks up—in an astonished voice.*] What's the matter,
Bartlett? It's all open. [*He starts to ascend.*]

NAT: [*In a voice of warning.*] Look out, man! Look out for them!

HIGGINS: [*Calls down from above.*] Them? Who? There's no one here. [*Suddenly—in alarm.*] Come up! Lend a hand here! He's fainted! [NAT *goes up slowly.* SUE *goes over and lights the lantern, then hurries back to the foot of the companionway with it. There is a scuffling noise from above. They reappear, carrying* CAPTAIN BART-LETT's *body.*]

HIGGINS: Easy now! [*They lay him on the couch in rear.* SUE *sets the lantern down by the couch.* HIGGINS *bends and listens for a heart-beat. Then he rises, shaking his head.*] I'm sorry—

SUE: [*Dully.*] Dead?

HIGGINS: [*Nodding.*] Heart failure, I should judge. [*With an attempt at consolation.*] Perhaps it's better so, if—

NAT: [*As if in a trance.*] There was something Horne handed him. Did you see?

SUE: [*Wringing her hands.*] Oh, Nat, be still! He's dead. [*To* HIGGINS *with pitiful appeal.*] Please go—go—

HIGGINS: There's nothing I can do?

SUE: Go—please— [HIGGINS *bows stiffly and goes out.* NAT *moves slowly to his father's body, as if attracted by some irresistible fascination.*]

NAT: Didn't you see? Horne handed him something.

SUE: [*Sobbing.*] Nat! Nat! Come away! Don't touch him, Nat! Come away. [*But her brother does not heed her. His gaze is fixed on his father's right hand, which hangs downward over the side of the couch. He pounces on it and forcing the clenched fingers open with a great effort, secures a crumpled ball of paper.*]

NAT: [*Flourishing it above his head with a shout of triumph.*] See! [*He bends down and spreads it out in the light of the lantern.*] The map of the island! Look! It isn't lost for me after all! There's still a chance—*my* chance! [*With mad, solemn decision.*] When the house is sold I'll go—and I'll find it! Look! It's written here in his hand writing: "The treasure is buried where the cross is made."

SUE: [*Covering her face with her hands—brokenly.*] Oh, God! Come away, Nat! Come away!

[*The Curtain Falls*]

THE ROPE

A PLAY IN ONE ACT

CHARACTERS

ABRAHAM BENTLEY

ANNIE, *his daughter*

PAT SWEENEY, *her husband*

MARY, *their child*

LUKE BENTLEY, *Abe's son by a second marriage*

THE ROPE

SCENE—*The interior of an old barn situated on top of a high headland of the seacoast. In the rear, to the left, a stall in which lumber is stacked up. To the right of it, an open double doorway looking out over the ocean. Outside the doorway, the faint trace of what was once a road leading to the barn. Beyond the road, the edge of a cliff which rises sheer from the sea below. On the right of the doorway, three stalls with mangers and hay-ricks. The first of these is used as a woodbin and is half full of piled-up cordwood. Near this bin, a chopping block with an ax driven into the top of it.*

The left section of the barn contains the hay loft, which extends at a height of about twelve feet from the floor as far to the right as the middle of the doorway. The loft is bare except for a few scattered mounds of dank-looking hay. From the edge of the loft, half way from the door, a rope about five feet long with an open running noose at the end is hanging. A rusty plow and various other farming implements, all giving evidence of long disuse, are lying on the floor near the left wall. Farther forward an old cane-bottomed chair is set back against the wall.

In front of the stalls on the right stands a long, roughly constructed carpenter's table, evidently home-made. Saws, a lathe, a hammer, chisel, a keg containing nails and other tools of the carpentry trade are on the table. Two benches are placed, one in front, one to the left of it.

The right side of the barn is a bare wall.

It is between six and half-past in the evening of a day in early spring. At the rising of the curtain some trailing clouds near the horizon, seen through the open doorway, are faintly tinged with gold by the first glow of the sunset. As the action progresses this reflected light gradually becomes brighter, and then slowly fades into a smoky crimson. The sea is a dark slate color. From the rocks below the headland sounds the muffled monotone of breaking waves.

As the curtain rises MARY *is discovered squatting cross-legged on the floor, her back propped against the right side of the doorway, her face in profile. She is a skinny, over-grown girl of ten with thin, carroty hair worn in a pig-tail. She wears a shabby gingham dress. Her face is stupidly expressionless. Her hands flutter about aimlessly in relaxed, flabby gestures.*

She is staring fixedly at a rag doll which she has propped up against the doorway opposite her. She hums shrilly to herself.

At a sudden noise from outside she jumps to her feet, peeks out, and quickly snatches up the doll, which she hugs fiercely to her breast. Then, after a second's fearful hesitation, she runs to the carpenter's table and crawls under it.

As she does so ABRAHAM BENTLEY *appears in the doorway and stands, blinking into the shadowy barn. He is a tall, lean stoop-shouldered old man of sixty-five. His thin legs, twisted by rheumatism, totter feebly under him as he shuffles slowly along by the aid of a thick cane. His face is gaunt, chalky-white, furrowed with wrinkles, surmounted by a shiny bald scalp fringed with scanty wisps of white hair. His eyes peer weakly from beneath bushy, black brows. His mouth is a sunken line drawn in under his large, beak-like nose. A two weeks' growth of stubby patches of beard covers his jaws and chin. He has on a threadbare brown overcoat but wears no hat.*

BENTLEY: [*Comes slowly into the barn, peering around him suspiciously. As he reaches the table and leans one hand on it for support,* MARY *darts from underneath and dashes out through the doorway.* BENTLEY *is startled; then shakes his cane after her.*] Out o' my sight, you Papist brat! Spawn o' Satan! Spyin' on me! They set her to it. Spyin' to watch me! [*He limps to the door and looks out cautiously. Satisfied, he turns back into the barn.*] Spyin' to see—what they'll never know. [*He stands staring up at the rope and taps it testingly several times with his stick, talking to himself as he does so.*] It's tied strong—strong as death— [*He cackles with satisfaction.*] They'll see, then! They'll see! [*He laboriously creeps over to the bench and sits down wearily. He looks toward the sea and his voice quavers in a doleful chant:*] "Woe unto us! for the day goeth away, for the shadows of the evening are stretched out." [*He mumbles to himself for a moment—then speaks clearly.*] Spyin' on me! Spawn o' the Pit! [*He renews his chant.*] "They hunt our steps that we cannot go in our streets: our end is near, our days are fulfilled; for our end is come."

[*As he finishes* ANNIE *enters. She is a thin, slovenly, worn-out looking woman of about forty with a drawn, pasty face. Her habitual expression is one of a dulled irritation. She talks in a high-pitched, sing-song whine. She wears a faded gingham dress and a torn sunbonnet.*]

ANNIE: [*Comes over to her father but warily keeps out of range of his stick.*] Paw! [*He doesn't answer or appear to see her.*] Paw! You ain't fergittin' what the doctor told you when he was here last, be you?

He said you was to keep still and not go a-walkin' round. Come on back to the house, Paw. It's gittin' near supper time and you got to take your medicine b'fore it, like he says.

BENTLEY: [*His eyes fixed in front of him.*] "The punishment of thine iniquity is accomplished, O daughter of Zion: he will visit thine iniquity, O daughter of Edom; he will discover thy sins."

ANNIE: [*Waiting resignedly until he has finished—wearily.*] You better take watch on your health, Paw, and not be sneakin' up to this barn no more. Lord sakes, soon 's ever my back is turned you goes sneakin' off agen. It's enough to drive a body outa their right mind.

BENTLEY: "Behold, every one that useth proverbs shall use this proverb against thee, saying, As is the mother, so is her daughter!" [*He cackles to himself.*] So is her daughter!

ANNIE: [*Her face flushing with anger.*] And if I am, I'm glad I take after her and not you, y'old wizard! [*Scornfully.*] A fine one you be to be shoutin' Scripture in a body's ears all the live-long day—you that druv Maw to her death with your naggin', and pinchin', and miser stinginess. If you've a mind to pray, it's down in the medder you ought to go, and kneel down by her grave, and ask God to forgive you for the meanness you done to her all her life.

BENTLEY: [*Mumbling.*] "As is the mother, so is her daughter."

ANNIE: [*Enraged by the repetition of this quotation.*] *You* quotin' Scripture! Why, Maw wasn't cold in the earth b'fore you was down in the port courtin' agen—courtin' that harlot that was the talk o' the whole town! And then you disgraces yourself and me by marryin' her—*her*—and bringin' her back home with you; and me still goin' every day to put flowers on Maw's grave that you'd fergotten. [*She glares at him vindictively, pausing for breath.*] And between you you'd have druv me into the grave like you done Maw if I hadn't married Pat Sweeney so's I could git away and live in peace. Then you took on so high and mighty 'cause he was a Cath'lic—*you* gittin' religion all of a moment just for spite on me 'cause I'd left—and b'cause she egged you on against me; *you* sayin' it was a sin to marry a Papist, after not bein' at Sunday meetin' yourself for more'n twenty years!

BENTLEY: [*Loudly.*] "He will visit thine iniquity—"

ANNIE: [*Interrupting.*] And the carryin's-on you had the six years at home after I'd left you—the shame of the whole county! Your wife, indeed, with a child she *claimed* was your'n, and her goin' with this farmer and that, and even men off the ships in the port, and you blind to it! And then when she got sick of you and ran away—only to meet her end at the hands of God a year after—she leaves you alone with that—*your* son, Luke, *she* called him—and him only five years old!

BENTLEY: [*Babbling.*] Luke? Luke?

ANNIE: [*Tauntingly.*] Yes, Luke! "As is the mother, so is her son"— that's what you ought to preach 'stead of puttin' curses on me. You was glad enough to git me back home agen, and Pat with me, to tend the place, and help bring up that brat of hers. [*Jealously.*] You was fond enough of him all them years—and how did he pay you back? Stole your money and ran off and left you just when he was sixteen and old enough to help. Told you to your face he'd stolen and was leavin'. He only laughed when you was took crazy and cursed him; and he only laughed harder when you hung up that silly rope there [*She points.*] and told him to hang himself on it when he ever came home agen.

BENTLEY: [*Mumbling.*] You'll see, then. You'll see!

ANNIE: [*Wearily—her face becoming dull and emotionless again.*] I s'pose I'm a bigger fool than you be to argy with a half-witted body. But I tell you agen that Luke of yours ain't comin' back; and if he does he ain't the kind to hang himself, more's the pity. He's like her. He'd hang *you* more likely if he s'pected you had any money. So you might 's well take down that ugly rope you've had tied there since he run off. He's probably dead anyway by this.

BENTLEY: [*Frightened.*] No! No!

ANNIE: Them as bad as him comes to a sudden end. [*Irritably.*] Land sakes, Paw, here I am argyin' with your lunatic notions and the supper not ready. Come on and git your medicine. You can see no one ain't touched your old rope. Come on! You can sit 'n' read your Bible. [*He makes no movement. She comes closer to him and peers into his face—uncertainly.*] Don't you hear me? I do hope you ain't off in one of your fits when you don't know nobody. D'you know who's talkin'? This is Annie—your Annie, Paw.

BENTLEY: [*Bursting into senile rage.*] None o' mine! Spawn o' the Pit! [*With a quick movement he hits her viciously over the arm with his stick. She gives a cry of pain and backs away from him, holding her arm.*]

ANNIE: [*Weeping angrily.*] That's what I git for tryin' to be kind to you, you ugly old devil! [*The sound of a man's footsteps is heard from outside, and* SWEENEY *enters. He is a stocky, muscular, sandy-haired Irishman dressed in patched corduroy trousers shoved down into high laced boots, and a blue flannel shirt. The bony face of his bullet head has a pressed-in appearance except for his heavy jaw, which sticks out pugnaciously. There is an expression of mean cunning and cupidity about his mouth and his small, round, blue eyes. He has evidently been drinking and his face is flushed and set in an angry scowl.*]

SWEENEY: Have ye no supper at all made, ye lazy slut? [*Seeing that she has been crying.*] What're you blubberin' about?

ANNIE: It's all his fault. I was tryin' to git him home but he's that set I couldn't budge him; and he hit me on the arm with his cane when I went near him.

SWEENEY: He did, did he? I'll soon learn him better. [*He advances toward* BENTLEY *threateningly.*]

ANNIE: [*Grasping his arm.*] Don't touch him, Pat. He's in one of his fits and you might kill him.

SWEENEY: An' good riddance!

BENTLEY: [*Hissing.*] Papist! [*Chants.*] "Pour out thy fury upon the heathen that know thee not, and upon the families that call not on thy name: for they have eaten up Jacob, and devoured him, and consumed him, and made his habitation desolate."

SWEENEY: [*Instinctively crosses himself—then scornfully.*] Spit curses on me till ye choke. It's not likely the Lord God'll be listenin' to a wicked auld sinner the like of you. [*To* ANNIE.] What's got into him to be roamin' up here? When I left for the town he looked too weak to lift a foot.

ANNIE: Oh, it's the same crazy notion he's had ever since Luke left. He wanted to make sure the rope was still here.

BENTLEY: [*Pointing to the rope with his stick.*] He-he! Luke'll come back. Then you'll see. You'll see!

SWEENEY: [*Nervously.*] Stop that mad cacklin' for the love of heaven! [*With a forced laugh.*] It's great laughter I should be havin' at you, mad as you are, for thinkin' that thief of a son of yours would come back to hang himself on account of your curses. It's five years he's been gone, and not a sight of him; an' you cursin' an' callin' down the wrath o' God on him by day an' by night. That shows you what God thinks of your curses—an' Him deaf to you!

ANNIE: It's no use talkin' to him, Pat.

SWEENEY: I've small doubt but that Luke is hung long since—by the police. He's come to no good end, that lad. [*His eyes on the rope.*] I'll be pullin' that thing down, so I will; an' the auld loon'll stay in the house, where he belongs, then, maybe. [*He reaches up for the rope as if to try and yank it down.* BENTLEY *waves his stick frantically in the air, and groans with rage.*]

ANNIE: [*Frightened.*] Leave it alone, Pat. Look at him. He's liable to hurt himself. Leave his rope be. It don't do no harm.

SWEENEY: [*Reluctantly moves away.*] It looks ugly hangin' there open like a mouth. [*The old man sinks back into a relieved immobility.* SWEENEY *speaks to his wife in a low tone.*] Where's the child? Get her to take him out o' this. I want a word with you he'll not be hearin'. [*She goes to the door and calls out:*] Ma-ry! Ma-ry! [*A faint, answering cry is heard and a moment later* MARY *rushes breathlessly into the barn.* SWEENEY *grabs her roughly by the arm. She shrinks away, looking at him with terrified eyes.*] You're to take your grandfather back to the house—an' see to it he stays there.

ANNIE: And give him his medicine.

SWEENEY: [*As the child continues to stare at him silently with eyes stupid from fear, he shakes her impatiently.*] D'you hear me, now? [*To his wife.*] It's soft-minded she is, like I've always told you, an' stupid; and you're not too firm in the head yourself at times, God help you! An' look at him! It's the curse is in the wits of your family, not mine.

ANNIE: You've been drinkin' in town or you wouldn't talk that way.

MARY: [*Whining.*] Maw! I'm skeered!

SWEENEY: [*Lets go of her arm and approaches* BENTLEY.] Get up out o' this, ye auld loon, an' go with Mary. She'll take you to the house. [BENTLEY *tries to hit him with the cane.*] Oho, ye would, would ye? [*He wrests the cane from the old man's hands.*] Bad cess to ye, you're the treach'rous one! Get up, now! [*He jerks the old man to his feet.*] Here, Mary, take his hand. Quick now! [*She does so tremblingly.*] Lead him to the house.

ANNIE: Go on, Paw! I'll come and git your supper in a minute.

BENTLEY: [*Stands stubbornly and begins to intone.*] "O Lord, thou hast seen my wrong; judge thou my cause. Thou hast seen all their vengeance and all their imaginations against me—"

SWEENEY: [*Pushing him toward the door.* BENTLEY *tries to resist.* MARY *pulls at his hand in a sudden fit of impish glee, and laughs shrilly.*] Get on now an' stop your cursin'.

BENTLEY: "Render unto them a recompense, O Lord, according to the work of their hands."

SWEENEY: Shut your loud quackin'! Here's your cane. [*He gives it to the old man as they come to the doorway and quickly steps back out of reach.*] An' mind you don't touch the child with it or I'll beat you to a jelly, old as ye are.

BENTLEY: [*Resisting* MARY's *efforts to pull him out, stands shaking his stick at* SWEENEY *and his wife.*] "Give them sorrow of heart, thy curse unto them. Persecute and destroy them in anger from under the heavens of the Lord."

MARY: [*Tugging at his hand and bursting again into shrill laughter.*] Come on, gran'paw. [*He allows himself to be led off, right.*]

SWEENEY: [*Making the sign of the cross furtively—with a sigh of relief.*] He's gone, thank God! What a snake's tongue he has in him! [*He sits down on the bench to the left of table.*] Come here, Annie, till I speak to you. [*She sits down on the bench in front of table.* SWEENEY *winks mysteriously.*] Well, I saw him, sure enough.

ANNIE: [*Stupidly.*] Who?

SWEENEY: [*Sharply.*] Who? Who but Dick Waller, the lawyer, that I went to see. [*Lowering his voice.*] An' I've found out what we was wishin' to know. [*With a laugh.*] Ye said I'd been drinkin'—which is true; but 'twas all in the plan I'd made. I've a head for strong drink, as ye know, but he hasn't. [*He winks cunningly.*] An' the whiskey loosened his tongue till he'd told all he knew.

ANNIE: He told you—about Paw's will?

SWEENEY: He did. [*Disappointedly.*] But for all the good it does us we might as well be no wiser than we was before. [*He broods for a moment in silence—then hits the table furiously with his fist.*] God's curse on the auld miser!

ANNIE: What did he tell you?

SWEENEY: Not much at the first. He's a cute one, an' he'd be askin' a fee to tell you your own name, if he could get it. His practice is all dribbled away from him lately on account of the drink. So I let on I was only payin' a friendly call, havin' known him for years. Then I asked him out to have a drop o' drink, knowin' his weakness; an' we had rashers of them, an' I payin' for it. Then I come out with it straight and asked him about the will—because the auld man was crazy an' on his last legs, I told him, an' he was the lawyer made out the will when Luke was gone. So he winked at me an' grinned—he was drunk by this—an' said: "It's no use, Pat. He left the farm to the boy." "To hell with the farm," I spoke back. "It's mortgaged to the teeth; but how about the money?" "The money?" an' he looks at me in surprise, "What money?" "The cash he has," I says. "You're crazy," he says. "There wasn't any cash—only the farm." "D'you mean to say he made no mention of money in his will?" I asked. You could have knocked me down with a feather. "He did not—on my oath," he says. [SWEENEY *leans over to his wife—indignantly.*] Now what d'you make o' that? The auld divil!

ANNIE: Maybe Waller was lyin'.

SWEENEY: He was not. I could tell by his face. He was surprised to hear me talkin' of money.

ANNIE: But the thousand dollars Paw got for the mortgage just before that woman ran away—

SWEENEY: An' that I've been slavin' me hands off to pay the int'rist on!

ANNIE: What could he have done with that? He ain't spent it. It was in twenty dollar gold pieces he got it, I remember Mr. Kellar of the bank tellin' me once.

SWEENEY: Divil a penny he's spent. Ye know as well as I do if it wasn't for my hammerin', an' sawin', an' nailin', he'd be in the poor house this minute—or the mad house, more likely.

ANNIE: D'you suppose that harlot ran off with it?

SWEENEY: I do not; I know better—an' so do you. D'you not remember the letter she wrote tellin' him he could support Luke on the money he'd got on the mortgage she'd signed with him; for he'd made the farm over to her when he married her. An' where d'you suppose Luke got the hundred dollars he stole? The auld loon must have had cash with him then, an' it's only five years back.

ANNIE: He's got it hid some place in the house most likely.

SWEENEY: Maybe you're right. I'll dig in the cellar this night when he's sleepin'. He used to be down there a lot recitin' Scripture in his fits.

ANNIE: What else did Waller say?

SWEENEY: Nothin' much; except that we should put notices in the papers for Luke, an' if he didn't come back by sivin years from when he'd left—two years from now, that'd be—the courts would say he was dead an' give us the farm. Divil a lot of use it is to us now with no money to fix it up; an' himself ruinin' it years ago by sellin' everythin' to buy that slut new clothes.

ANNIE: Don't folks break wills like his'n in the courts?

SWEENEY: Waller said 'twas no use. The auld divil was plain in his full senses when he made it; an' the courts cost money.

ANNIE: [*Resignedly.*] There ain't nothin' we can do then.

SWEENEY: No—except wait an' pray that young thief is dead an' won't come back; an' try an' find where it is the auld man has the gold hid, if he has it yet. I'd take him by the neck an' choke him till he told it, if he wasn't your father. [*He takes a full quart flask of whiskey from the pocket of his coat and has a big drink.*] Aahh! If we'd on'y the thousand we'd stock the farm good an' I'd give up this dog's game [*He indicates the carpentry outfit scornfully.*] an' we'd both work hard with a man or two to help, an' in a few years we'd be rich; for 'twas always a payin' place in the auld days.

ANNIE: Yes, yes, it was always a good farm then.

SWEENEY: He'll not last long in his senses, the doctor told me. His next attack will be very soon an' after it he'll be a real lunatic with no legal claims to anythin'. If we on'y had the money— 'Twould be the divil an' all if the auld fool should forget where he put it, an' him takin' leave of his senses altogether. [*He takes another nip at the bottle and puts it back in his pocket—with a sigh.*] Ah, well, I'll save what I can an' at the end of two years, with good luck in the trade, maybe we'll have enough. [*They are both startled by the heavy footsteps of some one approaching outside. A shrill burst of* MARY'*s laughter can be heard and the deep voice of a man talking to her.*]

SWEENEY: [*Uneasily.*] It's Mary; but who could that be with her? It's not himself. [*As he finishes speaking* LUKE *appears in the doorway, holding the dancing* MARY *by the hand. He is a tall, strapping young fellow about twenty-five with a coarse-featured, rather handsome face bronzed by the sun. What his face lacks in intelligence is partly forgiven for his good-natured, half-foolish grin, his hearty laugh, his curly dark hair, a certain devil-may-care recklessness and irresponsible youth in voice and gesture. But his mouth is weak and characterless; his brown eyes are large but shifty and acquisitive. He wears a dark blue jersey, patched blue pants, rough sailor shoes, and a gray cap. He advances into the stable with a mocking smile on his lips until he stands directly under the rope. The man and woman stare at him in petrified amazement.*]

ANNIE: Luke!

SWEENEY: [*Crossing himself.*] Glory be to God—it's him!

MARY: [*Hopping up and down wildly.*] It's Uncle Luke, Uncle Luke, Uncle Luke! [*She runs to her mother, who pushes her away angrily.*]

LUKE: [*Regarding them both with an amused grin.*] Sure, it's Luke—back after five years of bummin' round the rotten old earth in ships and things. Paid off a week ago—had a bust-up—and then took a notion to come out here—bummed my way—and here I am. And you're both of you tickled to death to see me, ain't yuh?—like hell! [*He laughs and walks over to* ANNIE.] Don't yuh even want to shake flippers with your dear, long-lost brother, Annie? I remember you and me used to git on so fine together—like hell!

ANNIE: [*Giving him a venomous look of hatred.*] Keep your hands to yourself.

LUKE: [*Grinning.*] You ain't changed, that's sure—on'y yuh're homlier'n ever. [*He turns to the scowling Sweeney.*] How about you, brother Pat?

SWEENEY: I'd not lower myself to take the hand of a—

LUKE: [*With a threat in his voice.*] Easy goes with that talk! I'm not so soft to lick as I was when I was a kid; and don't forget it.

ANNIE: [*To* MARY, *who is playing catch with a silver dollar which she has had clutched in her hand—sharply.*] Mary! What have you got there? Where did you get it? Bring it here to me this minute! [MARY *presses the dollar to her breast and remains standing by the doorway in stubborn silence.*]

LUKE: Aw, let her alone! What's bitin' yuh? That's on'y a silver dollar I give her when I met her front of the house. She told me you was up here; and I give her that as a present to buy candy with. I got it in Frisco—cart-wheels, they call 'em. There ain't none of them in these parts I ever seen, so I brung it along on the voyage.

ANNIE: [*Angrily.*] I don't know or care where you got it—but I know you ain't come by it honest. Mary! Give that back to him this instant! [*As the child hesitates, she stamps her foot furiously.*] D'you hear me? [MARY *starts to cry softly, but comes to* LUKE *and hands him the dollar.*]

LUKE: [*Taking it—with a look of disgust at his half-sister.*] I was right when I said you ain't changed, Annie. You're as stinkin' mean as ever. [*To* MARY, *consolingly.*] Quit bawlin', kid. You 'n' me'll go out on the edge of the cliff here and chuck some stones in the ocean same's we useter, remember? [MARY's *tears immediately cease. She looks up at him with shining eyes, and claps her hands.*]

MARY: [*Pointing to the dollar he has in his hand.*] Throw that! It's flat 'n' it'll skip.

LUKE: [*With a grin.*] That's the talk, kid. That's all it's good for—to throw away; not buryin' it like your miser folks'd tell you. Here! You take it and chuck it away. It's your'n. [*He gives her the dollar and she hops to the doorway. He turns to* PAT *with a grin.*] I'm learnin' your kid to be a sport, Tight-Wad. I hope you ain't got no objections.

MARY: [*Impatiently.*] Come on, Uncle Luke. Watch me throw it.

LUKE: Aw right. [*To* PAT.] I'll step outside a second and give you two a chanct to git all the dirty things yuh're thinkin' about me off your chest. [*Threateningly.*] And then I'm gointer come and talk turkey to you, see? I didn't come back here for fun, and the sooner you gets that in your beans, the better.

MARY: Come on and watch me!

LUKE: Aw right, I'm comin'. [*He walks out and stands, leaning his back against the doorway, left.* MARY *is about six feet beyond him on the*

*other side of the road. She is leaning down, peering over the edge of
the cliff and laughing excitedly.*]

MARY: Can I throw it now? Can I?

LUKE: Don't git too near the edge, kid. The water's deep down there,
and you'd be a drowned rat if you slipped. [*She shrinks back a step.*]
You chuck it when I say three. Ready, now! [*She draws back her
arm.*] One! Two! Three! [*She throws the dollar away and bends
down to see it hit the water.*]

MARY: [*Clapping her hands and laughing.*] I seen it! I seen it splash! It's
deep down now, ain't it?

LUKE: Yuh betcher it is! Now watch how far I kin chuck rocks. [*He
picks up a couple and goes to where she is standing. During the following conversation between* SWEENEY *and his wife he continues to
play this way with* MARY. *Their voices can be heard but the words
are indistinguishable.*]

SWEENEY: [*Glancing apprehensively toward the door—with a great
sigh.*] Speak of the divil an' here he is! [*Furiously.*] Flingin' away dollars, the dirty thief, an' us without—

ANNIE: [*Interrupting him.*] Did you hear what he said? A thief like him
ain't come back for no good. [*Lowering her voice.*] D'you s'pose he
knows about the farm bein' left to him?

SWEENEY: [*Uneasily.*] How could he? An' yet—I dunno—[*With sudden
decision.*] You'd best lave him to me to watch out for. It's small sense
you have to hide your hate from him. You're as looney as the rist of
your breed. An' he needs to be blarneyed round to fool him an' find
out what he's wantin'. I'll pritind to make friends with him, God
roast his soul! An' do you run to the house an' break the news to the
auld man; for if he seen him suddin its likely the little wits he has left
would leave him; an' the thief could take the farm from us tomorrow
if himself turned a lunatic.

ANNIE: [*Getting up.*] I'll tell him a little at a time till he knows.

SWEENEY: Be careful, now, or we'll lose the farm this night. [*She starts
towards the doorway.* SWEENEY *speaks suddenly in a strange, awed
voice.*] Did you see Luke when he first came in to us? He stood there
with the noose of the rope almost touchin' his head. I was almost
wishin'— [*He hesitates.*]

ANNIE: [*Viciously.*] I was wishin' it was round his neck chokin' him,
that's what I was—hangin' him just as Paw says.

SWEENEY: Ssshh! He might hear ye. Go along, now. He's comin' back.

MARY: [*Pulling at* LUKE'S *arm as he comes back to the doorway.*]
Lemme throw 'nother! Lemme throw 'nother!

LUKE: [*Enters just as* ANNIE *is going out and stops her.*] Goin' to the house? Do we get any supper? I'm hungry.

ANNIE: [*Glaring at him but restraining her rage.*] Yes.

LUKE: [*Jovially.*] Good work! And tell the old man I'm here and I'll see him in a while. He'll be glad to see me, too—like hell! [*He comes forward.* ANNIE *goes off, right.*]

MARY: [*In an angry whine, tugging at his hand.*] Lemme throw 'nother. Lemme—

LUKE: [*Shaking her away.*] There's lots of rocks, kid. Throw them. Dollars ain't so plentiful.

MARY: [*Screaming.*] No! No! I don't wanter throw rocks. Lemme throw 'nother o' them.

SWEENEY: [*Severely.*] Let your uncle in peace, ye brat! [*She commences to cry.*] Run help your mother now or I'll give ye a good hidin'. [MARY *runs out of the door, whimpering.* PAT *turns to* LUKE *and holds out his hand.*]

LUKE: [*Looking at it in amazement.*] Ahoy, there! What's this?

SWEENEY: [*With an ingratiating smile.*] Let's let by-gones be by-gones. I'm harborin' no grudge agen you these past years. Ye was only a lad when ye ran away an' not to be blamed for it. I'd have taken your hand a while back, an' glad to, but for her bein' with us. She has the divil's own tongue, as ye know, an' she can't forget the rowin' you an' her used to be havin'.

LUKE: [*Still looking at* SWEENEY'*s hand.*] So that's how the wind blows! [*With a grin.*] Well, I'll take a chanct. [*They shake hands and sit down by the table,* SWEENEY *on the front bench and* LUKE *on the left one.*]

SWEENEY: [*Pulls the bottle from his coat pocket—with a wink.*] Will ye have a taste? It's real stuff.

LUKE: Yuh betcher I will! [*He takes a big gulp and hands the bottle back.*]

SWEENEY: [*After taking a drink himself, puts bottle on table.*] I wasn't wishin' herself to see it or I'd have asked ye sooner. [*There is a pause, during which each measures the other with his eyes.*]

LUKE: Say, how's the old man now?

SWEENEY: [*Cautiously.*] Oh, the same as ivir—older an' uglier, maybe.

LUKE: I thought he might be in the bug-house by this time.

SWEENEY: [*Hastily.*] Indeed not; he's foxy to pritind he's looney, but he's his wits with him all the time.

LUKE: [*Insinuatingly.*] Is he as stingy with his coin as he used to be?

SWEENEY: If he owned the ocean he wouldn't give a fish a drink; but I doubt if he's any money left at all. Your mother got rid of it all, I'm thinkin'. [LUKE *smiles a superior, knowing smile.*] He has on'y the farm, an' that mortgaged. I've been payin' the int'rist an' supportin' himself an' his doctor's bills by the carpentryin' these five years past.

LUKE: [*With a grin.*] Huh! Yuh're slow. Yuh oughter get wise to yourself.

SWEENEY: [*Inquisitively.*] What d'ye mean by that?

LUKE: [*Aggravatingly.*] Aw, nothin'. [*He turns around and his eyes fix themselves on the rope.*] What the hell— [*He is suddenly convulsed with laughter and slaps his thigh.*] Hahaha! If that don't beat the Dutch! The old nut!

SWEENEY: What?

LUKE: That rope. Say, has he had that hangin' there ever since I skipped?

SWEENEY: [*Smiling.*] Sure; an' he thinks you'll be comin' home to hang yourself.

LUKE: Hahaha! Not this chicken! And you say he ain't crazy! Gee, that's too good to keep. I got to have a drink on that. [SWEENEY *pushes the bottle toward him. He raises it toward the rope.*] Here's how, old chum! [*He drinks.* SWEENEY *does likewise.*] Say, I'd a'most forgotten about that. Remember how hot he was that day when he hung that rope up and cussed me for pinchin' the hundred? He was standin' there shakin' his stick at me, and I was laughin' 'cause he looked so funny with the spit dribblin' outa his mouth like he was a mad dog. And when I turned round and beat it he shouted after me: "Remember, when you come home again there's a rope waitin' for yuh to hang yourself on, yuh bastard!" [*He spits contemptuously.*] What a swell chanct. [*His manner changes and he frowns.*] The old slave-driver! That's a hell of a fine old man for a guy to have!

SWEENEY: [*Pushing the bottle toward him.*] Take a sup an' forget it. 'Twas a long time past.

LUKE: But the rope's there yet, ain't it? And he keeps it there. [*He takes a large swallow.* SWEENEY *also drinks.*] But I'll git back at him aw right, yuh wait 'n' see. I'll git every cent he's got this time.

SWEENEY: [*Slyly.*] If he has a cent. I'm not wishful to discourage ye, but— [*He shakes his head doubtfully, at the same time fixing* LUKE *with a keen glance out of the corner of his eye.*]

LUKE: [*With a cunning wink.*] Aw, he's got it aw right. You watch me! [*He is beginning to show the effects of the drink he has had. He pulls out tobacco and a paper and rolls a cigarette and lights it. As he puffs he continues boastfully.*] You country jays oughter wake up and see what's goin' on. Look at me. I was green as grass when I left here, but bummin' round the world, and bein' in cities, and meetin' all kinds, and keepin' your two eyes open—that's what'll learn yuh a cute trick or two.

SWEENEY: No doubt but you're right. Us country folks is stupid in most ways. We've no chance to learn the things a travelin' lad like you'd be knowin'.

LUKE: [*Complacently.*] Well, you watch me and I'll learn yuh. [*He snickers.*] So yuh think the old man's flat broke, do yuh?

SWEENEY: I do so.

LUKE: Then yuh're simple; that's what—simple! You're lettin' him kid yuh.

SWEENEY: If he has any, it's well hid, I know that. He's a sly old bird.

LUKE: And I'm a slyer bird. D'yuh hear that? I c'n beat his game any time. You watch me! [*He reaches out his hand for the bottle. They both drink again.* SWEENEY *begins to show signs of getting drunk. He hiccoughs every now and then and his voice grows uncertain and husky.*]

SWEENEY: It'd be a crafty one who'd find where he'd hidden it, sure enough.

LUKE: You watch me! I'll find it. I betcher anything yuh like I find it. You watch me! Just wait till he's asleep and I'll show yuh—ternight. [*There is a noise of shuffling footsteps outside and* ANNIE's *whining voice raised in angry protest.*]

SWEENEY: Ssshh! It's himself comin' now. [LUKE *rises to his feet and stands, waiting in a defensive attitude, a surly expression on his face. A moment later* BENTLEY *appears in the doorway, followed by* ANNIE. *He leans against the wall, in an extraordinary state of excitement, shaking all over, gasping for breath, his eyes devouring* LUKE *from head to foot.*]

ANNIE: I couldn't do nothin' with him. When I told him *he'd* come back there was no holdin' him. He was a'most frothin' at the mouth till I let him out. [*Whiningly.*] You got to see to him, Pat, if you want any supper. I can't—

SWEENEY: Shut your mouth! We'll look after him.

ANNIE: See that you do. I'm goin' back. [*She goes off, right.* LUKE *and his father stand looking at each other. The surly expression disappears from* LUKE's *face, which gradually expands in a broad grin.*]

LUKE: [*Jovially.*] Hello, old sport! I s'pose yuh're tickled to pieces to see me—like hell! [*The old man stutters and stammers incoherently as if the very intensity of his desire for speech had paralyzed all power of articulation.* LUKE *turns to Pat.*] I see he ain't lost the old stick. Many a crack on the nut I used to get with that.

BENTLEY: [*Suddenly finding his voice—chants.*] "Bring forth the best robe, and put it on him; and put a ring on his hand, and shoes on his feet: And bring hither the fatted calf, and kill it; and let us eat, and be merry: For this my son was dead, and is alive again; he was lost, and is found." [*He ends up with a convulsive sob.*]

LUKE: [*Disapprovingly.*] Yuh're still spoutin' the rotten old Word o' God same's ever, eh? Say, give us a rest on that stuff, will yuh? Come on and shake hands like a good sport. [*He holds out his hand. The old man totters over to him, stretching out a trembling hand.* LUKE *seizes it and pumps it up and down.*] That's the boy!

SWEENEY: [*Genuinely amazed.*] Look at that, would ye—the two-faced auld liar. [BENTLEY *passes his trembling hand all over* LUKE, *feeling of his arms, his chest, his back. An expression of overwhelming joy suffuses his worn features.*]

LUKE: [*Grinning at* SWEENEY.] Say, watch this. [*With tolerant good-humor.*] On the level I b'lieve the old boy's glad to see me at that. He looks like he was tryin' to grin; and I never seen him grin in my life, I c'n remember. [*As* BENTLEY *attempts to feel of his face.*] Hey, cut it out! [*He pushes his hand away, but not roughly.*] I'm all here, yuh needn't worry. Yuh needn't be scared I'm a ghost. Come on and sit down before yuh fall down. Yuh ain't got your sea-legs workin' right. [*He guides the old man to the bench at left of table.*] Squat here for a spell and git your wind. [BENTLEY *sinks down on the bench.* LUKE *reaches for the bottle.*] Have a drink to my makin' port. It'll buck yuh up.

SWEENEY: [*Alarmed.*] Be careful, Luke. It might likely end him.

LUKE: [*Holds the bottle up to the old man's mouth, supporting his head with the other hand.* BENTLEY *gulps, the whiskey drips over his chin, and he goes into a fit of convulsive coughing.* LUKE *laughs.*] Hahaha! Went down the wrong way, did it? I'll show yuh the way to do it. [*He drinks.*] There yuh are—smooth as silk. [*He hands the bottle to* SWEENEY, *who drinks and puts it back on the table.*]

SWEENEY: He must be glad to see ye or he'd not drink. 'Tis dead against it he's been these five years past. [*Shaking his head.*] An' him cursin' you day an' night! I can't put head or tail to it. Look out he ain't meanin' some bad to ye underneath. He's crafty at pretendin'.

LUKE: [*As the old man makes signs to him with his hand.*] What's he af-ter now? He's lettin' on he's lost his voice again. What d'yuh want? [BENTLEY *points with his stick to the rope. His lips move convul-sively as he makes a tremendous effort to utter words.*]

BENTLEY: [*Mumbling incoherently.*] Luke—Luke—rope—Luke—hang.

SWEENEY: [*Appalled.*] There ye are! What did I tell you? It's to see you hang yourself he's wishin', the auld fiend!

BENTLEY: [*Nodding.*] Yes—Luke—hang.

LUKE: [*Taking it as a joke—with a loud guffaw.*] Hahaha! If that don't beat the Dutch! The old nanny-goat! Aw right, old sport. Anything to oblige. Hahaha! [*He takes the chair from left and places it under the rope. The old man watches him with eager eyes and seems to be trying to smile.* LUKE *stands on the chair.*]

SWEENEY: Have a care, now! I'd not be foolin' with it in your place.

LUKE: All out for the big hangin' of Luke Bentley by hisself. [*He puts the noose about his neck with an air of drunken bravado and grins at his father. The latter makes violent motions for him to go on.*] Look at him, Pat. By God, he's in a hurry. Hahaha! Well, old sport, here goes nothin'. [*He makes a movement as if he were going to jump and kick the chair from under him.*]

SWEENEY: [*Half starts to his feet—horrified.*] Luke! Are ye gone mad?

LUKE: [*Stands staring at his father, who is still making gestures for him to jump. A scowl slowly replaces his good-natured grin.*] D'yuh really mean it—that yuh want to see me hangin' myself? [BENTLEY *nods vigorously in the affirmative.* LUKE *glares at him for a moment in silence.*] Well, I'll be damned! [*To Pat.*] An' I thought he was only kiddin'. [*He removes the rope gingerly from his neck. The old man stamps his foot and gesticulates wildly, groaning with disappointment.* LUKE *jumps to the floor and looks at his father for a second. Then his face grows white with a vicious fury.*] I'll fix your hash, you stinkin' old murderer! [*He grabs the chair by its back and swings it over his head as if he were going to crush* BENTLEY'*s skull with it. The old man cowers on the bench in abject terror.*]

SWEENEY: [*Jumping to his feet with a cry of alarm.*] Luke! For the love of God! [LUKE *hesitates; then hurls the chair in back of him under the loft, and stands menacingly in front of his father, his hands on his hips.*]

LUKE: [*Grabbing* BENTLEY'*s shoulder and shaking him—hoarsely.*] Yuh wanted to see me hangin' there in real earnest, didn't yuh? You'd hang me yourself if yuh could, wouldn't yuh? And you my own father! Yuh damned son of a gun! Yuh would, would yuh? I'd smash your brains out for a nickel! [*He shakes the old man more and more furiously.*]

SWEENEY: Luke! Look out! You'll be killin' him next.

LUKE: [*Giving his father one more shake, which sends him sprawling on the floor.*] Git outa here! Git outa this b'fore I kill yuh dead! [SWEENEY *rushes over and picks the terrified old man up.*] Take him outa here, Pat! [*His voice rises to a threatening roar.*] Take him outa here or I'll break every bone in his body! [*He raises his clenched fists over his head in a frenzy of rage.*]

SWEENEY: Ssshh! Don't be roarin'! I've got him. [*He steers the whimpering, hysterical* BENTLEY *to the doorway.*] Come out o' this, now. Get down to the house! Hurry now! Ye've made enough trouble for one night. [*They disappear off right.* LUKE *flings himself on a bench, breathing heavily. He picks up the bottle and takes a long swallow.* SWEENEY *reënters from rear. He comes over and sits down in his old place.*] Thank God he's off down to the house, scurryin' like a frightened hare as if he'd never a kink in his legs in his life. He was moanin' out loud so you could hear him a long ways. [*With a sigh.*] It's a murd'rous auld loon he is, sure enough.

LUKE: [*Thickly.*] The damned son of a gun!

SWEENEY: I thought you'd be killin' him that time with the chair.

LUKE: [*Violently.*] Serve him damn right if I done it.

SWEENEY: An' you laughin' at him a moment sooner! I thought 'twas jokin' ye was.

LUKE: [*Sullenly.*] So I was kiddin'; but I thought he was tryin' to kid me, too. And then I seen by the way he acted he really meant it. [*Banging the table with his fist.*] Ain't that a hell of a fine old man for yuh!

SWEENEY: He's a mean auld swine.

LUKE: He meant it aw right, too. Yuh shoulda seen him lookin' at me. [*With sudden lugubriousness.*] Ain't he a hell of a nice old man for a guy to have? Ain't he?

SWEENEY: [*Soothingly.*] Hush! It's all over now. Don't be thinkin' about it.

LUKE: [*On the verge of drunken tears.*] How kin I help thinkin'—and him my own father? After me bummin' and starvin' round the rotten earth, and workin' myself to death on ships and things—and when I come home he tries to make me bump off—wants to see me a corpse—my own father, too! Ain't he a hell of an old man to have? The rotten son of a gun!

SWEENEY: It's past an' done. Forgit it. [*He slaps* LUKE *on the shoulder and pushes the bottle toward him.*] Let's take a drop more. We'll be goin' to supper soon.

LUKE: [*Takes a big drink—huskily.*] Thanks. [*He wipes his mouth on his sleeve with a snuffle.*] But I'll tell yuh something you can put in your pipe and smoke. It ain't past and done, and it ain't goin' to be! [*More and more aggressively.*] And I ain't goin' to forget it, either! Yuh kin betcher life on that, pal. And *he* ain't goin' to forget it—not if he lives a million—not by a damned sight! [*With sudden fury.*] I'll

fix his hash! I'll git even with him, the old skunk! You watch me!
And this very night, too!

SWEENEY: How d'you mean?

LUKE: You just watch me, I tell yuh! [*Banging the table.*] I said I'd git
even and I will git even—this same night, with no long waits, either!
[*Frowning.*] Say, you don't stand up for him, do yuh?

SWEENEY: [*Spitting—vehemently.*] That's child's talk. There's not a day
passed I've not wished him in his grave.

LUKE: [*Excitedly.*] Then we'll both git even on him—you 'n' me. We're
pals, ain't we?

SWEENEY: Sure.

LUKE: And yuh kin have half what we gits. That's the kinda feller I am!
That's fair enough, ain't it?

SWEENEY: Surely.

LUKE: I don't want no truck with this rotten farm. You kin have my
share of that. I ain't made to be no damned dirt puncher—not me!
And I ain't goin' to loaf round here more'n I got to, and when I goes
this time I ain't never comin' back. Not me! Not to punch dirt and
milk cows. You kin have the rotten farm for all of me. What I wants
is cash—regular coin yuh kin spend—not dirt. I want to show the
gang a real time, and then ship away to sea agen or go bummin'
agen. I want coin yuh kin throw away—same's your kid chucked
that dollar of mine overboard, remember? A real dollar, too! She's a
sport, aw right!

SWEENEY: [*Anxious to bring him back to the subject.*] But where d'you
think to find his money?

LUKE: [*Confidently.*] Don't yuh fret. I'll show yuh. You watch me! I
know his hidin' places. I useter spy on him when I was a kid— Maw
used to make me—and I seen him many a time at his sneakin'. [*Indignantly.*] He used to hide stuff from the old lady. What d'yuh
know about him—the mean skunk.

SWEENEY: That was a long time back. You don't know—

LUKE: [*Assertively.*] But I do know, see! He's got two places. One was
where I swiped the hundred.

SWEENEY: It'll not be there, then.

LUKE: No; but there's the other place; and he never knew I was wise to
that. I'd have left him clean on'y I was a kid and scared to pinch
more. So you watch me! We'll git even on him, you 'n' me, and go
halfs, and yuh kin start the rotten farm goin' agen and I'll beat it
where there's some life.

SWEENEY: But if there's no money in that place, what'll you be doin' to
find out where it is, then?

LUKE: Then you 'n' me 'ull make him tell!

SWEENEY: Oho, don't think it! 'Tis not him'd be tellin'.

LUKE: Aw, say, you're simple! You watch me! I know a trick or two about makin' people tell what they don't wanter. [*He picks up the chisel from the table.*] Yuh see this? Well, if he don't answer up nice and easy we'll show him! [*A ferocious grin settles over his face.*] We'll git even on him, you 'n' me—and he'll tell where it's hid. We'll just shove this into the stove till it's red hot and take off his shoes and socks and warm the bottoms of his feet for him. [*Savagely.*] He'll tell then—anything we wants him to tell.

SWEENEY: But Annie?

LUKE: We'll shove a rag in her mouth so's she can't yell. That's easy.

SWEENEY: [*His head lolling drunkenly—with a cruel leer.*] 'Twill serve him right to heat up his hoofs for him, the limpin', auld miser!—if ye don't hurt him too much.

LUKE: [*With a savage scowl.*] We won't hurt him—more'n enough. [*Suddenly raging.*] I'll pay him back aw right! He won't want no more people to hang themselves when I git through with him. I'll fix his hash! [*He sways to his feet, the chisel in his hand.*] Come on! Let's git to work. Sooner we starts the sooner we're rich. [SWEENEY *rises. He is steadier on his feet than* LUKE. *At this moment* MARY *appears in the doorway.*]

MARY: Maw says supper's ready. I had mine. [*She comes into the room and jumps up, trying to grab hold of the rope.*] Lift me, Uncle Luke. I wanter swing.

LUKE: [*Severely.*] Don't yuh dare touch that rope, d'yuh hear?

MARY: [*Whining.*] I wanter swing.

LUKE: [*With a shiver.*] It's bad, kid. Yuh leave it alone, take it from me.

SWEENEY: She'll get a good whalin' if I catch her jumpin' at it.

LUKE: Come on, pal. T'hell with supper. We got work to do first. [*They go to the doorway.*]

SWEENEY: [*Turning back to the sulking Mary.*] And you stay here, d'you hear, ye brat, till we call ye—or I'll skin ye alive.

LUKE: And termorrer mornin', kid, I'll give yuh a whole handful of them shiny, bright things yuh chucked in the ocean—and yuh kin be a real sport.

MARY: [*Eagerly.*] Gimme 'em now! Gimme 'em now, Uncle Luke. [*As he shakes his head—whiningly.*] Gimme one! Gimme one!

LUKE: Can't be done, kid. Termorrer. Me 'n' your old man is goin' to git even now—goin' to make him pay for—

SWEENEY: [*Interrupting—harshly.*] Hist with your noise! D'you think she's no ears? Don't be talkin' so much. Come on, now.

LUKE: [*Permitting himself to be pulled out the doorway.*] Aw right! I'm
with yuh. We'll git even—you 'n' me. The damned son of a gun!
[*They lurch off to the right.*]

[MARY *skips to the doorway and peeps after them for a moment.
Then she comes back to the center of the floor and looks around her
with an air of decision. She sees the chair in under the loft and runs
over to it, pulling it back and setting it on its legs directly underneath
the noose of the rope. She climbs and stands on the top of the chair and
grasps the noose with both her upstretched hands. Then with a shriek
of delight she kicks the chair from under her and launches herself for a
swing. The rope seems to part where it is fixed to the beam. A dirty
gray bag tied to the end of the rope falls to the floor with a muffled,
metallic thud.* MARY *sprawls forward on her hands and knees, whimpering. Straggly wisps from the pile of rank hay fall silently to the floor
in a mist of dust.* MARY, *discovering she is unhurt, glances quickly
around and sees the bag. She pushes herself along the floor and, untying
the string at the top, puts in her hand. She gives an exclamation of joy
at what she feels and, turning the bag upside down, pours its contents
in her lap. Giggling to herself, she gets to her feet and goes to the doorway, where she dumps what she has in her lap in a heap on the floor
just inside the barn. They lie there in a little glittering pile, shimmering
in the faint sunset glow—fifty twenty-dollar gold pieces.* MARY *claps
her hands and sings to herself:* "Skip—skip—skip." *Then she quickly
picks up four or five of them and runs out to the edge of the cliff. She
throws them one after another into the ocean as fast as she can and
bends over to see them hit the water. Against the background of horizon clouds still tinted with blurred crimson she hops up and down in a
sort of grotesque dance, clapping her hands and laughing shrilly. After
the last one is thrown she rushes back into the barn to get more.*]

MARY: [*Picking up a handful—giggling ecstatically.*] Skip! Skip! [*She
turns and runs out to throw them as*

[*The Curtain Falls*]

BEYOND THE HORIZON

A PLAY IN THREE ACTS

CHARACTERS

JAMES MAYO, *a farmer*

KATE MAYO, *his wife*

CAPTAIN DICK SCOTT, *of the bark* Sundra, *her brother*

ANDREW MAYO
ROBERT MAYO } *sons of* JAMES MAYO

RUTH ATKINS

MRS. ATKINS, *her widowed mother*

MARY

BEN, *a farm hand*

DOCTOR FAWCETT

ACT I

ACT II

(Three years later)

ACT III

(Five years later)

BEYOND THE HORIZON

ACT ONE

SCENE ONE

A section of country highway. The road runs diagonally from the left, forward, to the right, rear, and can be seen in the distance winding toward the horizon like a pale ribbon between the low, rolling hills with their freshly plowed fields clearly divided from each other, checker-board fashion, by the lines of stone walls and rough snake fences.

The forward triangle cut off by the road is a section of a field from the dark earth of which myriad bright-green blades of fall-sown rye are sprouting. A straggling line of piled rocks, too low to be called a wall, separates this field from the road.

To the rear of the road is a ditch with a sloping, grassy bank on the far side. From the center of this an old, gnarled apple tree, just budding into leaf, strains its twisted branches heavenwards, black against the pallor of distance. A snake-fence sidles from left to right along the top of the bank, passing beneath the apple tree.

The hushed twilight of a day in May is just beginning. The horizon hills are still rimmed by a faint line of flame, and the sky above them glows with the crimson flush of the sunset. This fades gradually as the action of the scene progresses.

At the rise of the curtain, ROBERT MAYO *is discovered sitting on the fence. He is a tall, slender young man of twenty-three. There is a touch of the poet about him expressed in his high forehead and wide, dark eyes. His features are delicate and refined, leaning to weakness in the mouth and chin. He is dressed in gray corduroy trousers pushed into high laced boots, and a blue flannel shirt with a bright colored tie. He is reading a book by the fading sunset light. He shuts this, keeping a fin-ger in to mark the place, and turns his head toward the horizon, gazing out over the fields and hills. His lips move as if he were reciting some-thing to himself.*

His brother ANDREW *comes along the road from the right, returning from his work in the fields. He is twenty-seven years old, an opposite type to* ROBERT—*husky, sun-bronzed, handsome in a large-featured, manly fashion—a son of the soil, intelligent in a shrewd way, but with nothing of the intellectual about him. He wears overalls, leather boots, a gray flannel shirt open at the neck, and a soft, mud-stained hat pushed back on his head. He stops to talk to* ROBERT, *leaning on the hoe he carries.*

ANDREW: [*Seeing* ROBERT *has not noticed his presence—in a loud shout.*] Hey there! [ROBERT *turns with a start. Seeing who it is, he smiles.*] Gosh, you do take the prize for daydreaming! And I see you've toted one of the old books along with you. [*He crosses the ditch and sits on the fence near his brother.*] What is it this time—poetry, I'll bet. [*He reaches for the book.*] Let me see.

ROBERT: [*Handing it to him rather reluctantly.*] Look out you don't get it full of dirt.

ANDREW: [*Glancing at his hands.*] That isn't dirt—it's good clean earth. [*He turns over the pages. His eyes read something and he gives an exclamation of disgust.*] Hump! [*With a provoking grin at his brother he reads aloud in a doleful, sing-song voice.*] "I have loved wind and light and the bright sea. But holy and most sacred night, not as I love and have loved thee." [*He hands the book back.*] Here! Take it and bury it. I suppose it's that year in college gave you a liking for that kind of stuff. I'm darn glad I stopped at High School, or maybe I'd been crazy too. [*He grins and slaps* ROBERT *on the back affectionately.*] Imagine me reading poetry and plowing at the same time! The team'd run away, I'll bet.

ROBERT: [*Laughing.*] Or picture me plowing.

ANDREW: You should have gone back to college last fall, like I know you wanted to. You're fitted for that sort of thing—just as I ain't.

ROBERT: You know why I didn't go back, Andy. Pa didn't like the idea, even if he didn't say so; and I know he wanted the money to use improving the farm. And besides, I'm not keen on being a student, just because you see me reading books all the time. What I want to do now is keep on moving so that I won't take root in any one place.

ANDREW: Well, the trip you're leaving on tomorrow will keep you moving all right. [*At this mention of the trip they both fall silent. There is a pause. Finally* ANDREW *goes on, awkwardly, attempting to speak casually.*] Uncle says you'll be gone three years.

ROBERT: About that, he figures.

ANDREW: [*Moodily.*] That's a long time.

ROBERT: Not so long when you come to consider it. You know the *Sunda* sails around the Horn for Yokohama first, and that's a long voyage on a sailing ship; and if we go to any of the other places Uncle Dick mentions—India, or Australia, or South Africa, or South America—they'll be long voyages, too.

ANDREW: You can have all those foreign parts for all of me. [*After a pause.*] Ma's going to miss you a lot, Rob.

ROBERT: Yes—and I'll miss her.

ANDREW: And Pa ain't feeling none too happy to have you go—though he's been trying not to show it.

ROBERT: I can see how he feels.

ANDREW: And you can bet that I'm not giving any cheers about it. [*He puts one hand on the fence near* ROBERT.]

ROBERT: [*Putting one hand on top of* ANDREW's *with a gesture almost of shyness.*] I know that, too, Andy.

ANDREW: I'll miss you as much as anybody, I guess. You see, you and I ain't like most brothers—always fighting and separated a lot of the time, while we've always been together—just the two of us. It's different with us. That's why it hits so hard, I guess.

ROBERT: [*With feeling.*] It's just as hard for me, Andy—believe that! I hate to leave you and the old folks—but—I feel I've got to. There's something calling me— [*He points to the horizon*] Oh, I can't just explain it to you, Andy.

ANDREW: No need to, Rob. [*Angry at himself.*] Hell! You want to go—that's all there is to it; and I wouldn't have you miss this chance for the world.

ROBERT: It's fine of you to feel that way, Andy.

ANDREW: Huh! I'd be a nice son-of-a-gun if I didn't, wouldn't I? When I know how you need this sea trip to make a new man of you—in the body, I mean—and give you your full health back.

ROBERT: [*A trifle impatiently.*] All of you seem to keep harping on my health. You were so used to seeing me lying around the house in the old days that you never will get over the notion that I'm a chronic invalid. You don't realize how I've bucked up in the past few years. If I had no other excuse for going on Uncle Dick's ship but just my health, I'd stay right here and start in plowing.

ANDREW: Can't be done. Farming ain't your nature. There's all the difference shown in just the way us two feel about the farm. You—well, you like the home part of it, I expect; but as a place to work and grow things, you hate it. Ain't that right?

ROBERT: Yes, I suppose it is. For you it's different. You're a Mayo through and through. You're wedded to the soil. You're as much a product of it as an ear of corn is, or a tree. Father is the same. This farm is his life-work, and he's happy in knowing that another Mayo, inspired by the same love, will take up the work where he leaves off. I can understand your attitude, and Pa's; and I think it's wonderful and sincere. But I—well, I'm not made that way.

ANDREW: No, you ain't; but when it comes to understanding, I guess I realize that you've got your own angle of looking at things.

ROBERT: [*Musingly.*] I wonder if you do, really.

ANDREW: [*Confidently.*] Sure I do. You've seen a bit of the world, enough to make the farm seem small, and you've got the itch to see it all.

ROBERT: It's more than that, Andy.

ANDREW: Oh, of course. I know you're going to learn navigation, and all about a ship, so's you can be an officer. That's natural, too. There's fair pay in it, I expect, when you consider that you've always got a home and grub thrown in; and if you're set on traveling, you can go anywhere you're a mind to without paying fare.

ROBERT: [*With a smile that is half sad.*] It's more than that, Andy.

ANDREW: Sure it is. There's always a chance of a good thing coming your way in some of those foreign ports or other. I've heard there are great opportunities for a young fellow with his eyes open in some of those new countries that are just being opened up. [*Jovially.*] I'll bet that's what you've been turning over in your mind under all your quietness! [*He slaps his brother on the back with a laugh.*] Well, if you get to be a millionaire all of a sudden, call 'round once in a while and I'll pass the plate to you. We could use a lot of money right here on the farm without hurting it any.

ROBERT: [*Forced to laugh.*] I've never considered that practical side of it for a minute, Andy.

ANDREW: Well, you ought to.

ROBERT: No, I oughtn't. [*Pointing to the horizon—dreamily.*] Supposing I was to tell you that it's just Beauty that's calling me, the beauty of the far off and unknown, the mystery and spell of the East which lures me in the books I've read, the need of the freedom of great wide spaces, the joy of wandering on and on—in quest of the secret which is hidden over there, beyond the horizon? Suppose I told you that was the one and only reason for my going?

ANDREW: I should say you were nutty.

ROBERT: [*Frowning.*] Don't, Andy. I'm serious.

ANDREW: Then you might as well stay here, because we've got all you're looking for right on this farm. There's wide space enough, Lord knows; and you can have all the sea you want by walking a mile down to the beach; and there's plenty of horizon to look at, and

beauty enough for anyone, except in the winter. [*He grins.*] As for
the mystery and spell, I haven't met 'em yet, but they're probably lying around somewheres. I'll have you understand this is a first class
farm with all the fixings. [*He laughs.*]

ROBERT: [*Joining in the laughter in spite of himself.*] It's no use talking
to you, you chump!

ANDREW: You'd better not say anything to Uncle Dick about spells and
things when you're on the ship. He'll likely chuck you overboard for
a Jonah. [*He jumps down from fence.*] I'd better run along. I've got
to wash up some as long as Ruth's Ma is coming over for supper.

ROBERT: [*Pointedly—almost bitterly.*] And Ruth.

ANDREW: [*Confused—looking everywhere except at* ROBERT—*trying
to appear unconcerned.*] Yes, Ruth'll be staying too. Well, I better
hustle, I guess, and— [*He steps over the ditch to the road while he is
talking.*]

ROBERT: [*Who appears to be fighting some strong inward emotion—
impulsively.*] Wait a minute, Andy! [*He jumps down from the fence.*]
There is something I want to— [*He stops abruptly, biting his lips, his
face coloring.*]

ANDREW: [*Facing him; half-defiantly.*] Yes?

ROBERT: [*Confusedly.*] No— never mind— it doesn't matter, it was
nothing.

ANDREW: [*After a pause, during which he stares fixedly at* ROBERT's
averted face.] Maybe I can guess— what you were going to say—
but I guess you're right not to talk about it. [*He pulls* ROBERT's *hand
from his side and grips it tensely; the two brothers stand looking into
each other's eyes for a minute.*] We can't help those things, Rob. [*He
turns away, suddenly releasing* ROBERT'S *hand.*] You'll be coming
along shortly, won't you?

ROBERT: [*Dully.*] Yes.

ANDREW: See you later, then. [*He walks off down the road to the left.*
ROBERT *stares after him for a moment; then climbs to the fence rail
again, and looks out over the hills, an expression of deep grief on his
face. After a moment or so,* RUTH *enters hurriedly from the left. She
is a healthy, blonde, out-of-door girl of twenty, with a graceful, slender figure. Her face, though inclined to roundness, is undeniably
pretty, its large eyes of a deep blue set off strikingly by the sun-
bronzed complexion. Her small, regular features are marked by a
certain strength—an underlying, stubborn fixity of purpose hidden
in the frankly-appealing charm of her fresh youthfulness. She wears
a simple white dress but no hat.*]

RUTH: [*Seeing him.*] Hello, Rob!

ROBERT: [*Startled.*] Hello, Ruth!

RUTH: [*Jumps the ditch and perches on the fence beside him.*] I was looking for you.

ROBERT: [*Pointedly.*] Andy just left here.

RUTH: I know. I met him on the road a second ago. He told me you were here. [*Tenderly playful.*] I wasn't looking for Andy, Smarty, if that's what you mean. I was looking for *you*.

ROBERT: Because I'm going away tomorrow?

RUTH: Because your mother was anxious to have you come home and asked me to look for you. I just wheeled Ma over to your house.

ROBERT: [*Perfunctorily.*] How is your mother?

RUTH: [*A shadow coming over her face.*] She's about the same. She never seems to get any better or any worse. Oh, Rob, I do wish she'd try to make the best of things that can't be helped.

ROBERT: Has she been nagging at you again?

RUTH: [*Nods her head, and then breaks forth rebelliously.*] She never stops nagging. No matter what I do for her she finds fault. If only Pa was still living— [*She stops as if ashamed of her outburst.*] I suppose I shouldn't complain this way. [*She sighs.*] Poor Ma, Lord knows it's hard enough for her. I suppose it's natural to be cross when you're not able ever to walk a step. Oh, I'd like to be going away some place—like you!

ROBERT: It's hard to stay—and equally hard to go, sometimes.

RUTH: There! If I'm not the stupid body! I swore I wasn't going to speak about your trip—until after you'd gone; and there I go, first thing!

ROBERT: Why didn't you want to speak of it?

RUTH: Because I didn't want to spoil this last night you're here. Oh, Rob, I'm going to—we're all going to miss you so awfully. Your mother is going around looking as if she'd burst out crying any minute. You ought to know how I feel. Andy and you and I—why it seems as if we'd always been together.

ROBERT: [*With a wry attempt at a smile.*] You and Andy will still have each other. It'll be harder for me without anyone.

RUTH: But you'll have new sights and new people to take your mind off; while we'll be here with the old, familiar place to remind us every minute of the day. It's a shame you're going—just at this time, in spring, when everything is getting so nice. [*With a sigh.*] I oughtn't to talk that way when I know going's the best thing for you. You're bound to find all sorts of opportunities to get on, your father says.

ROBERT: [*Heatedly.*] I don't give a damn about that! I wouldn't take a voyage across the road for the best opportunity in the world of the kind Pa thinks of. [*He smiles at his own irritation.*] Excuse me, Ruth, for getting worked up over it; but Andy gave me an overdose of the practical considerations.

RUTH: [*Slowly, puzzled.*] Well, then, if it isn't— [*With sudden intensity.*] Oh, Rob, why *do* you want to go?

ROBERT: [*Turning to her quickly, in surprise—slowly.*] Why do you ask that, Ruth?

RUTH: [*Dropping her eyes before his searching glance.*] Because— [*Lamely.*] It seems such a shame.

ROBERT: [*Insistently.*] Why?

RUTH: Oh, because—everything.

ROBERT: I could hardly back out now, even if I wanted to. And I'll be forgotten before you know it.

RUTH: [*Indignantly.*] You won't! I'll never forget— [*She stops and turns away to hide her confusion.*]

ROBERT: [*Softly.*] Will you promise me that?

RUTH: [*Evasively.*] Of course. It's mean of you to think that any of us would forget so easily.

ROBERT: [*Disappointedly.*] Oh!

RUTH: [*With an attempt at lightness.*] But you haven't told me your reason for leaving yet?

ROBERT: [*Moodily.*] I doubt if you'll understand. It's difficult to explain, even to myself. Either you feel it, or you don't. I can remember being conscious of it first when I was only a kid—you haven't forgotten what a sickly specimen I was then, in those days, have you?

RUTH: [*With a shudder.*] Let's not think about them.

ROBERT: You'll have to, to understand. Well, in those days, when Ma was fixing meals, she used to get me out of the way by pushing my chair to the west window and telling me to look out and be quiet. That wasn't hard. I guess I was always quiet.

RUTH: [*Compassionately.*] Yes, you always were—and you suffering so much, too!

ROBERT: [*Musingly.*] So I used to stare out over the fields to the hills, out there— [*He points to the horizon.*] and somehow after a time I'd forget any pain I was in, and start dreaming. I knew the sea was over beyond those hills,—the folks had told me—and I used to wonder what the sea was like, and try to form a picture of it in my mind. [*With a smile.*] There was all the mystery in the world to me then about that—far-off sea—and there still is! It called to me then just as it does now. [*After a slight pause.*] And other times my eyes would follow this road, winding off into the distance, toward the hills, as if it, too, was searching for the sea. And I'd promise myself that when I grew up and was strong, I'd follow that road, and it and I would find the sea together. [*With a smile.*] You see, my making this trip is only keeping that promise of long ago.

RUTH: [*Charmed by his low, musical voice telling the dreams of his childhood.*] Yes, I see.

ROBERT: Those were the only happy moments of my life then, dreaming there at the window. I liked to be all alone—those times. I got to know all the different kinds of sunsets by heart. And all those sunsets took place over there—[*He points.*] beyond the horizon. So gradually I came to believe that all the wonders of the world happened on the other side of those hills. There was the home of the good fairies who performed beautiful miracles. I believed in fairies then. [*With a smile.*] Perhaps I still do believe in them. Anyway, in those days they were real enough, and sometimes I could actually hear them calling to me to come out and play with them, dance with them down the road in the dusk in a game of hide-and-seek to find out where the sun was hiding himself. They sang their little songs to me, songs that told of all the wonderful things they had in their home on the other side of the hills; and they promised to show me all of them, if I'd only come, come! But I couldn't come then, and I used to cry sometimes and Ma would think I was in pain. [*He breaks off suddenly with a laugh.*] That's why I'm going now, I suppose. For I can still hear them calling. But the horizon is as far away and as luring as ever. [*He turns to her—softly.*] Do you understand now, Ruth?

RUTH: [*Spellbound, in a whisper.*] Yes.

ROBERT: You feel it then?

RUTH: Yes, yes, I do! [*Unconsciously she snuggles close against his side. His arm steals about her as if he were not aware of the action.*] Oh, Rob, how could I help feeling it? You tell things so beautifully!

ROBERT: [*Suddenly realizing that his arm is around her, and that her head is resting on his shoulder, gently takes his arm away.* RUTH, *brought back to herself, is overcome with confusion.*] So now you know why I'm going. It's for that reason—that and one other.

RUTH: You've another? Then you must tell me that, too.

ROBERT: [*Looking at her searchingly. She drops her eyes before his gaze.*] I wonder if I ought to! You'll promise not to be angry—whatever it is?

RUTH: [*Softly, her face still averted.*] Yes, I promise.

ROBERT: [*Simply.*] I love you. That's the other reason.

RUTH: [*Hiding her face in her hands.*] Oh, Rob!

ROBERT: I wasn't going to tell you, but I feel I have to. It can't matter now that I'm going so far away, and for so long—perhaps forever. I've loved you all these years, but the realization never came 'til I agreed to go away with Uncle Dick. Then I thought of leaving you, and the pain of that thought revealed to me in a flash—that I loved you, had loved you as long as I could remember. [*He gently pulls one of* RUTH's *hands away from her face.*] You mustn't mind my telling you this, Ruth. I realize how impossible it all is—and I understand; for the revelation of my own love seemed to open my eyes to the love of others. I saw Andy's love for you—and I knew that you must love him.

RUTH: [*Breaking out stormily.*] I don't! I don't love Andy! I don't! [ROBERT *stares at her in stupid astonishment.* RUTH *weeps hysterically.*] Whatever—put such a fool notion into—into your head? [*She suddenly throws her arms about his neck and hides her head on his shoulder.*] Oh, Rob! Don't go away! Please! You mustn't, now! You can't! I won't let you! It'd break my—my heart!

ROBERT: [*The expression of stupid bewilderment giving way to one of overwhelming joy. He presses her close to him—slowly and tenderly.*] Do you mean that—that you love me?

RUTH: [*Sobbing.*] Yes, yes—of course I do—what d'you s'pose? [*She lifts up her head and looks into his eyes with a tremulous smile.*] You stupid thing! [*He kisses her.*] I've loved you right along.

ROBERT: [*Mystified.*] But you and Andy were always together!

RUTH: Because you never seemed to want to go any place with me. You were always reading an old book, and not paying any attention to me. I was too proud to let you see I cared because I thought the year you had away to college had made you stuck-up, and you thought yourself too educated to waste any time on me.

ROBERT: [*Kissing her.*] And I was thinking— [*With a laugh.*] What fools we've both been!

RUTH: [*Overcome by a sudden fear.*] You won't go away on the trip, will you, Rob? You'll tell them you can't go on account of me, won't you? You can't go now! You can't!

ROBERT: [*Bewildered.*] Perhaps—you can come too.

RUTH: Oh, Rob, don't be so foolish. You know I can't. Who'd take care of ma? Don't you see I couldn't go—on her account? [*She clings to him imploringly.*] Please don't go—not now. Tell them you've decided not to. They won't mind. I know your mother and father'll be glad. They'll all be. They don't want you to go so far away from them. Please, Rob! We'll be so happy here together where it's natural and we know things. Please tell me you won't go!

ROBERT: [*Face to face with a definite, final decision, betrays the conflict going on within him.*] But—Ruth—I—Uncle Dick—

RUTH: He won't mind when he knows it's for your happiness to stay. How could he? [*As* ROBERT *remains silent she bursts into sobs again.*] Oh, Rob! And you said—you loved me!

ROBERT: [*Conquered by this appeal—an irrevocable decision in his voice.*] I won't go, Ruth. I promise you. There! Don't cry! [*He presses her to him, stroking her hair tenderly. After a pause he speaks with happy hopefulness.*] Perhaps after all Andy was right—righter than he knew—when he said I could find all the things I was seeking for here, at home on the farm. I think love must have been the secret—the secret that called to me from over the world's rim—the secret beyond every horizon; and when I did not come, it came to me. [*He clasps* RUTH *to him fiercely.*] Oh, Ruth, our love is sweeter than any distant dream! [*He kisses her passionately and steps to the ground, lifting* RUTH *in his arms and carrying her to the road where he puts her down.*]

RUTH: [*With a happy laugh.*] My, but you're strong!

ROBERT: Come! We'll go and tell them at once.

RUTH: [*Dismayed.*] Oh, no, don't, Rob, not 'til after I've gone. There'd be bound to be such a scene with them all together.

ROBERT: [*Kissing her—gayly.*] As you like—little Miss Common Sense!

RUTH: Let's go, then. [*She takes his hand, and they start to go off left.* ROBERT *suddenly stops and turns as though for a last look at the hills and the dying sunset flush.*]

ROBERT: [*Looking upward and pointing.*] See! The first star. [*He bends down and kisses her tenderly.*] Our star!

RUTH: [*In a soft murmur.*] Yes. Our very own star. [*They stand for a moment looking up at it, their arms around each other. Then* RUTH *takes his hand again and starts to lead him away.*] Come, Rob, let's go. [*His eyes are fixed again on the horizon as he half turns to follow her.* RUTH *urges.*] We'll be late for supper, Rob.

ROBERT: [*Shakes his head impatiently, as though he were throwing off some disturbing thought—with a laugh.*] All right. We'll run then. Come on! [*They run off laughing as*

[*The Curtain Falls*]

ACT ONE

SCENE TWO

The sitting room of the Mayo farm house about nine o'clock the same night. On the left, two windows looking out on the fields. Against the wall between the windows, an old-fashioned walnut desk. In the left corner, rear, a sideboard with a mirror. In the rear wall to the right of the sideboard, a window looking out on the road. Next to the window a door leading out into the yard. Farther right, a black horse-hair sofa, and another door opening on a bedroom. In the corner, a straight-backed chair. In the right wall, near the middle, an open doorway leading to the kitchen. Farther forward a double-heater stove with coal scuttle, etc. In the center of the newly carpeted floor, an oak dining-room table with a red cover. In the center of the table, a large oil reading lamp. Four chairs, three rockers with crocheted tidies on their backs, and one straight-backed, are placed about the table. The walls are papered a dark red with a scrolly-figured pattern.

Everything in the room is clean, well-kept, and in its exact place, yet there is no suggestion of primness about the whole. Rather the atmosphere is one of the orderly comfort of a simple, hard-earned prosperity, enjoyed and maintained by the family as a unit.

JAMES MAYO, his wife, her brother, CAPTAIN DICK SCOTT, and AN-DREW are discovered. MAYO is his son ANDREW over again in body and face—an ANDREW sixty-five years old with a short, square, white beard. MRS. MAYO is a slight, round-faced, rather prim-looking woman of fifty-five who had once been a school teacher. The labors of a farmer's wife have bent but not broken her, and she retains a certain refinement of movement and expression foreign to the MAYO part of the family. Whatever of resemblance ROBERT has to his parents may be traced to her. Her brother, the CAPTAIN, is short and stocky, with a weather-beaten, jovial face and a white mustache—a typical old salt, loud of voice and given to gesture. He is fifty-eight years old.

JAMES MAYO sits in front of the table. He wears spectacles, and a farm journal which he has been reading lies in his lap. THE CAPTAIN leans forward from a chair in the rear, his hands on the table in front of him. ANDREW is tilted back on the straight-backed chair to the left, his chin sunk forward on his chest, staring at the carpet, preoccupied and frowning.

As the Curtain rises the CAPTAIN is just finishing the relation of some sea episode. The others are pretending an interest which is belied by the absent-minded expressions on their faces.

THE CAPTAIN: [*Chuckling.*] And that mission woman, she hails me on the dock as I was acomin' ashore, and she says—with her silly face all screwed up serious as judgment—"Captain," she says, "would you be so kind as to tell me where the sea-gulls sleeps at nights?" Blow me if them warn't her exact words! [*He slaps the table with the palm of his hands and laughs loudly. The others force smiles.*] Ain't that just like a fool woman's question? And I looks at her serious as I could, "Ma'm," says I, "I couldn't rightly answer that question. I ain't never seed a sea-gull in his bunk yet. The next time I hears one snorin'," I says, "I'll make a note of where he's turned in, and write you a letter 'bout it." And then she calls me a fool real spiteful and tacks away from me quick. [*He laughs again uproariously.*] So I got rid of her that way. [*The others smile but immediately relapse into expressions of gloom again.*]

MRS. MAYO: [*Absent-mindedly—feeling that she has to say something.*] But when it comes to that, where *do* sea-gulls sleep, Dick?

SCOTT: [*Slapping the table.*] Ho! Ho! Listen to her, James. 'Nother one! Well, if that don't beat all hell—'scuse me for cussin', Kate.

MAYO: [*With a twinkle in his eyes.*] They unhitch their wings, Katey, and spreads 'em out on a wave for a bed.

SCOTT: And then they tells the fish to whistle to 'em when it's time to turn out. Ho! Ho!

MRS. MAYO: [*With a forced smile.*] You men folks are too smart to live, aren't you? [*She resumes her knitting.* MAYO *pretends to read his paper;* ANDREW *stares at the floor.*]

SCOTT: [*Looks from one to the other of them with a puzzled air. Finally he is unable to bear the thick silence a minute longer, and blurts out.*] You folks look as if you was settin' up with a corpse. [*With exaggerated concern.*] God A'mighty, there ain't anyone dead, be there?

MAYO: [*Sharply.*] Don't play the dunce, Dick! You know as well as we do there ain't no great cause to be feelin' chipper.

SCOTT: [*Argumentatively.*] And there ain't no cause to be wearin' mourning, either, I can make out.

MRS. MAYO: [*Indignantly.*] How can you talk that way, Dick Scott, when you're taking our Robbie away from us, in the middle of the night, you might say, just to get on that old boat of yours on time! I think you might wait until morning when he's had his breakfast.

SCOTT: [*Appealing to the others hopelessly.*] Ain't that a woman's way o' seein' things for you? God A'mighty, Kate, I can't give orders to the tide that it's got to be high just when it suits me to have it. I ain't gettin' no fun out o' missin' sleep and leavin' here at six bells myself.

[*Protestingly.*] And the *Sunda* ain't an old ship—leastways, not very old—and she's good's she ever was.

MRS. MAYO: [*Her lips trembling.*] I wish Robbie weren't going.

MAYO: [*Looking at her over his glasses—consolingly.*] There, Katey!

MRS. MAYO: [*Rebelliously.*] Well, I *do* wish he wasn't!

SCOTT: You shouldn't be taking it so hard, 's far as I kin see. This vige'll make a man of him. I'll see to it he learns how to navigate, 'n' study for a mate's c'tificate right off—and it'll give him a trade for the rest of his life, if he wants to travel.

MRS. MAYO: But I don't want him to travel all his life. You've got to see he comes home when this trip is over. Then he'll be all well, and he'll want to—to marry—[ANDREW *sits forward in his chair with an abrupt movement.*]—and settle down right here. [*She stares down at the knitting in her lap—after a pause.*] I never realized how hard it was going to be for me to have Robbie go—or I wouldn't have considered it a minute.

SCOTT: It ain't no good goin' on that way, Kate, now it's all settled.

MRS. MAYO: [*On the verge of tears.*] It's all right for *you* to talk. You've never had any children. You don't know what it means to be parted from them—and Robbie my youngest, too. [ANDREW *frowns and fidgets in his chair.*]

ANDREW: [*Suddenly turning to them.*] There's one thing none of you seem to take into consideration—that Rob wants to go. He's dead set on it. He's been dreaming over this trip ever since it was first talked about. It wouldn't be fair to him not to have him go. [*A sudden uneasiness seems to strike him.*] At least, not if he still feels the same way about it he did when he was talking to me this evening.

MAYO: [*With an air of decision.*] Andy's right, Katey. That ends all argyment, you can see that. [*Looking at his big silver watch.*] Wonder what's happened to Robert? He's been gone long enough to wheel the widder to home, certain. He can't be out dreamin' at the stars his last night.

MRS. MAYO: [*A bit reproachfully.*] Why didn't you wheel Mrs. Atkins back tonight, Andy? You usually do when she and Ruth come over.

ANDREW: [*Avoiding her eyes.*] I thought maybe Robert wanted to tonight. He offered to go right away when they were leaving.

MRS. MAYO: He only wanted to be polite.

ANDREW: [*Gets to his feet.*] Well, he'll be right back, I guess. [*He turns to his father.*] Guess I'll go take a look at the black cow, Pa—see if she's ailing any.

MAYO: Yes—better had, son. [ANDREW *goes into the kitchen on the right.*]

SCOTT: [*As he goes out—in a low tone.*] There's the boy that would make a good, strong sea-farin' man—if he'd a mind to.

MAYO: [*Sharply.*] Don't you put no such fool notions in Andy's head, Dick—or you 'n' me's goin' to fall out. [*Then he smiles.*] You couldn't tempt him, no ways. Andy's a Mayo bred in the bone, and he's a born farmer, and a damn good one, too. He'll live and die right here on this farm, like I expect to. [*With proud confidence.*] And he'll make this one of the slickest, best-payin' farms in the state, too, afore he gits through!

SCOTT: Seems to me it's a pretty slick place right now.

MAYO: [*Shaking his head.*] It's too small. We need more land to make it amount to much, and we ain't got the capital to buy it. [ANDREW *enters from the kitchen. His hat is on, and he carries a lighted lantern in his hand. He goes to the door in the rear leading out.*]

ANDREW: [*Opens the door and pauses.*] Anything else you can think of to be done, Pa?

MAYO: No, nothin' I know of. [ANDREW *goes out, shutting the door.*]

MRS. MAYO: [*After a pause.*] What's come over Andy tonight, I wonder? He acts so strange.

MAYO: He does seem sort o' glum and out of sorts. It's 'count o' Robert leavin', I s'pose. [*To* SCOTT.] Dick, you wouldn't believe how them boys o' mine sticks together. They ain't like most brothers. They've been thick as thieves all their lives, with nary a quarrel I kin remember.

SCOTT: No need to tell me that. I can see how they take to each other.

MRS. MAYO: [*Pursuing her train of thought.*] Did you notice, James, how queer everyone was at supper? Robert seemed stirred up about something; and Ruth was so flustered and giggly; and Andy sat there dumb, looking as if he'd lost his best friend; and all of them only nibbled at their food.

MAYO: Guess they was all thinkin' about tomorrow, same as us.

MRS. MAYO: [*Shaking her head.*] No. I'm afraid somethin's happened— somethin' else.

MAYO: You mean—'bout Ruth?

MRS. MAYO: Yes.

MAYO: [*After a pause—frowning.*] I hope her and Andy ain't had a serious fallin'-out. I always sorter hoped they'd hitch up together sooner or later. What d'you say, Dick? Don't you think them two'd pair up well?

SCOTT: [*Nodding his head approvingly.*] A sweet, wholesome couple they'd make.

MAYO: It'd be a good thing for Andy in more ways than one. I ain't what you'd call calculatin' generally, and I b'lieve in lettin' young folks run their affairs to suit themselves; but there's advantages for both o' them in this match you can't overlook in reason. The Atkins farm is right next to ourn. Jined together they'd make a jim-dandy of a place, with plenty o' room to work in. And bein' a widder with only a daughter, and laid up all the time to boot, Mrs. Atkins can't do nothin' with the place as it ought to be done. She needs a man, a first-class farmer, to take hold o' things; and Andy's just the one.

MRS. MAYO: [*Abruptly.*] I don't think Ruth loves Andy.

MAYO: You don't? Well, maybe a woman's eyes is sharper in such things, but—they're always together. And if she don't love him now, she'll likely come around to it in time. [*As* MRS. MAYO *shakes her head.*] You seem mighty fixed in your opinion, Katey. How d'you know?

MRS. MAYO: It's just—what I feel.

MAYO: [*A light breaking over him.*] You don't mean to say— [MRS. MAYO *nods.* MAYO *chuckles scornfully.*] Shucks! I'm losin' my respect for your eyesight, Katey. Why, Robert ain't got no time for Ruth, 'cept as a friend!

MRS. MAYO: [*Warningly.*] Sss-h-h! [*The door from the yard opens, and* ROBERT *enters. He is smiling happily, and humming a song to himself, but as he comes into the room an undercurrent of nervous uneasiness manifests itself in his bearing.*]

MAYO: So here you be at last! [ROBERT *comes forward and sits on* ANDY's *chair.* MAYO *smiles slyly at his wife.*] What have you been doin' all this time—countin' the stars to see if they all come out right and proper?

ROBERT: There's only one I'll ever look for any more, Pa.

MAYO: [*Reproachfully.*] You might've even not wasted time lookin' for that one—your last night.

MRS. MAYO: [*As if she were speaking to a child.*] You ought to have worn your coat a sharp night like this, Robbie.

SCOTT: [*Disgustedly.*] God A'mighty, Kate, you treat Robert as if he was one year old!

MRS. MAYO: [*Notices* ROBERT's *nervous uneasiness.*] You look all worked up over something, Robbie. What is it?

ROBERT: [*Swallowing hard, looks quickly from one to the other of them—then begins determinedly.*] Yes, there *is* something—something I must tell you—all of you. [*As he begins to talk* ANDREW *enters quietly from the rear, closing the door behind him, and setting the lighted lantern on the floor. He remains standing by the door, his arms folded, listening to* ROBERT *with a repressed expression of pain on his face.* ROBERT *is so much taken up with what he is going to say that he does not notice* ANDREW's *presence.*] Something I discovered only this evening—very beautiful and wonderful—something I did not take into consideration previously because I hadn't dared to hope that such happiness could ever come to me. [*Appealingly.*] You must all remember that fact, won't you?

MAYO: [*Frowning.*] Let's get to the point, son.

ROBERT: [*With a trace of defiance.*] Well, the point is this, Pa: I'm not going—I mean—I can't go tomorrow with Uncle Dick—or at any future time, either.

MRS. MAYO: [*With a sharp sigh of joyful relief.*] Oh, Robbie, I'm so glad!

MAYO: [*Astounded.*] You ain't serious, be you, Robert? [*Severely.*] Seems to me it's a pretty late hour in the day for you to be upsettin' all your plans so sudden!

ROBERT: I asked you to remember that until this evening I didn't know myself. I had never dared to dream—

MAYO: [*Irritably.*] What is this foolishness you're talkin' of?

ROBERT: [*Flushing.*] Ruth told me this evening that—she loved me. It was after I'd confessed I loved her. I told her I hadn't been conscious of my love until after the trip had been arranged, and I realized it would mean—leaving her. That was the truth. I *didn't* know until then. [*As if justifying himself to the others.*] I hadn't intended telling her anything but—suddenly—I felt I must. I didn't think it would matter, because I was going away. And I thought she loved—someone else. [*Slowly—his eyes shining.*] And then she cried and said it was I she'd loved all the time, but I hadn't seen it.

MRS. MAYO: [*Rushes over and throws her arms about him.*] I knew it! I was just telling your father when you came in—and, Oh, Robbie, I'm so happy you're not going!

ROBERT: [*Kissing her.*] I knew you'd be glad, Ma.

MAYO: [*Bewilderedly.*] Well, I'll be damned! You do beat all for gettin' folks' minds all tangled up, Robert. And Ruth too! Whatever got into her of a sudden? Why, I was thinkin'—

MRS. MAYO: [*Hurriedly—in a tone of warning.*] Never mind what you were thinking, James. It wouldn't be any use telling us that now. [*Meaningly.*] And what you were hoping for turns out just the same almost, doesn't it?

MAYO: [*Thoughtfully—beginning to see this side of the argument.*] Yes; I suppose you're right, Katey. [*Scratching his head in puzzlement.*]

But how it ever come about! It do beat anything ever I heard. [*Finally he gets up with a sheepish grin and walks over to* ROBERT.] We're glad you ain't goin', your Ma and I, for we'd have missed you terrible, that's certain and sure; and we're glad you've found happiness. Ruth's a fine girl and'll make a good wife to you.

ROBERT: [*Much moved.*] Thank you, Pa. [*He grips his father's hand in his.*]

ANDREW: [*His face tense and drawn comes forward and holds out his hand, forcing a smile.*] I guess it's my turn to offer congratulations, isn't it?

ROBERT: [*With a startled cry when his brother appears before him so suddenly.*] Andy! [*Confused.*] Why—I—I didn't see you. Were you here when—

ANDREW: I heard everything you said; and here's wishing you every happiness, you and Ruth. You both deserve the best there is.

ROBERT: [*Taking his hand.*] Thanks, Andy, it's fine of you to— [*His voice dies away as he sees the pain in* ANDREW'*s eyes.*]

ANDREW: [*Giving his brother's hand a final grip.*] Good luck to you both! [*He turns away and goes back to the rear where he bends over the lantern, fumbling with it to hide his emotion from the others.*]

MRS. MAYO: [*To the* CAPTAIN, *who has been too flabbergasted by* ROBERT'*s decision to say a word.*] What's the matter, Dick? Aren't you going to congratulate Robbie?

SCOTT: [*Embarrassed.*] Of course I be! [*He gets to his feet and shakes* ROBERT'*s hand, muttering a vague.*] Luck to you, boy. [*He stands beside* ROBERT *as if he wanted to say something more but doesn't know how to go about it.*]

ROBERT: Thanks, Uncle Dick.

SCOTT: So you're not acomin' on the *Sunda* with me? [*His voice indicates disbelief.*]

ROBERT: I can't, Uncle—not now. I wouldn't miss it for anything else in the world under any other circumstances. [*He sighs unconsciously.*] But you see I've found—a bigger dream. [*Then with joyous high spirits.*] I want you all to understand one thing—I'm not going to be a loafer on your hands any longer. This means the beginning of a new life for me in every way. I'm going to settle right down and take a real interest in the farm, and do my share. I'll prove to you, Pa, that I'm as good a Mayo as you are—or Andy, when I want to be.

MAYO: [*Kindly but skeptically.*] That's the right spirit, Robert. Ain't none of us doubts your willin'ness, but you ain't never learned—

ROBERT: Then I'm going to start learning right away, and you'll teach me, won't you?

MAYO: [*Mollifyingly.*] Of course I will, boy, and be glad to, only you'd best go easy at first.

SCOTT: [*Who has listened to this conversation in mingled consternation and amazement.*] You don't mean to tell me you're goin' to let him stay, do you, James?

MAYO: Why, things bein' as they be, Robert's free to do as he's a mind to.

MRS. MAYO: *Let him!* The very idea!

SCOTT: [*More and more ruffled.*] Then all I got to say is, you're a soft, weak-willed critter to be permittin' a boy—and women, too—to be layin' your course for you wherever they damn pleases.

MAYO: [*Slyly amused.*] It's just the same with me as 'twas with you, Dick. You can't order the tides on the seas to suit you, and I ain't pretendin' I can reg'late love for young folks.

SCOTT: [*Scornfully.*] Love! They ain't old enough to know love when they sight it! Love! I'm ashamed of you, Robert, to go lettin' a little huggin' and kissin' in the dark spile your chances to make a man out o' yourself. It ain't common sense—no siree, it ain't—not by a hell of a sight! [*He pounds the table with his fists in exasperation.*]

MRS. MAYO: [*Laughing provokingly at her brother.*] A fine one you are to be talking about love, Dick—an old cranky bachelor like you. Goodness sakes!

SCOTT: [*Exasperated by their joking.*] I've never been a damn fool like most, if that's what you're steerin' at.

MRS. MAYO: [*Tauntingly.*] Sour grapes, aren't they, Dick? [*She laughs. ROBERT and his father chuckle. SCOTT sputters with annoyance.*] Good gracious, Dick, you do act silly, flying into a temper over nothing.

SCOTT: [*Indignantly.*] Nothin'! You talk as if I wasn't concerned nohow in this here business. Seems to me I've got a right to have my say. Ain't I made all arrangements with the owners and stocked up with some special grub all on Robert's account?

ROBERT: You've been fine, Uncle Dick; and I appreciate it. Truly.

MAYO: 'Course; we all does, Dick.

SCOTT: [*Unplacated.*] I've been countin' sure on havin' Robert for company on this vige—to sorta talk to and show things to, and teach, kinda, and I got my mind so set on havin' him I'm goin' to be double lonesome this vige. [*He pounds on the table, attempting to cover up this confession of weakness.*] Darn all this silly lovin' business, anyway. [*Irritably.*] But all this talk ain't tellin' me what I'm to do with that sta'b'd cabin I fixed up. It's all painted white, an' a bran

new mattress on the bunk, 'n' new sheets 'n' blankets 'n' things. And
Chips built in a book-case so's Robert could take his books along—
with a slidin' bar fixed across't it, mind, so's they couldn't fall out no
matter how she rolled. [*With excited consternation.*] What d'you
suppose my officers is goin' to think when there's no one comes
aboard to occupy that sta'b'd cabin? And the men what did the
work on it—what'll *they* think? [*He shakes his finger indignantly.*]
They're liable as not to suspicion it was a *woman* I'd planned to ship
along, and that she gave me the go-by at the last moment! [*He wipes
his perspiring brow in anguish at this thought.*] Gawd A'mighty!
They're only lookin' to have the laugh on me for something like that.
They're liable to b'lieve anything, those fellers is!

MAYO: [*With a wink.*] Then there's nothing to it but for you to get right
out and hunt up a wife somewheres for that spick 'n' span cabin.
She'll have to be a pretty one, too, to match it. [*He looks at his
watch with exaggerated concern.*] You ain't got much time to find
her, Dick.

SCOTT: [*As the others smile—sulkily.*] You kin go to thunder, Jim
Mayo!

ANDREW: [*Comes forward from where he has been standing by the
door, rear, brooding. His face is set in a look of grim determination.*]
You needn't worry about that spare cabin, Uncle Dick, if you've a
mind to take me in Robert's place.

ROBERT: [*Turning to him quickly.*] Andy! [*He sees at once the fixed re-
solve in his brother's eyes, and realizes immediately the reason for
it—in consternation.*] Andy, you mustn't!

ANDREW: You've made your decision, Rob, and now I've made mine.
You're out of this, remember.

ROBERT: [*Hurt by his brother's tone.*] But Andy—

ANDREW: Don't interfere, Rob—that's all I ask. [*Turning to his uncle.*]
You haven't answered my question, Uncle Dick.

SCOTT: [*Clearing his throat, with an uneasy side glance at* JAMES MAYO
*who is staring at his elder son as if he thought he had suddenly gone
mad.*] O' course, I'd be glad to have you, Andy.

ANDREW: It's settled then. I can pack the little I want to take in a few
minutes.

MRS. MAYO: Don't be a fool, Dick. Andy's only joking you.

SCOTT: [*Disgruntedly.*] It's hard to tell who's jokin' and who's not in
this house.

ANDREW: [*Firmly.*] I'm not joking, Uncle Dick. [*As* SCOTT *looks at him
uncertainly.*] You needn't be afraid I'll go back on my word.

ROBERT: [*Hurt by the insinuation he feels in* ANDREW's *tone.*] Andy! That isn't fair!

MAYO: [*Frowning.*] Seems to me this ain't no subject to joke over—not for Andy.

ANDREW: [*Facing his father.*] I agree with you, Pa, and I tell you again, once and for all, that I've made up my mind to go.

MAYO: [*Dumbfounded—unable to doubt the determination in* AN-DREW's *voice—helplessly.*] But why, son? Why?

ANDREW: [*Evasively.*] I've always wanted to go.

ROBERT: Andy!

ANDREW: [*Half angrily.*] You shut up, Rob! [*Turning to his father again.*] I didn't ever mention it because as long as Rob was going I knew it was no use; but now Rob's staying on here, there isn't any reason for me not to go.

MAYO: [*Breathing hard.*] No reason? Can you stand there and say that to me, Andrew?

MRS. MAYO: [*Hastily—seeing the gathering storm.*] He doesn't mean a word of it, James.

MAYO: [*Making a gesture to her to keep silence.*] Let me talk, Katey. [*In a more kindly tone.*] What's come over you so sudden, Andy? You know's well as I do that it wouldn't be fair o' you to run off at a moment's notice right now when we're up to our necks in hard work.

ANDREW: [*Avoiding his eyes.*] Rob'll hold his end up as soon as he learns.

MAYO: Robert was never cut out for a farmer, and you was.

ANDREW: You can easily get a man to do my work.

MAYO: [*Restraining his anger with an effort.*] It sounds strange to hear you, Andy, that I always thought had good sense, talkin' crazy like that. [*Scornfully.*] Get a man to take your place! You ain't been workin' here for no hire, Andy, that you kin give me your notice to quit like you've done. The farm is your'n as well as mine. You've always worked on it with that understanding; and what you're sayin' you intend doin' is just skulkin' out o' your rightful responsibility.

ANDREW: [*Looking at the floor—simply.*] I'm sorry, Pa. [*After a slight pause.*] It's no use talking any more about it.

MRS. MAYO: [*In relief.*] There! I knew Andy'd come to his senses!

ANDREW: Don't get the wrong idea, Ma. I'm not backing out.

MAYO: You mean you're goin' in spite of—everythin'?

ANDREW: Yes. I'm going. I've got to. [*He looks at his father defiantly.*] I feel I oughn't to miss this chance to go out into the world and see things, and—I want to go.

MAYO: [*With bitter scorn.*] So—you want to go out into the world and see thin's! [*His voice raised and quivering with anger.*] I never thought I'd live to see the day when a son o' mine 'd look me in the face and tell a bare-faced lie! [*Bursting out.*] You're a liar, Andy Mayo, and a mean one to boot!

MRS. MAYO: James!

ROBERT: Pa!

SCOTT: Steady there, Jim!

MAYO: [*Waving their protests aside.*] He is and he knows it.

ANDREW: [*His face flushed.*] I won't argue with you, Pa. You can think as badly of me as you like.

MAYO: [*Shaking his finger at* ANDY, *in a cold rage.*] You know I'm speakin' truth—that's why you're afraid to argy! You lie when you say you want to go 'way—and see thin's! You ain't got no likin' in the world to go. I've watched you grow up, and I know your ways, and they're my ways. You're runnin' against your own nature, and you're goin' to be a'mighty sorry for it if you do. 'S if I didn't know your real reason for runnin' away! And runnin' away's the only words to fit it. You're runnin' away 'cause you're put out and riled 'cause your own brother's got Ruth 'stead o' you, and—

ANDREW: [*His face crimson—tensely.*] Stop, Pa! I won't stand hearing that—not even from you!

MRS. MAYO: [*Rushing to* ANDY *and putting her arms about him protectingly.*] Don't mind him, Andy dear. He don't mean a word he's saying! [ROBERT *stands rigidly, his hands clenched, his face contracted by pain.* SCOTT *sits dumbfounded and open-mouthed.* ANDREW *soothes his mother who is on the verge of tears.*]

MAYO: [*In angry triumph.*] It's the truth, Andy Mayo! And you ought to be bowed in shame to think of it!

ROBERT: [*Protestingly.*] Pa!

MRS. MAYO: [*Coming from* ANDREW *to his father; puts her hands on his shoulders as though to try and push him back in the chair from which he has risen.*] Won't you be still, James? Please won't you?

MAYO: [*Looking at* ANDREW *over his wife's shoulder—stubbornly.*] The truth—God's truth!

MRS. MAYO: Sh-h-h! [*She tries to put a finger across his lips, but he twists his head away.*]

ANDREW: [*Who has regained control over himself.*] You're wrong, Pa, it isn't truth. [*With defiant assertiveness.*] I don't love Ruth. I never loved her, and the thought of such a thing never entered my head.

MAYO: [*With an angry snort of disbelief.*] Hump! You're pilin' lie on lie!

ANDREW: [*Losing his temper—bitterly.*] I suppose it'd be hard for you to explain anyone's wanting to leave this blessed farm except for some outside reason like that. But I'm sick and tired of it—whether you want to believe me or not—and that's why I'm glad to get a chance to move on.

ROBERT: Andy! Don't! You're only making it worse.

ANDREW: [*Sulkily.*] I don't care. I've done my share of work here. I've earned my right to quit when I want to. [*Suddenly overcome with anger and grief; with rising intensity.*] I'm sick and tired of the whole damn business. I hate the farm and every inch of ground in it. I'm sick of digging in the dirt and sweating in the sun like a slave without getting a word of thanks for it. [*Tears of rage starting to his eyes—hoarsely.*] I'm through, through for good and all; and if Uncle Dick won't take me on his ship, I'll find another. I'll get away somewhere, somehow.

MRS. MAYO: [*In a frightened voice.*] Don't you answer him, James. He doesn't know what he's saying. Don't say a word to him 'til he's in his right senses again. Please James, don't—

MAYO: [*Pushes her away from him; his face is drawn and pale with the violence of his passion. He glares at* ANDREW *as if he hated him.*] You dare to—you dare to speak like that to me? You talk like that 'bout this farm—the Mayo farm—where you was born—you—you— [*He clenches his fist above his head and advances threateningly on* ANDREW.] You damned whelp!

MRS. MAYO: [*With a shriek.*] James! [*She covers her face with her hands and sinks weakly into* MAYO's *chair.* ANDREW *remains standing motionless, his face pale and set.*]

SCOTT: [*Starting to his feet and stretching his arms across the table toward* MAYO.] Easy there, Jim!

ROBERT: [*Throwing himself between father and brother.*] Stop! Are you mad?

MAYO: [*Grabs* ROBERT's *arm and pushes him aside—then stands for a moment gasping for breath before* ANDREW. *He points to the door with a shaking finger.*] Yes—go!—go!—You're no son o' mine—no son o' mine! You can go to hell if you want to! Don't let me find you here—in the mornin'—or—or—I'll *throw* you out!

ROBERT: Pa! For God's sake! [MRS. MAYO *bursts into noisy sobbing.*]

MAYO: [*He gulps convulsively and glares at* ANDREW.] You go—tomorrow mornin'—and by God—don't come back—don't dare come back—by God, not while I'm livin'—or I'll—I'll— [*He shakes over his muttered threat and strides toward the door rear, right.*]

MRS. MAYO: [*Rising and throwing her arms around him—hysterically.*] James! James! Where are you going?

MAYO: [*Incoherently.*] I'm goin'—to bed, Katey. It's late, Katey—it's late. [*He goes out.*]

MRS. MAYO: [*Following him, pleading hysterically.*] James! Take back what you've said to Andy. James! [*She follows him out.* ROBERT *and the* CAPTAIN *stare after them with horrified eyes.* ANDREW *stands rigidly looking straight in front of him, his fists clenched at his sides.*]

SCOTT: [*The first to find his voice—with an explosive sigh.*] Well, if he ain't the devil himself when he's roused! You oughtn't to have talked to him that way, Andy, 'bout the damn farm, knowin' how touchy he is about it. [*With another sigh.*] Well, you won't mind what he's said in anger. He'll be sorry for it when he's calmed down a bit.

ANDREW: [*In a dead voice.*] You don't know him. [*Defiantly.*] What's said is said and can't be unsaid; and I've chosen.

ROBERT: [*With violent protest.*] Andy! You can't go! This is all so stupid—and terrible!

ANDREW: [*Coldly.*] I'll talk to you in a minute, Rob. [*Crushed by his brother's attitude* ROBERT *sinks down into a chair, holding his head in his hands.*]

SCOTT: [*Comes and slaps* ANDREW *on the back.*] I'm damned glad you're shippin' on, Andy. I like your spirit, and the way you spoke up to him. [*Lowering his voice to a cautious whisper.*] The sea's the place for a young feller like you that isn't half dead 'n' alive. [*He gives* ANDY *a final approving slap.*] You 'n' me 'll get along like twins, see if we don't. I'm goin' aloft to turn in. Don't forget to pack your dunnage. And git some sleep, if you kin. We'll want to sneak out extra early b'fore they're up. It'll do away with more argyments. Robert can drive us down to the town, and bring back the team. [*He goes to the door in the rear, left.*] Well, good night.

ANDREW: Good night. [SCOTT *goes out. The two brothers remain silent for a moment. Then* ANDREW *comes over to his brother and puts a hand on his back. He speaks in a low voice, full of feeling.*] Buck up, Rob. It ain't any use crying over spilt milk; and it'll all turn out for the best—let's hope. It couldn't be helped—what's happened.

ROBERT: [*Wildly.*] But it's a lie, Andy, a lie!

ANDREW: Of course it's a lie. You know it and I know it,—but that's all ought to know it.

ROBERT: Pa'll never forgive you. Oh, the whole affair is so senseless— and tragic. Why did you think you must go away?

ANDREW: You know better than to ask that. You know why. [*Fiercely.*] I can wish you and Ruth all the good luck in the world, and I do, and I mean it; but you can't expect me to stay around here and watch you two together, day after day—and me alone. I couldn't stand it—not after all the plans I'd made to happen on this place thinking— [*His voice breaks.*] thinking she cared for me.

ROBERT: [*Putting a hand on his brother's arm.*] God! It's horrible! I feel so guilty—to think that I should be the cause of your suffering, after we've been such pals all our lives. If I could have foreseen what'd happen, I swear to you I'd have never said a word to Ruth. I swear I wouldn't have, Andy!

ANDREW: I know you wouldn't; and that would've been worse, for Ruth would've suffered then. [*He pats his brother's shoulder.*] It's best as it is. It had to be, and I've got to stand the gaff, that's all. Pa'll see how I felt—after a time. [*As* ROBERT *shakes his head.*]—and if he don't—well, it can't be helped.

ROBERT: But think of Ma! God, Andy, you can't go! You can't!

ANDREW: [*Fiercely.*] I've got to go—to get away! I've got to, I tell you. I'd go crazy here, bein' reminded every second of the day what a fool I'd made of myself. I've got to get away and try and forget, if I can. And I'd hate the farm if I stayed, hate it for bringin' things back. I couldn't take interest in the work any more, work with no purpose in sight. Can't you see what a hell it'd be? You love her too, Rob. Put yourself in my place, and remember I haven't stopped loving her, and couldn't if I was to stay. Would that be fair to you or to her? Put yourself in my place. [*He shakes his brother fiercely by the shoulder.*] What'd you do then? Tell me the truth! You love her. What'd you do?

ROBERT: [*Chokingly.*] I'd—I'd go, Andy! [*He buries his face in his hands with a shuddering sob.*] God!

ANDREW: [*Seeming to relax suddenly all over his body—in a low, steady voice.*] Then you know why I got to go; and there's nothing more to be said.

ROBERT: [*In a frenzy of rebellion.*] Why did this have to happen to us? It's damnable! [*He looks about him wildly, as if his vengeance were seeking the responsible fate.*]

ANDREW: [*Soothingly—again putting his hands on his brother's shoulder.*] It's no use fussing any more, Rob. It's done. [*Forcing a smile.*] I guess Ruth's got a right to have who she likes. She made a good choice—and God bless her for it!

ROBERT: Andy! Oh, I wish I could tell you half I feel of how fine you are!

ANDREW: [*Interrupting him quickly.*] Shut up! Let's go to bed. I've got to be up long before sun-up. You, too, if you're going to drive us down.

ROBERT: Yes. Yes.

ANDREW: [*Turning down the lamp.*] And I've got to pack yet. [*He yawns with utter weariness.*] I'm as tired as if I'd been plowing twenty-four hours at a stretch. [*Dully.*] I feel—dead. [ROBERT *covers his face again with his hands.* ANDREW *shakes his head as if to get rid of his thoughts, and continues with a poor attempt at cheery briskness.*] I'm going to douse the light. Come on. [*He slaps his brother on the back.* ROBERT *does not move.* ANDREW *bends over and blows out the lamp. His voice comes from the darkness.*] Don't sit there mourning, Rob. It'll all come out in the wash. Come on and get some sleep. Everything'll turn out all right in the end. [ROBERT *can be heard stumbling to his feet, and the dark figures of the two brothers can be seen groping their way toward the doorway in the rear as*

[*The Curtain Falls*]

ACT TWO

SCENE ONE

Same as Act One, Scene Two. Sitting room of the farm house about half past twelve in the afternoon of a hot, sun-baked day in midsummer, three years later. All the windows are open, but no breeze stirs the soiled white curtains. A patched screen door is in the rear. Through it the yard can be seen, its small stretch of lawn divided by the dirt path leading to the door from the gate in the white picket fence which borders the road.

The room has changed, not so much in its outward appearance as in its general atmosphere. Little significant details give evidence of carelessness, of inefficiency, of an industry gone to seed. The chairs appear shabby from lack of paint; the table cover is spotted and askew; holes show in the curtains; a child's doll, with one arm gone, lies under the table; a hoe stands in a corner; a man's coat is flung on the couch in the rear; the desk is cluttered up with odds and ends; a number of books are piled carelessly on the sideboard. The noon enervation of the sultry, scorching day seems to have penetrated indoors, causing even inanimate objects to wear an aspect of despondent exhaustion.

A place is set at the end of the table, left, for someone's dinner. Through the open door to the kitchen comes the clatter of dishes being washed, interrupted at intervals by a woman's irritated voice and the peevish whining of a child.

At the rise of the curtain MRS. MAYO *and* MRS. ATKINS *are discovered sitting facing each other,* MRS. MAYO *to the rear,* MRS. ATKINS *to the right of the table.* MRS. MAYO's *face has lost all character, disintegrated, become a weak mask wearing a helpless, doleful expression of being constantly on the verge of comfortless tears. She speaks in an uncertain voice, without assertiveness, as if all power of willing had deserted her.* MRS. ATKINS *is in her wheel chair. She is a thin, pale-faced, unintelligent looking woman of about forty-eight, with hard, bright eyes. A victim of partial paralysis for many years, condemned to be pushed from day to day of her life in a wheel chair, she has developed the selfish, irritable nature of the chronic invalid. Both women are dressed in black.* MRS. ATKINS *knits nervously as she talks. A ball of unused yarn, with needles stuck through it, lies on the table before* MRS. MAYO.

MRS. ATKINS: [*With a disapproving glance at the place set on the table.*] Robert's late for his dinner again, as usual. I don't see why Ruth puts up with it, and I've told her so. Many's the time I've said to her "It's about time you put a stop to his nonsense. Does he suppose you're runnin' a hotel—with no one to help with things?" But she don't pay no attention. She's as bad as he is, a'most—thinks she knows better than an old, sick body like me.

MRS. MAYO: [*Dully.*] Robbie's always late for things. He can't help it, Sarah.

MRS. ATKINS: [*With a snort.*] Can't help it! How you do go on, Kate, findin' excuses for him! Anybody can help anything they've a mind to—as long as they've got health, and ain't rendered helpless like me— [*She adds as a pious afterthought.*]—through the will of God.

MRS. MAYO: Robbie can't.

MRS. ATKINS: Can't! It do make me mad, Kate Mayo, to see folks that God gave all the use of their limbs to potterin' round and wastin' time doin' everything the wrong way—and me powerless to help and at their mercy, you might say. And it ain't that I haven't pointed the right way to 'em. I've talked to Robert thousands of times and told him how things ought to be done. You know that, Kate Mayo. But d'you s'pose he takes any notice of what I say? Or Ruth, either—my own daughter? No, they think I'm a crazy, cranky old woman, half dead a'ready, and the sooner I'm in the grave and out o' their way the better it'd suit them.

MRS. MAYO: You mustn't talk that way, Sarah. They're not as wicked as that. And you've got years and years before you.

MRS. ATKINS: You're like the rest, Kate. You don't know how near the

end I am. Well, at least I can go to my eternal rest with a clear conscience. I've done all a body could do to avert ruin from this house.
On their heads be it!

MRS. MAYO: [*With hopeless indifference.*] Things might be worse.
Robert never had any experience in farming. You can't expect him to
learn in a day.

MRS. ATKINS: [*Snappily.*] He's had three years to learn, and he's gettin'
worse 'stead of better. Not on'y your place but mine too is driftin' to
rack and ruin, and I can't do nothin' to prevent.

MRS. MAYO: [*With a spark of assertiveness.*] You can't say but Robbie
works hard, Sarah.

MRS. ATKINS: What good's workin' hard if it don't accomplish anythin',
I'd like to know?

MRS. MAYO: Robbie's had bad luck against him.

MRS. ATKINS: Say what you've a mind to, Kate, the proof of the pud-
din's in the eatin'; and you can't deny that things have been goin'
from bad to worse ever since your husband died two years back.

MRS. MAYO: [*Wiping tears from her eyes with her handkerchief.*] It was
God's will that he should be taken.

MRS. ATKINS: [*Triumphantly.*] It was God's punishment on James Mayo
for the blasphemin' and denyin' of God he done all his sinful life!
[MRS. MAYO *begins to weep softly.*] There, Kate, I shouldn't be re-
mindin' you, I know. He's at peace, poor man, and forgiven, let's
pray.

MRS. MAYO: [*Wiping her eyes—simply.*] James was a good man.

MRS. ATKINS: [*Ignoring this remark.*] What I was sayin' was that since
Robert's been in charge things've been goin' down hill steady. You
don't know *how* bad they are. Robert don't let on to you what's
happenin'; and you'd never see it yourself if 'twas under your nose.
But, thank the Lord, Ruth still comes to me once in a while for advice when she's worried near out of her senses by his goin's-on. Do
you know what she told me last night? But I forgot, she said not to
tell you—still I think you've got a right to know, and it's my duty not
to let such things go on behind your back.

MRS. MAYO: [*Wearily.*] You can tell me if you want to.

MRS. ATKINS: [*Bending over toward her—in a low voice.*] Ruth was almost crazy about it. Robert told her he'd have to mortgage the
farm—said he didn't know how he'd pull through 'til harvest without it, and he can't get money any other way. [*She straightens up—
indignantly.*] Now what do you think of your Robert?

MRS. MAYO: [*Resignedly.*] If it has to be—

MRS. ATKINS: You don't mean to say you're goin' to sign away your farm, Kate Mayo—after me warnin' you?

MRS. MAYO: —I'll do what Robbie says is needful.

MRS. ATKINS: [Holding up her hands.] Well, of all the foolishness!—well, it's your farm, not mine, and I've nothin' more to say.

MRS. MAYO: Maybe Robbie'll manage till Andy gets back and sees to things. It can't be long now.

MRS. ATKINS: [With keen interest.] Ruth says Andy ought to turn up any day. When does Robert figger he'll get here?

MRS. MAYO: He says he can't calculate exactly on account o' the Sunda being a sail boat. Last letter he got was from England, the day they were sailing for home. That was over a month ago, and Robbie thinks they're overdue now.

MRS. ATKINS: We can give praise to God then that he'll be back in the nick o' time. He ought to be tired of travelin' and anxious to get home and settle down to work again.

MRS. MAYO: Andy has been working. He's head officer on Dick's boat, he wrote Robbie. You know that.

MRS. ATKINS: That foolin' on ships is all right for a spell, but he must be right sick of it by this.

MRS. MAYO: [Musingly.] I wonder if he's changed much. He used to be so fine-looking and strong. [With a sigh.] Three years! It seems more like three hundred. [Her eyes filling—piteously.] Oh, if James could only have lived 'til he came back—and forgiven him!

MRS. ATKINS: He never would have—not James Mayo! Didn't he keep his heart hardened against him till the last in spite of all you and Robert did to soften him?

MRS. MAYO: [With a feeble flash of anger.] Don't you dare say that! [Brokenly.] Oh, I know deep down in his heart he forgave Andy, though he was too stubborn ever to own up to it. It was that brought on his death—breaking his heart just on account of his stubborn pride. [She wipes her eyes with her handkerchief and sobs.]

MRS. ATKINS: [Piously.] It was the will of God. [The whining crying of the child sounds from the kitchen. MRS. ATKINS frowns irritably.] Drat that young one! Seems as if she cries all the time on purpose to set a body's nerves on edge.

MRS. MAYO: [Wiping her eyes.] It's the heat upsets her. Mary doesn't feel any too well these days, poor little child!

MRS. ATKINS: She gets it right from her Pa—bein' sickly all the time. You can't deny Robert was always ailin' as a child. [She sighs heavily.] It was a crazy mistake for them two to get married. I argyed

against it at the time, but Ruth was so spelled with Robert's wild poetry notions she wouldn't listen to sense. Andy was the one would
have been the match for her.

MRS. MAYO: I've often thought since it might have been better the other
way. But Ruth and Robbie seem happy enough together.

MRS. ATKINS: At any rate it was God's work—and His will be done.
[*The two women sit in silence for a moment.* RUTH *enters from the
kitchen, carrying in her arms her two year old daughter,* MARY, *a
pretty but sickly and ænemic looking child with a tear-stained face.*
RUTH *has aged appreciably. Her face has lost its youth and fresh-
ness. There is a trace in her expression of something hard and spiteful. She sits in the rocker in front of the table and sighs wearily. She
wears a gingham dress with a soiled apron tied around her waist.*]

RUTH: Land sakes, if this isn't a scorcher! That kitchen's like a furnace.
Phew! [*She pushes the damp hair back from her forehead.*]

MRS. MAYO: Why didn't you call me to help with the dishes?

RUTH: [*Shortly.*] No. The heat in there'd kill you.

MARY: [*Sees the doll under the table and struggles on her mother's lap.*]
Dolly, Mama! Dolly!

RUTH: [*Pulling her back.*] It's time for your nap. You can't play with
Dolly now.

MARY: [*Commencing to cry whiningly.*] Dolly!

MRS. ATKINS: [*Irritably.*] Can't you keep that child still? Her racket's
enough to split a body's ears. Put her down and let her play with the
doll if it'll quiet her.

RUTH: [*Lifting* MARY *to the floor.*] There! I hope you'll be satisfied and
keep still. [MARY *sits down on the floor before the table and plays
with the doll in silence.* RUTH *glances at the place set on the table.*]
It's a wonder Rob wouldn't try to get to meals on time once in a
while.

MRS. MAYO: [*Dully.*] Something must have gone wrong again.

RUTH: [*Wearily.*] I s'pose so. Something's always going wrong these
days, it looks like.

MRS. ATKINS: [*Snappily.*] It wouldn't if you possessed a bit of spunk.
The idea of you permittin' him to come in to meals at all hours—and
you doin' the work! I never heard of such a thin'. You're too easy
goin', that's the trouble.

RUTH: Do stop your nagging at me, Ma! I'm sick of hearing you. I'll do
as I please about it; and thank you for not interfering. [*She wipes her
moist forehead—wearily.*] Phew! It's too hot to argue. Let's talk of
something pleasant. [*Curiously.*] Didn't I hear you speaking about
Andy a while ago?

MRS. MAYO: We were wondering when he'd get home.

RUTH: [*Brightening.*] Rob says any day now he's liable to drop in and surprise us—him and the Captain. It'll certainly look natural to see him around the farm again.

MRS. ATKINS: Let's hope the farm'll look more natural, too, when he's had a hand at it. The way thin's are now!

RUTH: [*Irritably.*] Will you stop harping on that, Ma? We all know things aren't as they might be. What's the good of your complaining all the time?

MRS. ATKINS: There, Kate Mayo! Ain't that just what I told you? I can't say a word of advice to my own daughter even, she's that stubborn and self-willed.

RUTH: [*Putting her hands over her ears—in exasperation.*] For goodness sakes, Ma!

MRS. MAYO: [*Dully.*] Never mind. Andy'll fix everything when he comes.

RUTH: [*Hopefully.*] Oh, yes, I know he will. He always did know just the right thing ought to be done. [*With weary vexation.*] It's a shame for him to come home and have to start in with things in such a topsy-turvy.

MRS. MAYO: Andy'll manage.

RUTH: [*Sighing.*] I s'pose it isn't Rob's fault things go wrong with him.

MRS. ATKINS: [*Scornfully.*] Hump! [*She fans herself nervously.*] Land o' Goshen, but it's bakin' in here! Let's go out in under the trees in back where there's a breath of fresh air. Come, Kate. [MRS. MAYO *gets up obediently and starts to wheel the invalid's chair toward the screen door.*] You better come too, Ruth. It'll do you good. Learn him a lesson and let him get his own dinner. Don't be such a fool.

RUTH: [*Going and holding the screen door open for them—listlessly.*] He wouldn't mind. He doesn't eat much. But I can't go anyway. I've got to put baby to bed.

MRS. ATKINS: Let's go, Kate. I'm boilin' in here. [MRS. MAYO *wheels her out and off left.* RUTH *comes back and sits down in her chair.*]

RUTH: [*Mechanically.*] Come and let me take off your shoes and stockings, Mary, that's a good girl. You've got to take your nap now. [*The child continues to play as if she hadn't heard, absorbed in her doll. An eager expression comes over* RUTH's *tired face. She glances toward the door furtively—then gets up and goes to the desk. Her movements indicate a guilty fear of discovery. She takes a letter from a pigeonhole and retreats swiftly to her chair with it. She opens the envelope and reads the letter with great interest, a flush of excitement coming to her cheeks.* ROBERT *walks up the path and opens*] *the screen door quietly and comes into the room. He, too, has aged. His shoulders are stooped as if under too great a burden. His eyes are dull and lifeless, his face burned by the sun and unshaven for days. Streaks of sweat have smudged the layer of dust on his cheeks. His lips drawn down at the corners, give him a hopeless, resigned expression. The three years have accentuated the weakness of his mouth and chin. He is dressed in overalls, laced boots, and a flannel shirt open at the neck.*]

ROBERT: [*Throwing his hat over on the sofa—with a great sigh of exhaustion.*] Phew! The sun's hot today! [RUTH *is startled. At first she makes an instinctive motion as if to hide the letter in her bosom. She immediately thinks better of this and sits with the letter in her hands looking at him with defiant eyes. He bends down and kisses her.*]

RUTH: [*Feeling of her cheek—irritably.*] Why don't you shave? You look awful.

ROBERT: [*Indifferently.*] I forgot—and it's too much trouble this weather.

MARY: [*Throwing aside her doll, runs to him with a happy cry.*] Dada! Dada!

ROBERT: [*Swinging her up above his head—lovingly.*] And how's this little girl of mine this hot day, eh?

MARY: [*Screeching happily.*] Dada! Dada!

RUTH: [*In annoyance.*] Don't do that to her! You know it's time for her nap and you'll get her all waked up; then I'll be the one that'll have to sit beside her till she falls asleep.

ROBERT: [*Sitting down in the chair on the left of table and cuddling* MARY *on his lap.*] You needn't bother. I'll put her to bed.

RUTH: [*Shortly.*] You've got to get back to your work, I s'pose.

ROBERT: [*With a sigh.*] Yes, I was forgetting. [*He glances at the open letter on* RUTH's *lap.*] Reading Andy's letter again? I should think you'd know it by heart by this time.

RUTH: [*Coloring as if she'd been accused of something—defiantly.*] I've got a right to read it, haven't I? He says it's meant for all of us.

ROBERT: [*With a trace of irritation.*] Right? Don't be so silly. There's no question of right. I was only saying that you must know all that's in it after so many readings.

RUTH: Well, I don't. [*She puts the letter on the table and gets wearily to her feet.*] I s'pose you'll be wanting your dinner now.

ROBERT: [*Listlessly.*] I don't care. I'm not hungry.

RUTH: And here I been keeping it hot for you!

ROBERT: [*Irritably.*] Oh, all right then. Bring it in and I'll try to eat.

RUTH: I've got to get her to bed first. [*She goes to lift* MARY *off his lap.*] Come, dear. It's after time and you can hardly keep your eyes open now.

MARY: [*Crying.*] No, no! [*Appealing to her father.*] Dada! No!

RUTH: [*Accusingly to* ROBERT.] There! Now see what you've done! I told you not to—

ROBERT: [*Shortly.*] Let her alone, then. She's all right where she is. She'll fall asleep on my lap in a minute if you'll stop bothering her.

RUTH: [*Hotly.*] She'll not do any such thing! She's got to learn to mind me! [*Shaking her finger at* MARY.] You naughty child! Will you come with Mama when she tells you for your own good?

MARY: [*Clinging to her father.*] No, Dada!

RUTH: [*Losing her temper.*] A good spanking's what you need, my young lady—and you'll get one from me if you don't mind better, d'you hear? [MARY *starts to whimper frightenedly.*]

ROBERT: [*With sudden anger.*] Leave her alone! How often have I told you not to threaten her with whipping? I won't have it. [*Soothing the wailing* MARY.] There! There, little girl! Baby mustn't cry. Dada won't like you if you do. Dada'll hold you and you must promise to go to sleep like a good little girl. Will you when Dada asks you?

MARY: [*Cuddling up to him.*] Yes, Dada.

RUTH: [*Looking at them, her pale face set and drawn.*] A fine one you are to be telling folks how to do things! [*She bites her lips. Husband and wife look into each other's eyes with something akin to hatred in their expressions; then* RUTH *turns away with a shrug of affected indifference.*] All right, take care of her then, if you think it's so easy. [*She walks away into the kitchen.*]

ROBERT: [*Smoothing* MARY's *hair—tenderly.*] We'll show Mama you're a good little girl, won't we?

MARY: [*Crooning drowsily.*] Dada, Dada.

ROBERT: Let's see: Does your mother take off your shoes and stockings before your nap?

MARY: [*Nodding with half-shut eyes.*] Yes, Dada.

ROBERT: [*Taking off her shoes and stockings.*] We'll show Mama we know how to do those things, won't we? There's one old shoe off—and there's the other old shoe—and here's one old stocking—and there's the other old stocking. There we are, all nice and cool and comfy. [*He bends down and kisses her.*] And now will you promise to go right to sleep if Dada takes you to bed? [MARY *nods sleepily.*] That's the good little girl. [*He gathers her up in his arms carefully and carries her into the bedroom. His voice can be heard faintly as he lulls the child to sleep.* RUTH *comes out of the kitchen and gets the plate from the table. She hears the voice from the room and tiptoes to the door to look in. Then she starts for the kitchen but stands for a moment thinking, a look of ill-concealed jealousy on her face. At a noise from inside she hurriedly disappears into the kitchen. A moment later* ROBERT *re-enters. He comes forward and picks up the shoes and stockings which he shoves carelessly under the table. Then, seeing no one about, he goes to the sideboard and selects a book. Coming back to his chair, he sits down and immediately becomes absorbed in reading.* RUTH *returns from the kitchen bringing his plate heaped with food, and a cup of tea. She sets those before him and sits down in her former place.* ROBERT *continues to read, oblivious to the food on the table.*]

RUTH: [*After watching him irritably for a moment.*] For heaven's sakes, put down that old book! Don't you see your dinner's getting cold?

ROBERT: [*Closing his book.*] Excuse me, Ruth. I didn't notice. [*He picks up his knife and fork and begins to eat gingerly, without appetite.*]

RUTH: I should think you might have some feeling for me, Rob, and not always be late for meals. If you think it's fun sweltering in that oven of a kitchen to keep things warm for you, you're mistaken.

ROBERT: I'm sorry, Ruth, really I am. Something crops up every day to delay me. I mean to be here on time.

RUTH: [*With a sigh.*] Mean-tos don't count.

ROBERT: [*With a conciliating smile.*] Then punish me, Ruth. Let the food get cold and don't bother about me.

RUTH: I'd have to wait just the same to wash up after you.

ROBERT: But I can wash up.

RUTH: A nice mess there'd be then!

ROBERT: [*With an attempt at lightness.*] The food is lucky to be able to get cold this weather. [*As* RUTH *doesn't answer or smile he opens his book and resumes his reading, forcing himself to take a mouthful of food every now and then.* RUTH *stares at him in annoyance.*]

RUTH: And besides, you've got your own work that's got to be done.

ROBERT: [*Absent-mindedly, without taking his eyes from the book.*] Yes, of course.

RUTH: [*Spitefully.*] Work you'll never get done by reading books all the time.

ROBERT: [*Shutting the book with a snap.*] Why do you persist in nagging at me for getting pleasure out of reading? Is it because— [*He checks himself abruptly.*]

RUTH: [*Coloring.*] Because I'm too stupid to understand them, I s'pose you were going to say.

ROBERT: [*Shame-facedly.*] No—no. [*In exasperation.*] Why do you goad me into saying things I don't mean? Haven't I got my share of troubles trying to work this cursed farm without your adding to them? You know how hard I've tried to keep things going in spite of bad luck—

RUTH: [*Scornfully.*] Bad luck!

ROBERT: And my own very apparent unfitness for the job, I was going to add; but you can't deny there's been bad luck to it, too. Why don't you take things into consideration? Why can't we pull together? We used to. I know it's hard on you also. Then why can't we help each other instead of hindering?

RUTH: [*Sullenly.*] I do the best I know how.

ROBERT: [*Gets up and puts his hand on her shoulder.*] I know you do. But let's both of us try to do better. We can both improve. Say a word of encouragement once in a while when things go wrong, even if it is my fault. You know the odds I've been up against since Pa died. I'm not a farmer. I've never claimed to be one. But there's nothing else I can do under the circumstances, and I've got to pull things through somehow. With your help, I can do it. With you against me— [*He shrugs his shoulders. There is a pause. Then he bends down and kisses her hair—with an attempt at cheerfulness.*] So you promise that; and I'll promise to be here when the clock strikes—and anything else you tell me to. Is it a bargain?

RUTH: [*Dully.*] I s'pose so. [*They are interrupted by the sound of a loud knock at the kitchen door.*] There's someone at the kitchen door. [*She hurries out. A moment later she reappears.*] It's Ben.

ROBERT: [*Frowning.*] What's the trouble now, I wonder? [*In a loud voice.*] Come on in here, Ben. [BEN *slouches in from the kitchen. He is a hulking, awkward young fellow with a heavy, stupid face and shifty, cunning eyes. He is dressed in overalls, boots, etc., and wears a broad-brimmed hat of coarse straw pushed back on his head.*] Well, Ben, what's the matter?

BEN: [*Drawlingly.*] The mowin' machine's bust.

ROBERT: Why, that can't be. The man fixed it only last week.

BEN: It's bust just the same.

ROBERT: And can't you fix it?

BEN: No. Don't know what's the matter with the goll-darned thing. 'Twon't work, anyhow.

ROBERT: [*Getting up and going for his hat.*] Wait a minute and I'll go look it over. There can't be much the matter with it.

BEN: [*Impudently.*] Don't make no diff'rence t' me whether there be or not. I'm quittin'.

ROBERT: [*Anxiously.*] You don't mean you're throwing up your job here?

BEN: That's what! My month's up today and I want what's owin' t' me.

ROBERT: But why are you quitting now, Ben, when you know I've so much work on hand? I'll have a hard time getting another man at such short notice.

BEN: That's for you to figger. I'm quittin'.

ROBERT: But what's your reason? You haven't any complaint to make about the way you've been treated, have you?

BEN: No. 'Tain't that. [*Shaking his finger.*] Look-a-here. I'm sick o' being made fun at, that's what; an' I got a job up to Timms' place; an' I'm quittin' here.

ROBERT: Being made fun of? I don't understand you. Who's making fun of you?

BEN: They all do. When I drive down with the milk in the mornin' they all laughs and jokes at me—that boy up to Harris' and the new feller up to Slocum's, and Bill Evans down to Meade's, and all the rest on 'em.

ROBERT: That's a queer reason for leaving me flat. Won't they laugh at you just the same when you're working for Timms?

BEN: They wouldn't dare to. Timms is the best farm hereabouts. They was laughin' at me for workin' for *you*, that's what! "How're things up to the Mayo place?" they hollers every mornin'. "What's Robert doin' now—pasturin' the cattle in the cornlot? Is he seasonin' his hay with rain this year, same as last?" they shouts. "Or is he inventin' some 'lectrical milkin' engine to fool them dry cows o' his into givin' hard cider?" [*Very much ruffled.*] That's like they talks; and I ain't goin' to put up with it no longer. Everyone's always knowed me as a first-class hand hereabouts, and I ain't wantin' 'em to get no different notion. So I'm quittin' you. And I wants what's comin' to me.

ROBERT: [*Coldly.*] Oh, if that's the case, you can go to the devil. You'll get your money tomorrow when I get back from town—not before!

BEN: [*Turning to doorway to kitchen.*] That suits me. [*As he goes out he speaks back over his shoulder.*] And see that I do get it, or there'll be trouble. [*He disappears and the slamming of the kitchen door is heard.*]

ROBERT: [*As* RUTH *comes from where she has been standing by the doorway and sits down dejectedly in her old place.*] The stupid damn fool! And now what about the haying? That's an example of what I'm up against. No one can say I'm responsible for that.

RUTH: He wouldn't dare act that way with anyone else! [*Spitefully, with *a glance at* ANDREW's *letter on the table.*] It's lucky Andy's coming back.

ROBERT: [*Without resentment.*] Yes, Andy'll see the right thing to do in a jiffy. [*With an affectionate smile.*] I wonder if the old chump's changed much? He doesn't seem to from his letters, does he? [*Shaking his head.*] But just the same I doubt if he'll want to settle down to a hum-drum farm life, after all he's been through.

RUTH: [*Resentfully.*] Andy's not like you. He likes the farm.

ROBERT: [*Immersed in his own thoughts—enthusiastically.*] Gad, the things he's seen and experienced! Think of the places he's been! All the wonderful far places I used to dream about! God, how I envy him! What a trip! [*He springs to his feet and instinctively goes to the window and stares out at the horizon.*]

RUTH: [*Bitterly.*] I s'pose you're sorry now you didn't go?

ROBERT: [*Too occupied with his own thoughts to hear her—vindictively.*] Oh, those cursed hills out there that I used to think promised me so much! How I've grown to hate the sight of them! They're like the walls of a narrow prison yard shutting me in from all the freedom and wonder of life! [*He turns back to the room with a gesture of loathing.*] Sometimes I think if it wasn't for you, Ruth, and— [*His voice softening.*]—little Mary, I'd chuck everything up and walk down the road with just one desire in my heart—to put the whole rim of the world between me and those hills, and be able to breathe freely once more! [*He sinks down into his chair and smiles with bitter self-scorn.*] There I go dreaming again—my old fool dreams.

RUTH: [*In a low, repressed voice—her eyes smoldering.*] You're not the only one!

ROBERT: [*Buried in his own thoughts—bitterly.*] And Andy, who's had the chance—what has he got out of it? His letters read like the diary of a—of a farmer! "We're in Singapore now. It's a dirty hole of a place and hotter than hell. Two of the crew are down with fever and we're short-handed on the work. I'll be damn glad when we sail again, although tacking back and forth in these blistering seas is a rotten job too!" [*Scornfully.*] That's about the way he summed up his impressions of the East.

RUTH: [*Her repressed voice trembling.*] You needn't make fun of Andy.

ROBERT: When I think—but what's the use? You know I wasn't making fun of Andy personally, but his attitude toward things is—

RUTH: [*Her eyes flashing—bursting into uncontrollable rage.*] You was too making fun of him! And I ain't going to stand for it! You ought to be ashamed of yourself! [ROBERT *stares at her in amazement. She continues furiously.*] A fine one to talk about anyone else—after the way you've ruined everything with your lazy loafing!—and the stupid way you do things!

ROBERT: [*Angrily.*] Stop that kind of talk, do you hear?

RUTH: You findin' fault—with your own brother who's ten times the man you ever was or ever will be! You're jealous, that's what! Jealous because he's made a man of himself, while you're nothing but a—but a— [*She stutters incoherently, overcome by rage.*]

ROBERT: Ruth! Ruth! You'll be sorry for talking like that.

RUTH: I won't! I won't never be sorry! I'm only saying what I've been thinking for years.

ROBERT: [*Aghast.*] Ruth! You can't mean that!

RUTH: What do you think—living with a man like you—having to suffer all the time because you've never been man enough to work and do things like other people. But no! You never own up to that. You think you're so much better than other folks, with your college education, where you never learned a thing, and always reading your stupid books instead of working. I s'pose you think I ought to be *proud* to be your wife—a poor, ignorant thing like me! [*Fiercely.*] But I'm not. I hate it! I hate the sight of you. Oh, if I'd only known! If I hadn't been such a fool to listen to your cheap, silly, poetry talk that you learned out of books! If I could have seen how you were in your true self—like you are now—I'd have killed myself before I'd have married you! I was sorry for it before we'd been together a month. I knew what you were really like—when it was too late.

ROBERT: [*His voice raised loudly.*] And now—I'm finding out what you're really like—what a—a creature I've been living with. [*With a harsh laugh.*] God! It wasn't that I haven't guessed how mean and small you are—but I've kept on telling myself that I must be wrong—like a fool!—like a damned fool!

RUTH: You were saying you'd go out on the road if it wasn't for me. Well, you can go, and the sooner the better! I don't care! I'll be glad to get rid of you! The farm'll be better off too. There's been a curse on it ever since you took hold. So go! Go and be a tramp like you've always wanted. It's all you're good for. I can get along without you, don't you worry. [*Exulting fiercely.*] Andy's coming back, don't forget that! He'll attend to things like they should be. He'll show what a man can do! I don't need you. Andy's coming!

ROBERT: [*They are both standing.* ROBERT *grabs her by the shoulders and glares into her eyes.*] What do you mean? [*He shakes her violently.*] What are you thinking of? What's in your evil mind, you— you— [*His voice is a harsh shout.*]

RUTH: [*In a defiant scream.*] Yes I do mean it! I'd say it if you was to kill me! I do love Andy. I do! I do! I always loved him. [*Exultantly.*] And he loves me! He loves me! I know he does. He always did! And you know he did, too! So go! Go if you want to!

ROBERT: [*Throwing her away from him. She staggers back against the table—thickly.*] You—you slut! [*He stands glaring at her as she leans back, supporting herself by the table, gasping for breath. A loud frightened whimper sounds from the awakened child in the bedroom. It continues. The man and woman stand looking at one another in horror, the extent of their terrible quarrel suddenly brought home to them. A pause. The noise of a horse and carriage comes from the road before the house. The two, suddenly struck by the same premonition, listen to it breathlessly, as to a sound heard in a dream. It stops. They hear* ANDY's *voice from the road shouting a long hail—"Ahoy there!"*]

RUTH: [*With a strangled cry of joy.*] Andy! Andy! [*She rushes and grabs the knob of the screen door, about to fling it open.*]

ROBERT: [*In a voice of command that forces obedience.*] Stop! [*He goes to the door and gently pushes the trembling* RUTH *away from it. The child's crying rises to a louder pitch.*] I'll meet Andy. You better go in to Mary, Ruth. [*She looks at him defiantly for a moment, but there is something in his eyes that makes her turn and walk slowly into the bedroom.*]

ANDY's VOICE: [*In a louder shout.*] Ahoy there, Rob!

ROBERT: [*In an answering shout of forced cheeriness.*] Hello, Andy! [*He opens the door and walks out as*

[*The Curtain Falls*]

ACT TWO

SCENE TWO

The top of a hill on the farm. It is about eleven o'clock the next morning. The day is hot and cloudless. In the distance the sea can be seen.

The top of the hill slopes downward slightly toward the left. A big boulder stands in the center toward the rear. Further right, a large oak tree. The faint trace of a path leading upward to it from the left foreground can be detected through the bleached, sun-scorched grass.

ROBERT *is discovered sitting on the boulder, his chin resting on his hands, staring out toward the horizon seaward. His face is pale and haggard, his expression one of utter despondency.* MARY *is sitting on the grass near him in the shade, playing with her doll, singing happily to herself. Presently she casts a curious glance at her father, and, propping her doll up against the tree, comes over and clambers to his side.*

MARY: [*Pulling at his hand—solicitously.*] Dada sick?

ROBERT: [*Looking at her with a forced smile.*] No, dear. Why?

MARY: Play wif Mary.

ROBERT: [*Gently.*] No, dear, not today. Dada doesn't feel like playing today.

MARY: [*Protestingly.*] Yes, Dada!

ROBERT: No, dear. Dada does feel sick—a little. He's got a bad headache.

MARY: Mary see. [*He bends his head. She pats his hair.*] Bad head.

ROBERT: [*Kissing her—with a smile.*] There! It's better now, dear, thank you. [*She cuddles up close against him. There is a pause during which each of them looks out seaward. Finally* ROBERT *turns to her tenderly.*] Would you like Dada to go away?—far, far away?

MARY: [*Tearfully.*] No! No! No, Dada, no!

ROBERT: Don't you like Uncle Andy—the man that came yesterday— not the old man with the white mustache—the other?

MARY: Mary loves Dada.

ROBERT: [*With fierce determination.*] He won't go away, baby. He was only joking. He couldn't leave his little Mary. [*He presses the child in his arms.*]

MARY: [*With an exclamation of pain.*] Oh! Hurt!

ROBERT: I'm sorry, little girl. [*He lifts her down to the grass.*] Go play with Dolly, that's a good girl; and be careful to keep in the shade. [*She reluctantly leaves him and takes up her doll again. A moment later she points down the hill to the left.*]

MARY: Mans, Dada.

ROBERT: [*Looking that way.*] It's your Uncle Andy. [*A moment later* ANDREW *comes up from the left, whistling cheerfully. He has changed but little in appearance, except for the fact that his face has been deeply bronzed by his years in the tropics; but there is a decided change in his manner. The old easy-going good-nature seems to have been partly lost in a breezy, business-like briskness of voice and gesture. There is an authoritative note in his speech as though he were accustomed to give orders and have them obeyed as a matter of course. He is dressed in the simple blue uniform and cap of a merchant ship's officer.*]

ANDREW: Here you are, eh?

ROBERT: Hello, Andy.

ANDREW: [*Going over to* MARY.] And who's this young lady I find you all alone with, eh? Who's this pretty young lady? [*He tickles the laughing, squirming* MARY, *then lifts her up at arm's length over his head.*] Upsy—daisy! [*He sets her down on the ground again.*] And there you are! [*He walks over and sits down on the boulder beside* ROBERT *who moves to one side to make room for him.*] Ruth told me I'd probably find you up top-side here; but I'd have guessed it, anyway. [*He digs his brother in the ribs affectionately.*] Still up to your old tricks, you old beggar! I can remember how you used to come up here to mope and dream in the old days.

ROBERT: [*With a smile.*] I come up here now because it's the coolest place on the farm. I've given up dreaming.

ANDREW: [*Grinning.*] I don't believe it. You can't have changed that much. [*After a pause—with boyish enthusiasm.*] Say, it sure brings back old times to be up here with you having a chin all by our lone-somes again. I feel great being back home.

ROBERT: It's great for us to have you back.

ANDREW: [*After a pause—meaningly.*] I've been looking over the old place with Ruth. Things don't seem to be—

ROBERT: [*His face flushing—interrupts his brother shortly.*] Never mind the damn farm! Let's talk about something interesting. This is the first chance I've had to have a word with you alone. Tell me about your trip.

ANDREW: Why, I thought I told you everything in my letters.

ROBERT: [*Smiling.*] Your letters were—sketchy, to say the least.

ANDREW: Oh, I know I'm no author. You needn't be afraid of hurting my feelings. I'd rather go through a typhoon again than write a letter.

ROBERT: [*With eager interest.*] Then you were through a typhoon?

ANDREW: Yes—in the China sea. Had to run before it under bare poles for two days. I thought we were bound down for Davy Jones, sure. Never dreamed waves could get so big or the wind blow so hard. If it hadn't been for Uncle Dick being such a good skipper we'd have gone to the sharks, all of us. As it was we came out minus a main top-mast and had to beat back to Hong-Kong for repairs. But I must have written you all this.

ROBERT: You never mentioned it.

ANDREW: Well, there was so much dirty work getting things ship-shape again I must have forgotten about it.

ROBERT: [*Looking at* ANDREW—*marveling.*] Forget a typhoon? [*With a trace of scorn.*] You're a strange combination, Andy. And is what you've told me all you remember about it?

ANDREW: Oh, I could give you your bellyful of details if I wanted to turn loose on you. It was all-wool-and-a-yard-wide-Hell, I'll tell you. You ought to have been there. I remember thinking about you at the worst of it, and saying to myself: "This'd cure Rob of them ideas of his about the beautiful sea, if he could see it." And it would have too, you bet! [*He nods emphatically.*]

ROBERT: [*Dryly.*] The sea doesn't seem to have impressed you very favorably.

ANDREW: I should say it didn't! I'll never set foot on a ship again if I can help it—except to carry me some place I can't get to by train.

ROBERT: But you studied to become an officer!

ANDREW: Had to do something or I'd gone mad. The days were like years. [*He laughs.*] And as for the East you used to rave about—well, you ought to see it, and *smell* it! One walk down one of their filthy narrow streets with the tropic sun beating on it would sicken you for life with the "wonder and mystery" you used to dream of.

ROBERT: [*Shrinking from his brother with a glance of aversion.*] So all you found in the East was a stench?

ANDREW: *A* stench! Ten thousand of them!

ROBERT: But you did like some of the places, judging from your letters—Sydney, Buenos Aires—

ANDREW: Yes, Sydney's a good town. [*Enthusiastically.*] But Buenos Aires—there's the place for you. Argentine's a country where a fellow has a chance to make good. You're right I like it. And I'll tell you, Rob, that's right where I'm going just as soon as I've seen you folks a while and can get a ship. I can get a berth as second officer, and I'll jump the ship when I get there. I'll need every cent of the wages Uncle's paid me to get a start at something in B. A.

ROBERT: [*Staring at his brother—slowly.*] So you're not going to stay on the farm?

ANDREW: Why sure not! Did you think I was? There wouldn't be any sense. One of us is enough to run this little place.

ROBERT: I suppose it does seem small to you now.

ANDREW: [*Not noticing the sarcasm in* ROBERT'*s tone.*] You've no idea, Rob, what a splendid place Argentine is. I had a letter from a marine insurance chap that I'd made friends with in Hong-Kong to his brother, who's in the grain business in Buenos Aires. He took quite a fancy to me, and what's more important, he offered me a job if I'd come back there. I'd have taken it on the spot, only I couldn't leave

Uncle Dick in the lurch, and I'd promised you folks to come home. But I'm going back there, you bet, and then you watch me get on! [*He slaps* ROBERT *on the back.*] But don't you think it's a big chance, Rob?

ROBERT: It's fine—for you, Andy.

ANDREW: We call this a farm—but you ought to hear about the farms down there—ten square miles where we've got an acre. It's a new country where big things are opening up—and I want to get in on something big before I die. I'm no fool when it comes to farming, and I know something about grain. I've been reading up a lot on it, too, lately. [*He notices* ROBERT'*s absent-minded expression and laughs.*] Wake up, you old poetry book worm, you! I know my talking about business makes you want to choke me, doesn't it?

ROBERT: [*With an embarrassed smile.*] No, Andy, I—I just happened to think of something else. [*Frowning.*] There've been lots of times lately that I've wished I had some of your faculty for business.

ANDREW: [*Soberly.*] There's something I want to talk about, Rob,—the farm. You don't mind, do you?

ROBERT: No.

ANDREW: I walked over it this morning with Ruth—and she told me about things— [*Evasively.*] I could see the place had run down; but you mustn't blame yourself. When luck's against anyone—

ROBERT: Don't, Andy! It *is* my fault. You know it as well as I do. The best I've ever done was to make ends meet.

ANDREW: [*After a pause.*] I've got over a thousand saved, and you can have that.

ROBERT: [*Firmly.*] No. You need that for your start in Buenos Aires.

ANDREW: I don't. I can—

ROBERT: [*Determinedly.*] No, Andy! Once and for all, no! I won't hear of it!

ANDREW: [*Protestingly.*] You obstinate old son of a gun!

ROBERT: Oh, everything'll be on a sound footing after harvest. Don't worry about it.

ANDREW: [*Doubtfully.*] Maybe. [*After a pause.*] It's too bad Pa couldn't have lived to see things through. [*With feeling.*] It cut me up a lot— hearing he was dead. He never—softened up, did he—about me, I mean?

ROBERT: He never understood, that's a kinder way of putting it. He does now.

ANDREW: [*After a pause.*] You've forgotten all about what—caused me to go, haven't you, Rob? [ROBERT *nods but keeps his face averted.*] I was a slushier damn fool in those days than you were. But it was an act of Providence I did go. It opened my eyes to how I'd been fooling myself. Why, I'd forgotten all about—that—before I'd been at sea six months.

ROBERT: [*Turns and looks into* ANDREW's *eyes searchingly.*] You're speaking of—Ruth?

ANDREW: [*Confused.*] Yes. I didn't want you to get false notions in your head, or I wouldn't say anything. [*Looking* ROBERT *squarely in the eyes.*] I'm telling you the truth when I say I'd forgotten long ago. It don't sound well for me, getting over things so easy, but I guess it never really amounted to more than a kid idea I was letting rule me. I'm certain now I never was in love—I was getting fun out of thinking I was—and being a hero to myself. [*He heaves a great sigh of relief.*] There! Gosh, I'm glad that's off my chest. I've been feeling sort of awkward ever since I've been home, thinking of what you two might think. [*A trace of appeal in his voice.*] You've got it all straight now, haven't you, Rob?

ROBERT: [*In a low voice.*] Yes, Andy.

ANDREW: And I'll tell Ruth, too, if I can get up the nerve. She must feel kind of funny having me round—after what used to be—and not knowing how I feel about it.

ROBERT: [*Slowly.*] Perhaps—for her sake—you'd better not tell her.

ANDREW: For her sake? Oh, you mean she wouldn't want to be reminded of my foolishness? Still, I think it'd be worse if—

ROBERT: [*Breaking out—in an agonized voice.*] Do as you please, Andy; but for God's sake, let's not talk about it! [*There is a pause.* ANDREW *stares at* ROBERT *in hurt stupefaction.* ROBERT *continues after a moment in a voice which he vainly attempts to keep calm.*] Excuse me, Andy. This rotten headache has my nerves shot to pieces.

ANDREW: [*Mumbling.*] It's all right, Rob—long as you're not sore at me.

ROBERT: Where did Uncle Dick disappear to this morning?

ANDREW: He went down to the port to see to things on the *Sunda.* He said he didn't know exactly when he'd be back. I'll have to go down and tend to the ship when he comes. That's why I dressed up in these togs.

MARY: [*Pointing down the hill to the left.*] See! Mama! Mama! [*She struggles to her feet.* RUTH *appears at left. She is dressed in white, shows she has been fixing up. She looks pretty, flushed and full of life.*]

MARY: [*Running to her mother.*] Mama!

RUTH: [*Kissing her.*] Hello, dear! [*She walks toward the rock and addresses* ROBERT *coldly.*] Jake wants to see you about something. He finished working where he was. He's waiting for you at the road.

ROBERT: [*Getting up—wearily.*] I'll go down right away. [*As he looks at* RUTH, *noting her changed appearance, his face darkens with pain.*]

RUTH: And take Mary with you, please. [*To* MARY.] Go with Dada, that's a good girl. Grandma has your dinner almost ready for you.

ROBERT: [*Shortly.*] Come, Mary!

MARY: [*Taking his hand and dancing happily beside him.*] Dada! Dada! [*They go down the hill to the left.* RUTH *looks after them for a moment, frowning—then turns to* ANDY *with a smile.*] I'm going to sit down. Come on, Andy. It'll be like old times. [*She jumps lightly to the top of the rock and sits down.*] It's so fine and cool up here after the house.

ANDREW: [*Half-sitting on the side of the boulder.*] Yes. It's great.

RUTH: I've taken a holiday in honor of your arrival. [*Laughing excitedly.*] I feel so free I'd like to have wings and fly over the sea. You're a man. You can't know how awful and stupid it is—cooking and washing dishes all the time.

ANDREW: [*Making a wry face.*] I can guess.

RUTH: Besides, your mother just insisted on getting your first dinner to home, she's that happy at having you back. You'd think I was planning to poison you the flurried way she shooed me out of the kitchen.

ANDREW: That's just like Ma, bless her!

RUTH: She's missed you terrible. We all have. And you can't deny the farm has, after what I showed you and told you when we was looking over the place this morning.

ANDREW: [*With a frown.*] Things are run down, that's a fact! It's too darn hard on poor old Rob.

RUTH: [*Scornfully.*] It's his own fault. He never takes any interest in things.

ANDREW: [*Reprovingly.*] You can't blame him. He wasn't born for it; but I know he's done his best for your sake and the old folks and the little girl.

RUTH: [*Indifferently.*] Yes, I suppose he has. [*Gayly.*] But thank the Lord, all those days are over now. The "hard luck" Rob's always blaming won't last long when you take hold, Andy. All the farm's ever needed was someone with the knack of looking ahead and preparing for what's going to happen.

ANDREW: Yes, Rob hasn't got that. He's frank to own up to that himself. I'm going to try and hire a good man for him—an experienced farmer—to work the place on a salary and percentage. That'll take it off of Rob's hands, and he needn't be worrying himself to death any more. He looks all worn out, Ruth. He ought to be careful.

RUTH: [*Absent-mindedly.*] Yes, I s'pose. [*Her mind is filled with premonitions by the first part of his statement.*] Why do you want to hire a man to oversee things? Seems as if now that you're back it wouldn't be needful.

ANDREW: Oh, of course I'll attend to everything while I'm here. I mean after I'm gone.

RUTH: [*As if she couldn't believe her ears.*] Gone!

ANDREW: Yes. When I leave for the Argentine again.

RUTH: [*Aghast.*] You're going away to sea!

ANDREW: Not to sea, no; I'm through with the sea for good as a job. I'm going down to Buenos Aires to get in the grain business.

RUTH: But—that's far off—isn't it?

ANDREW: [*Easily.*] Six thousand miles more or less. It's quite a trip. [*With enthusiasm.*] I've got a peach of a chance down there, Ruth. Ask Rob if I haven't. I've just been telling him all about it.

RUTH: [*A flush of anger coming over her face.*] And didn't he try to stop you from going?

ANDREW: [*In surprise.*] No, of course not. Why?

RUTH: [*Slowly and vindictively.*] That's just like him—not to.

ANDREW: [*Resentfully.*] Rob's too good a chum to try and stop me when he knows I'm set on a thing. And he could see just as soon's I told him what a good chance it was.

RUTH: [*Dazedly.*] And you're bound on going?

ANDREW: Sure thing. Oh, I don't mean right off. I'll have to wait for a ship sailing there for quite a while, likely. Anyway, I want to stay to home and visit with you folks a spell before I go.

RUTH: [*Dumbly.*] I s'pose. [*With sudden anguish.*] Oh, Andy, you can't go! You can't. Why we've all thought—we've all been hoping and praying you was coming home to stay, to settle down on the farm and see to things. You mustn't go! Think of how your Ma'll take on if you go—and how the farm'll be ruined if you leave it to Rob to look after. You can see that.

ANDREW: [*Frowning.*] Rob hasn't done so bad. When I get a man to direct things the farm'll be safe enough.

RUTH: [*Insistently.*] But your Ma—think of her.

ANDREW: She's used to me being away. She won't object when she knows it's best for her and all of us for me to go. You ask Rob. In a couple of years down there I'll make my pile, see if I don't; and then I'll come back and settle down and turn this farm into the crackiest place in the whole state. In the meantime, I can help you both from down there. [*Earnestly.*] I tell you, Ruth, I'm going to make good right from the minute I land, if working hard and a determination to get on can do it; and I *know* they can! [*Excitedly—in a rather boastful tone.*] I tell you, I feel ripe for bigger things than settling down here. The trip did that for me, anyway. It showed me the world is a larger proposition than ever I thought it was in the old days. I couldn't be content any more stuck here like a fly in molasses. It all seems trifling, somehow. You ought to be able to understand what I feel.

RUTH: [*Dully.*] Yes—I s'pose I ought. [*After a pause—a sudden suspicion forming in her mind.*] What did Rob tell you—about me?

ANDREW: Tell? About you? Why, nothing.

RUTH: [*Staring at him intensely.*] Are you telling me the truth, Andy Mayo? Didn't he say—I— [*She stops confusedly.*]

ANDREW: [*Surprised.*] No, he didn't mention you, I can remember. Why? What made you think he did?

RUTH: [*Wringing her hands.*] Oh, I wish I could tell if you're lying or not!

ANDREW: [*Indignantly.*] What're you talking about? I didn't used to lie to you, did I? And what in the name of God is there to lie for?

RUTH: [*Still unconvinced.*] Are you sure—will you swear—it isn't the reason— [*She lowers her eyes and half turns away from him.*] The same reason that made you go last time that's driving you away again? 'Cause if it is—I was going to say—you mustn't go—on that account. [*Her voice sinks to a tremulous, tender whisper as she finishes.*]

ANDREW: [*Confused—forces a laugh.*] Oh, is *that* what you're driving at? Well, you needn't worry about that no more— [*Soberly.*] I don't blame you, Ruth, feeling embarrassed having me around again, after the way I played the dumb fool about going away last time.

RUTH: [*Her hope crushed—with a gasp of pain.*] Oh, Andy!

ANDREW: [*Misunderstanding.*] I know I oughtn't to talk about such foolishness to you. Still I figure it's better to get it out of my system so's we three can be together same's years ago, and not be worried thinking one of us might have the wrong notion.

RUTH: Andy! Please! Don't!

ANDREW: Let me finish now that I've started. It'll help clear things up. I don't want you to think once a fool always a fool, and be upset all the time I'm here on my fool account. I want you to believe I put all that silly nonsense back of me a long time ago—and now—it seems—well—as if you'd always been my sister, that's what, Ruth.

RUTH: [*At the end of her endurance—laughing hysterically.*] For God's sake, Andy—won't you please stop talking! [*She again hides her face in her hands, her bowed shoulders trembling.*]

ANDREW: [*Ruefully.*] Seem's if I put my foot in it whenever I open my mouth today. Rob shut me up with almost the same words when I tried speaking to him about it.

RUTH: [*Fiercely.*] You told him—what you've told me?

ANDREW: [*Astounded.*] Why sure! Why not?

RUTH: [*Shuddering.*] Oh, my God!

ANDREW: [*Alarmed.*] Why? Shouldn't I have?

RUTH: [*Hysterically.*] Oh, I don't care what you do! I don't care! Leave me alone! [ANDREW *gets up and walks down the hill to the left, embarrassed, hurt, and greatly puzzled by her behavior.*]

ANDREW: [*After a pause—pointing down the hill.*] Hello! Here they come back—and the Captain's with them. How'd he come to get back so soon, I wonder? That means I've got to hustle down to the port and get on board. Rob's got the baby with him. [*He comes back to the boulder.* RUTH *keeps her face averted from him.*] Gosh, I never saw a father so tied up in a kid as Rob is! He just watches every move she makes. And I don't blame him. You both got a right to feel proud of her. She's surely a little winner. [*He glances at* RUTH *to see if this very obvious attempt to get back in her good graces is having any effect.*] I can see the likeness to Rob standing out all over her, can't you? But there's no denying she's your young one, either. There's something about her eyes—

RUTH: [*Piteously.*] Oh, Andy, I've a headache! I don't want to talk! Leave me alone, won't you please?

ANDREW: [*Stands staring at her for a moment—then walks away saying in a hurt tone.*] Everybody hereabouts seems to be on edge today. I begin to feel as if I'm not wanted around. [*He stands near the path, left, kicking at the grass with the toe of his shoe. A moment later* CAPTAIN DICK SCOTT *enters, followed by* ROBERT *carrying* MARY. *The* CAPTAIN *seems scarcely to have changed at all from the jovial, booming person he was three years before. He wears a uniform similar to* ANDREW'*s. He is puffing and breathless from his climb and mops wildly at his perspiring countenance.* ROBERT *casts a quick glance at* ANDREW, *noticing the latter's discomfited look, and then turns his eyes on* RUTH *who, at their approach, has moved so her back is toward them, her chin resting on her hands as she stares out seaward.*]

MARY: Mama! Mama! [ROBERT *puts her down and she runs to her mother.* RUTH *turns and grabs her up in her arms with a sudden fierce tenderness, quickly turning away again from the others. During the following scene she keeps* MARY *in her arms.*]

SCOTT: [*Wheezily.*] Phew! I got great news for you, Andy. Let me get my wind first. Phew! God A'mighty, mountin' this damned hill is worser'n goin' aloft to the skys'l yard in a blow. I got to lay to a while. [*He sits down on the grass, mopping his face.*]

ANDREW: I didn't look for you this soon, Uncle.

SCOTT: I didn't figger it, neither; but I run across a bit o' news down to the Seamen's Home made me 'bout ship and set all sail back here to find you.

ANDREW: [*Eagerly.*] What is it, Uncle?

SCOTT: Passin' by the Home I thought I'd drop in an' let 'em know I'd be lackin' a mate next trip count o' your leavin'. Their man in charge o' the shippin' asked after you 'special curious. "Do you think he'd consider a berth as Second on a steamer, Captain?" he asks. I was goin' to say no when I thinks o' you wantin' to get back down south to the Plate agen; so I asks him: "What is she and where's she bound?" "She's the *El Paso,* a brand new tramp," he says, "and she's bound for Buenos Aires."

ANDREW: [*His eyes lighting up—excitedly.*] Gosh, that is luck! When does she sail?

SCOTT: Tomorrow mornin'. I didn't know if you'd want to ship away agen so quick an' I told him so. "Tell him I'll hold the berth open for him until late this afternoon," he says. So there you be, an' you can make your own choice.

ANDREW: I'd like to take it. There may not be another ship for Buenos Aires with a vacancy in months. [*His eyes roving from* ROBERT *to* RUTH *and back again—uncertainly.*] Still—damn it all—tomorrow morning *is* soon. I wish she wasn't leaving for a week or so. That'd give me a chance—it seems hard to go right away again when I've just got home. And yet it's a chance in a thousand— [*Appealing to* ROBERT.] What do you think, Rob? What would you do?

ROBERT: [*Forcing a smile.*] He who hesitates, you know. [*Frowning.*] It's a piece of good luck thrown in your way—and—I think you owe it to yourself to jump at it. But don't ask me to decide for you.

RUTH: [*Turning to look at* ANDREW—*in a tone of fierce resentment.*] Yes, go, Andy! [*She turns quickly away again. There is a moment of embarrassed silence*].

ANDREW: [*Thoughtfully.*] Yes, I guess I will. It'll be the best thing for all of us in the end, don't you think so, Rob? [ROBERT *nods but remains silent.*]

SCOTT: [*Getting to his feet.*] Then, that's settled.

ANDREW: [*Now that he has definitely made a decision his voice rings with hopeful strength and energy.*] Yes, I'll take the berth. The sooner I go the sooner I'll be back, that's a certainty; and I won't come back with empty hands next time. You bet I won't!

SCOTT: You ain't got so much time, Andy. To make sure you'd best leave here soon's you kin. I got to get right back aboard. You'd best come with me.

ANDREW: I'll go to the house and repack my bag right away.

ROBERT: [*Quietly.*] You'll both be here for dinner, won't you?

ANDREW: [*Worriedly.*] I don't know. Will there be time? What time is it now, I wonder?

ROBERT: [*Reproachfully.*] Ma's been getting dinner especially for you, Andy.

ANDREW: [*Flushing—shamefacedly.*] Hell! And I was forgetting! Of course I'll stay for dinner if I missed every damned ship in the world. [*He turns to the* CAPTAIN—*briskly.*] Come on, Uncle. Walk down with me to the house and you can tell me about this berth on the way. I've got to pack before dinner. [*He and the* CAPTAIN *start down to the left.* ANDREW *calls back over his shoulder.*] You're coming soon, aren't you, Rob?

ROBERT: Yes. I'll be right down. [ANDREW *and the* CAPTAIN *leave.* RUTH *puts* MARY *on the ground and hides her face in her hands. Her shoulders shake as if she were sobbing.* ROBERT *stares at her with a grim, somber expression.* MARY *walks backward toward* ROBERT, *her wondering eyes fixed on her mother.*]

MARY: [*Her voice vaguely frightened, taking her father's hand.*] Dada, Mama's cryin', Dada.

ROBERT: [*Bending down and stroking her hair—in a voice he endeavors to keep from being harsh.*] No, she isn't, little girl. The sun hurts her eyes, that's all. Aren't you beginning to feel hungry, Mary?

MARY: [*Decidedly.*] Yes, Dada.

ROBERT: [*Meaningly.*] It must be your dinner time now.

RUTH: [*In a muffled voice.*] I'm coming, Mary. [*She wipes her eyes quickly and, without looking at* ROBERT, *comes and takes* MARY's *hand—in a dead voice.*] Come on and I'll get your dinner for you. [*She walks out left, her eyes fixed on the ground, the skipping* MARY *tugging at her hand.* ROBERT *waits a moment for them to get ahead and then slowly follows as*

[*The Curtain Falls*]

ACT THREE

SCENE ONE

Same as Act Two, Scene One—The sitting room of the farm house about six o'clock in the morning of a day toward the end of October five years later. It is not yet dawn, but as the action progresses the darkness outside the windows gradually fades to gray.

The room, seen by the light of the shadeless oil lamp with a smoky chimney which stands on the table, presents an appearance of decay, of dissolution. The curtains at the windows are torn and dirty and one of them is missing. The closed desk is gray with accumulated dust as if it had not been used in years. Blotches of dampness disfigure the wall paper. Threadbare trails, leading to the kitchen and outer doors, show in the faded carpet. The top of the coverless table is stained with the imprints of hot dishes and spilt food. The rung of one rocker has been clumsily mended with a piece of plain board. A brown coating of rust covers the unblacked stove. A pile of wood is stacked up carelessly against the wall by the stove.

The whole atmosphere of the room, contrasted with that of former years, is one of an habitual poverty too hopelessly resigned to be any longer ashamed or even conscious of itself.

At the rise of the curtain RUTH *is discovered sitting by the stove, with hands outstretched to the warmth as if the air in the room were damp and cold. A heavy shawl is wrapped about her shoulders, half-concealing her dress of deep mourning. She has aged horribly. Her pale, deeply lined face has the stony lack of expression of one to whom nothing more can ever happen, whose capacity for emotion has been exhausted. When she speaks her voice is without timbre, low and monotonous. The negligent disorder of her dress, the slovenly arrangement of her hair, now streaked with gray, her muddied shoes run down at the heel, give full evidence of the apathy in which she lives.*

Her mother is asleep in her wheel chair beside the stove toward the rear, wrapped up in a blanket.

There is a sound from the open bedroom door in the rear as if someone were getting out of bed. RUTH *turns in that direction with a look of dull annoyance. A moment later* ROBERT *appears in the doorway, leaning weakly against it for support. His hair is long and unkempt, his face and body emaciated. There are bright patches of crimson over his cheek bones and his eyes are burning with fever. He is dressed in corduroy pants, a flannel shirt, and wears worn carpet slippers on his bare feet.*

RUTH: [*Dully.*] S-s-s-h-! Ma's asleep.

ROBERT: [*Speaking with an effort.*] I won't wake her. [*He walks weakly to a rocker by the side of the table and sinks down in it exhausted.*]

RUTH: [*Staring at the stove.*] You better come near the fire where it's warm.

ROBERT: No. I'm burning up now.

RUTH: That's the fever. You know the doctor told you not to get up and move round.

ROBERT: [*Irritably.*] That old fossil! He doesn't know anything. Go to bed and stay there—that's his only prescription.

RUTH: [*Indifferently.*] How are you feeling now?

ROBERT: [*Buoyantly.*] Better! Much better than I've felt in ages. Really I'm fine now—only very weak. It's the turning point, I guess. From now on I'll pick up so quick I'll surprise you—and no thanks to that old fool of a country quack, either.

RUTH: He's always tended to us.

ROBERT: Always helped us to die, you mean! He "tended" to Pa and Ma and—[*His voice breaks.*]—and to—Mary.

RUTH: [*Dully.*] He did the best he knew, I s'pose. [*After a pause.*] Well, Andy's bringing a specialist with him when he comes. That ought to suit you.

ROBERT: [*Bitterly.*] Is that why you're waiting up all night?

RUTH: Yes.

ROBERT: For Andy?

RUTH: [*Without a trace of feeling.*] Somebody had got to. It's only right for someone to meet him after he's been gone five years.

ROBERT: [*With bitter mockery.*] Five years! It's a long time.

RUTH: Yes.

ROBERT: [*Meaningly.*] To *wait!*

RUTH: [*Indifferently.*] It's past now.

ROBERT: Yes, it's past. [*After a pause.*] Have you got his two telegrams with you? [RUTH *nods.*] Let me see them, will you? My head was so full of fever when they came I couldn't make head or tail to them. [*Hastily.*] But I'm feeling fine now. Let me read them again. [RUTH *takes them from the bosom of her dress and hands them to him.*]

RUTH: Here. The first one's on top.

ROBERT: [*Opening it.*] New York. "Just landed from steamer. Have important business to wind up here. Will be home as soon as deal is completed." [*He smiles bitterly.*] Business first was always Andy's motto. [*He reads.*] "Hope you are all well. Andy." [*He repeats ironically.*] "Hope you are all well!"

RUTH: [*Dully.*] He couldn't know you'd been took sick till I answered that and told him.

ROBERT: [*Contritely.*] Of course he couldn't. I'm a fool. I'm touchy about nothing lately. Just what did you say in your reply?

RUTH: [*Inconsequentially.*] I had to send it collect.

ROBERT: [*Irritably.*] What did you say was the matter with me?

RUTH: I wrote you had lung trouble.

ROBERT: [*Flying into a petty temper.*] You *are* a fool! How often have I explained to you that it's *pleurisy* is the matter with me. You can't seem to get it in your head that the pleura is outside the lungs, not in them!

RUTH: [*Callously.*] I only wrote what Doctor Smith told me.

ROBERT: [*Angrily.*] He's a damned ignoramus!

RUTH: [*Dully.*] Makes no difference. I had to tell Andy something, didn't I?

ROBERT: [*After a pause, opening the other telegram.*] He sent this last evening. Let's see. [*He reads.*] "Leave for home on midnight train. Just received your wire. Am bringing specialist to see Rob. Will motor to farm from Port." [*He calculates.*] What time is it now?

RUTH: Round six, must be.

ROBERT: He ought to be here soon. I'm glad he's bringing a doctor who knows something. A specialist will tell you in a second that there's nothing the matter with my lungs.

RUTH: [*Stolidly.*] You've been coughing an awful lot lately.

ROBERT: [*Irritably.*] What nonsense! For God's sake, haven't you ever had a bad cold yourself? [RUTH *stares at the stove in silence.* ROBERT *fidgets in his chair. There is a pause. Finally* ROBERT's *eyes are fixed on the sleeping* MRS. ATKINS.] Your mother is lucky to be able to sleep so soundly.

RUTH: Ma's tired. She's been sitting up with me most of the night.

ROBERT: [*Mockingly.*] Is she waiting for Andy, too? [*There is a pause.* ROBERT *sighs.*] I couldn't get to sleep to save my soul. I counted ten million sheep if I counted one. No use! I gave up trying finally and just laid there in the dark thinking. [*He pauses, then continues in a tone of tender sympathy.*] I was thinking about you, Ruth—of how hard these last years must have been for you. [*Appealingly.*] I'm sorry, Ruth.

RUTH: [*In a dead voice.*] I don't know. They're past now. They were hard on all of us.

ROBERT: Yes; on all of us but Andy. [*With a flash of sick jealousy.*] Andy's made a big success of himself—the kind he wanted. [*Mock-*

ingly.] And now he's coming home to let us admire his greatness. [*Frowning—irritably.*] What am I talking about? My brain must be sick, too. [*After a pause.*] Yes, these years have been terrible for both of us. [*His voice is lowered to a trembling whisper.*] Especially the last eight months since Mary—died. [*He forces back a sob with a convulsive shudder—then breaks out in a passionate agony.*] Our last hope of happiness! I could curse God from the bottom of my soul—if there was a God! [*He is racked by a violent fit of coughing and hurriedly puts his handkerchief to his lips.*]

RUTH: [*Without looking at him.*] Mary's better off—being dead.

ROBERT: [*Gloomily.*] We'd all be better off for that matter. [*With a sudden exasperation.*] You tell that mother of yours she's got to stop saying that Mary's death was due to a weak constitution inherited from me. [*On the verge of tears of weakness.*] It's got to stop, I tell you!

RUTH: [*Sharply.*] S-h-h! You'll wake her; and then she'll nag at me—not you.

ROBERT: [*Coughs and lies back in his chair weakly—a pause.*] It's all because your mother's down on me for not begging Andy for help.

RUTH: [*Resentfully.*] You might have. He's got plenty.

ROBERT: How can *you* of all people think of taking money from *him*?

RUTH: [*Dully.*] I don't see the harm. He's your own brother.

ROBERT: [*Shrugging his shoulders.*] What's the use of talking to you? Well, *I* couldn't. [*Proudly.*] And I've managed to keep things going, thank God. You can't deny that without help I've succeeded in— [*He breaks off with a bitter laugh.*] My God, what am I boasting of? Debts to this one and that, taxes, interest unpaid! I'm a fool! [*He lies back in his chair closing his eyes for a moment, then speaks in a low voice.*] I'll be frank, Ruth. I've been an utter failure, and I've dragged you with me. I couldn't blame you in all justice—for hating me.

RUTH: [*Without feeling.*] I don't hate you. It's been my fault too, I s'pose.

ROBERT: No. You couldn't help loving—Andy.

RUTH: [*Dully.*] I don't love anyone.

ROBERT: [*Waving her remark aside.*] You needn't deny it. It doesn't matter. [*After a pause—with a tender smile.*] Do you know Ruth, what I've been dreaming back there in the dark? [*With a short laugh.*] I was planning our future when I get well. [*He looks at her with appealing eyes as if afraid she will sneer at him. Her expression does not change. She stares at the stove. His voice takes on a note of eagerness.*] After all, why shouldn't we have a future? We're young yet. If we can only shake off the curse of this farm! It's the farm that's ruined our lives, damn it! And now that Andy's coming back—

I'm going to sink my foolish pride, Ruth! I'll borrow the money from him to give us a good start in the city. We'll go where people live instead of stagnating, and start all over again. [*Confidently.*] I won't be the failure there that I've been here, Ruth. You won't need to be ashamed of me there. I'll prove to you the reading I've done can be put to some use. [*Vaguely.*] I'll write, or something of that sort. I've always wanted to write. [*Pleadingly.*] You'll want to do that, won't you, Ruth?

RUTH: [*Dully.*] There's Ma.

ROBERT: She can come with us.

RUTH: She wouldn't.

ROBERT: [*Angrily.*] So that's your answer! [*He trembles with violent passion. His voice is so strange that* RUTH *turns to look at him in alarm.*] You're lying, Ruth! Your mother's just an excuse. You want to stay here. You think that because Andy's coming back that— [*He chokes and has an attack of coughing.*]

RUTH: [*Getting up—in a frightened voice.*] What's the matter? [*She goes to him.*] I'll go with you, Rob. Stop that coughing for goodness' sake! It's awful bad for you. [*She soothes him in dull tones.*] I'll go with you to the city—soon's you're well again. Honest I will, Rob, I promise! [ROBERT *lies back and closes his eyes. She stands looking down at him anxiously.*] Do you feel better now?

ROBERT: Yes. [RUTH *goes back to her chair. After a pause he opens his eyes and sits up in his chair. His face is flushed and happy.*] Then you *will* go, Ruth?

RUTH: Yes.

ROBERT: [*Excitedly.*] We'll make a new start, Ruth—just you and I. Life owes us some happiness after what we've been through. [*Vehemently.*] It must! Otherwise our suffering would be meaningless—and that is unthinkable.

RUTH: [*Worried by his excitement.*] Yes, yes, of course, Rob, but you mustn't—

ROBERT: Oh, don't be afraid. I feel completely well, really I do—now that I can hope again. Oh if you knew how glorious it feels to have something to look forward to! Can't you feel the thrill of it, too—the vision of a new life opening up after all the horrible years?

RUTH: Yes, yes, but do be—

ROBERT: Nonsense! I won't be careful. I'm getting back all my strength. [*He gets lightly to his feet.*] See! I feel light as a feather. [*He walks to her chair and bends down to kiss her smilingly.*] One kiss—the first in years, isn't it?—to greet the dawn of a new life together.

RUTH: [*Submitting to his kiss—worriedly.*] Sit down, Rob, for goodness' sake!

ROBERT: [*With tender obstinacy—stroking her hair.*] I won't sit down. You're silly to worry. [*He rests one hand on the back of her chair.*] Listen. All our suffering has been a test through which we had to pass to prove ourselves worthy of a finer realization. [*Exultingly.*] And we did pass through it! It hasn't broken us! And now the dream is to come true! Don't you see?

RUTH: [*Looking at him with frightened eyes as if she thought he had gone mad.*] Yes, Rob, I see; but won't you go back to bed now and rest?

ROBERT: No. I'm going to see the sun rise. It's an augury of good fortune. [*He goes quickly to the window in the rear left, and pushing the curtains aside, stands looking out. RUTH springs to her feet and comes quickly to the table, left, where she remains watching ROBERT in a tense, expectant attitude. As he peers out his body seems gradually to sag, to grow limp and tired. His voice is mournful as he speaks.*] No sun yet. It isn't time. All I can see is the black rim of the damned hills outlined against a creeping grayness. [*He turns around; letting the curtains fall back, stretching a hand out to the wall to support himself. His false strength of a moment has evaporated leaving his face drawn and hollow-eyed. He makes a pitiful attempt to smile.*] That's not a very happy augury, is it? But the sun'll come— soon. [*He sways weakly.*]

RUTH: [*Hurrying to his side and supporting him.*] Please go to bed, won't you, Rob? You don't want to be all wore out when the specialist comes, do you?

ROBERT: [*Quickly.*] No. That's right. He mustn't think I'm sicker than I am. And I feel as if I could sleep now—[*Cheerfully.*]—a good, sound, restful sleep.

RUTH: [*Helping him to the bedroom door.*] That's what you need most. [*They go inside. A moment later she reappears calling back.*] I'll shut this door so's you'll be quiet. [*She closes the door and goes quickly to her mother and shakes her by the shoulder.*] Ma! Ma! Wake up!

MRS. ATKINS: [*Coming out of her sleep with a start.*] Glory be! What's the matter with you?

RUTH: It was Rob. He's just been talking to me out here. I put him back to bed. [*Now that she is sure her mother is awake her fear passes and she relapses into dull indifference. She sits down in her chair and stares at the stove—dully.*] He acted—funny; and his eyes looked so—so wild like.

MRS. ATKINS: [*With asperity.*] And is that all you woke me out of a sound sleep for, and scared me near out of my wits?

RUTH: I was afraid. He talked so crazy. I couldn't quiet him. I didn't want to be alone with him that way. Lord knows what he might do.

MRS. ATKINS: [*Scornfully.*] Humph! A help I'd be to you and me not able to move a step! Why didn't you run and get Jake?

RUTH: [*Dully.*] Jake isn't here. He quit last night. He hasn't been paid in three months.

MRS. ATKINS: [*Indignantly.*] I can't blame him. What decent person'd want to work on a place like this? [*With sudden exasperation.*] Oh, I wish you'd never married that man!

RUTH: [*Wearily.*] You oughtn't to talk about him now when he's sick in his bed.

MRS. ATKINS: [*Working herself into a fit of rage.*] You know very well, Ruth Mayo, if it wasn't for me helpin' you on the sly out of my savin's, you'd both been in the poor house—and all 'count of his pigheaded pride in not lettin' Andy know the state thin's were in. A nice thin' for me to have to support him out of what I'd saved for my last days—and me an invalid with no one to look to!

RUTH: Andy'll pay you back, Ma. I can tell him so's Rob'll never know.

MRS. ATKINS: [*With a snort.*] What'd Rob think you and him was livin' on, I'd like to know?

RUTH: [*Dully.*] He didn't think about it, I s'pose. [*After a slight pause.*] He said he'd made up his mind to ask Andy for help when he comes. [*As a clock in the kitchen strikes six.*] Six o'clock. Andy ought to get here directly.

MRS. ATKINS: D'you think this special doctor'll do Rob any good?

RUTH: [*Hopelessly.*] I don't know. [*The two women remain silent for a time staring dejectedly at the stove.*]

MRS. ATKINS: [*Shivering irritably.*] For goodness' sake put some wood on that fire. I'm most freezin'!

RUTH: [*Pointing to the door in the rear.*] Don't talk so loud. Let him sleep if he can. [*She gets wearily from the chair and puts a few pieces of wood in the stove.*] This is the last of the wood. I don't know who'll cut more now that Jake's left. [*She sighs and walks to the window in the rear, left, pulls the curtains aside, and looks out.*] It's getting gray out. [*She comes back to the stove.*] Looks like it'd be a nice day. [*She stretches out her hands to warm them.*] Must've been a heavy frost last night. We're paying for the spell of warm weather we've been having. [*The throbbing whine of a motor sounds from the distance outside.*]

MRS. ATKINS: [*Sharply.*] S-h-h! Listen! Ain't that an auto I hear?

RUTH: [*Without interest.*] Yes. It's Andy, I s'pose.

MRS. ATKINS: [*With nervous irritation.*] Don't sit there like a silly goose. Look at the state of this room! What'll this strange doctor think of us? Look at the lamp chimney all smoke! Gracious sakes, Ruth—

RUTH: [*Indifferently.*] I've got a lamp all cleaned up in the kitchen.

MRS. ATKINS: [*Peremptorily.*] Wheel me in there this minute. I don't want him to see me looking a sight. I'll lay down in the room the other side. You don't need me now and I'm dead for sleep. [RUTH *wheels her mother off right. The noise of the motor grows louder and finally ceases as the car stops on the road before the farmhouse.* RUTH *returns from the kitchen with a lighted lamp in her hand which she sets on the table beside the other. The sound of footsteps on the path is heard—then a sharp rap on the door.* RUTH *goes and opens it.* ANDREW *enters, followed by* DOCTOR FAWCETT *carrying a small black bag.* ANDREW *has changed greatly. His face seems to have grown highstrung, hardened by the look of decisiveness which comes from being constantly under a strain where judgments on the spur of the moment are compelled to be accurate. His eyes are keener and more alert. There is even a suggestion of ruthless cunning about them. At present, however, his expression is one of tense anxiety.* DOCTOR FAWCETT *is a short, dark, middle-aged man with a Vandyke beard. He wears glasses.*]

RUTH: Hello, Andy! I've been waiting—

ANDREW: [*Kissing her hastily.*] I got here as soon as I could. [*He throws off his cap and heavy overcoat on the table, introducing* RUTH *and the* DOCTOR *as he does so. He is dressed in an expensive business suit and appears stouter.*] My sister-in-law, Mrs. Mayo—Doctor Fawcett. [*They bow to each other silently.* ANDREW *casts a quick glance about the room.*] Where's Rob?

RUTH: [*Pointing.*] In there.

ANDREW: I'll take your coat and hat, Doctor. [*As he helps the* DOCTOR *with his things.*] Is he very bad, Ruth?

RUTH: [*Dully.*] He's been getting weaker.

ANDREW: Damn! This way, Doctor. Bring the lamp, Ruth. [*He goes into the bedroom, followed by the* DOCTOR *and* RUTH *carrying the clean lamp.* RUTH *reappears almost immediately closing the door behind her, and goes slowly to the outside door, which she opens, and stands in the doorway looking out. The sound of* ANDREW's *and* ROBERT's *voices comes from the bedroom. A moment later* ANDREW *re-enters, closing the door softly. He comes forward and sinks down*

*in the rocker on the right of table, leaning his head on his hand. His
face is drawn in a shocked expression of great grief. He sighs heavily,
staring mournfully in front of him.* RUTH *turns and stands watching
him. Then she shuts the door and returns to her chair by the stove,
turning it so she can face him.*]

ANDREW: [*Glancing up quickly—in a harsh voice.*] How long has this
been going on?

RUTH: You mean—how long has he been sick?

ANDREW: [*Shortly.*] Of course! What else?

RUTH: It was last summer he had a bad spell first, but he's been ailin'
ever since Mary died—eight months ago.

ANDREW: [*Harshly.*] Why didn't you let me know—cable me? Do you
want him to die, all of you? I'm damned if it doesn't look that way!
[*His voice breaking.*] Poor old chap! To be sick in this out-of-the-
way hole without anyone to attend to him but a country quack! It's
a damned shame!

RUTH: [*Dully.*] I wanted to send you word once, but he only got mad
when I told him. He was too proud to ask anything, he said.

ANDREW: Proud? To ask *me*? [*He jumps to his feet and paces nervously
back and forth.*] I can't understand the way you've acted. Didn't you
see how sick he was getting? Couldn't you realize—why, I nearly
dropped in my tracks when I saw him! He looks—[*He shudders.*]—
terrible! [*With fierce scorn.*] I suppose you're so used to the idea of
his being delicate that you took his sickness as a matter of course.
God, if I'd only known!

RUTH: [*Without emotion.*] A letter takes so long to get where you
were—and we couldn't afford to telegraph. We owed everyone already, and I couldn't ask Ma. She'd been giving me money out of her
savings till she hadn't much left. Don't say anything to Rob about it.
I never told him. He'd only be mad at me if he knew. But I had to,
because—God knows how we'd have got on if I hadn't.

ANDREW: You mean to say— [*His eyes seem to take in the poverty-
stricken appearance of the room for the first time.*] You sent that
telegram to me collect. Was it because— [RUTH *nods silently.* AN-
DREW *pounds on the table with his fist.*] Good God! And all this
time I've been—why I've had everything! [*He sits down in his chair
and pulls it close to* RUTH's—*impulsively.*] But—I can't get it
through my head. Why? Why? What has happened? How did it ever
come about? Tell me!

RUTH: [*Dully.*] There's nothing much to tell. Things kept getting worse,
that's all—and Rob didn't seem to care. He never took any interest

since way back when your Ma died. After that he got men to take
charge, and they nearly all cheated him—he couldn't tell—and left
one after another. Then after Mary died he didn't pay no heed to
anything any more—just stayed indoors and took to reading books
again. So I had to ask Ma if she wouldn't help us some.

ANDREW: [*Surprised and horrified.*] Why, damn it, this is frightful! Rob
must be mad not to have let me know. Too proud to ask help of *me*!
What's the matter with him in God's name? [*A sudden, horrible suspicion entering his mind.*] Ruth! Tell me the truth. His mind hasn't
gone back on him, has it?

RUTH: [*Dully.*] I don't know. Mary's dying broke him up terrible—but
he's used to her being gone by this, I s'pose.

ANDREW: [*Looking at her queerly.*] Do you mean to say *you're* used
to it?

RUTH: [*In a dead tone.*] There's a time comes—when you don't mind
any more—anything.

ANDREW: [*Looks at her fixedly for a moment—with great pity.*] I'm
sorry, Ruth—if I seemed to blame you. I didn't realize— The sight of
Rob lying in bed there, so gone to pieces—it made me furious at
everyone. Forgive me, Ruth.

RUTH: There's nothing to forgive. It doesn't matter.

ANDREW: [*Springing to his feet again and pacing up and down.*] Thank
God I came back before it was too late. This doctor will know exactly what to do. That's the first thing to think of. When Rob's on
his feet again we can get the farm working on a sound basis once
more. I'll see to that—before I leave.

RUTH: You're going away again?

ANDREW: I've got to.

RUTH: You wrote Rob you was coming back to stay this time.

ANDREW: I expected to—until I got to New York. Then I learned certain facts that make it necessary. [*With a short laugh.*] To be candid,
Ruth, I'm not the rich man you've probably been led to believe by
my letters—not now. I was when I wrote them. I made money hand
over fist as long as I stuck to legitimate trading; but I wasn't content
with that. I wanted it to come easier, so like all the rest of the idiots,
I tried speculation. Oh, I won all right! Several times I've been almost a millionaire—on paper—and then come down to earth again
with a bump. Finally the strain was too much. I got disgusted with
myself and made up my mind to get out and come home and forget
it and really live again. [*He gives a harsh laugh.*] And now comes the
funny part. The day before the steamer sailed I saw what I thought

was a chance to become a millionaire again. [*He snaps his fingers.*] That easy! I plunged. Then, before things broke, I left—I was so confident I couldn't be wrong. But when I landed in New York—I wired you I had business to wind up, didn't I? Well, it was the business that wound me up! [*He smiles grimly, pacing up and down, his hands in his pockets.*]

RUTH: [*Dully.*] You found—you'd lost everything?

ANDREW: [*Sitting down again.*] Practically. [*He takes a cigar from his pocket, bites the end off, and lights it.*] Oh, I don't mean I'm dead broke. I've saved ten thousand from the wreckage, maybe twenty. But that's a poor showing for five years' hard work. That's why I'll have to go back. [*Confidently.*] I can make it up in a year or so down there—and I don't need but a shoestring to start with. [*A weary expression comes over his face and he sighs heavily.*] I wish I didn't have to. I'm sick of it all.

RUTH: It's too bad—things seem to go wrong so.

ANDREW: [*Shaking off his depression—briskly.*] They might be much worse. There's enough left to fix the farm O. K. before I go. I won't leave 'til Rob's on his feet again. In the meantime I'll make things fly around here. [*With satisfaction.*] I need a rest, and the kind of rest I need is hard work in the open—just like I used to do in the old days. [*Stopping abruptly and lowering his voice cautiously.*] Not a word to Rob about my losing money! Remember that, Ruth! You can see why. If he's grown so touchy he'd never accept a cent if he thought I was hard up; see?

RUTH: Yes, Andy. [*After a pause, during which* ANDREW *puffs at his cigar abstractedly, his mind evidently busy with plans for the future, the bedroom door is opened and* DOCTOR FAWCETT *enters, carrying a bag. He closes the door quietly behind him and comes forward, a grave expression on his face.* ANDREW *springs out of his chair.*]

ANDREW: Ah, Doctor! [*He pushes a chair between his own and* RUTH's.] Won't you have a chair?

FAWCETT: [*Glancing at his watch.*] I must catch the nine o'clock back to the city. It's imperative. I have only a moment. [*Sitting down and clearing his throat—in a perfunctory, impersonal voice.*] The case of your brother, Mr. Mayo, is— [*He stops and glances at* RUTH *and says meaningly to* ANDREW.] Perhaps it would be better if you and I—

RUTH: [*With dogged resentment.*] I know what you mean, Doctor. [*Dully.*] Don't be afraid I can't stand it. I'm used to bearing trouble by this; and I can guess what you've found out. [*She hesitates for a moment—then continues in a monotonous voice.*] Rob's going to die.

ANDREW: [*Angrily.*] Ruth!

FAWCETT: [*Raising his hand as if to command silence.*] I am afraid my diagnosis of your brother's condition forces me to the same conclusion as Mrs. Mayo's.

ANDREW: [*Groaning.*] But, Doctor, surely—

FAWCETT: [*Calmly.*] Your brother hasn't long to live—perhaps a few days, perhaps only a few hours. It's a marvel that he's alive at this moment. My examination revealed that both of his lungs are terribly affected.

ANDREW: [*Brokenly.*] Good God! [RUTH *keeps her eyes fixed on her lap in a trance-like stare.*]

FAWCETT: I am sorry I have to tell you this. If there was anything that could be done—

ANDREW: There isn't anything?

FAWCETT: [*Shaking his head.*] It's too late. Six months ago there might have—

ANDREW: [*In anguish.*] But if we were to take him to the mountains—or to Arizona—or—

FAWCETT: That might have prolonged his life six months ago. [AN-DREW *groans.*] But now— [*He shrugs his shoulders significantly.*]

ANDREW: [*Appalled by a sudden thought.*] Good heavens, you haven't told him this, have you, Doctor?

FAWCETT: No. I lied to him. I said a change of climate— [*He looks at his watch again nervously.*] I must leave you. [*He gets up.*]

ANDREW: [*Getting to his feet—insistently.*] But there must still be some chance—

FAWCETT: [*As if he were reassuring a child.*] There is always that last chance—the miracle. [*He puts on his hat and coat—bowing to* RUTH.] Good-by, Mrs. Mayo.

RUTH: [*Without raising her eyes—dully.*] Good-by.

ANDREW: [*Mechanically.*] I'll walk to the car with you, Doctor. [*They go out of the door.* RUTH *sits motionlessly. The motor is heard starting and the noise gradually recedes into the distance.* ANDREW *re-enters and sits down in his chair, holding his head in his hands.*] Ruth! [*She lifts her eyes to his.*] Hadn't we better go in and see him? God! I'm afraid to! I know he'll read it in my face. [*The bedroom door is noiselessly opened and* ROBERT *appears in the doorway. His cheeks are flushed with fever, and his eyes appear unusually large and brilliant.* ANDREW *continues with a groan.*] It can't be, Ruth. It can't be as hopeless as he said. There's always a fighting chance. We'll take Rob to Arizona. He's got to get well. There *must* be a chance!

ROBERT: [*In a gentle tone.*] Why must there, Andy? [RUTH *turns and stares at him with terrified eyes.*]

ANDREW: [*Whirling around.*] Rob! [*Scoldingly.*] What are you doing out of bed? [*He gets up and goes to him.*] Get right back now and obey the Doc, or you're going to get a licking from me!

ROBERT: [*Ignoring these remarks.*] Help me over to the chair, please, Andy.

ANDREW: Like hell I will! You're going right back to bed, that's where you're going, and stay there! [*He takes hold of* ROBERT's *arm.*]

ROBERT: [*Mockingly.*] Stay there 'til I die, eh, Andy? [*Coldly.*] Don't behave like a child. I'm sick of lying down. I'll be more rested sitting up. [*As* ANDREW *hesitates—violently.*] I swear I'll get out of bed every time you put me there. You'll have to sit on my chest, and that wouldn't help my health any. Come on, Andy. Don't play the fool. I want to talk to you, and I'm going to. [*With a grim smile.*] A dying man has some rights, hasn't he?

ANDREW: [*With a shudder.*] Don't talk that way, for God's sake! I'll only let you sit down if you'll promise that. Remember. [*He helps* ROBERT *to the chair between his own and* RUTH's.] Easy now! There you are! Wait, and I'll get a pillow for you. [*He goes into the bedroom.* ROBERT *looks at* RUTH *who shrinks away from him in terror.* ROBERT *smiles bitterly.* ANDREW *comes back with the pillow which he places behind* ROBERT's *back.*] How's that?

ROBERT: [*With an affectionate smile.*] Fine! Thank you! [*As* ANDREW *sits down.*] Listen, Andy. You've asked me not to talk—and I won't after I've made my position clear. [*Slowly.*] In the first place I know I'm dying. [RUTH *bows her head and covers her face with her hands. She remains like this all during the scene between the two brothers.*]

ANDREW: Rob! That isn't so!

ROBERT: [*Wearily.*] It *is* so! Don't lie to me. After Ruth put me to bed before you came, I saw it clearly for the first time. [*Bitterly.*] I'd been making plans for our future—Ruth's and mine—so it came hard at first—the realization. Then when the doctor examined me, I knew—although he tried to lie about it. And then to make sure I listened at the door to what he told you. So don't mock me with fairy tales about Arizona, or any such rot as that. Because I'm dying is no reason you should treat me as an imbecile or a coward. Now that I'm sure what's happening I can say Kismet to it with all my heart. It was only the silly uncertainty that hurt. [*There is a pause.* ANDREW *looks around in impotent anguish, not knowing what to say.* ROBERT *regards him with an affectionate smile.*]

ANDREW: [*Finally blurts out.*] It isn't foolish. You *have* got a chance. If you heard all the Doctor said that ought to prove it to you.

ROBERT: Oh, you mean when he spoke of the miracle? [*Dryly.*] I don't believe in miracles—in my case. Besides, I know more than any doctor on earth *could* know—because I *feel* what's coming. [*Dismissing the subject.*] But we've agreed not to talk of it. Tell me about yourself, Andy. That's what I'm interested in. Your letters were too brief and far apart to be illuminating.

ANDREW: I meant to write oftener.

ROBERT: [*With a faint trace of irony.*] I judge from them you've accomplished all you set out to do five years ago?

ANDREW: That isn't much to boast of.

ROBERT: [*Surprised.*] Have you really, honestly reached that conclusion?

ANDREW: Well, it doesn't seem to amount to much now.

ROBERT: But you're rich, aren't you?

ANDREW: [*With a quick glance at* RUTH.] Yes, I s'pose so.

ROBERT: I'm glad. You can do to the farm all I've undone. But what did you do down there? Tell me. You went in the grain business with that friend of yours?

ANDREW: Yes. After two years I had a share in it. I sold out last year. [*He is answering* ROBERT's *questions with great reluctance.*]

ROBERT: And then?

ANDREW: I went in on my own.

ROBERT: Still in grain?

ANDREW: Yes.

ROBERT: What's the matter? You look as if I were accusing you of something.

ANDREW: I'm proud enough of the first four years. It's after that I'm not boasting of. I took to speculating.

ROBERT: In wheat?

ANDREW: Yes.

ROBERT: And you made money—gambling?

ANDREW: Yes.

ROBERT: [*Thoughtfully.*] I've been wondering what the great change was in you. [*After a pause.*] You—a farmer—to gamble in a wheat pit with scraps of paper. There's a spiritual significance in that picture, Andy. [*He smiles bitterly.*] I'm a failure, and Ruth's another—but we can both justly lay some of the blame for our stumbling on God. But you're the deepest-dyed failure of the three, Andy. You've spent eight years running away from yourself. Do you see what I mean? You used to be a creator when you loved the farm. You and life were in harmonious partnership. And now— [*He stops as if seeking vainly for words.*] My brain is muddled. But part of what I mean is that your gambling with the thing you used to love to create proves how far astray— So you'll be punished. You'll have to suffer to win back— [*His voice grows weaker and he sighs wearily.*] It's no use. I can't say it. [*He lies back and closes his eyes, breathing pantingly.*]

ANDREW: [*Slowly.*] I think I know what you're driving at, Rob—and it's true, I guess. [ROBERT *smiles gratefully and stretches out his hand, which* ANDREW *takes in his.*]

ROBERT: I want you to promise me to do one thing, Andy, after—

ANDREW: I'll promise anything, as God is my Judge!

ROBERT: Remember, Andy, Ruth has suffered double her share. [*His voice faltering with weakness.*] Only through contact with suffering, Andy, will you—awaken. Listen. You must marry Ruth—afterwards.

RUTH: [*With a cry.*] Rob! [ROBERT *lies back, his eyes closed, gasping heavily for breath.*]

ANDREW: [*Making signs to her to humor him—gently.*] You're tired out, Rob. You better lie down and rest a while, don't you think? We can talk later on.

ROBERT: [*With a mocking smile.*] Later on! You always were an optimist, Andy! [*He sighs with exhaustion.*] Yes, I'll go and rest a while. [*As* ANDREW *comes to help him.*] It must be near sunrise, isn't it?

ANDREW: It's after six.

ROBERT: [*As* ANDREW *helps him into the bedroom.*] Shut the door, Andy. I want to be alone. [ANDREW *reappears and shuts the door softly. He comes and sits down on his chair again, supporting his head on his hands. His face is drawn with the intensity of his dry-eyed anguish.*]

RUTH: [*Glancing at him—fearfully.*] He's out of his mind now, isn't he?

ANDREW: He may be a little delirious. The fever would do that. [*With impotent rage.*] God, what a shame! And there's nothing we can do but sit and—wait! [*He springs from his chair and walks to the stove.*]

RUTH: [*Dully.*] He was talking—wild—like he used to—only this time it sounded—unnatural, don't you think?

ANDREW: I don't know. The things he said to me had truth in them— even if he did talk them way up in the air, like he always sees things. Still— [*He glances down at* RUTH *keenly.*] Why do you suppose he wanted us to promise we'd— [*Confusedly.*] You know what he said.

RUTH: [*Dully.*] His mind was wandering, I s'pose.

ANDREW: [*With conviction.*] No—there was something back of it.

RUTH: He wanted to make sure I'd be all right—after he'd gone, I expect.

ANDREW: No, it wasn't that. He knows very well I'd naturally look after you without—anything like that.

RUTH: He might be thinking of—something happened five years back, the time you came home from the trip.

ANDREW: What happened? What do you mean?

RUTH: [*Dully.*] We had a fight.

ANDREW: A fight? What has that to do with me?

RUTH: It was about you—in a way.

ANDREW: [*Amazed.*] About *me*?

RUTH: Yes, mostly. You see I'd found out I'd made a mistake about Rob soon after we were married—when it was too late.

ANDREW: Mistake? [*Slowly.*] You mean—you found out you didn't love Rob?

RUTH: Yes.

ANDREW: Good God!

RUTH: And then I thought that when Mary came it'd be different, and I'd love him; but it didn't happen that way. And I couldn't bear with his blundering and book-reading—and I grew to hate him, almost.

ANDREW: Ruth!

RUTH: I couldn't help it. No woman could. It had to be because I loved someone else, I'd found out. [*She sighs wearily.*] It can't do no harm to tell you now—when it's all past and gone—and dead. *You* were the one I really loved—only I didn't come to the knowledge of it 'til too late.

ANDREW: [*Stunned.*] Ruth! Do you know what you're saying?

RUTH: It was true—then. [*With sudden fierceness.*] How could I help it? No woman could.

ANDREW: Then—you loved me—that time I came home?

RUTH: [*Doggedly.*] I'd known your real reason for leaving home the first time—everybody knew it—and for three years I'd been thinking—

ANDREW: That I loved you?

RUTH: Yes. Then that day on the hill you laughed about what a fool you'd been for loving me once—and I knew it was all over.

ANDREW: Good God, but I never thought— [*He stops, shuddering at his remembrance.*] And did Rob—

RUTH: That was what I'd started to tell. We'd had a fight just before you came and I got crazy mad—and I told him all I've told you.

ANDREW: [*Gaping at her speechlessly for a moment.*] You told Rob—you loved me?

RUTH: Yes.

ANDREW: [*Shrinking away from her in horror.*] You—you—you mad fool, you! How could you do such a thing?

RUTH: I couldn't help it. I'd got to the end of bearing things—without talking.

ANDREW: Then Rob must have known every moment I stayed here! And yet he never said or showed—God, how he must have suffered! Didn't you know how much he loved you?

RUTH: [*Dully.*] Yes. I knew he liked me.

ANDREW: Liked you! What kind of a woman are you? Couldn't you have kept silent? Did you have to torture him? No wonder he's dying! And you've lived together for five years with this between you?

RUTH: We've lived in the same house.

ANDREW: Does he still think—

RUTH: I don't know. We've never spoke a word about it since that day. Maybe, from the way he went on, he s'poses I care for you yet.

ANDREW: But you don't. It's outrageous. It's stupid! You don't love me!

RUTH: [*Slowly.*] I wouldn't know how to feel love, even if I tried, any more.

ANDREW: [*Brutally.*] And I don't love you, that's sure! [*He sinks into his chair, his head between his hands.*] It's damnable such a thing should be between Rob and me. Why, I love Rob better'n anybody in the world and always did. There isn't a thing on God's green earth I wouldn't have done to keep trouble away from him. And I have to be the very one—it's damnable! How am I going to face him again? What can I say to him now? [*He groans with anguished rage. After a pause.*] He asked me to promise—what am I going to do?

RUTH: You can promise—so's it'll ease his mind—and not mean anything.

ANDREW: What? Lie to him now—when he's dying? [*Determinedly.*] No! It's *you* who'll have to do the lying, since it must be done. You've got a chance now to undo some of all the suffering you've brought on Rob. Go in to him! Tell him you never loved me—it was all a mistake. Tell him you only said so because you were mad and didn't know what you were saying! Tell him something, anything, that'll bring him peace!

RUTH: [*Dully.*] He wouldn't believe me.

ANDREW: [*Furiously.*] You've got to make him believe you, do you hear? You've got to—now—hurry—you never know when it may be too late. [*As she hesitates—imploringly.*] For God's sake, Ruth! Don't you see you owe it to him? You'll never forgive yourself if you don't.

RUTH: [*Dully.*] I'll go. [*She gets wearily to her feet and walks slowly toward the bedroom.*] But it won't do any good. [ANDREW's *eyes are fixed on her anxiously. She opens the door and steps inside the room. She remains standing there for a minute. Then she calls in a frightened voice.*] Rob! Where are you? [*Then she hurries back, trembling with fright.*] Andy! Andy! He's gone!

ANDREW: [*Misunderstanding her—his face pale with dread.*] He's not—
RUTH: [*Interrupting him—hysterically.*] He's gone! The bed's empty.
The window's wide open. He must have crawled out into the yard!
ANDREW: [*Springing to his feet. He rushes into the bedroom and returns immediately with an expression of alarmed amazement on his
face.*] Come! He can't have gone far! [*Grabbing his hat he takes
RUTH's arm and shoves her toward the door.*] Come on! [*Opening
the door.*] Let's hope to God— [*The door closes behind them, cutting
off his words as*

[*The Curtain Falls*]

ACT THREE

SCENE TWO

*Same as Act One, Scene One—A section of country highway. The
sky to the east is already alight with bright color and a thin, quivering
line of flame is spreading slowly along the horizon rim of the dark hills.
The roadside, however, is still steeped in the grayness of the dawn,
shadowy and vague. The field in the foreground has a wild uncultivated
appearance as if it had been allowed to remain fallow the preceding
summer. Parts of the snake-fence in the rear have been broken down.
The apple tree is leafless and seems dead.*

*ROBERT staggers weakly in from the left. He stumbles into the ditch
and lies there for a moment; then crawls with a great effort to the top
of the bank where he can see the sun rise, and collapses weakly. RUTH
and ANDREW come hurriedly along the road from the left.*

ANDREW: [*Stopping and looking about him.*] There he is! I knew it! I
knew we'd find him here.
ROBERT: [*Trying to raise himself to a sitting position as they hasten to
his side—with a wan smile.*] I thought I'd given you the slip.
ANDREW: [*With kindly bullying.*] Well you didn't, you old scoundrel,
and we're going to take you right back where you belong—in bed.
[*He makes a motion to lift ROBERT.*]
ROBERT: Don't, Andy. Don't, I tell you!
ANDREW: You're in pain?
ROBERT: [*Simply.*] No. I'm dying. [*He falls back weakly. RUTH sinks
down beside him with a sob and pillows his head on her lap. AN-

DREW *stands looking down at him helplessly.* ROBERT *moves his head restlessly on* RUTH's *lap.*] I couldn't stand it back there in the room. It seemed as if all my life—I'd been cooped in a room. So I thought I'd try to end as I might have—if I'd had the courage— alone—in a ditch by the open road—watching the sun rise.

ANDREW: Rob! Don't talk. You're wasting your strength. Rest a while and then we'll carry you—

ROBERT: Still hoping, Andy? Don't. I know. [*There is a pause during which he breathes heavily, straining his eyes toward the horizon.*] The sun comes so slowly. [*With an ironical smile.*] The doctor told me to go to the far-off places—and I'd be cured. He was right. That was always the cure for me. It's too late—for this life—but— [*He has a fit of coughing which racks his body.*]

ANDREW: [*With a hoarse sob.*] Rob! [*He clenches his fists in an impotent rage against Fate.*] God! God! [RUTH *sobs brokenly and wipes* ROBERT's *lips with her handkerchief.*]

ROBERT: [*In a voice which is suddenly ringing with the happiness of hope.*] You mustn't feel sorry for me. Don't you see I'm happy at last—free—free!—freed from the farm—free to wander on and on— eternally! [*He raises himself on his elbow, his face radiant, and points to the horizon.*] Look! Isn't it beautiful beyond the hills? I can hear the old voices calling me to come— [*Exultantly.*] And this time I'm going! It isn't the end. It's a free beginning—the start of my voyage! I've won to my trip—the right of release—beyond the horizon! Oh, you ought to be glad—glad—for my sake! [*He collapses weakly.*] Andy! [ANDREW *bends down to him.*] Remember Ruth—

ANDREW: I'll take care of her, I swear to you, Rob!

ROBERT: Ruth has suffered—remember, Andy—only through sacrifice— the secret beyond there— [*He suddenly raises himself with his last remaining strength and points to the horizon where the edge of the sun's disc is rising from the rim of the hills.*] The sun! [*He remains with his eyes fixed on it for a moment. A rattling noise throbs from his throat. He mumbles.*] Remember! [*And falls back and is still.* RUTH *gives a cry of horror and springs to her feet, shuddering, her hands over her eyes.* ANDREW *bends on one knee beside the body, placing a hand over* ROBERT's *heart, then he kisses his brother reverentially on the forehead and stands up.*]

ANDREW: [*Facing* RUTH, *the body between them—in a dead voice.*] He's dead. [*With a sudden burst of fury.*] God damn you, you never told him!

RUTH: [*Piteously.*] He was so happy without my lying to him.

ANDREW: [*Pointing to the body—trembling with the violence of his rage.*] This is your doing, you damn woman, you coward, you murderess!

RUTH: [*Sobbing.*] Don't, Andy! I couldn't help it—and he knew how I'd suffered, too. He told you—to remember.

ANDREW: [*Stares at her for a moment, his rage ebbing away, an expression of deep pity gradually coming over his face. Then he glances down at his brother and speaks brokenly in a compassionate voice.*] Forgive me, Ruth—for his sake—and I'll remember— [RUTH *lets her hands fall from her face and looks at him, uncomprehendingly. He lifts his eyes to hers and forces out falteringly.*] I—you—we've both made a mess of things! We must try to help each other—and—in time—we'll come to know what's right— [*Desperately.*] And perhaps we— [*But* RUTH, *if she is aware of his words, gives no sign. She remains silent, gazing at him dully with the sad humility of exhaustion, her mind already sinking back into that spent calm beyond the further troubling of any hope.*]

[*The Curtain Falls*]

THE STRAW

A PLAY IN THREE ACTS

CHARACTERS

BILL CARMODY

MARY
NORA
TOM
BILLY
} *his children*

DOCTOR GAYNOR

FRED NICHOLLS

EILEEN CARMODY, *Bill's eldest child*

STEPHEN MURRAY

MISS HOWARD, *a nurse in training*

MISS GILPIN, *superintendent of the Infirmary*

DOCTOR STANTON, *of the Hill Farm Sanatorium*

DOCTOR SIMMS, *his assistant*

MR. SLOAN

PETERS, *a patient*

MRS. TURNER, *matron of the Sanatorium*

MISS BAILEY
MRS. ABNER
FLYNN
} *Patients*

OTHER PATIENTS OF THE SANATORIUM

MRS. BRENNAN

SCENES

ACT I

SCENE I: The Kitchen of the Carmody Home—Evening.
SCENE II: The Reception Room of the Infirmary, Hill Farm
Sanatorium—An Evening a Week Later.

ACT II

SCENE I: Assembly Room of the Main Building at the Sanatorium—
A Morning Four Months Later.
SCENE II: A Crossroads Near the Sanatorium—Midnight of the
Same Day.

ACT III

An Isolation Room and Porch at the Sanatorium—An Afternoon Four
Months Later.

THE STRAW

ACT ONE

SCENE ONE

The kitchen of the Carmody home on the outskirts of a manufacturing town in Connecticut. On the left, forward, the sink. Farther back,
two windows looking out on the yard. In the left corner, rear, the ice-
box. Immediately to the right of it, in the rear wall, a window opening
on the side porch. To the right of this, a dish closet, and a door leading
into the hall where the main front entrance to the house and the stairs
to the floor above are situated. On the right, to the rear, a door opening
on the dining room. Farther forward, the kitchen range with scuttle,
wood box, etc. In the center of the room, a table with a red and white
cover. Four cane-bottomed chairs are pushed under the table. In front
of the stove, two battered, wicker rocking chairs. The floor is partly
covered by linoleum strips. The walls are papered a light cheerful color.
Several old framed picture-supplement prints hang from nails. Everything has a clean, neatly-kept appearance. The supper dishes are piled
in the sink ready for washing. A dish pan of water simmers on the
stove.

It is about eight o'clock in the evening of a bitter cold day in late
February.

As the curtain rises, BILL CARMODY is discovered sitting in a rocker
by the stove, reading a newspaper and smoking a blackened clay
pipe. He is a man of fifty, heavy-set and round-shouldered, with long
muscular arms and swollen-veined, hairy hands. His face is bony
and ponderous; his nose, short and squat; his mouth large, thick-lipped
and harsh; his complexion mottled—red, purple-streaked, and freckled;
his hair, short and stubby with a bald spot on the crown. The expression of his small, blue eyes is one of selfish cunning. His voice is loud
and hoarse. He wears a flannel shirt, open at the neck, criss-crossed
by red suspenders; black, baggy trousers gray with dust; muddy
brogans.

His youngest daughter, MARY, is sitting on a chair by the table, front,
turning over the pages of a picture book. She is a delicate, dark-haired,
blue-eyed, quiet little girl about eight years old.

CARMODY: [*After watching the child's preoccupation for a moment, in a tone of half-exasperated amusement.*] Well, but you're the quiet one, surely! It's the dead spit and image of your sister, Eileen, you are, with your nose always in a book; and you're like your mother, too, God rest her soul. [*He crosses himself with pious unction and* MARY *also does so.*] It's Nora and Tom has the high spirits in them like their father; and Billy, too,—if he is a lazy shiftless divil—has the fightin' Carmody blood like me. You're a Cullen like your mother's people. They always was dreamin' their lives out. [*He lights his pipe and shakes his head with ponderous gravity.*] It's out rompin' and playin' you ought to be at your age, not carin' a fig for books. [*With a glance at the clock.*] Is that auld fool of a doctor stayin' the night? Run out in the hall, Mary, and see if you hear him.

MARY: [*Goes out into the hall, rear, and comes back.*] He's upstairs. I heard him talking to Eileen.

CARMODY: Close the door, ye little divil! There's a freezin' draught comin' in. [*She does so and comes back to her chair.* CARMODY *continues with a sneer.*] I've no use for their drugs at all. They only keep you sick to pay more visits. I'd not have sent for this bucko if Eileen didn't scare me by faintin'.

MARY: [*Anxiously.*] Is Eileen very sick, Papa?

CARMODY: [*Spitting—roughly.*] If she is, it's her own fault entirely— weakenin' her health by readin' here in the house. [*Irritably.*] Put down that book on the table and leave it be. I'll have no more readin' or I'll take the strap to you!

MARY: [*Laying the book on the table.*] It's only pictures.

CARMODY: No back talk! Pictures or not, it's all the same mopin' and lazin' in it. [*After a pause—morosely.*] Who's to do the work and look after Nora and Tom and yourself, if Eileen is bad took and has to stay in her bed? All that I've saved from slavin' and sweatin' in the sun with a gang of lazy Dagoes'll be up the spout in no time. [*Bitterly.*] What a fool a man is to be raisin' a raft of children and him not a millionaire! [*With lugubrious self-pity.*] Mary, dear, it's a black curse God put on me when he took your mother just when I needed her most. [MARY *commences to sob.* CARMODY *starts and looks at her angrily.*] What are you snifflin' at?

MARY: [*Tearfully.*] I was thinking—of Mama.

CARMODY: [*Scornfully.*] It's late you are with your tears, and her cold in her grave for a year. Stop it, I'm tellin' you! [MARY *gulps back her sobs.*]

[*There is a noise of childish laughter and screams from the street in*

*front. The outside door is opened and slammed, footsteps pound along
the hall. The door in the rear is shoved open, and* NORA *and* TOM *rush
in breathlessly.* NORA *is a bright, vivacious, red-haired girl of eleven—
pretty after an elfish, mischievous fashion—light-hearted and robust.*]

[TOM *resembles* NORA *in disposition and appearance. A healthy,
good-humored youngster with a shock of sandy hair. He is a year
younger than* NORA. *They are followed into the room, a moment later,
by their brother,* BILLY, *who is evidently loftily disgusted with their an-
tics.* BILLY *is a fourteen-year-old replica of his father, whom he imitates
even to the hoarse, domineering tone of voice.*]

CARMODY: [*Grumpily.*] Ah, here you are, the lot of you. Shut that door
after you! What's the use in me spendin' money for coal if all you do
is to let the cold night in the room itself?

NORA: [*Hopping over to him—teasingly.*] Me and Tom had a race,
Papa. I beat him. [*She sticks her tongue out at her younger brother.*]
Slow poke!

TOM: You didn't beat me, neither!

NORA: I did, too!

TOM: You tripped me comin' up the steps. Brick-top! Cheater!

NORA: [*Flaring up.*] You're a liar! I beat you fair. Didn't I, Papa?

CARMODY: [*With a grin.*] You did, darlin'. [TOM *slinks back to the
chair in the rear of the table, sulking.* CARMODY *pats* NORA's *red
hair with delighted pride.*] Sure it's you can beat the divil himself!

NORA: [*Sticks out her tongue again at* TOM.] See? Liar! [*She goes and
perches on the table near* MARY *who is staring sadly in front of her.*]

CARMODY: [*To* BILLY—*irritably.*] Did you get the plug I told you?

BILLY: Sure. [*He takes a plug of tobacco from his pocket and hands it to
his father.* NORA *slides down off her perch and disappears, unno-
ticed, under the table.*]

CARMODY: It's a great wonder you didn't forget it—and me without a
chew. [*He bites off a piece and tucks it into his cheek.*]

TOM: [*Suddenly clutching at his leg with a yell.*] Ouch! Darn you! [*He
kicks frantically at something under the table, but* NORA *scrambles
out at the other end, grinning.*]

CARMODY: [*Angrily.*] Shut your big mouth!

TOM: [*Indignantly.*] She pinched me—hard as she could, too—and look
at her laughin'!

NORA: [*Hopping on the table again.*] Cry-baby!

TOM: I'll tell Eileen, wait 'n' see!

NORA: Tattle-tale! Eileen's sick.

TOM: That's why you dast do it. You dasn't if she was up.

CARMODY: [*Exasperated.*] Go up to bed, the two of you, and no more talk, and you go with them, Mary.

NORA: [*Giving a quick tug at* MARY'*s hair.*] Come on, Mary.

MARY: Ow! [*She begins to cry.*]

CARMODY: [*Raising his voice furiously.*] Hush your noise! It's nothin' but blubberin' you do be doin' all the time. [*He stands up threateningly.*] I'll have a moment's peace, I will! Go on, now! [*They scurry out of the rear door.*]

NORA: [*Sticks her head back in the door.*] Can I say good-night to Eileen, papa?

CARMODY: No. The doctor's with her yet. [*Then he adds hastily.*] Yes, go in to her, Nora. It'll drive himself out of the house maybe, bad cess to him, and him stayin' half the night. [NORA *waits to hear no more but darts back, shutting the door behind her.* BILLY *takes the chair in front of the table.* CARMODY *sits down again with a groan.*] The rheumatics are in my leg again. [*Shakes his head.*] If Eileen's in bed long those brats'll have the house down. Ara, well, it's God's will, I suppose, but where the money'll come from, I dunno. [*With a disparaging glance at his son.*] They'll not be raisin' your wages soon, I'll be bound.

BILLY: [*Surlily.*] Naw.

CARMODY: [*Still scanning him with contempt.*] A divil of a lot of good it was for me to go against Eileen's wish and let you leave off your schoolin' this year thinkin' the money you'd earn would help with the house.

BILLY: Aw, goin' to school didn't do me no good. The teachers was all down on me. I couldn't learn nothin' there.

CARMODY: [*Disgustedly.*] Nor any other place, I'm thinkin', you're that thick. [*There is a noise from the stairs in the hall.*] Wisht! It's the doctor comin' down from Eileen. [*The door in the rear is opened and Doctor Gaynor enters. He is a stout, bald, middle-aged man, forceful of speech, who in the case of patients of the* CARMODYS' *class dictates rather than advises.* CARMODY *adopts a whining tone.*] Aw, Doctor, and how's Eileen now?

GAYNOR: [*Does not answer this but comes forward into the room holding out two slips of paper—dictatorially.*] Here are two prescriptions that'll have to be filled immediately.

CARMODY: [*Frowning.*] You take them, Billy, and run round to the drug store. [GAYNOR *hands them to* BILLY.]

BILLY: Give me the money, then.

CARMODY: [*Reaches down into his pants pocket with a sigh.*] How much will they come to, Doctor?

GAYNOR: About a dollar, I guess.

CARMODY: [*Protestingly.*] A dollar! Sure it's expensive medicines you're givin' her for a bit of a cold. [*He meets the doctor's cold glance of contempt and he wilts—grumblingly, as he peels a dollar bill off a small roll and gives it to* BILLY.] Bring back the change—if there is any. And none of your tricks!

BILLY: Aw, what do you think I am? [*He takes the money and goes out.*]

CARMODY: [*Grudgingly.*] Take a chair, Doctor, and tell me what's wrong with Eileen.

GAYNOR: [*Seating himself by the table—gravely.*] Your daughter is very seriously ill.

CARMODY: [*Irritably.*] Aw, Doctor, didn't I know you'd be sayin' that, anyway!

GAYNOR: [*Ignoring this remark—coldly.*] She has tuberculosis of the lungs.

CARMODY: [*With puzzled awe.*] Too-ber-c'losis?

GAYNOR: Consumption, if that makes it plainer to you.

CARMODY: [*With dazed terror—after a pause.*] Consumption? Eileen? [*With sudden anger.*] What lie is it you're tellin' me?

GAYNOR: [*Icily.*] Look here, Carmody!

CARMODY: [*Bewilderedly.*] Don't be angry, now. Sure I'm out of my wits entirely. Ah, Doctor, sure you must be mistaken!

GAYNOR: There's no chance for a mistake, I'm sorry to say. Her right lung is badly affected.

CARMODY: [*Desperately.*] It's a cold only, maybe.

GAYNOR: [*Curtly.*] Don't talk nonsense. [CARMODY *groans.* GAYNOR *continues authoritatively.*] She'll have to go to a sanatorium at once. She ought to have been sent to one months ago. [*Casts a look of indignant scorn at* CARMODY *who is sitting staring at the floor with an expression of angry stupor on his face.*] It's a wonder to me you didn't see the condition she was in and force her to take care of herself.

CARMODY: [*With vague fury.*] God blast it!

GAYNOR: She kept on doing her work, I suppose—taking care of her brothers and sisters, washing, cooking, sweeping, looking after your comfort—worn out—when she should have been in bed—and— [*He gets to his feet with a harsh laugh.*] But what's the use of talking? The damage is done. We've got to set to work to repair it at once. I'll write tonight to Dr. Stanton of the Hill Farm Sanatorium and find out if he has a vacancy.

CARMODY: [*His face growing red with rage.*] Is it sendin' Eileen away to a hospital you'd be? [*Exploding.*] Then you'll not! You'll get that notion out of your head damn quick. It's all nonsense you're stuffin' me with, and lies, makin' things out to be the worst in the world. She'll not move a step out of here, and I say so, and I'm her father!

GAYNOR: [*Who has been staring at him with contempt—coldly angry.*] You refuse to let her go to a sanatorium?

CARMODY: I do.

GAYNOR: [*Threateningly.*] Then I'll have to report her case to the Society for the Prevention of Tuberculosis of this county and tell them of your refusal to help her.

CARMODY: [*Wavering a bit.*] Report all you like, and be damned to you!

GAYNOR: [*Ignoring the interruption—impressively.*] A majority of the most influential men of this city are back of the Society. [*Grimly.*] We'll find a way to move you, Carmody, if you try to be stubborn.

CARMODY: [*Thoroughly frightened but still protesting.*] Ara, Doctor, you don't see the way of it at all. If Eileen goes to the hospital, who's to be takin' care of the others, and mindin' the house when I'm off to work?

GAYNOR: You can easily hire some woman.

CARMODY: [*At once furious again.*] Hire? D'you think I'm a millionaire itself?

GAYNOR: [*Contemptuously.*] That's where the shoe pinches, eh? [*In a rage.*] I'm not going to waste any more words on you, Carmody, but I'm damn well going to see this thing through! You might as well give in first as last.

CARMODY: [*Wailing.*] But where's the money comin' from?

GAYNOR: The weekly fee at the Hill Farm is only seven dollars. You can easily afford that—the price of a few rounds of drinks.

CARMODY: Seven dollars! And I'll have to pay a woman to come in— and the four of the children eatin' their heads off! Glory be to God, I'll not have a penny saved for me old age—and then it's the poor house!

GAYNOR: Well, perhaps I can get the Society to pay half for your daughter—if you're really as hard up as you pretend.

CARMODY: [*Brightening.*] Ah, Doctor, thank you.

GAYNOR: [*Abruptly.*] Then it's all settled?

CARMODY: [*Grudgingly—trying to make the best of it.*] I'll do my best for Eileen, if it's needful—and you'll not be tellin' them people about it at all, Doctor?

GAYNOR: Not unless you force me to.

CARMODY: And they'll pay the half, surely?

GAYNOR: I'll see what I can do.

CARMODY: God bless you, Doctor! [*Grumblingly.*] It's the whole of it they ought to be payin', I'm thinkin', and them with sloos of money. 'Tis them builds the hospitals and why should they be wantin' the poor like me to support them?

GAYNOR: [*Disgustedly.*] Bah! [*Abruptly.*] I'll telephone to Doctor Stanton tomorrow morning. Then I'll know something definite when I come to see your daughter in the afternoon.

CARMODY: [*Darkly.*] You'll be comin' again tomorrow? [*Half to himself.*] Leave it to the likes of you to be drainin' a man dry. [GAYNOR *has gone out to the hall in rear and does not hear this last remark. There is a loud knock from the outside door. The Doctor comes back into the room carrying his hat and overcoat.*]

GAYNOR: There's someone knocking.

CARMODY: Who'll it be? Ah, it's Fred Nicholls, maybe. [*In a low voice to* GAYNOR *who has started to put on his overcoat.*] Eileen's young man, Doctor, that she's engaged to marry, as you might say.

GAYNOR: [*Thoughtfully.*] Hmm—yes—she spoke of him. [*As another knock sounds* CARMODY *hurries to the rear.* GAYNOR, *after a moment's indecision, takes off his overcoat again and sits down. A moment later* CARMODY *reënters followed by* FRED NICHOLLS, *who has left his overcoat and hat in the hallway.* NICHOLLS *is a young fellow of twenty-three, stockily built, fair-haired, handsome in a commonplace, conventional mold. His manner is obviously an attempt at suave gentility; he has an easy, taking smile and a ready laugh, but there is a petty, calculating expression in his small, observing, blue eyes. His well-fitting, readymade clothes are carefully pressed. His whole get-up suggests an attitude of man-about-small-town complacency.*]

CARMODY: [*As they enter.*] I had a mind to phone to your house but I wasn't wishful to disturb you, knowin' you'd be comin' to call tonight.

NICHOLLS: [*With disappointed concern.*] It's nothing serious, I hope.

CARMODY: [*Grumblingly.*] Ah, who knows? Here's the doctor. You've not met him?

NICHOLLS: [*Politely, looking at* GAYNOR *who inclines his head stiffly.*] I haven't had the pleasure. Of course I've heard—

CARMODY: It's Doctor Gaynor. This is Fred Nicholls, Doctor. [*The two men shake hands with conventional pleased-to-meet yous.*] Sit down, Fred, that's a good lad, and be talkin' to the Doctor a moment while I go upstairs and see how is Eileen.

NICHOLLS: Certainly, Mr. Carmody—and tell her how sorry I am to learn she's under the weather.

CARMODY: I will so. [*He goes out.*]

GAYNOR: [*After a pause in which he is studying* NICHOLLS.] Do you happen to be any relative to Albert Nicholls over at the Downs Manufacturing Company?

NICHOLLS: [*Smiling.*] He's sort of a near relative—my father.

GAYNOR: Ah, yes?

NICHOLLS: [*With satisfaction.*] I work for the Downs Company myself—bookkeeper.

GAYNOR: Miss Carmody had a position there also, didn't she, before her mother died?

NICHOLLS: Yes. She had a job as stenographer for a time. When she graduated from the business college—I was already working at the Downs—and through my father's influence—you understand. [GAYNOR *nods curtly.*] She was getting on finely, too, and liked the work. It's too bad—her mother's death, I mean—forcing her to give it up and come home to take care of those kids.

GAYNOR: It's a damn shame. That's the main cause of her breakdown.

NICHOLLS: [*Frowning.*] I've noticed she's been looking badly lately. Well, it's all her father's fault—and her own, too, because whenever I raised a kick about his making a slave of her, she always defended him. [*With a quick glance at the Doctor—in a confidential tone.*] Between us, Carmody's as selfish as they make 'em, if you want my opinion.

GAYNOR: [*With a growl.*] He's a hog on two legs.

NICHOLLS: [*With a gratified smile.*] You bet! [*With a patronizing air.*] I hope to get Eileen away from all this as soon as—things pick up a little. [*Making haste to explain his connection with the dubious household.*] Eileen and I have gone around together for years—went to Grammar and High School together—in different classes, of course. She's really a corker—very different from the rest of the family you've seen—like her mother. My folks like her awfully well. Of course, they'd never stand for him.

GAYNOR: You'll excuse my curiosity, but you and Miss Carmody are engaged, aren't you? Carmody said you were.

NICHOLLS: [*Embarrassed.*] Why, yes, in a way—but nothing definite— no official announcement or anything of that kind. [*With a sentimental smile.*] It's always been sort of understood between us. [*He laughs awkwardly.*]

GAYNOR: [*Gravely.*] Then I can be frank with you. I'd like to be because I may need your help. Besides, you're bound to know anyway. She'd tell you.

NICHOLLS: [*A look of apprehension coming over his face.*] Is it—about her sickness?

GAYNOR: Yes.

NICHOLLS: Then—it's serious?

GAYNOR: It's pulmonary tuberculosis—consumption.

NICHOLLS: [*Stunned.*] Consumption? Good heavens! [*After a dazed pause—lamely.*] Are you sure, Doctor?

GAYNOR: Positive. [NICHOLLS *stares at him with vaguely frightened eyes.*] It's had a good start—thanks to her father's blind selfishness— but let's hope that can be overcome. The important thing is to ship her off to a sanatorium immediately. That's where you can be of help. It's up to you to help me convince Carmody that it's imperative she be sent away at once—for the safety of those around her as well as her own.

NICHOLLS: [*Confusedly.*] I'll do my best, Doctor. [*As if he couldn't yet believe his ears—shuddering.*] Good heavens! She never said a word about—being so ill. She's had a cold. But Doctor,—do you think this sanatorium will—?

GAYNOR: [*With hearty hopefulness.*] She has every chance. The Hill Farm has a really surprising record of arrested cases. Of course, she'll never be able to live as carelessly as before, even after the most favorable results. [*Apologetically.*] I'm telling you all this as being the one most intimately concerned. You're the one who'll have to assume responsibility when she returns to everyday life.

NICHOLLS: [*Answering as if he were merely talking to screen the thoughts in his mind.*] Yes—certainly— Where is this sanatorium, Doctor?

GAYNOR: Half an hour by train to the town. The sanatorium is two miles out on the hills. You'll be able to see her whenever you've a day off.

NICHOLLS: [*A look of horrified realization has been creeping into his eyes.*] You said—Eileen ought to be sent away—for the sake of those around her—?

GAYNOR: T. B. is extremely contagious, you must know that. Yet I'll bet she's been fondling and kissing those brothers and sisters of hers regardless. [NICHOLLS *fidgets uneasily on his chair.*]

NICHOLLS: [*His eyes shiftily avoiding the doctor's face.*] Then the kids might have gotten it—by kissing Eileen?

GAYNOR: It stands to reason that's a common means of communication.

NICHOLLS: [*Very much shaken.*] Yes. I suppose it must be. But that's terrible, isn't it? [*With sudden volubility, evidently extremely anxious to wind up this conversation and conceal his thoughts from* GAYNOR.] I'll promise you, Doctor, I'll tell Carmody straight what's what. He'll pay attention to me or I'll know the reason why.

GAYNOR: [*Getting to his feet and picking up his overcoat.*] Good boy! Tell him I'll be back tomorrow with definite information about the sanatorium.

NICHOLLS: [*Helping him on with his overcoat, anxious to have him go.*] All right, Doctor.

GAYNOR: [*Puts on his hat.*] And do your best to cheer the patient up. Give her confidence in her ability to get well. That's half the battle.

NICHOLLS: [*Hastily.*] I'll do all I can.

GAYNOR: [*Turns to the door and shakes* NICHOLLS' *hand sympathetically.*] And don't take it to heart too much yourself. In six months she'll come back to you her old self again.

NICHOLLS: [*Nervously.*] It's hard on a fellow—so suddenly but I'll remember—and—[*Abruptly.*] Good-night, Doctor.

GAYNOR: Good-night. [*He goes out. The outer door is heard shutting behind him.* NICHOLLS *closes the door, rear, and comes back and sits in the chair in front of table. He rests his chin on his hands and stares before him, a look of desperate, frightened calculation coming into his eyes.* CARMODY *is heard clumping heavily down the stairs. A moment later he enters. His expression is glum and irritated.*]

CARMODY: [*Coming forward to his chair by the stove.*] Has he gone away?

NICHOLLS: [*Turning on him with a look of repulsion.*] Yes. He said to tell you he'd be back tomorrow with definite information—about the sanatorium business.

CARMODY: [*Darkly.*] Oho, he did, did he? Maybe I'll surprise him. I'm thinkin' it's lyin' he is about Eileen's sickness, and her lookin' as fresh as a daisy with the high color in her cheeks when I saw her now.

NICHOLLS: [*Impatiently.*] Gaynor knows his business. [*After a moment's hesitation.*] He told me all about Eileen's sickness.

CARMODY: [*Resentfully.*] Small thanks to him to be tellin' our secrets to the town.

NICHOLLS: [*Exasperated.*] He only told me because you'd said I and Eileen were engaged. You're the one who was telling—secrets.

CARMODY: [*Irritated.*] Ara, don't be talkin'! That's no secret at all with the whole town watchin' Eileen and you spoonin' together from the time you was kids.

NICHOLLS: [*Vindictively.*] Well, the whole town is liable to find out—
[*He checks himself.*]

CARMODY: [*Too absorbed in his own troubles to notice this threat.*] So
he told you he'd send Eileen away to the hospital? I've half a mind
not to let him—and let him try to make me! [*With a frown.*] But
Eileen herself says she's wantin' to go, now. [*Angrily.*] It's all that
divil's notion he put in her head that the children'd be catchin' her
sickness that makes her willin' to go.

NICHOLLS: [*With a superior air.*] From what he told me, I should say
it's the only thing for Eileen to do if she wants to get well quickly.
[*Spitefully.*] And I'd certainly not go against Gaynor, if I was you.

CARMODY: [*Worriedly.*] But what can he do—him and his Sasiety? I'm
her father.

NICHOLLS: [*Seeing* CARMODY's *uneasiness with revengeful satisfaction.*] You'll make a mistake if you think he's bluffing. It'd probably
get in all the papers about you refusing. Everyone would be down on
you. [*As a last jab—spitefully.*] You might even lose your job over it,
people would be so sore.

CARMODY: [*Jumping to his feet.*] Ah, divil take him! Let him send her
where he wants, then.

NICHOLLS: [*As an afterthought.*] And, honestly, Mr. Carmody, I don't
see how you can object for a second. [*Seeing* CARMODY's *shaken
condition, he finishes boldly.*] You've some feeling for your own
daughter, haven't you?

CARMODY: [*Apprehensively.*] Whisht! She might hear you. Let her do
what she's wishful.

NICHOLLS: [*Complacently—feeling his duty in the matter well done.*]
That's the right spirit. And you and I'll do all we can to help her. [*He
gets to his feet.*] Well, I guess I'll have to go. Tell Eileen—

CARMODY: You're not goin'? Sure, Eileen is puttin' on her clothes to
come down and have a look at you.

NICHOLLS: [*Suddenly panic-stricken by the prospect of facing her.*] No—
no—I can't stay—I only came for a moment—I've got an ap-
pointment—honestly. Besides, it isn't right for her to be up. You
should have told her. [*The door in the rear is opened and* EILEEN *enters. She is just over eighteen. Her wavy mass of dark hair is parted in
the middle and combed low on her forehead, covering her ears, to a
knot at the back of her head. The oval of her face is spoiled by a long,
rather heavy, Irish jaw contrasting with the delicacy of her other features. Her eyes are large and blue, confident in their compelling candor
and sweetness; her lips, full and red, half-open, over strong even teeth,
droop at the corners into an expression of wistful sadness; her clear*

complexion is unnaturally striking in its contrasting colors, rose and white; her figure is slight and undeveloped. She wears a plain black dress with a bit of white at the neck and wrists. She stands looking appealingly at NICHOLLS *who avoids her glance. Her eyes have a startled, stunned expression as if the doctor's verdict were still in her ears.*]

EILEEN: [*Faintly—forcing a smile.*] Good-evening, Fred. [*Her eyes search his face anxiously.*]

NICHOLLS: [*Confusedly.*] Hello, Eileen. I'm so sorry to— [*Clumsily trying to cover up his confusion, he goes over and leads her to a chair.*] You sit down. You've got to take care of yourself. You never ought to have gotten up tonight.

EILEEN: [*Sits down.*] I wanted to talk to you. [*She raises her face with a pitiful smile.* NICHOLLS *hurriedly moves back to his own chair.*]

NICHOLLS: [*Almost brusquely.*] I could have talked to you from the hall. You're silly to take chances just now. [EILEEN'*s eyes show her hurt at his tone.*]

CARMODY: [*Seeing his chance—hastily.*] You'll be stayin' a while now, Fred? I'll take a walk down the road. I'm needin' a drink to clear my wits. [*He goes to the door in rear.*]

EILEEN: [*Reproachfully.*] You won't be long, Father? And please don't—you know.

CARMODY: [*Exasperated.*] Sure who wouldn't get drunk with all the sorrows of the world piled on him? [*He stamps out. A moment later the outside door bangs behind him.* EILEEN *sighs.* NICHOLLS *walks up and down with his eyes on the floor.*]

NICHOLLS: [*Furious at* CARMODY *for having left him in this situation.*] Honestly, Eileen, your father is the limit. I don't see how you stand for him. He's the most selfish—

EILEEN: [*Gently.*] Sssh! You mustn't, Fred. He just doesn't understand. [NICHOLLS *snorts disdainfully.*] Don't! Let's not talk about him now. We won't have many more evenings together for a long, long time. Did Father or the doctor tell you— [*She falters.*]

NICHOLLS: [*Not looking at her—glumly.*] Everything there was to tell, I guess.

EILEEN: [*Hastening to comfort him.*] You mustn't worry, Fred. Please don't! It'd make it so much worse for me if I thought you did. I'll be all right. I'll do exactly what they tell me, and in a few months I'll be back so fat and healthy you won't know me.

NICHOLLS: [*Lamely.*] Oh, there's no doubt of that. No one's worrying about your not getting well quick.

EILEEN: It won't be long. We can write often, and it isn't far away. You can come out and see me every Sunday—if you want to.

NICHOLLS: [*Hastily.*] Of course I will!

EILEEN: [*Looking at his face searchingly.*] Why do you act so funny? Why don't you sit down—here, by me? Don't you want to?

NICHOLLS: [*Drawing up a chair by hers—flushing guiltily.*] I—I'm all bawled up, Eileen. I don't know what I'm doing.

EILEEN: [*Putting her hand on his knee.*] Poor Fred! I'm so sorry I have to go. I didn't want to at first. I knew how hard it would be on Father and the kids—especially little Mary. [*Her voice trembles a bit.*] And then the doctor said if I stayed I'd be putting them all in danger. He even ordered me not to kiss them any more. [*She bites her lips to restrain a sob—then coughs, a soft, husky cough.* NICHOLLS *shrinks away from her to the edge of his chair, his eyes shifting nervously with fright.* EILEEN *continues gently.*] So I've got to go and get well, don't you see?

NICHOLLS: [*Wetting his dry lips.*] Yes—it's better.

EILEEN: [*Sadly.*] I'll miss the kids so much. Taking care of them has meant so much to me since Mother died. [*With a half-sob she suddenly throws her arms about his neck and hides her face on his shoulder. He shudders and fights against an impulse to push her away.*] But I'll miss you most of all, Fred. [*She lifts her lips towards his, expecting a kiss. He seems about to kiss her—then averts his face with a shrinking movement, pretending he hasn't seen.* EILEEN's *eyes grow wide with horror. She throws herself back into her own chair, staring accusingly at* NICHOLLS. *She speaks chokingly.*] Fred! Why—why didn't you kiss—what is it? Are you—afraid? [*With a moaning sound.*] Oooh!

NICHOLLS: [*Goaded by this accusation into a display of manhood, seizes her fiercely by the arms.*] No! What—what d'you mean? [*He tries to kiss her but she hides her face.*]

EILEEN: [*In a muffled voice of hysterical self-accusation, pushing his head away.*] No, no, you mustn't! The doctor told you not to, didn't he? Please don't, Fred! It would be awful if anything happened to you—through me. [NICHOLLS *gives up his attempts, recalled to caution by her words. She raises her face and tries to force a smile through her tears.*] But you can kiss me on the forehead, Fred. That can't do any harm. [*His face crimson, he does so. She laughs hysterically.*] It seems so silly—being kissed that way—by you. [*She gulps back a sob and continues to attempt to joke.*] I'll have to get used to it, won't I?

[*The Curtain Falls*]

ACT ONE

SCENE TWO

The reception room of the Infirmary, a large, high-ceilinged room painted white, with oiled, hardwood floor. In the left wall, forward, a row of four windows. Farther back, the main entrance from the driveway, and another window. In the rear wall left, a glass partition looking out on the sleeping porch. A row of white beds, with the faces of patients barely peeping out from under piles of heavy bedclothes, can be seen. To the right of this partition, a bookcase, and a door leading to the hall past the patients' rooms. Farther right, another door opening on the examining room. In the right wall, rear, a door to the office. Farther forward, a row of windows. In front of the windows, a long dining table with chairs. On the left of the table, toward the center of the room, a chimney with two open fireplaces, facing left and right. Several wicker armchairs are placed around the fireplace on the left in which a cheerful wood fire is crackling. To the left of center, a round reading and writing table with a green-shaded electric lamp. Other electric lights are in brackets around the walls. Easy chairs stand near the table which is stacked with magazines. Rocking chairs are placed here and there about the room, near the windows, etc. A Victrola stands near the left wall, forward.

It is nearing eight o'clock of a cold evening about a week later.

At the rise of the curtain STEPHEN MURRAY *is discovered sitting in a chair in front of the fireplace, left.* MURRAY *is thirty years old—a tall, slender, rather unusual looking fellow with a pale face, sunken under high cheek bones, lined about the eyes and mouth, jaded and worn for one still so young. His intelligent, large hazel eyes have a tired, dispirited expression in repose, but can quicken instantly with a concealment mechanism of mocking, careless humor whenever his inner privacy is threatened. His large mouth aids this process of protection by a quick change from its set apathy to a cheerful grin of cynical good nature. He gives off the impression of being somehow dissatisfied with himself but not yet embittered enough by it to take it out on others. His manner, as revealed by his speech—nervous, inquisitive, alert—seems more an acquired quality than any part of his real nature. He stoops a trifle, giving him a slightly round-shouldered appearance. He is dressed in a shabby dark suit, baggy at the knees. He is staring into the fire, dreaming, an open book lying unheeded on the arm of his chair. The Victrola is whining out the last strains of Dvorak's Humoresque. In the doorway to the office,* MISS GILPIN *stands talking to* MISS HOWARD. *The former is a slight, middle-aged woman with black hair, and a strong, intelligent face, its expression of resolute efficiency softened and made kindly by her warm, sympathetic gray eyes.* MISS HOWARD *is tall, slender and blond—decidedly pretty and provokingly conscious of it, yet with a certain air of seriousness underlying her apparent frivolity. She is twenty years old. The elder woman is dressed in the all white of a full-fledged nurse.* MISS HOWARD *wears the gray-blue uniform of one still in training. The record peters out.* MURRAY *sighs with relief but makes no move to get up and stop the grinding needle.* MISS HOWARD *hurries across to the machine.* MISS GILPIN *goes back into the office.*

MISS HOWARD: [*Takes off the record, glancing at* MURRAY *with amused vexation.*] It's a wonder you wouldn't stop this machine grinding itself to bits, Mr. Murray.

MURRAY: [*With a smile.*] I was hoping the darn thing would bust. [MISS HOWARD *sniffs.* MURRAY *grins at her teasingly.*] It keeps you from talking to me. That's the real music.

MISS HOWARD: [*Comes over to his chair laughing.*] I think you're a natural born kidder. All newspaper reporters are like that, I've heard.

MURRAY: You wrong me terribly. [*Then frowning.*] And it isn't charitable to remind me of my job.

MISS HOWARD: [*Surprised.*] I think it's great to be able to write. You ought to be proud of it.

MURRAY: [*Glumly.*] I'm not. You can't call it writing—not what I did— small town stuff. [*Changing the subject.*] Do you know when I'm to be moved to the shacks?

MISS HOWARD: In a few days, I guess. [MURRAY *grunts and moves nervously on his chair.*] What's the matter? Don't you like us here at the Infirmary?

MURRAY: [*Smiling.*] Oh—you—yes! [*Then seriously.*] I don't care for the atmosphere, though. [*He waves his hand toward the partition looking out on the porch.*] All those people in bed out there on the porch seem so sick. It's depressing.

MISS HOWARD: All the patients have to come here first until Doctor Stanton finds out whether they're well enough to be sent out to the shacks and cottages. And remember you're a patient.

MURRAY: I know it. But I don't feel as if I were—really sick like them.

MISS HOWARD: [*Wisely.*] None of them do, either.

MURRAY: [*After a moment's reflection—cynically.*] Yes, I suppose it's that pipe dream keeps us all going, eh?

MISS HOWARD: Well, you ought to be thankful. [*Lowering her voice.*] Shall I tell you a secret? I've seen your chart and *you've* no cause to worry. Doctor Stanton joked about it. He said you were too uninteresting—there was so little the matter with you.

MURRAY: [*Pleased but pretending indifference.*] Humph! He's original in that opinion.

MISS HOWARD: I know it's hard you're being the only one up the week you've been here; but there's another patient due today. Maybe she'll be well enough to be around with you. [*With a quick glance at her wrist watch.*] She can't be coming unless she got in on the last train.

MURRAY: [*Interestedly.*] It's a she, eh?

MISS HOWARD: Yes.

MURRAY: [*Grinning provokingly.*] Young?

MISS HOWARD: Eighteen, I believe. [*Seeing his grin—with feigned pique.*] I suppose you'll be asking if she's pretty next! Her name is Carmody, that's the only other thing I know. So there!

MISS GILPIN: [*Appearing in the office doorway.*] Miss Howard.

MISS HOWARD: Yes, Miss Gilpin. [*In an aside to* MURRAY *as she leaves him.*] It's time for those horrid diets. [*She hurries back into the office.* MURRAY *stares into the fire.* MISS HOWARD *reappears from the office and goes out by the door to the hall, rear. Carriage wheels are heard from the driveway in front of the house on the left. They stop. After a pause there is a sharp rap on the door and a bell rings insistently. Men's muffled voices are heard in argument.* MURRAY *turns curiously in his chair.* MISS GILPIN *comes from the office and walks quickly to the door, unlocking and opening it.* EILEEN *enters, followed by* NICHOLLS, *who is carrying her suit-case, and by her father.*]

EILEEN: I'm Miss Carmody. I believe Doctor Gaynor wrote—

MISS GILPIN: [*Taking her hand—with kind affability.*] We've been expecting you all day. How do you do? I'm Miss Gilpin. You came on the last train, didn't you?

EILEEN: [*Heartened by the other woman's kindness.*] Yes. This is my father, Miss Gilpin—and Mr. Nicholls. [MISS GILPIN *shakes hands cordially with the two men who are staring about the room in embarrassment.* CARMODY *has very evidently been drinking. His voice is thick and his face puffed and stupid.* NICHOLLS' *manner is that of one who is accomplishing a necessary but disagreeable duty with the best grace possible, but is frightfully eager to get it over and done with.* CARMODY's *condition embarrasses him acutely and when he glances at him it is with hatred and angry disgust.*]

MISS GILPIN: [*Indicating the chairs in front of the windows on the left, forward.*] Won't you gentlemen sit down? [CARMODY *grunts sullenly and plumps himself into the one nearest the door.* NICHOLLS *hesitates, glancing down at the suit-case he carries.* MISS GILPIN *turns to* EILEEN.] And now we'll get you settled immediately. Your room is all ready for you. If you'll follow me— [*She turns toward the door in rear, center.*]

EILEEN: Let me take the suit-case now, Fred.

MISS GILPIN: [*As he is about to hand it to her—decisively.*] No, my dear, you mustn't. Put the case right down there, Mr. Nicholls. I'll have it taken to Miss Carmody's room in a moment. [*She shakes her finger at* EILEEN *with kindly admonition.*] That's the first rule you'll have to learn. Never exert yourself or tax your strength. You'll find laziness is a virtue instead of a vice with us.

EILEEN: [*Confused.*] I— I didn't know—

MISS GILPIN: [*Smiling.*] Of course you didn't. And now if you'll come with me I'll show you your room. We'll have a little chat there and I can explain all the other important rules in a second. The gentlemen can make themselves comfortable in the meantime. We won't be gone more than a moment.

NICHOLLS: [*Feeling called upon to say something.*] Yes—we'll wait— certainly, we're all right. [CARMODY *remains silent, glowering at the fire.* NICHOLLS *sits down beside him.* MISS GILPIN *and* EILEEN *go out.* MURRAY *switches his chair so he can observe the two men out of the corner of his eye while pretending to be absorbed in his book.*]

CARMODY: [*Looking about shiftily and reaching for the inside pocket of his overcoat.*] I'll be havin' a nip now we're alone, and that cacklin' hen gone. [*He pulls out a pint flask, half full.*]

NICHOLLS: [*Excitedly.*] Put that bottle away! [*In a whisper*] Don't you see that fellow in the chair there?

CARMODY: [*Taking a big drink.*] Ah, I'm not mindin' a man at all. Sure I'll bet it's himself would be likin' a taste of the same. [*He appears about to get up and invite* MURRAY *to join him but* NICHOLLS *grabs his arm.*]

NICHOLLS: [*With a frightened look at* MURRAY *who appears buried in his book.*] Stop it, you— Don't you know he's probably a patient and they don't allow them—

CARMODY: [*Scornfully.*] It's queer they'd be allowin' the sick ones to read books when I'll bet it's the same lazy readin' in the house brought the half of them down with the consumption itself. [*Raising his voice.*] I'm thinkin' this whole shebang is a big, thievin' fake— and I've always thought so.

NICHOLLS: [*Furiously.*] Put that bottle away, damn it! And don't shout. You're not in a barrel-house.

CARMODY: [*With provoking calm.*] I'll put it back when I'm ready, not before, and no lip from you!

NICHOLLS: [*With fierce disgust.*] You're drunk now.

CARMODY: [*Raging.*] Drunk, am I? Is it the like of a young jackass like you that's still wet behind the ears to be tellin' me I'm drunk?

NICHOLLS: [*Half-rising from his chair—pleadingly.*] For heaven's sake, Mr. Carmody, remember where we are and don't raise any rumpus. What'll Eileen say?

CARMODY: [*Puts the bottle away hastily, mumbling to himself—then glowers about the room scornfully with blinking eyes.*] It's a grand hotel this is, I'm thinkin', for the rich to be takin' their ease, and not a hospital for the poor, but the poor has to pay for it.

NICHOLLS: [*Fearful of another outbreak.*] Sshh!

CARMODY: Don't be shshin' at me? I'd make Eileen come back out of this tonight if that divil of a doctor didn't have me by the throat.

NICHOLLS: [*Glancing at him nervously.*] I wonder how soon she'll be back? We'll have to hurry to make that last train.

CARMODY: [*Angrily.*] Is it anxious to get out of her sight you are, and you engaged to marry her? [NICHOLLS *flushes guiltily.* MURRAY *pricks up his ears and stares over at* NICHOLLS. *The latter meets his glance, scowls, and hurriedly averts his eyes.* CARMODY *goes on accusingly.*] Sure, it's no heart at all you have—and her your sweetheart for years—and her sick with the consumption—and you wild to run away and leave her alone.

NICHOLLS: [*Springing to his feet—furiously.*] That's a—! [*He controls himself with an effort. His voice trembles.*] You're not responsible for the idiotic things you're saying or I'd— [*He turns away, seeking some escape from the old man's tongue.*] I'll see if the man is still there with the rig. [*He goes to the door on left and goes out.*]

CARMODY: [*Following him with his eyes.*] Go to hell, for all I'm preventin'. You've got no guts of a man in you. [*He addresses* MURRAY *with the good nature inspired by the flight of* NICHOLLS.] Is it true you're one of the consumptives, young fellow?

MURRAY: [*Delighted by this speech—with a grin.*] Yes, I'm one of them.

CARMODY: My name's Carmody. What's yours, then?

MURRAY: Murray.

CARMODY: [*Slapping his thigh.*] Irish as Paddy's pig! [MURRAY *nods.* CARMODY *brightens and grows confidential.*] I'm glad to be knowin' you're one of us. You can keep an eye on Eileen.

MURRAY: I'll be glad to do all I can.

CARMODY: Thanks to you—though it's a grand life she'll be havin' here from the fine look of the place. [*With whining self-pity.*] It's me it's hard on, God help me, with four small children and me widowed, and havin' to hire a woman to come in and look after them and the house now that Eileen's sick; and payin' for her curin' in this place, and me with only a bit of money in the bank for my old age. That's hard, now, on a man, and who'll say it isn't?

MURRAY: [*Made uncomfortable by this confidence.*] Hard luck always comes in bunches. [*To head off* CARMODY *who is about to give vent to more woe—quickly, with a glance toward the door from the hall.*] If I'm not mistaken, here comes your daughter now.

CARMODY: [*As* EILEEN *comes into the room.*] I'll make you acquainted. Eileen! [*She comes over to them, embarrassed to find her father in his condition so chummy with a stranger.* MURRAY *rises to his feet.*] This is Mr. Murray, Eileen. He's Irish and he'll put you on to the ropes of the place. He's got the consumption, too, God pity him.

EILEEN: [*Distressed.*] Oh, Father, how can you— [*With a look at* MUR-RAY *which pleads for her father.*] I'm glad to meet you, Mr. Murray.

MURRAY: [*With a straight glance at her which is so frankly admiring that she flushes and drops her eyes.*] I'm glad to meet you. [*The front door is opened and* NICHOLLS *re-appears, shivering with the cold. He stares over at the others with ill-concealed irritation.*]

CARMODY: [*Noticing him—with malicious satisfaction.*] Oho, here you are again. [NICHOLLS *scowls and turns away.* CARMODY *addresses his daughter with a sly wink at* MURRAY.] I thought Fred was slidin' down hill to the train, and him so desperate hurried to get away from here. Look at the knees on him clappin' together with the great fear he'll be catchin' a sickness in this place! [NICHOLLS, *his guilty conscience stabbed to the quick, turns pale with impotent rage.*]

EILEEN: [*Remonstrating pitifully.*] Father! Please! [*She hurries over to* NICHOLLS.] Oh, please don't mind him, Fred! You know what he is when he's drinking.

NICHOLLS: [*Thickly.*] That's all right—for you to say. But I won't forget—I'm sick and tired standing for—I'm not used to—such people.

EILEEN: [*Shrinking from him.*] Fred!

NICHOLLS: [*With a furious glance at* MURRAY.] Before that cheap slob, too.

EILEEN: [*Faintly.*] He seems—very nice.

NICHOLLS: You've got your eyes set on him already, have you?

EILEEN: Fred!

NICHOLLS: Well, go ahead if you want to. I don't care. I'll— [*Startled by the look of anguish which comes over her face, he hastily swallows his words. He takes out watch—fiercely.*] We'll miss that train, damn it!

EILEEN: [*In a stricken tone.*] Oh, Fred! [*Then forcing back her tears she calls to* CARMODY *in a strained voice.*] Father! You'll have to go now.

CARMODY: [*Shaking hands with* MURRAY.] Keep your eye on her. I'll be out soon to see her and you and me'll have another chin.

MURRAY: Glad to. Good-by for the present. [*He walks to windows on the far right, turning his back considerately on their leave-taking.*]

EILEEN: [*Comes to* CARMODY *and hangs on his arm as they proceed to the door.*] Be sure and kiss them all for me—and bring them out to see me as soon as you can, Father, please! And don't forget to tell Mrs. Brennan all the directions I gave you coming out on the train. I told her but she mightn't remember—about Mary's bath—and to give Tom his—

CARMODY: [*Impatiently.*] Hasn't she brought up brats of her own, and doesn't she know the way of it?

EILEEN: [*Helplessly.*] Never mind telling her, then. I'll write to her.

CARMODY: You'd better not. She'll not wish you mixin' in with her work and tellin' her how to do it.

EILEEN: [*Aghast.*] Her work! [*She seems at the end of her tether—wrung too dry for any further emotion. She kisses her father at the door with indifference and speaks calmly.*] Good-by, Father.

CARMODY: [*In a whining tone of injury.*] A cold kiss! Is your heart a stone? [*Drunken tears well from his eyes and he blubbers.*] And your own father going back to a lone house with a stranger in it!

EILEEN: [*Wearily in a dead voice.*] You'll miss your train, Father.

CARMODY: [*Raging in a second.*] I'm off, then! Come on, Fred. It's no welcome we have with her here in this place—and a great curse on this day I brought her to it! [*He stamps out.*]

EILEEN: [*In the same dead tone.*] Good-by, Fred.

NICHOLLS: [*Repenting his words of a moment ago—confusedly.*] I'm sorry, Eileen—for what I said. I didn't mean—you know what your father is—excuse me, won't you?

EILEEN: [*Without feeling.*] Yes.

NICHOLLS: And I'll be out soon—in a week if I can make it. Well then—good-by for the present. [*He bends down as if to kiss her but she shrinks back out of his reach.*]

EILEEN: [*A faint trace of mockery in her weary voice.*] No, Fred. Remember you mustn't now.

NICHOLLS: [*In an instant huff.*] Oh, if that's the way you feel about—
[*He strides out and slams the door viciously behind him.* EILEEN
*walks slowly back toward the fireplace, her face fixed in the dead
calm of despair. As she sinks into one of the armchairs, the strain becomes too much. She breaks down, hiding her face in her hands, her
frail shoulders heaving with the violence of her sobs. As this sound,*
MURRAY *turns from the windows and comes over near her chair.*]

MURRAY: [*After watching her for a moment—in an embarrassed tone
of sympathy.*] Come on, Miss Carmody, that'll never do. I know it's
hard at first—but— It isn't so bad up here—really—once you get
used to it! [*The shame she feels at giving way in the presence of a
stranger only adds to her loss of control and she sobs heartbrokenly.*
MURRAY *walks up and down nervously, visibly nonplussed and upset. Finally he hits upon something.*] One of the nurses will be in any
minute. You don't want them to see you like this.

EILEEN: [*Chokes back her sobs and finally raises her face and attempts
a smile.*] I'm sorry—to make such a sight of myself.

MURRAY: [*Jocularly.*] Well, they say a cry does you a lot of good.

EILEEN: [*Forcing a smile.*] I do feel—better.

MURRAY: [*Staring at her with a quizzical smile—cynically.*] You shouldn't
take those lovers' squabbles so seriously. Tomorrow he'll be sorry.
He'll write begging forgiveness. Result—all serene again.

EILEEN: [*A shadow of pain on her face—with dignity.*] Don't—please.

MURRAY: [*Angry at himself—hanging his head contritely.*] Pardon me.
I'm rude sometimes—before I know it. [*He shakes off his confusion
with a renewed attempt at a joking tone.*] You can blame your father
for any breaks I make. He told me to see that you behaved.

EILEEN: [*With a genuine smile.*] Oh, Father! [*Flushing.*] You mustn't
mind anything he said tonight.

MURRAY: [*Thoughtlessly.*] Yes, he was well lit up. I envied him. [EILEEN
looks very shame-faced. MURRAY *sees it and exclaims in exasperation at himself.*] Darn! There I go again putting my foot in it! [*With
an irrepressible grin.*] I ought to have my tongue operated on—that's
what's the matter with me. [*He laughs and throws himself in a chair.*]

EILEEN: [*Forced in spite of herself to smile with him.*] You're candid, at
any rate, Mr. Murray.

MURRAY: I said I envied him his jag and that's the truth. The same candor compels me to confess that I was pickled to the gills myself when
I arrived here. Fact! I made love to all the nurses and generally dis-
graced myself—and had a wonderful time.

EILEEN: I suppose it does make you forget your troubles.

MURRAY: [*Waving this aside.*] I didn't want to forget—not for a second. I wasn't drowning my sorrow. I was hilariously celebrating.

EILEEN: [*Astonished—by this time quite interested in this queer fellow to the momentary forgetfulness of her own grief.*] Celebrating—coming here? But—aren't you sick?

MURRAY: Yes, of course. [*Confidentially.*] But it's only a matter of time when I'll be all right again. I hope it won't be too soon.

EILEEN: [*With wide eyes.*] I wonder if you really mean—

MURRAY: I sure do—every word of it!

EILEEN: [*Puzzled.*] I can't understand how anyone could— [*With a worried glance over her shoulder.*] I think I'd better look for Miss Gilpin, hadn't I? She may wonder— [*She half rises from her chair.*]

MURRAY: [*Quickly.*] No. Please don't go yet. [*She glances at him irresolutely, then resumes her chair.*] I'll see to it that you don't fracture any rules. [*Hitching his chair nearer hers,—impulsively.*] In all charity to me you've got to stick awhile. I haven't had a chance to really talk to a soul for a week. You found what I said a while ago hard to believe, didn't you?

EILEEN: [*With a smile.*] You said you hoped you wouldn't get well too soon!

MURRAY: And I meant it! This place is honestly like heaven to me—a lonely heaven till your arrival. [EILEEN *looks embarrassed.*] And why wouldn't it be? Just let me tell you what I was getting away from— [*With a sudden laugh full of a weary bitterness.*] Do you know what it means to work from seven at night till three in the morning on a morning newspaper in a town of twenty thousand people—for *ten* years? No. You don't. You can't. But what it did to me—it made me happy—yes, happy!—to get out here!

EILEEN: [*Looking at him curiously.*] But I always thought being a reporter was so interesting.

MURRAY: [*With a cynical laugh.*] On a small town rag? A month of it, perhaps, when you're new to the game. But ten years! With only a raise of a couple of dollars every blue moon or so, and a weekly spree on Saturday night to vary the monotony. [*He laughs again.*] Interesting, eh? Getting the dope on the Social of the Queen Esther Circle in the basement of the Methodist Episcopal Church, unable to sleep through a meeting of the Common Council on account of the noisy oratory caused by John Smith's application for a permit to build a house; making a note that a tug boat towed two barges loaded with coal up the river, that Mrs. Perkins spent a week-end with relatives in Hickville, that John Jones—Oh help! Why go on? I'm a broken man. God, how I used to pray that our Congressman would commit suicide, or the Mayor murder his wife—just to be able to write a real story!

EILEEN: [*With a smile.*] Is it as bad as that? But weren't there other things that were interesting?

MURRAY: [*Decidedly.*] Nope. Never anything new—and I knew everyone and everything in town by heart years ago. [*With sudden bitterness.*] Oh, it was my own fault. Why didn't I get out of it? Well, I was always going to—tomorrow—and tomorrow never came. I got in a rut—and stayed put. People seem to get that way, somehow—in that town. It took T. B. to blast me loose.

EILEEN: [*Wonderingly.*] But—your family—

MURRAY: I haven't much of a family left. My mother died when I was a kid. My father—he was a lawyer—died when I was nineteen, just about to go to college. He left nothing, so I went to work instead. I've two sisters, respectably married and living in another part of the state. We don't get along—but they're paying for me here, so I suppose I've no kick. [*Cynically.*] A family wouldn't have changed things. From what I've seen that blood-thicker-than-water dope is all wrong. It's thinner than table-d'hôte soup. You may have seen a bit of that truth in your own case already.

EILEEN: [*Shocked.*] How can you say that? You don't know—

MURRAY: Don't I, though? Wait till you've been here three months or four. You'll see then!

EILEEN: [*Angrily, her lips trembling.*] You must be crazy to say such things! [*Fighting back her tears.*] Oh, I think it's hateful—when you see how badly I feel!

MURRAY: [*In acute confusion. Stammering.*] Look here, Miss Carmody, I didn't mean to— Listen—don't feel mad at me, please. I was only talking. I'm like that. You mustn't take it seriously.

EILEEN: [*Still resentful.*] I don't see how you can talk—when you've just said you had no family of your own, really.

MURRAY: [*Eager to return to her good graces.*] Of course I don't know. I was just talking regardless for the fun of it.

EILEEN: [*After a pause.*] Hasn't either of your sisters any children?

MURRAY: One of them has—two squally little brats.

EILEEN: [*Disapprovingly.*] You don't like babies?

MURRAY: [*Bluntly.*] No. [*Then with a grin at her shocked face.*] I don't get them. They're something I can't seem to get acquainted with.

EILEEN: [*With a smile, indulgently.*] You're a funny person. [*Then with a superior motherly air.*] No wonder you couldn't understand how badly I feel. [*With a tender smile.*] I've four of them—my brothers and sisters—though they're not what you'd call babies, except to me. I've been a mother to them now for a whole year—ever since our mother died. [*Sadly.*] And I don't know how they'll ever get along while I'm away.

MURRAY: [*Cynically.*] Oh, they'll— [*He checks what he was going to say and adds lamely.*] —get along somehow.

EILEEN: [*With the same superior tone.*] It's easy for you to say that. You don't know how children grow to depend on you for everything. You're not a woman.

MURRAY: [*With a grin.*] Are you? [*Then with a chuckle.*] You're as old as the pyramids, aren't you? I feel like a little boy. Won't you adopt me, too?

EILEEN: [*Flushing, with a shy smile.*] Someone ought to. [*Quickly changing the subject.*] Do you know, I can't get over what you said about hating your work so. I should think it would be wonderful—to be able to write things.

MURRAY: My job had nothing to do with writing. To write—really write—yes, that's something worth trying for. That's what I've always meant to have a stab at. I've run across ideas enough for stories—that sounded good to me, anyway. [*With a forced laugh*] But—like everything else—I never got down to it. I started one or two—but—either I thought I didn't have the time or— [*He shrugs his shoulders.*]

EILEEN: Well, you've plenty of time now, haven't you?

MURRAY: [*Instantly struck by this suggestion.*] You mean—I could write up here? [*She nods. His face lights up with enthusiasm.*] Say! That is an idea! Thank you! I'd never have had sense enough to have thought of that myself. [EILEEN *flushes with pleasure.*] Sure there's time—nothing but time up here—

EILEEN: Then you seriously think you'll try it?

MURRAY: [*Determinedly.*] Yes. Why not? I've got to try and do something real sometime, haven't I? I've no excuse not to, now. My mind isn't sick.

EILEEN: [*Excitedly.*] That'll be wonderful!

MURRAY: [*Confidently.*] Listen. I've had ideas for a series of short stories for the last couple of years—small town experiences, some of them actual. I know that life too darn well. I ought to be able to write about it. And if I can sell one—to the *Post*, say—I'm sure they'd take the others, too. And then— I should worry! It'd be easy sailing. But you must promise to help—play critic for me—read them and tell me where they're rotten.

EILEEN: [*Pleased but protesting.*] Oh, no, I'd never dare. I don't know anything—

MURRAY: Yes, you do. And you started me off on this thing, so you've got to back me up now. [*Suddenly.*] Say, I wonder if they'd let me have a typewriter up here?

EILEEN: It'd be fine if they would. I'd like to have one, too—to practice.

MURRAY: I don't see why they wouldn't allow it. You're not sick enough to be kept in bed, I'm sure of that.

EILEEN: I— I don't know—

MURRAY: Here! None of that! You just think you're not and you won't be. Say, I'm keen on that typewriter idea.

EILEEN: [*Eagerly.*] And I could type your stories after you've written them! I *could* help that way.

MURRAY: [*Smiling.*] But I'm quite able— [*Then seeing how interested she is he adds hurriedly.*] That'd be great! I've always been a bum at a machine. And I'd be willing to pay whatever— [MISS GILPIN *enters from the rear and walks toward them.*]

EILEEN: [*Quickly.*] Oh, no! I'd be glad to get the practice. I wouldn't accept— [*She coughs slightly.*]

MURRAY: [*With a laugh.*] Maybe, after you've read my stuff, you won't type it at any price.

MISS GILPIN: Miss Carmody, may I speak to you for a moment, please. [*She takes* EILEEN *aside and talks to her in low tones of admonition.* EILEEN's *face falls. She nods a horrified acquiescence.* MISS GILPIN *leaves her and goes into the office, rear.*]

MURRAY: [*As* EILEEN *comes back. Noticing her perturbation. Kindly.*] Well? Now, what's the trouble?

EILEEN: [*Her lips trembling.*] She told me I mustn't forget to shield my mouth with my handkerchief when I cough.

MURRAY: [*Consolingly.*] Yes, that's one of the rules, you know.

EILEEN: [*Falteringly.*] She said they'd give me—a—cup to carry around— [*She stops, shuddering.*]

MURRAY: [*Easily.*] It's not as bad as it sounds. They're only little paste-board things you carry in your pocket.

EILEEN: [*As if speaking to herself.*] It's so horrible. [*She holds out her hand to* MURRAY.] I'm to go to my room now. Good-night, Mr. Murray.

MURRAY: [*Holding her hand for a moment—earnestly.*] Don't mind your first impressions here. You'll look on everything as a matter of course in a few days. I felt your way at first. [*He drops her hand and shakes his finger at her.*] Mind your guardian, now! [*She forces a trembling smile.*] See you at breakfast. Good-night. [EILEEN *goes out to the hall in rear.* MISS HOWARD *comes in from the door just after her, carrying a glass of milk.*]

MISS HOWARD: Almost bedtime, Mr. Murray. Here's your diet. [*He takes the glass. She smiles at him provokingly.*] Well, is it love at first sight?

MURRAY: [*With a grin.*] Sure thing! You can consider yourself heartlessly jilted. [*He turns and raises his glass toward the door through which* EILEEN *has just gone, as if toasting her.*]

> "A glass of milk, and thou
>   Coughing beside me in the wilderness—
>   Ah—wilderness were Paradise enow!"

[*He takes a sip of milk.*]

MISS HOWARD: [*Peevishly.*] That's old stuff, Mr. Murray. A patient at Saranac wrote that parody.

MURRAY: [*Maliciously.*] Aha, you've discovered it's a parody, have you, you sly minx! [MISS HOWARD *turns from him huffily and walks back towards the office, her chin in the air.*]

[*The Curtain Falls*]

ACT TWO

SCENE ONE

The assembly room of the main building of the sanatorium—early in the morning of a fine day in June, four months later. The room is large, light and airy, painted a fresh white. On the left forward, an armchair. Farther back, a door opening on the main hall. To the rear of this door a pianola on a raised platform. In back of the pianola, a door leading into the office. In the rear wall, a long series of French windows looking out on the lawn, with wooded hills in the far background. Shrubs in flower grow immediately outside the windows. Inside, there is a row of potted plants. In the right wall, rear, four windows. Farther forward, a long, well-filled bookcase, and a doorway leading into the dining room. Following the walls, but about five feet out from them a stiff line of chairs placed closely against each other forms a sort of right-angled auditorium of which the large, square table that stands at center, forward, would seem to be the stage.

*From the dining room comes the clatter of dishes, the confused mur-
mur of many voices, male and female—all the mingled sounds of a
crowd of people at a meal.*

After the curtain rises, DOCTOR STANTON *enters from the hall, followed by a visitor,* MR. SLOAN, *and the assistant physician,* DOCTOR
SIMMS. DOCTOR STANTON *is a handsome man of forty-five or so with
a grave, care-lined, studious face lightened by a kindly, humorous smile.
His gray eyes, saddened by the suffering they have witnessed, have the
sympathetic quality of real understanding. The look they give is full of
companionship, the courage-renewing, human companionship of a
hope which is shared. He speaks with a slight Southern accent, soft and
slurring.* DOCTOR SIMMS *is a tall, angular young man with a long, sallow face and a sheepish, self-conscious grin.* MR. SLOAN *is fifty, short
and stout, well dressed—one of the successful business men whose en-
dowments have made the Hill Farm a possibility.*

STANTON: [*As they enter.*] This is the general assembly room, Mr.
Sloan—where the patients of both sexes are allowed to congregate
together after meals, for diets, and in the evening.

SLOAN: [*Looking around him.*] Couldn't be more pleasant, I must say.
[*He walks where he can take a peep into the dining room.*] Ah,
they're all at breakfast, I see.

STANTON: [*Smiling.*] Yes, and with no lack of appetite, let me tell you.
[*With a laugh of proud satisfaction.*] They'd sure eat us out of house
and home at one sitting, if we'd give them the opportunity.

SLOAN: [*With a smile.*] That's fine. [*With a nod toward the dining
room.*] The ones in there are the sure cures, aren't they?

STANTON: [*A shadow coming over his face.*] Strictly speaking, there are
no sure cures in this disease, Mr. Sloan. When we permit a patient to
return to take up his or her activities in the world, the patient is
what we call an arrested case. The disease is overcome, quiescent;
the wound is healed over. It's then up to the patient to so take care of
himself that this condition remains permanent. It isn't hard for them
to do this, usually. Just ordinary, bull-headed common sense—added
to what they've learned here—is enough. And the precautions we
teach them to take don't diminish their social usefulness in the slightest, either, as I can prove by our statistics of former patients. [*With a
smile.*] It's rather early in the morning for statistics, though.

MR. SLOAN: [*With a wave of the hand.*] Oh, you needn't. Your reputation in that respect, Doctor— [STANTON *inclines his head in ac-
knowledgment.* SLOAN *jerks his thumb toward the dining room.*]
But the ones in there *are* getting well, aren't they?

STANTON: To all appearances, yes. You don't dare swear to it, though. Sometimes, just when a case looks most favorable, there's a sudden, unforeseen breakdown and they have to be sent back to bed, or, if it's very serious, back to the Infirmary again. These are the exceptions, however, not the rule. You can bank on most of those eaters being out in the world and usefully employed within six months.

SLOAN: You couldn't say more than that. [*Abruptly.*] But—the unfortunate ones—do you have many deaths?

STANTON: [*With a frown.*] No. We're under a very hard, almost cruel imperative which prevents that. If, at the end of six months, a case shows no response to treatment, continues to go down hill—if, in a word, it seems hopeless—we send them away, to one of the State Farms if they have no private means. [*Apologetically.*] You see, this sanatorium is overcrowded and has a long waiting list most of the time of others who demand their chance for life. We have to make places for them. We have no time to waste on incurables. There are other places for them—and sometimes, too, a change is beneficial and they pick up in new surroundings. You never can tell. But we're bound by the rule. It may seem cruel—but it's as near justice to all concerned as we can come.

SLOAN: [*Soberly.*] I see. [*His eyes fall on the pianola—in surprise.*] Ah—a piano.

STANTON: [*Replying to the other's thought.*] Yes, the patients play and sing. [*With a smile.*] If you'd call the noise they make by those terms. They'd dance, too, if we permitted it. There's only one song taboo—Home, Sweet Home—for obvious reasons.

SLOAN: I see. [*With a final look around.*] Did I understand you to say this is the only place where the sexes are permitted to mingle?

STANTON: Yes, sir.

SLOAN: [*With a smile.*] Not much chance for a love affair, then.

STANTON: [*Seriously.*] We do our best to prevent them. We even have a strict rule which allows us to step in and put a stop to any intimacy which grows beyond the casual. People up here, Mr. Sloan, are expected to put aside all ideas except the one—getting well.

SLOAN: [*Somewhat embarrassed.*] A damn good rule, too, under the circumstances.

STANTON: [*With a laugh.*] Yes, we're strictly anti-Cupid, sir, from top to bottom. [*Turning to the door to the hall.*] And now, if you don't mind, Mr. Sloan, I'm going to turn you footloose to wander about the grounds on an unconducted tour. Today is my busy morning—Saturday. We weigh each patient immediately after breakfast.

SLOAN: Every week?

STANTON: Every Saturday. You see we depend on fluctuations in weight to tell us a lot about the patient's condition. If they gain, or stay at normal, all's usually well. If they lose week after week, we keep careful watch. It's a sign that something's wrong.

SLOAN: [*With a smile.*] Well, you just shoo me off wherever you please and go on with the good work. I'll be glad of a ramble in the open.

STANTON: After the weighing is over, sir, I'll be free to— [*His words are lost as the three go out. A moment later,* EILEEN *enters from the dining room. She has grown stouter, her face has more of a healthy, out-of-door color, but there is still about her the suggestion of being worn down by a burden too oppressive for her strength. She is dressed in shirtwaist and dark skirt. She goes to the armchair, left forward, and sinks down on it. She is evidently in a state of nervous depression; she twists her fingers together in her lap; her eyes stare sadly before her; she clenches her upper lip with her teeth to prevent its trembling. She has hardly regained control over herself when* STEPHEN MURRAY *comes in hurriedly from the dining room and, seeing her at his first glance, walks quickly over to her chair. He is the picture of health, his figure has filled out solidly, his tanned face beams with suppressed exultation.*]

MURRAY: [*Excitedly.*] Eileen! I saw you leave your table. I've something to tell you. I didn't get a chance last night after the mail came. Just listen, Eileen—it's too good to be true—but on that mail—guess what?

EILEEN: [*Forgetting her depression—with an excited smile.*] I know! You've sold your story!

MURRAY: [*Triumphantly.*] Go to the head of the class. What d'you know about that for luck! My first, too—and only the third magazine I sent it to! [*He cuts a joyful caper.*]

EILEEN: [*Happily.*] Isn't that wonderful, Stephen! But I knew all the time you would. The story's so good.

MURRAY: Well, you might have known but I didn't think there was a chance in the world. And as for being good— [*With superior air.*]— wait till I turn loose with the real big ones, the kind I'm going to write. Then I'll make them sit up and take notice. They can't stop me now. And I haven't told you the best part. The editor wrote saying how much he liked the yarn and asked me for more of the same kind.

EILEEN: And you've the three others about the same person—just as good, too! [*She claps her hands delightedly.*]

MURRAY: And I can send them out right away. They're all typed, thanks to you. That's what's brought me luck, I know. I never had a bit by myself. [*Then, after a quick glance around to make sure they are alone, he bends down and kisses her.*] There! A token of gratitude—even if it is against the rules.

EILEEN: [*Flushing—with timid happiness.*] Stephen! You mustn't! They'll see.

MURRAY: [*Boldly.*] Let them!

EILEEN: But you know—they've warned us against being so much together, already.

MURRAY: Let them! We'll be out of this prison soon. [EILEEN *shakes her head sadly but he does not notice.*] Oh, I wish you could leave when I do. We'd have some celebration together.

EILEEN: [*Her lips trembling.*] I was thinking last night—that you'd be going away. You look so well. Do you think—they'll let you go—soon?

MURRAY: You bet I do. I caught Stanton in the hall last night and asked him if I could go.

EILEEN: [*Anxiously.*] What did he say?

MURRAY: He only smiled and said: "We'll see if you gain weight tomorrow." As if that mattered now! Why, I'm way above normal as it is! But you know Stanton—always putting you off.

EILEEN: [*Slowly.*] Then—if you gain today—

MURRAY: He'll let me go. I'm going to insist on it.

EILEEN: Then—you'll leave—?

MURRAY: The minute I can get packed.

EILEEN: [*Trying to force a smile.*] Oh, I'm so glad—for your sake; but—I'm selfish—it'll be so lonely here without you.

MURRAY: [*Consolingly.*] You'll be going away yourself before long. [EILEEN *shakes her head. He goes on without noticing, wrapped in his own success.*] Oh, Eileen, you can't imagine all it opens up for me—selling that story. I can go straight to New York, and live, and meet real people who are doing things. I can take my time, and try and do the work I hope to. [*Feelingly.*] You don't know how grateful I am to you, Eileen—how you've helped me. Oh, I don't mean just the typing, I mean your encouragement, your faith! The stories would never have been written if it hadn't been for you.

EILEEN: [*Choking back a sob.*] I didn't do—anything.

MURRAY: [*Staring down at her—with rough kindliness.*] Here, here, that'll never do! You're not weeping about it, are you, silly? [*He pats her on the shoulder.*] What's the matter, Eileen? You didn't eat a thing this morning. I was watching you. [*With kindly severity.*] That's no way to gain weight you know. You'll have to feed up. Do you hear what your guardian commands, eh?

EILEEN: [*With dull hopelessness.*] I know I'll lose again. I've been losing steadily the past three weeks.

MURRAY: Here! Don't you dare talk that way! Why, you've been picking up wonderfully—until just lately. Even the old Doc has told you how much he admired your pluck, and how much better you were getting. You're not going to quit now, are you?

EILEEN: [*Despairingly.*] Oh, I don't care! I don't care—now.

MURRAY: Now? What do you mean by that? What's happened to make things any different?

EILEEN: [*Evasively.*] Oh—nothing. Don't ask me, Stephen.

MURRAY: [*With sudden anger.*] I don't have to ask you. I can guess. Another letter from home—or from that ass, eh?

EILEEN: [*Shaking her head.*] No, it isn't that. [*She looks at him as if imploring him to comprehend.*]

MURRAY: [*Furiously.*] Of course, you'd deny it. You always do. But don't you suppose I've got eyes? It's been the same damn thing all the time you've been here. After every nagging letter—thank God they don't write often any more!—you've been all in; and after their Sunday visits—you can thank God they've been few, too—you're utterly knocked out. It's a shame!

EILEEN: Stephen!

MURRAY: [*Relentlessly.*] They've done nothing but worry and torment you and do their best to keep you from getting well.

EILEEN: [*Faintly.*] You're not fair, Stephen.

MURRAY: Rot! When it isn't your father grumbling about expense, it's the kids, or that stupid housekeeper, or that slick Aleck, Nicholls, with his cowardly lies. Which is it this time?

EILEEN: [*Pitifully.*] None of them.

MURRAY: [*Explosively.*] But him, especially—the dirty cad! Oh, I've got a rich notion to pay a call on that gentleman when I leave and tell him what I think of him.

EILEEN: [*Quickly.*] No—you mustn't ever! He's not to blame. If you knew— [*She stops, lowering her eyes in confusion.*]

MURRAY: [*Roughly.*] Knew what? You make me sick, Eileen—always finding excuses for him. I never could understand what a girl like you could see— But what's the use? I've said all this before. You're wasting yourself on a— [*Rudely.*] Love must be blind. And yet you say you don't love him, really?

EILEEN: [*Shaking her head—helplessly.*] But I do—like Fred. We've been good friends so many years. I don't want to hurt him—his pride—

MURRAY: That's the same as answering no to my question. Then, if you don't love him, why don't you write and tell him to go to— break it off? [EILEEN *bows her head but doesn't reply. Irritated,* MURRAY *continues brutally.*] Are you afraid it would break his heart? Don't be a fool! The only way you could do that would be to deprive him of his meals.

EILEEN: [*Springing to her feet—distractedly.*] Please stop, Stephen! You're cruel! And you've been so kind—the only real friend I've had up here. Don't spoil it all now.

MURRAY: [*Remorsefully.*] I'm sorry, Eileen. I won't say another word. [*Irritably.*] Still someone ought to say or do something to put a stop to—

EILEEN: [*With a broken laugh.*] Never mind. Everything will stop— soon, now!

MURRAY: [*Suspiciously.*] What do you mean?

EILEEN: [*With an attempt at a careless tone.*] Nothing. If you can't see— [*She turns to him with sudden intensity.*] Oh, Stephen, if you only knew how wrong you are about everything you've said. It's all true; but it isn't that—any of it—any more— that's— Oh, I can't tell you!

MURRAY: [*With great interest.*] Please do, Eileen!

EILEEN: [*With a helpless laugh.*] No.

MURRAY: Please tell me what it is! Let me help you.

EILEEN: No. It wouldn't be any use, Stephen.

MURRAY: [*Offended.*] Why do you say that? Haven't I helped before?

EILEEN: Yes—but this—

MURRAY: Come now! 'Fess up! What is "this"?

EILEEN: No. I couldn't speak of it here, anyway. They'll all be coming out soon.

MURRAY: [*Insistently.*] Then when? Where?

EILEEN: Oh, I don't know—perhaps never, nowhere. I don't know— Sometime before you leave, maybe.

MURRAY: But I may go tomorrow morning—if I gain weight and Stanton lets me.

EILEEN: [*Sadly.*] Yes, I was forgetting—you were going right away. [*Dully.*] Then nowhere I suppose—never. [*Glancing toward the dining room.*] They're all getting up. Let's not talk about it any more—now.

MURRAY: [*Stubbornly.*] But you'll tell me later, Eileen? You must.

EILEEN: [*Vaguely.*] Perhaps. It depends— [*The patients, about forty in number, straggle in from the dining room by twos and threes, chatting in low tones. The men and women with few exceptions separate*

into two groups, the women congregating in the left right angle of
chairs, the men sitting or standing in the right right angle. In appearance, most of the patients are tanned, healthy, and cheerful looking.
The great majority are under middle age. Their clothes are of the
cheap, readymade variety. They are all distinctly of the wage-earning
class. They might well be a crowd of cosmopolitan factory workers
gathered together after a summer vacation. A hollow-chestedness
and a tendency to round shoulders may be detected as a common
characteristic. A general air of tension, marked by frequent bursts of
laughter in too high a key, seems to pervade the throng. MURRAY
and EILEEN, as if to avoid contact with the others, come over to the
right in front of the dining-room door.]

MURRAY: [In a low voice.] Listen to them laugh. Did you ever notice—
perhaps it's my imagination—how forced they act on Saturday
mornings before they're weighed?

EILEEN: [Dully.] No.

MURRAY: Can't you tell me that secret now? No one'll hear.

EILEEN: [Vehemently.] No, no, how could I? Don't speak of it! [A sudden silence falls on all the groups at once. Their eyes, by a common
impulse turn quickly toward the door to the hall.]

A WOMAN: [Nervously—as if this moment's silent pause oppressed her.]
Play something, Peters. They ain't coming yet. [PETERS, a stupid-
looking young fellow with a sly, twisted smirk which gives him the
appearance of perpetually winking his eye, detaches himself from a
group on the right. All join in with urging exclamations: "Go on,
Peters! Go to it! Pedal up, Pete! Give us a rag! That's the boy, Peters!" etc.]

PETERS: Sure, if I got time. [He goes to the pianola and puts in a roll.
The mingled conversation and laughter bursts forth again as he sits
on the bench and starts pedaling.]

MURRAY: [Disgustedly.] It's sure good to think I won't have to listen to
that old tin-pan being banged much longer! [The music interrupts
him—a quick rag. The patients brighten, hum, whistle, sway their
heads or tap their feet in time to the tune. DOCTOR STANTON and
DOCTOR SIMMS appear in the doorway from the hall. All eyes are
turned on them.]

STANTON: [Raising his voice.]—They all seem to be here, Doctor. We
might as well start. [MRS. TURNER, the matron, comes in behind
them—a stout, motherly, capable-looking woman with gray hair. She
hears STANTON's remark.]

MRS. TURNER: And take temperatures after, Doctor?

STANTON: Yes, Mrs. Turner. I think that's better today.

MRS. TURNER: All right, Doctor. [STANTON *and the assistant go out.* MRS. TURNER *advances a step or so into the room and looks from one group of patients to the other, inclining her head and smiling benevolently. All force smiles and nod in recognition of her greeting.* PETERS, *at the pianola, lets the music slow down, glancing questioningly at the matron to see if she is going to order it stopped. Then, encouraged by her smile, his feet pedal harder than ever.*]

MURRAY: Look at old Mrs. Grundy's eyes pinned on us! She'll accuse us of being too familiar again, the old wench!

EILEEN: Ssshh. You're wrong. She's looking at me, not at us.

MURRAY: At you? Why?

EILEEN: I ran a temperature yesterday. It must have been over a hundred last night.

MURRAY: [*With consoling scepticism.*] You're always suffering for trouble, Eileen. How do you know you ran a temp? You didn't see the stick, I suppose?

EILEEN: No—but—I could tell. I felt feverish and chilly. It must have been way up.

MURRAY: Bosh! If it was you'd have been sent to bed.

EILEEN: That's why she's looking at me. [*Piteously.*] Oh, I do hope I won't be sent back to bed! I don't know what I'd do. If I could only gain this morning. If my temp has only gone down! [*Hopelessly.*] But I feel— I didn't sleep a wink—thinking—

MURRAY: [*Roughly.*] You'll persuade yourself you've got leprosy in a second. Don't be a nut! It's all imagination, I tell you. You'll gain. Wait and see if you don't. [EILEEN *shakes her head. A metallic rumble and jangle comes from the hallway. Everyone turns in that direction with nervous expectancy.*]

MRS. TURNER: [*Admonishingly.*] Mr. Peters!

PETERS: Yes, ma'am. [*He stops playing and rejoins the group of men on the right. In the midst of a silence broken only by hushed murmurs of conversation,* DOCTOR STANTON *appears in the hall doorway. He turns to help his assistant wheel in a Fairbanks scale on castors. They place the scale against the wall immediately to the rear of the doorway.* DOCTOR SIMMS *adjusts it to a perfect balance.*]

DOCTOR STANTON: [*Takes a pencil from his pocket and opens the record book he has in his hand.*] All ready, Doctor?

DOCTOR SIMMS: Just a second, sir.

MURRAY: [*With a nervous smile.*] Well, we're all set. Here's hoping!

EILEEN: You'll gain, I'm sure you will. You look so well.

MURRAY: Oh—I—I wasn't thinking of myself, I'm a sure thing. I was betting on you. I've simply got to gain today, when so much depends on it.

EILEEN: Yes, I hope you— [*She falters brokenly and turns away from him.*]

DOCTOR SIMMS: [*Straightening up.*] All ready, Doctor.

STANTON: [*Nods and glances at his book—without raising his voice— distinctly.*] Mrs. Abner. [*A middle-aged woman comes and gets on the scales.* SIMMS *adjusts it to her weight of the previous week which* STANTON *reads to him from the book in a low voice, and weighs her.*]

MURRAY: [*With a relieved sigh.*] They're off. [*Noticing* EILEEN's *downcast head and air of dejection.*] Here! Buck up, Eileen! Old Lady Grundy's watching you—and it's your turn in a second. [EILEEN *raises her head and forces a frightened smile.* MRS. ABNER *gets down off the scales with a pleased grin. She has evidently gained. She rejoins the group of women, chattering volubly in low tones. Her exultant "gained half a pound" can be heard. The other women smile their perfunctory congratulations, their eyes absent-minded, intent on their own worries.* STANTON *writes down the weight in the book.*]

STANTON: Miss Bailey. [*A young girl goes to the scales.*]

MURRAY: Bailey looks badly, doesn't she?

EILEEN: [*Her lips trembling.*] She's been losing, too.

MURRAY: Well, *you're* going to gain today. Remember, now!

EILEEN: [*With a feeble smile.*] I'll try to obey your orders. [MISS BAILEY *gets down off the scales. Her eyes are full of despondency although she tries to make a brave face of it, forcing a laugh as she joins the women. They stare at her with pitying looks and murmur consoling phrases.*]

EILEEN: She's lost again. Oh, I wish I didn't have to get weighed—

STANTON: Miss Carmody. [EILEEN *starts nervously.*]

MURRAY: [*As she leaves him.*] Remember now! Break the scales! [*She walks quickly to the scales, trying to assume an air of defiant indifference. The balance stays down as she steps up.* EILEEN's *face shows her despair at this.* SIMMS *weighs her and gives the poundage in a low voice to* STANTON. EILEEN *steps down mechanically, then hesitates as if not knowing where to turn, her anguished eyes flitting from one group to another.*]

MURRAY: [*Savagely.*] Damn! [DOCTOR STANTON *writes the figures in his book, glances sharply at* EILEEN, *and then nods significantly to* MRS. TURNER *who is standing beside him.*]

STANTON: [*Calling the next.*] Miss Doeffler. [*Another woman comes to be weighed.*]

MRS. TURNER: Miss Carmody! Will you come here a moment, please?

EILEEN: [*Her face growing very pale.*] Yes, Mrs. Turner. [*The heads of the different groups bend together. Their eyes follow* EILEEN *as they whisper.* MRS. TURNER *leads her down front, left. Behind them the weighing of the women continues briskly. The great majority have gained. Those who have not have either remained stationary or lost a negligible fraction of a pound. So, as the weighing proceeds, the general air of smiling satisfaction rises among the groups of women. Some of them, their ordeal over, go out through the hall doorway by twos and threes with suppressed laughter and chatter. As they pass behind* EILEEN *they glance at her with pitying curiosity.* DOCTOR STANTON's *voice is heard at regular intervals calling the names in alphabetical order: Mrs. Elbing, Miss Finch, Miss Grimes, Miss Haines, Miss Hayes, Miss Jutner, Miss Linowski, Mrs. Marini, Mrs. McCoy, Miss McElroy, Miss Nelson, Mrs. Nott, Mrs. O'Brien, Mrs. Olson, Miss Paul, Miss Petrovski, Mrs. Quinn, Miss Robersi, Mrs. Stattler, Miss Unger.*]

MRS. TURNER: [*Putting her hand on* EILEEN's *shoulder—kindly.*] You're not looking so well, lately, my dear, do you know it?

EILEEN [*Bravely.*] I feel—fine. [*Her eyes, as if looking for encouragement, seek* MURRAY *who is staring at her worriedly.*]

MRS. TURNER: [*Gently.*] You lost weight again, you know.

EILEEN: I know—but—

MRS. TURNER: This is the fourth week.

EILEEN: I— I know it is—

MRS. TURNER: I've been keeping my eye on you. You seem—worried. Are you upset about—something we don't know?

EILEEN: [*Quickly.*] No, no! I haven't slept much lately. That must be it.

MRS. TURNER: Are you worrying about your condition? Is that what keeps you awake?

EILEEN: No.

MRS. TURNER: You're sure it's not that?

EILEEN: Yes, I'm sure it's not, Mrs. Turner.

MRS. TURNER: I was going to tell you if you were: Don't do it! You can't expect it to be all smooth sailing. Even the most favorable cases have to expect these little setbacks. A few days' rest in bed will start you on the right trail again.

EILEEN: [*In anguish, although she has realized this was coming.*] Bed? Go back to bed? Oh, Mrs. Turner!

MRS. TURNER: [*Gently.*] Yes, my dear, Doctor Stanton thinks it best. So when you go back to your cottage—

EILEEN: Oh, please—not today—not right away!

MRS. TURNER: You had a temperature and a high pulse yesterday, didn't you realize it? And this morning you look quite feverish. [*She tries to put her hand on* EILEEN'*s forehead but the latter steps away defensively.*]

EILEEN: It's only—not sleeping last night. Oh, I'm sure it'll go away.

MRS. TURNER: [*Consolingly.*] When you lie still and have perfect rest, of course it will.

EILEEN: [*With a longing look over at* MURRAY.] But not today—please, Mrs. Turner.

MRS. TURNER: [*Looking at her keenly.*] There is something upsetting you. You've something on your mind that you can't tell me, is that it? [EILEEN *maintains a stubborn silence.*] But think—*can't* you tell me? [*With a kindly smile.*] I'm used to other people's troubles. I've been playing mother-confessor to the patients for years now, and I think I've usually been able to help them. Can't you confide in me, child? [EILEEN *drops her eyes but remains silent.* MRS. TURNER *glances meaningly over at* MURRAY *who is watching them whenever he thinks the matron is not aware of it—a note of sharp rebuke in her voice.*] I think I can guess your secret. You've let other notions become more important to you than the idea of getting well. And you've no excuse for it. After I had to warn you a month ago, I expected *that* silliness to stop instantly.

EILEEN: [*Her face flushed—protesting.*] Nothing like that has anything to do with it.

MRS. TURNER: [*Sceptically.*] What is it that has, then?

EILEEN: [*Lying determinedly.*] It's my family. They keep writing—and worrying me—and— That's what it is, Mrs. Turner.

MRS. TURNER: [*Not exactly knowing whether to believe this or not—probing the girl with her eyes.*] Your father?

EILEEN: Yes, all of them. [*Suddenly seeing a way to discredit all of the matron's suspicions—excitedly.*] And principally the young man I'm engaged to—the one who came to visit me several times—

MRS. TURNER: [*Surprised.*] So—you're engaged? [EILEEN *nods.* MRS. TURNER *immediately dismisses her suspicions.*] Oh, pardon me. I didn't know that, you see, or I wouldn't— [*She pats* EILEEN *on the shoulder comfortingly.*] Never mind. You'll tell me all about it, won't you?

EILEEN: [*Desperately.*] Yes. [*She seems about to go on but the matron interrupts her.*]

MRS. TURNER: Oh, not here, my dear. Not now. Come to my room—let me see—I'll be busy all morning—sometime this afternoon. Will you do that?

EILEEN: Yes. [*Joyfully.*] Then I needn't go to bed right away?

MRS. TURNER: No—on one condition. You mustn't take any exercise. Stay in your recliner all day and rest and remain in bed tomorrow morning.

EILEEN: I promise, Mrs. Turner.

MRS. TURNER: [*Smiling in dismissal.*] Very well, then. I'll see you this afternoon.

EILEEN: Yes, Mrs. Turner. [*The matron goes to the rear where* MISS BAILEY *is sitting with* MRS. ABNER. *She beckons to* MISS BAILEY *who gets up with a scared look, and they go to the far left corner of the room.* EILEEN *stands for a moment hesitating—then starts to go to* MURRAY, *but just at this moment* PETERS *comes forward and speaks to* MURRAY.]

PETERS: [*With his sly twisted grin.*] Say, Carmody musta lost fierce. Did yuh see the Old Woman handin' her an earful? Sent her back to bed, I betcha. What d'yuh think?

MURRAY: [*Impatiently, showing his dislike.*] How the hell do I know?

PETERS: [*Sneeringly.*] Huh, you don't know nothin' 'bout her, I s'pose? Where d'yuh get that stuff?

MURRAY: [*With cold rage before which the other slinks away.*] If it wasn't for other people losing weight you couldn't get any joy out of life, could you? [*Roughly.*] Get away from me! [*He makes a threatening gesture.*]

PETERS: [*Beating a snarling retreat.*] Wait 'n' see if yuh don't lose too, yuh stuck-up boob! [*Seeing that* MURRAY *is alone again,* EILEEN *starts toward him but this time she is intercepted by* MRS. ABNER *who stops on her way out. The weighing of the women is now finished, and that of the men, which proceeds much quicker, begins.*]

DOCTOR STANTON: Anderson! [ANDERSON *comes to the scales. The men all move down to the left to wait their turn, with the exception of* MURRAY, *who remains by the dining room door, fidgeting impatiently, anxious for a word with* EILEEN.]

MRS. ABNER: [*Taking* EILEEN's *arm.*] Coming over to the cottage, dearie?

EILEEN: Not just this minute, Mrs. Abner. I have to wait—

MRS. ABNER: For the Old Woman? You lost today, didn't you? Is she sendin' you to bed, the old devil?

EILEEN: Yes, I'm afraid I'll have to—

MRS. ABNER: She's a mean one, ain't she? I gained this week—half a pound. Lord, I'm gettin' fat! All my clothes are gittin' too small for me. Don't know what I'll do. Did you lose much, dearie?

EILEEN: Three pounds.

MRS. ABNER: Ain't that awful! [*Hastening to make up for this thought-less remark.*] All the same, what's three pounds! You can git them back in a week after you're resting more. You've been runnin' a temp, too, ain't you? [EILEEN *nods.*] Don't worry about it, dearie. It'll go down. Worryin's the worst. Me, I don't never worry none. [*She chuckles with satisfaction—then soberly.*] I just been talkin' with Bailey. She's got to go to bed, too, I guess. She lost two pounds. She ain't runnin' no temp though.

STANTON: Barnes! [*Another man comes to the scales.*] MRS. ABNER: [*In a mysterious whisper.*] Look at Mr. Murray, dearie. Ain't he nervous today? I don't know as I blame him, either. I heard the doctor said he'd let him go home if he gained today. Is it true, d'you know?

EILEEN: [*Dully.*] I don't know.

MRS. ABNER: Gosh, I wish it was me! My old man's missin' me like the dickens, he writes. [*She starts to go.*] You'll be over to the cottage in a while, won't you? Me'n' you'll have a game of casino, eh?

EILEEN: [*Happy at this deliverance.*] Yes, I'll be glad to.

STANTON: Cordero! [MRS. ABNER *goes out.* EILEEN *again starts toward* MURRAY *but this time* FLYNN, *a young fellow with a brick-colored, homely, good-natured face, and a shaven-necked haircut, slouches back to* MURRAY. EILEEN *is brought to a halt in front of the table where she stands, her face working with nervous strain, clasping and unclasping her trembling hands.*]

FLYNN: [*Curiously.*] Say, Steve, what's this bull about the Doc lettin' yuh beat it if yuh gain today? Is it straight goods?

MURRAY: He said he might, that's all. [*Impatiently.*] How the devil did that story get traveling around?

FLYNN: [*With a grin.*] Wha' d'yuh expect with this gang of skirts chewin' the fat? Well, here's hopin' yuh come home a winner, Steve.

MURRAY: [*Gratefully.*] Thanks. [*With confidence.*] Oh, I'll gain all right; but whether he'll let me go or not— [*He shrugs his shoulders.*]

FLYNN: Make 'em behave. I wisht Stanton'd ask waivers on me. [*With a laugh.*] I oughter gain a ton today. I ate enough spuds for breakfast to plant a farm.

STANTON: Flynn!

FLYNN: Me to the plate! [*He strides to the scales.*]

MURRAY: Good luck! [*He starts to join* EILEEN *but* MISS BAILEY, *who has finished her talk with* MRS. TURNER, *who goes out to the hall, approaches* EILEEN *at just this moment.* MURRAY *stops in his tracks, fuming. He and* EILEEN *exchange a glance of helpless annoyance.*]

MISS BAILEY: [*Her thin face full of the satisfaction of misery finding company—plucks at* EILEEN's *sleeve.*] Say, Carmody, she sent you back to bed, too, didn't she?

EILEEN: [*Absent-mindedly.*] I suppose—

MISS BAILEY: You suppose? Of course she did. I got to go, too. [*Pulling* EILEEN's *sleeve.*] Come on. Let's get out of here. I hate this place, don't you?

STANTON: [*Calling the next.*] Hopper!

FLYNN: [*Shouts to* MURRAY *as he is going out to the hall.*] I hit 'er for a two-bagger, Steve. Come on now, Bo, and bring me home! 'Atta boy! [*Grinning gleefully, he slouches out.* DOCTOR STANTON *and all the patients laugh.*]

MISS BAILEY: [*With irritating persistence.*] Come on, Carmody. You've got to go to bed, too.

EILEEN: [*At the end of her patience—releasing her arm from the other's grasp.*] Let me alone, will you? I don't have to go to bed now—not till tomorrow morning.

MISS BAILEY: [*In a whining rage.*] Why not? You've been running a temp, too, and I haven't! You must have a pull, that's what! It isn't fair. I'll bet you lost more than I did, too! What right have you got— Well, I'm not going to bed if you don't. Wait 'n' see!

EILEEN: [*Turning away revolted.*] Go away! Leave me alone, please.

STANTON: Lowenstein!

MISS BAILEY: [*Turns to the hall door, whining.*] All right for you! I'm going to find out. It isn't square. I'll write home. [*She disappears in the hallway.* MURRAY *strides over to* EILEEN *whose strength seems to have left her and who is leaning weakly against the table.*]

MURRAY: Thank God—at last! Isn't it hell—all these fools! I couldn't get to you. What did Old Lady Grundy have to say to you? I saw her giving me a hard look. Was it about us—the old stuff? [EILEEN *nods with downcast eyes.*] What did she say? Never mind now. You can tell me in a minute. It's my turn next. [*His eyes glance toward the scales.*]

EILEEN: [*Intensely.*] Oh, Stephen, I wish you weren't going away!

MURRAY: [*Excitedly.*] Maybe I'm not. It's like gambling—if I win—

STANTON: Murray!

MURRAY: Wait here, Eileen. [*He goes to the scales.* EILEEN *keeps her back turned. Her body stiffens rigidly in the intensity of her conflicting emotions. She stares straight ahead, her eyes full of anguish.* MURRAY *steps on the scales nervously. The balance rod hits the top smartly. He has gained. His face lights up and he heaves a great sigh of relief.* EILEEN *seems to sense this outcome and her head sinks, her*

body sags weakly and seems to shrink to a smaller size. MURRAY
gets off the scales, his face beaming with a triumphant smile. DOC-
TOR STANTON *smiles and murmurs something to him in a low voice.*
MURRAY *nods brightly; then turns back to* EILEEN.]

STANTON: Nathan! [*Another patient advances to the scales.*]

MURRAY: [*Trying to appear casual.*] Well—three rousing cheers! Stanton told me to come to his office at eleven. That means a final
exam—and release!

EILEEN: [*Dully.*] So you gained?

MURRAY: Three pounds.

EILEEN: Funny—I lost three. [*With a pitiful effort at a smile.*] I hope
you gained the ones I lost. [*Her lips tremble.*] So you're surely going
away.

MURRAY: [*His joy fleeing as he is confronted with her sorrow—slowly.*]
It looks that way, Eileen.

EILEEN: [*In a trembling whisper broken by rising sobs.*] Oh—I'm so
glad—you gained—the ones I lost, Stephen— So glad! [*She breaks
down, covering her face with her hands, stifling her sobs.*]

MURRAY: [*Alarmed.*] Eileen! What's the matter? [*Desperately.*] Stop it!
Stanton'll see you!

[*The Curtain Falls*]

ACT TWO

SCENE TWO

*Midnight of the same day. A crossroads near the sanatorium. The
main road comes down forward from the right. A smaller road, leading
down from the left, joins it toward left, center.*

*Dense woods rise sheer from the grass and bramble-grown ditches at
the road's sides. At the junction of the two roads there is a signpost, its
arms pointing toward the right and the left, rear. A pile of round stones
is at the road corner, left forward. A full moon, riding high overhead,
throws the roads into white shadowless relief and masses the woods
into walls of compact blackness. The trees lean heavily together, their
branches motionless, unstirred by any trace of wind.*

As the curtain rises, EILEEN *is discovered standing in the middle of
the road, front center. Her face shows white and clear in the bright
moonlight as she stares with anxious expectancy up the road to the left.*

*Her body is fixed in an attitude of rigid immobility as if she were afraid
a slightest movement would break the spell of silence and awaken the
unknown. She has shrunk instinctively as far away as she can from the
mysterious darkness which rises at the road's sides like an imprisoning
wall. A sound of hurried footfalls, muffled by the dust, comes from the
road she is watching. She gives a startled gasp. Her eyes strain to iden-
tify the oncomer. Uncertain, trembling, with fright, she hesitates a second; then darts to the side of the road and crouches down in the
shadow.*

STEPHEN MURRAY *comes down the road from the left. He stops by
the sign post and peers about him. He wears a cap, the peak of which
casts his face into shadow. Finally he calls in a low voice:*

MURRAY: Eileen!

EILEEN: [*Coming out quickly from her hiding place—with a glad little
cry.*] Stephen! At last! [*She runs to him as if she were going to fling
her arms about him but stops abashed. He reaches out and takes her
hands.*]

MURRAY: It can't be twelve yet. [*He leads her to the pile of stones to the
left.*] I haven't heard the village clock.

EILEEN: I must have come early. It seemed as if I'd been waiting for
ages.

MURRAY: How your hands tremble! Were you frightened?

EILEEN: [*Forcing a smile.*] A little. The woods are so black and queer
looking. I'm all right now.

MURRAY: Sit down. You must rest. [*In a tone of annoyed reproof.*] I am
going to read you a lecture, young lady. You shouldn't ever have
done this—running a temp and— Good heavens, don't you want to
get well?

EILEEN: [*Dully.*] I don't know—

MURRAY: [*Irritably.*] You make me ill when you talk that way, Eileen. It
doesn't sound like you at all. What's come over you lately? I was—
knocked out—when I read the note you slipped me after supper. I
didn't get a chance to read it until late, I was so busy packing, and
by that time you'd gone to your cottage. If I could have reached you
any way I'd have refused to come here, I tell you straight. But I
couldn't—and I knew you'd be here waiting—and—still, I feel guilty.
Damn it, this isn't the thing for you! You ought to be in bed asleep.

EILEEN: [*Humbly.*] Please, Stephen, don't scold me.

MURRAY: How the devil did you ever get the idea—meeting me here at
this ungodly hour?

EILEEN: You'd told me about your sneaking out to go to the village, and I thought there'd be no harm this one night—the last night.

MURRAY: But I'm well. I've been well. It's different. You— Honest, Eileen, you shouldn't lose sleep and tax your strength.

EILEEN: Don't scold me, please. I'll make up for it. I'll rest all the time—after you're gone. I just had to see you some way. [*A clock in the distant village begins striking.*] Ssshh! Listen.

MURRAY: That's twelve now. You see I was early. [*In a pause of silence they wait motionlessly until the last mournful note dies in the hushed woods.*]

EILEEN: [*In a stifled voice.*] It isn't tomorrow now, is it? It's today—the day you're going.

MURRAY: [*Something in her voice making him avert his face and kick at the heap of stones on which she is sitting—brusquely.*] Well, I hope you took precautions so you wouldn't be caught sneaking out.

EILEEN: I did just what you'd told me you did—stuffed the pillows under the clothes so the watchman would think I was there.

MURRAY: None of the patients on your porch saw you leave, did they?

EILEEN: No. They were all asleep.

MURRAY: That's all right, then. I wouldn't trust any of that bunch of women. They'd be only too tickled to squeal on you. [*There is an uncomfortable pause.* MURRAY *seems waiting for her to speak. He looks about him at the trees, up into the moonlit sky, breathing in the fresh night air with a healthy delight.* EILEEN *remains with downcast head, staring at the road.*] It's beautiful tonight, isn't it? Worth losing sleep for.

EILEEN: [*Dully.*] Yes. [*Another pause—finally she murmurs faintly.*] Are you leaving early?

MURRAY: The ten-forty. Leave the San at ten, I guess.

EILEEN: You're going home?

MURRAY: Home? No. But I'm going to see my sisters—just to say hello. I've got to, I suppose.

EILEEN: I'm sure—I've often felt—you're unjust to your sisters. [*With conviction.*] I'm sure they must both love you.

MURRAY: [*Frowning.*] Maybe, in their own way. But what's love without a glimmer of understanding—a nuisance! They've never seen the real me and never wanted to.

EILEEN: [*As if to herself.*] What is—the real you? [MURRAY *kicks at the stones impatiently without answering.* EILEEN *hastens to change the subject.*] And then you'll go to New York?

MURRAY: [*Interested at once.*] Yes. You bet.

EILEEN: And write more?

MURRAY: Not in New York, no. I'm going there to take a vacation and really enjoy myself for a while. I've enough money for that as it is and if the other stories you typed sell—I'll be as rich as Rockefeller. I might even travel— No, I've got to make good with my best stuff first. I know what I'll do. When I've had enough of New York, I'll rent a place in the country—some old farmhouse—and live alone there and work. [*Lost in his own plans—with pleasure.*] That's the right idea, isn't it?

EILEEN: [*Trying to appear enthused.*] It ought to be fine for your work. [*After a pause.*] They're fine, those stories you wrote here. They're— so much like you. I'd know it was you wrote them even if—I didn't know.

MURRAY: [*Pleased.*] Wait till you read the others I'm going to do! [*After a slight pause—with a good-natured grin.*] Here I am talking about myself again! But you don't know how good it is to have your dreams coming true. It'd make an egotist out of anyone.

EILEEN: [*Sadly.*] No. I don't know. But I love to hear you talk of yours.

MURRAY: [*With an embarrassed laugh.*] Thanks. Well, I've certainly told you all of them. You're the only one— [*He stops and abruptly changes the subject.*] You said in your note that you had something important to tell me. [*He sits down beside her, crossing his legs.*] Is it about your interview with Old Mrs. Grundy this afternoon?

EILEEN: No, that didn't amount to anything. She seemed mad because I told her so little. I think she guessed I only told her what I did so she'd let me stay, maybe—your last day,—and to keep her from thinking what she did—about us.

MURRAY: [*Quickly, as if he wishes to avoid this subject.*] What is it you wanted to tell me, then?

EILEEN: [*Sadly.*] It doesn't seem so important now, somehow. I suppose it was silly of me to drag you out here, just for that. It can't mean anything to you—much.

MURRAY: [*Encouragingly.*] How do you know it can't?

EILEEN: [*Slowly.*] I only thought—you might like to know.

MURRAY: [*Interestedly.*] Know what? What is it? If I can help—

EILEEN: No. [*After a moment's hesitation.*] I wrote to him this afternoon.

MURRAY: Him?

EILEEN: The letter you've been advising me to write.

MURRAY: [*As if the knowledge of this alarmed him—haltingly.*] You mean—Fred Nicholls?

EILEEN: Yes.

MURRAY: [*After a pause—uncomfortably.*] You mean—you broke it all off?

EILEEN: Yes—for good. [*She looks up at his averted face. He remains silent. She continues apprehensively.*] You don't say anything. I thought—you'd be glad. You've always told me it was the honorable thing to do.

MURRAY: [*Gruffly.*] I know. I say more than my prayers, damn it! [*With sudden eagerness.*] Have you mailed the letter yet?

EILEEN: Yes. Why?

MURRAY: [*Shortly.*] Humph. Oh—nothing.

EILEEN: [*With pained disappointment.*] Oh, Stephen, you don't think I did wrong, do you—now—after all you've said?

MURRAY: [*Hurriedly.*] Wrong? No, not if you were convinced it was the right thing to do yourself—if you know you don't love him. But I'd hate to think you did it just on my say-so. I shouldn't— I didn't mean to interfere. I don't know enough about your relations for my opinion to count.

EILEEN: [*Hurt.*] You know all there is to know.

MURRAY: I know you've been frank. But him—I don't know him. He may be quite different from my idea. That's what I'm getting at. I don't want to be unfair to him.

EILEEN: [*Bitterly scornful.*] You needn't worry. You weren't unfair. And you needn't be afraid you were responsible for my writing. I'd been going to for a long time before you ever spoke.

MURRAY: [*With a relieved sigh.*] I'm glad of that—honestly, Eileen. I felt guilty. I shouldn't have knocked him behind his back without knowing him at all.

EILEEN: You said you could read him like a book from his letters I showed you.

MURRAY: [*Apolegetically.*] I know. I'm a fool.

EILEEN: [*Angrily.*] What makes you so considerate of Fred Nicholls all of a sudden? What you thought about him was right.

MURRAY: [*Vaguely.*] I don't know. One makes mistakes.

EILEEN: [*Assertively.*] Well, I know! You needn't waste pity on him. He'll be only too glad to get my letter. He's been anxious to be free of me ever since I was sent here, only he thought it wouldn't be decent to break it off himself while I was sick. He was afraid of what people would say about him when they found it out. So he's just gradually stopped writing and coming for visits, and waited for me to realize. And if I didn't, I know he'd have broken it off himself the first day I got home. I've kept persuading myself that, in spite of the way he's acted, he did love me as much as he could love anyone, and that it would hurt him if I— But now I know that he never loved me, that he couldn't love anyone but himself. Oh, I don't hate him for it. He can't help being what he is. And all people seem to be—like that, mostly. I'm only going to remember that he and I grew up together, and that he was kind to me then when he thought he liked me—and forget all the rest. [*With agitated impatience.*] Oh, Stephen, you know all this I've said about him. Why don't you admit it? You've read his letters.

MURRAY: [*Haltingly.*] Yes, I'll admit that was my opinion—only I wanted to be sure you'd found out for yourself.

EILEEN: [*Defiantly.*] Well, I have! You see that now, don't you?

MURRAY: Yes; and I'm glad you're free of him, for your own sake. I knew he wasn't the person. [*With an attempt at a joking tone.*] You must get one of the right sort—next time.

EILEEN: [*Springing to her feet with a cry of pain.*] Stephen! [*He avoids her eyes which search his face pleadingly.*]

MURRAY: [*Mumbling.*] He wasn't good enough—to lace your shoes— nor anyone else, either.

EILEEN: [*With a nervous laugh.*] Don't be silly. [*After a pause during which she waits hungrily for some words from him—with a sigh of despair—faintly.*] Well, I've told you—all there is. I might as well go back.

MURRAY: [*Not looking at her—indistinctly.*] Yes. You mustn't lose too much sleep. I'll come to your cottage in the morning to say good-by. They'll permit that, I guess.

EILEEN: [*Stands looking at him imploringly, her face convulsed with anguish, but he keeps his eyes fixed on the rocks at his feet. Finally she seems to give up and takes a few uncertain steps up the road toward the right—in an exhausted whisper.*] Good night, Stephen.

MURRAY: [*His voice choked and husky.*] Good night, Eileen.

EILEEN: [*Walks weakly up the road but, as she passes the signpost, she suddenly stops and turns to look again at* MURRAY *who has not moved or lifted his eyes. A great shuddering sob shatters her pent-up emotions. She runs back to* MURRAY, *her arms outstretched, with a choking cry.*] Stephen!

MURRAY: [*Startled, whirls to face her and finds her arms thrown around his neck—in a terrified tone.*] Eileen!

EILEEN: [*Brokenly.*] I love you, Stephen—you! That's what I wanted to tell! [*She gazes up into his eyes, her face transfigured by the joy and pain of this abject confession.*]

MURRAY: [*Wincing as if this were the thing he had feared to hear.*] Eileen!

EILEEN: [*Pulling down his head with fierce strength and kissing him passionately on the lips.*] I love you! I will say it! There! [*With sudden horror.*] Oh, I know I shouldn't kiss you! I mustn't! You're all well—and I—

MURRAY: [*Protesting frenziedly.*] Eileen! Damn it! Don't say that! What do you think I am! [*He kisses her fiercely two or three times until she forces a hand over her mouth.*]

EILEEN: [*With a hysterically happy laugh.*] No! Just hold me in your arms—just a little while—before—

MURRAY: [*His voice trembling.*] Eileen! Don't talk that way! You're—it's killing me. I can't stand it!

EILEEN: [*With soothing tenderness.*] Listen, dear—listen—and you won't say a word— I've so much to say—till I get through—please, will you promise?

MURRAY: [*Between clenched teeth.*] Yes—anything, Eileen!

EILEEN: Then I want to say—I know your secret. You don't love me— Isn't that it? [MURRAY *groans.*] Ssshh! It's all right, dear. You can't help what you don't feel. I've guessed you didn't—right along. And I've loved you—such a long time now—always, it seems. And you've sort of guessed—that I did—didn't you? No, don't speak! I am sure you've guessed—only you didn't want to know—that—did you?— when you didn't love me. That's why you were lying—but I saw, I knew! Oh, I'm not blaming you, darling. How could I—never! You mustn't look so—so frightened. I know how you felt, dear. I've—I've watched you. It was just a flirtation for you at first. Wasn't it? Oh, I know. It was just fun, and— Please don't look at me so. I'm not hurting you, am I? I wouldn't for worlds, dear—you know—hurt you! And then afterwards—you found we could be such good friends—helping each other—and you wanted it to stay just like that always, didn't you?—I know—and then I had to spoil it all—and fall in love with you—didn't I? Oh, it was stupid— I shouldn't—I couldn't help it, you were so kind and—and different—and I wanted to share in your work and—and everything. I knew you wouldn't want to know I loved you—when you didn't—and I tried hard to be fair and hide my love so you wouldn't see—and I did, didn't I, dear? You never knew till just lately—maybe not till just today—did you?—when I knew you were going away so soon—and couldn't help showing it. You never knew before, did you? Did you?

MURRAY: [*Miserably.*] No. Oh, Eileen—Eileen, I'm so sorry!

EILEEN: [*In heart-broken protest.*] Sorry? Oh no, Stephen, you mustn't be! It's been beautiful—all of it—for me! That's what makes your going— so hard. I had to see you tonight—I'd have gone—crazy—if I didn't know you knew, if I hadn't made you guess. And I thought— if you knew about my writing to Fred—that—maybe—it'd make some difference. [MURRAY *groans—and she laughs hysterically.*] I must have been crazy—to think that—mustn't I? As if that could— when you don't love me. Sshh! Please! Let me finish. You mustn't feel sad—or anything. It's made me happier than I've ever been— loving you—even when I did know—you didn't. Only now—you'll forgive me telling you all this, won't you, dear? Now, it's so terrible to think I won't see you any more. I'll feel so—without anybody.

MURRAY: [*Brokenly.*] But I'll—come back. And you'll be out soon—and then—

EILEEN: [*Brokenly.*] Sshh! Let me finish. You don't know how alone I am now. Father—he'll marry that housekeeper—and the children— they've forgotten me. None of them need me any more. They've found out how to get on without me—and I'm a drag—dead to them—no place for me home any more—and they'll be afraid to have me back—afraid of catching—I know she won't want me back. And Fred—he's gone—he never mattered, anyway. Forgive me, dear—worrying you—only I want you to know how much you've meant to me—so you won't forget—ever—after you've gone.

MURRAY: [*In grief-stricken tones.*] Forget? Eileen! I'll do anything in God's world—

EILEEN: I know—you like me a lot even if you can't love me—don't you? [*His arms tighten about her as he bends down and forces a kiss on her lips again.*] Oh, Stephen! That was for good-by. You mustn't come tomorrow morning. I couldn't bear having you—with people watching. But you'll write after—often—won't you? [*Heart-brokenly.*] Oh, please do that, Stephen!

MURRAY: I will! I swear! And when you get out I'll—we'll—I'll find something— [*He kisses her again.*]

EILEEN: [*Breaking away from him with a quick movement and stepping back a few feet.*] Good-by, darling. Remember me—and perhaps— you'll find out after a time—I'll pray God to make it so! Oh, what am I saying? Only—I'll hope—I'll hope—till I die!

MURRAY: I*in anguish.*] Eileen!

EILEEN: [*Her breath coming in tremulous heaves of her bosom.*] Remember, Stephen—if ever you want—I'll do anything—anything you want—no matter what—I don't care—there's just you and—don't hate me, dear. I love you—love you—remember! [*She suddenly turns and runs away up the road.*]

MURRAY: Eileen! [*He starts to run after her but stops by the signpost and stamps on the ground furiously, his fists clenched in impotent rage at himself and at Fate.*] Christ!

[*The Curtain Falls*]

ACT THREE

SCENE—*Four months later. An isolation room at the Infirmary with a sleeping porch at the right of it. Late afternoon of a Sunday toward the end of October. The room, extending two-thirds of the distance from left to right, is, for reasons of space economy, scantily furnished with the bare necessities—a bureau with mirror in the left corner, rear—two straight-backed chairs—a table with a glass top in the center. The floor is varnished hardwood. The walls and furniture are painted white. On the left, forward, a door to the hallway. On the right, rear, a double glass door opening on the porch. Farther front two windows. The porch, a screened-in continuation of the room, contains only a single iron bed painted white, and a small table placed beside the bed.*

The woods, the leaves of the trees rich in their autumn coloring, rise close about this side of the Infirmary. Their branches almost touch the porch on the right. In the rear of the porch they have been cleared away from the building for a narrow space, and through this opening the distant hills can be seen with the tree tops glowing in the sunlight.

As the curtain rises, EILEEN *is discovered lying in the bed on the porch, propped up into a half-sitting position by pillows under her back and head. She seems to have grown much thinner. Her face is pale and drawn with deep hollows under her cheek-bones. Her eyes are dull and lusterless. She gazes straight before her into the wood with the unseeing stare of apathetic indifference. The door from the hall in the room behind her is opened and* MISS HOWARD *enters followed by* BILL CAR-MODY, MRS. BRENNAN, *and* MARY. CARMODY's *manner is unwontedly sober and subdued. This air of respectable sobriety is further enhanced by a black suit, glaringly new and stiffly pressed, a new black derby hat, and shoes polished like a mirror. His expression is full of a bitter, if suppressed, resentment. His gentility is evidently forced upon him in spite of himself and correspondingly irksome.* MRS. BRENNAN *is a tall, stout woman of fifty, lusty and loud-voiced, with a broad, snub-nosed, florid* face, a large mouth, the upper lip darkened by a suggestion of mustache, and little round blue eyes, hard and restless with a continual fuming irritation. She is got up regardless in her ridiculous Sunday-best. MARY appears tall and skinny-legged in a starched, outgrown frock. The sweetness of her face has disappeared, giving way to a hangdog sullenness, a stubborn silence, with sulky, furtive glances of rebellion directed at her stepmother.

MISS HOWARD: [Pointing to the porch.] She's out there on the porch.

MRS. BRENNAN: [With dignity.] Thank you, ma'am.

MISS HOWARD: [With a searching glance at the visitors as if to appraise their intentions.] Eileen's been very sick lately, you know, so be careful not to worry her about anything. Do your best to cheer her up.

CARMODY: [Mournfully.] We'll try to put life in her spirits, God help her. [With an uncertain look at MRS. BRENNAN.] Won't we, Maggie?

MRS. BRENNAN: [Turning sharply on MARY who has gone over to examine the things on the bureau.] Come away from that, Mary. Curiosity killed a cat. Don't be touchin' her things. Remember what I told you. Or is it admirin' your mug in the mirror you are? [Turning to MISS HOWARD as MARY moves away from the bureau, hanging her head—shortly.] Don't you worry, ma'am. We won't trouble Eileen at all.

MISS HOWARD: Another thing. You mustn't say anything to her of what Miss Gilpin just told you about her being sent away to the State Farm in a few days. Eileen isn't to know till the very last minute. It would only disturb her.

CARMODY: [Hastily.] We'll not say a word of it.

MISS HOWARD: [Turning to the hall door.] Thank you. [She goes out, shutting the door.]

MRS. BRENNAN: [Angrily.] She has a lot of impudent gab, that one, with her don't do this and don't do that! [Gazing about the room critically.] Two sticks of chairs and a table! They don't give much for the money.

CARMODY: Catch them! It's a good thing she's clearin' out of this and her worse off after them curin' her eight months than she was when she came. She'll maybe get well in the new place.

MRS. BRENNAN: [Indifferently.] It's God will, what'll happen. [Irritably.] And I'm thinkin' it's His punishment she's under now for having no heart in her and never writin' home a word to you or the children in two months or more. If the doctor hadn't wrote us himself to come see her, we'd have been no wiser.

CARMODY: Whisht. Don't be blamin' a sick girl.

MARY: [*Who has drifted to one of the windows at right—curiously.*] There's somebody in bed out there. Is it Eileen?

MRS. BRENNAN: Don't be goin' out there till I tell you, you imp! [*Coming closer to him and lowering her voice.*] Are you going to tell her about it?

CARMODY: [*Pretending ignorance.*] About what?

MRS. BRENNAN: About what, indeed! About our marryin' two weeks back, of course. What else?

CARMODY: [*Uncertainly.*] Yes—I disremembered she didn't know. I'll have to tell her, surely.

MRS. BRENNAN: [*Flaring up.*] You speak like you wouldn't. Are you afraid of a slip of a girl? Well, then, I'm not! I'll tell her to her face soon enough.

CARMODY: [*Angry in his turn—assertively.*] You'll not, now! Keep your mouth out of this and your rough tongue! I tell you I'll tell her.

MRS. BRENNAN: [*Satisfied.*] Let's be going out to her, then. [*They move toward the door to the porch.*] And keep your eye on your watch. We mustn't miss the train. Come with us, Mary, and remember to keep your mouth shut. [*They go out on the porch and stand just outside the door waiting for* EILEEN *to notice them; but the girl in bed continues to stare into the woods, oblivious to their presence.*]

MRS. BRENNAN: [*Nudging* CARMODY *with her elbow—in a harsh whisper.*] Glory be, it's bad she's lookin'. The look on her face'd frighten you. Speak to her, you! [EILEEN *stirs uneasily as if this whisper had disturbed her unconsciously.*]

CARMODY: [*Wetting his lips and clearing his throat huskily.*] Eileen.

EILEEN: [*Startled, turns and stares at them with frightened eyes. After a pause she ventures uncertainly as if she were not sure but what these figures might be creatures of her dream.*] Father. [*Her eyes shift to* MRS. BRENNAN'*s face and she shudders.*] Mrs. Brennan.

MRS. BRENNAN: [*Quickly—in a voice meant to be kindly.*] Here we are, all of us, come to see you. How is it you're feelin' now, Eileen? [*While she is talking she advances to the bedside, followed by* CARMODY, *and takes one of the sick girl's hands in hers.* EILEEN *withdraws it as if stung and holds it out to her father.* MRS. BRENNAN'*s face flushes angrily and she draws back from the bedside.*]

CARMODY: [*Moved—with rough tenderness patting her hand.*] Ah, Eileen, sure it's a sight for sore eyes to see you again! [*He bends down as if to kiss her, but, struck by a sudden fear, hesitates, straightens himself, and shamed by the understanding in* EILEEN'*s *eyes, grows red and stammers confusedly.*] How are you now? Sure it's the picture of health you're lookin'. [EILEEN *sighs and turns her eyes away from his with a resigned sadness.*]

MRS. BRENNAN: What are you standin' there for like a stick, Mary? Haven't you a word to say to your sister?

EILEEN: [*Twisting her head around and seeing* MARY *for the first time—with a glad cry.*] Mary! I—why I didn't see you before! Come here. [MARY *approaches gingerly with apprehensive side glances at* MRS. BRENNAN *who watches her grimly.* EILEEN's *arms reach out for her hungrily. She grasps her about the waist and seems trying to press the unwilling child to her breast.*]

MARY: [*Fidgeting nervously—suddenly in a frightened whine.*] Let me go! [EILEEN *releases her, looks at her face dazedly for a second, then falls back limply with a little moan and shuts her eyes.* MARY, *who has stepped back a pace, remains fixed there as if fascinated with fright by her sister's face. She stammers.*] Eileen—you look so—so funny.

EILEEN: [*Without opening her eyes—in a dead voice.*] You, too! I never thought you— Go away, please.

MRS. BRENNAN: [*With satisfaction.*] Come here to me, Mary, and don't be botherin' your sister. [MARY *avoids her stepmother but retreats to the far end of the porch where she stands shrunk back against the wall, her eyes fixed on* EILEEN *with the same fascinated horror.*]

CARMODY: [*After an uncomfortable pause, forcing himself to speak.*] Is the pain bad, Eileen?

EILEEN: [*Dully—without opening her eyes.*] There's no pain. [*There is another pause—then she murmurs indifferently.*] There are chairs in the room you can bring out if you want to sit down.

MRS. BRENNAN: [*Sharply.*] We've not time to be sittin'. We've the train back to catch.

EILEEN: [*In the same lifeless voice.*] It's a disagreeable trip. I'm sorry you had to come.

CARMODY: [*Fighting against an oppression he cannot understand, bursts into a flood of words.*] Don't be talking of the trip. Sure we're glad to take it to get a sight of you. It's three months since I've had a look at you and I was anxious. Why haven't you written a line to us? You could do that without trouble, surely. Don't you ever think of us at all any more? [*He waits for an answer but* EILEEN *remains silent with her eyes closed.* CARMODY *starts to walk up and down talking with an air of desperation.*] You're not asking a bit of news from home. I'm thinkin' the people out here have taken all the thought of us out of your head. We're all well, thank God. I've another good job on the streets from Murphy and one that'll last a long time, praise be! I'm needin' it surely, with all the expenses—but no matter. Billy had a raise from his old skinflint of a boss a month back. He's gettin' seven a week now and proud as a turkey. He was comin' out with us today but he'd a date with his girl. Sure, he's got a girl now, the young bucko! What d'you think of him? It's old Malloy's girl he's after—the pop-eyed one with glasses, you remember—as ugly as a blind sheep, only he don't think so. He said to give you his love. [EILEEN *stirs and sighs wearily, a frown appearing for an instant on her forehead.*] And Tom and Nora was comin' out too, but Father Fitz had some doin's or other up to the school, and he told them to be there, so they wouldn't come with us, but they sent their love to you too. They're growin' so big you'd not know them. Tom's no good at the school. He's like Billy was. I've had to take the strap to him often. He's always playin' hooky and roamin' the streets. And Nora— [*With pride.*] There's the divil for you! Up to everything she is and no holdin' her high spirits. As pretty as a picture, and the smartest girl in her school, Father Fitz says. Am I lyin', Maggie?

MRS. BRENNAN: [*Grudgingly.*] She's smart enough—and too free with her smartness.

CARMODY: [*Pleased.*] Ah, don't be talkin! She'll know more than the lot of us before she's grown even. [*He pauses in his walk and stares down at* EILEEN, *frowning.*] Are you sick, Eileen, that you're keepin' your eyes shut without a word out of you?

EILEEN: [*Wearily.*] No. I'm tired, that's all.

CARMODY: [*Resuming his walk.*] And who else is there, let me think? Oh, Mary—she's the same as ever, you can see for yourself.

EILEEN: [*Bitterly.*] The same? Oh, no!

CARMODY: She's grown, you mean? I suppose. You'd notice, not seeing her so long? [*He can think of nothing else to say but walks up and down with a restless, uneasy expression.*]

MRS. BRENNAN: [*Sharply.*] What time is it gettin'?

CARMODY: [*Fumbles for his watch.*] Half past four, a bit after.

MRS. BRENNAN: We'll have to leave soon. It's a long jaunt down the hill in that buggy. [*She catches his eye and makes violent signs to him to tell* EILEEN *what he has come to tell.*]

CARMODY: [*After an uncertain pause—clenching his fists and clearing his throat.*] Eileen.

EILEEN: Yes.

CARMODY: [*Irritably.*] Can't you open your eyes on me? It's like talkin' to myself I am.

EILEEN: [*Looking at him—dully.*] What is it?

CARMODY: [*Stammering—avoiding her glance.*] It's this, Eileen—me and Maggie—Mrs. Brennan, that is—we—

EILEEN: [*Without surprise.*] You're going to marry her?

CARMODY: [*With an effort.*] Not goin' to. It's done.

EILEEN: [*Without a trace of feeling.*] Oh, so you've been married already? [*Without further comment, she closes her eyes.*]

CARMODY: Two weeks back we were, by Father Fitz. [*He stands staring down at his daughter, irritated, perplexed and confounded by her silence, looking as if he longed to shake her.*]

MRS. BRENNAN: [*Angry at the lack of enthusiasm shown by* EILEEN.] Let us get out of this, Bill. It's little she's caring about you, and little thanks she has for all you've done for her and the money you've spent.

CARMODY: [*With a note of pleading.*] Is that a proper way to be treatin' your father, Eileen, after what I've told you? Is it nothin' to you you've a good, kind woman now for mother?

EILEEN: [*Fiercely, her eyes flashing open on him.*] No, No! Never!

MRS. BRENNAN: [*Plucking at* CARMODY's *elbow. He stands looking at* EILEEN *helplessly, his mouth open, a guilty flush spreading over his face.*] Come out of here, you big fool, you! Is it to listen to insults to your livin' wife you're waiting?

CARMODY: [*Turning on her threateningly.*] Will you shut your gab?

EILEEN: [*With a moan.*] Oh, go away. Father! Please! Take her away!

MRS. BRENNAN: [*Pulling at his arm.*] Take me away this second or I'll never speak again to you till the day I die!

CARMODY: [*Pushes her violently away from him—raging, his fist uplifted.*] Shut your gab, I'm saying!

MRS. BRENNAN: The devil mend you and yours then! I'm leavin' you. [*She starts for the door.*]

CARMODY: [*Hastily.*] Wait a bit, Maggie. I'm coming. [*She goes into the room, slamming the door, but once inside she stands still, trying to listen.* CARMODY *glares down at his daughter's pale twitching face with closed eyes. Finally he croaks in a whining tone of fear.*] Is your last word a cruel one to me this day, Eileen? [*She remains silent. His face darkens. He turns and strides out of the door.* MARY *darts after him with a frightened cry of* "Papa." EILEEN *covers her face with her hands and a shudder of relief runs over her body.*]

MRS. BRENNAN: [*As* CARMODY *enters the room—in a mollified tone.*] So you've come, have you? Let's go, then! [CARMODY *stands looking at her in silence, his expression full of gloomy rage. She bursts out impatiently.*] Are you comin' or are you goin' back to her? [*She grabs*

MARY's *arm and pushes her toward the door to the hall.*] Are you comin' or not. I'm asking?

CARMODY: [*Somberly—as if to himself.*] There's something wrong in the whole of this—that I can't make out. [*With sudden fury he brandishes his fists as though defying someone and growls threateningly.*] And I'll get drunk this night—dead, rotten drunk! [*He seems to detect disapproval in* MRS. BRENNAN's *face for he shakes his fist at her and repeats like a solemn oath.*] I'll get drunk if my soul roasts for it—and no one in the whole world is strong enough to stop me! [MRS. BRENNAN *turns from him with a disgusted shrug of her shoulders and hustles* MARY *out of the door.* CARMODY, *after a second's pause, follows them.* EILEEN *lies still, looking out into the woods with empty, desolate eyes.* MISS HOWARD *comes into the room from the hall and goes to the porch, carrying a glass of milk in her hand.*]

MISS HOWARD: Here's your diet, Eileen. I forgot it until just now. Did you have a nice visit with your folks?

EILEEN: [*Forcing a smile.*] Yes.

MISS HOWARD: I hope they didn't worry you over home affairs?

EILEEN: No. [*She sips her milk and sets it back on the table with a shudder of disgust.*]

MISS HOWARD: [*With a smile.*] What a face! You'd think you were taking poison.

EILEEN: [*With deep passion.*] I wish it was poison!

MISS HOWARD: [*Jokingly.*] Oh, come now! That isn't a nice way to feel on the Sabbath. [*With a meaning smile.*] I've some news that'll cheer you up, I bet. [*Archly.*] Guess who's here on a visit?

EILEEN: [*Startled—in a frightened whisper.*] Who?

MISS HOWARD: Mr. Murray. [EILEEN *closes her eyes wincingly for a moment and a shadow of pain comes over her face.*] He came just about the time your folks did. I saw him for a moment, not to speak to. [*Beaming—with a certain curiosity.*] What do you think of that for news?

EILEEN: [*Trying to conceal her agitation and assume a casual tone.*] He must have come to be examined.

MISS HOWARD: [*With a meaning laugh.*] Oh, I'd hardly say that was his main reason. [*In business-like tones.*] Well, I've got to get back on the job. [*She turns to the door calling back jokingly.*] He'll be in to see you of course, so look your prettiest. [*She goes out and shuts the door to the porch.* EILEEN *gives a frightened gasp and struggles up in bed as if she wanted to call the nurse to return. Then she lies back in a state of great nervous excitement, twisting her head with eager, fearful glances toward the door, listening, clasping and unclasping her thin fingers on the white spread. As* MISS HOWARD *walks across the room to the hall door, it is opened and* STEPHEN MURRAY *enters. A great change is visible in his face. It is much thinner and the former healthy tan has faded to a sallow pallor. Puffy shadows of sleeplessness and dissipation are marked under his heavy-lidded eyes. He is dressed in a well-fitting, expensive, dark suit, a white shirt with a soft collar and bright-colored tie.*]

MISS HOWARD: [*With pleased surprise, holding out her hand.*] Hello, Mr. Murray.

MURRAY: [*Shaking her hand—with a forced pleasantness.*] How are you, Miss Howard?

MISS HOWARD: Fine as ever. It certainly looks natural to see you around here again—not that I hope you're here to stay, though. [*With a smile.*] I suppose you're on your way to Eileen now. Well, I won't keep you. I've oodles of work to do. [*She opens the hall door. He starts for the porch.*] Oh, I was forgetting—Congratulations! I've read those stories—all of us have. They're great. We're all so proud of you. You're one of our graduates, you know.

MURRAY: [*Indifferently.*] Oh,—that stuff.

MISS HOWARD: [*Gayly.*] Don't be so modest. Well, see you later, I hope.

MURRAY: Yes. Doctor Stanton invited me to stay for supper and I may—

MISS HOWARD: Fine! Be sure to! [*She goes out.* MURRAY *walks to porch door and steps out. He finds* EILEEN's *eyes waiting for him. As their eyes meet she gasps involuntarily and he stops short in his tracks. For a moment they remain looking at each other in silence.*]

EILEEN: [*Dropping her eyes—faintly.*] Stephen.

MURRAY: [*Much moved, strides to her bedside and takes her hands awkwardly.*] Eileen. [*Then after a second's pause in which he searches her face and is shocked by the change illness has made—anxiously.*] How are you feeling, Eileen? [*He grows confused by her gaze and his eyes shift from hers, which search his face with wild yearning.*]

EILEEN: [*Forcing a smile.*] Oh, I'm all right. [*Eagerly.*] But you, Stephen? How are you? [*Excitedly.*] Oh, it's good to see you again! [*Her eyes continue fixed on his face pleadingly, questioningly.*]

MURRAY: [*Haltingly.*] And it's sure great to see you again, Eileen. [*He releases her hand and turns away.*] And I'm fine and dandy. I look a little done up, I guess, but that's only the result of too much New York.

EILEEN: [*Sensing from his manner that whatever she has hoped for from his visit is not to be, sinks back on the pillows, shutting her eyes hopelessly, and cannot control a sigh of pain.*]

MURRAY: [*Turning to her anxiously.*] What's the matter, Eileen? You're not in pain, are you?

EILEEN: [*Wearily.*] No.

MURRAY: You haven't been feeling badly lately, have you? Your letters suddenly stopped—not a line for the past three weeks—and I—

EILEEN: [*Bitterly.*] I got tired of writing and never getting any answer, Stephen.

MURRAY: [*Shame-faced.*] Come, Eileen, it wasn't as bad as that. You'd think I never—and I did write, didn't I?

EILEEN: Right after you left here, you did, Stephen. Lately—

MURRAY: I'm sorry, Eileen. It wasn't that I didn't mean to—but—in New York it's so hard. You start to do one thing and something else interrupts you. You never seem to get any one thing done when it ought to be. You can understand that, can't you, Eileen?

EILEEN: [*Sadly.*] Yes. I understand everything now.

MURRAY: [*Offended.*] What do you mean by everything? You said that so strangely. You mean you don't believe— [*But she remains silent with her eyes shut. He frowns and takes to pacing up and down beside the bed.*] Why have they got you stuck out here on this isolation porch, Eileen?

EILEEN: [*Dully.*] There was no room on the main porch, I suppose.

MURRAY: You never mentioned in any of your letters—

EILEEN: It's not very cheerful to get letters full of sickness. I wouldn't like to, I know.

MURRAY: [*Hurt.*] That isn't fair, Eileen. You know I— How long have you been back in the Infirmary?

EILEEN: About a month.

MURRAY: [*Shocked.*] A month! But you were up and about—on exercise, weren't you—before that?

EILEEN: No. I had to stay in bed while I was at the cottage.

MURRAY: You mean—ever since that time they sent you back—the day before I left?

EILEEN: Yes.

MURRAY: But I thought from the cheery tone of your letters that you were—

EILEEN: [*Uneasily.*] Getting better? I am, Stephen. I'm strong enough to be up now but Doctor Stanton wants me to take a good long rest this time so that when I get up again I'll be sure— [*She breaks off impatiently.*] But don't let's talk about it. I'm all right. [MURRAY

glances down at her face worriedly. She changes the subject.] You've
been over to see Doctor Stanton, haven't you?

MURRAY: Yes.

EILEEN: Did he examine you?

MURRAY: Yes. [*Carelessly.*] Oh, he found me O. K.

EILEEN: I'm glad, Stephen. [*After a pause.*] Tell about yourself—what
you've been doing. You've written a lot lately, haven't you?

MURRAY: [*Frowning.*] No. I haven't been able to get down to it—somehow.
There's so little time to yourself once you get to know people in New
York. The sale of the stories you typed put me on easy street as far as
money goes, so I've felt no need— [*He laughs weakly.*] I guess I'm
one of those who have to get down to hard pan before they get the
kick to drive them to hard work.

EILEEN: [*Surprised.*] Was it hard work writing them up here? You used
to seem so happy just in doing them.

MURRAY: I was—happier than I've been before or afterward. [*Cynically.*] But—I don't know—it was a new game to me then and I was
chuck full of illusions about the glory of it. [*He laughs half-
heartedly.*] Now I'm hardly a bit more enthusiastic over it than I
used to be over newspaper work. It's like everything else, I guess.
When you've got it, you find you don't want it.

EILEEN: [*Looking at him wonderingly—disturbed.*] But isn't just the
writing itself worth while?

MURRAY: [*As if suddenly ashamed of himself—quickly.*] Yes. Of course
it is. I'm talking like a fool. I'm sore at everything because I'm dissatisfied with my own cussedness and laziness—and I want to pass
the buck. [*With a smile of cheerful confidence.*] It's only a fit. I'll
come out of it all right and get down to brass tacks again.

EILEEN: [*With an encouraging smile.*] That's the way you ought to feel.
It'd be wrong—I've read the two stories that have come out so far
over and over. They're fine, I think. Every line in them sounds like
you, and at the same time sounds natural and like people and things
you see every day. Everybody thinks they're fine, Stephen.

MURRAY: [*Pleased but pretending cynicism.*] Then they must be rotten.
[*Then with self-assurance.*] Well, I've plenty more of those stories in
my head. [*Spiritedly.*] And I'll make them so much better than what
I've done so far, you won't recognize them. [*Smiling.*] Darn it, do
you know just talking about it makes me feel as if I could sit right
down now and start in on one. Is it the fact I've worked here before—or is it seeing you, Eileen? [*Gratefully.*] I really believe it's you.
I haven't forgotten how you helped me before.

EILEEN: [*In a tone of pain.*] Don't, Stephen. I didn't do anything.

MURRAY: [*Eagerly.*] Yes, you did. You made it possible. And since I've left the San, I've looked forward to your letters to boost up my spirits. When I felt down in the mouth over my own idiocy, I used to reread them, and they always were good medicine. I can't tell you how grateful I've felt, honestly!

EILEEN: [*Faintly.*] You're kind to say so, Stephen—but it was nothing, really.

MURRAY: And I can't tell you how I've missed those letters for the past three weeks. They left a big hole in things. I was worried about you—not having heard a word. [*With a smile.*] So I came to look you up.

EILEEN: [*Faintly. Forcing an answering smile.*] Well, you see now I'm all right.

MURRAY: [*Concealing his doubt.*] Yes, of course you are. Only I'd a darn sight rather see you up and about. We could take a walk, then—through the woods. [*A wince of pain shadows* EILEEN's *face. She closes her eyes.* MURRAY *continues softly, after a pause.*] You haven't forgotten that last night—out there—Eileen?

EILEEN: [*Her lips trembling—trying to force a laugh.*] Please please don't remind me of that, Stephen. I was so silly and so sick, too. My temp was so high it must have made me—completely crazy—or I'd never dreamed of doing such a stupid thing. My head must have been full of wheels because I don't remember anything I did or said, hardly.

MURRAY: [*His pride taken down a peg by this—in a hurt tone.*] Oh! Well—I haven't forgotten and I never will, Eileen. [*Then his face clears up as if a weight had been taken off his conscience.*] Well—I rather thought you wouldn't take it seriously—afterward. You were all up in the air that night. And you never mentioned it in your letters—

EILEEN: [*Pleadingly.*] Don't talk about it! Forget it ever happened. It makes me feel—[*With a half-hysterical laugh.*]—like a fool!

MURRAY: [*Worried.*] All right, Eileen. I won't. Don't get worked up over nothing. That isn't resting, you know. [*Looking down at her closed eyes—solicitously.*] Perhaps all my talking has tired you out? Do you feel done up? Why don't you try and take a nap now?

EILEEN: [*Dully.*] Yes, I'd like to sleep.

MURRAY: [*Clasps her hands gently.*] I'll leave you then. I'll drop back to say good-by and stay awhile before I go. I won't leave until the last train. [*As she doesn't answer.*] Do you hear, Eileen?

EILEEN: [*Weakly.*] Yes. You'll come back—to say good-by.

MURRAY: Yes. I'll be back sure. [*He presses her hand and after a kindly glance of sympathy down at her face, tiptoes to the door and goes into the room, shutting the door behind him. When she hears the door shut* EILEEN *struggles up in bed and stretches her arms after him with an agonized sob* "Stephen!" *She hides her face in her hands and sobs brokenly.* MURRAY *walks across to the hall door and is about to go out when the door is opened and* MISS GILPIN *enters.*]

MISS GILPIN: [*Hurriedly.*] How do you do, Mr. Murray. Doctor Stanton just told me you were here.

MURRAY: [*As they shake hands—smiling.*] How are you, Miss Gilpin?

MISS GILPIN: He said he'd examined you, and that you were O.K. I'm glad. [*Glancing at him keenly.*] You've been talking to Eileen?

MURRAY: Just left her this second. She wanted to sleep for a while.

MISS GILPIN: [*Wonderingly.*] Sleep? [*Then hurriedly.*] It's too bad. I wish I'd known you were here sooner. I wanted very much to talk to you before you saw Eileen. [*With a worried smile.*] I still think I ought to have a talk with you.

MURRAY: Certainly, Miss Gilpin.

MISS GILPIN: [*Takes a chair and places it near the hall door.*] Sit down. She can't hear us here. Goodness knows this is hardly the place for confidences, but there are visitors all over and it'll have to do. Did you close the door tightly? She mustn't hear me above all. [*She goes to the porch door and peeps out for a moment; then comes back to him with flashing eyes.*] She's crying! What have you been saying to her? Oh, it's too late, I know! What has happened out there? Tell me!

MURRAY: [*Stammering.*] Nothing. She's crying? Why Miss Gilpin—you know I wouldn't hurt her for worlds.

MISS GILPIN: [*More calmly.*] Intentionally, I know you wouldn't. But something has happened. [*Then briskly.*] Since you don't seem inclined to confide in me, I'll have to in you. You noticed how badly she looks, didn't you?

MURRAY: Yes, I did.

MISS GILPIN: [*Gravely.*] She's been going down hill steadily— [*Meaningly.*]—ever since you left. She's in a very serious state, let me impress you with that. Doctor Stanton has given up hope of her improving here, and her father is unwilling to pay for her elsewhere now he knows there's a cheaper place—the State Farm. So she's to be sent there in a day or so.

MURRAY: [*Springing to his feet—horrified.*] To the State Farm!

MISS GILPIN: Her time here is long past. You know the rule—and she isn't getting better.

MURRAY: [*Appalled.*] That means—!

MISS GILPIN: [*Forcibly.*] Death! That's what it means for her!

MURRAY: [*Stunned.*] Good God, I never dreamed—

MISS GILPIN: In her case, it's certain. She'll die. And it wouldn't do any good to keep her here, either. She'd die here. She'll die anywhere because lately she's given up hope, she hasn't wanted to live any more. She's let herself go—and now it's too late.

MURRAY: Too late? You mean there's no chance—now? [MISS GILPIN *nods.* MURRAY *is overwhelmed—after a pause—stammering.*] Isn't there—anything—we can do?

MISS GILPIN: [*Sadly.*] I don't know. I should have talked to you before. You see, she's seen you now. She knows. [*As he looks mystified she continues slowly.*] I suppose you know that Eileen loves you, don't you?

MURRAY: [*As if defending himself against an accusation—with confused alarm.*] No—Miss Gilpin. She may have felt something like that—once—but that was long ago before I left the San. She's forgotten all about it since, I know she has. [MISS GILPIN *smiles bitterly.*] Why—just now—she said that part of it had all been so silly she felt she'd acted like a fool and didn't ever want to be reminded of it.

MISS GILPIN: She saw that you didn't love her—any more than you did in the days before you left. Oh, I used to watch you then. I sensed what was going on between you. I would have stopped it then out of pity for her, if I could have, if I didn't know that any interference would only make matters worse. [*She sighs—then after a pause.*] You'll have to forgive me for speaking to you so boldly on a delicate subject. But, don't you see, it's for her sake. I love Eileen. We all do. [*Averting her eyes from his—in a low voice.*] I know how Eileen feels, Mr. Murray. Once—a long time ago—I suffered as she is suffering—from the same mistake. But I had resources to fall back upon that Eileen hasn't got—a family who loved me and understood—friends—so I pulled through. But it spoiled my life for a long time. [*Looking at him again and forcing a smile.*] So I feel that perhaps I have a right to speak for Eileen who has no one else.

MURRAY: [*Huskily—much moved.*] Say anything you like, Miss Gilpin.

MISS GILPIN: [*After a pause—sadly.*] You don't love her—do you?

MURRAY: No—I— I don't believe I've ever thought much of loving anyone—that way.

MISS GILPIN: [*Sadly.*] Oh, it's too late, I'm afraid. If we had only had this talk before you had seen her! I meant to talk to you frankly and if I found out you didn't love Eileen—there was always the forlorn hope that you might—I was going to tell you not to see her, for her sake—not to let her face the truth. For I'm sure she continued to hope in spite of everything, and always would—to the end—if she didn't see you. I was going to implore you to stay away, to write her letters that would encourage her hope, and in that way she'd never learn the truth. I thought of writing you all this—but—it's so delicate a matter—I didn't have the courage. [*With intense grief.*] And now Doctor Stanton's decision to send her away makes everything doubly hard. When she knows *that*—she'll throw everything that holds her to life—out of the window! And think of it—her dying there alone!

MURRAY: [*Very pale.*] Don't! That shan't happen. I have money enough—I'll make more—to send her any place you think—

MISS GILPIN: That's something—but it doesn't touch the source of her unhappiness. If there were only some way to make her happy in the little time that's left to her! She has suffered so much through you. Oh, Mr. Murray, can't you tell her you love her?

MURRAY: [*After a pause—slowly.*] But she'll never believe me, I'm afraid, now.

MISS GILPIN: [*Eagerly.*] But you must make her believe! And you must ask her to marry you. If you're engaged it will give you the right in her eyes to take her away. You can take her to some private San. There's a small place but a very good one at White Lake. It's not too expensive, and it's a beautiful spot, out of the world, and you can live and work nearby. And she'll be happy to the very last. Don't you think that's something you can give in return for her love for you?

MURRAY: [*Slowly—deeply moved.*] Yes. [*Then determinedly.*] But I won't go into this thing by halves. It isn't fair to her. I'm going to marry her—yes, I mean it. I owe her that if it will make her happy.

MISS GILPIN: [*With a sad smile.*] She'll never consent—for your sake—until she's well again. And stop and think, Mr. Murray. Even if she did consent to marry you right now the shock—it'd be suicide for her. I'd have to warn her against it myself. I've talked with Dr. Stanton. God knows I'd be the first one to hold out hope if there was any. There isn't. It's merely a case of prolonging the short time left to her and making it happy. You must bear that in mind—as a fact!

MURRAY: [*Dully.*] All right. I'll remember. But it's hell to realize— [*He turns suddenly toward the porch door.*] I'll go out to her now while I feel—that—yes, I know I can make her believe me now.

MISS GILPIN: You'll tell me—later on?

MURRAY: Yes. [*He opens the door to the porch and goes out.* MISS GILPIN *stands for a moment looking after him worriedly. Then she sighs helplessly and goes out to the hall.* MURRAY *steps noiselessly out on the porch.* EILEEN *is lying motionless with her eyes closed.* MURRAY *stands looking at her, his face showing the emotional stress he is under, a great pitying tenderness in his eyes. Then he seems to come to a revealing decision on what is best to do for he tiptoes to the bedside and bending down with a quick movement, takes her in his arms, and kisses her.*] Eileen!

EILEEN: [*Startled at first, resists automatically for a moment.*] Stephen! [*Then she succumbs and lies back in his arms with a happy sigh, putting both hands to the sides of his face and staring up at him adoringly.*] Stephen, dear!

MURRAY: [*Quickly questioning her before she can question him.*] You were fibbing—about that night—weren't you? You do love me, don't you. Eileen?

EILEEN: [*Breathlessly.*] Yes—I—but you, Stephen—you don't love me. [*She makes a movement as if to escape from his embrace.*]

MURRAY: [*Genuinely moved—with tender reassurance.*] Why do you suppose I came away up here if not to tell you I did? But they warned me—Miss Gilpin—that you were still weak and that I mustn't excite you in any way. And I—I didn't want—but I had to come back and tell you.

EILEEN: [*Convinced—with a happy laugh.*] And is that why you acted so strange—and cold? Aren't they silly to tell you that! As if being happy could hurt me! Why, it's just that, just you I've needed!

MURRAY: [*His voice trembling.*] And you'll marry me, Eileen?

EILEEN: [*A shadow of doubt crossing her face momentarily.*] Are you sure—you want me, Stephen?

MURRAY: [*A lump in his throat—huskily.*] Yes. I do want you, Eileen.

EILEEN: [*Happily.*] Then I will—after I'm well again, of course. [*She kisses him.*]

MURRAY: [*Chokingly.*] That won't be long now, Eileen.

EILEEN: [*Joyously.*] No—not long—now that I'm happy for once in my life. I'll surprise you, Stephen, the way I'll pick up and grow fat and healthy. You won't know me in a month. How can you ever love such a skinny homely thing as I am now! [*With a laugh.*] I couldn't if I was a man—love such a fright.

MURRAY: Ssshh!

EILEEN: [*Confidently.*] But you'll see now. I'll make myself get well. We won't have to wait long, dear. And can't you move up to the town near here where you can see me every day, and you can work and I can help you with your stories just as I used to—and I'll soon be strong enough to do your typing again. [*She laughs.*] Listen to me—talking about helping you—as if they weren't all your own work, those blessed stories!—as if I had anything to do with it!

MURRAY: [*Hoarsely.*] You had! You did! They're yours. [*Trying to calm himself.*] But you mustn't stay here, Eileen. You'll let me take you away, won't you?—to a better place—not far away—White Lake, it's called. There's a small private sanatorium there. Doctor Stanton says it's one of the best. And I'll live nearby—it's a beautiful spot—and see you every day.

EILEEN: [*In the seventh heaven.*] And did you plan out all this for me beforehand, Stephen? [*He nods with averted eyes. She kisses his hair.*] You wonderful, kind dear! And it's a small place—this White Lake? Then we won't have so many people around to disturb us, will we? We'll be all to ourselves. And you ought to work so well up there. I know New York wasn't good for you—alone—without me. And I'll get well and strong so quick! And you say it's a beautiful place? [*Intensely.*] Oh, Stephen, any place in the world would be beautiful to me—if you were with me! [*His face is hidden in the pillow beside her. She is suddenly startled by a muffled sob—anxiously.*] Why—Stephen—you're—you're crying! [*The tears start to her own eyes.*]

MURRAY: [*Raising his face which is this time alight with a passionate awakening—a revelation.*] Oh, I do love you, Eileen! I do! I love you, love you!

EILEEN: [*Thrilled by the depths of his present sincerity—but with a teasing laugh.*] Why, you say that as if you'd just made the discovery, Stephen!

MURRAY: Oh, what does it matter, Eileen! Oh, what a blind selfish ass I've been! You are my life—everything! I love you, Eileen! I do! I do! And we'll be married— [*Suddenly his face grows frozen with horror as he remembers the doom. For the first time Death confronts him face to face as a menacing reality.*]

EILEEN: [*Terrified by the look in his eyes.*] What is it, Stephen? What—?

MURRAY: [*With a groan—protesting half-aloud in a strangled voice.*] No! No! It can't be—! My God! [*He clutches her hands and hides his face in them.*]

EILEEN: [*With a cry.*] Stephen! What is the matter? [*Her face suddenly betrays an awareness, an intuitive sense of the truth.*] Oh—Stephen— [*Then with a childish whimper of terror.*] Oh, Stephen, I'm going to die! I'm going to die!

MURRAY: [*Lifting his tortured face—wildly.*] No!

EILEEN: [*Her voice sinking to a dead whisper.*] I'm going to die.

MURRAY: [*Seizing her in his arms in a passionate frenzy and pressing his lips to hers.*] No, Eileen, no, my love, no! What are you saying? What could have made you think it? You—die? Why, of course, we're all going to die—but— Good God! What damned nonsense! You're getting well—every day. Everyone—Miss Gilpin—Stanton— everyone told me that. I swear before God, Eileen, they did! You're still weak, that's all. They said—it won't be long. You mustn't think that—not now.

EILEEN: [*Miserably—unconvinced.*] But why did you look at me—that way—with that awful look in your eyes—? [*While she is speaking* MISS GILPIN *enters the room from the hallway. She appears worried, agitated. She hurries toward the porch but stops inside the doorway, arrested by* MURRAY's *voice.*]

MURRAY: [*Takes* EILEEN *by the shoulders and forces her to look into his eyes.*] I wasn't thinking about you then— No, Eileen—not you. I didn't mean you—but me—yes, me! I couldn't tell you before. They'd warned me—not to excite you—and I knew that would—if you loved me.

EILEEN: [*Staring at him with frightened amazement.*] You mean you— you're sick again?

MURRAY: [*Desperately striving to convince her.*] Yes. I saw Stanton. I lied to you before—about that. It's come back on me, Eileen—you see how I look—I've let myself go. I don't know how to live without you, don't you see? And you'll—marry me now—without waiting— and help me to get well—you and I together—and not mind their lies—what they say to prevent you? You'll do that, Eileen?

EILEEN: I'll do anything for you— And I'd be so happy— [*She breaks down.*] But, Stephen, I'm so afraid. I'm all mixed up. Oh, Stephen, I don't know what to believe!

MISS GILPIN: [*Who has been listening thunderstruck to* MURRAY's *wild pleading, at last summons up the determination to interfere—steps out on the porch—in a tone of severe remonstrance.*] Mr. Murray!

MURRAY: [*Starts to his feet with wild, bewildered eyes—confusedly.*] Oh—you— [MISS GILPIN *cannot restrain an exclamation of dismay as she sees his face wrung by despair.* EILEEN *turns her head away with a little cry as if she would hide her face in the bedclothes. A sudden fierce resolution lights up* MURRAY's *countenance— hoarsely.*] You're just in time, Miss Gilpin! Eileen! Listen! You'll be- lieve Miss Gilpin, won't you? She knows all about it. [EILEEN *turns her eyes questioningly on the bewildered nurse.*]

MISS GILPIN: What—?

MURRAY: [*Determinedly.*] Doctor Stanton—he must have told you about me. Eileen doesn't believe me—when I tell her I got T. B. again. She thinks—I don't know what. I know you're not supposed to, but—can't you tell her—?

MISS GILPIN: [*Stunned by being thus defiantly confronted—stammeringly.*] Mr. Murray! I—I—how can you ask—

MURRAY: [*Quickly.*] She loves me—and I—I—love her! [*He holds her eyes and speaks with a passion of sincerity that compels belief.*] I love her, do you hear?

MISS GILPIN: [*Falteringly.*] You—love—Eileen?

MURRAY: Yes! I do! [*Entreatingly.*] So—tell her—won't you?

MISS GILPIN: [*Swallowing hard, her eyes full of pity and sorrow fixed on EILEEN.*] Yes—Eileen— [*She turns away slowly toward the door.*]

EILEEN: [*With a little cry of alarmed concern, stretches out her hands to MURRAY protectingly.*] Poor Stephen—dear! [*He grasps her hands and kisses them.*]

MISS GILPIN: [*In a low voice.*] Mr. Murray. May I speak to you?

MURRAY: [*With a look of questioning defiance at her.*] Certainly.

MISS GILPIN: [*Turns to EILEEN with a forced smile.*] I won't steal him away for more than a moment, Eileen. [EILEEN *smiles happily.*]

MURRAY: [*Follows MISS GILPIN into the room. She leads him to the far end of the room near the door to the hall, after shutting the porch door carefully behind him. He looks at her defiantly.*] Well?

MISS GILPIN: [*In low, agitated tones.*] What has happened? I feel as if I may have done a great wrong to myself—to you—to her—by that lie. And yet—something forced me.

MURRAY: [*Moved.*] It has saved her—us. Oh, how can I explain what happened? I suddenly saw—how beautiful and sweet and good she is—how I couldn't bear the thought of life without her— That's all. [*Determinedly.*] She must marry me at once and I'll take her away—the far West—any place Stanton thinks can help. And she can take care of me—as she thinks—and I know she'll grow well as I seem to grow well. Oh Miss Gilpin, don't you see? No half and half measures can help us—help her. [*Fiercely as if defying her.*] But we'll win together. We can! We must! There are things doctors can't value—can't know the strength of! [*Exultantly.*] You'll see! I'll make Eileen get well, I tell you! Happiness will cure! Love is stronger than— [*He suddenly breaks down before the pitying negation she cannot keep from her eyes. He sinks on a chair, shoulders bowed, face hidden in his hands, with a groan of despair.*] Oh, why did you give me a hopeless hope?

MISS GILPIN: [*Putting her hand on his shoulder—with tender compas-*

sion—sadly.] Isn't all life just that—when you think of it? [*Her face lighting up with a consoling revelation.*] But there must be something back of it—some promise of fulfillment,—somehow—somewhere—in the spirit of hope itself.

MURRAY: [*Dully.*] What do words mean to me now? [*Then suddenly starting to his feet and flinging off her hand with disdainful strength—violently and almost insultingly.*] What damned rot! I tell you we'll win! We must! All the verdicts of all the doctors—what do they matter? This is—beyond you! And we'll win in spite of you! [*Scornfully.*] How dare you use the word hopeless—as if it were the last! Come now, confess, damn it! There's always hope, isn't there? What do you *know?* Can you say you *know* anything?

MISS GILPIN: [*Taken aback by his violence for a moment, finally bursts into a laugh of helplessness which is close to tears.*] I? I know nothing—absolutely nothing! God bless you both! [*She raises her handkerchief to her eyes and hurries out to the hallway without turning her head.* MURRAY *stands looking after her for a moment; then strides out to the porch.*]

EILEEN: [*Turning and greeting him with a shy smile of happiness as he comes and kneels by her bedside.*] Stephen! [*He kisses her. She strokes his hair and continues in a tone of motherly, self-forgetting solicitude.*] I'll have to look out for you, Stephen, won't I? From now on? And see that you rest so many hours a day—and drink your milk when I drink mine—and go to bed at nine sharp when I do—and obey everything I tell you—and—

[*The Curtain Falls*]

THE EMPEROR JONES

CHARACTERS

BRUTUS JONES, *Emperor.*

HENRY SMITHERS, *A Cockney Trader.*

AN OLD NATIVE WOMAN.

LEM, *A Native Chief.*

SOLDIERS, *Adherents of Lem.*
The Little Formless Fears; Jeff; The Negro Convicts; The Prison Guard;
The Planters; The Auctioneer; The Slaves; The Congo Witch-Doctor;
The Crocodile God.

The action of the play takes place on an island in the West Indies as yet not self-determined by White Marines. The form of native government is, for the time being, an Empire.

SCENE—*The audience chamber in the palace of the Emperor—a spacious, high-ceilinged room with bare, white-washed walls. The floor is of white tiles. In the rear, to the left of center, a wide archway giving out on a portico with white pillars. The palace is evidently situated on high ground for beyond the portico nothing can be seen but a vista of distant hills, their summits crowned with thick groves of palm trees. In the right wall, center, a smaller arched doorway leading to the living quarters of the palace. The room is bare of furniture with the exception of one huge chair made of uncut wood which stands at center, its back to rear. This is very apparently the Emperor's throne. It is painted a dazzling, eye-smiting scarlet. There is a brilliant orange cushion on the seat and another smaller one is placed on the floor to serve as a footstool. Strips of matting, dyed scarlet, lead from the foot of the throne to the two entrances.*

It is late afternoon but the sunlight still blazes yellowly beyond the portico and there is an oppressive burden of exhausting heat in the air.

As the curtain rises, a native negro woman sneaks in cautiously from the entrance on the right. She is very old, dressed in cheap calico, bare-footed, a red bandana handkerchief covering all but a few stray wisps of white hair. A bundle bound in colored cloth is carried over her shoulder on the end of a stick. She hesitates beside the doorway, peering back as if in extreme dread of being discovered. Then she begins to glide noiselessly, a step at a time, toward the doorway in the rear. At this moment, SMITHERS *appears beneath the portico.*

SMITHERS *is a tall, stoop-shouldered man about forty. His bald head, perched on a long neck with an enormous Adam's apple, looks like an egg. The tropics have tanned his naturally pasty face with its small, sharp features to a sickly yellow, and native rum has painted his pointed nose to a startling red. His little, washy-blue eyes are red-rimmed and dart about him like a ferret's. His expression is one of unscrupulous meanness, cowardly and dangerous. He is dressed in a worn riding suit of dirty white drill, puttees, spurs, and wears a white cork helmet. A cartridge belt with an automatic revolver is around his waist. He carries a riding whip in his hand. He sees the woman and stops to watch her suspiciously. Then, making up his mind, he steps quickly on tiptoe into the room. The woman, looking back over her shoulder continually, does not see him until it is too late. When she does* SMITHERS *springs forward and grabs her firmly by the shoulder. She struggles to get away, fiercely but silently.*

SMITHERS: [*Tightening his grasp—roughly.*] Easy! None o' that, me birdie. You can't wriggle out now. I got me 'ooks on yer.

WOMAN: [*Seeing the uselessness of struggling, gives way to frantic terror, and sinks to the ground, embracing his knees supplicatingly.*] No tell him! No tell him, Mister!

SMITHERS: [*With great curiosity.*] Tell 'im? [*Then scornfully.*] Oh, you mean 'is bloomin' Majesty. What's the gaime, any 'ow? What are you sneakin' away for? Been stealin' a bit, I s'pose. [*He taps her bundle with his riding whip significantly.*]

WOMAN: [*Shaking her head vehemently.*] No, me no steal.

SMITHERS: Bloody liar! But tell me what's up. There's somethin' funny goin' on. I smelled it in the air first thing I got up this mornin'. You blacks are up to some devilment. This palace of 'is is is like a bleedin' tomb. Where's all the 'ands? [*The woman keeps sullenly silent. SMITHERS raises his whip threateningly.*] Ow, yer won't, won't yer? I'll show yer what's what.

WOMAN: [*Coweringly.*] I tell, Mister. You no hit. They go—all go. [*She makes a sweeping gesture toward the hills in the distance.*]

SMITHERS: Run away—to the 'ills?

WOMAN: Yes, Mister. Him Emperor—Great Father. [*She touches her forehead to the floor with a quick mechanical jerk.*] Him sleep after eat. Then they go—all go. Me old woman. Me left only. Now me go too.

SMITHERS: [*His astonishment giving way to an immense, mean satisfaction.*] Ow! So that's the ticket! Well, I know bloody well wot's in the air—when they runs orf to the 'ills. The tom-tom 'll be thumping out there bloomin' soon. [*With extreme vindictiveness.*] And I'm bloody glad of it, for one! Serve 'im right! Puttin' on airs, the stinkin' nigger! 'Is Majesty! Gawd blimey! I only 'opes I'm there when they takes 'im out to shoot 'im. [*Suddenly.*] 'E's still 'ere all right, ain't 'e?

WOMAN: Yes. Him sleep.

SMITHERS: 'E's bound to find out soon as 'e wakes up. 'E's cunnin' enough to know when 'is time's come. [*He goes to the doorway on right and whistles shrilly with his fingers in his mouth. The old woman springs to her feet and runs out of the doorway, rear. SMITHERS goes after her, reaching for his revolver.*] Stop or I'll shoot! [*Then stopping—indifferently.*] Pop orf then, if yer like, yer black cow. [*He stands in the doorway, looking after her.*]

[JONES *enters from the right. He is a tall, powerfully-built, full-blooded negro of middle age. His features are typically negroid, yet there is something decidedly distinctive about his face—an underlying strength of will, a hardy, self-reliant confidence in himself that inspires respect. His eyes are alive with a keen, cunning intelligence. In manner he is shrewd, suspicious, evasive. He wears a light blue uniform coat, sprayed with brass buttons, heavy gold chevrons on his shoulders, gold braid on the collar, cuffs, etc. His pants are bright red with a light blue stripe down the side. Patent leather laced boots with brass spurs, and a belt with a long-barreled, pearl-handled revolver in a holster complete his make up. Yet there is something not altogether ridiculous about his grandeur. He has a way of carrying it off.*]

JONES: [*Not seeing anyone—greatly irritated and blinking sleepily—shouts.*] Who dare whistle dat way in my palace? Who dare wake up de Emperor? I'll git de hide frayled off some o' you niggers sho'!

SMITHERS: [*Showing himself—in a manner half-afraid and half-defiant.*] It was me whistled to yer. [*As* JONES *frowns angrily.*] I got news for yer.

JONES: [*Putting on his suavest manner, which fails to cover up his contempt for the white man.*] Oh, it's you, Mister Smithers. [*He sits down on his throne with easy dignity.*] What news you got to tell me?

SMITHERS: [*Coming close to enjoy his discomfiture.*] Don't yer notice nothin' funny today?

JONES: [*Coldly.*] Funny? No. I ain't perceived nothin' of de kind!

SMITHERS: Then yer ain't so foxy as I thought yer was. Where's all your court? [*Sarcastically*] the Generals and the Cabinet Ministers and all?

JONES: [*Imperturbably.*] Where dey mostly runs to minute I closes my eyes—drinkin' rum and talkin' big down in de town. [*Sarcastically.*] How come you don't know dat? Ain't you sousin' with 'em most every day?

SMITHERS: [*Stung but pretending indifference—with a wink.*] That's part of the day's work. I got ter—ain't I—in my business?

JONES: [*Contemptuously.*] Yo' business!

SMITHERS: [*Imprudently enraged.*] Gawd blimey, you was glad enough for me ter take yer in on it when you landed here first. You didn' 'ave no 'igh and mighty airs in them days!

JONES: [*His hand going to his revolver like a flash—menacingly.*] Talk polite, white man! Talk polite, you heah me! I'm boss heah now, is you fergettin'? [*The Cockney seems about to challenge this last statement with the facts but something in the other's eyes holds and cows him.*]

SMITHERS: [*In a cowardly whine.*] No 'arm meant, old top.

JONES: [*Condescendingly.*] I accepts yo' apology. [*Lets his hand fall from his revolver.*] No use'n you rakin' up ole times. What I was den is one thing. What I is now 's another. You didn't let me in on yo' crooked work out o' no kind feelin's dat time. I done de dirty work fo' you—and most o' de brain work, too, fo' dat matter—and I was wu'th money to you, dat's de reason.

SMITHERS: Well, blimey, I give yer a start, didn't I—when no one else would. I wasn't afraid to 'ire yer like the rest was—'count of the story about your breakin' jail back in the States.

JONES: No, you didn't have no s'cuse to look down on me fo' dat. You been in jail you'self more'n once.

SMITHERS: [*Furiously.*] It's a lie! [*Then trying to pass it off by an attempt at scorn.*] Garn! Who told yer that fairy tale?

JONES: Dey's some tings I ain't got to be tole. I kin see 'em in folk's eyes. [*Then after a pause—meditatively.*] Yes, you sho' give me a start. And it didn't take long from dat time to git dese fool, woods' niggers right where I wanted dem. [*With pride.*] From stowaway to Emperor in two years! Dat's goin' some!

SMITHERS: [*With curiosity.*] And I bet you got yer pile o' money 'id safe some place.

JONES: [*With satisfaction.*] I sho' has! And it's in a foreign bank where no pusson don't ever git it out but me no matter what come. You didn't s'pose I was holdin' down dis Emperor job for de glory in it, did you? Sho'! De fuss and glory part of it, dat's only to turn de heads o' de low-flung, bush niggers dat's here. Dey wants de big circus show for deir money. I gives it to 'em an' I gits de money. [*With a grin.*] De long green, dat's me every time! [*Then rebukingly.*] But you ain't got no kick agin me, Smithers. I'se paid you back all you done for me many times. Ain't I pertected you and winked at all de crooked tradin' you been doin' right out in de broad day. Sho' I has—and me makin' laws to stop it at de same time! [*He chuckles.*]

SMITHERS: [*Grinning.*] But, meanin' no' 'arm, you been grabbin' right and left yourself, ain't yer? Look at the taxes you've put on 'em! Blimey! You've squeezed 'em dry!

JONES: [*Chuckling.*] No, dey ain't *all* dry yet. I'se still heah, ain't I?

SMITHERS: [*Smiling at his secret thought.*] They're dry right now, you'll

find out. [*Changing the subject abruptly.*] And as for me breakin'
laws, you've broke 'em all yerself just as fast as yer made 'em.

JONES: Ain't I de Emperor? De laws don't go for him. [*Judicially.*] You
heah what I tells you, Smithers. Dere's little stealin' like you does,
and dere's big stealin' like I does. For de little stealin' dey gits you in
jail soon or late. For de big stealin' dey makes you Emperor and puts
you in de Hall o' Fame when you croaks. [*Reminiscently.*] If dey's
one thing I learns in ten years on de Pullman ca's listenin' to de white
quality talk, it's dat same fact. And when I gits a chance to use it I
winds up Emperor in two years.

SMITHERS: [*Unable to repress the genuine admiration of the small fry
for the large.*] Yes, yer turned the bleedin' trick, all right. Blimey, I
never seen a bloke 'as 'ad the bloomin' luck you 'as.

JONES: [*Severely.*] Luck? What you mean—luck?

SMITHERS: I suppose you'll say as that swank about the silver bullet
ain't luck—and that was what first got the fool blacks on yer side the
time of the revolution, wasn't it?

JONES: [*With a laugh.*] Oh, dat silver bullet! Sho' was luck! But I makes
dat luck, you heah? I loads de dice! Yessuh! When dat murderin' nigger ole Lem hired to kill me takes aim ten feet away and his gun
misses fire and I shoots him dead, what you heah me say?

SMITHERS: You said yer'd got a charm so's no lead bullet'd kill yer. You
was so strong only a silver bullet could kill yer, you told 'em. Blimey,
wasn't that swank for yer—and plain, fat-'eaded luck?

JONES: [*Proudly.*] I got brains and I uses 'em quick. Dat ain't luck.

SMITHERS: Yer know they wasn't 'ardly liable to get no silver bullets.
And it was luck 'e didn't 'it you that time.

JONES: [*Laughing.*] And dere all dem fool, bush niggers was kneelin'
down and bumpin' deir heads on de ground like I was a miracle out
o' de Bible. Oh Lawd, from dat time on I has dem all eatin' out of
my hand. I cracks de whip and dey jumps through.

SMITHERS: [*With a sniff.*] Yankee bluff done it.

JONES: Ain't a man's talkin' big what makes him big—long as he makes
folks believe it? Sho', I talks large when I ain't got nothin' to back it
up, but I ain't talkin' wild just de same. I knows I kin fool 'em—I
knows it—and dat's backin' enough fo' my game. And ain't I got to
learn deir lingo and teach some of dem English befo' I kin talk to
'em? Ain't dat wuk? You ain't never learned ary word er it, Smithers,
in de ten years you been heah, dough you' knows it's money in yo'
pocket tradin' wid 'em if you does. But you'se too shiftless to take de
trouble.

SMITHERS: [*Flushing.*] Never mind about me. What's this I've 'eard about yer really 'avin' a silver bullet moulded for yourself?

JONES: It's playin' out my bluff. I has de silver bullet moulded and I tells 'em when de time comes I kills myself wid it. I tells 'em dat's 'cause I'm de on'y man in de world big enuff to git me. No use'n deir tryin'. And dey falls down and bumps deir heads. [*He laughs.*] I does dat so's I kin take a walk in peace widout no jealous nigger gunnin' at me from behind de trees.

SMITHERS: [*Astonished.*] Then you 'ad it made—'onest?

JONES: Sho' did. Heah she be. [*He takes out his revolver, breaks it, and takes the silver bullet out of one chamber.*] Five lead an' dis silver baby at de last. Don't she shine pretty? [*He holds it in his hand, looking at it admiringly, as if strangely fascinated.*]

SMITHERS: Let me see. [*Reaches out his hand for it.*]

JONES: [*Harshly.*] Keep yo' hands whar dey b'long, white man. [*He replaces it in the chamber and puts the revolver back on his hip.*]

SMITHERS: [*Snarling.*] Gawd blimey! Think I'm a bleedin' thief, you would.

JONES: No, 'tain't dat. I knows you'se scared to steal from me. On'y I ain't 'lowin' nary body to touch dis baby. She's my rabbit's foot.

SMITHERS: [*Sneering.*] A bloomin' charm, wot? [*Venomously.*] Well, you'll need all the bloody charms you 'as before long, s' 'elp me!

JONES: [*Judicially.*] Oh, I'se good for six months yit 'fore dey gits sick o' my game. Den, when I sees trouble comin', I makes my getaway.

SMITHERS: Ho! You got it all planned, ain't yer?

JONES: I ain't no fool. I knows dis Emperor's time is sho't. Dat why I make hay when de sun shine. Was you thinkin' I'se aimin' to hold down dis job for life? No, suh! What good is gittin' money if you stays back in dis raggedy country? I wants action when I spends. And when I sees dese niggers gittin' up deir nerve to tu'n me out, and I'se got all de money in sight, I resigns on de spot and beats it quick.

SMITHERS: Where to?

JONES: None o' yo' business.

SMITHERS: Not back to the bloody States, I'll lay my oath.

JONES: [*Suspiciously.*] Why don't I? [*Then with an easy laugh.*] You mean 'count of dat story 'bout me breakin' from jail back dere? Dat's all talk.

SMITHERS: [*Skeptically.*] Ho, yes!

JONES: [*Sharply.*] You ain't 'sinuatin' I'se a liar, is you?

SMITHERS: [*Hastily.*] No, Gawd strike me! I was only thinkin' o' the bloody lies you told the blacks 'ere about killin' white men in the States.

JONES: [*Angered.*] How come dey're lies?

SMITHERS: You'd 'ave been in jail if you 'ad, wouldn't yer then? [*With venom.*] And from what I've 'eard, it ain't 'ealthy for a black to kill a white man in the States. They burns 'em in oil, don't they?

JONES: [*With cool deadliness.*] You mean lynchin' 'd scare me? Well, I tells you, Smithers, maybe I does kill one white man back dere. Maybe I does. And maybe I kills another right heah 'fore long if he don't look out.

SMITHERS: [*Trying to force a laugh.*] I was on'y spoofin' yer. Can't yer take a joke? And you was just sayin' you'd never been in jail.

JONES: [*In the same tone—slightly boastful.*] Maybe I goes to jail dere for gettin' in an argument wid razors ovah a crap game. Maybe I gits twenty years when dat colored man die. Maybe I gits in 'nother argument wid de prison guard was overseer ovah us when we're wukin' de roads. Maybe he hits me wid a whip and I splits his head wid a shovel and runs away and files de chain off my leg and gits away safe. Maybe I does all dat an' maybe I don't. It's a story I tells you so's you knows I'se de kind of man dat if you evah repeats one words of it, I ends yo' stealin' on dis yearth mighty damn quick!

SMITHERS: [*Terrified.*] Think I'd peach on yer? Not me! Ain't I always been yer friend?

JONES: [*Suddenly relaxing.*] Sho' you has—and you better be.

SMITHERS: [*Recovering his composure—and with it his malice.*] And just to show yer I'm yer friend, I'll tell yer that bit o' news I was goin' to.

JONES: Go ahead! Shoot de piece. Must be bad news from de happy way you look.

SMITHERS: [*Warningly.*] Maybe it's gettin' time for you to resign—with that bloomin' silver bullet, wot? [*He finishes with a mocking grin.*]

JONES: [*Puzzled.*] What's dat you say? Talk plain.

SMITHERS: Ain't noticed any of the guards or servants about the place today, I 'aven't.

JONES: [*Carelessly.*] Dey're all out in de garden sleepin' under de trees. When I sleeps, dey sneaks a sleep, too, and I pretends I never suspicions it. All I got to do is to ring de bell and dey come flyin', makin' a bluff dey was wukin' all de time.

SMITHERS: [*In the same mocking tone.*] Ring the bell now an' you'll bloody well see what I means.

JONES: [*Startled to alertness, but preserving the same careless tone.*] Sho' I rings. [*He reaches below the throne and pulls out a big, common dinner bell which is painted the same vivid scarlet as the throne. He rings this vigorously—then stops to listen. Then he goes to both doors, rings again, and looks out.*]

SMITHERS: [*Watching him with malicious satisfaction, after a pause— mockingly.*] The bloody ship is sinkin' an' the bleedin' rats 'as slung their 'ooks.

JONES: [*In a sudden fit of anger flings the bell clattering into a corner.*] Low-flung, woods' niggers! [*Then catching Smithers' eye on him, he controls himself and suddenly bursts into a low chuckling laugh.*] Reckon I overplays my hand dis once! A man can't take de pot on a bob-tailed flush all de time. Was I sayin' I'd sit in six months mo'? Well, I'se changed my mind den. I cashes in and resigns de job of Emperor right dis minute.

SMITHERS: [*With real admiration.*] Blimey, but you're a cool bird, and no mistake.

JONES: No use'n fussin'. When I knows de game's up I kisses it goodbye widout no long waits. Dey've all run off to de hills, ain't dey?

SMITHERS: Yes—every bleedin' man jack of 'em.

JONES: Den de revolution is at de post. And de Emperor better git his feet smokin' up de trail. [*He starts for the door in rear.*]

SMITHERS: Goin' out to look for your 'orse? Yer won't find any. They steals the 'orses first thing. Mine was gone when I went for 'im this mornin'. That's wot first give me a suspicion of wot was up.

JONES: [*Alarmed for a second, scratches his head, then philosophically.*] Well, den I hoofs it. Feet, do yo' duty! [*He pulls out a gold watch and looks at it.*] Three-thuty. Sundown's at six-thuty or dereabouts. [*Puts his watch back—with cool confidence.*] I got plenty o' time to make it easy.

SMITHERS: Don't be so bloomin' sure of it. They'll be after you 'ot and 'eavy. Ole Lem is at the bottom o' this business an' 'e 'ates you like 'ell. 'E'd rather do for you than eat 'is dinner, 'e would!

JONES: [*Scornfully.*] Dat fool no-count nigger! Does you think I'se scared o' him? I stands him on his thick head more'n once befo' dis, and I does it again if he come in my way— [*Fiercely.*] And dis time I leave him a dead nigger fo' sho'!

SMITHERS: You'll 'ave to cut through the big forest—an' these blacks 'ere can sniff and follow a trail in the dark like 'ounds. You'd 'ave to 'ustle to get through that forest in twelve hours even if you knew all the bloomin' trails like a native.

JONES: [*With indignant scorn.*] Look-a-heah, white man! Does you think I'se a natural bo'n fool? Give me credit fo' havin' some sense, fo' Lawd's sake! Don't you s'pose I'se looked ahead and made sho' of all de chances? I'se gone out in dat big forest, pretendin' to hunt, so many times dat I knows it high an' low like a book. I could go through on dem trails wid my eyes shut. [*With great contempt.*]

Think dese ig'nerent bush niggers dat ain't got brains enuff to know deir own names even can catch Brutus Jones? Huh, I s'pects not! Not on yo' life! Why, man, de white men went after me wid bloodhounds where I come from an' I jes' laughs at 'em. It's a shame to fool dese black trash around heah, dey're so easy. You watch me, man'. I'll make dem look sick, I will. I'll be 'cross de plain to de edge of de forest by time dark comes. Once in de woods in de night, dey got a swell chance o' findin' dis baby! Dawn tomorrow I'll be out at de oder side and on de coast whar dat French gunboat is stayin'. She picks me up, take me to the Martinique when she go dar, and dere I is safe wid a mighty big bankroll in my jeans. It's easy as rollin' off a log.

SMITHERS: [*Maliciously.*] But s'posin' somethin' 'appens wrong an' they do nab yer?

JONES: [*Decisively.*] Dey don't—dat's de answer.

SMITHERS: But, just for argyment's sake—what'd you do?

JONES: [*Frowning.*] I'se got five lead bullets in dis gun good enuff fo' common bush niggers—and after dat I got de silver bullet left to cheat 'em out o' gittin' me.

SMITHERS: [*Jeeringly.*] Ho, I was fergettin' that silver bullet. You'll bump yourself orf in style, won't yer? Blimey!

JONES: [*Gloomily.*] You kin bet yo' whole roll on one thing, white man. Dis baby plays out his string to de end and when he quits, he quits wid a bang de way he ought. Silver bullet ain't none too good for him when he go, dat's a fac'! [*Then shaking off his nervousness—with a confident laugh.*] Sho'! What is I talkin' about? Ain't come to dat yit and I never will—not wid trash niggers like dese yere. [*Boastfully.*] Silver bullet bring me luck anyway. I kin outguess, outrun, outfight, an' out-play de whole lot o' dem all ovah de board any time o' de day er night! You watch me! [*From the distant hills comes the faint, steady thump of a tom-tom, low and vibrating. It starts at a rate exactly corresponding to normal pulse beat—72 to the minute—and continues at a gradually accelerating rate from this point uninterruptedly to the very end of the play.*]

[JONES *starts at the sound. A strange look of apprehension creeps into his face for a moment as he listens. Then he asks, with an attempt to regain his most casual manner.*] What's dat drum beatin' fo'?

SMITHERS: [*With a mean grin.*] For you. That means the bleedin' ceremony 'as started. I've 'eard it before and I knows.

JONES: Cer'mony? What cer'mony?

SMITHERS: The blacks is 'oldin' a bloody meetin', 'avin' a war dance, gettin' their courage worked up b'fore they starts after you.

JONES: Let dem! Dey'll sho' need it!

SMITHERS: And they're there 'oldin' their 'eathen religious service— makin' no end of devil spells and charms to 'elp 'em against your sil- ver bullet. [*He guffaws loudly.*] Blimey, but they're balmy as 'ell!

JONES: [*A tiny bit awed and shaken in spite of himself.*] Huh! Takes more'n dat to scare dis chicken!

SMITHERS: [*Scenting the other's feeling—maliciously.*] Ternight when it's pitch black in the forest, they'll 'ave their pet devils and ghosts 'oundin' after you. You'll find yer bloody 'air 'll be standin' on end before termorrow mornin'. [*Seriously.*] It's a bleedin' queer place, that stinkin' forest, even in daylight. Yer don't know what might 'ap- pen in there, it's that rotten still. Always sends the cold shivers down my back minute I gets in it.

JONES: [*With a contemptuous sniff.*] I ain't no chicken-liver like you is. Trees an' me, we'se friends, and dar's a full moon comin' bring me light. And let dem po' niggers make all de fool spells dey'se a min' to. Does yo' s'pect I'se silly enuff to b'lieve in ghosts an' ha'nts an' all dat ole woman's talk? G'long, white man! You ain't talkin' to me. [*With a chuckle.*] Doesn't you know dey's got to do wid a man was member in good standin' o' de Baptist Church? Sho' I was dat when I was porter on de Pullmans, befo' I gits into my little trouble. Let dem try deir heathen tricks. De Baptist Church done pertect me and land dem all in hell. [*Then with more confident satisfaction.*] And I'se got little silver bullet o' my own, don't forgit.

SMITHERS: Ho! You 'aven't give much 'eed to your Baptist Church since you been down 'ere. I've 'eard myself you 'ad turned yer coat an' was takin' up with their blarsted witch-docters, or whatever the 'ell yer calls the swine.

JONES: [*Vehemently.*] I pretends to! Sho' I pretends! Dat's part o' my game from de fust. If I finds out dem niggers believes dat black is white, den I yells it out louder 'n deir loudest. It don't git me nothin' to do missionary work for de Baptist Church. I'se after de coin, an' I lays my Jesus on de shelf for de time bein'. [*Stops abruptly to look at his watch—alertly.*] But I ain't got de time to waste no more fool talk wid you. I'se gwine away from heah dis secon'. [*He reaches in under the throne and pulls out an expensive Panama hat with a bright multi-colored band and sets it jauntily on his head.*] So long, white man! [*With a grin.*] See you in jail sometime, maybe!

SMITHERS: Not me, you won't. Well, I wouldn't be in yer bloody boots for no bloomin' money, but 'ere's wishin' yer luck just the same.

JONES: [*Contemptuously.*] You're de frightenedest man evah I see! I tells you I'se safe's 'f I was in New York City. It takes dem niggers from now to dark to git up de nerve to start somethin'. By dat time, I'se got a head start dey never kotch up wid.

SMITHERS: [*Maliciously.*] Give my regards to any ghosts yer meets up with.

JONES: [*Grinning.*] If dat ghost got money, I'll tell him never ha'nt you less'n he wants to lose it.

SMITHERS: [*Flattered.*] Garn! [*Then curiously.*] Ain't yer takin' no luggage with yer?

JONES: I travels light when I wants to move fast. And I got tinned grub buried on de edge o' de forest. [*Boastfully.*] Now say dat I don't look ahead an' use my brains! [*With a wide, liberal gesture.*] I will all dat's left in de palace to you—and you better grab all you kin sneak away wid befo' dey gits here.

SMITHERS: [*Gratefully.*] Righto—and thanks ter yer. [*As* JONES *walks toward the door in rear—cautioningly.*] Say! Look 'ere, you ain't goin' out that way, are yer?

JONES: Does you think I'd slink out de back door like a common nigger? I'se Emperor yit, ain't I? And de Emperor Jones leaves de way he comes, and dat black trash don't dare stop him—not yit, leastways. [*He stops for a moment in the doorway, listening to the far-off but insistent beat of the tom-tom.*] Listen to dat roll-call, will you? Must be mighty big drum carry dat far. [*Then with a laugh.*] Well, if dey ain't no whole brass band to see me off, I sho' got de drum part of it. So long, white man. [*He puts his hands in his pockets and with studied carelessness, whistling a tune, he saunters out of the doorway and off to the left.*]

SMITHERS: [*Looks after him with a puzzled admiration.*] 'E's got 'is bloomin' nerve with 'im, s'elp me! [*Then angrily.*] Ho—the bleedin' nigger—puttin' an 'is bloody airs! I 'opes they nabs 'im an' gives 'im what's what! [*Then putting business before the pleasure of this thought, looking around him with cupidity.*] A bloke ought to find a 'ole lot in this palace that'd go for a bit of cash. Let's take a look, 'Arry, me lad. [*He starts for the doorway on right as*

[*The Curtain Falls.*]

SCENE TWO: NIGHTFALL

SCENE—*The end of the plain where the Great Forest begins. The foreground is sandy, level ground dotted by a few stones and clumps of stunted bushes cowering close against the earth to escape the buffeting of the trade wind. In the rear the forest is a wall of darkness dividing the world. Only when the eye becomes accustomed to the gloom can the outlines of separate trunks of the nearest trees be made out, enormous pillars of deeper blackness. A somber monotone of wind lost in the leaves moans in the air. Yet this sound serves but to intensify the impression of the forest's relentless immobility, to form a background throwing into relief its brooding, implacable silence.*

*[*JONES *enters from the left, walking rapidly. He stops as he nears the edge of the forest, looks around him quickly, peering into the dark as if searching for some familiar landmark. Then, apparently satisfied that he is where he ought to be, he throws himself on the ground, dog-tired.]*

Well, heah I is. In de nick o' time, too! Little mo' an' it'd be black-er'n de ace of spades heah-abouts. [*He pulls a bandana handkerchief from his hip pocket and mops off his perspiring face.*] Sho'! Gimme air! I'se tuckered out sho' 'nuff. Dat soft Emperor job ain't no trainin' for a long hike ovah dat plain in de brilin' sun. [*Then with a chuckle.*] Cheah up, nigger, de worst is yet to come. [*He lifts his head and stares at the forest. His chuckle peters out abruptly. In a tone of awe.*] My goodness, look at dem woods, will you? Dat no-count Smithers said dey'd be black an' he sho' called de turn. [*Turning away from them quickly and looking down at his feet, he snatches at a chance to change the subject—solicitously.*] Feet, you is holdin' up yo' end fine an' I sutinly hopes you ain't blisterin' none. It's time you git a rest. [*He takes off his shoes, his eyes studiously avoiding the forest. He feels of the soles of his feet gingerly.*] You is still in de pink—on'y a little mite feverish. Cool yo'selfs. Remember you done got a long journey yit befo' you. [*He sits in a weary attitude, listening to the rhythmic beating of the tom-tom. He grumbles in a loud tone to cover up a growing uneasiness.*] Bush niggers! Wonder dey wouldn' git sick o' beatin' dat drum. Sound louder, seem like. I wonder if dey's startin' after me? [*He scrambles to his feet, looking back across the plain.*] Couldn't see dem now, nohow, if dey was hundred feet away. [*Then shaking himself like a wet dog to get rid of these depressing thoughts.*] Sho', dey's miles an' miles behind. What you gittin' fidgetty about? [*But he sits down and begins to lace up his shoes in great haste, all the time muttering reassuringly.*] You know what? Yo' belly is empty, dat's what's de matter wid you. Come time to eat! Wid nothin' but wind on yo' stumach, o' course you feels jiggedy. Well, we eats right heah an' now soon's I gits dese pesky shoes laced up. [*He finishes lacing up his shoes.*] Dere! Now le's see! [*Gets on his hands and knees and searches the ground around him with his eyes.*] White stone, white stone, where is you? [*He sees the first white stone and crawls to it—with satisfaction.*] Heah you is! I knowed dis was de right place. Box of grub, come to me. [*He turns over the stone and feels in under it—in a tone of dismay.*] Ain't heah! Gorry, is I in de right place or isn't I? Dere's 'nother stone. Guess dat's it. [*He scrambles to the next stone and turns it over.*] Ain't heah, neither! Grub, whar is you? Ain't heah. Gorry, has I got to go hungry into dem woods—all de night? [*While he is talking he scrambles from one stone to another, turning them over in frantic haste. Finally, he jumps to his feet excitedly.*] Is I lost de place? Must have! But how dat happen when I was followin' de trail across de plain in broad daylight? [*Almost plaintively.*] I'se hungry, I is! I gotta git my feed. Whar's my strength gonna come from if I doesn't? Gorry, I gotta find dat grub high an' low somehow! Why it come dark so quick like dat? Can't see nothin'. [*He scratches a match on his trousers and peers about him. The rate of the beat of the far-off tom-tom increases perceptibly as he does so. He mutters in a bewildered voice.*] How come all dese white stones come heah when I only remembers one? [*Suddenly, with a frightened gasp, he flings the match on the ground and stamps on it.*] Nigger, is you gone crazy mad? Is you lightin' matches to show dem whar you is? Fo' Lawd's sake, use yo' haid. Gorry, I'se got to be careful! [*He stares at the plain behind him apprehensively, his hand on his revolver.*] But how come all dese white stones? And whar's dat tin box o' grub I hid all wrapped up in oil cloth?

[*While his back is turned, the* LITTLE FORMLESS FEARS *creep out from the deeper blackness of the forest. They are black, shapeless, only their glittering little eyes can be seen. If they have any describable form at all it is that of a grubworm about the size of a creeping child. They move noiselessly, but with deliberate, painful effort, striving to raise themselves on end, failing and sinking prone again.* JONES *turns about to face the forest. He stares up at the tops of the trees, seeking vainly to discover his whereabouts by their conformation.*]

Can't tell nothin' from dem trees! Gorry, nothin' 'round heah look like I evah seed it befo'. I'se done lost de place sho' 'nuff! [*With mournful foreboding.*] It's mighty queer! It's mighty queer! [*With sudden forced defiance—in an angry tone.*] Woods, is you tryin' to put somethin' ovah on me?

[*From the formless creatures on the ground in front of him comes a tiny gale of low mocking laughter like a rustling of leaves. They squirm upward toward him in twisted attitudes.* JONES *looks down, leaps backward with a yell of terror, yanking out his revolver as he does so—in a quavering voice.*] What's dat? Who's dar? What is you? Git away from me befo' I shoots you up! You don't?—

[*He fires. There is a flash, a loud report, then silence broken only by the far-off, quickened throb of the tom-tom. The formless creatures have scurried back into the forest.* JONES *remains fixed in his position, listening intently. The sound of the shot, the reassuring feel of the revolver in his hand, have somewhat restored his shaken nerve. He addresses himself with renewed confidence.*]

Dey're gone. Dat shot fix 'em. Dey was only little animals—little wild pigs, I reckon. Dey've maybe rooted out yo' grub an' eat it. Sho', you fool nigger, what you think dey is—ha'nts? [*Excitedly.*] Gorry, you give de game away when you fire dat shot. Dem niggers heah dat fo' su'tin! Time you beat it in de woods widout no long waits. [*He starts for the forest—hesitates before the plunge—then urging himself in with manful resolution.*] Git in, nigger! What you skeered at? Ain't nothin' dere but de trees! Git in! [*He plunges boldly into the forest.*]

SCENE THREE

SCENE—*Nine o'clock. In the forest. The moon has just risen. Its beams, drifting through the canopy of leaves, make a barely perceptible, suffused, eerie glow. A dense low wall of underbrush and creepers is in the nearer foreground, fencing in a small triangular clearing. Beyond this is the massed blackness of the forest like an encompassing barrier. A path is dimly discerned leading down to the clearing from left, rear, and winding away from it again toward the right. As the scene opens nothing can be distinctly made out. Except for the beating of the tom-tom, which is a trifle louder and quicker than in the previous scene, there is silence, broken every few seconds by a queer, clicking sound. Then gradually the figure of the negro,* JEFF, *can be discerned crouching on his haunches at the rear of the triangle. He is middle-aged, thin, brown in color, is dressed in a Pullman porter's uniform, cap, etc. He is throwing a pair of dice on the ground before him, picking them up, shaking them, casting them out with the regular, rigid, mechanical movements of an automaton. The heavy, plodding footsteps of someone approaching along the trail from the left are heard and* JONES' *voice, pitched in a slightly higher key and strained in a cheering effort to overcome its own tremors.*

De moon's rizen. Does you heah dat, nigger? You gits more light from dis out. No mo' buttin' yo' fool head agin' de trunks an' scratchin' de hide off yo' legs in de bushes. Now you sees whar yo'se gwine. So cheer up! From now on you has a snap. [*He steps just to the rear of the triangular clearing and mops off his face on his sleeve. He has lost his Panama hat. His face is scratched, his brilliant uniform shows several large rents.*] What time's it gittin' to be, I wonder? I dassent light no match to find out. Phoo'. It's wa'm an' dats a fac'! [*Wearily.*] How long I been makin' tracks in dese woods? Must be hours an' hours. Seems like fo'evah! Yit can't be, when de moon's jes' riz. Dis am a long night fo' yo', yo' Majesty! [*With a mournful chuckle.*] Majesty! Der ain't much majesty 'bout dis baby now. [*With attempted cheerfulness.*] Never min'. It's all part o' de game. Dis night come to an end like everything else. And when you gits dar safe and has dat bankroll in yo' hands you laughs at all dis. [*He starts to whistle but checks himself abruptly.*] What yo' whistlin' for, you po' dope! Want all de worl' to heah you? [*He stops talking to listen.*] Heah dat ole drum! Sho' gits nearer from de sound. Dey're packin' it along wid 'em. Time fo' me to move. [*He takes a step forward, then stops—worriedly.*] What's dat odder queer clicketty sound I heah? Dere it is! Sound close! Sound like—sound like—Fo' God sake, sound like some nigger was shootin' crap! [*Frightenedly.*] I better beat it quick when I gits dem notions. [*He walks quickly into the clear space—then stands transfixed as he sees* JEFF—*in a terrified gasp.*] Who dar? Who dat? Is dat you, Jeff? [*Starting toward the other, forgetful for a moment of his surroundings and really believing it is a living man that he sees—in a tone of happy relief.*] Jeff! I'se sho' mighty glad to see you! Dey tol' me you done died from dat razor cut I gives you. [*Stopping suddenly, bewilderedly.*] But how you come to be heah, nigger? [*He stares fascinatedly at the other who continues his mechanical play with the dice.* JONES' *eyes begin to roll wildly. He stutters.*] Ain't you gwine—look up—can't you speak to me? Is you—is you—a ha'nt? [*He jerks out his revolver in a frenzy of terrified rage.*] Nigger, I kills you dead once. Has I got to kill you agin? You take it den. [*He fires. When the smoke clears away* JEFF *has disappeared.* JONES *stands trembling—then with a certain reassurance.*] He's gone, anyway. Ha'nt or no ha'nt, dat shot fix him. [*The beat of the far-off tom-tom is perceptibly louder and more rapid.* JONES *becomes conscious of it—with a start, looking back over his shoulder.*] Dey's gittin' near! Dey'se comin' fast! And heah I is shootin' shots to let 'em know jes' whar I is. Oh, Gorry, I'se got to run. [*Forgetting the path he plunges wildly into the underbrush in the rear and disappears in the shadow.*]

SCENE FOUR

SCENE—*Eleven o'clock. In the forest. A wide dirt road runs diagonally from right, front, to left, rear. Rising sheer on both sides the forest walls it in. The moon is now up. Under its light the road glimmers ghastly and unreal. It is as if the forest had stood aside momentarily to let the road pass through and accomplish its veiled purpose. This done, the forest will fold in upon itself again and the road will be no more.* JONES *stumbles in from the forest on the right. His uniform is ragged and torn. He looks about him with numbed surprise when he sees the road, his eyes blinking in the bright moonlight. He flops down exhaustedly and pants heavily for a while. Then with sudden anger.*

I'm meltin' wid heat! Runnin' an' runnin' an' runnin'! Damn dis heah coat! Like a strait jacket! [*He tears off his coat and flings it away from him, revealing himself stripped to the waist.*] Dere! Dat's better! Now I kin breathe! [*Looking down at his feet, the spurs catch his eye.*] And to hell wid dese high-fangled spurs. Dey're what's been a-trippin' me up an' breakin' my neck. [*He unstraps them and flings them away disgustedly.*] Dere! I gits rid o' dem frippety Emperor trappin's an' I travels lighter. Lawd! I'se tired! [*After a pause, listening to the insistent beat of the tom-tom in the distance.*] I must 'a put some distance between myself an' dem—runnin' like dat—and yit—dat damn drum sound jes' de same—nearer, even. Well, I guess I a'most holds my lead anyhow. Dey won't never catch up. [*With a sigh.*] If on'y my fool legs stands up. Oh, I'se sorry I evah went in for dis. Dat Emperor job is sho' hard to shake. [*He looks around him suspiciously.*] How'd dis road evah git heah? Good level road, too. I never remembers seein' it befo'. [*Shaking his head apprehensively.*] Dese woods is sho' full o' de queerest things at night. [*With a sudden terror.*] Lawd God, don't let me see no more o' dem ha'nts! Dey gits my goat! [*Then trying to talk himself into confidence.*] Ha'nts! You fool nigger, dey ain't no such things! Don't de Baptist parson tell you dat many time? Is you civilized, or is you like dese ign'rent black niggers heah? Sho'! Dat was all in yo' own head. Wasn't nothin' dere. Wasn't no Jeff! Know what? You jus' get seein' dem things 'cause yo' belly's empty and you's sick wid hunger inside. Hunger 'fects yo' head and yo' eyes. Any fool know dat. [*Then pleading fervently.*] But bless God, I don't come across no more o' dem, whatever dey is! [*Then cautiously.*] Rest! Don't talk! Rest! You needs it. Den you gits on yo' way again. [*Looking at the moon.*] Night's half gone a'most. You hits de coast in de mawning! Den you'se all safe.

[*From the right forward a small gang of negroes enter. They are dressed in striped convict suits, their heads are shaven, one leg drags limpingly, shackled to a heavy ball and chain. Some carry picks, the others shovels. They are followed by a white man dressed in the uniform of a prison guard. A Winchester rifle is slung across his shoulders and he carries a heavy whip. At a signal from the* GUARD *they stop on the road opposite where* JONES *is sitting.* JONES, *who has been staring up at the sky, unmindful of their noiseless approach, suddenly looks down and sees them. His eyes pop out, he tries to get to his feet and fly, but sinks back, too numbed by fright to move. His voice catches in a choking prayer.*]

Lawd Jesus!

[*The* PRISON GUARD *cracks his whip—noiselessly—and at that signal all the convicts start to work on the road. They swing their picks, they shovel, but not a sound comes from their labor. Their movements, like those of* JEFF *in the preceding scene, are those of automatons,—rigid, slow, and mechanical. The* PRISON GUARD *points sternly at* JONES *with his whip, motions him to take his place among the other shovellers.* JONES *gets to his feet in a hypnotized stupor. He mumbles subserviently.*]

Yes, suh! Yes, suh! I'se comin'.

[*As he shuffles, dragging one foot, over to his place, he curses under his breath with rage and hatred.*]

God damn yo' soul, I gits even wid you yit, sometime.

[*As if there were a shovel in his hands he goes through weary, mechanical gestures of digging up dirt, and throwing it to the roadside. Suddenly the* GUARD *approaches him angrily, threateningly.
He raises his whip and lashes* JONES *viciously across the shoulders
with it.* JONES *winces with pain and cowers abjectly. The* GUARD
turns his back on him and walks away contemptuously. Instantly
JONES *straightens up. With arms upraised as if his shovel were a
club in his hands he springs murderously at the unsuspecting*
GUARD. *In the act of crashing down his shovel on the white man's
skull,* JONES *suddenly becomes aware that his hands are empty. He
cries despairingly.*]

Whar's my shovel? Gimme my shovel 'till I splits his damn head!
[*Appealing to his fellow convicts.*] Gimme a shovel, one o' you, fo'
God's sake!

[*They stand fixed in motionless attitudes, their eyes on the
ground. The* GUARD *seems to wait expectantly, his back turned
to the attacker.* JONES *bellows with baffled, terrified rage, tugging
frantically at his revolver.*]

I kills you, you white debil, if it's de last thing I evah does! Ghost
or debil, I kill you agin!

[*He frees the revolver and fires point blank at the* GUARD'*s back.
Instantly the walls of the forest close in from both sides, the road
and the figures of the convict gang are blotted out in an en-
shrouding darkness. The only sounds are a crashing in the underbrush as* JONES *leaps away in mad flight and the throbbing of the
tom-tom, still far distant, but increased in volume of sound and
rapidity of beat.*]

SCENE FIVE

SCENE—*One o'clock. A large circular clearing, enclosed by the serried
ranks of gigantic trunks of tall trees whose tops are lost to view. In the
center is a big dead stump worn by time into a curious resemblance to
an auction block. The moon floods the clearing with a clear light.*
JONES *forces his way in through the forest on the left. He looks wildly
about the clearing with hunted, fearful glances. His pants are in tatters,*

his shoes cut and misshapen, flapping about his feet. He slinks cautiously to the stump in the center and sits down in a tense position, ready for instant flight. Then he holds his head in his hands and rocks back and forth, moaning to himself miserably.]

Oh Lawd, Lawd! Oh Lawd, Lawd! [*Suddenly he throws himself on his knees and raises his clasped hands to the sky—in a voice of agonized pleading.*] Lawd Jesus, heah my prayer! I'se a po' sinner, a po' sinner! I knows I done wrong, I knows it! When I cotches Jeff cheatin' wid loaded dice my anger overcomes me and I kills him dead! Lawd, I done wrong! When dat guard hits me wid de whip, my anger overcomes me, and I kills him dead. Lawd, I done wrong! And down heah whar dese fool bush niggers raises me up to the seat o' de mighty, I steals all I could grab. Lawd, I done wrong! I knows it! I'se sorry! Forgive me, Lawd! Forgive dis po' sinner! [*Then beseeching terrifiedly.*] And keep dem away, Lawd! Keep dem away from me! And stop dat drum soundin' in my ears! Dat begin to sound ha'nted, too. [*He gets to his feet, evidently slightly reassured by his prayer—with attempted confidence.*] De Lawd'll preserve me from dem ha'nts after dis. [*Sits down on the stump again.*] I ain't skeered o' real men. Let dem come. But dem odders— [*He shudders—then looks down at his feet, working his toes inside the shoes—with a groan.*] Oh, my po' feet! Dem shoes ain't no use no more 'ceptin' to hurt. I'se better off widout dem. [*He unlaces them and pulls them off—holds the wrecks of the shoes in his hands and regards them mournfully.*] You was real, A-one patin' leather, too. Look at you now. Emperor, you'se gittin' mighty low!

[*He sighs dejectedly and remains with bowed shoulders, staring down at the shoes in his hands as if reluctant to throw them away. While his attention is thus occupied, a crowd of figures silently enter the clearing from all sides. All are dressed in Southern costumes of the period of the fifties of the last century. There are middle-aged men who are evidently well-to-do planters. There is one spruce, authoritative individual—the AUCTIONEER. There are a crowd of curious spectators, chiefly young belles and dandies who have come to the slave-market for diversion. All exchange courtly greetings in dumb show and chat silently together. There is something stiff, rigid, unreal, marionettish about their movements. They group themselves about the stump. Finally a batch of slaves are led in from the left by an attendant—three men of different ages, two women, one with a baby in her arms, nursing. They are placed to the left of the stump, beside* JONES.

The white planters look them over appraisingly as if they were cattle, and exchange judgments on each. The dandies point with their fingers and make witty remarks. The belles titter bewitchingly. All this in silence save for the ominous throb of the tom-tom. The AUCTIONEER *holds up his hand, taking his place at the stump. The groups strain forward attentively. He touches* JONES *on the shoulder peremptorily, motioning for him to stand on the stump—the auction block.*

JONES *looks up, sees the figures on all sides, looks wildly for some opening to escape, sees none, screams and leaps madly to the top of the stump to get as far away from them as possible. He stands there, cowering, paralyzed with horror. The* AUCTIONEER *begins his silent spiel. He points to* JONES, *appeals to the planters to see for themselves. Here is a good field hand, sound in wind and limb as they can see. Very strong still in spite of his being middle-aged. Look at that back. Look at those shoulders. Look at the muscles in his arms and his sturdy legs. Capable of any amount of hard labor. Moreover, of a good disposition, intelligent and tractable. Will any gentleman start the bidding? The* PLANTERS *raise their fingers, make their bids. They are apparently all eager to possess* JONES. *The bidding is lively, the crowd interested. While this has been going on,* JONES *has been seized by the courage of desperation. He dares to look down and around him. Over his face abject terror gives way to mystification, to gradual realization—stutteringly.*]

What you all doin', white folks? What's all dis? What you all lookin' at me fo'? What you doin' wid me, anyhow? [*Suddenly convulsed with raging hatred and fear.*] Is dis a auction? Is you sellin' me like dey uster befo' de war? [*Jerking out his revolver just as the* AUCTIONEER *knocks him down to one of the planters—glaring from him to the purchaser.*] And *you* sells me? And *you* buys me? I shows you I'se a free nigger, damn yo' souls! [*He fires at the* AUCTIONEER *and at the* PLANTER *with such rapidity that the two shots are almost simultaneous. As if this were a signal the walls of the forest fold in. Only blackness remains and silence broken by* JONES *as he rushes off, crying with fear—and by the quickened, ever louder beat of the tom-tom.*]

SCENE SIX

SCENE—*Three o'clock. A cleared space in the forest. The limbs of the trees meet over it forming a low ceiling about five feet from the ground. The interlocked ropes of creepers reaching upward to entwine the tree trunks gives an arched appearance to the sides. The space thus enclosed is like the dark, noisome hold of some ancient vessel. The moonlight is almost completely shut out and only a vague, wan light filters through. There is the noise of someone approaching from the left, stumbling and crawling through the undergrowth.* JONES' *voice is heard between chattering moans.*

Oh, Lawd, what I gwine do now? Ain't got no bullet left on'y de silver one. If mo' o' dem ha'nts come after me, how I gwine skeer dem away? Oh, Lawd, on'y de silver one left—an' I gotta save dat fo' luck. If I shoots dat one I'm a goner sho'! Lawd, it's black heah! Whar's de moon? Oh, Lawd, don't dis night evah come to an end? [*By the sounds, he is feeling his way cautiously forward.*] Dere! Dis feels like a clear space. I gotta lie down an' rest. I don't care if dem niggers does cotch me. I gotta rest.

[*He is well forward now where his figure can be dimly made out. His pants have been so torn away that what is left of them is no better than a breech cloth. He flings himself full length, face downward on the ground, panting with exhaustion. Gradually it seems to grow lighter in the enclosed space and two rows of seated figures can be seen behind* JONES. *They are sitting in crumpled, despairing attitudes, hunched, facing one another with their backs touching the forest walls as if they were shackled to them. All are negroes, naked save for loin cloths. At first they are silent and motionless. Then they begin to sway slowly forward toward each and back again in unison, as if they were laxly letting themselves follow the long roll of a ship at sea. At the same time, a low, melancholy murmur rises among them, increasing gradually by rhythmic degrees which seem to be directed and controlled by the throb of the tom-tom in the distance, to a long, tremulous wail of despair that reaches a certain pitch, unbearably acute, then falls by slow graduations of tone into silence and is taken up again.* JONES *starts, looks up, sees the figures, and throws himself down again to shut out the sight. A shudder of terror shakes his whole body as the wail rises up about him again. But the next time, his voice, as if under some uncanny compulsion, starts with the others. As their chorus lifts he rises to a sitting posture similar to the others, swaying back and forth. His voice reaches the highest pitch of sorrow, of desolation. The light fades out, the other voices cease, and only darkness is left.* JONES *can be heard scrambling to his feet and running off, his voice sinking down the scale and receding as he moves farther and farther away in the forest. The tom-tom beats louder, quicker, with a more insistent, triumphant pulsation.*]

SCENE SEVEN

SCENE—*Five o'clock. The foot of a gigantic tree by the edge of a great river. A rough structure of boulders, like an altar, is by the tree. The raised river bank is in the nearer background. Beyond this the surface of the river spreads out, brilliant and unruffled in the moonlight, blotted out and merged into a veil of bluish mist in the distance.* JONES' *voice is heard from the left rising and falling in the long, despairing wail of the chained slaves, to the rhythmic beat of the tom-tom. As his voice sinks into silence, he enters the open space. The expression of his face is fixed and stony, his eyes have an obsessed glare, he moves with a strange deliberation like a sleep-walker or one in a trance. He looks around at the tree, the rough stone altar, the moonlit surface of the river beyond, and passes his hand over his head with a vague gesture of puzzled bewilderment. Then, as if in obedience to some obscure impulse, he sinks into a kneeling, devotional posture before the altar. Then he seems to come to himself partly, to have an uncertain realization of what he is doing, for he straightens up and stares about him horrifiedly—in an incoherent mumble.*

What—what is I doin? What is—dis place? Seems like—seems like I know dat tree—an' dem stones—an' de river. I remember—seems like I been heah befo'. [*Tremblingly.*] Oh, Gorry, I'se skeered in dis place! I'se skeered! Oh, Lawd, pertect dis sinner!

[*Crawling away from the altar, he cowers close to the ground, his face hidden, his shoulders heaving with sobs of hysterical fright. From behind the trunk of the tree, as if he had sprung out of it, the figure of the* CONGO WITCH-DOCTOR *appears. He is wizened and old, naked except for the fur of some small animal tied about*

*his waist, its bushy tail hanging down in front. His body is
stained all over a bright red. Antelope horns are on each side of
his head, branching upward. In one hand he carries a bone rattle,
in the other a charm stick with a bunch of white cockatoo feath-
ers tied to the end. A great number of glass beads and bone ornaments are about his neck, ears, wrists, and ankles. He struts
noiselessly with a queer prancing step to a position in the clear
ground between* JONES *and the altar. Then with a preliminary,
summoning stamp of his foot on the earth, he begins to dance and
to chant. As if in response to his summons the beating of the tom-
tom grows to a fierce, exultant boom whose throbs seem to fill
the air with vibrating rhythm.* JONES *looks up, starts to spring to
his feet, reaches a half-kneeling, half-squatting position and remains rigidly fixed there, paralyzed with awed fascination by this
new apparition. The* WITCH-DOCTOR *sways, stamping with his
foot, his bone rattle clicking the time. His voice rises and falls in a
weird, monotonous croon, without articulate word divisions.
Gradually his dance becomes clearly one of a narrative in pan-
tomime, his croon is an incantation, a charm to allay the fierceness of some implacable deity demanding sacrifice. He flees, he is
pursued by devils, he hides, he flees again. Ever wilder and wilder
becomes his flight, nearer and nearer draws the pursuing evil,
more and more the spirit of terror gains possession of him. His
croon, rising to intensity, is punctuated by shrill cries.* JONES *has
become completely hypnotized. His voice joins in the incantation,
in the cries, he beats time with his hands and sways his body to
and fro from the waist. The whole spirit and meaning of the
dance has entered into him, has become his spirit. Finally the
theme of the pantomine halts on a howl of despair, and is taken
up again in a note of savage hope. There is a salvation. The forces
of evil demand sacrifice. They must be appeased. The* WITCH-
DOCTOR *points with his wand to the sacred tree, to the river beyond, to the altar, and finally to* JONES *with a ferocious
command.* JONES *seems to sense the meaning of this. It is he who
must offer himself for sacrifice. He beats his forehead abjectly to
the ground, moaning hysterically.*]

Mercy, Oh Lawd! Mercy! Mercy on dis po' sinner.

[*The* WITCH-DOCTOR *springs to the river bank. He stretches out
his arms and calls to some God within its depths. Then he starts*

*backward slowly, his arms remaining out. A huge head of a croc-
odile appears over the bank and its eyes, glittering greenly, fasten
upon* JONES. *He stares into them fascinatedly. The* WITCH-
DOCTOR *prances up to him, touches him with his wand, motions
with hideous command toward the waiting monster.* JONES
squirms on his belly nearer and nearer, moaning continually.]

Mercy, Lawd! Mercy!

[*The crocodile heaves more of his enormous hulk onto the land.*
JONES *squirms toward him. The* WITCH-DOCTOR'S *voice shrills
out in furious exultation, the tom-tom beats madly.* JONES *cries
out in a fierce, exhausted spasm of anguished pleading.*]

Lawd, save me! Lawd Jesus, heah my prayer!

[*Immediately, in answer to his prayer, comes the thought of the
one bullet left him. He snatches at his hip, shouting defiantly.*]

De silver bullet! You don't git me yit!

[*He fires at the green eyes in front of him. The head of the crocodile sinks back behind the river bank, the* WITCH-DOCTOR
springs behind the sacred tree and disappears. JONES *lies with his
face to the ground, his arms outstretched, whimpering with fear
as the throb of the tom-tom fills the silence about him with a
somber pulsation, a baffled but revengeful power.*]

SCENE EIGHT

SCENE—*Dawn. Same as Scene Two, the dividing line of forest and
plain. The nearest tree trunks are dimly revealed but the forest behind
them is still a mass of glooming shadow. The tom-tom seems on the
very spot, so loud and continuously vibrating are its beats.* LEM *enters
from the left, followed by a small squad of his soldiers, and by the
Cockney trader,* SMITHERS. LEM *is a heavy-set, ape-faced old savage of
the extreme African type, dressed only in a loin cloth. A revolver and
cartridge belt are about his waist. His soldiers are in different degrees of
rag-concealed nakedness. All wear broad palm-leaf hats. Each one carries a rifle.* SMITHERS *is the same as in Scene One. One of the soldiers,
evidently a tracker, is peering about keenly on the ground. He grunts*

and points to the spot where JONES *entered the forest.* LEM *and*
SMITHERS *come to look.*

SMITHERS: [*After a glance, turns away in disgust.*] That's where 'e went
in right enough. Much good it'll do yer. 'E's miles orf by this an' safe
to the Coast damn 's 'ide! I tole yer yer'd lose 'im, didn't I?—wastin'
the 'ole bloomin' night beatin' yer bloody drum and castin' yer silly
spells! Gawd blimey, wot a pack!

LEM: [*Gutturally.*] We cotch him. You see. [*He makes a motion to his
soldiers who squat down on their haunches in a semi-circle.*]

SMITHERS: [*Exasperatedly.*] Well, ain't yer goin' in an' 'unt 'im in the
woods? What the 'ell's the good of waitin'?

LEM: [*Imperturbably—squatting down himself.*] We cotch him.

SMITHERS: [*Turning away from him contemptuously.*] Aw! Garn! 'E's a
better man than the lot o' you put together. I 'ates the sight o' 'im
but I'll say that for 'im. [*A sound of snapping twigs comes from the
forest. The soldiers jump to their feet, cocking their rifles alertly.*
LEM *remains sitting with an imperturbable expression, but listening
intently. The sound from the woods is repeated.* LEM *makes a quick
signal with his hand. His followers creep quickly but noiselessly into
the forest, scattering so that each enters at a different spot.*]

SMITHERS: [*In the silence that follows—in a contemptuous whisper.*]
You ain't thinkin' that would be 'im, I 'ope?

LEM: [*Calmly.*] We cotch him.

SMITHERS: Blarsted fat 'eads! [*Then after a second's thought—
wonderingly.*] Still an' all, it might 'appen. If 'e lost 'is bloody way in
these stinkin' woods 'e'd likely turn in a circle without 'is knowin' it.
They all does.

LEM: [*Peremptorily.*] Sssh! [*The reports of several rifles sound from the
forest, followed a second later by savage, exultant yells. The beating
of the tom-tom abruptly ceases.* LEM *looks up at the white man with
a grin of satisfaction.*] We cotch him. Him dead.

SMITHERS: [*With a snarl.*] 'Ow d'yer know it's 'im an' 'ow d'yer know
'e's dead?

LEM: My mens dey got 'um silver bullets. Dey kill him shore.

SMITHERS: [*Astonished.*] They got silver bullets?

LEM: Lead bullet no kill him. He got um strong charm. I cook um
money, make um silver bullet, make um strong charm, too.

SMITHERS: [*Light breaking upon him.*] So that's wot you was up to all
night, wot? You was scared to put after 'im till you'd moulded silver
bullets, eh?

LEM: [*Simply stating a fact.*] Yes. Him got strong charm. Lead no good.

SMITHERS: [*Slapping his thigh and guffawing.*] Haw-haw! If yer don't beat all 'ell! [*Then recovering himself—scornfully.*] I'll bet yer it ain't 'im they shot at all, yer bleedin' looney!

LEM: [*Calmly.*] Dey come bring him now. [*The soldiers come out of the forest, carrying* JONES' *limp body. There is a little reddish-purple hole under his left breast. He is dead. They carry him to* LEM, *who examines his body with great satisfaction.* SMITHERS *leans over his shoulder—in a tone of frightened awe.*] Well, they did for yer right enough, Jonsey, me lad! Dead as a 'erring! [*Mockingly.*] Where's yer 'igh an' mighty airs now, yer bloomin' Majesty? [*Then with a grin.*] Silver bullets! Gawd blimey, but yer died in the 'eighth o' style, any'ow! [LEM *makes a motion to the soldiers to carry the body out left.* SMITHERS *speaks to him sneeringly.*]

SMITHERS: And I s'pose you think it's yer bleedin' charms and yer silly beatin' the drum that made 'im run in a circle when 'e'd lost 'imself, don't yer? [*But* LEM *makes no reply, does not seem to hear the question, walks out left after his men.* SMITHERS *looks after him with contemptuous scorn.*] Stupid as 'ogs, the lot of 'em! Blarsted niggers!

[*Curtain Falls.*]

ANNA CHRISTIE

A PLAY IN FOUR ACTS

CHARACTERS

"JOHNNY-THE-PRIEST"

TWO LONGSHOREMEN

A POSTMAN

LARRY, *bartender*

CHRIS. CHRISTOPHERSON, *captain of the barge* Simeon Winthrop

MARTHY OWEN

ANNA CHRISTOPHERSON, *Chris's daughter*

THREE MEN OF A STEAMER'S CREW

MAT BURKE, *a stoker*

JOHNSON, *deckhand on the barge*

ACT I

SCENE—"JOHNNY-THE-PRIEST'S" *saloon near South Street, New York City. The stage is divided into two sections, showing a small back room on the right. On the left, forward, of the barroom, a large window looking out on the street. Beyond it, the main entrance—a double swinging door. Farther back, another window. The bar runs from left to right nearly the whole length of the rear wall. In back of the bar, a small showcase displaying a few bottles of case goods, for which there is evidently little call. The remainder of the rear space in front of the large mirrors is occupied by half-barrels of cheap whiskey of the "nickel-a-shot" variety, from which the liquor is drawn by means of spigots. On the right is an open doorway leading to the back room. In the back room are four round wooden tables with five chairs grouped about each. In the rear, a family entrance opening on a side street.*

It is late afternoon of a day in fall.

As the curtain rises, JOHNNY *is discovered.* "JOHNNY-THE-PRIEST" *deserves his nickname. With his pale, thin, clean-shaven face, mild blue eyes and white hair, a cassock would seem more suited to him than the apron he wears. Neither his voice nor his general manner dispel this illusion which has made him a personage of the water front. They are soft and bland. But beneath all his mildness one senses the man behind the mask—cynical, callous, hard as nails. He is lounging at ease behind the bar, a pair of spectacles on his nose, reading an evening paper.*

Two longshoremen enter from the street, wearing their working aprons, the button of the union pinned conspicuously on the caps pulled sideways on their heads at an aggressive angle.

FIRST LONGSHOREMAN: [*As they range themselves at the bar.*] Gimme a shock. Number Two. [*He tosses a coin on the bar.*]

SECOND LONGSHOREMAN: Same here. [JOHNNY *sets two glasses of barrel whiskey before them.*]

FIRST LONGSHOREMAN: Here's luck! [*The other nods. They gulp down their whiskey.*]

SECOND LONGSHOREMAN: [*Putting money on the bar.*] Give us another.

FIRST LONGSHOREMAN: Gimme a scoop this time—lager and porter. I'm dry.

SECOND LONGSHOREMAN: Same here. [JOHNNY *draws the lager and*

*porter and sets the big, foaming schooners before them. They drink
down half the contents and start to talk together hurriedly in low
tones. The door on the left is swung open and* LARRY *enters. He is a
boyish, red-cheeked, rather good-looking young fellow of twenty
or so.*]

LARRY: [*Nodding to Johnny—cheerily.*] Hello, boss.

JOHNNY: Hello, Larry. [*With a glance at his watch.*] Just on time.
[*Larry goes to the right behind the bar, takes off his coat, and puts
on an apron.*]

FIRST LONGSHOREMAN: [*Abruptly.*] Let's drink up and get back to it.
[*They finish their drinks and go out left. The Postman enters as they
leave. He exchanges nods with Johnny and throws a letter on
the bar.*]

THE POSTMAN: Addressed care of you, Johnny. Know him?

JOHNNY: [*Picks up the letter, adjusting his spectacles.* LARRY *comes
and peers over his shoulders.* JOHNNY *reads very slowly.*] Christopher Christopherson.

THE POSTMAN: [*Helpfully.*] Square-head name.

LARRY: Old Chris—that's who.

JOHNNY: Oh, sure. I was forgetting Chris carried a hell of a name like
that. Letters come here for him sometimes before, I remember now.
Long time ago, though.

THE POSTMAN: It'll get him all right then?

JOHNNY: Sure thing. He comes here whenever he's in port.

THE POSTMAN: [*Turning to go.*] Sailor, eh?

JOHNNY: [*With a grin.*] Captain of a coal barge.

THE POSTMAN: [*Laughing.*] Some job! Well, s'long.

JOHNNY: S'long. I'll see he gets it. [*The Postman goes out.* JOHNNY
scrutinizes the letter.] You got good eyes, Larry. Where's it from?

LARRY: [*After a glance.*] St. Paul. That'll be in Minnesota, I'm thinkin'.
Looks like a woman's writing, too, the old divil!

JOHNNY: He's got a daughter somewheres out West, I think he told me
once. [*He puts the letter on the cash register.*] Come to think of it, I
ain't seen old Chris in a dog's age. [*Putting his overcoat on, he comes
around the end of the bar.*] Guess I'll be gettin' home. See you tomorrow.

LARRY: Good-night to ye, boss. [*As* JOHNNY *goes toward the street
door, it is pushed open and* CHRISTOPHER CHRISTOPHERSON *enters.
He is a short, squat, broad-shouldered man of about fifty, with a
round, weather-beaten, red face from which his light blue eyes peer
short-sightedly, twinkling with a simple good humor. His large*

mouth, overhung by a thick, drooping, yellow mustache, is child-
ishly self-willed and weak, of an obstinate kindliness. A thick neck is
jammed like a post into the heavy trunk of his body. His arms with
their big, hairy, freckled hands, and his stumpy legs terminating in
large flat feet, are awkwardly short and muscular. He walks with a
clumsy, rolling gait. His voice, when not raised in a hollow boom,
is toned down to a sly, confidential half-whisper with something
vaguely plaintive in its quality. He is dressed in a wrinkled, ill-fitting
dark suit of shore clothes, and wears a faded cap of gray cloth over
his mop of grizzled, blond hair. Just now his face beams with a too-
blissful happiness, and he has evidently been drinking. He reaches
his hand out to Johnny.]

CHRIS: Hello, Yohnny! Have drink on me. Come on, Larry. Give us
drink. Have one yourself. [*Putting his hand in his pocket.*] Ay gat
money—plenty money.

JOHNNY: [*Shakes Chris by the hand.*] Speak of the devil. We was just
talkin' about you.

LARRY: [*Coming to the end of the bar.*] Hello, Chris. Put it there. [*They
shake hands.*]

CHRIS: [*Beaming.*] Give us drink.

JOHNNY: [*With a grin.*] You got a half-snootful now. Where'd you
get it?

CHRIS: [*Grinning.*] Oder fallar on oder barge—Irish fallar—he gat bottle vhiskey and we drank it, yust us two. Dot vhiskey gat kick, by
yingo! Ay yust come ashore. Give us drink, Larry. Ay vas little
drunk, not much. Yust feel good. [*He laughs and commences to sing
in a nasal, high-pitched quaver.*]

"My Yosephine, come board de ship. Long time Ay vait for you.

De moon, she shi-i-i-ine. She looka yust like you.

Tchee-tchee, tchee-tchee, tchee-tchee, tchee-tchee."

[*To the accompaniment of this last he waves his hand as if he were con-
ducting an orchestra.*]

JOHNNY: [*With a laugh.*] Same old Yosie, eh, Chris?

CHRIS: You don't know good song when you hear him. Italian fallar on
oder barge, he learn me dat. Give us drink. [*He throws change on
the bar.*]

LARRY: [*With a professional air.*] What's your pleasure, gentlemen?

JOHNNY: Small beer, Larry.

CHRIS: Vhiskey—Number Two.

LARRY: [*As he gets their drinks.*] I'll take a cigar on you.

CHRIS: [*Lifting his glass.*] Skoal! [*He drinks.*]

JOHNNY: Drink hearty.

CHRIS: [*Immediately.*] Have oder drink.

JOHNNY: No. Some other time. Got to go home now. So you've just landed? Where are you in from this time?

CHRIS: Norfolk. Ve make slow voyage—dirty vedder—yust fog, fog, fog, all bloody time! [*There is an insistent ring from the doorbell at the family entrance in the back room. Chris gives a start—hurriedly.*] Ay go open, Larry. Ay forgat. It vas Marthy. She come with me. [*He goes into the back room.*]

LARRY: [*With a chuckle.*] He's still got that same cow livin' with him, the old fool!

JOHNNY: [*With a grin.*] A sport, Chris is. Well, I'll beat it home. S'long. [*He goes to the street door.*]

LARRY: So long, boss.

JOHNNY: Oh—don't forget to give him his letter.

LARRY: I won't. [JOHNNY *goes out. In the meantime,* CHRIS *has opened the family entrance door, admitting* MARTHY. *She might be forty or fifty. Her jowly, mottled face, with its thick red nose, is streaked with interlacing purple veins. Her thick, gray hair is piled anyhow in a greasy mop on top of her round head. Her figure is flabby and fat; her breath comes in wheezy gasps; she speaks in a loud, mannish voice, punctuated by explosions of hoarse laughter. But there still twinkles in her blood-shot blue eyes a youthful lust for life which hard usage has failed to stifle, a sense of humor mocking, but good-tempered. She wears a man's cap, double-breasted man's jacket, and a grimy, calico skirt. Her bare feet are encased in a man's brogans several sizes too large for her, which gives her a shuffling, wobbly gait.*]

MARTHY: [*Grumblingly.*] What yuh tryin' to do, Dutchy—keep me standin' out there all day? [*She comes forward and sits at the table in the right corner, front.*]

CHRIS: [*Mollifyingly.*] Ay'm sorry, Marthy. Ay talk to Yohnny. Ay forgat. What you goin' take for drink?

MARTHY: [*Appeased.*] Gimme a scoop of lager an' ale.

CHRIS: Ay go bring him back. [*He returns to the bar.*] Lager and ale for Marthy, Larry. Vhiskey for me. [*He throws change on the bar.*]

LARRY: Right you are. [*Then remembering, he takes the letter from in back of the bar.*] Here's a letter for you—from St. Paul, Minnesota— and a lady's writin'. [*He grins.*]

CHRIS: [*Quickly—taking it.*] Oh, den it come from my daughter, Anna. She live dere. [*He turns the letter over in his hands uncertainly.*] Ay don't gat letter from Anna—must be a year.

LARRY: [*Jokingly.*] That's a fine fairy tale to be tellin'—your daughter! Sure I'll bet it's some bum.

CHRIS: [*Soberly.*] No. Dis come from Anna. [*Engrossed by the letter in his hand—uncertainly.*] By golly, Ay tank Ay'm too drunk for read dis letter from Anna. Ay tank Ay sat down for a minute. You bring drinks in back room, Larry. [*He goes into the room on right.*]

MARTHY: [*Angrily.*] Where's my lager an' ale, yuh big stiff?

CHRIS: [*Preoccupied.*] Larry bring him. [*He sits down opposite her. Larry brings in the drinks and sets them on the table. He and Marthy exchange nods of recognition. Larry stands looking at Chris curiously. Marthy takes a long draught of her schooner and heaves a huge sigh of satisfaction, wiping her mouth with the back of her hand. Chris stares at the letter for a moment—slowly opens it, and, squinting his eyes, commences to read laboriously, his lips moving as he spells out the words. As he reads his face lights up with an expression of mingled joy and bewilderment.*]

LARRY: Good news?

MARTHY: [*Her curiosity also aroused.*] What's that yuh got—a letter, fur Gawd's sake?

CHRIS: [*Pauses for a moment, after finishing the letter, as if to let the news sink in—then suddenly pounds his fist on the table with happy excitement.*] Py yiminy! Yust tank, Anna say she's comin' here right avay! She gat sick on yob in St. Paul, she say. It's short letter, don't tal me much more'n dat. [*Beaming.*] Py golly, dat's good news all at one time for ole fallar! [*Then turning to Marthy, rather shame-facedly.*] You know, Marthy, Ay've tole you Ay don't see my Anna since she vas little gel in Sveden five year ole.

MARTHY: How old'll she be now?

CHRIS: She must be—lat me see—she must be twenty year ole, py Yo!

LARRY: [*Surprised.*] You've not seen her in fifteen years?

CHRIS: [*Suddenly growing somber—in a low tone.*] No. Ven she vas little gel, Ay vas bo'sun on vindjammer. Ay never gat home only few time dem year. Ay'm fool sailor fallar. My voman—Anna's mother—she gat tired vait all time Sveden for me ven Ay don't never come. She come dis country, bring Anna, dey go out Minnesota, live with her cousins on farm. Den ven her mo'der die ven Ay vas on voyage, Ay tank it's better dem cousins keep Anna. Ay tank it's better Anna live on farm, den she don't know dat ole davil, sea, she don't know fader like me.

LARRY: [*With a wink at MARTHY.*] This girl, now, 'll be marryin' a sailor herself, likely. It's in the blood.

CHRIS: [*Suddenly springing to his feet and smashing his fist on the table in a rage.*] No, py God! She don't do dat!

MARTHY: [*Grasping her schooner hastily—angrily.*] Hey, look out, yuh nut! Wanta spill my suds for me?

LARRY: [*Amazed.*] Oho, what's up with you? Ain't you a sailor yourself now, and always been?

CHRIS: [*Slowly.*] Dat's yust vhy Ay say it. [*Forcing a smile.*] Sailor vas all right fallar, but not for marry gel. No. Ay know dat. Anna's mo'der, she know it, too.

LARRY: [*As Chris remains sunk in gloomy reflection.*] When is your daughter comin'? Soon?

CHRIS: [*Roused.*] Py yiminy, Ay forgat. [*Reads through the letter hurriedly.*] She say she come right avay, dat's all.

LARRY: She'll maybe be comin' here to look for you, I s'pose. [*He returns to the bar, whistling. Left alone with* MARTHY, *who stares at him with a twinkle of malicious humor in her eyes,* CHRIS *suddenly becomes desperately ill-at-ease. He fidgets, then gets up hurriedly.*]

CHRIS: Ay gat speak with Larry. Ay be right back. [*Mollifyingly.*] Ay bring you oder drink.

MARTHY: [*Emptying her glass.*] Sure. That's me. [*As he retreats with the glass she guffaws after him derisively.*]

CHRIS: [*To* LARRY *in an alarmed whisper.*] Py yingo, Ay gat gat Marthy shore off barge before Anna come! Anna raise hell if she find dat out. Marthy raise hell, too, for go, py golly!

LARRY: [*With a chuckle.*] Serve ye right, ye old divil—havin' a woman at your age!

CHRIS: [*Scratching his head in a quandary.*] You tal me lie for tal Marthy, Larry, so's she gat off barge quick.

LARRY: She knows your daughter's comin'. Tell her to get the hell out of it.

CHRIS: No. Ay don't like make her feel bad.

LARRY: You're an old mush! Keep your girl away from the barge, then. She'll likely want to stay ashore anyway. [*Curiously.*] What does she work at, your Anna?

CHRIS: She stay on dem cousins' farm 'till two year ago. Dan she gat yob nurse gel in St. Paul. [*Then shaking his head resolutely.*] But Ay don't vant for her gat yob now. Ay vant for her stay with me.

LARRY: [*Scornfully.*] On a coal barge! She'll not like that, I'm thinkin'.

MARTHY: [*Shouts from next room.*] Don't I get that bucket o' suds, Dutchy?

CHRIS: [*Startled—in apprehensive confusion.*] Yes, Ay come, Marthy.

LARRY: [*Drawing the lager and ale, hands it to* CHRIS—*laughing.*] Now you're in for it! You'd better tell her straight to get out!

CHRIS: [*Shaking in his boots.*] Py golly. [*He takes her drink in to* MARTHY *and sits down at the table. She sips it in silence.* LARRY *moves quietly close to the partition to listen, grinning with expectation.* CHRIS *seems on the verge of speaking, hesitates, gulps down his whiskey desperately as if seeking for courage. He attempts to whistle a few bars of "Yosephine" with careless bravado, but the whistle peters out futilely.* MARTHY *stares at him keenly, taking in his embarrassment with a malicious twinkle of amusement in her eye.* CHRIS *clears his throat.*] Marthy—

MARTHY: [*Aggressively.*] Wha's that? [*Then, pretending to fly into a rage, her eyes enjoying* CHRIS' *misery.*] I'm wise to what's in back of your nut, Dutchy. Yuh want to git rid o' me, huh?—now she's comin'. Gimme the bum's rush ashore, huh? Lemme tell yuh, Dutchy, there ain't a square-head workin' on a boat man enough to git away with that. Don't start nothin' yuh can't finish!

CHRIS: [*Miserably.*] Ay don't start nutting, Marthy.

MARTHY: [*Glares at him for a second—then cannot control a burst of laughter.*] Ho-ho! Yuh're a scream, Square-head—an honest-ter-Gawd knockout! Ho-ho! [*She wheezes, panting for breath.*]

CHRIS: [*With childish pique.*] Ay don't see nutting for laugh at.

MARTHY: Take a slant in the mirror and yuh'll see. Ho-ho! [*Recovering from her mirth—chuckling, scornfully.*] A square-head tryin' to kid Marthy Owen at this late day!—after me campin' with barge men the last twenty years. I'm wise to the game, up, down, and sideways. I ain't been born and dragged up on the water front for nothin'. Think I'd make trouble, huh? Not me! I'll pack up me duds an' beat it. I'm quittin' yuh, get me? I'm tellin' yuh I'm sick of stickin' with yuh, and I'm leavin' yuh flat, see? There's plenty of other guys on other barges waitin' for me. Always was, I always found. [*She claps the astonished* CHRIS *on the back.*] So cheer up, Dutchy! I'll be offen the barge before she comes. You'll be rid o' me for good—and me o' you—good riddance for both of us. Ho-ho!

CHRIS: [*Seriously.*] Ay don' tank dat. You vas good gel, Marthy.

MARTHY: [*Grinning.*] Good girl? Aw, can the bull! Well, yuh treated me square, yuhself. So it's fifty-fifty. Nobody's sore at nobody. We're still good frien's, huh? [LARRY *returns to bar.*]

CHRIS: [*Beaming now that he sees his troubles disappearing.*] Yes, py golly.

MARTHY: That's the talkin'! In all my time I tried never to split with a guy with no hard feelin's. But what was yuh so scared about—that

I'd kick up a row? That ain't Marthy's way. [*Scornfully.*] Think I'd break my heart to loose yuh? Commit suicide, huh? Ho-ho! Gawd! The world's full o' men if that's all I'd worry about! [*Then with a grin, after emptying her glass.*] Blow me to another scoop, huh? I'll drink your kid's health for yuh.

CHRIS: [*Eagerly.*] Sure tang. Ay go gat him. [*He takes the two glasses into the bar.*] Oder drink. Same for both.

LARRY: [*Getting the drinks and putting them on the bar.*] She's not such a bad lot, that one.

CHRIS: [*Jovially.*] She's good gel, Ay tal you! Py golly, Ay calabrate now! Give me vhiskey here at bar, too. [*He puts down money. LARRY serves him.*] You have drink, Larry.

LARRY: [*Virtuously.*] You know I never touch it.

CHRIS: You don't know what you miss. Skoal! [*He drinks—then begins to sing loudly.*]

"My Yosephine, come board de ship—"

[*He picks up the drinks for MARTHY and himself and walks unsteadily into the back room, singing.*]

"De moon, she shi-i-i-ine. She looks yust like you.

Tche-tchee, tchee-tchee, tchee-tchee, tchee-tchee."

MARTHY: [*Grinning, hands to ears.*] Gawd!

CHRIS: [*Sitting down.*] Ay'm good singer, yes? Ve drink, eh? Skoal! Ay calabrate! [*He drinks.*] Ay calabrate 'cause Anna's coming home. You know, Marthy, Ay never write for her to come, 'cause Ay tank Ay'm no good for her. But all time Ay hope like hell some day she vant for see me and den she come. And dat's vay it happen now, py yiminy! [*His face beaming.*] What you tank she look like, Marthy? Ay bet you she's fine, good, strong gel, pooty like hell! Living on farm made her like dat. And Ay bet you some day she marry good, steady land fallar here in East, have home all her own, have kits— and dan Ay'm ole grandfader, py golly! And Ay go visit dem every time Ay gat in port near! [*Bursting with joy.*] By yiminy crickens, Ay calabrate dat! [*Shouts.*] Bring oder drink, Larry! [*He smashes his fist on the table with a bang.*]

LARRY: [*Coming in from bar—irritably.*] Easy there! Don't be breakin' the table, you old goat!

CHRIS: [*By way of reply, grins foolishly and begins to sing.*] "My Yosephine comes board de ship—"

MARTHY: [*Touching CHRIS' arm persuasively.*] You're soused to the ears, Dutchy. Go out and put a feed into you. It'll sober you up. [*Then as CHRIS shakes his head obstinately.*] Listen, yuh old nut!

Yuh don't know what time your kid's liable to show up. Yuh want to be sober when she comes, don't yuh?

CHRIS: [*Aroused—gets unsteadily to his feet.*] Py golly, yes.

LARRY: That's good sense for you. A good beef stew'll fix you. Go round the corner.

CHRIS: All right. Ay be back soon, Marthy. [CHRIS *goes through the bar and out the street door.*]

LARRY: He'll come round all right with some grub in him.

MARTHY: Sure. [LARRY *goes back to the bar and resumes his newspaper.* MARTHY *sips what is left of her schooner reflectively. There is the ring of the family entrance bell.* LARRY *comes to the door and opens it a trifle—then, with a puzzled expression, pulls it wide.* ANNA CHRISTOPHERSON *enters. She is a tall, blond, fully-developed girl of twenty, handsome after a large, Viking-daughter fashion but now run down in health and plainly showing all the outward evidences of belonging to the world's oldest profession. Her youthful face is already hard and cynical beneath its layer of make-up. Her clothes are the tawdry finery of peasant stock turned prostitute. She comes and sinks wearily in a chair by the table, left front.*]

ANNA: Gimme a whiskey—ginger ale on the side. [*Then, as* LARRY *turns to go, forcing a winning smile at him.*] And don't be stingy, baby.

LARRY: [*Sarcastically.*] Shall I serve it in a pail?

ANNA: [*With a hard laugh.*] That suits me down to the ground. [LARRY *goes into the bar. The two women size each other up with frank stares.* LARRY *comes back with the drink which he sets before* ANNA *and returns to the bar again.* ANNA *downs her drink at a gulp. Then, after a moment, as the alcohol begins to rouse her, she turns to* MARTHY *with a friendly smile.*] Gee, I needed that bad, all right, all right!

MARTHY: [*Nodding her head sympathetically.*] Sure—yuh look all in. Been on a bat?

ANNA: No—travelling—day and a half on the train. Had to sit up all night in the dirty coach, too. Gawd, I thought I'd never get here!

MARTHY: [*With a start—looking at her intently.*] Where'd yuh come from, huh?

ANNA: St. Paul—out in Minnesota.

MARTHY: [*Staring at her in amazement—slowly.*] So—yuh're— [*She suddenly burst out into hoarse, ironical laughter.*] Gawd!

ANNA: All the way from Minnesota, sure. [*Flaring up.*] What you laughing at? Me?

MARTHY: [*Hastily.*] No, honest, kid. I was thinkin' of somethin' else.

ANNA: [*Mollified—with a smile.*] Well, I wouldn't blame you, at that. Guess I do look rotten—yust out of the hospital two weeks. I'm going to have another 'ski. What d'you say? Have something on me?

MARTHY: Sure I will. T'anks. [*She calls.*] Hey, Larry! Little service! [*He comes in.*]

ANNA: Same for me.

MARTHY: Same here. [LARRY *takes their glasses and goes out.*]

ANNA: Why don't you come sit over here, be sociable. I'm a dead stranger in this burg—and I ain't spoke a word with no one since day before yesterday.

MARTHY: Sure thing. [*She shuffles over to* ANNA'*s table and sits down opposite her.* LARRY *brings the drinks and* ANNA *pays him.*]

ANNA: Skoal! Here's how! [*She drinks.*]

MARTHY: Here's luck! [*She takes a gulp from her schooner.*]

ANNA: [*Taking a package of Sweet Caporal cigarettes from her bag.*] Let you smoke in here, won't they?

MARTHY: [*Doubtfully.*] Sure. [*Then with evident anxiety.*] On'y trow it away if yuh hear someone comin'.

ANNA: [*Lighting one and taking a deep inhale.*] Gee, they're fussy in this dump, ain't they? [*She puffs, staring at the table top.* MARTHY *looks her over with a new penetrating interest, taking in every detail of her face.* ANNA *suddenly becomes conscious of this appraising stare—resentfully.*] Ain't nothing wrong with me, is there? You're looking hard enough.

MARTHY: [*Irritated by the other's tone—scornfully.*] Ain't got to look much. I got your number the minute you stepped in the door.

ANNA: [*Her eyes narrowing.*] Ain't you smart! Well, I got yours, too, without no trouble. You're me forty years from now. That's you! [*She gives a hard little laugh.*]

MARTHY: [*Angrily.*] Is that so? Well, I'll tell you straight, kiddo, that Marthy Owen never— [*She catches herself up short—with a grin.*] What are you and me scrappin' over? Let's cut it out, huh? Me, I don't want no hard feelin's with no one. [*Extending her hand.*] Shake and forget it, huh?

ANNA: [*Shakes her hand gladly.*] Only too glad to. I ain't looking for trouble. Let's have 'nother. What d'you say?

MARTHY: [*Shaking her head.*] Not for mine. I'm full up. And you— Had anythin' to eat lately?

ANNA: Not since this morning on the train.

MARTHY: Then yuh better go easy on it, hadn't yuh?

ANNA: [*After a moment's hesitation.*] Guess you're right. I got to meet someone, too. But my nerves is on edge after that rotten trip.

MARTHY: Yuh said yuh was just outa the hospital?

ANNA: Two weeks ago. [*Leaning over to* MARTHY *confidentially.*] The joint I was in out in St. Paul got raided. That was the start. The judge give all us girls thirty days. The others didn't seem to mind being in the cooler much. Some of 'em was used to it. But me, I couldn't stand it. It got my goat right—couldn't eat or sleep or nothing. I never could stand being caged up nowheres. I got good and sick and they had to send me to the hospital. It was nice there. I was sorry to leave it, honest!

MARTHY: [*After a slight pause.*] Did yuh say yuh got to meet someone here?

ANNA: Yes. Oh, not what you mean. It's my Old Man I got to meet. Honest! It's funny, too. I ain't seen him since I was a kid—don't even know what he looks like—yust had a letter every now and then. This was always the only address he give me to write him back. He's yanitor of some building here now—used to be a sailor.

MARTHY: [*Astonished.*] Janitor!

ANNA: Sure. And I was thinking maybe, seeing he ain't never done a thing for me in my life, he might be willing to stake me to a room and eats till I get rested up. [*Wearily.*] Gee, I sure need that rest! I'm knocked out. [*Then resignedly.*] But I ain't expecting much from him. Give you a kick when you're down, that's what all men do. [*With sudden passion.*] Men, I hate 'em—all of 'em! And I don't expect he'll turn out no better than the rest. [*Then with sudden interest.*] Say, do you hang out around this dump much?

MARTHY: Oh, off and on.

ANNA: Then maybe you know him—my Old Man—or at least seen him?

MARTHY: It ain't old Chris, is it?

ANNA: Old Chris?

MARTHY: Chris Christopherson, his full name is.

ANNA: [*Excitedly.*] Yes, that's him! Anna Christopherson—that's my real name—only out there I called myself Anna Christie. So you know him, eh?

MARTHY: [*Evasively.*] Seen him about for years.

ANNA: Say, what's he like, tell me, honest?

MARTHY: Oh, he's short and—

ANNA: [*Impatiently.*] I don't care what he looks like. What kind is he?

MARTHY: [*Earnestly.*] Well, yuh can bet your life, kid, he's as good an old guy as ever walked on two feet. That goes!

ANNA: [*Pleased.*] I'm glad to hear it. Then you think's he'll stake me to that rest cure I'm after?

MARTHY: [*Emphatically.*] Surest thing you know. [*Disgustedly.*] But where'd yuh get the idea he was a janitor?

ANNA: He wrote me he was himself.

MARTHY: Well, he was lyin'. He ain't. He's captain of a barge—five men under him.

ANNA: [*Disgusted in her turn.*] A barge? What kind of a barge?

MARTHY: Coal, mostly.

ANNA: A coal barge! [*With a harsh laugh.*] If that ain't a swell job to find your long lost Old Man working at! Gee, I knew something'd be bound to turn out wrong—always does with me. That puts my idea of his giving me a rest on the bum.

MARTHY: What d'yuh mean?

ANNA: I s'pose he lives on the boat, don't he?

MARTHY: Sure. What about it? Can't you live on it, too?

ANNA: [*Scornfully.*] Me? On a dirty coal barge! What d'you think I am?

MARTHY: [*Resentfully.*] What d'yuh know about barges, huh? Bet yuh ain't never seen one. That's what comes of his bringing yuh up inland—away from the old devil sea—where yuh'd be safe—Gawd! [*The irony of it strikes her sense of humor and she laughs hoarsely.*]

ANNA: [*Angrily.*] His bringing me up! Is that what he tells people! I like his nerve! He let them cousins of my Old Woman's keep me on their farm and work me to death like a dog.

MARTHY: Well, he's got queer notions on some things. I've heard him say a farm was the best place for a kid.

ANNA: Sure. That's what he'd always answer back—and a lot of crazy stuff about staying away from the sea—stuff I couldn't make head or tail to. I thought he must be nutty.

MARTHY: He is on that one point. [*Casually.*] So yuh didn't fall for life on the farm, huh?

ANNA: I should say not! The old man of the family, his wife, and four sons—I had to slave for all of 'em. I was only a poor relation, and they treated me worse than they dare treat a hired girl. [*After a moment's hesitation—somberly.*] It was one of the sons—the youngest—started me—when I was sixteen. After that, I hated 'em so I'd killed 'em all if I'd stayed. So I run away—to St. Paul.

MARTHY: [*Who has been listening sympathetically.*] I've heard Old Chris talkin' about your bein' a nurse girl out there. Was that all a bluff yuh put up when yuh wrote him?

ANNA: Not on your life, it wasn't. It was true for two years. I didn't go wrong all at one jump. Being a nurse girl was yust what finished me. Taking care of other people's kids, always listening to their bawling and crying, caged in, when you're only a kid yourself and want to go out and see things. At last I got the chance—to get into that house. And you bet your life I took it! [*Defiantly.*] And I ain't sorry neither. [*After a pause—with bitter hatred.*] It was all men's fault—the whole business. It was men on the farm ordering and beating me—and giving me the wrong start. Then when I was a nurse, it was men again hanging around, bothering me, trying to see what they could get. [*She gives a hard laugh.*] And now it's men all the time. Gawd, I hate 'em all, every mother's son of 'em! Don't you?

MARTHY: Oh, I dunno. There's good ones and bad ones, kid. You've just had a run of bad luck with 'em, that's all. Your Old Man, now—old Chris—he's a good one.

ANNA: [*Sceptically.*] He'll have to show me.

MARTHY: Yuh kept right on writing him yuh was a nurse girl still, even after yuh was in the house, didn't yuh?

ANNA: Sure. [*Cynically.*] Not that I think he'd care a darn.

MARTHY: Yuh're all wrong about him, kid. [*Earnestly.*] I know Old Chris well for a long time. He's talked to me 'bout you lots o' times. He thinks the world o' you, honest he does.

ANNA: Aw, quit the kiddin'!

MARTHY: Honest! Only, he's a simple old guy, see? He's got nutty notions. But he means well, honest. Listen to me, kid— [*She is interrupted by the opening and shutting of the street door in the bar and by hearing Chris's voice.*] Ssshh!

ANNA: What's up?

CHRIS: [*Who has entered the bar. He seems considerably sobered up.*] Py golly, Larry, dat grub taste good. Marthy in back?

LARRY: Sure—and another tramp with her. [CHRIS *starts for the entrance to the back room.*]

MARTHY: [*To* ANNA *in a hurried, nervous whisper.*] That's him now. He's comin' in here. Brace up!

ANNA: Who? [*Chris opens the door.*]

MARTHY: [*As if she were greeting him for the first time.*] Why hello, Old Chris. [*Then before he can speak, she shuffles hurriedly past him into the bar, beckoning him to follow her.*] Come here. I wanta tell yuh somethin'. [*He goes out to her. She speaks hurriedly in a low voice.*] Listen! I'm goin' to beat it down to the barge—pack up me duds and blow. That's her in there—your Anna—just come—waitin' for yuh. Treat her right, see? She's been sick. Well, s'long! [*She goes into the back room—to* ANNA.] S'long, kid. I gotta beat it now. See yuh later.

ANNA: [*Nervously.*] So long. [MARTHA *goes quickly out of the family entrance.*]

LARRY: [*Looking at the stupefied* CHRIS *curiously.*] Well, what's up now?

CHRIS: [*Vaguely.*] Nutting—nutting. [*He stands before the door to the back room in an agony of embarrassed emotion—then he forces himself to a bold decision, pushes open the door and walks in. He stands there, casts a shy glance at Anna, whose brilliant clothes, and, to him, high-toned appearance, awe him terribly. He looks about him with pitiful nervousness as if to avoid the appraising look with which she takes in his face, his clothes, etc.—his voice seeming to plead for her forebearance.*] Anna!

ANNA: [*Acutely embarrassed in her turn.*] Hello—father. She told me it was you. I yust got here a little while ago.

CHRIS: [*Goes slowly over to her chair.*] It's good—for see you—after all dem years, Anna. [*He bends down over her. After an embarrassed struggle they manage to kiss each other.*]

ANNA: [*A trace of genuine feeling in her voice.*] It's good to see you, too.

CHRIS: [*Grasps her arms and looks into her face—then overcome by a wave of fierce tenderness.*] Anna lilla! Anna lilla! [*Takes her in his arms.*]

ANNA: [*Shrinks away from him, half-frightened.*] What's that—Swedish? I don't know it. [*Then as if seeking relief from the tension in a voluble chatter.*] Gee, I had an awful trip coming here. I'm all in. I had to sit up in the dirty coach all night—couldn't get no sleep, hardly—and then I had a hard job finding this place. I never been in New York before, you know, and—

CHRIS: [*Who has been staring down at her face admiringly, not hearing what she says—impulsively.*] You know you vas awful pooty gel, Anna? Ay bet all men see you fall in love with you, py yiminy!

ANNA: [*Repelled—harshly.*] Cut it! You talk same as they all do.

CHRIS: [*Hurt—humbly.*] Ain't no harm for your fader talk dat vay, Anna.

ANNA: [*Forcing a short laugh.*] No—course not. Only—it's funny to see you and not remember nothing. You're like—a stranger.

CHRIS: [*Sadly.*] Ay s'pose. Ay never come home only few times ven you vas kit in Sveden. You don't remember dat?

ANNA: No. [*Resentfully.*] But why didn't you never come home them days? Why didn't you never come out West to see me?

CHRIS: [*Slowly.*] Ay tank, after your mo'der die, ven Ay vas avay on voyage, it's better for you you don't never see me! [*He sinks down in the chair opposite her dejectedly—then turns to her—sadly.*] Ay don't know, Anna, vhy Ay never come home Sveden in ole year. Ay vant come home end of every voyage. Ay vant see your mo'der, your two bro'der before dey vas drowned, you ven you vas born—but—Ay—don't go. Ay sign on oder ships—go South America, go Australia, go China, go every port all over world many times—but Ay never go aboard ship sail for Sveden. Ven Ay gat money for pay passage home as passenger den— [*He bows his head guiltily.*] Ay forgat and Ay spend all money. Ven Ay tank again, it's too late. [*He sighs.*] Ay don't know vhy but dat's vay with most sailor fallar, Anna. Dat ole davil sea make dem crazy fools with her dirty tricks. It's so.

ANNA: [*Who has watched him keenly while he has been speaking—with a trace of scorn in her voice.*] Then you think the sea's to blame for everything, eh? Well, you're still workin' on it, ain't you, spite of all you used to write me about hating it. That dame was here told me you was captain of a coal barge—and you wrote me you was yanitor of a building!

CHRIS: [*Embarrassed but lying glibly.*] Oh, Ay work on land long time as yanitor. Yust short time ago Ay got dis yob cause Ay vas sick, need open air.

ANNA: [*Sceptically.*] Sick? You? You'd never think it.

CHRIS: And, Anna, dis ain't real sailor yob. Dis ain't real boat on sea. She's yust ole tub—like piece of land with house on it dat float. Yob on her ain't sea yob. No. Ay don't gat yob on sea, Anna, if Ay die first. Ay swear dat, ven your mo'der die. Ay keep my word, py yingo!

ANNA: [*Perplexed.*] Well, I can't see no difference. [*Dismissing the subject.*] Speaking of being sick, I been there myself—yust out of the hospital two weeks ago.

CHRIS: [*Immediately all concern.*] You, Anna? Py golly! [*Anxiously.*] You feel better now, dough, don't you? You look little tired, dat's all!

ANNA: [*Wearily.*] I am. Tired to death. I need a long rest and I don't see much chance of getting it.

CHRIS: What you mean, Anna?

ANNA: Well, when I made up my mind to come to see you, I thought you was a yanitor—that you'd have a place where, maybe, if you didn't mind having me, I could visit a while and rest up—till I felt able to get back on the job again.

CHRIS: [*Eagerly.*] But Ay gat place, Anna—nice place. You rest all you want, py yiminy! You don't never have to vork as nurse gel no more. You stay with me, py golly!

ANNA: [*Surprised and pleased by his eagerness—with a smile.*] Then you're really glad to see me—honest?

CHRIS: [*Pressing one of her hands in both of his.*] Anna, Ay like see you like hell, Ay tal you! And don't you talk no more about gatting yob. You stay with me. Ay don't see you for long time, you don't forgat dat. [*His voice trembles.*] Ay'm gatting ole. Ay gat no one in vorld but you.

ANNA: [*Touched—embarrassed by this unfamiliar emotion.*] Thanks. It sounds good to hear someone—talk to me that way. Say, though—if you're so lonely—it's funny—why ain't you ever married again?

CHRIS: [*Shaking his head emphatically—after a pause.*] Ay love your mo'der too much for ever do dat, Anna.

ANNA: [*Impressed—slowly.*] I don't remember nothing about her. What was she like? Tell me.

CHRIS: Ay tal you all about everytang—and you tal me all tangs happen to you. But not here now. Dis ain't good place for young gel, anyway. Only no good sailor fallar come here for gat drunk. [*He gets to his feet quickly and picks up her bag.*] You come with me, Anna. You need lie down, gat rest.

ANNA: [*Half rises to her feet, then sits down again.*] Where're you going?

CHRIS: Come. Ve gat on board.

ANNA: [*Disappointedly.*] On board your barge, you mean? [*Dryly.*] Nix for mine! [*Then seeing his crestfallen look—forcing a smile.*] Do you think that's a good place for a young girl like me—a coal barge?

CHRIS: [*Dully.*] Yes, Ay tank. [*He hesitates—then continues more and more pleadingly.*] You don't know how nice it's on barge, Anna. Tug come and ve gat towed out on voyage—yust water all round, and sun, and fresh air, and good grub for make you strong, healthy gel. You see many tangs you don't see before. You gat moonlight at night, maybe; see steamer pass; see schooner make sail—see everytang dat's pooty. You need take rest like dat. You work too hard for young gel already. You need vacation, yes!

ANNA: [*Who has listened to him with a growing interest—with an uncertain laugh.*] It sounds good to hear you tell it. I'd sure like a trip on the water, all right. It's the barge idea has me stopped. Well, I'll go down with you and have a look—and maybe I'll take a chance. Gee, I'd do anything once.

CHRIS: [*Picks up her bag again.*] Ve go, eh?

ANNA: What's the rush? Wait a second. [*Forgetting the situation for a moment, she relapses into the familiar form and flashes one of her winning trade smiles at him.*] Gee, I'm thirsty.

CHRIS: [*Sets down her bag immediately—hastily.*] Ay'm sorry, Anna. What you tank you like for drink, eh?

ANNA: [*Promptly.*] I'll take a— [*Then suddenly reminded—confusedly.*] I don't know. What'a they got here?

CHRIS: [*With a grin.*] Ay don't tank dey got much fancy drink for young gel in dis place, Anna. Yinger ale—sas'prilla, maybe.

ANNA: [*Forcing a laugh herself.*] Make it sas, then.

CHRIS: [*Coming up to her—with a wink.*] Ay tal you, Anna, ve calabrate, yes—dis one time because ve meet after many year. [*In a half whisper, embarrassedly.*] Dey gat good port wine, Anna. It's good for you, Ay tank—little bit—for give you appetite. It ain't strong, neider. One glass don't go to your head, Ay promise.

ANNA: [*With a half hysterical laugh.*] All right. I'll take port.

CHRIS: Ay go gat him. [*He goes out to the bar. As soon as the door closes, Anna starts to her feet.*]

ANNA: [*Picking up her bag—half-aloud—stammeringly.*] Gawd, I can't stand this! I better beat it. [*Then she lets her bag drop, stumbles over to her chair again, and covering her face with her hands, begins to sob.*]

LARRY: [*Putting down his paper as* CHRIS *comes up—with a grin.*] Well, who's the blond?

CHRIS: [*Proudly.*] Dat vas Anna, Larry.

LARRY: [*In amazement.*] Your daughter, Anna? [CHRIS *nods.* LARRY *lets a long, low whistle escape him and turns away embarrassedly.*]

CHRIS: Don't you tank she vas pooty gel, Larry?

LARRY: [*Rising to the occasion.*] Sure! A peach!

CHRIS: You bet you! Give me drink for take back—one port vine for Anna—she calabrate dis one time with me—and small beer for me.

LARRY: [*As he gets the drinks.*] Small beer for you, eh? She's reformin' you already.

CHRIS: [*Pleased.*] You bet! [*He takes the drinks. As she hears him coming,* ANNA *hastily dries her eyes, tries to smile.* CHRIS *comes in and sets the drinks down on the table—stares at her for a second anxiously—patting her hand.*] You look tired, Anna. Vell, Ay make you take good long rest now. [*Picking up his beer.*] Come, you drink vine. It put new life in you. [*She lifts her glass—he grins.*] Skoal, Anna! You know dat Svedish word?

ANNA: Skoal! [*Downing her port at a gulp like a drink of whiskey—her lips trembling.*] Skoal? Guess I know that word, all right, all right!

[*The Curtain Falls*]

ACT TWO

SCENE—*Ten days later. The stern of the deeply-laden barge, "SIMEON WINTHROP," at anchor in the outer harbor of Provincetown, Mass. It is ten o'clock at night. Dense fog shrouds the barge on all sides, and she floats motionless on a calm. A lantern set up on an immense coil of thick hawser sheds a dull, filtering light on objects near it—the heavy steel bits for making fast the tow lines, etc. In the rear is the cabin, its misty windows glowing wanly with the light of a lamp inside. The chimney of the cabin stove rises a few feet above the roof. The doleful tolling of bells, on Long Point, on ships at anchor, breaks the silence at regular intervals.*

As the curtain rises, ANNA *is discovered standing near the coil of rope on which the lantern is placed. She looks healthy, transformed, the natural color has come back to her face. She has on a black, oilskin coat, but wears no hat. She is staring out into the fog astern with an expression of awed wonder. The cabin door is pushed open and* CHRIS *appears. He is dressed in yellow oilskins—coat, pants, sou'wester—and wears high sea-boots.*

CHRIS: [*The glare from the cabin still in his eyes, peers blinkingly astern.*] Anna! [*Receiving no reply, he calls again, this time with apparent apprehension.*] Anna!

ANNA: [*With a start—making a gesture with her hand as if to impose silence—in a hushed whisper.*] Yes, here I am. What d'you want?

CHRIS: [*Walks over to her—solicitously.*] Don't you come turn in, Anna? It's late—after four bells. It ain't good for you stay out here in fog, Ay tank.

ANNA: Why not? [*With a trace of strange exultation.*] I love this fog! Honest! It's so— [*She hesitates, groping for a word.*]—Funny and still. I feel as if I was—out of things altogether.

CHRIS: [*Spitting disgustedly.*] Fog's vorst one of her dirty tricks, py yingo!

ANNA: [*With a short laugh.*] Beefing about the sea again? I'm getting so's I love it, the little I've seen.

CHRIS: [*Glancing at her moodily.*] Dat's foolish talk, Anna. You see her more, you don't talk dat vay. [*Then seeing her irritation, he hastily adopts a more cheerful tone.*] But Ay'm glad you like it on barge. Ay'm glad it makes you feel good again. [*With a placating grin.*] You like live like dis alone with ole fa'der, eh?

ANNA: Sure I do. Everything's been so different from anything I ever come across before. And now—this fog—Gee, I wouldn't have missed it for nothing. I never thought living on ships was so different from land. Gee, I'd yust love to work on it, honest I would, if I was a man. I don't wonder you always been a sailor.

CHRIS: [*Vehemently.*] Ay ain't sailor, Anna. And dis ain't real sea. You only see nice part. [*Then as she doesn't answer, he continues hopefully.*] Vell, fog lift in morning, Ay tank.

ANNA: [*The exultation again in her voice.*] I love it! I don't give a rap if it never lifts! [CHRIS *fidgets from one foot to the other worriedly.* ANNA *continues slowly, after a pause.*] It makes me feel clean—out here—'s if I'd taken a bath.

CHRIS: [*After a pause.*] You better go in cabin—read book. Dat put you to sleep.

ANNA: I don't want to sleep. I want to stay out here—and think about things.

CHRIS: [*Walks away from her toward the cabin—then comes back.*] You act funny tonight, Anna.

ANNA: [*Her voice rising angrily.*] Say, what're you trying to do—make things rotten? You been kind as kind can be to me and I certainly appreciate it—only don't spoil it all now. [*Then, seeing the hurt expression on her father's face, she forces a smile.*] Let's talk of something else. Come. Sit down here. [*She points to the coil of rope.*]

CHRIS: [*Sits down beside her with a sigh.*] It's gatting pooty late in night, Anna. Must be near five bells.

ANNA: [*Interestedly.*] Five bells? What time is that?

CHRIS: Half past ten.

ANNA: Funny I don't know nothing about sea talk—but those cousins was always talking crops and that stuff. Gee, wasn't I sick of it—and of them!

CHRIS: You don't like live on farm, Anna?

ANNA: I've told you a hundred times I hated it. [*Decidedly.*] I'd rather have one drop of ocean than all the farms in the world! Honest! And you wouldn't like a farm, neither. Here's where you belong. [*She makes a sweeping gesture seaward.*] But not on a coal barge. You belong on a real ship, sailing all over the world.

CHRIS: [*Moodily.*] Ay've done dat many year, Anna, when Ay vas damn fool.

ANNA: [*Disgustedly.*] Oh, rats! [*After a pause she speaks musingly.*] Was the men in our family always sailors—as far back as you know about?

CHRIS: [*Shortly.*] Yes. Damn fools! All men in our village on coast, Sveden, go to sea. Ain't nutting else for dem to do. My fa'der die on board ship in Indian Ocean. He's buried at sea. Ay don't never know him only little bit. Den my tree bro'der, older'n me, dey go on ships. Den Ay go, too. Den my mo'der she's left all 'lone. She die pooty quick after dat—all 'lone. Ve vas all avay on voyage when she die. [*He pauses sadly.*] Two my bro'der dey gat lost on fishing boat same like your bro'ders vas drowned. My oder bro'der, he save money, give up sea, den he die home in bed. He's only one dat ole davil don't kill. [*Defiantly.*] But me, Ay bet you Ay die ashore in bed, too!

ANNA: Were all of 'em yust plain sailors?

CHRIS: Able body seaman, most of dem. [*With a certain pride.*] Dey vas all smart seaman, too—A one. [*Then after hesitating a moment— shyly.*] Ay vas bo'sun.

ANNA: Bo'sun?

CHRIS: Dat's kind of officer.

ANNA: Gee, that was fine. What does he do?

CHRIS: [*After a second's hesitation, plunged into gloom again by his fear of her enthusiasm.*] Hard vork all time. It's rotten, Ay tal you, for go to sea. [*Determined to disgust her with sea life—volubly.*] Dey're all fool fallar, dem fallar in our family. Dey all vork rotten yob on sea for nutting, don't care nutting but yust gat big pay day in pocket, gat drunk, gat robbed, ship avay again on oder voyage. Dey don't come home. Dey don't do anytang like good man do. And dat ole davil, sea, sooner, later she svallow dem up.

ANNA: [*With an excited laugh.*] Good sports, I'd call 'em. [*Then hastily.*] But say—listen—did all the women of the family marry sailors?

CHRIS: [*Eagerly—seeing a chance to drive home his point.*] Yes—and it's bad on dem like hell vorst of all. Dey don't see deir men only once in long while. Dey set and vait all 'lone. And vhen deir boys grows up, go to sea, dey sit and vait some more. [*Vehemently.*] Any gel marry sailor, she's crazy fool! Your mo'der she tal you same tang if she vas alive. [*He relapses into an attitude of somber brooding.*]

ANNA: [*After a pause—dreamily.*] Funny! I do feel sort of—nutty, to-night. I feel old.

CHRIS: [*Mystified.*] Ole?

ANNA: Sure—like I'd been living a long, long time—out here in the fog. [*Frowning perplexedly.*] I don't know how to tell you yust what I mean. It's like I'd come home after a long visit away some place. It all seems like I'd been here before lots of times—on boats—in this same fog. [*With a short laugh.*] You must think I'm off my base.

CHRIS: [*Gruffly.*] Anybody feel funny dat vay in fog.

ANNA: [*Persistently.*] But why d'you s'pose I feel so—so—like I'd found something I'd missed and been looking for—'s if this was the right place for me to fit in? And I seem to have forgot—everything that's happened—like it didn't matter no more. And I feel clean, somehow—like you feel yust after you've took a bath. And I feel happy for once—yes, honest!—happier than I ever been anywhere before! [*As* CHRIS *makes no comment but a heavy sigh, she continues wonderingly.*] It's nutty for me to feel that way, don't you think?

CHRIS: [*A grim foreboding in his voice.*] Ay tank Ay'm damn fool for bring you on voyage, Anna.

ANNA: [*Impressed by his tone.*] You talk—nutty tonight yourself. You act 's if you was scared something was going to happen.

CHRIS: Only God know dat, Anna.

ANNA: [*Half-mockingly.*] Then it'll be Gawd's will, like the preachers say—what does happen.

CHRIS: [*Starts to his feet with fierce protest.*] No! Dat ole davil, sea, she ain't God! [*In the pause of silence that comes after his defiance a hail in a man's husky, exhausted voice comes faintly out of the fog to port.*] "Ahoy!" [CHRIS *gives a startled exclamation.*]

ANNA: [*Jumping to her feet.*] What's that?

CHRIS: [*Who has regained his composure—sheepishly.*] Py golly, dat scare me for minute. It's only some fallar hail, Anna—loose his course in fog. Must be fisherman's power boat. His engine break down, Ay guess. [*The "ahoy" comes again through the wall of fog, sounding much nearer this time.* CHRIS *goes over to the port bulwark.*] Sound from dis side. She come in from open sea. [*He holds his hands to his mouth, megaphone-fashion, and shouts back.*] Ahoy, dere! Vhat's trouble?

THE VOICE: [*This time sounding nearer but up forward toward the bow.*] Heave a rope when we come alongside. [*Then irritably.*] Where are ye, ye scut?

CHRIS: Ay hear dem rowing. Dey come up by bow, Ay tank. [*Then shouting out again.*] Dis vay!

THE VOICE: Right ye are! [*There is a muffled sound of oars in oarlocks.*]

ANNA: [*Half to herself—resentfully.*] Why don't that guy stay where he belongs?

CHRIS: [*Hurriedly.*] Ay go up bow. All hands asleep 'cepting fallar on vatch. Ay gat heave line to dat fallar. [*He picks up a coil of rope and hurries off toward the bow.* ANNA *walks back toward the extreme stern as if she wanted to remain as much isolated as possible. She turns her back on the proceedings and stares out into the fog.* THE VOICE *is heard again shouting "Ahoy" and* CHRIS *answering "Dis vay." Then there is a pause—the murmur of excited voices—then the scuffling of feet.* CHRIS *appears from around the cabin to port. He is supporting the limp form of a man dressed in dungarees, holding one of the man's arms around his neck. The deckhand,* JOHNSON, *a young, blond Swede, follows him, helping along another exhausted man similar fashion.* ANNA *turns to look at them.* CHRIS *stops for a second—volubly.*] Anna! You come help, vill you? You find vhiskey in cabin. Dese fallars need drink for fix dem. Dey vas near dead.

ANNA: [*Hurrying to him.*] Sure—but who are they? What's the trouble?

CHRIS: Sailor fallars. Deir steamer gat wrecked. Dey been five days in open boat—four fallars—only one left able stand up. Come, Anna. [*She precedes him into the cabin, holding the door open while he and* JOHNSON *carry in their burdens. The door is shut, then opened again as* JOHNSON *comes out.* CHRIS'S *voice shouts after him.*] Go gat oder fallar, Yohnson.

JOHNSON: Yes, sir. [*He goes. The door is closed again.* MAT BURKE *stumbles in around the port side of the cabin. He moves slowly, feeling his way uncertainly, keeping hold of the port bulwark with his right hand to steady himself. He is stripped to the waist, has on nothing but a pair of dirty dungaree pants. He is a powerful, broad-chested six-footer, his face handsome in a hard, rough, bold, defiant way. He is about thirty, in the full power of his heavy-muscled, immense strength. His dark eyes are bloodshot and wild from sleeplessness. The muscles of his arms and shoulders are lumped in knots and bunches, the veins of his forearms stand out like blue cords. He finds his way to the coil of hawser and sits down on it facing the cabin, his back bowed, head in his hands, in an attitude of spent weariness.*]

BURKE: [*Talking aloud to himself.*] Row, ye divil! Row! [*Then lifting his head and looking about him.*] What's this tub? Well, we're safe anyway—with the help of God. [*He makes the sign of the cross mechanically.* JOHNSON *comes along the deck to port, supporting the fourth man, who is babbling to himself incoherently.* BURKE *glances at him disdainfully.*] Is it losing the small wits ye iver had, ye are? Deck-scrubbing scut! [*They pass him and go into the cabin, leaving the door open.* BURKE *sags forward wearily.*] I'm bate out—bate out entirely.

ANNA: [*Comes out of the cabin with a tumbler quarter-full of whiskey in her hand. She gives a start when she sees* BURKE *so near her, the light from the open door falling full on him. Then, overcoming what is evidently a feeling of repulsion, she comes up beside him.*] Here you are. Here's a drink for you. You need it, I guess.

BURKE: [*Lifting his head slowly—confusedly.*] Is it dreaming I am?

ANNA: [*Half smiling.*] Drink it and you'll find it ain't no dream.

BURKE: To hell with the drink—but I'll take it just the same. [*He tosses it down.*] Aah! I'm needin' that—and 'tis fine stuff. [*Looking up at her with frank, grinning admiration.*] But 'twasn't the booze I meant when I said, was I dreaming. I thought you was some mermaid out of the sea come to torment me. [*He reaches out to feel of her arm.*] Aye, rale flesh and blood, divil a less.

ANNA: [*Coldly. Stepping back from him.*] Cut that.

BURKE: But tell me, isn't this a barge I'm on—or isn't it?

ANNA: Sure.

BURKE: And what is a fine handsome woman the like of you doing on this scow?

ANNA: [*Coldly.*] Never you mind. [*Then half-amused in spite of herself.*] Say, you're a great one, honest—starting right in kidding after what you been through.

BURKE: [*Delighted—proudly.*] Ah, it was nothing—aisy for a rale man with guts to him, the like of me. [*He laughs.*] All in the day's work, darlin'. [*Then, more seriously but still in a boastful tone, confidentially.*] But I won't be denying 'twas a damn narrow squeak. We'd all ought to be with Davy Jones at the bottom of the sea, be rights. And only for me, I'm telling you, and the great strength and guts is in me, we'd be being scoffed by the fishes this minute!

ANNA: [*Contemptuously.*] Gee, you hate yourself, don't you? [*Then turning away from him indifferently.*] Well, you'd better come in and lie down. You must want to sleep.

BURKE: [*Stung—rising unsteadily to his feet with chest out and head thrown back—resentfully.*] Lie down and sleep, is it? Divil a wink I'm after having for two days and nights and divil a bit I'm needing now. Let you not be thinking I'm the like of them three weak scuts come in the boat with me. I could lick the three of them sitting down with one hand tied behind me. They may be bate out, but I'm not— and I've been rowing the boat with them lying in the bottom not able to raise a hand for the last two days we was in it. [*Furiously, as he sees this is making no impression on her.*] And I can lick all hands on this tub, wan be wan, tired as I am!

ANNA: [*Sarcastically.*] Gee, ain't you a hard guy! [*Then, with a trace of sympathy, as she notices him swaying from weakness.*] But never mind that fight talk. I'll take your word for all you've said. Go on and sit down out here, anyway, if I can't get you to come inside. [*He sits down weakly.*] You're all in, you might as well own up to it.

BURKE: [*Fiercely.*] The hell I am!

ANNA: [*Coldly.*] Well, be stubborn then for all I care. And I must say I don't care for your language. The men I know don't pull that rough stuff when ladies are around.

BURKE: [*Getting unsteadily to his feet again—in a rage.*] Ladies! Ho-ho! Divil mend you! Let you not be making game of me. What would ladies be doing on this bloody hulk? [*As ANNA attempts to go to the cabin, he lurches into her path.*] Aisy, now! You're not the old Square-head's woman, I suppose you'll be telling me next—living in his cabin with him, no less! [*Seeing the cold, hostile expression on ANNA's face, he suddenly changes his tone to one of boisterous joviality.*] But I do be thinking, iver since the first look my eyes took at you, that it's a fool you are to be wasting yourself—a fine, handsome girl—on a stumpy runt of a man like that old Swede. There's too many strapping great lads on the sea would give their heart's blood for one kiss of you!

ANNA: [*Scornfully.*] Lads like you, eh?

BURKE: [*Grinning.*] Ye take the words out o' my mouth. I'm the proper lad for you, if it's meself do be saying it. [*With a quick movement he puts his arms about her waist.*] Whisht, now, me daisy! Himself's in the cabin. It's wan of your kisses I'm needing to take the tiredness from me bones. Wan kiss, now! [*He presses her to him and attempts to kiss her.*]

ANNA: [*Struggling fiercely.*] Leggo of me, you big mut! [*She pushes him away with all her might. BURKE, weak and tottering, is caught off his guard. He is thrown down backward and, in falling, hits his head a hard thump against the bulwark. He lies there still, knocked out for the moment. ANNA stands for a second, looking down at him frightenedly. Then she kneels down beside him and raises his head to her knee, staring into his face anxiously for some sign of life.*]

BURKE: [*Stirring a bit—mutteringly.*] God stiffen it! [*He opens his eyes and blinks up at her with vague wonder.*]

ANNA: [*Letting his head sink back on the deck, rising to her feet with a sigh of relief.*] You're coming to all right, eh? Gee, I was scared for a moment I'd killed you.

BURKE: [*With difficulty rising to a sitting position—scornfully.*] Killed, is it? It'd take more than a bit of a blow to crack my thick skull. [*Then looking at her with the most intense admiration.*] But, glory be, it's a power of strength is in them two fine arms of yours. There's not a man in the world can say the same as you, that he seen Mat Burke lying at his feet and him dead to the world.

ANNA: [*Rather remorsefully.*] Forget it. I'm sorry it happened, see? [*Burke rises and sits on bench. Then severely.*] Only you had no right to be getting fresh with me. Listen, now, and don't go getting any more wrong notions. I'm on this barge because I'm making a trip with my father. The captain's my father. Now you know.

BURKE: The old square—the old Swede, I mean?

ANNA: Yes.

BURKE: [*Rising—peering at her face.*] Sure I might have known it, if I wasn't a bloody fool from birth. Where else'd you get that fine yellow hair is like a golden crown on your head.

ANNA: [*With an amused laugh.*] Say, nothing stops you, does it? [*Then attempting a severe tone again.*] But don't you think you ought to be apologizing for what you said and done yust a minute ago, instead of trying to kid me with that mush?

BURKE: [*Indignantly.*] Mush! [*Then bending forward toward her with very intense earnestness.*] Indade and I will ask your pardon a thousand times—and on my knees, if ye like. I didn't mean a word of what I said or did. [*Resentful again for a second.*] But divil a woman in all the ports of the world has iver made a great fool of me that way before!

ANNA: [*With amused sarcasm.*] I see. You mean you're a lady-killer and they all fall for you.

BURKE: [*Offended. Passionately.*] Leave off your fooling! 'Tis that is after getting my back up at you. [*Earnestly.*] 'Tis no lie I'm telling you about the women. [*Ruefully.*] Though it's a great jackass I am to be mistaking you, even in anger, for the like of them cows on the waterfront is the only women I've met up with since I was growed to a man. [*As ANNA shrinks away from him at this, he hurries on pleadingly.*] I'm a hard, rough man and I'm not fit, I'm thinking, to be kissing the shoe-soles of a fine, dacent girl the like of yourself. 'Tis only the ignorance of your kind made me see you wrong. So you'll forgive me, for the love of God, and let us be friends from this out. [*Passionately.*] I'm thinking I'd rather be friends with you than have my wish for anything else in the world. [*He holds out his hand to her shyly.*]

ANNA: [*Looking queerly at him, perplexed and worried, but moved and pleased in spite of herself—takes his hand uncertainly.*] Sure.

BURKE: [*With boyish delight.*] God bless you! [*In his excitement he squeezes her hand tight.*]

ANNA: Ouch!

BURKE: [*Hastily dropping her hand—ruefully.*] Your pardon, Miss. 'Tis a clumsy ape I am. [*Then simply—glancing down his arm proudly.*] It's great power I have in my hand and arm, and I do be forgetting it at times.

ANNA: [*Nursing her crushed hand and glancing at his arm, not without a trace of his own admiration.*] Gee, you're some strong, all right.

BURKE: [*Delighted.*] It's no lie, and why shouldn't I be, with me shovel-ing a million tons of coal in the stokeholes of ships since I was a lad only. [*He pats the coil of hawser invitingly.*] Let you sit down, now, Miss, and I'll be telling you a bit of myself, and you'll be telling me a bit of yourself, and in an hour we'll be as old friends as if we was born in the same house. [*He pulls at her sleeve shyly.*] Sit down now, if you plaze.

ANNA: [*With a half laugh.*] Well— [*She sits down.*] But we won't talk about me, see? You tell me about yourself and about the wreck.

BURKE: [*Flattered.*] I'll tell you, surely. But can I be asking you one question, Miss, has my head in a puzzle?

ANNA: [*Guardedly.*] Well—I dunno—what is it?

BURKE: What is it you do when you're not taking a trip with the Old Man? For I'm thinking a fine girl the like of you ain't living always on this tub.

ANNA: [*Uneasily.*] No—of course I ain't. [*She searches his face suspi-ciously, afraid there may be some hidden insinuation in his words. Seeing his simple frankness, she goes on confidently.*] Well, I'll tell you. I'm a governess, see? I take care of kids for people and learn them things.

BURKE: [*Impressed.*] A governess, is it? You must be smart, surely.

ANNA: But let's not talk about me. Tell me about the wreck, like you promised me you would.

BURKE: [*Importantly.*] 'Twas this way, Miss. Two weeks out we ran into the divil's own storm, and she sprang wan hell of a leak up for'ard. The skipper was hoping to make Boston before another blow would finish her, but ten days back we met up with another storm the like of the first, only worse. Four days we was in it with green seas rak-ing over her from bow to stern. That was a terrible time, God help us. [*Proudly.*] And if 'twasn't for me and my great strength, I'm telling you—and it's God's truth—there'd been mutiny itself in the stokehole. 'Twas me held them to it, with a kick to wan and a clout to another, and they not caring a damn for the engineers any more, but fearing a clout of my right arm more than they'd fear the sea it-self. [*He glances at her anxiously, eager for her approval.*]

ANNA: [*Concealing a smile—amused by this boyish boasting of his.*] You did some hard work, didn't you?

BURKE: [*Promptly.*] I did that! I'm a divil for sticking it out when them that's weak give up. But much good it did anyone! 'Twas a mad, fightin' scramble in the last seconds with each man for himself. I disremember how it come about, but there was the four of us in wan boat and when we was raised high on a great wave I took a look about and divil a sight there was of ship or men on top of the sea.

ANNA: [*In a subdued voice.*] Then all the others was drowned?

BURKE: They was, surely.

ANNA: [*With a shudder.*] What a terrible end!

BURKE: [*Turns to her.*] A terrible end for the like of them swabs does live on land, maybe. But for the like of us does be roaming the seas, a good end, I'm telling you—quick and clane.

ANNA: [*Struck by the word.*] Yes, clean. That's yust the word for—all of it—the way it makes me feel.

BURKE: The sea, you mean? [*Interestedly.*] I'm thinking you have a bit of it in your blood, too. Your Old Man wasn't only a barge rat—begging your pardon—all his life, by the cut of him.

ANNA: No, he was bo'sun on sailing ships for years. And all the men on both sides of the family have gone to sea as far back as he remembers, he says. All the women have married sailors, too.

BURKE: [*With intense satisfaction.*] Did they, now? They had spirit in them. It's only on the sea you'd find rale men with guts is fit to wed with fine, high-tempered girls [*Then he adds half-boldly*] the like of yourself.

ANNA: [*With a laugh.*] There you go kiddin' again. [*Then seeing his hurt expression—quickly.*] But you was going to tell me about yourself. You're Irish, of course I can tell that.

BURKE: [*Stoutly.*] Yes, thank God, though I've not seen a sight of it in fifteen years or more.

ANNA: [*Thoughtfully.*] Sailors never do go home hardly, do they? That's what my father was saying.

BURKE: He wasn't telling no lie. [*With sudden melancholy.*] It's a hard and lonesome life, the sea is. The only women you'd meet in the ports of the world who'd be willing to speak you a kind word isn't women at all. You know the kind I mane, and they're a poor, wicked lot, God forgive them. They're looking to steal the money from you only.

ANNA: [*Her face averted—rising to her feet—agitatedly.*] I think—I guess I'd better see what's doing inside.

BURKE: [*Afraid he has offended her—beseechingly.*] Don't go, I'm saying! Is it I've given you offence with my talk of the like of them? Don't heed it at all! I'm clumsy in my wits when it comes to talking proper with a girl the like of you. And why wouldn't I be? Since the day I left home for to go to sea punching coal, this is the first time I've had a word with a rale, dacent woman. So don't turn your back on me now, and we beginning to be friends.

ANNA: [*Turning to him again—forcing a smile.*] I'm not sore at you, honest.

BURKE: [*Gratefully.*] God bless you!

ANNA: [*Changing the subject abruptly.*] But if you honestly think the sea's such a rotten life, why don't you get out of it?

BURKE: [*Surprised.*] Work on land, is it? [*She nods. He spits scornfully.*] Digging spuds in the muck from dawn to dark, I suppose? [*Vehemently.*] I wasn't made for it, Miss.

ANNA: [*With a laugh.*] I thought you'd say that.

BURKE: [*Argumentatively.*] But there's good jobs and bad jobs at sea, like there'd be on land. I'm thinking if it's in the stokehole of a proper liner I was, I'd be able to have a little house and be home to it wan week out of four. And I'm thinking that maybe then I'd have the luck to find a fine dacent girl—the like of yourself, now—would be willing to wed with me.

ANNA: [*Turning away from him with a short laugh—uneasily.*] Why sure. Why not?

BURKE: [*Edging up close to her—exultantly.*] Then you think a girl the like of yourself might maybe not mind the past at all but only be seeing the good herself put in me?

ANNA: [*In the same tone.*] Why, sure.

BURKE: [*Passionately.*] She'd not be sorry for it, I'd take my oath! 'Tis no more drinking and roving about I'd be doing then, but giving my pay day into her hand and staying at home with her as meek as a lamb each night of the week I'd be in port.

ANNA: [*Moved in spite of herself and troubled by this half-concealed proposal—with a forced laugh.*] All you got to do is find the girl.

BURKE: I have found her!

ANNA: [*Half-frightenedly—trying to laugh it off.*] You have? When? I thought you was saying—

BURKE: [*Boldly and forcefully.*] This night. [*Hanging his head—humbly.*] If she'll be having me. [*Then raising his eyes to hers—simply.*] 'Tis you I mean.

ANNA: [*Is held by his eyes for a moment—then shrinks back from him *with a strange, broken laugh.*] Say—are you—going crazy? Are you trying to kid me? Proposing—to me!—for Gawd's sake!—on such short acquaintance? [CHRIS *comes out of the cabin and stands staring blinkingly astern. When he makes out* ANNA *in such intimate proximity to this strange sailor, an angry expression comes over his face.*]

BURKE: [*Following her—with fierce, pleading insistence.*] I'm telling you there's the will of God in it that brought me safe through the storm and fog to the wan spot in the world where you was! Think of that now, and isn't it queer—

CHRIS: Anna! [*He comes toward them, raging, his fists clenched.*] Anna, you gat in cabin, you hear!

ANNA: [*All her emotions immediately transformed into resentment at his bullying tone.*] Who d'you think you're talking to—a slave?

CHRIS: [*Hurt—his voice breaking—pleadingly.*] You need gat rest, Anna. You gat sleep. [*She does not move. He turns on* BURKE *furiously*]. What you doing here, you sailor fallar? You ain't sick like odors. You gat in fo'c's'tle. Dey give you bunk. [*Threateningly.*] You hurry, Ay tal you!

ANNA: [*Impulsively.*] But he is sick. Look at him. He can hardly stand up.

BURKE: [*Straightening and throwing out his chest—with a bold laugh.*] Is it giving me orders ye are, me bucko? Let you look out, then! With wan hand, weak as I am, I can break ye in two and fling the pieces over the side—and your crew after you. [*Stopping abruptly.*] I was forgetting. You're her Old Man and I'd not raise a fist to you for the world. [*His knees sag, he wavers and seems about to fall.* ANNA *utters an exclamation of alarm and hurries to his side.*]

ANNA: [*Taking one of his arms over her shoulder.*] Come on in the cabin. You can have my bed if there ain't no other place.

BURKE: [*With jubilant happiness—as they proceed toward the cabin.*] Glory be to God, is it holding my arm about your neck you are! Anna! Anna! Sure it's a sweet name is suited to you.

ANNA: [*Guiding him carefully.*] Sssh! Sssh!

BURKE: Whisht, is it? Indade, and I'll not. I'll be roaring it out like a fog horn over the sea! You're the girl of the world and we'll be marrying soon and I don't care who knows it!

ANNA: [*As she guides him through the cabin door.*] Ssshh! Never mind that talk. You go to sleep. [*They go out of sight in the cabin.* CHRIS, *who has been listening to* BURKE's *last words with open-mouthed amazement stands looking after them helplessly.*]

CHRIS: [*Turns suddenly and shakes his fist out at the sea—with bitter hatred.*] Dat's your dirty trick, damn ole davil, you! [*Then in a frenzy of rage.*] But, py God, you don't do dat! Not while Ay'm living! No, py God, you don't!

[*The Curtain Falls*]

ACT THREE

SCENE—*The interior of the cabin on the barge,* "SIMEON WINTHROP" (*at dock in Boston*)—*a narrow, low-ceilinged compartment the walls of which are painted a light brown with white trimmings. In the rear on the left, a door leading to the sleeping quarters. In the far left corner, a large locker-closet, painted white, on the door of which a mirror hangs on a nail. In the rear wall, two small square windows and a door opening out on the deck toward the stern. In the right wall, two more windows looking out on the port deck. White curtains, clean and stiff, are at the windows. A table with two cane-bottomed chairs stands in the center of the cabin. A dilapidated, wicker rocker, painted brown, is also by the table.*

It is afternoon of a sunny day about a week later. From the harbor and docks outside, muffled by the closed door and windows, comes the sound of steamers' whistles and the puffing snort of the donkey engines of some ship unloading nearby.

As the curtain rises, CHRIS *and* ANNA *are discovered.* ANNA *is seated in the rocking-chair by the table, with a newspaper in her hands. She is not reading but staring straight in front of her. She looks unhappy, troubled, frowningly concentrated on her thoughts.* CHRIS *wanders about the room, casting quick, uneasy side glances at her face, then stopping to peer absentmindedly out of the window. His attitude betrays an overwhelming, gloomy anxiety which has him on tenter hooks. He pretends to be engaged in setting things shipshape, but this occupation is confined to picking up some object, staring at it stupidly for a second, then aimlessly putting it down again. He clears his throat and starts to sing to himself in a low, doleful voice:* "My Yosephine, come aboard de ship. Long time Ay vait for you."

ANNA: [*Turning on him, sarcastically.*] I'm glad someone's feeling good. [*Wearily.*] Gee, I sure wish we was out of this dump and back in New York.
CHRIS: [*With a sigh.*] Ay'm glad ven ve sail again, too. [*Then, as she*

*makes no comment, he goes on with a ponderous attempt at sar-
casm.*] Ay don't see vhy you don't like Boston, dough. You have
good time here, Ay tank. You go ashore all time, every day and night
veek ve've been here. You go to movies, see show, gat all kinds fun—
[*His eyes hard with hatred.*] All with that damn Irish fallar!

ANNA: [*With weary scorn.*] Oh, for heaven's sake, are you off on that
again? Where's the harm in his taking me around? D'you want me to
sit all day and night in this cabin with you—and knit? Ain't I got a
right to have as good a time as I can?

CHRIS: It ain't right kind of fun—not with that fallar, no.

ANNA: I been back on board every night by eleven, ain't I? [*Then struck
by some thought—looks at him with keen suspicion—with rising
anger.*] Say, look here, what d'you mean by what you yust said?

CHRIS: [*Hastily.*] Nutting but what Ay say, Anna.

ANNA: You said "ain't right" and you said it funny. Say, listen here, you
ain't trying to insinuate that there's something wrong between us,
are you?

CHRIS: [*Horrified.*] No, Anna! No, Ay svear to God, Ay never tank dat!

ANNA: [*Mollified by his very evident sincerity—sitting down again.*]
Well, don't you never think it neither if you want me ever to speak to
you again. [*Angrily again.*] If I ever dreamt you thought that, I'd get
the hell out of this barge so quick you couldn't see me for dust.

CHRIS: [*Soothingly.*] Ay wouldn't never dream—[*Then, after a second's
pause, reprovingly.*] You vas gatting learn to svear. Dat ain't nice for
young gel, you tank?

ANNA: [*With a faint trace of a smile.*] Excuse me. You ain't used to such
language, I know. [*Mockingly.*] That's what your taking me to sea
has done for me.

CHRIS: [*Indignantly.*] No, it ain't me. It's dat damn sailor fallar learn
you bad tangs.

ANNA: He ain't a sailor. He's a stoker.

CHRIS: [*Forcibly.*] Dat vas million times vorse, Ay tal you! Dem fallars
dat vork below shoveling coal vas de dirtiest, rough gang of no-good
fallars in vorld!

ANNA: I'd hate to hear you say that to Mat.

CHRIS: Oh, Ay tal him same tang. You don't gat it in head Ay'm scared
of him yust 'cause he vas stronger'n Ay vas. [*Menacingly.*] You don't
gat for fight with fists with dem fallars. Dere's oder vay for fix him.

ANNA: [*Glancing at him with sudden alarm.*] What d'you mean?

CHRIS: [*Sullenly.*] Nutting.

ANNA: You'd better not. I wouldn't start no trouble with him if I was

you. He might forget some time that you was old and my father—
and then you'd be out of luck.

CHRIS: [*With smouldering hatred.*] Vell, yust let him! Ay'm ole bird
maybe, but Ay bet Ay show him trick or two.

ANNA: [*Suddenly changing her tone—persuasively.*] Aw come on, be
good. What's eating you, anyway? Don't you want no one to be nice
to me except yourself?

CHRIS: [*Placated—coming to her—eagerly.*] Yes, Ay do, Anna—only
not fallar on sea. But Ay like for you marry steady fallar got good
yob on land. You have little home in country all your own—

ANNA: [*Rising to her feet—brusquely.*] Oh, cut it out! [*Scornfully.*] Little home in the country! I wish you could have seen the little home in
the country where you had me in jail till I was sixteen! [*With rising
irritation.*] Some day you're going to get me so mad with that talk,
I'm going to turn loose on you and tell you—a lot of things that'll
open your eyes.

CHRIS: [*Alarmed.*] Ay don't vant—

ANNA: I know you don't; but you keep on talking yust the same.

CHRIS: Ay don't talk no more den, Anna.

ANNA: Then promise me you'll cut out saying nasty things about Mat
Burke every chance you get.

CHRIS: [*Evasive and suspicious.*] Vhy? You like dat fallar—very much,
Anna?

ANNA: Yes, I certainly do! He's a regular man, no matter what faults
he's got. One of his fingers is worth all the hundreds of men I met
out there—inland.

CHRIS: [*His face darkening.*] Maybe you tank you love him, den?

ANNA: [*Defiantly.*] What of it if I do?

CHRIS: [*Scowling and forcing out the words.*] Maybe—you tank you—
marry him?

ANNA: [*Shaking her head.*] No! [CHRIS' *face lights up with relief.* ANNA
continues slowly, a trace of sadness in her voice.] If I'd met him four
years ago—or even two years ago—I'd have jumped at the chance, I
tell you that straight. And I would now—only he's such a simple
guy—a big kid—and I ain't got the heart to fool him. [*She breaks off
suddenly.*] But don't never say again he ain't good enough for me. It's
me ain't good enough for him.

CHRIS: [*Snorts scornfully.*] Py yiminy, you go crazy, Ay tank!

ANNA: [*With a mournful laugh.*] Well, I been thinking I was myself the
last few days. [*She goes and takes a shawl from a hook near the door
and throws it over her shoulders.*] Guess I'll take a walk down to the

end of the dock for a minute and see what's doing. I love to watch the ships passing. Mat'll be along before long, I guess. Tell him where I am, will you?

CHRIS: [*Despondently.*] All right, Ay tal him. [ANNA *goes out the doorway on rear.* CHRIS *follows her out and stands on the deck outside for a moment looking after her. Then he comes back inside and shuts the door. He stands looking out of the window—mutters—"Dirty ole davil, you." Then he goes to the table, sets the cloth straight mechanically, picks up the newspaper* ANNA *has let fall to the floor and sits down in the rocking-chair. He stares at the paper for a while, then puts it on table, holds his head in his hands and sighs drearily. The noise of a man's heavy footsteps comes from the deck outside and there is a loud knock on the door.* CHRIS *starts, makes a move as if to get up and go to the door, then thinks better of it and sits still. The knock is repeated—then as no answer comes, the door is flung open and* MAT BURKE *appears.* CHRIS *scowls at the intruder and his hand instinctively goes back to the sheath knife on his hip.* BURKE *is dressed up—wears a cheap blue suit, a striped cotton shirt with a black tie, and black shoes newly shined. His face is beaming with good humor.*]

BURKE: [*As he sees* CHRIS—*in a jovial tone of mockery.*] Well, God bless who's here! [*He bends down and squeezes his huge form through the narrow doorway.*] And how is the world treating you this afternoon, Anna's father?

CHRIS: [*Sullenly.*] Pooty goot—if it ain't for some fallars.

BURKE: [*With a grin.*] Meaning me, do you? [*He laughs.*] Well, if you ain't the funny old crank of a man! [*Then soberly.*] Where's herself? [CHRIS *sits dumb, scowling, his eyes averted.* BURKE *is irritated by this silence.*] Where's Anna, I'm after asking you?

CHRIS: [*Hesitating—then grouchily.*] She go down end of dock.

BURKE: I'll be going down to her, then. But first I'm thinking I'll take this chance when we're alone to have a word with you. [*He sits down opposite* CHRIS *at the table and leans over toward him.*] And that word is soon said. I'm marrying your Anna before this day is out, and you might as well make up your mind to it whether you like it or no.

CHRIS: [*Glaring at him with hatred and forcing a scornful laugh.*] Ho-ho! Dat's easy for say!

BURKE: You mean I won't? [*Scornfully.*] Is it the like of yourself will stop me, are you thinking?

CHRIS: Yes, Ay stop it, if it come to vorst.

BURKE: [*With scornful pity.*] God help you!

CHRIS: But ain't no need for me do dat. Anna—

BURKE: [*Smiling confidently.*] Is it Anna you think will prevent me?

CHRIS: Yes.

BURKE: And I'm telling you she'll not. She knows I'm loving her, and she loves me the same, and I know it.

CHRIS: Ho-ho! She only have fun. She make big fool of you, dat's all!

BURKE: [*Unshaken—pleasantly.*] That's a lie in your throat, divil mend you!

CHRIS: No, it ain't lie. She tal me yust before she go out she never marry fallar like you.

BURKE: I'll not believe it. 'Tis a great old liar you are, and a divil to be making a power of trouble if you had your way. But 'tis not trouble I'm looking for, and me sitting down here. [*Earnestly.*] Let us be talking it out now as man to man. You're her father, and wouldn't it be a shame for us to be at each other's throats like a pair of dogs, and I married with Anna. So out with the truth, man alive. What is it you're holding against me at all?

CHRIS: [*A bit placated, in spite of himself, by* BURKE's *evident sincerity— but puzzled and suspicious.*] Vell—Ay don't vant for Anna gat married. Listen, you fallar. Ay'm a ole man. Ay don't see Anna for fifteen year. She vas all Ay gat in vorld. And now ven she come on first trip—you tank Ay vant her leave me 'lone again?

BURKE: [*Heartily.*] Let you not be thinking I have no heart at all for the way you'd be feeling.

CHRIS: [*Astonished and encouraged—trying to plead persuasively.*] Den you do right tang, eh? You ship avay again, leave Anna alone. [*Cajolingly.*] Big fallar like you dat's on sea, he don't need vife. He gat new gel in every port, you know dat.

BURKE: [*Angry for a second.*] God stiffen you! [*Then controlling himself—calmly.*] I'll not be giving you the lie on that. But divil take you, there's a time comes to every man, on sea or land, that isn't a born fool, when he's sick of the lot of them cows, and wearing his heart out to meet up with a fine dacent girl, and have a home to call his own and be rearing up children in it. 'Tis small use you're asking me to leave Anna. She's the wan woman of the world for me, and I can't live without her now, I'm thinking.

CHRIS: You forgat all about her in one veek out of port, Ay bet you!

BURKE: You don't know the like I am. Death itself wouldn't make me forget her. So let you not be making talk to me about leaving her. I'll not, and be damned to you! It won't be so bad for you as you'd make out at all. She'll be living here in the States, and her married to me. And you'd be seeing her often so—a sight more often than ever you saw her the fifteen years she was growing up in the West. It's quare you'd be the one to be making great trouble about her leaving you when you never laid eyes on her once in all them years.

CHRIS: [*Guiltily.*] Ay taught it vas better Anna stay avay, grow up inland where she don't ever know ole davil, sea.

BURKE: [*Scornfully.*] Is it blaming the sea for your troubles ye are again, God help you? Well, Anna knows it now. 'Twas in her blood, anyway.

CHRIS: And Ay don't vant she ever know no-good fallar on sea—

BURKE: She knows one now.

CHRIS: [*Banging the table with his fist—furiously.*] Dat's yust it! Dat's yust what you are—no-good, sailor fallar! You tank Ay lat her life be made sorry by you like her mo'der's vas by me! No, Ay svear! She don't marry you if Ay gat kill you first!

BURKE: [*Looks at him a moment, in astonishment—then laughing uproariously.*] Ho-ho! Glory be to God, it's bold talk you have for a stumpy runt of a man!

CHRIS: [*Threateningly.*] Vell—you see!

BURKE: [*With grinning defiance.*] I'll see, surely! I'll see myself and Anna married this day, I'm telling you! [*Then with contemptuous exasperation.*] It's quare fool's blather you have about the sea done this and the sea done that. You'd ought to be shamed to be saying the like, and you an old sailor yourself. I'm after hearing a lot of it from you and a lot more that Anna's told me you do be saying to her, and I'm thinking it's a poor weak thing you are, and not a man at all!

CHRIS: [*Darkly.*] You see if Ay'm man—maybe quicker'n you tank.

BURKE: [*Contemptuously.*] Yerra, don't be boasting. I'm thinking 'tis out of your wits you've got with fright of the sea. You'd be wishing Anna married to a farmer, she told me. That'd be a swate match, surely! Would you have a fine girl the like of Anna lying down at nights with a muddy scut stinking of pigs and dung? Or would you have her tied for life to the like of them skinny, shrivelled swabs does be working in cities?

CHRIS: Dat's lie, you fool!

BURKE: 'Tis not. 'Tis your own mad notions I'm after telling. But you know the truth in your heart, if great fear of the sea has made you a liar and coward itself. [*Pounding the table.*] The sea's the only life for a man with guts in him isn't afraid of his own shadow! 'Tis only on the sea he's free, and him roving the face of the world, seeing all things, and not giving a damn for saving up money, or stealing from his friends, or any of the black tricks that a landlubber'd waste his life on. 'Twas yourself knew it once, and you a bo'sun for years.

CHRIS: [*Sputtering with rage.*] You vas crazy fool, Ay tal you!

BURKE: You've swallowed the anchor. The sea give you a clout once knocked you down, and you're not man enough to get up for another, but lie there for the rest of your life howling bloody murder. [*Proudly.*] Isn't it myself the sea has nearly drowned, and me battered and bate till I was that close to hell I could hear the flames roaring, and never a groan out of me till the sea gave up and it seeing the great strength and guts of a man was in me?

CHRIS: [*Scornfully.*] Yes, you vas hell of fallar, hear you tal it!

BURKE: [*Angrily.*] You'll be calling me a liar once too often, me old bucko! Wasn't the whole story of it and my picture itself in the newspapers of Boston a week back? [*Looking* CHRIS *up and down belittlingly.*] Sure I'd like to see you in the best of your youth do the like of what I done in the storm and after. 'Tis a mad lunatic, screeching with fear, you'd be this minute!

CHRIS: Ho-ho! You vas young fool! In ole years when Ay was on windyammer, Ay vas through hundred storms vorse'n dat! Ships vas ships den—and men dat sail on dem vas real men. And now what you gat on steamers? You gat fallars on deck don't know ship from mudscow. [*With a meaning glance at* BURKE.] And below deck you gat fallars yust know how for shovel coal—might yust as vell vork on coal vagon ashore!

BURKE: [*Stung—angrily.*] Is it casting insults at the men in the stokehole ye are, ye old ape? God stiffen you! Wan of them is worth any ten stock-fish-swilling Square-heads ever shipped on a windbag!

CHRIS: [*His face working with rage, his hand going back to the sheath-knife on his hip.*] Irish svine, you!

BURKE: [*Tauntingly.*] Don't ye like the Irish, ye old babboon? 'Tis that you're needing in your family, I'm telling you—an Irishman and a man of the stoke-hole—to put guts in it so that you'll not be having grandchildren would be fearful cowards and jackasses the like of yourself!

CHRIS: [*Half rising from his chair—in a voice choked with rage.*] You look out!

BURKE: [*Watching him intently—a mocking smile on his lips.*] And it's that you'll be having, no matter what you'll do to prevent; for Anna and me'll be married this day, and no old fool the like of you will stop us when I've made up my mind.

CHRIS: [*With a hoarse cry.*] You don't! [*He throws himself at* BURKE, *knife in hand, knocking his chair over backwards.* BURKE *springs to his feet quickly in time to meet the attack. He laughs with the pure love of battle. The old Swede is like a child in his hands.* BURKE *does not strike or mistreat him in any way, but simply twists his right hand behind his back and forces the knife from his fingers. He throws the knife into a far corner of the room—tauntingly.*]

BURKE: Old men is getting childish shouldn't play with knives. [*Holding the struggling* CHRIS *at arm's length—with a sudden rush of anger, drawing back his fist.*] I've half a mind to hit you a great clout will put sense in your square head. Kape off me now, I'm warning you! [*He gives* CHRIS *a push with the flat of his hand which sends the old Swede staggering back against the cabin wall, where he remains standing, panting heavily, his eyes fixed on* BURKE *with hatred, as if he were only collecting his strength to rush at him again.*]

BURKE: [*Warningly.*] Now don't be coming at me again, I'm saying, or I'll flatten you on the floor with a blow, if 'tis Anna's father you are itself! I've no patience left for you. [*Then with an amused laugh.*] Well, 'tis a bold old man you are just the same, and I'd never think it was in you to come tackling me alone. [*A shadow crosses the cabin windows. Both men start.* ANNA *appears in the doorway.*]

ANNA: [*With pleased surprise as she sees* BURKE.] Hello, Mat. Are you here already? I was down—[*She stops, looking from one to the other, sensing immediately that something has happened.*] What's up? [*Then noticing the overturned chair—in alarm.*] How'd that chair get knocked over? [*Turning on* BURKE *reproachfully.*] You ain't been fighting with him, Mat—after you promised?

BURKE: [*His old self again.*] I've not laid a hand on him, Anna. [*He goes and picks up the chair, then turning on the still questioning* ANNA— *with a reassuring smile.*] Let you not be worried at all. 'Twas only a bit of an argument we was having to pass the time till you'd come.

ANNA: It must have been some argument when you got to throwing chairs. [*She turns on* CHRIS.] Why don't you say something? What was it about?

CHRIS: [*Relaxing at last—avoiding her eyes—sheepishly.*] Ve vas talking about ships and fallars on sea.

ANNA: [*With a relieved smile.*] Oh—the old stuff, eh?

BURKE: [*Suddenly seeming to come to a bold decision—with a defiant grin at* CHRIS.] He's not after telling you the whole of it. We was arguing about you mostly.

ANNA: [*With a frown.*] About me?

BURKE: And we'll be finishing it out right here and now in your presence if you're willing. [*He sits down at the left of table.*]

ANNA: [*Uncertainly—looking from him to her father.*] Sure. Tell me what it's all about.

CHRIS: [*Advancing toward the table—protesting to* BURKE.] No! You don't do dat, you! You tal him you don't vant for hear him talk, Anna.

ANNA: But I do. I want this cleared up.

CHRIS: [*Miserably afraid now.*] Vell, not now, anyvay. You vas going ashore, yes? You ain't got time—

ANNA: [*Firmly.*] Yes, right here and now. [*She turns to* BURKE.] You tell me, Mat, since he don't want to.

BURKE: [*Draws a deep breath—then plunges in boldly.*] The whole of it's in a few words only. So's he'd make no mistake, and him hating the sight of me, I told him in his teeth I loved you. [*Passionately.*] And that's God truth, Anna, and well you know it!

CHRIS: [*Scornfully—forcing a laugh.*] Ho-ho! He tal same tang to gel every port he go!

ANNA: [*Shrinking from her father with repulsion—resentfully.*] Shut up, can't you? [*Then to* BURKE—*feelingly.*] I know it's true, Mat. I don't mind what he says.

BURKE: [*Humbly grateful.*] God bless you!

ANNA: And then what?

BURKE: And then—[*Hesitatingly.*] And then I said— [*He looks at her pleadingly.*] I said I was sure—I told him I thought you have a bit of love for me, too. [*Passionately.*] Say you do, Anna! Let you not destroy me entirely, for the love of God! [*He grasps both her hands in his two.*]

ANNA: [*Deeply moved and troubled—forcing a trembling laugh.*] So you told him that, Mat? No wonder he was mad. [*Forcing out the words.*] Well, maybe it's true, Mat. Maybe I do. I been thinking and thinking—I didn't want to, Mat, I'll own up to that—I tried to cut it out—but— [*She laughs helplessly.*] I guess I can't help it anyhow. So I guess I do, Mat. [*Then with a sudden joyous defiance.*] Sure I do! What's the use of kidding myself different? Sure I love you, Mat!

CHRIS: [*With a cry of pain.*] Anna! [*He sits crushed.*]

BURKE: [*With a great depth of sincerity in his humble gratitude.*] God be praised!

ANNA: [*Assertively.*] And I ain't never loved a man in my life before, you can always believe that—no matter what happens.

BURKE: [*Goes over to her and puts his arms around her.*] Sure I do be believing ivery word you iver said or iver will say. And 'tis you and me will be having a grand, beautiful life together to the end of our days! [*He tries to kiss her. At first she turns away her head—then,* overcome by a fierce impulse of passionate love, she takes his head in both her hands and holds his face close to hers, staring into his eyes. Then she kisses him full on the lips.]

ANNA: [Pushing him away from her—forcing a broken laugh.] Good-bye. [She walks to the doorway in rear—stands with her back toward them, looking out. Her shoulders quiver once or twice as if she were fighting back her sobs.]

BURKE: [Too in the seventh heaven of bliss to get any correct interpretation of her word—with a laugh.] Good-by, is it? The divil you say! I'll be coming back at you in a second for more of the same! [To CHRIS, who has quickened to instant attention at his daughter's good-by, and has looked back at her with a stirring of foolish hope in his eyes.] Now, me old bucko, what'll you be saying? You heard the words from her own lips. Confess I've bate you. Own up like a man when you're bate fair and square. And here's my hand to you— [Holds out his hand.] And let you take it and we'll shake and forget what's over and done, and be friends from this out.

CHRIS: [With implacable hatred.] Ay don't shake hands with you fallar—not vile Ay live!

BURKE: [Offended.] The back of my hand to you then, if that suits you better. [Growling.] 'Tis a rotten bad loser you are, divil mend you!

CHRIS: Ay don't lose— [Trying to be scornful and self-convincing.] Anna say she like you little bit but you don't hear her say she marry you, Ay bet. [At the sound of her name ANNA has turned round to them. Her face is composed and calm again, but it is the dead calm of despair.]

BURKE: [Scornfully.] No, and I wasn't hearing her say the sun is shining either.

CHRIS: [Doggedly.] Dat's all right. She don't say it, yust same.

ANNA: [Quietly—coming forward to them.] No, I didn't say it, Mat.

CHRIS: [Eagerly.] Dere! You hear!

BURKE: [Misunderstanding her—with a grin.] You're waiting till you do be asked, you mane? Well, I'm asking you now. And we'll be married this day, with the help of God!

ANNA: [Gently.] You heard what I said, Mat—after I kissed you?

BURKE: [Alarmed by something in her manner.] No—I disremember.

ANNA: I said good-by. [Her voice trembling.] That kiss was for good-by, Mat.

BURKE: [Terrified.] What d'you mane?

ANNA: I can't marry you, Mat—and we've said good-by. That's all.

CHRIS: [Unable to hold back his exultation.] Ay know it! Ay know dat vas so!

BURKE: [Jumping to his feet—unable to believe his ears.] Anna! Is it making game of me you'd be? 'Tis a quare time to joke with me, and don't be doing it, for the love of God.

ANNA: [*Looking him in the eyes—steadily.*] D'you think I'd kid you now? No, I'm not joking, Mat. I mean what I said.

BURKE: Ye don't! Ye can't! 'Tis mad you are, I'm telling you!

ANNA: [*Fixedly.*] No I'm not.

BURKE: [*Desperately.*] But what's come over you so sudden? You was saying you loved me—

ANNA: I'll say that as often as you want me to. It's true.

BURKE: [*Bewilderedly.*] Then why—what, in the divil's name— Oh, God help me, I can't make head or tail to it at all!

ANNA: Because it's the best way out I can figure, Mat. [*Her voice catching.*] I been thinking it over and thinking it over day and night all week. Don't think it ain't hard on me, too, Mat.

BURKE: For the love of God, tell me then, what is it that's preventing you wedding me when the two of us has love? [*Suddenly getting an idea and pointing at* CHRIS—*exasperately.*] Is it giving heed to the like of that old fool ye are, and him hating me and filling your ears full of bloody lies against me?

CHRIS: [*Getting to his feet—raging triumphantly before* ANNA *has a chance to get in a word.*] Yes, Anna believe me, not you! She know her old fa'der don't lie like you.

ANNA: [*Turning on her father angrily.*] You sit down, d'you hear? Where do you come in butting in and making things worse? You're like a devil, you are! [*Harshly.*] Good Lord, and I was beginning to like you, beginning to forget all I've got held up against you!

CHRIS: [*Crushed—feebly.*] You ain't got nutting for hold against me, Anna.

ANNA: Ain't I yust! Well, lemme tell you— [*She glances at* BURKE *and stops abruptly.*] Say, Mat, I'm s'prised at you. You didn't think anything he'd said—

BURKE: [*Glumly.*] Sure, what else would it be?

ANNA: Think I've ever paid any attention to all his crazy bull? Gee, you must take me for a five-year-old kid.

BURKE: [*Puzzled and beginning to be irritated at her, too.*] I don't know how to take you, with your saying this one minute and that the next.

ANNA: Well, he has nothing to do with it.

BURKE: Then what is it has? Tell me, and don't keep me waiting and sweating blood.

ANNA: [*Resolutely.*] I can't tell you—and I won't. I got a good reason— and that's all you need to know. I can't marry you, that's all there is to it. [*Distractedly.*] So, for Gawd's sake, let's talk of something else.

BURKE: I'll not! [*Then fearfully.*] Is it married to someone else you are—in the West maybe?

ANNA: [*Vehemently.*] I should say not.

BURKE: [*Regaining his courage.*] To the divil with all other reasons then. They don't matter with me at all. [*He gets to his feet confidently, assuming a masterful tone.*] I'm thinking you're the like of them women can't make up their mind till they're drove to it. Well, then, I'll make up your mind for you bloody quick. [*He takes her by the arms, grinning to soften his serious bullying.*] We've had enough of talk! Let you be going into your room now and be dressing in your best and we'll be going ashore.

CHRIS: [*Aroused—angrily.*] No, py God, she don't do that! [*Takes hold of her arm.*]

ANNA: [*Who has listened to BURKE in astonishment. She draws away from him, instinctively repelled by his tone, but not exactly sure if he is serious or not—a trace of resentment in her voice.*] Say, where do you get that stuff?

BURKE: [*Imperiously.*] Never mind, now! Let you go get dressed, I'm saying. [*Then turning to CHRIS.*] We'll be seeing who'll win in the end—me or you.

CHRIS: [*To ANNA—also in an authoritative tone.*] You stay right here, Anna, you hear! [*ANNA stands looking from one to the other of them as if she thought they had both gone crazy. Then the expression of her face freezes into the hardened sneer of her experience.*]

BURKE: [*Violently.*] She'll not! She'll do what I say! You've had your hold on her long enough. It's my turn now.

ANNA: [*With a hard laugh.*] Your turn? Say, what am I, anyway?

BURKE: 'Tis not what you are, 'tis what you're going to be this day—and that's wedded to me before night comes. Hurry up now with your dressing.

CHRIS: [*Commandingly.*] You don't do one tang he say, Anna! [*ANNA laughs mockingly.*]

BURKE: She will, so!

CHRIS: Ay tal you she don't! Ay'm her fa'der.

BURKE: She will in spite of you. She's taking my orders from this out, not yours.

ANNA: [*Laughing again.*] Orders is good!

BURKE: [*Turning to her impatiently.*] Hurry up now, and shake a leg. We've no time to be wasting. [*Irritated as she doesn't move.*] Do you hear what I'm telling you?

CHRIS: You stay dere, Anna!

ANNA: [*At the end of her patience—blazing out at them passionately.*] You can go to hell, both of you! [*There is something in her tone that makes them forget their quarrel and turn to her in a stunned amazement.* ANNA *laughs wildly.*] You're just like all the rest of them—you two! Gawd, you'd think I was a piece of furniture! I'll show you! Sit down now! [*As they hesitate—furiously.*] Sit down and let me talk for a minute. You're all wrong, see? Listen to me! I'm going to tell you something—and then I'm going to beat it. [*To* BURKE—*with a harsh laugh.*] I'm going to tell you a funny story, so pay attention. [*Pointing to* CHRIS.] I've been meaning to turn it loose on him every time he'd get my goat with his bull about keeping me safe inland. I wasn't going to tell you, but you've forced me into it. What's the dif? It's all wrong anyway, and you might as well get cured that way as any other. [*With hard mocking.*] Only don't forget what you said a minute ago about it not mattering to you what other reason I got so long as I wasn't married to no one else.

BURKE: [*Manfully.*] That's my word, and I'll stick to it!

ANNA: [*Laughing bitterly.*] What a chance! You make me laugh, honest! Want to bet you will? Wait 'n see! [*She stands at the table rear, looking from one to the other of the two men with her hard, mocking smile. Then she begins, fighting to control her emotion and speak calmly.*] First thing is, I want to tell you two guys something. You was going on 's if one of you had got to own me. But nobody owns me, see?—'cepting myself. I'll do what I please and no man, I don't give a hoot who he is, can tell me what to do! I ain't asking either of you for a living. I can make it myself—one way or other. I'm my own boss. So put that in your pipe and smoke it! You and your orders!

BURKE: [*Protestingly.*] I wasn't meaning it that way at all and well you know it. You've no call to be raising this rumpus with me. [*Pointing to* CHRIS.] 'Tis him you've a right—

ANNA: I'm coming to him. But you—you did mean it that way, too. You sounded—yust like all the rest. [*Hysterically.*] But, damn it, shut up! Let me talk for a change!

BURKE: 'Tis quare, rough talk, that—for a dacent girl the like of you!

ANNA: [*With a hard laugh.*] Decent? Who told you I was? [CHRIS *is sitting with bowed shoulders, his head in his hands. She leans over in exasperation and shakes him violently by the shoulder.*] Don't go to sleep, Old Man! Listen here, I'm talking to you now!

CHRIS: [*Straightening up and looking about as if he were seeking a way to escape—with frightened foreboding in his voice.*] Ay don't vant for hear it. You vas going out of head, Ay tank, Anna.

ANNA: [*Violently.*] Well, living with you is enough to drive anyone off their nut. Your bunk about the farm being so fine! Didn't I write you year after year how rotten it was and what a dirty slave them cousins made of me? What'd you care? Nothing! Not even enough to come out and see me! That crazy bull about wanting to keep me away from the sea don't go down with me! You yust didn't want to be bothered with me! You're like all the rest of 'em!

CHRIS: [*Feebly.*] Anna! It ain't so—

ANNA: [*Not heeding his interruption—revengefully.*] But one thing I never wrote you. It was one of them cousins that you think is such nice people—the youngest son—Paul—that started me wrong. [*Loudly.*] It wasn't none of my fault. I hated him worse'n hell and he knew it. But he was big and strong—[*Pointing to Burke*]—like you!

BURKE: [*Half springing to his feet—his fists clenched.*] God blarst it! [*He sinks slowly back in his chair again, the knuckles showing white on his clenched hands, his face tense with the effort to suppress his grief and rage.*]

CHRIS: [*In a cry of horrified pain.*] Anna!

ANNA: [*To him—seeming not to have heard their interruptions.*] That was why I run away from the farm. That was what made me get a yob as nurse girl in St. Paul. [*With a hard, mocking laugh.*] And you think that was a nice yob for a girl, too, don't you? [*Sarcastically.*] With all them nice inland fellers yust looking for a chance to marry me, I s'pose. Marry me? What a chance! They wasn't looking for marrying. [*As* BURKE *lets a groan of fury escape him—desperately.*] I'm owning up to everything fair and square. I was caged in, I tell you—yust like in yail—taking care of other people's kids—listening to 'em bawling and crying day and night—when I wanted to be out—and I was lonesome—lonesome as hell! [*With a sudden weariness in her voice.*] So I give up finally. What was the use? [*She stops and looks at the two men. Both are motionless and silent.* CHRIS *seems in a stupor of despair, his house of cards fallen about him.* BURKE's *face is livid with the rage that is eating him up, but he is too stunned and bewildered yet to find a vent for it. The condemnation she feels in their silence goads* ANNA *into a harsh, strident defiance.*] You don't say nothing—either of you—but I know what you're thinking. You're like all the rest! [*To* CHRIS—*furiously.*] And who's to blame for it, me or you? If you'd even acted like a man—if you'd even been a regular father and had me with you—maybe things would be different!

CHRIS: [*In agony.*] Don't talk dat vay, Anna! Ay go crazy! Ay von't listen! [*Puts his hands over his ears.*]

ANNA: [*Infuriated by his action—stridently.*] You will too listen! [*She leans over and pulls his hands from his ears—with hysterical rage.*] You—keeping me safe inland—I wasn't no nurse girl the last two years—I lied when I wrote you—I was in a house, that's what!—yes, that kind of a house—the kind sailors like you and Mat goes to in port—and your nice inland men, too—and all men, God damn 'em! I hate 'em! Hate 'em! [*She breaks into hysterical sobbing, throwing herself into the chair and hiding her face in her hands on the table. The two men have sprung to their feet.*]

CHRIS: [*Whimpering like a child.*] Anna! Anna! It's lie! It's lie! [*He stands wringing his hands together and begins to weep.*]

BURKE: [*His whole great body tense like a spring—dully and gropingly.*] So that's what's in it!

ANNA: [*Raising her head at the sound of his voice—with extreme mocking bitterness.*] I s'pose you remember your promise, Mat? No other reason was to count with you so long as I wasn't married already. So I s'pose you want me to get dressed and go ashore, don't you? [*She laughs.*] Yes, you do!

BURKE: [*On the verge of his outbreak—stammeringly.*] God stiffen you!

ANNA: [*Trying to keep up her hard, bitter tone, but gradually letting a note of pitiful pleading creep in.*] I s'pose if I tried to tell you I wasn't—that—no more you'd believe me, wouldn't you? Yes, you would! And if I told you that yust getting out in this barge, and being on the sea had changed me and made me feel different about things, 's if all I'd been through wasn't me and didn't count and was yust like it never happened—you'd laugh, wouldn't you? And you'd die laughing sure if I said that meeting you that funny way that night in the fog, and afterwards seeing that you was straight goods stuck on me, had got me to thinking for the first time, and I sized you up as a different kind of man—a sea man as different from the ones on land as water is from mud—and that was why I got stuck on you, too. I wanted to marry you and fool you, but I couldn't. Don't you see how I'd changed? I couldn't marry you with you believing a lie— and I was shamed to tell you the truth—till the both of you forced my hand, and I seen you was the same as all the rest. And now, give me a bawling out and beat it, like I can tell you're going to. [*She stops, looking at* BURKE. *He is silent, his face averted, his features beginning to work with fury. She pleads passionately.*] Will you believe it if I tell you that loving you has made me—clean? It's the straight goods, honest! [*Then as he doesn't reply—bitterly.*] Like hell you will! You're like all the rest!

BURKE: [*Blazing out—turning on her in a perfect frenzy of rage—his voice trembling with passion.*] The rest, is it? God's curse on you! Clane, is it? You slut, you, I'll be killing you now! [*He picks up the chair on which he has been sitting and, swinging it high over his shoulder, springs toward her.* CHRIS *rushes forward with a cry of alarm, trying to ward off the blow from his daughter.* ANNA *looks up into* BURKE's *eyes with the fearlessness of despair.* BURKE *checks himself, the chair held in the air.*]

CHRIS: [*Wildly.*] Stop, you crazy fool! You vant for murder her!

ANNA: [*Pushing her father away brusquely, her eyes still holding* BURKE's.] Keep out of this, you! [*To* BURKE—*dully.*] Well, ain't you got the nerve to do it? Go ahead! I'll be thankful to you, honest. I'm sick of the whole game.

BURKE: [*Throwing the chair away into a corner of the room— helplessly.*] I can't do it, God help me, and your two eyes looking at me. [*Furiously.*] Though I do be thinking I'd have a good right to smash your skull like a rotten egg. Was there iver a woman in the world had the rottenness in her that you have, and was there iver a man the like of me was made the fool of the world, and me thinking thoughts about you, and having great love for you, and dreaming dreams of the fine life we'd have when we'd be wedded! [*His voice high pitched in a lamentation that is like a keen*]. Yerra, God help me! I'm destroyed entirely and my heart is broken in bits! I'm asking God Himself, was it for this He'd have me roaming the earth since I was a lad only, to come to black shame in the end, where I'd be giving a power of love to a woman is the same as others you'd meet in any hooker-shanty in port, with red gowns on them and paint on their grinning mugs, would be sleeping with any man for a dollar or two!

ANNA: [*In a scream.*] Don't, Mat! For Gawd's sake! [*Then raging and pounding on the table with her hands.*] Get out of here! Leave me alone! Get out of here!

BURKE: [*His anger rushing back on him.*] I'll be going, surely! And I'll be drinking sloos of whiskey will wash that black kiss of yours off my lips; and I'll be getting dead rotten drunk so I'll not remember if 'twas iver born you was at all; and I'll be shipping away on some boat will take me to the other end of the world where I'll never see your face again! [*He turns toward the door.*]

CHRIS: [*Who has been standing in a stupor—suddenly grasping* BURKE *by the arm—stupidly.*] No, you don't go. Ay tank maybe it's better Anna marry you now.

BURKE: [*Shaking* CHRIS *off—furiously.*] Lave go of me, ye old ape!

Marry her, is it? I'd see her roasting in hell first! I'm shipping away out of this, I'm telling you! [*Pointing to Anna—passionately.*] And my curse on you and the curse of Almighty God and all the Saints! You've destroyed me this day and may you lie awake in the long nights, tormented with thoughts of Mat Burke and the great wrong you've done him!

ANNA: [*In anguish.*] Mat! [*But he turns without another word and strides out of the doorway.* ANNA *looks after him wildly, starts to run after him, then hides her face in her outstretched arms, sobbing.* CHRIS *stands in a stupor, staring at the floor.*]

CHRIS: [*After a pause, dully.*] Ay tank Ay go ashore, too.

ANNA: [*Looking up, wildly.*] Not after him! Let him go! Don't you dare—

CHRIS: [*Somberly.*] Ay go for gat drink.

ANNA: [*With a harsh laugh.*] So I'm driving you to drink, too, eh? I s'pose you want to get drunk so's you can forget—like him?

CHRIS: [*Bursting out angrily.*] Yes, Ay vant! You tank Ay like hear dem tangs. [*Breaking down—weeping.*] Ay tank you vasn't dat kind of gel, Anna.

ANNA: [*Mockingly.*] And I s'pose you want me to beat it, don't you? You don't want me here disgracing you, I s'pose?

CHRIS: No, you stay here! [*Goes over and pats her on the shoulder, the tears running down his face.*] Ain't your fault, Anna, Ay know dat. [*She looks up at him, softened. He bursts into rage.*] It's dat ole davil, sea, do this to me! [*He shakes his fist at the door.*] It's her dirty tricks! It vas all right on barge with yust you and me. Den she bring dat Irish fallar in fog, she make you like him, she make you fight with me all time! If dat Irish fallar don't never come, you don't never tal me dem tangs, Ay don't never know, and everytang's all right. [*He shakes his fist again.*] Dirty ole davil!

ANNA: [*With spent weariness.*] Oh, what's the use? Go on ashore and get drunk.

CHRIS: [*Goes into room on left and gets his cap. He goes to the door, silent and stupid—then turns.*] You vait here, Anna?

ANNA: [*Dully.*] Maybe—and maybe not. Maybe I'll get drunk, too. Maybe I'll— But what the hell do you care what I do? Go on and beat it. [CHRIS *turns stupidly and goes out.* ANNA *sits at the table, staring straight in front of her.*]

[*The Curtain Falls*]

ACT FOUR

SCENE—*Same as Act Three, about nine o'clock of a foggy night two days later. The whistles of steamers in the harbor can be heard. The cabin is lighted by a small lamp on the table. A suit case stands in the middle of the floor. ANNA is sitting in the rocking-chair. She wears a hat, is all dressed up as in Act One. Her face is pale, looks terribly tired and worn, as if the two days just past had been ones of suffering and sleepless nights. She stares before her despondently, her chin in her hands. There is a timid knock on the door in rear. ANNA jumps to her feet with a startled exclamation and looks toward the door with an expression of mingled hope and fear.*

ANNA: [*Faintly.*] Come in. [*Then summoning her courage—more resolutely.*] Come in. [*The door is opened and CHRIS appears in the doorway. He is in a very bleary, bedraggled condition, suffering from the after effects of his drunk. A tin pail full of foaming beer is in his hand. He comes forward, his eyes avoiding ANNA's. He mutters stupidly.*] It's foggy.

ANNA: [*Looking him over with contempt.*] So you come back at last, did you? You're a fine looking sight! [*Then jeeringly.*] I thought you'd beaten it for good on account of the disgrace I'd brought on you.

CHRIS: [*Wincing—faintly.*] Don't say dat, Anna, please! [*He sits in a chair by the table, setting down the can of beer, holding his head in his hands.*]

ANNA: [*Looks at him with a certain sympathy.*] What's the trouble? Feeling sick?

CHRIS: [*Dully.*] Inside my head feel sick.

ANNA: Well, what d'you expect after being soused for two days? [*Resentfully.*] It serves you right. A fine thing—you leaving me alone on this barge all that time!

CHRIS: [*Humbly.*] Ay'm sorry, Anna.

ANNA: [*Scornfully.*] Sorry!

CHRIS: But Ay'm not sick inside head vay you mean. Ay'm sick from tank too much about you, about me.

ANNA: And how about me? D'you suppose I ain't been thinking, too?

CHRIS: Ay'm sorry, Anna. [*He sees her bag and gives a start.*] You pack your bag, Anna? You vas going—?

ANNA: [*Forcibly.*] Yes, I was going right back to what you think.

CHRIS: Anna!

ANNA: I went ashore to get a train for New York. I'd been waiting and waiting 'till I was sick of it. Then I changed my mind and decided not to go today. But I'm going first thing tomorrow, so it'll all be the same in the end.

CHRIS: [*Raising his head—pleadingly.*] No, you never do dat, Anna!

ANNA: [*With a sneer.*] Why not, I'd like to know?

CHRIS: You don't never gat to do—dat vay—no more, Ay tal you. Ay fix dat up all right.

ANNA: [*Suspiciously.*] Fix what up?

CHRIS: [*Not seeming to have heard her question—sadly.*] You vas vaiting, you say? You vasn't vaiting for me, Ay bet.

ANNA: [*Callously.*] You'd win.

CHRIS: For dat Irish fallar?

ANNA: [*Defiantly.*] Yes—if you want to know! [*Then with a forlorn laugh.*] If he did come back it'd only be 'cause he wanted to beat me up or kill me, I suppose. But even if he did, I'd rather have him come than not show up at all. I wouldn't care what he did.

CHRIS: Ay guess it's true you vas in love with him all right.

ANNA: You guess!

CHRIS: [*Turning to her earnestly.*] And Ay'm sorry for you like hell he don't come, Anna!

ANNA: [*Softened.*] Seems to me you've changed your tune a lot.

CHRIS: Ay've been tanking, and Ay guess it vas all my fault—all bad tangs dat happen to you. [*Pleadingly.*] You try for not hate me, Anna. Ay'm crazy ole fool, dat's all.

ANNA: Who said I hated you?

CHRIS: Ay'm sorry for everytang Ay do wrong for you, Anna. Ay vant for you be happy all rest of your life for make up! It make you happy marry dat Irish fallar, Ay vant it, too.

ANNA: [*Dully.*] Well, there ain't no chance. But I'm glad you think different about it, anyway.

CHRIS: [*Supplicatingly.*] And you tank—maybe—you forgive me sometime?

ANNA: [*With a wan smile.*] I'll forgive you right now.

CHRIS: [*Seizing her hand and kissing it—brokenly.*] Anna lilla! Anna lilla!

ANNA: [*Touched but a bit embarrassed.*] Don't bawl about it. There ain't nothing to forgive, anyway. It ain't your fault, and it ain't mine, and it ain't his neither. We're all poor nuts, and things happen, and we yust get mixed in wrong, that's all.

CHRIS: [*Eagerly.*] You say right tang, Anna, py golly! It ain't nobody's fault! [*Shaking his fist.*] It's dat ole davil, sea!

ANNA: [*With an exasperated laugh.*] Gee, won't you ever can that stuff? [CHRIS *relapses into injured silence. After a pause* ANNA *continues curiously.*] You said a minute ago you'd fixed something up—about me. What was it?

CHRIS: [*After a hesitating pause.*] Ay'm shipping avay on sea again, Anna.

ANNA: [*Astounded.*] You're—what?

CHRIS: Ay sign on steamer sail tomorrow. Ay gat my ole yob—bo'sun. [ANNA *stares at him. As he goes on, a bitter smile comes over her face.*] Ay tank dat's best tang for you. Ay only bring you bad luck, Ay tank. Ay make your mo'der's life sorry. Ay don't vant make yours dat way, but Ay do yust same. Dat ole davil, sea, she make me Yonah man ain't no good for nobody. And Ay tank now it ain't no use fight with sea. No man dat live going to beat her, py yingo!

ANNA: [*With a laugh of helpless bitterness.*] So that's how you've fixed me, is it?

CHRIS: Yes, Ay tank if dat ole davil gat me back she leave you alone den.

ANNA: [*Bitterly.*] But, for Gawd's sake, don't you see, you're doing the same thing you've always done? Don't you see—? [*But she sees the look of obsessed stubbornness on her father's face and gives it up helplessly.*] But what's the use of talking. You ain't right, that's what. I'll never blame you for nothing no more. But how you could figure out that was fixing me—!

CHRIS: Dat ain't all. Ay gat dem fallars in steamship office to pay you all money coming to me every month vhile Ay'm avay.

ANNA: [*With a hard laugh.*] Thanks. But I guess I won't be hard up for no small change.

CHRIS: [*Hurt—humbly.*] It ain't much, Ay know, but it's plenty for keep you so you never gat go back—

ANNA: [*Shortly.*] Shut up, will you? We'll talk about it later, see?

CHRIS: [*After a pause—ingratiatingly.*] You like Ay go ashore look for dat Irish fallar, Anna?

ANNA: [*Angrily.*] Not much! Think I want to drag him back?

CHRIS: [*After a pause—uncomfortably.*] Py golly, dat booze don't go vell. Give me fever, Ay tank. Ay feel hot like hell. [*He takes off his coat and lets it drop on the floor. There is a loud thud.*]

ANNA: [*With a start.*] What you got in your pocket, for Pete's sake—a ton of lead? [*She reaches down, takes the coat and pulls out a revolver—looks from it to him in amazement.*] A gun? What were you doing with this?

CHRIS: [*Sheepishly.*] Ay forgat. Ain't nutting. Ain't loaded, anyvay.

ANNA: [*Breaking it open to make sure—then closing it again—looking at him suspiciously.*] That ain't telling me why you got it?

CHRIS: [*Sheepishly.*] Ay'm ole fool. Ay gat it vhen Ay go ashore first. Ay tank den it's all fault of dat Irish fallar.

ANNA: [*With a shudder.*] Say, you're crazier than I thought. I never dreamt you'd go that far.

CHRIS: [*Quickly.*] Ay don't. Ay gat better sense right avay. Ay don't never buy bullets even. It ain't his fault, Ay know.

ANNA: [*Still suspicious of him.*] Well, I'll take care of this for a while, loaded or not. [*She puts it in the drawer of table and closes the drawer.*]

CHRIS: [*Placatingly.*] Throw it overboard if you vant. Ay don't care. [*Then after a pause.*] Py golly, Ay tank Ay go lie down. Ay feel sick. [ANNA *takes a magazine from the table.* CHRIS *hesitates by her chair.*] Ve talk again before Ay go, yes?

ANNA: [*Dully.*] Where's this ship going to?

CHRIS: Cape Town. Dat's in South Africa. She's British steamer called Londonderry. [*He stands hesitatingly—finally blurts out.*] Anna— you forgive me sure?

ANNA: [*Wearily.*] Sure I do. You ain't to blame. You're yust—what you are—like me.

CHRIS: [*Pleadingly.*] Den—you lat me kiss you again once?

ANNA: [*Raising her face—forcing a wan smile.*] Sure. No hard feelings.

CHRIS: [*Kisses her—brokenly.*] Anna lilla! Ay— [*He fights for words to express himself, but finds none—miserably—with a sob.*] Ay can't say it. Good-night, Anna.

ANNA: Good-night. [*He picks up the can of beer and goes slowly into the room on left, his shoulders bowed, his head sunk forward deject-edly. He closes the door after him.* ANNA *turns over the pages of the magazine, trying desperately to banish her thoughts by looking at the pictures. This fails to distract her, and flinging the magazine back on the table, she springs to her feet and walks about the cabin dis-tractedly, clenching and unclenching her hands. She speaks aloud to herself in a tense, trembling voice.*] Gawd, I can't stand this much longer! What am I waiting for anyway?—like a damn fool! [*She laughs helplessly, then checks herself abruptly, as she hears the sound of heavy footsteps on the deck outside. She appears to recognize these and her face lights up with joy. She gasps:*] Mat! [*A strange ter-ror seems suddenly to seize her. She rushes to the table, takes the re-volver out of drawer and crouches down in the corner, left, behind the cupboard. A moment later the door is flung open and* MAT

BURKE *appears in the doorway. He is in bad shape—his clothes torn and dirty, covered with sawdust as if he had been grovelling or sleeping on barrom floors. There is a red bruise on his forehead over one of his eyes, another over one cheekbone, his knuckles are skinned and raw—plain evidence of the fighting he has been through on his "bat." His eyes are bloodshot and heavy-lidded, his face has a bloated look. But beyond these appearances—the results of heavy drinking—there is an expression in his eyes of wild mental turmoil, of impotent animal rage baffled by its own abject misery.*]

BURKE: [*Peers blinkingly about the cabin—hoarsely.*] Let you not be hiding from me, whoever's here—though 'tis well you know I'd have a right to come back and murder you. [*He stops to listen. Hearing no sound, he closes the door behind him and comes forward to the table. He throws himself into the rocking-chair—despondently.*] There's no one here, I'm thinking, and 'tis a great fool I am to be coming. [*With a sort of dumb, uncomprehending anguish.*] Yerra, Mat Burke, 'tis a great jackass you've become and what's got into you at all, at all? She's gone out of this long ago, I'm telling you, and you'll never see her face again. [ANNA *stands up, hesitating, struggling between joy and fear.* BURKE's *eyes fall on* ANNA's *bag. He leans over to examine it.*] What's this? [*Joyfully.*] It's hers. She's not gone! But where is she? Ashore? [*Darkly.*] What would she be doing ashore on this rotten night? [*His face suddenly convulsed with grief and rage.*] 'Tis that, is it? Oh, God's curse on her! [*Raging.*] I'll wait 'till she comes and choke her dirty life out. [ANNA *starts, her face grows hard. She steps into the room, the revolver in her right hand by her side.*]

ANNA: [*In a cold, hard tone.*] What are you doing here?

BURKE: [*Wheeling about with a terrified gasp.*] Glory be to God! [*They remain motionless and silent for a moment, holding each other's eyes.*]

ANNA: [*In the same hard voice.*] Well, can't you talk?

BURKE: [*Trying to fall into an easy, careless tone.*] You've a year's growth scared out of me, coming at me so sudden and me thinking I was alone.

ANNA: You've got your nerve butting in here without knocking or nothing. What d'you want?

BURKE: [*Airily.*] Oh, nothing much. I was wanting to have a last word with you, that's all. [*He moves a step toward her.*]

ANNA: [*Sharply—raising the revolver in her hand.*] Careful now! Don't try getting too close. I heard what you said you'd do to me.

BURKE: [*Noticing the revolver for the first time.*] Is it murdering me you'd be now, God forgive you? [*Then with a contemptuous laugh.*] Or is it thinking I'd be frightened by that old tin whistle? [*He walks straight for her.*]

ANNA: [*Wildly.*] Look out, I tell you!

BURKE: [*Who has come so close that the revolver is almost touching his chest.*] Let you shoot, then! [*Then with sudden wild grief.*] Let you shoot, I'm saying, and be done with it! Let you end me with a shot and I'll be thanking you, for it's a rotten dog's life I've lived the past two days since I've known what you are, 'til I'm after wishing I was never born at all!

ANNA: [*Overcome—letting the revolver drop to the floor, as if her fingers had no strength to hold it—hysterically.*] What d'you want coming here? Why don't you beat it? Go on! [*She passes him and sinks down in the rocking-chair.*]

BURKE: [*Following her—mournfully.*] 'Tis right you'd be asking why did I come. [*Then angrily.*] 'Tis because 'tis a great weak fool of the world I am, and me tormented with the wickedness you'd told of yourself, and drinking oceans of booze that'd make me forget. Forget? Divil a word I'd forget, and your face grinning always in front of my eyes, awake or asleep, 'til I do be thinking a madhouse is the proper place for me.

ANNA: [*Glancing at his hands and face—scornfully.*] You look like you ought to be put away some place. Wonder you wasn't pulled in. You been scrapping, too, ain't you?

BURKE:—I have—with every scut would take off his coat to me! [*Fiercely.*] And each time I'd be hitting one a clout in the mug, it wasn't his face I'd be seeing at all, but yours, and me wanting to drive you a blow would knock you out of this world where I wouldn't be seeing or thinking more of you.

ANNA: [*Her lips trembling pitifully.*] Thanks!

BURKE: [*Walking up and down—distractedly.*] That's right, make game of me! Oh, I'm a great coward surely, to be coming back to speak with you at all. You've a right to laugh at me.

ANNA: I ain't laughing at you, Mat.

BURKE: [*Unheeding.*] You to be what you are, and me to be Mat Burke, and me to be drove back to look at you again! 'Tis black shame is on me!

ANNA: [*Resentfully.*] Then get out. No one's holding you!

BURKE: [*Bewilderedly.*] And me to listen to that talk from a woman like you and be frightened to close her mouth with a slap! Oh, God help me, I'm a yellow coward for all men to spit at! [*Then furiously.*] But

I'll not be getting out of this 'till I've had me word. [*Raising his fist threateningly.*] And let you look out how you'd drive me! [*Letting his fist fall helplessly.*] Don't be angry now! I'm raving like a real lunatic, I'm thinking, and the sorrow you put on me has my brains drownded in grief. [*Suddenly bending down to her and grasping her arm intensely.*] Tell me it's a lie, I'm saying! That's what I'm after coming to hear you say.

ANNA: [*Dully.*] A lie? What?

BURKE: [*With passionate entreaty.*] All the badness you told me two days back. Sure it must be a lie! You was only making game of me, wasn't you? Tell me 'twas a lie, Anna, and I'll be saying prayers of thanks on my two knees to the Almighty God!

ANNA: [*Terribly shaken—faintly.*] I can't, Mat. [*As he turns away—imploringly.*] Oh, Mat, won't you see that no matter what I was I ain't that any more? Why, listen! I packed up my bag this afternoon and went ashore. I'd been waiting here all alone for two days, thinking maybe you'd come back—thinking maybe you'd think over all I'd said—and maybe—oh, I don't know what I was hoping! But I was afraid to even go out of the cabin for a second, honest—afraid you might come and not find me here. Then I gave up hope when you didn't show up and I went to the railroad station. I was going to New York. I was going back—

BURKE: [*Hoarsely.*] God's curse on you!

ANNA: Listen, Mat! You hadn't come, and I'd gave up hope. But—in the station—I couldn't go. I'd bought my ticket and everything. [*She takes the ticket from her dress and tries to hold it before his eyes.*] But I got to thinking about you—and I couldn't take the train—I couldn't! So I come back here—to wait some more. Oh, Mat, don't you see I've changed? Can't you forgive what's dead and gone—and forget it?

BURKE:—[*Turning on her—overcome by rage again.*] Forget, is it? I'll not forget 'til my dying day, I'm telling you, and me tormented with thoughts. [*In a frenzy.*] Oh, I'm wishing I had wan of them fornenst me this minute and I'd beat him with my fists 'till he'd be a bloody corpse! I'm wishing the whole lot of them will roast in hell 'til the Judgment Day—and yourself along with them, for you're as bad as they are.

ANNA: [*Shuddering.*] Mat! [*Then after a pause—in a voice of dead, stony calm.*] Well, you've had your say. Now you better beat it.

BURKE: [*Starts slowly for the door—hesitates—then after a pause.*] And what'll you be doing?

ANNA:—What difference does it make to you?

BURKE: I'm asking you!

ANNA: [*In the same tone.*] My bag's packed and I got my ticket. I'll go to New York tomorrow.

BURKE:[*Helplessly.*] You mean—you'll be doing the same again?

ANNA: [*Stonily.*] Yes.

BURKE: [*In anguish.*] You'll not! Don't torment me with that talk! 'Tis a she-divil you are sent to drive me mad entirely!

ANNA: [*Her voice breaking.*] Oh, for Gawd's sake, Mat, leave me alone! Go away! Don't you see I'm licked? Why d'you want to keep on kicking me?

BURKE: [*Indignantly.*] And don't you deserve the worst I'd say, God forgive you?

ANNA: All right. Maybe I do. But don't rub it in. Why ain't you done what you said you was going to? Why ain't you got that ship was going to take you to the other side of the earth where you'd never see me again?

BURKE: I have.

ANNA: [*Startled.*] What—then you're going—honest?

BURKE: I signed on today at noon, drunk as I was—and she's sailing tomorrow.

ANNA: And where's she going to?

BURKE: Cape Town.

ANNA: [*The memory of having heard that name a little while before coming to her—with a start, confusedly.*] Cape Town? Where's that. Far away?

BURKE: 'Tis at the end of Africa. That's far for you.

ANNA: [*Forcing a laugh.*] You're keeping your word all right, ain't you? [*After a slight pause—curiously.*] What's the boat's name?

BURKE: The Londonderry.

ANNA: [*It suddenly comes to her that this is the same ship her father is sailing on.*] The Londonderry! It's the same—Oh, this is too much! [*With wild, ironical laughter.*] Ha-ha-ha!

BURKE: What's up with you now?

ANNA: Ha-ha-ha! It's funny, funny! I'll die laughing!

BURKE: [*Irritated.*] Laughing at what?

ANNA: It's a secret. You'll know soon enough. It's funny. [*Controlling herself—after a pause—cynically.*] What kind of a place is this Cape Town? Plenty of dames there, I suppose?

BURKE: To hell with them! That I may never see another woman to my dying hour!

ANNA: That's what you say now, but I'll bet by the time you get there
   you'll have forgot all about me and start in talking the same old bull
   you talked to me to the first one you meet.

BURKE: [*Offended.*] I'll not, then! God mend you, is it making me out
   to be the like of yourself you are, and you taking up with this one
   and that all the years of your life?

ANNA: [*Angrily assertive.*] Yes, that's yust what I do mean! You been
   doing the same thing all your life, picking up a new girl in every
   port. How're you any better than I was?

BURKE: [*Thoroughly exasperated.*] Is it no shame you have at all? I'm a
   fool to be wasting talk on you and you hardened in badness. I'll go
   out of this and lave you alone forever. [*He starts for the door—then
   stops to turn on her furiously.*] And I suppose 'tis the same lies you
   told them all before that you told to me?

ANNA: [*Indignantly.*] That's a lie! I never did!

BURKE: [*Miserably.*] You'd be saying that, anyway.

ANNA: [*Forcibly, with growing intensity.*] Are you trying to accuse
   me—of being in love—really in love—with them?

BURKE: I'm thinking you were, surely.

ANNA: [*Furiously, as if this were the last insult—advancing on him
   threateningly.*] You mutt, you! I've stood enough from you. Don't
   you dare. [*With scornful bitterness.*] Love 'em! Oh, my Gawd! You
   damn thick-head! Love 'em? [*Savagely.*] I hated 'em, I tell you!
   Hated 'em, hated 'em, hated 'em! And may Gawd strike me dead
   this minute and my mother, too, if she was alive, if I ain't telling you
   the honest truth!

BURKE: [*Immensely pleased by her vehemence—a light beginning to
   break over his face—but still uncertain, torn between doubt and the
   desire to believe—helplessly.*] If I could only be believing you now!

ANNA: [*Distractedly.*] Oh, what's the use? What's the use of me talking?
   What's the use of anything? [*Pleadingly.*] Oh, Mat, you mustn't
   think that for a second! You mustn't! Think all the other bad about
   me you want to, and I won't kick, 'cause you've a right to. But don't
   think that! [*On the point of tears.*] I couldn't bear it! It'd be yust too
   much to know you was going away where I'd never see you again—
   thinking that about me!

BURKE: [*After an inward struggle—tensely—forcing out the words with
   difficulty.*] If I was believing—that you'd never had love for any
   other man in the world but me—I could be forgetting the rest,
   maybe.

ANNA: [*With a cry of joy.*] Mat!

BURKE: [*Slowly.*] If 'tis truth you're after telling, I'd have a right, maybe, to believe you'd changed—and that I'd changed you myself 'til the thing you'd been all your life wouldn't be you any more at all.

ANNA: [*Hanging on his words—breathlessly.*] Oh, Mat! That's what I been trying to tell you all along!

BURKE: [*Simply.*] For I've a power of strength in me to lead men the way I want, and women, too, maybe, and I'm thinking I'd change you to a new woman entirely, so I'd never know, or you either, what kind of woman you'd been in the past at all.

ANNA: Yes, you could, Mat! I know you could!

BURKE: And I'm thinking 'twasn't your fault, maybe, but having that old ape for a father that left you to grow up alone, made you what you was. And if I could be believing 'tis only me you—

ANNA: [*Distractedly.*] You got to believe it, Mat! What can I do? I'll do anything, anything you want to prove I'm not lying!

BURKE: [*Suddenly seems to have a solution. He feels in the pocket of his coat and grasps something—solemnly.*] Would you be willing to swear an oath, now—a terrible, fearful oath would send your soul to the divils in hell if you was lying?

ANNA: [*Eagerly.*] Sure, I'll swear, Mat—on anything!

BURKE: [*Takes a small, cheap old crucifix from his pocket and holds it up for her to see.*] Will you swear on this?

ANNA: [*Reaching out for it.*] Yes. Sure I will. Give it to me.

BURKE: [*Holding it away.*] 'Tis a cross was given me by my mother, God rest her soul. [*He makes the sign of the cross mechanically.*] I was a lad only, and she told me to keep it by me if I'd be waking or sleeping and never lose it, and it'd bring me luck. She died soon after. But I'm after keeping it with me from that day to this, and I'm telling you there's great power in it, and 'tis great bad luck it's saved me from and me roaming the seas, and I having it tied round my neck when my last ship sunk, and it bringing me safe to land when the others went to their death. [*Very earnestly.*] And I'm warning you now, if you'd swear an oath on this, 'tis my old woman herself will be looking down from Hivin above, and praying Almighty God and the Saints to put a great curse on you if she'd hear you swearing a lie!

ANNA: [*Awed by his manner—superstitiously.*] I wouldn't have the nerve—honest—if it was a lie. But it's the truth and I ain't scared to swear. Give it to me.

BURKE: [*Handing it to her—almost frightenedly, as if he feared for her safety.*] Be careful what you'd swear, I'm saying.

ANNA: [*Holding the cross gingerly.*] Well—what do you want me to swear? You say it.

BURKE: Swear I'm the only man in the world ivir you felt love for.

ANNA: [*Looking into his eyes steadily.*] I swear it.

BURKE: And that you'll be forgetting from this day all the badness you've done and never do the like of it again.

ANNA: [*Forcibly.*] I swear it! I swear it by God!

BURKE: And may the blackest curse of God strike you if you're lying. Say it now!

ANNA: And may the blackest curse of God strike me if I'm lying!

BURKE: [*With a stupendous sigh.*] Oh, glory be to God, I'm after believing you now! [*He takes the cross from her hand, his face beaming with joy, and puts it back in his pocket. He puts his arm about her waist and is about to kiss her when he stops, appalled by some terrible doubt.*]

ANNA: [*Alarmed.*] What's the matter with you?

BURKE: [*With sudden fierce questioning.*] Is it Catholic ye are?

ANNA: [*Confused.*] No. Why?

BURKE: [*Filled with a sort of bewildered foreboding.*] Oh, God, help me! [*With a dark glance of suspicion at her.*] There's some divil's trickery in it, to be swearing an oath on a Catholic cross and you wan of the others.

ANNA: [*Distractedly.*] Oh, Mat, don't you believe me?

BURKE: [*Miserably.*] If it isn't a Catholic you are—

ANNA: I ain't nothing. What's the difference? Didn't you hear me swear?

BURKE: [*Passionately.*] Oh, I'd a right to stay away from you—but I couldn't! I was loving you in spite of it all and wanting to be with you, God forgive me, no matter what you are. I'd go mad if I'd not have you! I'd be killing the world— [*He seizes her in his arms and kisses her fiercely.*]

ANNA: [*With a gasp of joy.*] Mat!

BURKE: [*Suddenly holding her away from him and staring into her eyes as if to probe into her soul—slowly.*] If your oath is no proper oath at all, I'll have to be taking your naked word for it and have you anyway, I'm thinking—I'm needing you that bad!

ANNA: [*Hurt—reproachfully.*] Mat! I swore, didn't I?

BURKE: [*Defiantly, as if challenging fate.*] Oath or no oath, 'tis no matter. We'll be wedded in the morning, with the help of God. [*Still more defiantly.*] We'll be happy now, the two of us, in spite of the divil! [*He crushes her to him and kisses her again. The door on the left is pushed open and CHRIS appears in the doorway. He stands blinking at them. At first the old expression of hatred of BURKE comes into his eyes instinctively. Then a look of resignation and relief takes its place. His face lights up with a sudden happy thought.*]

He turns back into the bedroom—reappears immediately with the tin can of beer in his hand—grinning.]

CHRIS: Ve have drink on this, py golly! [*They break away from each other with startled exclamations.*]

BURKE: [*Explosively.*] God stiffen it! [*He takes a step toward* CHRIS *threateningly.*]

ANNA: [*Happily—to her father.*] That's the way to talk! [*With a laugh.*] And say, it's about time for you and Mat to kiss and make up. You're going to be shipmates on the Londonderry, did you know it?

BURKE: [*Astounded.*] Shipmates— Has himself—

CHRIS: [*Equally astounded.*] Ay vas bo'sun on her.

BURKE: The divil! [*Then angrily.*] You'd be going back to sea and leaving her alone, would you?

ANNA: [*Quickly.*] It's all right, Mat. That's where he belongs, and I want him to go. You got to go, too; we'll need the money. [*With a laugh, as she gets the glasses.*] And as for me being alone, that runs in the family, and I'll get used to it. [*Pouring out their glasses.*] I'll get a little house somewhere and I'll make a regular place for you two to come back to,—wait and see. And now you drink up and be friends.

BURKE: [*Happily—but still a bit resentful against the old man.*] Sure! [*Clinking his glass against* CHRIS'.] Here's luck to you! [*He drinks.*]

CHRIS: [*Subdued—his face melancholy.*] Skoal. [*He drinks.*]

BURKE: [*To Anna, with a wink.*] You'll not be lonesome long. I'll see to that, with the help of God. 'Tis himself here will be having a grandchild to ride on his foot, I'm telling you!

ANNA: [*Turning away in embarrassment.*] Quit the kidding, now. [*She picks up her bag and goes into the room on left. As soon as she is gone* BURKE *relapses into an attitude of gloomy thought.* CHRIS *stares at his beer absent-mindedly. Finally* BURKE *turns on him.*]

BURKE: Is it any religion at all you have, you and your Anna?

CHRIS: [*Surprised.*] Vhy yes. Ve vas Lutheran in ole country.

BURKE: [*Horrified.*] Luthers, is it? [*Then with a grim resignation, slowly, aloud to himself.*] Well, I'm damned then surely. Yerra, what's the difference? 'Tis the will of God, anyway.

CHRIS: [*Moodily preoccupied with his own thoughts—speaks with somber premonition as* ANNA *re-enters from the left.*] It's funny. It's queer, yes—you and me shipping on same boat dat vay. It ain't right. Ay don't know—it's dat funny vay ole davil sea do her vorst dirty tricks, yes. It's so. [*He gets up and goes back and, opening the door, stares out into the darkness.*]

BURKE: [*Nodding his head in gloomy acquiescence—with a great sigh.*] I'm fearing maybe you have the right of it for once, divil take you.

ANNA: [*Forcing a laugh.*] Gee, Mat, you ain't agreeing with him, are you? [*She comes forward and puts her arm about his shoulder—with a determined gaiety.*] Aw say, what's the matter? Cut out the gloom. We're all fixed now, ain't we, me and you? [*Pours out more beer into his glass and fills one for herself—slaps him on the back.*] Come on! Here's to the sea, no matter what! Be a game sport and drink to that! Come on! [*She gulps down her glass. Burke banishes his superstitious premonitions with a defiant jerk of his head, grins up at her, and drinks to her toast.*]

CHRIS: [*Looking out into the night—lost in his somber preoccupation—shakes his head and mutters.*] Fog, fog, fog, all bloody time. You can't see vhere you vas going, no. Only dat ole davil, sea—she knows! [*The two stare at him. From the harbor comes the muffled, mournful wail of steamers' whistles.*]

[*The Curtain Falls*]

THE HAIRY APE

A COMEDY OF ANCIENT AND MODERN LIFE

IN EIGHT SCENES

CHARACTERS

ROBERT SMITH, "YANK"

PADDY

LONG

MILDRED DOUGLAS

HER AUNT

SECOND ENGINEER

A GUARD

A SECRETARY OF AN ORGANIZATION

STOKERS, LADIES, GENTLEMEN, ETC.

SCENES

TIME—The Modern.

SCENE—*The firemen's forecastle of a transatlantic liner an hour after sailing from New York for the voyage across. Tiers of narrow, steel bunks, three deep, on all sides. An entrance in rear. Benches on the floor before the bunks. The room is crowded with men, shouting, cursing, laughing, singing—a confused, inchoate uproar swelling into a sort of unity, a meaning—the bewildered, furious, baffled defiance of a beast in a cage. Nearly all the men are drunk. Many bottles are passed from hand to hand. All are dressed in dungaree pants, heavy ugly shoes. Some wear singlets, but the majority are stripped to the waist.*

The treatment of this scene, or of any other scene in the play, should by no means be naturalistic. The effect sought after is a cramped space in the bowels of a ship, imprisoned by white steel. The lines of bunks, the uprights supporting them, cross each other like the steel framework of a cage. The ceiling crushes down upon the men's heads. They cannot stand upright. This accentuates the natural stooping posture which shovelling coal and the resultant over-development of back and shoulder muscles have given them. The men themselves should resemble those pictures in which the appearance of Neanderthal Man is guessed at. All are hairy-chested, with long arms of tremendous power, and low, receding brows above their small, fierce, resentful eyes. All the civilized white races are represented, but except for the slight differentiation in color of hair, skin, eyes, all these men are alike.

The curtain rises on a tumult of sound. YANK *is seated in the foreground. He seems broader, fiercer, more truculent, more powerful, more sure of himself than the rest. They respect his superior strength—the grudging respect of fear. Then, too, he represents to them a self-expression, the very last word in what they are, their most highly developed individual.*

VOICES: Gif me trink dere, you!
     'Ave a wet!
     Salute!
     Gesundheit!
     Skoal!
     Drunk as a lord, God stiffen you!
     Here's how!
     Luck!

Pass back that bottle, damn you!
Pourin' it down his neck!
Ho, Froggy! Where the devil have you been?
La Touraine.
I hit him smash in yaw, py Gott!
Jenkins—the First—he's a rotten swine—
And the coppers nabbed him—and I run—
I like peer better. It don't pig head gif you.
A slut, I'm sayin'! She robbed me aslape—
To hell with 'em all!
You're a bloody liar!
Say dot again! [*Commotion. Two men about to fight are
    pulled apart.*]
No scrappin' now!
Tonight—
See who's the best man!
Bloody Dutchman!
Tonight on the for'ard square.
I'll bet on Dutchy.
He packa da wallop, I tella you!
Shut up, Wop!
No fightin', maties. We're all chums, ain't we?
[*A voice starts bawling a song.*]

"Beer, beer, glorious beer!
Fill yourselves right up to here."

YANK: [*For the first time seeming to take notice of the uproar about
him, turns around threateningly—in a tone of contemptuous author-
ity.*] Choke off dat noise! Where d'yuh get dat beer stuff? Beer, hell!
Beer's for goils—and Dutchmen. Me for somep'n wit a kick to it!
Gimme a drink, one of youse guys. [*Several bottles are eagerly offered. He takes a tremendous gulp at one of them; then, keeping the
bottle in his hand, glares belligerently at the owner, who hastens to
acquiesce in this robbery by saying:*] All righto, Yank. Keep it and
have another." [YANK *contemptuously turns his back on the crowd
again. For a second there is an embarrassed silence. Then—*]
VOICES: We must be passing the Hook.
    She's beginning to roll to it.
    Six days in hell—and then Southampton.
    Py Yesus, I vish somepody take my first vatch for me!

Gittin' seasick, Square-head?

Drink up and forget it!

What's in your bottle?

Gin.

Dot's nigger trink.

Absinthe? It's doped. You'll go off your chump, Froggy!

Cochon!

Whiskey, that's the ticket!

Where's Paddy?

Going asleep.

Sing us that whiskey song, Paddy. [*They all turn to an old, wizened Irishman who is dozing, very drunk, on the benches forward. His face is extremely monkey-like with all the sad, patient pathos of that animal in his small eyes.*]

Singa da song, Caruso Pat!

He's gettin' old. The drink is too much for him.

He's too drunk.

PADDY: [*Blinking about him, starts to his feet resentfully, swaying, holding on to the edge of a bunk.*] I'm never too drunk to sing. 'Tis only when I'm dead to the world I'd be wishful to sing at all. [*With a sort of sad contempt.*] "Whiskey Johnny," ye want? A chanty, ye want? Now that's a queer wish from the ugly like of you, God help you. But no matther. [*He starts to sing in a thin, nasal, doleful tone:*]

> Oh, whiskey is the life of man!
> > Whiskey! O Johnny! [*They all join in on this.*]
> Oh, whiskey is the life of man!
> > Whiskey for my Johnny! [*Again chorus*]
> Oh, whiskey drove my old man mad!
> > Whiskey! O Johnny!
> Oh, whiskey drove my old man mad!
> > Whiskey for my Johnny!

YANK: [*Again turning around scornfully.*] Aw hell! Nix on dat old sailing ship stuff! All dat bull's dead, see? And you're dead, too, yuh damned old Harp, on'y yuh don't know it. Take it easy, see. Give us a rest. Nix on de loud noise. [*With a cynical grin.*] Can't youse see I'm tryin' to t'ink?

ALL: [*Repeating the word after him as one with the same cynical amused mockery.*] Think! [*The chorused word has a brazen metallic quality as if their throats were phonograph horns. It is followed by a general uproar of hard, barking laughter.*]

VOICES: Don't be cracking your head wid ut, Yank.

You gat headache, py yingo!

One thing about it—it rhymes with drink!

Ha, ha, ha!

Drink, don't think!

Drink, don't think!

Drink, don't think! [*A whole chorus of voices has taken up this refrain, stamping on the floor, pounding on the benches with fists.*]

YANK: [*Taking a gulp from his bottle—good-naturedly.*] Aw right. Can de noise. I got yuh de foist time. [*The uproar subsides. A very drunken sentimental tenor begins to sing:*]

> "Far away in Canada,
> Far across the sea,
> There's a lass who fondly waits
> Making a home for me—"

YANK: [*Fiercely contemptuous.*] Shut up, yuh lousey boob! Where d'yuh get dat tripe? Home? Home, hell! I'll make a home for yuh! I'll knock yuh dead. Home! T'hell wit home! Where d'yuh get dat tripe? Dis is home, see? What d'yuh want wit home? [*Proudly.*] I runned away from mine when I was a kid. On'y too glad to beat it, dat was me. Home was lickings for me, dat's all. But yuh can bet your shoit noone ain't never licked me since! Wanter try it, any of youse? Huh! I guess not. [*In a more placated but still contemptuous tone.*] Goils waitin' for yuh, huh? Aw, hell! Dat's all tripe. Dey don't wait for noone. Dey'd double-cross yuh for a nickel. Dey're all tarts, get me? Treat 'em rough, dat's me. To hell wit 'em. Tarts, dat's what, de whole bunch of 'em.

LONG: [*Very drunk, jumps on a bench excitedly, gesticulating with a bottle in his hand.*] Listen 'ere, Comrades! Yank 'ere is right. 'E says this 'ere stinkin' ship is our 'ome. And 'e says as 'ome is 'ell. And 'e's right! This is 'ell. We lives in 'ell, Comrades—and right enough we'll die in it. [*Raging.*] And who's ter blame, I arsks yer? We ain't. We wasn't born this rotten way. All men is born free and ekal. That's in the bleedin' Bible, maties. But what d'they care for the Bible—them lazy, bloated swine what travels first cabin? Them's the ones. They dragged us down 'til we're on'y wage slaves in the bowels of a bloody ship, sweatin', burnin' up, eatin' coal dust! Hit's them's ter blame—the damned capitalist clarss! [*There had been a gradual murmur of contemptuous resentment rising among the men until now he is interrupted by a storm of catcalls, hisses, boos, hard laughter.*]

VOICES: Turn it off!

Shut up!

Sit down!

Closa da face!

Tamn fool! [*Etc.*]

YANK: [*Standing up and glaring at* LONG.] Sit down before I knock yuh down! [LONG *makes haste to efface himself.* YANK *goes on contemptuously.*] De Bible, huh? De Cap'tlist class, huh? Aw nix on dat Salvation Army-Socialist bull. Git a soapbox! Hire a hall! Come and be saved, huh? Jerk us to Jesus, huh? Aw g'wan! I've listened to lots of guys like you, see. Yuh're all wrong. Wanter know what I t'ink? Yuh ain't no good for noone. Yuh're de bunk. Yuh ain't got no noive, get me? Yuh're yellow, dat's what. Yellow, dat's you. Say! What's dem slobs in de foist cabin got to do wit us? We're better men dan dey are, ain't we? Sure! One of us guys could clean up de whole mob wit one mit. Put one of 'em down here for one watch in de stokehole, what'd happen? Dey'd carry him off on a stretcher. Dem boids don't amount to nothin'. Dey're just baggage. Who makes dis old tub run? Ain't it us guys? Well den, we belong, don't we? We belong and dey don't. Dat's all. [*A loud chorus of approval.* YANK *goes on.*] As for dis bein' hell—aw, nuts! Yuh lost your noive, dat's what. Dis is a man's job, get me? It belongs. It runs dis tub. No stiffs need apply. But yuh're a stiff, see? Yuh're yellow, dat's you.

VOICES: [*With a great hard pride in them.*]

Righto!

A man's job!

Talk is cheap, Long.

He never could hold up his end.

Divil take him!

Yank's right. We make it go.

Py Gott, Yank say right ting!

We don't need noone cryin' over us.

Makin' speeches.

Throw him out!

Yellow!

Chuck him overboard!

I'll break his jaw for him!

[*They crowd around* LONG *threateningly.*]

YANK: [*Half good-natured again—contemptuously.*] Aw, take it easy.

Leave him alone. He ain't woith a punch. Drink up. Here's how, whoever owns dis. [*He takes a long swallow from his bottle. All drink with him. In a flash all is hilarious amiability again, back-slapping, loud talk, etc.*]

PADDY: [*Who has been sitting in a blinking, melancholy daze— suddenly cries out in a voice full of old sorrow.*] We belong to this, you're saying? We make the ship to go, you're saying? Yerra then, that Almighty God have pity on us! [*His voice runs into the wail of a keen, he rocks back and forth on his bench. The men stare at him, startled and impressed in spite of themselves.*] Oh, to be back in the fine days of my youth, ochone! Oh, there was fine beautiful ships them days—clippers wid tall masts touching the sky—fine strong men in them—men that was sons of the sea as if 'twas the mother that bore them. Oh, the clean skins of them, and the clear eyes, the straight backs and full chests of them! Brave men they was, and bold men surely! We'd be sailing out, bound down round the Horn maybe. We'd be making sail in the dawn, with a fair breeze, singing a chanty song wid no care to it. And astern the land would be sink-ing low and dying out, but we'd give it no heed but a laugh, and never a look behind. For the day that was, was enough, for we was free men—and I'm thinking 'tis only slaves do be giving heed to the day that's gone or the day to come—until they're old like me. [*With a sort of religious exaltation.*] Oh, to be scudding south again wid the power of the Trade Wind driving her on steady through the nights and the days! Full sail on her! Nights and days! Nights when the foam of the wake would be flaming wid fire, when the sky'd be blazing and winking wid stars. Or the full of the moon maybe. Then you'd see her driving through the gray night, her sails stretching aloft all silver and white, not a sound on the deck, the lot of us dreaming dreams, till you'd believe 'twas no real ship at all you was on but a ghost ship like the Flying Dutchman they say does be roaming the seas forevermore widout touching a port. And there was the days, too. A warm sun on the clean decks. Sun warming the blood of you, and wind over the miles of shiny green ocean like strong drink to your lungs. Work—aye, hard work—but who'd mind that at all? Sure, you worked under the sky and 'twas work wid skill and daring to it. And wid the day done, in the dog watch, smoking me pipe at ease, the lookout would be raising land maybe, and we'd see the mountains of South Americy wid the red fire of the setting sun paint-ing their white tops and the clouds floating by them! [*His tone of ex-altation ceases. He goes on mournfully.*] Yerra, what's the use of

talking? 'Tis a dead man's whisper. [*To* YANK *resentfully.*] 'Twas
them days men belonged to ships, not now. 'Twas them days a ship
was part of the sea, and a man was part of a ship, and the sea joined
all together and made it one. [*Scornfully.*] Is it one wid this you'd be,
Yank—black smoke from the funnels smudging the sea, smudging
the decks—the bloody engines pounding and throbbing and shaking—
wid divil a sight of sun or a breath of clean air—choking our lungs
wid coal dust—breaking our backs and hearts in the hell of the
stokehole—feeding the bloody furnace—feeding our lives along wid
the coal, I'm thinking—caged in by steel from a sight of the sky like
bloody apes in the Zoo! [*With a harsh laugh.*] Ho-ho, divil mend
you! Is it to belong to that you're wishing? Is it a flesh and blood
wheel of the engines you'd be?

YANK: [*Who has been listening with a contemptuous sneer, barks out
the answer.*] Sure ting! Dat's me! What about it?

PADDY: [*As if to himself—with great sorrow.*] Me time is past due. That
a great wave wid sun in the heart of it may sweep me over the side
sometime I'd be dreaming of the days that's gone!

YANK: Aw, yuh crazy Mick! [*He springs to his feet and advances on
PADDY threateningly—then stops, fighting some queer struggle
within himself—lets his hands fall to his sides—contemptuously.*]
Aw, take it easy. Yuh're aw right, at dat. Yuh're bugs, dat's all—
nutty as a cuckoo. All dat tripe yuh been pullin'—Aw, dat's all right.
On'y it's dead, get me? Yuh don't belong no more, see. Yuh don't get
de stuff. Yuh're too old. [*Disgustedly.*] But aw say, come up for air
onct in a while, can't yuh? See what's happened since yuh croaked.
[*He suddenly bursts forth vehemently, growing more and more excited.*] Say! Sure! Sure I meant it! What de hell— Say, lemme talk!
Hey! Hey, you old Harp! Hey, youse guys! Say, listen to me—wait a
moment—I gotter talk, see. I belong and he don't. He's dead but I'm
livin'. Listen to me! Sure I'm part of de engines! Why de hell not!
Dey move, don't dey? Dey're speed, ain't dey? Dey smash trou, don't
dey? Twenty-five knots a hour! Dat's goin' some! Dat's new stuff!
Dat belongs! But him, he's too old. He gets dizzy. Say, listen. All dat
crazy tripe about nights and days; all dat crazy tripe about stars and
moons; all dat crazy tripe about suns and winds, fresh air and de rest
of it—Aw hell, dat's all a dope dream! Hittin' de pipe of de past,
dat's what he's doin'. He's old and don't belong no more. But me,
I'm young! I'm in de pink! I move wit it! It, get me! I mean de ting
dat's de guts of all dis. It ploughs trou all de tripe he's been sayin'. It
blows dat up! It knocks dat dead! It slams dat offen de face of de
oith! It, get me! De engines and de coal and de smoke and all de rest

of it! He can't breathe and swallow coal dust, but I kin, see? Dat's fresh air for me! Dat's food for me! I'm new, get me? Hell in de stokehole? Sure! It takes a man to work in hell. Hell, sure, dat's my fav'rite climate. I eat it up! I git fat on it! It's me makes it hot! It's me makes it roar! It's me makes it move! Sure, on'y for me everyting stops. It all goes dead, get me? De noise and smoke and all de engines movin' de woild, dey stop. Dere ain't nothin' no more! Dat's what I'm sayin'. Everything else dat makes de woild move, somep'n makes it move. It can't move witout somep'n else, see? Den yuh get down to me. I'm at de bottom, get me! Dere ain't nothin' foither. I'm de end! I'm de start! I start somep'n and de woild moves! It—dat's me!—de new dat's moiderin' de old! I'm de ting in coal dat makes it boin; I'm steam and oil for de engines; I'm de ting in noise dat makes yuh hear it; I'm smoke and express trains and steamers and factory whistles; I'm de ting in gold dat makes it money! And I'm what makes iron into steel! Steel, dat stands for de whole ting! And I'm steel—steel—steel! I'm de muscles in steel, de punch behind it! [*As he says this he pounds with his fist against the steel bunks. All the men, roused to a pitch of frenzied self-glorification by his speech, do likewise. There is a deafening metallic roar, through which* YANK'S *voice can be heard bellowing.*] Slaves, hell! We run de whole woiks. All de rich guys dat tink dey're somep'n, dey ain't nothin'! Dey don't belong. But us guys, we're in de move, we're at de bottom, de whole ting is us! [PADDY *from the start of* YANK'S *speech has been taking one gulp after another from his bottle, at first frightenedly, as if he were afraid to listen, then desperately, as if to drown his senses, but finally has achieved complete indifferent, even amused, drunkenness.* YANK *sees his lips moving. He quells the uproar with a shout.*] Hey, youse guys, take it easy! Wait a moment! De nutty Harp is sayin' somep'n.

PADDY: [*Is heard now—throws his head back with a mocking burst of laughter.*] Ho-ho-ho-ho-ho—

YANK: [*Drawing back his fist, with a snarl.*] Aw! Look out who yuh're givin' the bark!

PADDY: [*Begins to sing the "Miller of Dee" with enormous good-nature.*]

> "I care for nobody, no, not I,
> And nobody cares for me."

YANK: [*Good-natured himself in a flash, interrupts* PADDY *with a slap on the bare back like a report.*] Dat's de stuff! Now yuh're gettin' wise to somep'n. Care for nobody, dat's de dope! To hell wit 'em all! And nix on nobody else carin'. I kin care for myself, get me! [*Eight bells sound, muffled, vibrating through the steel walls as if some enormous brazen gong were imbedded in the heart of the ship. All the men jump up mechanically, file through the door silently close upon each other's heels in what is very like a prisoners' lockstep.* YANK *slaps* PADDY *on the back.*] Our watch, yuh old Harp! [*Mockingly.*] Come on down in hell. Eat up de coal dust. Drink in de heat. It's it, see! Act like yuh liked it, yuh better—or croak yuhself.

PADDY: [*With jovial defiance.*] To the divil wid it! I'll not report this watch. Let them log me and be damned. I'm no slave the like of you. I'll be sittin' here at me ease, and drinking, and thinking, and dreaming dreams.

YANK: [*Contemptuously.*] Tinkin' and dreamin', what'll that get yuh? What's tinkin' got to do wit it? We move, don't we? Speed, ain't it? Fog, dat's all you stand for. But we drive trou dat, don't we? We split dat up and smash trou—twenty-five knots a hour! [*Turns his back on* PADDY *scornfully.*] Aw, yuh make me sick! Yuh don't belong! [*He strides out the door in rear.* PADDY *hums to himself, blinking drowsily.*]

[*Curtain*]

SCENE TWO

SCENE—*Two days out. A section of the promenade deck.* MILDRED DOUGLAS *and her aunt are discovered reclining in deck chairs. The former is a girl of twenty, slender, delicate, with a pale, pretty face marred by a self-conscious expression of disdainful superiority. She looks fretful, nervous and discontented, bored by her own anemia. Her aunt is a pompous and proud—and fat—old lady. She is a type even to the point of a double chin and lorgnettes. She is dressed pretentiously, as if afraid her face alone would never indicate her position in life.* MILDRED *is dressed all in white.*

The impression to be conveyed by this scene is one of the beautiful, vivid life of the sea all about—sunshine on the deck in a great flood, the fresh sea wind blowing across it. In the midst of this, these two incongruous, artificial figures, inert and disharmonious, the elder like a gray lump of dough touched up with rouge, the younger looking as if the vitality of her stock had been sapped before she was conceived, so that

*she is the expression not of its life energy but merely of the artificialities
that energy had won for itself in the spending.*

MILDRED: [*Looking up with affected dreaminess.*] How the black
smoke swirls back against the sky! Is it not beautiful?

AUNT: [*Without looking up.*] I dislike smoke of any kind.

MILDRED: My great-grandmother smoked a pipe—a clay pipe.

AUNT: [*Ruffling.*] Vulgar!

MILDRED: She was too distant a relative to be vulgar. Time mellows
pipes.

AUNT: [*Pretending boredom but irritated.*] Did the sociology you took
up at college teach you that—to play the ghoul on every possible occasion, excavating old bones? Why not let your great-grandmother
rest in her grave?

MILDRED: [*Dreamily.*] With her pipe beside her—puffing in Paradise.

AUNT: [*With spite.*] Yes, you are a natural born ghoul. You are even
getting to look like one, my dear.

MILDRED: [*In a passionless tone.*] I detest you, Aunt. [*Looking at her
critically.*] Do you know what you remind me of? Of a cold pork
pudding against a background of linoleum tablecloth in the kitchen
of a—but the possibilities are wearisome. [*She closes her eyes.*]

AUNT: [*With a bitter laugh.*] Merci for your candor. But since I am and
must be your chaperone—in appearance, at least—let us patch up
some sort of armed truce. For my part you are quite free to indulge
any pose of eccentricity that beguiles you—as long as you observe
the amenities—

MILDRED: [*Drawling.*] The inanities?

AUNT: [*Going on as if she hadn't heard.*] After exhausting the morbid
thrills of social service work on New York's East Side—how they
must have hated you, by the way, the poor that you made so much
poorer in their own eyes!—you are now bent on making your slum-
ming international. Well, I hope Whitechapel will provide the needed
nerve tonic. Do not ask me to chaperone you there, however. I told
your father I would not. I loathe deformity. We will hire an army
of detectives and you may investigate everything—they allow you
to see.

MILDRED: [*Protesting with a trace of genuine earnestness.*] Please do
not mock at my attempts to discover how the other half lives. Give
me credit for some sort of groping sincerity in that at least. I would
like to help them. I would like to be some use in the world. Is it my
fault I don't know how? I would like to be sincere, to touch life

somewhere. [*With weary bitterness.*] But I'm afraid I have neither the vitality nor integrity. All that was burnt out in our stock before I was born. Grandfather's blast furnaces, flaming to the sky, melting steel, making millions—then father keeping those home fires burning, making more millions—and little me at the tail-end of it all. I'm a waste product in the Bessemer process—like the millions. Or rather, I inherit the acquired trait of the by-product, wealth, but none of the energy, none of the strength of the steel that made it. I am sired by gold and damed by it, as they say at the race track—damned in more ways than one. [*She laughs mirthlessly*].

AUNT: [*Unimpressed—superciliously.*] You seem to be going in for sincerity today. It isn't becoming to you, really—except as an obvious pose. Be as artificial as you are, I advise. There's a sort of sincerity in that, you know. And, after all, you must confess you like that better.

MILDRED: [*Again affected and bored.*] Yes, I suppose I do. Pardon me for my outburst. When a leopard complains of its spots, it must sound rather grotesque. [*In a mocking tone.*] Purr, little leopard. Purr, scratch, tear, kill, gorge yourself and be happy—only stay in the jungle where your spots are camouflage. In a cage they make you conspicuous.

AUNT: I don't know what you are talking about.

MILDRED: It would be rude to talk about anything to you. Let's just talk. [*She looks at her wrist watch.*] Well, thank goodness, it's about time for them to come for me. That ought to give me a new thrill, Aunt.

AUNT: [*Affectedly troubled.*] You don't mean to say you're really going? The dirt—the heat must be frightful—

MILDRED: Grandfather started as a puddler. I should have inherited an immunity to heat that would make a salamander shiver. It will be fun to put it to the test.

AUNT: But don't you have to have the captain's—or someone's—permission to visit the stokehole?

MILDRED: [*With a triumphant smile.*] I have it—both his and the chief engineer's. Oh, they didn't want to at first, in spite of my social service credentials. They didn't seem a bit anxious that I should investigate how the other half lives and works on a ship. So I had to tell them that my father, the president of Nazareth Steel, chairman of the board of directors of this line, had told me it would be all right.

AUNT: He didn't.

MILDRED: How naïve age makes one! But I said he did, Aunt. I even said he had given me a letter to them—which I had lost. And they were afraid to take the chance that I might be lying. [*Excitedly.*] So it's ho! for the stokehole. The second engineer is to escort me. [*Looking at her watch again.*] It's time. And here he comes, I think. [*The* SECOND ENGINEER *enters. He is a husky, fine-looking man of thirty-five or so. He stops before the two and tips his cap, visibly embarrassed and ill-at-ease.*]

SECOND ENGINEER: Miss Douglas?

MILDRED: Yes. [*Throwing off her rugs and getting to her feet.*] Are we all ready to start?

SECOND ENGINEER: In just a second, ma'am. I'm waiting for the Fourth. He's coming along.

MILDRED: [*With a scornful smile.*] You don't care to shoulder this responsibility alone, is that it?

SECOND ENGINEER: [*Forcing a smile.*] Two are better than one. [*Disturbed by her eyes, glances out to sea—blurts out.*] A fine day we're having.

MILDRED: Is it?

SECOND ENGINEER: A nice warm breeze—

MILDRED: It feels cold to me.

SECOND ENGINEER: But it's hot enough in the sun—

MILDRED: Not hot enough for me. I don't like Nature. I was never athletic.

SECOND ENGINEER: [*Forcing a smile.*] Well, you'll find it hot enough where you're going.

MILDRED: Do you mean hell?

SECOND ENGINEER: [*Flabbergasted, decides to laugh.*] Ho-ho! No, I mean the stokehole.

MILDRED: My grandfather was a puddler. He played with boiling steel.

SECOND ENGINEER: [*All at sea—uneasily.*] Is that so? Hum, you'll excuse me, ma'am, but are you intending to wear that dress?

MILDRED: Why not?

SECOND ENGINEER: You'll likely rub against oil and dirt. It can't be helped.

MILDRED: It doesn't matter. I have lots of white dresses.

SECOND ENGINEER: I have an old coat you might throw over—

MILDRED: I have fifty dresses like this. I will throw this one into the sea when I come back. That ought to wash it clean, don't you think?

SECOND ENGINEER: [*Doggedly.*] There's ladders to climb down that are none too clean—and dark alleyways—

MILDRED: I will wear this very dress and none other.

SECOND ENGINEER: No offence meant. It's none of my business. I was only warning you—

MILDRED: Warning? That sounds thrilling.

SECOND ENGINEER: [*Looking down the deck—with a sigh of relief.*]—
    There's the Fourth now. He's waiting for us. If you'll come—
MILDRED: Go on. I'll follow you. [*He goes.* MILDRED *turns a mocking
    smile on her aunt.*] An oaf—but a handsome, virile oaf.
AUNT: [*Scornfully.*] Poser!
MILDRED: Take care. He said there were dark alleyways—
AUNT: [*In the same tone.*] Poser!
MILDRED: [*Biting her lips angrily.*] You are right. But would that my
    millions were not so anemically chaste!
AUNT: Yes, for a fresh pose I have no doubt you would drag the name
    of Douglas in the gutter!
MILDRED: From which it sprang. Good-by, Aunt. Don't pray too hard
    that I may fall into the fiery furnace.
AUNT: Poser!
MILDRED: [*Viciously.*] Old hag! [*She slaps her aunt insultingly across
    the face and walks off, laughing gaily.*]
AUNT: [*Screams after her.*] I said poser!

[*Curtain*]

SCENE THREE

SCENE—*The stokehole. In the rear, the dimly-outlined bulks of the furnaces and boilers. High overhead one hanging electric bulb sheds just
enough light through the murky air laden with coal dust to pile up
masses of shadows everywhere. A line of men, stripped to the waist, is
before the furnace doors. They bend over, looking neither to right nor
left, handling their shovels as if they were part of their bodies, with a
strange, awkward, swinging rhythm. They use the shovels to throw
open the furnace doors. Then from these fiery round holes in the black
a flood of terrific light and heat pours full upon the men who are outlined in silhouette in the crouching, inhuman attitudes of chained gorillas. The men shovel with a rhythmic motion, swinging as on a pivot
from the coal which lies in heaps on the floor behind to hurl it into the
flaming mouths before them. There is a tumult of noise—the brazen
clang of the furnace doors as they are flung open or slammed shut, the
grating, teeth-gritting grind of steel against steel, of crunching coal.
This clash of sounds stuns one's ears with its rending dissonance. But
there is order in it, rhythm, a mechanical regulated recurrence, a tempo.
And rising above all, making the air hum with the quiver of liberated*

energy, the roar of leaping flames in the furnaces, the monotonous throbbing beat of the engines.

As the curtain rises, the furnace doors are shut. The men are taking a breathing spell. One or two are arranging the coal behind them, pulling it into more accessible heaps. The others can be dimly made out leaning on their shovels in relaxed attitudes of exhaustion.

PADDY: [*From somewhere in the line—plaintively.*] Yerra, will this divil's own watch nivir end? Me back is broke. I'm destroyed entirely.

YANK: [*From the center of the line—with exuberant scorn.*] Aw, yuh make me sick! Lie down and croak, why don't yuh? Always beefin', dat's you! Say, dis is a cinch! Dis was made for me! It's my meat, get me! [*A whistle is blown—a thin, shrill note from somewhere overhead in the darkness.* YANK *curses without resentment.*] Dere's de damn engineer crakin' de whip. He tinks we're loafin'.

PADDY: [*Vindictively.*] God stiffen him!

YANK: [*In an exultant tone of command.*] Come on, youse guys! Git into de game! She's gittin' hungry! Pile some grub in her! Trow it into her belly! Come on now, all of youse! Open her up! [*At this last all the men, who have followed his movements of getting into position, throw open their furnace doors with a deafening clang. The fiery light floods over their shoulders as they bend round for the coal. Rivulets of sooty sweat have traced maps on their backs. The enlarged muscles form bunches of high light and shadow.*]

YANK: [*Chanting a count as he shovels without seeming effort.*] One— two—tree— [*His voice rising exultantly in the joy of battle.*] Dat's de stuff! Let her have it! All togedder now! Sling it into her! Let her ride! Shoot de piece now! Call de toin on her! Drive her into it! Feel her move! Watch her smoke! Speed, dat's her middle name! Give her coal, youse guys! Coal, dat's her booze! Drink it up, baby! Let's see yuh sprint! Dig in and gain a lap! Dere she go-o-es [*This last in the chanting formula of the gallery gods at the six-day bike race. He slams his furnace door shut. The others do likewise with as much unison as their wearied bodies will permit. The effect is of one fiery eye after another being blotted out with a series of accompanying bangs.*]

PADDY: [*Groaning.*] Me back is broke. I'm bate out—bate— [*There is a pause. Then the inexorable whistle sounds again from the dim regions above the electric light. There is a growl of cursing rage from all sides.*]

YANK: [*Shaking his fist upward—contemptuously.*] Take it easy dere, you! Who d'yuh tinks runnin' dis game, me or you? When I git ready, we move. Not before! When I git ready, get me!

VOICES: [*Approvingly.*] That's the stuff!

                    Yank tal him, py golly!

                    Yank ain't affeerd.

                    Goot poy, Yank!

                    Give him hell!

                    Tell 'im 'e's a bloody swine!

                    Bloody slave-driver!

YANK: [*Contemptuously.*] He ain't got no noive. He's yellow, get me? All de engineers is yellow. Dey got streaks a mile wide. Aw, to hell wit him! Let's move, youse guys. We had a rest. Come on, she needs it! Give her pep! It ain't for him. Him and his whistle, dey don't belong. But we belong, see! We gotter feed de baby! Come on! [*He turns and flings his furnace door open. They all follow his lead. At this instant the* SECOND *and* FOURTH ENGINEERS *enter from the darkness on the left with* MILDRED *between them. She starts, turns paler, her pose is crumbling, she shivers with fright in spite of the blazing heat, but forces herself to leave the* ENGINEERS *and take a few steps nearer the men. She is right behind* YANK. *All this happens quickly while the men have their backs turned.*]

YANK: Come on, youse guys! [*He is turning to get coal when the whistle sounds again in a peremptory, irritating note. This drives* YANK *into a sudden fury. While the other men have turned full around and stopped dumfounded by the spectacle of* MILDRED *standing there in her white dress.* YANK *does not turn far enough to see her. Besides, his head is thrown back, he blinks upward through the murk trying to find the owner of the whistle, he brandishes his shovel murderously over his head in one hand, pounding on his chest, gorilla-like, with the other, shouting:*] Toin off dat whistle! Come down outa dere, yuh yellow, brass-buttoned, Belfast bum, yuh! Come down and I'll knock yer brains out! Yuh lousey, stinkin', yellow mut of a Catholic-moiderin' bastard! Come down and I'll moider yuh! Pullin' dat whistle on me, huh? I'll show yuh! I'll crash yer skull in! I'll drive yer teet' down yer troat! I'll slam yer nose trou de back of yer head! I'll cut yer guts out for a nickel, yuh lousey boob, yuh dirty, crummy, muck-eatin' son of a—[*Suddenly he becomes conscious of all the other men staring at something directly behind his back. He whirls defensively with a snarling, murderous growl, crouching to spring, his lips drawn back over his teeth, his small eyes gleaming fero-*

ciously. He sees MILDRED, *like a white apparition in the full light
from the open furnace doors. He glares into her eyes, turned to
stone. As for her, during his speech she has listened, paralyzed with
horror, terror, her whole personality crushed, beaten in, collapsed,
by the terrific impact of this unknown, abysmal brutality, naked and
shameless. As she looks at his gorilla face, as his eyes bore into hers,
she utters a low, choking cry and shrinks away from him, putting
both hands up before her eyes to shut out the sight of his face, to
protect her own. This startles* YANK *to a reaction. His mouth falls
open, his eyes grow bewildered.*]

MILDRED: [*About to faint—to the* ENGINEERS, *who now have her one
by each arm—whimperingly.*] Take me away! Oh, the filthy beast!
[*She faints. They carry her quickly back, disappearing in the darkness at the left, rear. An iron door clangs shut. Rage and bewildered
fury rush back on* YANK. *He feels himself insulted in some unknown
fashion in the very heart of his pride. He roars:*] God damn yuh!
[*And hurls his shovel after them at the door which has just closed. It
hits the steel bulkhead with a clang and falls clattering on the steel
floor. From overhead the whistle sounds again in a long, angry, insistent command.*]

[*Curtain*]

SCENE FOUR

SCENE—*The firemen's forecastle.* YANK's *watch has just come off duty
and had dinner. Their faces and bodies shine from a soap and water
scrubbing but around their eyes, where a hasty dousing does not touch,
the coal dust sticks like black make-up, giving them a queer, sinister expression.* YANK *has not washed either face or body. He stands out in
contrast to them, a blackened, brooding figure. He is seated forward on
a bench in the exact attitude of Rodin's "The Thinker." The others,
most of them smoking pipes, are staring at* YANK *half-apprehensively,
as if fearing an outburst; half-amusedly, as if they saw a joke somewhere that tickled them.*

VOICES: He ain't ate nothin'.
        Py golly, a fallar gat gat grub in him.
        Divil a lie.
        Yank feeda da fire, no feeda da face.

Ha-ha.

He ain't even washed hisself.

He's forgot.

Hey, Yank, you forgot to wash.

YANK: [*Sullenly.*] Forgot nothin'! To hell wit washin'.

VOICES: It'll stick to you.

It'll get under your skin.

Give yer the bleedin' itch, that's wot.

It makes spots on you—like a leopard.

Like a piebald nigger, you mean.

Better wash up, Yank.

You sleep better.

Wash up, Yank.

Wash up! Wash up!

YANK: [*Resentfully.*] Aw say, youse guys. Lemme alone. Can't youse see I'm tryin' to tink?

ALL: [*Repeating the word after him as one with cynical mockery.*] Think! [*The word has a brazen, metallic quality as if their throats were phonograph horns. It is followed by a chorus of hard, barking laughter.*]

YANK: [*Springing to his feet and glaring at them belligerently.*] Yes, tink! Tink, dat's what I said! What about it? [*They are silent, puzzled by his sudden resentment at what used to be one of his jokes.* YANK *sits down again in the same attitude of "The Thinker."*]

VOICES: Leave him alone.

He's got a grouch on.

Why wouldn't he?

PADDY: [*With a wink at the others.*] Sure I know what's the matther. 'Tis aisy to see. He's fallen in love, I'm telling you.

ALL: [*Repeating the word after him as one with cynical mockery.*] Love! [*The word has a brazen, metallic quality as if their throats were phonograph horns. It is followed by a chorus of hard, barking laughter.*]

YANK: [*With a contemptuous snort.*] Love, hell! Hate, dat's what. I've fallen in hate, get me?

PADDY: [*Philosophically.*] 'Twould take a wise man to tell one from the other. [*With a bitter, ironical scorn, increasing as he goes on.*] But I'm telling you it's love that's in it. Sure what else but love for us poor bastes in the stokehole would be bringing a fine lady, dressed like a white quane, down a mile of ladders and steps to be havin' a look at us? [*A growl of anger goes up from all sides.*]

LONG: [*Jumping on a bench—hecticly.*] Hinsultin' us! Hinsultin' us, the bloody cow! And them bloody engineers! What right 'as they got to be exhibitin' us 's if we was bleedin' monkeys in a menagerie? Did we sign for hinsults to our dignity as 'onest workers? Is that in the ship's articles? You kin bloody well bet it ain't! But I knows why they done it. I arsked a deck steward 'o she was and 'e told me. 'Er old man's a bleedin' millionaire, a bloody Capitalist! 'E's got enuf bloody gold to sink this bleedin' ship! 'E makes arf the bloody steel in the world! 'E owns this bloody boat! And you and me, comrades, we're 'is slaves! And the skipper and mates and engineers, they're 'is slaves! And she's 'is bloody daughter and we're all 'er slaves, too! And she gives 'er orders as 'ow she wants to see the bloody animals below decks and down they takes 'er! [*There is a roar of rage from all sides.*]

YANK: [*Blinking at him bewilderedly.*] Say! Wait a moment! Is all dat straight goods?

LONG: Straight as string! The bleedin' steward as waits on 'em, 'e told me about 'er. And what're we goin' ter do, I arsks yer? 'Ave we got ter swaller 'er hinsults like dogs? It ain't in the ship's articles. I tell yer we got a case. We kin go ter law—

YANK: [*With abysmal contempt.*] Hell! Law!

ALL: [*Repeating the word after him as one with cynical mockery.*] Law! [*The word has a brazen metallic quality as if their throats were phonograph horns. It is followed by a chorus of hard, barking laughter.*]

LONG: [*Feeling the ground slipping from under his feet—desperately.*] As voters and citizens we kin force the bloody governments—

YANK: [*With abysmal contempt.*] Hell! Governments!

ALL: [*Repeating the word after him as one with cynical mockery.*] Governments! [*The word has a brazen metallic quality as if their throats were phonograph horns. It is followed by a chorus of hard, barking laughter.*]

LONG: [*Hysterically.*] We're free and equal in the sight of God—

YANK: [*With abysmal contempt.*] Hell! God!

ALL: [*Repeating the word after him as one with cynical mockery.*] God! [*The word has a brazen metallic quality as if their throats were phonograph horns. It is followed by a chorus of hard, barking laughter.*]

YANK: [*Witheringly.*] Aw, join de Salvation Army!

ALL: Sit down! Shut up! Damn fool! Sea-lawyer! [LONG *slinks back out of sight.*]

PADDY: [*Continuing the trend of his thoughts as if he had never been interrupted—bitterly.*] And there she was standing behind us, and the Second pointing at us like a man you'd hear in a circus would be saying: In this cage is a queerer kind of baboon than ever you'd find in darkest Africy. We roast them in their own sweat—and be damned if you won't hear some of thim saying they like it! [*He glances scornfully at* YANK.]

YANK: [*With a bewildered uncertain growl.*] Aw!

PADDY: And there was Yank roarin' curses and turning round wid his shovel to brain her—and she looked at him, and him at her—

YANK: [*Slowly.*] She was all white. I tought she was a ghost. Sure.

PADDY: [*With heavy, biting sarcasm.*] 'Twas love at first sight, divil a doubt of it! If you'd seen the endearin' look on her pale mug when she shrivelled away with her hands over her eyes to shut out the sight of him! Sure, 'twas as if she'd seen a great hairy ape escaped from the Zoo!

YANK: [*Stung—with a growl of rage.*] Aw!

PADDY: And the loving way Yank heaved his shovel at the skull of her, only she was out the door! [*A grin breaking over his face.*] 'Twas touching, I'm telling you! It put the touch of home, swate home in the stokehole. [*There is a roar of laughter from all.*]

YANK: [*Glaring at* PADDY *menacingly.*] Aw, choke dat off, see!

PADDY: [*Not heeding him—to the others.*] And her grabbin' at the Second's arm for protection. [*With a grotesque imitation of a woman's voice.*] Kiss me, Engineer dear, for it's dark down here and me old man's in Wall Street making money! Hug me tight, darlin', for I'm afeerd in the dark and me mother's on deck makin' eyes at the skipper! [*Another roar of laughter.*]

YANK: [*Threateningly.*] Say! What yuh tryin' to do, kid me, yuh old Harp?

PADDY: Divil a bit! Ain't I wishin' myself you'd brained her?

YANK: [*Fiercely.*] I'll brain her! I'll brain her yet, wait 'n' see! [*Coming over to* PADDY—*slowly.*] Say, is dat what she called me—a hairy ape?

PADDY: She looked it at you if she didn't say the word itself.

YANK: [*Grinning horribly.*] Hairy ape, huh? Sure! Dat's de way she looked at me, aw right. Hairy ape! So dat's me, huh? [*Bursting into rage—as if she were still in front of him.*] Yuh skinny tart! Yuh white-faced bum, yuh! I'll show yuh who's a ape! [*Turning to the others, bewilderment seizing him again.*] Say, youse guys. I was bawlin' him out for pullin' de whistle on us. You heard me. And den I seen youse lookin' at somep'n and I tought he'd sneaked down to come up in back of me, and I hopped round to knock him dead wit de shovel. And dere she was wit de light on her! Christ, yuh coulda pushed me over with a finger! I was scared, get me? Sure! I tought she was a ghost, see? She was all in white like dey wrap around stiffs. You seen her. Kin yuh blame me? She didn't belong, dat's what. And den when I come to and seen it was a real skoit and seen de way she was lookin' at me—like Paddy said—Christ, I was sore, get me? I don't stand for dat stuff from nobody. And I flung de shovel—on'y she'd beat it. [*Furiously.*] I wished it'd banged her! I wished it'd knocked her block off!

LONG: And be 'anged for murder or 'lectrocuted? She ain't bleedin' well worth it.

YANK: I don't give a damn what! I'd be square wit her, wouldn't I? Tink I wanter let her put somep'n over on me? Tink I'm goin' to let her git away wit dat stuff? Yuh don't know me! Noone ain't never put nothin' over on me and got away wit it, see!—not dat kind of stuff— no guy and no skoit neither! I'll fix her! Maybe she'll come down again—

VOICE: No chance, Yank. You scared her out of a year's growth.

YANK: I scared her? Why de hell should I scare her? Who de hell is she? Ain't she de same as me? Hairy ape, huh? [*With his old confident bravado.*] I'll show her I'm better'n her, if she on'y knew it. I belong and she don't, see! I move and she's dead! Twenty-five knots a hour, dats me! Dat carries her but I make dat. She's on'y baggage. Sure! [*Again bewilderedly.*] But, Christ, she was funny lookin'! Did yuh pipe her hands? White and skinny. Yuh could see de bones trough 'em. And her mush, dat was dead white, too. And her eyes, dey was like dey'd seen a ghost. Me, dat was! Sure! Hairy ape! Ghost, huh? Look at dat arm! [*He extends his right arm, swelling out the great muscles.*] I coulda took her wit dat, wit' just my little finger even, and broke her in two. [*Again bewilderedly.*] Say, who is dat skoit, huh? What is she? What's she come from? Who made her? Who give her de noive to look at me like dat? Dis ting's got my goat right. I don't get her. She's new to me. What does a skoit like her mean, huh? She don't belong, get me! I can't see her. [*With growing anger.*] But one ting I'm wise to, aw right, aw right! Youse all kin bet your shoits I'll git even wit her. I'll show her if she tinks she— She grinds de organ and I'm on de string, huh? I'll fix her! Let her come down again and I'll fling her in de furnace! She'll move den! She won't shiver at nothin', den! Speed, dat'll be her! She'll belong den! [*He grins horribly.*]

PADDY: She'll never come. She's had her belly-full, I'm telling you. She'll be in bed now, I'm thinking, wid ten doctors and nurses feedin' her salts to clean the fear out of her.

YANK: [*Enraged.*] Yuh tink I made her sick, too, do yuh? Just lookin' at me, huh? Hairy ape, huh? [*In a frenzy of rage.*] I'll fix her! I'll tell her where to git off! She'll git down on her knees and take it back or I'll bust de face offen her! [*Shaking one fist upward and beating on his chest with the other.*] I'll find yuh! I'm comin', d'yuh hear? I'll fix yuh, God damn yuh! [*He makes a rush for the door.*]

VOICES: Stop him!
       He'll get shot!
       He'll murder her!
       Trip him up!
       Hold him!
       He's gone crazy!
       Gott, he's strong!
       Hold him down!
       Look out for a kick!
       Pin his arms!

[*They have all piled on him and, after a fierce struggle, by sheer weight of numbers have borne him to the floor just inside the door.*]

PADDY: [*Who has remained detached.*] Kape him down till he's cooled off. [*Scornfully.*] Yerra, Yank, you're a great fool. Is it payin' attention at all you are to the like of that skinny sow widout one drop of rale blood in her?

YANK: [*Frenziedly, from the bottom of the heap.*] She done me doit! She done me doit, didn't she? I'll git square wit her! I'll get her some way! Git offen me, youse guys! Lemme up! I'll show her who's a ape!

[*Curtain*]

SCENE FIVE

SCENE—*Three weeks later. A corner of Fifth Avenue in the Fifties on a fine, Sunday morning. A general atmosphere of clean, well-tidied, wide street; a flood of mellow, tempered sunshine; gentle, genteel breezes. In the rear, the show windows of two shops, a jewelry establishment on the corner, a furrier's next to it. Here the adornments of extreme wealth are tantalizingly displayed. The jeweler's window is gaudy with glittering diamonds, emeralds, rubies, pearls, etc., fashioned in ornate tiaras, crowns, necklaces, collars, etc. From each piece hangs an enormous tag*

*from which a dollar sign and numerals in intermittent electric lights
wink out the incredible prices. The same in the furrier's. Rich furs of all
varieties hang there bathed in a downpour of artificial light. The general effect is of a background of magnificence cheapened and made
grotesque by commercialism, a background in tawdry disharmony with
the clear light and sunshine on the street itself.*

Up the side street YANK *and* LONG *come swaggering.* LONG *is
dressed in shore clothes, wears a black Windsor tie, cloth cap.* YANK *is
in his dirty dungarees. A fireman's cap with black peak is cocked defiantly on the side of his head. He has not shaved for days and around
his fierce, resentful eyes—as around those of* LONG *to a lesser degree—
the black smudge of coal dust still sticks like make-up. They hesitate
and stand together at the corner, swaggering, looking about them with
a forced, defiant contempt.*

LONG: [*Indicating it all with an oratorical gesture.*] Well, 'ere we are.
Fif' Avenoo. This 'ere's their bleedin' private lane, as yer might say.
[*Bitterly.*] We're trespassers 'ere. Proletarians keep orf the grass!

YANK: [*Dully.*] I don't see no grass, yuh boob. [*Staring at the sidewalk.*]
Clean, ain't it? Yuh could eat a fried egg offen it. The white wings
got some job sweepin' dis up. [*Looking up and down the avenue—
surlily.*] Where's all de white-collar stiffs yuh said was here—and de
skoits—*her* kind?

LONG: In church, blarst 'em! Arskin' Jesus to give 'em more money.

YANK: Choich, huh? I useter go to choich onct—sure—when I was a
kid. Me old man and woman, dey made me. Dey never went dem-
selves, dough. Always got too big a head on Sunday mornin', dat
was dem. [*With a grin.*] Dey was scrappers for fair, bot' of dem. On
Satiday nights when dey bot' got a skinful dey could put up a bout
oughter been staged at de Garden. When dey got trough dere wasn't
a chair or table wit a leg under it. Or else dey bot' jumped on me for
somep'n. Dat was where I loined to take punishment. [*With a grin
and a swagger.*] I'm a chip offen de old block, get me?

LONG: Did yer old man follow the sea?

YANK: Naw. Worked along shore. I runned away when me old lady
croaked wit de tremens. I helped at truckin' and in de market. Den I
shipped in de stokehole. Sure. Dat belongs. De rest was nothin'.
[*Looking around him.*] I ain't never seen dis before. De Brooklyn
waterfront, dat was where I was dragged up. [*Taking a deep breath.*]
Dis ain't so bad at dat, huh?

LONG: Not bad? Well, we pays for it wiv our bloody sweat, if yer wants
to know!

YANK: [*With sudden angry disgust.*] Aw, hell! I don't see noone, see—like her. All dis gives me a pain. It don't belong. Say, ain't dere a backroom around dis dump? Let's go shoot a ball. All dis is too clean and quiet and dolled-up, get me! It gives me a pain.

LONG: Wait and yer'll bloody well see—

YANK: I don't wait for noone. I keep on de move. Say, what yuh drag me up here for, anyway? Tryin' to kid me, yuh simp, yuh?

LONG: Yer wants to get back at her, don't yer? That's what yer been saying' every bloomin' 'our since she hinsulted yer.

YANK: [*Vehemently.*] Sure ting I do! Didn't I try to git even wit her in Southampton? Didn't I sneak on de dock and wait for her by de gangplank? I was goin' to spit in her pale mug, see! Sure, right in her pop-eyes! Dat woulda made me even, see? But no chanct. Dere was a whole army of plain clothes bulls around. Dey spotted me and gimme de bum's rush. I never seen her. But I'll git square wit her yet, you watch! [*Furiously.*] De lousey tart! She tinks she kin get away wit moider—but not wit me! I'll fix her! I'll tink of a way!

LONG: [*As disgusted as he dares to be.*] Ain't that why I brought yer up 'ere—to show yer? Yer been lookin' at this 'ere 'ole affair wrong. Yer been actin' an' talkin' 's if it was all a bleedin' personal matter between yer and that bloody cow. I wants to convince yer she was on'y a representative of 'er clarss. I wants to awaken yer bloody clarss consciousness. Then yer'll see it's 'er clarss yer've got to fight, not 'er alone. There's a 'ole mob of 'em like 'er, Gawd blind 'em!

YANK: [*Spitting on his hands—belligerently.*] De more de merrier when I gits started. Bring on de gang!

LONG: Yer'll see 'em in arf a mo', when that church lets out. [*He turns and sees the window display in the two stores for the first time.*] Blimey! Look at that, will yer? [*They both walk back and stand looking in the jewelers.* LONG *flies into a fury.*] Just look at this 'ere bloomin' mess! Just look at it! Look at the bleedin' prices on 'em—more'n our 'old bloody stokehole makes in ten voyages sweatin' in 'ell! And they—her and her bloody clarss—buys 'em for toys to dangle on 'em! One of these 'ere would buy scoff for a starvin' family for a year!

YANK: Aw, cut de sob stuff! T' hell wit de starvin' family! Yuh'll be passin' de hat to me next. [*With naïve admiration.*] Say, dem tings is pretty, huh? Bet yuh dey'd hock for a piece of change aw right. [*Then turning away, bored.*] But, aw hell, what good are dey? Let her have 'em. Dey don't belong no more'n she does. [*With a gesture of sweeping the jewelers into oblivion.*] All dat don't count, get me?

LONG: [*Who has moved to the furriers—indignantly.*] And I s'pose this

'ere don't count neither—skins of poor, 'armless animals slaughtered
so as 'er and 'ers can keep their bleedin' noses warm!

YANK: [*Who has been staring at something inside—with queer excitement.*] Take a slant at dat! Give it de once-over! Monkey fur—two
t'ousand bucks! [*Bewilderedly.*] Is dat straight goods—monkey fur?
What de hell—?

LONG: [*Bitterly.*] It's straight enuf. [*With grim humor.*] They wouldn't
bloody well pay that for a 'airy ape's skin—no, nor for the 'ole livin'
ape with all 'is 'ead, and body, and soul thrown in!

YANK: [*Clenching his fists, his face growing pale with rage as if the skin
in the window were a personal insult.*] Trowin' it up in my face!
Christ! I'll fix her!

LONG: [*Excitedly.*] Church is out. 'Ere they come, the bleedin' swine. [*After a glance at* YANK's *lowering face—uneasily.*] Easy goes, Comrade.
Keep yer bloomin' temper. Remember force defeats itself. It ain't our
weapon. We must impress our demands through peaceful means—the
votes of the on-marching proletarians of the bloody world!

YANK: [*With abysmal contempt.*] Votes, hell! Votes is a joke, see. Votes
for women! Let dem do it!

LONG: [*Still more uneasily.*] Calm, now. Treat 'em wiv the proper contempt. Observe the bleedin' parasites but 'old yer 'orses.

YANK: [*Angrily.*] Git away from me! Yuh're yellow, dat's what. Force,
dat's me! De punch, dat's me every time, see! [*The crowd from
church enter from the right, sauntering slowly and affectedly, their
heads held stiffly up, looking neither to right nor left, talking in tone-
less, simpering voices. The women are rouged, calcimined, dyed,
overdressed to the nth degree. The men are in Prince Alberts, high
hats, spats, canes, etc. A procession of gaudy marionettes, yet with
something of the relentless horror of Frankensteins in their detached,
mechanical unawareness.*]

VOICES: Dear Doctor Caiaphas! He is so sincere!
What was the sermon? I dozed off.
About the radicals, my dear—and the false doctrines that are
being preached.
We must organize a hundred per cent American bazaar.
And let everyone contribute one one-hundredth percent of
their income tax.
What an original idea!
We can devote the proceeds to rehabilitating the veil of the
temple.
But that has been done so many times.

YANK: [*Glaring from one to the other of them—with an insulting snort of scorn.*] Huh! Huh! [*Without seeming to see him, they make wide detours to avoid the spot where he stands in the middle of the side-walk.*]

LONG: [*Frightenedly.*] Keep yer bloomin' mouth shut, I tells yer.

YANK: [*Viciously.*] G'wan! Tell it to Sweeney! [*He swaggers away and deliberately lurches into a top-hatted gentleman, then glares at him pugnaciously.*] Say, who d'yuh tink yuh're bumpin? Tink yuh own de oith?

GENTLEMAN: [*Coldly and affectedly.*] I beg your pardon. [*He has not looked at* YANK *and passes on without a glance, leaving him bewildered.*]

LONG: [*Rushing up and grabbing* YANK's *arm.*] 'Ere! Come away! This wasn't what I meant. Yer'll 'ave the bloody coppers down on us.

YANK: [*Savagely—giving him a push that sends him sprawling.*] G'wan!

LONG: [*Picks himself up—hysterically.*] I'll pop orf then. This ain't what I meant. And whatever 'appens, yer can't blame me. [*He slinks off left.*]

YANK: T' hell wit youse! [*He approaches a lady—with a vicious grin and a smirking wink.*] Hello, Kiddo. How's every little ting? Got anyting on for tonight? I know an old boiler down to de docks we kin crawl into. [*The lady stalks by without a look, without a change of pace.* YANK *turns to others—insultingly.*] Holy smokes, what a mug! Go hide yuhself before de horses shy at yuh. Gee, pipe de heinie on dat one! Say, youse, yuh look like de stoin of a ferryboat. Paint and powder! All dolled up to kill! Yuh look like stiffs laid out for de boneyard! Aw, g'wan, de lot of youse! Yuh give me de eye-ache. Yuh don't belong, get me! Look at me, why don't youse dare? I belong, dat's me! [*Pointing to a skyscraper across the street which is in process of construction—with bravado.*] See dat building goin' up dere? See de steel work? Steel, dat's me! Youse guys live on it and tink yuh're somep'n. But I'm *in* it, see! I'm de hoistin' engine dat makes it go up! I'm it—de inside and bottom of it! Sure! I'm steel and steam and smoke and de rest of it! It moves—speed—twenty-five stories up—and me at de top and bottom—movin'! Youse simps don't move. Yuh're on'y dolls I winds up to see 'm spin. Yuh're de garbage, get me—de leavins—de ashes we dump over de side! Now, whata yuh gotto say? [*But as they seem neither to see nor hear him, he flies into a fury.*] Bums! Pigs! Tarts! Bitches! [*He turns in a rage on the men, bumping viciously into them but not jarring them the least bit. Rather it is he who recoils after each collision. He keeps growling.*] Git off de oith! G'wan, yuh bum! Look where yuh're goin', can't yuh? Git outa here! Fight, why don't yuh? Put up yer mits! Don't be a dog! Fight or I'll knock yuh dead! [*But, without seeming to see him, they all answer with mechanical affected politeness:*] I beg your pardon. [*Then at a cry from one of the women, they all scurry to the furrier's window.*]

THE WOMAN: [*Ecstatically, with a gasp of delight.*] Monkey fur! [*The whole crowd of men and women chorus after her in the same tone of affected delight.*] Monkey fur!

YANK: [*With a jerk of his head back on his shoulders, as if he had received a punch full in the face—raging.*] I see yuh, all in white! I see yuh, yuh white-faced tart, yuh! Hairy ape, huh? I'll hairy ape yuh! [*He bends down and grips at the street curbing as if to pluck it out and hurl it. Foiled in this, snarling with passion, he leaps to the lamp-post on the corner and tries to pull it up for a club. Just at that moment a bus is heard rumbling up. A fat, high-hatted, spatted gentleman runs out from the side street. He calls out plaintively: "Bus! Bus! Stop there!" and runs full tilt into the bending, straining YANK, who is bowled off his balance.*]

YANK: [*Seeing a fight—with a roar of joy as he springs to his feet.*] At last! Bus, huh? I'll bust yuh! [*He lets drive a terrific swing, his fist landing full on the fat gentleman's face. But the gentleman stands unmoved as if nothing had happened.*]

GENTLEMAN: I beg your pardon. [*Then irritably.*] You have made me lose my bus. [*He claps his hands and begins to scream:*] Officer! Officer! [*Many police whistles shrill out on the instant and a whole platoon of policemen rush in on YANK from all sides. He tries to fight but is clubbed to the pavement and fallen upon. The crowd at the window have not moved or noticed this disturbance. The clanging gong of the patrol wagon approaches with a clamoring din.*]

[*Curtain*]

SCENE SIX

SCENE—*Night of the following day. A row of cells in the prison on Blackwells Island. The cells extend back diagonally from right front to left rear. They do not stop, but disappear in the dark background as if they ran on, numberless, into infinity. One electric bulb from the low ceiling of the narrow corridor sheds its light through the heavy steel bars of the cell at the extreme front and reveals part of the interior.*

YANK *can be seen within, crouched on the edge of his cot in the attitude of Rodin's "The Thinker." His face is spotted with black and blue bruises. A blood-stained bandage is wrapped around his head.*

YANK: [*Suddenly starting as if awakening from a dream, reaches out and shakes the bars—aloud to himself, wonderingly.*] Steel. Dis is de Zoo, huh? [*A burst of hard, barking laughter comes from the unseen occupants of the cells, runs back down the tier, and abruptly ceases.*]

VOICES: [*Mockingly.*] The Zoo? That's a new name for this coop—a damn good name!

Steel, eh? You said a mouthful. This is the old iron house.

Who is that boob talkin'?

He's the bloke they brung in out of his head.

The bulls had beat him up fierce.

YANK: [*Dully.*] I musta been dreamin'. I tought I was in a cage at de Zoo—but de apes don't talk, do dey?

VOICES: [*With mocking laughter.*] You're in a cage aw right.

A coop!

A pen!

A sty!

A kennel! [*Hard laughter—a pause.*]

Say, guy! Who are you? No, never mind lying. What are you?

Yes, tell us your sad story. What's your game?

What did they jug yuh for?

YANK: [*Dully.*] I was a fireman—stokin' on de liners. [*Then with sudden rage, rattling his cell bars.*] I'm a hairy ape, get me? And I'll bust youse all in de jaw if yuh don't lay off kiddin' me.

VOICES: Huh! You're a hard boiled duck ain't you!

When you spit, it bounces! [*Laughter.*]

Aw, can it. He's a regular guy. Ain't you?

What did he say he was—a ape?

YANK: [*Defiantly.*] Sure ting! Ain't dat what youse all are—apes? [*A silence. Then a furious rattling of bars from down the corridor.*]

A VOICE: [*Thick with rage.*] I'll show yuh who's a ape, yuh bum!

VOICES: Ssshh! Nix!

Can de noise!

Piano!

You'll have the guard down on us!

YANK: [*Scornfully.*] De guard? Yuh mean de keeper, don't yuh? [*Angry exclamations from all the cells.*]

VOICE: [*Placatingly.*] Aw, don't pay no attention to him. He's off his nut from the beatin'-up he got. Say, you guy! We're waitin' to hear what they landed you for—or ain't yuh tellin'?

YANK: Sure, I'll tell youse. Sure! Why de hell not? On'y—youse won't get me. Nobody gets me but me, see? I started to tell de Judge and all he says was: "Toity days to tink it over." Tink it over! Christ, dat's all I been doin' for weeks! [*After a pause.*] I was tryin' to git even wit someone, see?—someone dat done me doit.

VOICES: [*Cynically.*] De old stuff, I bet. Your goil, huh?

Give yuh the double-cross, huh?

That's them every time!

Did yuh beat up de odder guy?

YANK: [*Disgustedly.*] Aw, yuh're all wrong! Sure dere was a skoit in it— but not what youse mean, not dat old tripe. Dis was a new kind of skoit. She was dolled up all in white—in de stokehole. I tought she was a ghost. Sure. [*A pause.*]

VOICES: [*Whispering.*] Gee, he's still nutty.

Let him rave. It's fun listenin'.

YANK: [*Unheeding—groping in his thoughts.*] Her hands—dey was skinny and white like dey wasn't real but painted on somep'n. Dere was a million miles from me to her—twenty-five knots a hour. She was like some dead ting de cat brung in. Sure, dat's what. She didn't belong. She belonged in de window of a toy store, or on de top of a garbage can, see! Sure! [*He breaks out angrily.*] But would yuh believe it, she had de noive to do me doit. She lamped me like she was seein' somep'n broke loose from de menagerie. Christ, yuh'd oughter seen her eyes! [*He rattles the bars of his cell furiously.*] But I'll get back at her yet, you watch! And if I can't find her I'll take it out on de gang she runs wit. I'm wise to where dey hangs out now. I'll show her who belongs! I'll show her who's in de move and who ain't. You watch my smoke!

VOICES: [*Serious and joking.*] Dat's de talkin'!

Take her for all she's got!

What was this dame, anyway? Who was she, eh?

YANK: I dunno. First cabin stiff. Her old man's a millionaire, dey says— name of Douglas.

VOICES: Douglas? That's the president of the Steel Trust, I bet.

Sure. I seen his mug in de papers.

He's filthy with dough.

VOICE: Hey, feller, take a tip from me. If you want to get back at that dame, you better join the Wobblies. You'll get some action then.

YANK: Wobblies? What de hell's dat?

VOICE: Ain't you ever heard of the I. W. W.?

YANK: Naw. What is it?

VOICE: A gang of blokes—a tough gang. I been readin' about 'em to-day in the paper. The guard give me the *Sunday Times*. There's a long spiel about 'em. It's from a speech made in the Senate by a guy named Senator Queen. [*He is in the cell next to* YANK'*s. There is a rustling of paper.*] Wait'll I see if I got light enough and I'll read you. Listen. [*He reads:*] "There is a menace existing in this country today which threatens the vitals of our fair Republic—as foul a menace against the very life-blood of the American Eagle as was the foul conspiracy of Cataline against the eagles of ancient Rome!"

VOICE [*Disgustedly.*] Aw hell! Tell him to salt de tail of dat eagle!

VOICE: [*Reading:*] "I refer to that devil's brew of rascals, jailbirds, murderers and cutthroats who libel all honest working men by calling themselves the Industrial Workers of the World; but in the light of their nefarious plots, I call them the Industrious *Wreckers* of the World!"

YANK: [*With vengeful satisfaction.*] Wreckers, dat's de right dope! Dat belongs! Me for dem!

VOICE: Ssshh! [*Reading.*] "This fiendish organization is a foul ulcer on the fair body of our Democracy—"

VOICE: Democracy, hell! Give him the boid, fellers—the raspberry! [*They do.*]

VOICE: Ssshh! [*Reading:*] "Like Cato I say to this senate, the I. W. W. must be destroyed! For they represent an ever-present dagger pointed at the heart of the greatest nation the world has ever known, where all men are born free and equal, with equal opportunities to all, where the Founding Fathers have guaranteed to each one happiness, where Truth, Honor, Liberty, Justice, and the Brotherhood of Man are a religion absorbed with one's mother's milk, taught at our father's knee, sealed, signed, and stamped upon in the glorious Constitution of these United States!" [*A perfect storm of hisses, catcalls, boos, and hard laughter.*]

VOICES: [*Scornfully.*] Hurrah for de Fort' of July!

　　　　Pass de hat!

　　　　Liberty!

　　　　Justice!

　　　　Honor!

　　　　Opportunity!

　　　　Brotherhood!

ALL: [*With abysmal scorn.*] Aw, hell!

VOICE: Give that Queen Senator guy the bark! All togedder now—one—two—tree— [*A terrific chorus of barking and yapping.*]

GUARD: [*From a distance.*] Quiet there, youse—or I'll git the hose. [*The noise subsides.*]

YANK: [*With growling rage.*] I'd like to catch dat senator guy alone for a second. I'd loin him some trute!

VOICE: Ssshh! Here's where he gits down to cases on the Wobblies. [*Reads:*] "They plot with fire in one hand and dynamite in the other. They stop not before murder to gain their ends, nor at the outraging of defenceless womanhood. They would tear down society, put the lowest scum in the seats of the mighty, turn Almighty God's revealed plan for the world topsy-turvy, and make of our sweet and lovely civilization a shambles, a desolation where man, God's masterpiece, would soon degenerate back to the ape!"

VOICE: [*To* YANK.] Hey, you guy. There's your ape stuff again.

YANK: [*With a growl of fury.*] I got him. So dey blow up tings, do dey? Dey turn tings round, do dey? Hey, lend me dat paper, will yuh?

VOICE: Sure. Give it to him. On'y keep it to yourself, see. We don't wanter listen to no more of that slop.

VOICE: Here you are. Hide it under your mattress.

YANK: [*Reaching out.*] Tanks. I can't read much but I kin manage. [*He sits, the paper in the hand at his side, in the attitude of Rodin's "The Thinker." A pause. Several snores from down the corridor. Suddenly* YANK *jumps to his feet with a furious groan as if some appalling thought had crashed on him—bewilderedly.*] Sure—her old man—president of de Steel Trust—makes half de steel in de world—steel—where I tought I belonged—drivin' trou—movin'—in dat—to make her—and cage me in for her to spit on! Christ [*He shakes the bars of his cell door till the whole tier trembles. Irritated, protesting exclamations from those awakened or trying to get to sleep.*] He made dis—dis cage! Steel! *It* don't belong, dat's what! Cages, cells, locks, bolts, bars—dat's what it means!—holdin' me down wit him at de top! But I'll drive trou! Fire, dat melts it! I'll be fire—under de heap—fire dat never goes out—hot as hell—breakin' out in de night— [*While he has been saying this last he has shaken his cell door to a clanging accompaniment. As he comes to the "breakin' out" he seizes one bar with both hands and, putting his two feet up against the others so that his position is parallel to the floor like a monkey's, he gives a great wrench backwards. The bar bends like a licorice stick under his tremendous strength. Just at this moment the* PRISON GUARD *rushes in, dragging a hose behind him.*]

GUARD: [*Angrily.*] I'll loin youse bums to wake me up! [*Sees* YANK.]
   Hello, it's you, huh? Got the D. Ts., hey? Well, I'll cure 'em. I'll
   drown your snakes for yuh! [*Noticing the bar.*] Hell, look at dat bar
   bended! On'y a bug is strong enough for dat!
YANK: [*Glaring at him.*] Or a hairy ape, yuh big yellow bum! Look out!
   Here I come! [*He grabs another bar.*]
GUARD: [*Scared now—yelling off left.*] Toin de hoose on, Ben!—full
   pressure! And call de others—and a strait jacket! [*The curtain is
   falling. As it hides* YANK *from view, there is a splattering smash as
   the stream of water hits the steel of* YANK'*s cell.*]

[*Curtain*]

SCENE SEVEN

SCENE—*Nearly a month later. An I. W. W. local near the waterfront,
showing the interior of a front room on the ground floor, and the street
outside. Moonlight on the narrow street, buildings massed in black
shadow. The interior of the room, which is general assembly room, office, and reading room, resembles some dingy settlement boys club. A
desk and high stool are in one corner. A table with papers, stacks of
pamphlets, chairs about it, is at center. The whole is decidedly cheap,
banal, commonplace and unmysterious as a room could well be. The
secretary is perched on the stool making entries in a large ledger. An eye
shade casts his face into shadows. Eight or ten men, longshoremen, iron
workers, and the like, are grouped about the table. Two are playing
checkers. One is writing a letter. Most of them are smoking pipes. A big
signboard is on the wall at the rear, "Industrial Workers of the World—
Local No. 57."*

YANK: [*Comes down the street outside. He is dressed as in Scene Five.
   He moves cautiously, mysteriously. He comes to a point opposite the
   door; tiptoes softly up to it, listens, is impressed by the silence
   within, knocks carefully, as if he were guessing at the password to
   some secret rite. Listens. No answer. Knocks again a bit louder. No
   answer. Knocks impatiently, much louder.*]
SECRETARY: [*Turning around on his stool.*] What the devil is that—
   someone knocking? [*Shouts:*] Come in, why don't you? [*All the men
   in the room look up.* YANK *opens the door slowly, gingerly, as if
   afraid of an ambush. He looks around for secret doors, mystery, is*

taken aback by the commonplaceness of the room and the men in it, thinks he may have gotten in the wrong place, then sees the signboard on the wall and is reassured.]

YANK: [*Blurts out.*] Hello.

MEN: [*Reservedly.*] Hello.

YANK: [*More easily.*] I tought I'd bumped into de wrong dump.

SECRETARY: [*Scrutinizing him carefully.*] Maybe you have. Are you a member?

YANK: Naw, not yet. Dat's what I come for—to join.

SECRETARY: That's easy. What's your job—longshore?

YANK: Naw. Fireman—stoker on de liners.

SECRETARY: [*With satisfaction.*] Welcome to our city. Glad to know you people are waking up at last. We haven't got many members in your line.

YANK: Naw. Dey're all dead to de woild.

SECRETARY: Well, you can help to wake 'em. What's your name? I'll make out your card.

YANK: [*Confused.*] Name? Lemme tink.

SECRETARY: [*Sharply.*] Don't you know your own name?

YANK: Sure; but I been just Yank for so long—Bob, dat's it—Bob Smith.

SECRETARY: [*Writing.*] Robert Smith. [*Fills out the rest of card.*] Here you are. Cost you half a dollar.

YANK: Is dat all—four bits? Dat's easy. [*Gives the Secretary the money.*]

SECRETARY: [*Throwing it in drawer.*] Thanks. Well, make yourself at home. No introductions needed. There's literature on the table. Take some of those pamphlets with you to distribute aboard ship. They may bring results. Sow the seed, only go about it right. Don't get caught and fired. We got plenty out of work. What we need is men who can hold their jobs—and work for us at the same time.

YANK: Sure. [*But he still stands, embarrassed and uneasy.*]

SECRETARY: [*Looking at him—curiously.*] What did you knock for? Think we had a coon in uniform to open doors?

YANK: Naw. I tought it was locked—and dat yuh'd wanter give me the once-over trou a peep-hole or somep'n to see if I was right.

SECRETARY: [*Alert and suspicious but with an easy laugh.*] Think we were running a crap game? That door is never locked. What put that in your nut?

YANK: [*With a knowing grin, convinced that this is all camouflage, a part of the secrecy.*] Dis burg is full of bulls, ain't it?

SECRETARY: [*Sharply.*] What have the cops got to do with us? We're breaking no laws.

YANK: [*With a knowing wink.*] Sure. Youse wouldn't for woilds. Sure. I'm wise to dat.

SECRETARY: You seem to be wise to a lot of stuff none of us knows about.

YANK: [*With another wink.*] Aw, dat's aw right, see. [*Then made a bit resentful by the suspicious glances from all sides.*] Aw, can it! Youse needn't put me trou de toid degree. Can't youse see I belong? Sure! I'm reg'lar. I'll stick, get me? I'll shoot de woiks for youse. Dat's why I wanted to join in.

SECRETARY: [*Breezily, feeling him out.*] That's the right spirit. Only are you sure you understand what you've joined? It's all plain and above board; still, some guys get a wrong slant on us. [*Sharply.*] What's your notion of the purpose of the I. W. W.?

YANK: Aw, I know all about it.

SECRETARY: [*Sarcastically.*] Well, give us some of your valuable information.

YANK: [*Cunningly.*] I know enough not to speak outa my toin. [*Then resentfully again.*] Aw, say! I'm reg'lar. I'm wise to de game. I know yuh got to watch your step wit a stranger. For all youse know, I might be a plain-clothes dick, or somep'n, dat's what yuh're tinkin', huh? Aw, forget it! I belong, see? Ask any guy down to de docks if I don't.

SECRETARY: Who said you didn't?

YANK: After I'm 'nitiated, I'll show yuh.

SECRETARY: [*Astounded.*] Initiated? There's no initiation.

YANK: [*Disappointed.*] Ain't there no password—no grip nor nothin'?

SECRETARY: What'd you think this is—the Elks—or the Black Hand?

YANK: De Elks, hell! De Black Hand, dey're a lot of yellow backstickin' Ginees. Naw. Dis is a man's gang, ain't it?

SECRETARY: You said it! That's why we stand on our two feet in the open. We got no secrets.

YANK: [*Surprised but admiringly.*] Yuh mean to say yuh always run wide open—like dis?

SECRETARY: Exactly.

YANK: Den yuh sure got your noive wit youse!

SECRETARY: [*Sharply.*] Just what was it made you want to join us? Come out with that straight.

YANK: Yuh call me? Well, I got noive, too! Here's my hand. Yuh wanter blow tings up, don't yuh? Well, dat's me! I belong!

SECRETARY: [*With pretended carelessness.*] You mean change the unequal conditions of society by legitimate direct action—or with dynamite?

YANK: Dynamite! Blow it offen de oith—steel—all de cages—all de factories, steamers, buildings, jails—de Steel Trust and all dat makes it go.

SECRETARY: So—that's your idea, eh? And did you have any special job in that line you wanted to propose to us. [*He makes a sign to the men, who get up cautiously one by one and group behind* YANK.]

YANK: [*Boldly.*] Sure, I'll come out wit it. I'll show youse I'm one of de gang. Dere's dat millionaire guy, Douglas—

SECRETARY: President of the Steel Trust, you mean? Do you want to assassinate him?

YANK: Naw, dat don't get yuh nothin'. I mean blow up de factory, de woiks, where he makes de steel. Dat's what I'm after—to blow up de steel, knock all de steel in de woild up to de moon. Dat'll fix tings! [*Eagerly, with a touch of bravado.*] I'll do it by me lonesome! I'll show yuh! Tell me where his woiks is, how to git there, all de dope. Gimme de stuff, de old butter—and watch me do de rest! Watch de smoke and see it move! I don't give a damn if dey nab me—long as it's done! I'll soive life for it—and give 'em de laugh! [*Half to himself.*] And I'll write her a letter and tell her de hairy ape done it. Dat'll square tings.

SECRETARY: [*Stepping away from* YANK.] Very interesting. [*He gives a signal. The men, huskies all, throw themselves on* YANK *and before he knows it they have his legs and arms pinioned. But he is too flabbergasted to make a struggle, anyway. They feel him over for weapons.*]

MAN: No gat, no knife. Shall we give him what's what and put the boots to him?

SECRETARY: No. He isn't worth the trouble we'd get into. He's too stupid. [*He comes closer and laughs mockingly in* YANK'*s face.*] Ho-ho! By God, this is the biggest joke they've put up on us yet. Hey, you Joke! Who sent you—Burns or Pinkerton? No, by God, you're such a bonehead I'll bet you're in the Secret Service! Well, you dirty spy, you rotten agent provocator, you can go back and tell whatever skunk is paying you blood-money for betraying your brothers that he's wasting his coin. You couldn't catch a cold. And tell him that all he'll ever get on us, or ever has got, is just his own sneaking plots that he's framed up to put us in jail. We are what our manifesto says we are, neither more or less—and we'll give him a copy of that any time he calls. And as for you— [*He glares scornfully at* YANK, *who is sunk in an oblivious stupor.*] Oh, hell, what's the use of talking? You're a brainless ape.

YANK: [*Aroused by the word to fierce but futile struggles.*] What's dat, yuh Sheeny bum, yuh!

SECRETARY: Throw him out, boys. [*In spite of his struggles, this is done with gusto and éclat. Propelled by several parting kicks,* YANK *lands sprawling in the middle of the narrow cobbled street. With a growl he starts to get up and storm the closed door, but stops bewildered by the confusion in his brain, pathetically impotent. He sits there, brooding, in as near to the attitude of Rodin's "Thinker" as he can get in his position.*]

YANK: [*Bitterly.*] So dem boids don't tink I belong, neider. Aw, to hell wit 'em! Dey're in de wrong pew—de same old bull—soapboxes and Salvation Army—no guts! Cut out an hour offen de job a day and make me happy! Gimme a dollar more a day and make me happy! Tree square a day, and cauliflowers in de front yard—ekal rights—a woman and kids—a lousey vote—and I'm all fixed for Jesus, huh? Aw, hell! What does dat get yuh? Dis ting's in your inside, but it ain't your belly. Feedin' your face—sinkers and coffee—dat don't touch it. It's way down—at de bottom. Yuh can't grab it, and yuh can't stop it. It moves, and everyting moves. It stops and de whole woild stops. Dat's me now—I don't tick, see?—I'm a busted Ingersoll, dat's what. Steel was me, and I owned de woild. Now I ain't steel, and de woild owns me. Aw, hell! I can't see—it's all dark, get me? It's all wrong! [*He turns a bitter mocking face up like an ape gibbering at the moon.*] Say, youse up dere, Man in de Moon, yuh look so wise, gimme de answer, huh? Slip me de inside dope, de information right from de stable—where do I get off at, huh?

A POLICEMAN: [*Who has come up the street in time to hear this last— with grim humor.*] You'll get off at the station, you boob, if you don't get up out of that and keep movin'.

YANK: [*Looking up at him—with a hard, bitter laugh.*] Sure! Lock me up! Put me in a cage! Dat's de on'y answer yuh know. G'wan, lock me up!

POLICEMAN: What you been doin'?

YANK: Enuf to gimme life for! I was born, see? Sure, dat's de charge. Write it in de blotter. I was born, get me!

POLICEMAN: [*Jocosely.*] God pity your old woman! [*Then matter-of-fact.*] But I've no time for kidding. You're soused. I'd run you in but it's too long a walk to the station. Come on now, get up, or I'll fan your ears with this club. Beat it now! [*He hauls* YANK *to his feet.*]

YANK: [*In a vague mocking tone.*] Say, where do I go from here?

POLICEMAN: [*Giving him a push—with a grin, indifferently.*] Go to hell.

[*Curtain*]

SCENE EIGHT

SCENE—*Twilight of the next day. The monkey house at the Zoo. One spot of clear gray light falls on the front of one cage so that the interior can be seen. The other cages are vague, shrouded in shadow from which chatterings pitched in a conversational tone can be heard. On the one cage a sign from which the word "gorilla" stands out. The gigantic animal himself is seen squatting on his haunches on a bench in much the same attitude as Rodin's "Thinker." YANK enters from the left. Immediately a chorus of angry chattering and screeching breaks out. The gorilla turns his eyes but makes no sound or move.*

YANK: [*With a hard, bitter laugh.*] Welcome to your city, huh? Hail, hail, de gang's all here! [*At the sound of his voice the chattering dies away into an attentive silence.* YANK *walks up to the gorilla's cage and, leaning over the railing, stares in at its occupant, who stares back at him, silent and motionless. There is a pause of dead stillness. Then* YANK *begins to talk in a friendly confidential tone, half-mockingly, but with a deep undercurrent of sympathy.*] Say, yuh're some hard-lookin' guy, ain't yuh? I seen lots of tough nuts dat de gang called gorillas, but yuh're de foist real one I ever seen. Some chest yuh got, and shoulders, and dem arms and mits! I bet yuh got a punch in eider fist dat'd knock 'em all silly! [*This with genuine admiration. The gorilla, as if he understood, stands upright, swelling out his chest and pounding on it with his fist.* YANK *grins sympathetically.*] Sure, I get yuh. Yuh challenge de whole woild, huh? Yuh got what I was sayin' even if yuh muffed de woids. [*Then bitterness creeping in.*] And why wouldn't yuh get me? Ain't we both members of de same club—de Hairy Apes? [*They stare at each other—a pause—then* YANK *goes on slowly and bitterly.*] So yuh're what she seen when she looked at me, de white-faced tart! I was you to her, get me? On'y outa de cage—broke out—free to moider her, see? Sure! Dat's what she tought. She wasn't wise dat I was in a cage, too—worser'n yours—sure—a damn sight—'cause you got some chanct to bust loose—but me— [*He grows confused.*] Aw, hell! It's all wrong, ain't it? [*A pause.*] I s'pose yuh wanter know what I'm doin' here, huh? I been warmin' a bench down to de Battery—ever since last night. Sure. I seen de sun come up. Dat was pretty, too—all red and pink and green. I was lookin' at de skyscrapers—steel—and all de ships comin' in, sailin' out, all over de oith—and dey was steel, too. De sun was warm, dey wasn't no clouds, and dere was a breeze blowin'. Sure, it was great stuff. I got it aw right—what Paddy said about dat bein' de right dope—on'y I couldn't get *in* it, see? I couldn't belong in dat. It was over my head. And I kept tinkin'—and den I beat it up here to see what youse was like. And I waited till dey was all gone to git yuh alone. Say, how d'yuh feel sittin' in dat pen all de time, havin' to stand for 'em comin' and starin' at yuh—de white-faced, skinny tarts and de boobs what marry 'em—makin' fun of yuh, laughin' at yuh, gittin' scared of yuh—damn 'em! [*He pounds on the rail with his fist. The gorilla rattles the bars of his cage and snarls. All the other monkeys set up an angry chattering in the darkness.* YANK *goes on excitedly.*] Sure! Dat's de way it hits me, too. On'y yuh're lucky, see? Yuh don't belong wit 'em and yuh know it. But me, I belong wit 'em—but I don't, see? Dey don't belong wit me, dat's what. Get me? Tinkin' is hard— [*He passes one hand across his forehead with a painful gesture. The gorilla growls impatiently.* YANK *goes on gropingly.*] It's dis way, what I'm drivin' at. Youse can sit and dope dream in de past, green woods, de jungle and de rest of it. Den yuh belong and dey don't. Den yuh kin laugh at 'em, see? Yuh're de champ of de woild. But me—I ain't got no past to tink in, nor nothin' dat's coming', on'y what's now—and dat don't belong. Sure, you're de best off! Yuh can't tink, can yuh? Yuh can't talk neider. But I kin make a bluff at talkin' and tinkin'— a'most git away wit it—a'most!—and dat's where de joker comes in. [*He laughs.*] I ain't on oith and I ain't in heaven, get me? I'm in de middle tryin' to separate 'em, takin' all de woist punches from bot' of 'em. Maybe dat's what dey call hell, huh? But you, yuh're at de bottom. You belong! Sure! Yuh're de on'y one in de woild dat does, yuh lucky stiff! [*The gorilla growls proudly.*] And dat's why dey gotter put yuh in a cage, see? [*The gorilla roars angrily.*] Sure! Yuh get me. It beats it when you try to tink it or talk it—it's way down— deep—behind—you 'n' me we feel it. Sure! Bot' members of dis club! [*He laughs—then in a savage tone.*] What de hell! T' hell wit it! A little action, dat's our meat! Dat belongs! Knock 'em down and keep bustin' 'em till dey croaks yuh wit a gat—wit steel! Sure! Are yuh game? Dey've looked at youse, ain't dey—in a cage? Wanter git even? Wanter wind up like a sport 'stead of croakin' slow in dere? [*The gorilla roars an emphatic affirmative.* YANK *goes on with a sort of furious exaltation.*] Sure! Yuh're reg'lar! Yuh'll stick to de finish! Me 'n' you, huh?—bot' members of this club! We'll put up one last star bout dat'll knock 'em offen deir seats! Dey'll have to make de cages stronger after we're trou! [*The gorilla is straining at his bars, growling, hopping from one foot to the other.* YANK *takes a jimmy from under his coat and forces the lock on the cage door. He throws this open.*] Pardon from de governor! Step out and shake hands! I'll take yuh for a walk down Fif' Avenoo. We'll knock 'em offen de oith and croak wit de band playin'. Come on, Brother. [*The gorilla scrambles gingerly out of his cage. Goes to* YANK *and stands looking at him.* YANK *keeps his mocking tone—holds out his hand.*] Shake— de secret grip of our order. [*Something, the tone of mockery, perhaps, suddenly enrages the animal. With a spring he wraps his huge arms around* YANK *in a murderous hug. There is a crackling snap of crushed ribs—a gasping cry, still mocking, from* YANK.] Hey, I didn't say, kiss me. [*The gorilla lets the crushed body slip to the floor; stands over it uncertainly, considering; then picks it up, throws it in the cage, shuts the door, and shuffles off menacingly into the darkness at left. A great uproar of frightened chattering and whimpering comes from the other cages. Then* YANK *moves, groaning, opening his eyes, and there is silence. He mutters painfully.*] Say—dey oughter match him—wit Zybszko. He got me, aw right. I'm trou. Even him didn't tink I belonged. [*Then, with sudden passionate despair.*] Christ, where do I get off at? Where do I fit in? [*Checking himself as suddenly.*] Aw, what de hell! No squakin', see! No quittin', get me! Croak wit your boots on! [*He grabs hold of the bars of the cage and hauls himself painfully to his feet—looks around him bewilderedly—forces a mocking laugh.*] In de cage, huh? [*In the strident tones of a circus barker.*] Ladies and gents, step forward and take a slant at de one and only—[*His voice weakening*]—one and original—Hairy Ape from de wilds of— [*He slips in a heap on the floor and dies. The monkeys set up a chattering, whimpering wail. And, perhaps, the Hairy Ape at last belongs.*]

[*Curtain*]